# A WOMAN'S PLACE

JOANA COOK

# A Woman's Place

*US Counterterrorism Since 9/11*

# OXFORD
UNIVERSITY PRESS

Oxford University Press is a department of the
University of Oxford. It furthers the University's objective
of excellence in research, scholarship, and education
by publishing worldwide.

Oxford    New York
Auckland    Cape Town    Dar es Salaam    Hong Kong    Karachi
Kuala Lumpur    Madrid    Melbourne    Mexico City    Nairobi
New Delhi    Shanghai    Taipei    Toronto

With offices in
Argentina    Austria    Brazil    Chile    Czech Republic    France    Greece
Guatemala    Hungary    Italy    Japan    Poland    Portugal    Singapore
South Korea    Switzerland    Thailand    Turkey    Ukraine    Vietnam

Oxford is a registered trade mark of Oxford University Press
in the UK and certain other countries.

Published in the United States of America by
Oxford University Press
198 Madison Avenue, New York, NY 10016

Library of Congress Cataloging-in-Publication Data is available
Joana Cook.
A Woman's Place: US Counterterrorism Since 9/11.
ISBN: 9780197506554

Printed in the United Kingdom by Bell and Bain Ltd, Glasgow

*For Ian, Denise, Bobbie-Jo and Andrew.*
*For your never-ending love, support and inspiration: this is for you.*

# CONTENTS

# LIST OF ABBREVIATIONS

| | |
|---|---|
| ANA | Afghan National Army |
| ANP | Afghan National Police |
| ANSF | Afghan National Security Forces |
| AQAP | al-Qaeda in the Arabian Peninsula |
| AQI | al-Qaeda in Iraq |
| AQIM | al-Qaeda in the Islamic Maghreb |
| ATA | Anti-Terrorism Assistance |
| AUMF | Authorization for Use of Military Force |
| CBRN | chemical, biological, radiological and nuclear [weapons] |
| CEDAW | 1979 Convention on the Elimination of All Forms of Discrimination Against Women |
| CENTCOM | US Central Command |
| CIA | Central Intelligence Agency |
| COCOM | Combat Command |
| COIN | counterinsurgency |
| CST | Cultural Support Team |
| CVE | countering violent extremism |
| DDR | demobilization, disarmament and reintegration |
| DHS | Department of Homeland Security |
| DoD | US Department of Defense |
| FBI | Federal Bureau of Investigation |
| FET | Female Engagement Team |
| FSP | Family Support Platoon |
| FSS | feminist security studies |
| FTF | foreign terrorist fighter |

# LIST OF ABBREVIATIONS

| | |
|---|---|
| GBV | gender-based violence |
| GSCF | Global Security Contingency Fund |
| GWOT | Global War on Terror |
| HTS | Hayat Tahrir al-Sham/Human Terrain Systems [both are referenced in this book] |
| IDP | internally displaced person |
| IED | improvised explosive device |
| IRA | Irish Republican Army |
| ISAF | International Security Assistance Force (NATO-led Afghanistan mission) |
| ISIS | Islamic State in Iraq and Syria. Also referred to as Daesh, Islamic State (IS), and Islamic State in the Levant (ISIL) |
| IS-K | Islamic State in Khorasan Province |
| JP | Joint Publication |
| JSOC | Joint Special Operations Command |
| LGBTI | lesbian, gay, bisexual, transgender and intersex |
| MADD | Mothers Against Drunk Driving |
| MCC | Millennium Challenge Corporation |
| MENA | Middle East and North Africa |
| MEPI | Middle East Partnership Initiative |
| MP | military police |
| NAP | National Action Plan [on Women, Peace and Security] |
| NATO | North Atlantic Treaty Organization |
| NCTC | National Counterterrorism Center |
| NGO | non-governmental organization |
| NSCT | National Strategy for Combating Terrorism |
| NSS | National Security Strategy |
| PDD | Presidential Decision Directive |
| PDRY | People's Democratic Republic of Yemen |
| PKK | Kurdistan Workers' Party |
| POW | prisoner of war |
| PRT | Provincial Reconstruction Teams |
| QDDR | Quadrennial Diplomacy and Development Review |
| QDR | Quadrennial Defense Review |
| SAVE | Struggle Against Violent Extremism |
| SDF | Syrian Democratic Forces |

# LIST OF ABBREVIATIONS

| | |
|---|---|
| SEAL | US Navy Sea, Air and Land Forces |
| SGBV | sexual and gender-based violence |
| SOCOM | US Special Operations Command |
| SOF | Special Operations Forces |
| TSCTP | Trans-Sahara Counterterrorism Partnership |
| TTP | Tehrik-i-Taliban Pakistan, or Taliban Movement of Pakistan |
| UN | United Nations |
| UNSCR | UN Security Council Resolution |
| US State | US Department of State |
| USAID | US Agency for International Development |
| USIP | United States Institute of Peace |
| USMC | United States Marine Corps |
| VEO | violent extremist organization |
| WMD | weapon of mass destruction |
| WPS | women, peace and security |
| WWB | Women Without Borders |
| YPG | People's Protection Units |
| YPJ | Syrian Women's Protection Units |

# ACKNOWLEDGEMENTS

Where to even begin. Since starting this research in 2013, dozens of friends, colleagues and relations have played fundamental roles in helping me advance, shape and complete this project at different steps along the way.

Some of the first to support me were those who contributed to a crowdfunding campaign to raise funds for this research which began as a PhD, including Derek Anaquod, Ann and Edwin Cook, Kelly Donald, Imo Ekong, Lyndon Froese, Robert Lowther, Carmelle Pretzlaw, Michael Tochor Law Consulting Prof. Corp., Iryn Tushabe, Laura Wilcocks and the many who anonymously contributed. For your early support for this research and for helping me find my feet, I am humbled and forever thankful.

I have been fortunate enough to receive funding and support to carry out this research in various capacities from outstanding institutions such as Public Safety Canada, the Canadian Centennial Scholarship Fund, the Canadian Network for the Study of Terrorism, Security and Society, the British-Yemeni Society and the Gerda Henkel Foundation. Your support for emerging research was crucial to this process.

I am incredibly thankful to have met so many selfless colleagues and professionals in this field from around the world who have provided endless guidance and support over the years. For consistently being willing to put their name behind me in support of this research (and its required funding), I sincerely thank Dr Rudra Chaudhuri. My thanks also extend to General John de Chastelain, along with other professionals and practitioners such as David Page, Dr Chris Kolenda and Dr Bill

# ACKNOWLEDGEMENTS

Duff, who were willing to share their insights, opinions and experiences with me over many coffees and emails, and helped me better understand a side of this research I may not have otherwise.

This research would not have been possible without the interviews both on and off the record with the dozens of government officials, practitioners, academics and countless other hard-working professionals, non-governmental organizations and individuals who took the time to share their experiences and insights with me. While these cannot all be listed here (many are cited throughout this research and in other publications extending from this), there are a number that deserve special mention. For taking time out of their schedules for an early career researcher, special thanks must be given to General David Petraeus, Ambassador Melanne Verveer, Susan Markham, Sir David Omand, Richard Barrett and Farah Pandith. I acknowledge they may not agree with all that I have written, but I hope I have portrayed their insights and experiences as accurately as possible. Any errors in this book remain my own. Conversations with exceptional academics such as Dr Elisabeth Kendall, Dr Laura Sjoberg, Dr Katherine Brown and Dr Nelly Lahoud also helped inform diverse ways of conceiving of this topic, and your time for emerging researchers is greatly valued. Dr Rebekka Friedman, Dr Kieran Mitton and Professor Brooke Rogers have also helped inform and shape professional aspects over these years, and are thus owed thanks for their support and insights. Dr Shiraz Maher and the International Center for the Study of Radicalisation have my particular gratitude for providing the space, encouragement and support to allow me to carry out additional research and facilitate the completion of this book.

The constructive and valuable feedback by Professor Mia Bloom, Professor Jayne Huckerby and Dr Stephen Tankel for this book was greatly appreciated, and I could not have requested more knowledgeable and respected reviewers. Professor Peter Neumann, Whitney Grespin, Brett Van Ess, Oliver Mains, John Holland McCowan and Lorenzo Piras all deserve special thanks for their review and feedback on separate chapters of the book. The feedback and guidance provided by Dr Caron Gentry and Dr Jelke Boesten following my viva examination have also helped expand and strengthen this research: thank you. I am also particularly appreciative to Michael Dwyer at Hurst for his support of this book, and Farhaana Arefin, Daisy Leitch and Michael Eckhardt for their hard work bringing it from manuscript to publication. Mackenzie Hart also deserves thanks for her help with editing the final product.

As a (relatively) young female academic, I found myself at times intimidated to focus on the field of counterterrorism policy and practice. However, I discovered that not only was there a great willingness by policymakers and practitioners to engage with me as an academic, but there was also a desire to continue to bridge the academic–policy-practitioner gap where this relationship was often viewed as mutually beneficial. I only hope that more (particularly young, female) academics take an interest in this field and feel confident in reaching out to, and actively engaging with, actors involved in all aspects of this work. I hope policymakers, practitioners and other actors continue to share their experiences and insights with us as academics as well.

I am forever fortunate to share my life with so many relations, friends and colleagues who have helped and supported me throughout the process (whether they know it or not). Marion Daniel (aka "the war horse") is the embodiment of calm, endurance and dedication to helping those around her. Rod McDonald has forever been encouraging and inspirational, and deserves special thanks for his support. For always having wine at the ready and time to chat through any concept, theory or life matter, Claire Yorke has truly lived (and survived) this process with me. Michelle Schultz, Samina Thind, Ashley Major, Duygu Zoral, and Natalia Kammerer continue to be the best friends a girl could ask for, and helped carry me through the highs and lows of the research process. I'm particularly thankful for sharing the final stages of the book (and its rocky patches) with Andrew Galloway. My dearest Bianca Barton and Iona Ebben have helped ensure this research was also interspersed with a little adventure. Zoha Waseem, Maryam Mahmood, Sarah Katharina Kayß, Raphael Marcus, David Parker, Eugenio Lilli, Stefan Schilling, Samar Batrawi, Matt Heffler, Devorah Margolin, Elizabeth Pearson and Jill Russell have been incredibly supportive friends and colleagues who have selflessly offered their assistance, shared their valuable insights and contributed to a research experience par none. The "fig crew" gets special mention for the lasting friendships and memories formed throughout this process. Countless others have offered their friendship, support and spare couches for research trips throughout this process, including the Forsyth family, Dani Mario, the Earls girls, Andy Hariman, Jason Zhao, Thapelo Mokhathi, the Gates family, Craig Melhoff, Phyllis (and her garden), the WW gals, Simon Zekaria, Michael Hermann and Laurence Hargreaves. Thank you for all you have done.

This research, which has come out of my PhD, would not have been possible without the unparalleled Professor Vivienne Jabri. Her enduring patience, constructive feedback, unwavering support and encouragement set her apart as a PhD supervisor, and pushed this research further then I could have imagined. I could not have asked for a better supervisor, and Viv will have my eternal gratitude for all that she has done for me over these years.

# INTRODUCTION

## WOMEN AS AGENTS, PARTNERS AND TARGETS OF COUNTERTERRORISM

The events of 11 September 2001 have proven to be some of the most formative for the twenty-first-century global landscape. The four coordinated attacks perpetrated by al-Qaeda on 9/11 resulted in the deaths of 2,977 victims from over ninety countries, and led to unprecedented efforts by the United States and its partners to counter terrorism both at home and abroad as part of the Global War on Terror (GWOT). This GWOT has since continued in various incarnations up to today, and has had profound impacts and consequences around the world. As this book will show, this phenomenon has impacted the roles of women in relation to counterterrorism and terrorism in as yet largely unrecognized and undocumented ways, with profound effects on the efficacy, impacts and support of these efforts to prevent, address and recover from terrorism around the world.

It is the aim of this book to examine how, where and why women have become visible in the discourses and practices related to counterterrorism through the lens of US efforts since 2001. Through analyzing these discourses and practices, this book defines the roles and themes that women have been most emphasized in and their implications. It highlights the factors that have most visibly impacted and shaped these along the way, and discusses the justifications frequently used to explain women's participation in this space. In particular, it considers the specific discursive, operational and institutional factors:

namely, the language employed in policy discourses; the operational factors on the ground where the GWOT was being waged; and considerations of the diverse institutions and their histories who shaped and carried out this work. In short, it looks at how the discourses and practices related to women in counterterrorism have profoundly evolved in the years since the start of the GWOT, and what this has meant for the roles of women along the way. It thus provides a base from which to assess how women can be more meaningfully and comprehensively brought into all aspects of security today in both policy and practice, particularly that relating to countering terrorism.

The continued threat of infamous jihadist organizations such as al-Qaeda, the rise of new terrorist actors such as the Islamic State in Iraq and Syria (ISIS),[1] regional organizations such as Boko Haram or al-Shabaab, and an increasing number of attacks by lone actors perpetrated globally have only reinforced the evolving and transnational nature of this concern. Indeed, the twenty-first century can thus far unhappily regard terrorism and violent extremism as some of its core, defining features. Within these groups, women have also taken increased roles as terrorist actors themselves, both committing violence and acting in other diverse roles. While for jihadist groups this has not been common, it does reflect a longer history of women's roles in political violence. However, similar to women's participation in security historically, their roles and agency in terror groups have often been viewed as being at the margins, and have been neglected in the practices devised to manage and respond to these threats, and has led to serious gaps in how we understand and respond to these groups. Terrorism and violent extremism will remain a key topic of concern for decades to come, one that governments and international organizations will continue to formulate and enact policies, legislation, practices and responses to. This book thus examines counterterrorism holistically: from how women become visible in the responses devised to manage and respond to terrorism, to understanding how women too become viewed as actors present in terror groups. It argues that it is imperative to meaningfully engage and consider women at every step of the way as actors, partners and targets of this work.

Terrorism, and efforts to counter it, long preceded 9/11. Yet 9/11 represented the most significant terrorist attack in US history; indeed, the evolution of Salafi jihadism has remained a primary security focus for the US government since. National strategies to address terrorism have been vast and varied across the US government in both domestic and international initiatives, and have often been framed as "whole-of-government" or "comprehensive" approaches to dealing with end-to-end concerns related to terrorism. This includes, amongst others, the prevention of radicalization to political violence, managing active terrorist threats and stabilizing post-conflict societies so that terrorism does not re-emerge.

These strategies have utilized what are generally referred to as "hard" and "soft" power (sometimes referred to as "direct" and "indirect" power) approaches to terrorism. Hard power efforts are often those most visibly related to enemy-centric aspects of counterterrorism—the more offensive military, special forces operations, policing or intelligence efforts in place to stop a specific threat.[2] Hard power strategies are used to enforce national interests, and to emphasize military intervention, coercive diplomacy and economic sanctions.[3] These are the most commonly recognized actions against terrorist groups—including targeting terrorist actors, their leadership and their financing, destroying their training camps, and dismantling their networks—and are those most often associated with US counterterrorism actions.

Soft power efforts are more persuasive and population-centric in nature. They are considered the "capacity to persuade others to do what one wants," particularly through means other than military or economic power.[4] They can shape, influence and stabilize an environment where there is a perceived threat from violent extremism and terrorism, and are seen to help reduce support for, and potential membership of, these groups. This can include aspects such as capacity-building, economic development and counter-radicalization work in communities.[5] These more preventative efforts are often associated with aid and development, and, increasingly, with countering violent extremism (CVE) initiatives in areas such as education, political empowerment and employment creation. Moreover, they have been gaining increased focus in recent years as more emphasis has been placed on preventing the emergence of violent extremists, rather than just responding to these when it may be too late. As will be demonstrated in this book, women have been engaged in both old and new roles, and as actors, partners and recipients of these hard and soft power approaches to terrorism. Yet, as these approaches have often lacked clear aims and support, they have not been meaningfully engaged, and have even been instrumentalized to advance counterterrorism aims. These efforts are also gendered and have at times assumed idealized or relative roles for men and women, in some cases defining what a "woman's place" should look like in this space. The implications for this cannot be downplayed.

Though these terrorism concerns have notably never constituted an existential threat to the US, the scale of the campaign against terrorism cannot be understated. Due to the events of 9/11, at least 263 US organizations have been reorganized or created.[6] The US Congressional Research Service estimated that between 2001 and 2016, $1.6 trillion was appropriated for the US Department of Defense (DoD) for war-related activities, specifically those in Afghanistan and Iraq. The US Department of State (US State) and US Agency for International Development (USAID) also received significant appropriations for their activities and operations in support of these efforts that exceeded $123 billion. Since 9/11, US government figures note these three agencies alone have spent over $1.7 trillion on "activities and operations in support of the broad US government response to the 9/11 attack."[7] This figure does not even account for dozens of other agencies which have roles in counterterrorism efforts, or domestic responses such as the establishment of the Department of Homeland Security (DHS). Estimates that have attempted to account for these wars, homeland security and post-9/11 veteran care have placed this figure up to 2018 at $5.6 trillion.[8] The monetary figures alone neglect the human cost of this GWOT, where 6,949 US servicemen and women have lost their lives and 52,737 have been injured, primarily in Afghanistan and Iraq.[9] Countless others have suffered a second battle upon return home facing mental wounds such as post-traumatic stress disorder, depression or even suicide. In the countries most impacted by the GWOT (including Afghanistan, Pakistan and Iraq), 507,000 have died due to direct war violence.[10] There are thus multiple motivations for better accounting for women in this field, ranging from the security, financial, political and ethical, to implications for the public and the private roles that women hold in affected societies and international politics more broadly.

# INTRODUCTION

*Thinking about women and counterterrorism in the United States*

Globally, there has been a growing call to consider women and gender in relation to security, and increasingly (and much more recently) in relation to counterterrorism and terrorism in policy, practice and academic circles. In its most basic form, "women" refers to either of the two main biological categories (male/man and female/woman) into which humans and many other living things are divided on the basis of their reproductive functions—an individual's sex. Gender, however, is much more dynamic. It is a social construct that refers to relations between and among the sexes based on their relative roles. It encompasses the economic, political and sociocultural attributes, constraints and opportunities associated with being male or female.[11] It invokes curiosity about power relations and dynamics in a society, raises questions about who has access to roles, resources and opportunities, and how agency is enacted or restricted in a given context. As a social construct, gender varies across cultures, and is dynamic and open to change over time. "Gender" is not interchangeable with "women" or "sex." When discussing women, gender and counterterrorism, then, we can consider how the roles of women are understood in that society; in other words, how, where and why they participate in distinct spaces and ways. We can ask what roles they are assumed to have, and how they demonstrate agency through such positions based on their perceived gendered roles in that time and space. A number of academic fields have led this work, including feminist security studies (FSS) and terrorism studies, as well as the literature on women, peace and security based in feminist international relations.

This call to more comprehensively account for women and gender on the topic of security has also been emphasized at the international level. The most prominent example of this has been United Nations Security Council Resolution (UNSCR) 1325 on Women, Peace and Security from 2000, which was considered a global landmark resolution on women, peace and security. It was the first resolution at the United Nations (UN) Security Council that recognized "women and gender as a security issue."[12] As will be seen throughout this book, UNSCR 1325 had a notable impact on how the US considered and engaged with women in their own security practices in some instances, while in others this appeared to be largely neglected.

5

Nevertheless, UNSCR 1325, and the many UN resolutions that have been established since which recall UNSCR 1325 in their foundation, remains crucial for informing how and why women have been framed in certain ways in national and institutional discourses and practices in the US and worldwide.

The US has most directly informed and shaped their own discourses and practices around counterterrorism. While influenced to an extent by bodies like the UN and evidence from academic research (as discussed above), it is the strategic and policy approach devised by each presidential administration, and the design and implementation of that by the relevant government bodies and actors, that impacts what US counterterrorism looks like on the ground. Though dozens of US agencies have roles to play in these efforts,[13] three agencies in particular have increasingly cooperated and coordinated their work within a unified approach to international US security efforts, where countering international terrorism remains a prominent focus: they are the DoD, US State and USAID.

DoD, US State and USAID have been simultaneously and increasingly considering, engaging and impacting women in their efforts as agents, partners and targets of their work. These have evolved from new roles, units or programs established in distinct response to US counterterrorism efforts within their own activities, to those pertaining to partner nations. Examples have included Team Lioness, established in Iraq in 2003, which was comprised of units of US servicewomen tasked with engaging with and searching local women as part of support services to all-male combat units, who were restricted from engaging with Iraqi women. Others included training an all-female elite counterterrorism unit in Yemen in 2006, or establishing and training female Special Operations Forces (SOFs) in Afghanistan to help facilitate raids on terrorist targets where women and minors may be present. It has included supporting programming to alert women to signs of radicalization in their communities, and empowering women in political or socio-economic terms to undercut extremism by increasing societal stability and resilience. The emphasis, order and coordination of these across the full spectrum of efforts—from prevention, to interruption, elimination and recovery—are incredibly vast, complex and ever-changing. Looking at military presence and operations alone, global US efforts to counter terror now involve 39 per cent of the world's countries, whether through air and drone strikes, combat troops, military bases or training in counterterrorism, highlighting the breadth and impact of this work.[14] This figure does not account for the operations of US State and USAID, which reach even further.

Soon after 9/11, Tickner stated that war often creates new space for understanding women and gender in relation to security, and indeed noted how gendered relations "have become a key point of distinction between the West and groups like al-Qaeda."[15] Yet terrorist groups like al-Qaeda and ISIS that have been the primary focus of the GWOT have also demonstrated that the roles of women are also evolving in their own discourses and practices. This prompts us to consider if and how these gendered relations have shifted, how they remain distinct, and whether the evolving roles of women in terrorism have also impacted on women's roles in counterterrorism. Authors such as Crelinsten or Gentry and Sjoberg have rightly asserted that how we understand terrorism has a significant impact on how we counter it, and thus also impact on the programs, resources, institutional efforts and time that are utilized for these.[16] Crelinsten states that "[t]errorism and counterterrorism are obviously closely related and are best studied and analyzed together, not in isolation from each other."[17] It is important then that as we recognize how women and gender have been increasingly considered and engaged in counterterrorism efforts in the GWOT that their diverse roles in terrorist groups not be neglected either, as it is our understanding of these organizations and their actors, objectives, strategies and tactics that inform how responses to them are devised and executed.

Women have played expansive roles in terrorist groups throughout history. Groups such as the Liberation Tigers of Tamil Eelam (LTTE) have reportedly had women represent up to half of their membership,[18] similar to groups such as the Kurdistan Workers' Party (PKK). In one data set which considered women in terrorism, Davis recorded over 300 incidents of women carrying out terrorist attacks in groups such as al-Qaeda in Iraq (AQI), Boko Haram, al-Shabaab, LTTE, Tehrik-i-Taliban Pakistan (otherwise known as the Taliban Movement of Pakistan) and across various Palestinian organizations since 1968.[19] While women have played various roles in al-Qaeda over the years, ranging from the mothers and wives of militants, to fundraisers, propagandists and violent actors themselves, they have often been viewed as passive. As such, they have generally been neglected as threats and pushed to the margins of analysis. However, their roles in Salafi jihadist terrorist organizations have continued to evolve significantly, where they are now increasingly (though often too slowly) considered as potential threats. This has never been so visible, expansive or prominent as with ISIS.

Globally, women accounted for at least 13 per cent of the estimated 41,490 foreign ISIS affiliates who traveled to Iraq and Syria; in regions like Western Europe, they represented 17 per cent, and even up to 23 per cent in Eastern Europe. Nevertheless, this is still believed to be a significant underestimation due to lack of available data, and also neglects the thousands of women locally who became affiliated with the organization in some manner, whether forcibly or coercively.[20] This highlights the significance of female membership and activism in jihadist groups, and suggests that women as extremist actors would also have to be increasingly recognized and responded to in wider US efforts. This is particularly relevant where terrorist groups like al-Qaeda in the Arabian Peninsula (AQAP) and ISIS attempt to engage in governance in self-established proto-states, as women have been increasingly considered as "citizens" and constituents of these efforts. In fact, in places where these terrorist organizations have held and administered territory (as seen in Iraq and Syria in particular), how they viewed and engaged women became increasingly reflective of wider state efforts: women, too, could be seen as security actors such as "police" or militants, or as members of the community whose support various groups would compete for. Terrorist groups would utilize discourses which emphasized the rights that could be afforded to women in their organizations, and that they played important roles in the establishment of this community. This also suggested that even relationships between state actors and terrorist groups could be gendered; where they may draw off similar language, or where terror groups envisioned idealized roles for women in their groups that may be reflective of those of the state. In short, women have never been more emphasized in, active in or relevant to broad counterterrorism considerations. However, this emphasis on women in relation to comprehensive approaches to counterterrorism remains conspicuously undocumented and under-examined.

This thinking also reflects a theme that has appeared increasingly since 2001, and which has been driven by certain government, academic and non-governmental actors: namely, the growing chorus of voices demanding the recognition and support of women as empowered actors in efforts to prevent and counter terrorism and violent extremism, but also as potential security threats capable themselves of conducting violence. Alongside this is a demand to recognize women in all aspects of this security space. As the negative impacts and implications of counterterrorism efforts were also increasingly recognized, the gendered impacts of these specific to women also gained focus in legal and human rights circles. A heightened recognition of the violence (including sexual and gender-based violence [SGBV]) inflicted on women by terrorist organizations was gaining increased attention and had to be accounted for in responses to these groups. From AQI or Boko Haram kidnapping, raping and shaming women into becoming suicide bombers, to ISIS abducting thousands of Yazidi women and holding them in human slavery, or targeting lesbian, gay, bisexual, transgender and intersex persons in territory they controlled, SGBV has seen disproportional implications for women in relation to terrorism. Women themselves, and gendered considerations broadly related to them, were becoming increasingly visible in all aspects related to how terror groups were understood. This could be seen in terrorist strategies, tactics and operations, as well as in how they were being responded to by the diverse actors countering them.

Countless volumes have been written about various aspects of the GWOT, such as the wars, campaigns, doctrines, strategies, actors and other aspects that have extended from these. This book cannot replicate these and that is not its intent. Instead, this book attempts a humble effort to begin illuminating the various locations and roles in which women have become visible throughout the GWOT, and the diverse ways this became manifest in policy and practice. It examines how women have been featured in the discourses and practices of international US counterterrorism efforts between 2001 and early 2019. By mapping and interrogating the trajectory of the broad international counterterrorism responses of the United States—first through presidential-level and then institutional-level discourses and practices in the DoD, US State and USAID—it will demonstrate how women have been viewed, engaged and even securitized or instrumentalized by different departments and agencies for distinct purposes at various times.[21] By tracing how women have been discussed in the language and practices of counterterrorism, it argues that women have largely been overlooked in US counterterrorism efforts, or considered and included in flawed or limited ways. Yet, these three particular agencies who contribute to counterterrorism efforts have all, to various degrees and in different ways, increasingly engaged and considered women in their efforts, thereby offering reason for some cautious optimism.

Perhaps most critically, this book demonstrates how focusing on women in the GWOT illuminates a thus far neglected component of how the US has for almost two decades conceived of the terrorist threat and how it has responded to it. It takes this further by considering this through the lens of three of the most actively involved US departments and agencies in international US counterterrorism efforts, and considers how their own histories, mandates and personnel impact how and why this story has evolved as it has. It probes how the US approach has also affected diverse spaces and places around the world through the stories of women in the affected locations, namely Afghanistan, Iraq, Yemen, Syria and others. It tells us how, where and why women have been evident in the GWOT, and what this means for how we think about and respond to terrorism and violent extremism today. Finally, recognizing that terrorism and violent extremism will continue to be a key issue in the political agenda for the foreseeable future, it has established a framework by which to outline how and why women have been engaged in this field as they have, thereby providing a helpful tool for policymakers and practitioners, to try and avoid problematic practices of the past in future efforts.

## Women in US counterterrorism: The framework

As the primary initiator and actor in the GWOT, the US represents the most important case to assess how women have become visible in counterterrorism discourses and practices today. The US lead and impact global trends in this field, as well as in countries or institutions the country partners with. It also represents the most prominent case of how new language and practices related to counterterrorism have evolved since 9/11. Jackson posits that the US administration had to "construct a whole new world for its citizens" through public discourses after 9/11 in order to enact its political goals including "to normalise and legitimise the current counter-terrorist approach."[22] He further emphasized that "the language and practices of the war on terror—are interdependent and co-constitutive" whereby language informs and "makes possible" practice.[23] Richardson, meanwhile, pointed out that the act of terrorism itself did not change on 9/11; what changed was how the US dealt with terrorism: "in America's reaction to those forces,"[24] 9/11 "changed the scale and the nature of the violence that confronted the US"[25] It also "transformed the grand strategy debate and led to a sweeping re-evaluation of American security policy."[26] It was not necessarily a change in security threats themselves, but in the scale of the threat and how the threat was perceived, articulated and responded to in subsequent policies and actions extending from the events on 9/11. Former Vice President Dick Cheney pointedly stated: "9/11 changed everything. It changed the way we think about threats to the United States. It changed our recognition of our vulnerabilities. It changed in terms of the kind of national security strategy we need to pursue, in terms of guaranteeing the safety and security of the American people."[27]

New discourses and practices were developed in many global counterterrorism efforts based on the US's leadership, and more resources were invested. As such, it is critical to interrogate how "women" were discussed in relation to countering terrorism and what this meant in practice.

Dozens of US government bodies contribute to different aspects of counterterrorism, both domestically and abroad:[28] the Department of the Treasury focuses on extinguishing terrorist financing at both a group and state-sponsored level; the Department of Justice investigates and prosecutes terrorist actors; the National Counterterrorism Center integrates and analyzes interagency intelligence gathered from diverse government bodies; while the DHS focuses on the physical and information security infrastructure vital to protecting the US. Given this, why should focus be placed on the DoD, US State and USAID alone?

The US National Security Strategies (NSS) since 9/11—which high-light the interests, goals and foreign-policy objectives of each adminis-tration in relation to US security—consistently highlight terrorism as a primary concern. The NSS also consistently references defense, dip-lomatic and development streams, which fall largely under the purview of these three agencies. Most international counterterrorism cases discussed in this book also emphasized interaction or interagency efforts by DoD, US State and USAID in, for example, counterinsur-gency (COIN) or stabilization work, even as other departments and agencies also directly worked with, impacted and influenced their activities. These three agencies are furthermore key agencies of focus in the US National Action Plan (NAP) on Women, Peace and Security—an important US document which highlights how the US will consider women in all aspects of security. This is briefly expanded on in Chapter 2, where I discuss the broader multi-stream and multi-agency approach devised to counter terrorism since 9/11.

The international counterterrorism efforts discussed in this book first hones in on the cases of Afghanistan, Iraq and Yemen, and later Syria (and briefly others), though dozens of others have could be con-sidered since 9/11. This "comprehensive approach to security" which developed in response to 9/11 demonstrated the scope of what the GWOT would encompass. In these countries, counterterrorism efforts could not be viewed narrowly or exclusively. They became embedded in, and interlinked with, broader regional responses in which stabiliza-tion, political, development, COIN and CVE efforts (amongst count-less others) also played a connected role. While each of the concepts explored in this book are demonstrated to have been framed and uti-lized in their relation to the GWOT and concerns related to terrorism, this is not to say that they are themselves "counterterrorism" efforts per se. Nonetheless, while terrorism remained a concern in each of these countries, and the US continued to emphasize countering terrorism as a top government priority in its foreign policy, these concepts all became part of the unique approach developed for each specific loca-tion and context in broad response to managing terrorism concerns. The cases of Afghanistan, Iraq, Yemen and Syria all prove distinct cases for demonstrating how the GWOT unfolded over the years, and how women became manifest within these.

# INTRODUCTION

## *Countries of focus for the GWOT*

Afghanistan was the original destination for *mujahideen* during the fight against the Soviets in the 1980s, before becoming the base from which al-Qaeda was able to train and plot the events of 9/11 under sanctuary provided to it by the Taliban. The Taliban also became infamous around the world for its treatment of women, often encapsulated through images of women clad in burkas being executed in soccer stadiums, or girls being prevented from going to school. Immediately following 9/11, the US sought to prevent Afghanistan from ever again being used as a safe haven and base for terrorist activity. Simultaneously, from the very onset of the GWOT, discourses related to the protection and empowerment of women became visible, as the Taliban's treatment of women became utilized to justify the US's mission in the country. Initiating Operation Enduring Freedom in Afghanistan in October 2001, the US toppled the Taliban leadership within two months and subsequently focused on rebuilding Afghan institutions, restoring the legitimacy of the Afghan government and defeating Taliban insurgents throughout the country. Later, extensive focus was placed on getting girls back to school, giving women rights and empowering women throughout Afghan society. In December 2001, the UN Security Council established the International Security Assistance Force (ISAF) to support interim Afghan authorities; the North Atlantic Treaty Organization (NATO) joined and led ISAF from 2003, at which point it comprised forty-three countries.

Violence continued to escalate from the Taliban and other militant and insurgent groups after 2003, and following an increase in COIN operations, a surge of US troops was announced by President Obama in 2009. COIN doctrine emphasizes securing the population and gaining their support over that of insurgents, and women in local Afghan communities started to gain attention within COIN operations. The leadership of al-Qaeda maintained varied levels of support and partnership from different elements within the Taliban throughout this period, although a focus on the Taliban insurgency proved a primary focus for the US for much of the war. Al-Qaeda leadership under Bin Laden, and following his death under Ayman al-Zawahiri, has continued to use the mountainous Afghan-Pakistan border region as its base, though the capabilities of the group appear significantly depleted. ISIS entered onto the scene in January 2015 by announcing the formation of the Islamic State in Khorasan Province (IS-K) in the region, and has worked in active opposition to the Taliban and al-Qaeda there ever since. It has proven itself a deadly force in the country, conducting numerous large-scale attacks, and even become a destination for regional foreign fighters, including some of those fleeing Syria and Iraq.

Justification for the 2003 Iraq War was based on the perception that President Saddam Hussein had been developing a chemical weapons program (thereby contravening UN sanctions), as well as his support for terror groups like al-Qaeda—both of which proved to be largely false. However, the emergence of AQI in 2004 under Abu Musab al-Zarqawi, one of the most destructive forces in the war, maintained it as a counterterrorism concern even as a larger sectarian conflict and insurgency was taking hold across the country. AQI also proved to be the first branch of al-Qaeda that would use female suicide bombers on a significant and sustained scale, which also prompted increased attention on women as terrorist actors in the GWOT. Simultaneously, it prompted increased consideration of how to engage and train women (both US and Iraqi) as security actors, who were better positioned to search and engage with other women in Iraqi society.

Renaming itself Islamic State in Iraq (ISI) in 2006, the group and its activities were significantly diminished, due in large part to a loss of support from local tribes in the Sunni Awakening. A host of concerns related to the legitimacy and governance capabilities of the Iraqi government, alongside continued sectarian tensions and regional powerplay, saw Iraq remain vulnerable to conflict and instability. ISI group leadership transferred to Abu Bakr al-Baghdadi in 2010, and as the 2011 Arab Spring swept the region, ISI militants took advantage of the conflict to increase its presence and activity. Distinguishing itself from al-Qaeda initially, Jabhat al-Nusra was officially announced in January 2012, based off an attempt to expand al-Qaeda influence in Syria and highlighted an increasingly competitive, crowded and complex battle space. The rebranded Islamic State in Iraq and the Levant (or, ISIL) was unilaterally announced by Baghdadi in April 2013, and in spring 2014, from the pulpit of the al-Nuri mosque in Mosul, Baghdadi announced a so-called "caliphate," thus previewing the reign of terror and international foreign fighter mobilization ISIS would instigate.[29] This announcement initiated the most significant and expansive attempt at governance by a terrorist group in history, and women around the world who were attracted to this ideology now had an organization offering them clearly defined roles and a physical space where they could go and support this cause. Women across the region also mobilized with local YPJ and Kurdish forces fighting and dying on the front lines in the conflict with ISIS, while human slavery and SGBV saw unspeakable horrors inflicted on women under ISIS.

Al-Qaeda, its various incarnations and other jihadist groups also retained a strong presence throughout this period, including as Jabhat Fateh al-Sham (2016) and subsequently Hayat Tahrir al-Sham (2017). As such, Al-Qaeda and ISIS remain considerable concerns to this day: both have demonstrated they are not only terrorist organizations, but hybrid insurgencies and even conventional military actors necessitating a multi-stream approach to degrade and defeat them amidst troubled Iraqi and Syrian states. Moreover, where earlier emphasis had largely been placed on al-Qaeda, they also made clear that there was now competition between two transnational terrorist organizations for supremacy. Now, even vying for the support of female populations became a point of competition between jihadist organizations.

Yemen has additionally been chosen as a key country of interest in relation to this topic for several reasons. First, unlike in Iraq and Afghanistan, the US was not at war in Yemen, offering a distinct environment and case to consider. However, Yemen has also remained a key country of focus in terms of the terrorist threat posed from al-Qaeda and then ISIS.[30] It's also historically a country of significance for the US in counterterrorism. A dual attack in 1992 on the Gold Mohur and Aden Mövenpick hotels is considered to be the first al-Qaeda-linked attack against the US. A subsequent attack by al-Qaeda on the USS Cole in the Port of Aden in October 2000, which killed seventeen crew members and injured thirty-nine, remains the deadliest attack against US personnel in the country. After 9/11, numerous al-Qaeda links to the country also emerged. In 2006, twenty-three key al-Qaeda figures escaped from a Sanaa prison, and in 2009, Saudi and Yemeni al-Qaeda elements established AQAP.[31] The man credited with opening al-Qaeda propaganda to a Western, English-language audience was dual

American-Yemeni citizen Anwar al-Awlaki. He was linked to the November 2009 Fort Hood shooting and to Umar Farouk Abdul-mutallab, who attempted to detonate an explosive device aboard a Northwest Airlines flight on Christmas Day in 2009. Other persons inspired by al-Awlaki included Roshonara Choudhry, who attacked UK MP Stephen Timms in London in 2010, and al-Awlaki continues to act as a source of inspiration for many jihadists today. Al-Awlaki was killed by a US strike in Yemen in 2011—the first American citizen targeted in this way in the GWOT.[32]

AQAP has been responsible for countless deadly attacks in Yemen in attempts to destabilize and undermine an already weak and troubled state. It has often contended to be the most dangerous jihadist group globally, particularly due to the abilities and ambitions of its late key bomb-maker Ibrahim al-Asiri (d. 2018) to attack the "far enemy" of the US, thus highlighting the relationship between international and domestic counterterrorism concerns. Yemen has also been a key recipient of US security training and equipping, as well as economic and development funding and aid that has been framed in terms of its contribution to countering this threat. Whether establishing female counterterror units, or promoting women's education, employment or political participation, women have maintained consistent focus throughout this relationship. In 2014, ISIS announced the establishment of a province in Yemen, serving to compound these issues, as seen in its numerous attacks in the country since. Now embroiled in a civil and increasingly internationalized conflict since 2015, terrorist actors have continued to exploit ungoverned spaces and grievances in Yemen, and vie for supremacy in the country.

Due to the timescale of this book, Syria has also been highlighted as a more contemporary country of relevance, particularly due to events since 2011. The civil war that has raged in Syria has generated egregious violence and suffering for its people at the hands of the Assad regime. Yet the power vacuum that this conflict created has in part led to the emergence and success of ISIS and a range of other jihadist groups in the area, many of whom neglect international boundaries. This conflict also brought with it a combination of humanitarian, security and political concerns, and has triggered one of the largest refugee flows in history, internationalizing this conflict in ways as yet unseen. As such, Syria acts as an important case for today and going forward.

Afghanistan, Iraq, Yemen and Syria remain key countries for US counterterrorism interests. They have been significant recipients of everything from humanitarian aid, development funding and stabilization work, to conventional military operations, training and equipping efforts, amongst many others. Each of these has been conducted to deal directly with these terrorist groups, but also to manage the full spectrum of activities required to prevent their emergence and support in the first place, and to reinstitute accountable governance and stability both during operations to defeat them and following US drawdown. What is more, women have been visible in each country at every step of the way.

## The language and practice of counterterrorism

Considering the global breadth, complexity and evolution of US efforts relating to counterterrorism in this period, how does one even begin to map how women became visible in these? What can explain these changes or why these practices evolved as they did? For this research, the author reviewed government publications, speeches, testimonies, and reports, as well as texts and documents produced by al-Qaeda and ISIS, and conducted nearly forty interviews with key practitioners, policymakers and academics. By utilizing discourse analysis, I was then able to trace and identify how and where women became visible in the language of counterterrorism, and what this meant in practice in both direct and indirect counterterrorism efforts. Discourse analysis is a method that helps reveal how particular concepts and language related to women and counterterrorism were made visible, interpreted and enacted within different agencies.

According to Fairclough, discourses are three-dimensional and constitute a "piece of [written or spoken] text, an instance of discursive practice and an instance of social practice," and should be considered both constitutive and constituted.[33] The discourses of counterterrorism considers the strategies and practices devised in print in documents like the NSS or National Strategy for Counterterrorism/National Strategy for Combating Terrorism, and how these identify and prescribe roles for women. It considers the language used in these, how and where women are articulated, and to what aims, as well as how these discourses were practiced on the ground in the roles women took up. Policy discourses inform practice; for Shapiro, these discourses specifically construct "problems, objects, and subjects, but they are also simultaneously articulating policies to address them."[34] In other words, the language used in US security discourses has a direct impact on what concepts such as "women" and "security" mean in practice, and must be considered in the ever evolving post-9/11 environment in which they are articulated. In relation to the GWOT, the practice of counterterrorism is "predicated on and determined by the language of counterterrorism."[35] Such practices go hand in hand with an "accompanying series of assumptions, beliefs, justifications and narratives—it is an entire language or discourse."[36] Here, direct and indirect practices range from war-related military efforts to training and equipping partner nations, diplomatic efforts, democracy promotion, addressing underlying conditions conducive to extremism, CVE, and so forth. Each comes with its own assumptions, beliefs, justifications and narratives related to the roles of women within these. In addition, these practices have also evolved over the years throughout the GWOT.

This book focuses both on discourse and practice for a number of reasons. Counterterrorism discourses at the government level (sometimes referenced to as "high politics") that relate to women have a particular salience and impact on their relations with their populations, and often receive significant attention in the media. Furthermore, counterterrorism and its related discourses and practices impact government–community relations, who has access to (often significant) government resources and programming, and what roles certain actors (such as women) assumedly have in contributing to the security of their society. In this way, it is also gendered in how it either reinforces or challenges idealized gendered roles and assumptions for men and women in this space. Perhaps most importantly for those who formulate policy and carry out counterterrorism and related practices, these can have very real life or death consequences for the citizens under their jurisdiction, as well as for them and their colleagues, and can directly impact on social stability and cohesion more broadly. Considerations of women in counterterrorism and its related discourses and practices thus have direct impact on the legitimacy and efficacy of state security practices, government–community relations (whether the US community or communities abroad), and the rights and broader security of populations both in the US and in the countries it operates in and partners with.

In this book, the overarching strategies and policies developed by the Bush, Obama and Trump administrations will first be outlined. It will then consider the assessed practices and specific courses of action and programs designed and operationalized by DoD, US State and USAID. These practices prioritize those designed and led by the US internationally, as well as the limited cases of multilateral efforts (ISAF, the Global Coalition to Defeat Daesh, etc.). These practices have clear, demonstrable and stated links and contributions to "security" where some explicit counterterrorism aim (either direct or indirect) was articulated. As we shall see, this encompasses actors ranging from SOFs, to diplomats and development workers, and activities from COIN operations and CVE efforts, to programs focused on political empowerment and even healthcare. It considers how these interact and function as part of a holistic strategy and practice to counter and prevent terrorism.

This book doesn't offer definitions of key terms such as "women," "terrorism" and "counterterrorism." Indeed, the very basis of this book is to investigate how these were defined and interpreted by each agency, and the ways in which they were utilized and applied in practice. However, it is worth emphasizing that definitions of terrorism and terrorists,[37] and what constitutes counterterrorism,[38] continue to be heavily debated and expansive academically, institutionally and legally. For example, Pillar notes:

> Not everything that can be done to combat terrorism ordinarily bears the label of "counterterrorism". Anything that cuts the roots or attenuates the causes of terrorism is properly viewed as being at least partly a counterterrorist measure, even if it is not commonly called that and even if other policy goals are involved.[39]

Crelinsten states counterterrorism must "go beyond legal and military approaches, to include political, social, cultural, and economic initiatives aimed at underlining the viral spread of radicalizing and violence-glorifying ideas that fuel the use of terrorism in social and political life."[40] For Crenshaw, terrorism is a complex concern which engages numerous departments and actors to deal with terrorism; these are "widely distributed" whereby "lines of jurisdiction tend to be blurred and overlapping, with no clear institutional monopoly of the issue."[41] Historically, and still today, this can produce rivalries between parties who have an institutional role or interest in counterterrorism, particularly in terms of access to government funding and prioritization of programming, and is particularly visible in interagency efforts. This book does consider the roles of women in relation to counterterrorism through a gendered lens to identify how and where women have been emphasized in the GWOT in the roles they have played. A gendered lens queries "how, where, and by whom highly contested terms (such as gender, equality, rights, national security, terrorism, counter-terrorism) are constructed and deployed."[42] As will be demonstrated in Chapter 2, the US government has consistently stated they are taking a broad and expansive approach to counterterrorism and their policies reflect that generally, as outlined in the academic literature above.

Yet, how these unfolded on the ground in practice as the US moved into different regions and faced new challenges was much more complex, and at times disjointed and even problematic. Over the course of this research, the terrorist actors defined in official US discourses expanded beyond those of the Islamist terrorist groups al-Qaeda and then ISIS and their regional affiliates or partners. There were discussions of state sponsors of terrorism, and reference to right-wing or nationalist terrorist organization. This book has limited this scope: the primary recipients of counterterrorist actions examined in this book are al-Qaeda and ISIS largely as they functioned in Afghanistan, Iraq, Yemen and Syria. Yet it also recognizes that, particularly in the cases of Afghanistan and Iraq, what were limited terrorism-focused campaigns initially evolved into full-blown COIN campaigns, and thus actors like the Taliban must also be considered.

This research identified and analyzed over 500 publicly accessible, open-source policy and strategy documents and guides largely produced by each administration, the DoD, US State, and USAID, as well as those of al-Qaeda and ISIS. These also included congressional research reports, proceedings, presidential speeches, testimonies and public statements to support this. All texts were utilized to highlight three layers of discourse: (1) the government's stance towards the public and these agencies as expressed through the president and other senior persons in each administration; (2) the views of senior figures in the specific departments and agencies of interest; and (3) the exchanges of practitioners within these agencies. The most fundamental of the administrations' guides were the NSS (2002, 2006, 2010, 2015, 2017), the National Strategy for Combating Terrorism/National Strategy for Counterterrorism (2003, 2011, 2018) and the strategy document entitled Empowering Local Partners to Prevent Violent Extremism in the United States (2011). These documents laid out each administration's overarching security strategy, which was then interpreted and honed more concretely in each agency. These also defined who and what the administration viewed as threats, and how these should be broadly countered. The NAP on Women, Peace and Security (2011), and its subsequent implementation plans and updates from the DoD, US State and USAID, also proved crucial for highlighting how women were understood in counterterrorism discourses. These also outlined how unique defense, foreign policy, or development and humanitarian aid mandates were pulled together to address security cohesively in "whole-of-government" or "comprehensive" approaches, and what policies may be competing for resources and attention.

The second tier of documents assessed were those produced by DoD, US State and USAID and their staff. At this level, the agency-specific discourses, as well as policies which may pertain to women, became clearer. This intertextual chain informed how DoD, US State and USAID interpreted and applied the administration's policies, strategies and aims at the agency level (for example, how the president's NSS and statements were interpreted in US State and applied in practice on the ground).

The stated importance of recognizing how terrorism is understood when looking at counterterrorism efforts has been highlighted, and this book also considers how women have been conceived of in primary source material produced by al-Qaeda and ISIS in each chapter. This included their speeches, publications (especially AQAP's *Inspire* and ISIS's *Dabiq* and *Rumiyah*, and other localized publications) and reports of their practices and actions between 2001 and early 2019. These highlighted how these terror groups considered women in their own strategies and in practices that had to be accounted for in counterterrorism efforts.

21

These documents were also supported by the perspectives of practitioners, and between 2014 and 2019, nearly forty semi-structured, elite primary source interviews with four categories of professionals took place in the US and UK: political figures (senior diplomats, figures in the administration or government); security professionals and practitioners; academics; and non-governmental organizations (NGOs). These were chosen due to their active roles in relation to security and in the agencies of focus, including key figures who shaped and designed the counterterrorism practices being interrogated. This included interviews with General David Petraeus, who was the Commanding General in Iraq (2007–08), Commander of US Central Command (2008–10), Commander of ISAF Afghanistan (2010–11) and the Director of the Central Intelligence Agency (2011–12). It also included key figures such as Ambassador Melanne Verveer, the first US Ambassador-at-Large for Global Women's Issues in US State; Farah Pandith, the first US Special Representative to Muslim Communities; numerous US ambassadors to Yemen; and other senior and mid-level personnel in DoD, US State and USAID. These interviewees provided insights which academics simply may never have access to, and it was often their very experiences and insights in these environments which shaped and guided the policies and practices which emerge out of reviews, assessments, inquiries and debates.

To determine how these discourses and practices evolved specifically in the DoD, US State and USAID, it was first necessary to generally categorize how women became visible in national US counterterrorism discourses. This investigation thus begins at the national level, looking at presidential speeches and statements: how did Presidents Bush, Obama and Trump talk about women in relation to countering terrorism and violent extremism in their speeches and statements? How was this reflected in their administration's core strategy documents like the NSS or National Strategies for Combating Terrorism? Subsequently, it became easier to see how and why certain discourses trickled down into the DoD, US State and USAID. It became evident that the presidential administrations and these agencies shared a common set of categories by which women were discussed: namely that women were security actors or victims, and were discussed in terms of women's rights and equality as this related to terrorism and violent extremism, amongst others. However, the various factors that impacted how/why particular categories of "women" evolved in the discourses and practices of the DoD, US State and USAID were unique. There were often also specific thematic justifications stated for including women at the agency level, with persons in these agencies using different language and reasoning to justify why women should be involved in counterterrorism in diverse ways, and what or how they were understood to contribute to their strategic aims.

The remainder of this chapter will clarify this and outline the particular categories in which women became apparent in both national- and agency-level US discourses, before detailing the key factors that impacted how and why these categories evolved at the agency level. Finally, it will demonstrate that there were three common justifications for including women in counterterrorism policies and practices. In considering these categories, factors and justifications, it highlights three key things: first, how women were talked about in relation to counterterrorism; second, what impacted any changes in practice in the departments and agencies themselves and in the environments in which they were operating; and third, why including women seemingly mattered and was thus justified by different actors. These are first discussed below but are summarized in Figure 1. A full range of examples from throughout the book is summarized in the Appendix.

## Women in US counterterrorism discourses: The categories

This book surveyed these national-level and agency-specific texts and documents to identify and assess how the notion of "women" became apparent, and how these were understood in relation to counterterrorism. It determined there were seven categories that women were discussed in most frequently in counterterrorism-relevant discourses between 2001 and 2019: (1) security practitioners; (2) conflict prevention, reconciliation and reconstruction; (3) female rights, empowerment and equality; (4) members of the public or community; (5) the private/domestic sphere; (6) victimhood; and (7) terrorist actors. These categories are my own, and in practical terms quite general. Yet, they informed and guided how the DoD, US State and USAID generally perceived "women" in their own policies and practices in the pursuit of counterterrorism-related goals.

The first category was "security practitioners," which emphasized women's roles in formal security practices in the armed forces, police, intelligence services or other security-related roles, and proved to be one of the two most common categories related to women throughout this period. This category viewed women, particularly American women, in terms of their active roles and contributions to US security forces, and were almost without exception referenced alongside their male counterparts as the "men and women" in US forces. In references to foreign forces, the "men and women" label often disappeared, even as female security practitioners received training, equipping and other support, suggesting female security actors in forces the US partnered with may be viewed distinctly or even negligibly.

The second category—"conflict prevention, reconciliation, and reconstruction"—was based most pointedly off UNSCR 1325, the UN's landmark resolution on women, peace and security. This category emphasized women's roles in preventing conflict, or in post-conflict reconciliation or reconstruction efforts, highlighting how they serve as actors in preventative or post-conflict efforts which contribute to state stability and security. As the most prominent UNSCR relevant to women and security, UNSCR 1325 acts as the foundational document for NAPs on women, peace and security around the world, and therefore one would assume that it would be frequently referenced when discussing women and counterterrorism. Yet, UNSCR 1325 remained largely absent in US government discourses until 2011, when the first NAP was established, later influencing department-specific recommendations related to women's roles in counterterrorism.

The third category—"women's rights, empowerment and equality"—proved to be the second most emphasized in US discourses. This category suggested that women's rights, empowerment and equality could enable women to become effective actors and citizens in their societies. In turn, this could contribute to positive change and help prevent violence, and is also interlinked to concepts such as "women's dignity." This category has two distinguishable streams: women's status in terms of democracy promotion, which tended to emphasize women's legal rights, status and participation in governance (for example, training for political leadership, encouraging voter participation, etc.); and a focus on more traditional foreign assistance and humanitarian aid efforts to bolster women's status, emphasizing areas such as education, employment and health. This category most clearly reflected alignment with traditional women's rights and status efforts. It appeared to be influenced by UN declarations such as the 1979 Convention on the Elimination of All Forms of Discrimination Against Women (CEDAW), UNSCR 1325 and the UN Millennium Development goals. It also reflected US constitutional principles of the rights and equality of all citizens, and its leadership in promoting a liberal international order where democracy was viewed as the type of government most associated with global security and stability, stressing how women's rights and equal status were equated with "stable, peaceful and secure" states.[43] However, women's rights in relation to counterterrorism have also been noted to be instrumentalized in the pursuit of counterterrorism aims.

The fourth category was women as "members of the public [or] community," and emphasized women's roles in the wider (foreign) population as members of a community of interest. This consisted of two streams. The first was specific efforts focused on women in the local (often Muslim majority) community, and included engagement with women to attain cooperation, partnership, information or support in counterterrorism efforts, or which simply viewed women as access points into their communities. This category became visible particularly where COIN and stabilization operations were emphasized. The second related to women's positive status in their communities, which was understood to represent "good governance" and a healthy, stable society more generally where terrorism was less likely to take hold.

The fifth category—"the private/domestic sphere"—emphasized women's roles in the family, particularly as mothers and wives. This was linked to the ways in which women were seen to deter or interject when their loved ones were susceptible to violent extremism. In practice, this was often seen or utilized more in official discourses in countries such as the UK, as seen in their counter-extremism policy Prevent (where women were emphasized initially in their roles within the family or as "moderating influences" in their communities),[44] and was not as explicitly emphasized in US discourses at the senior administration level. However, it was also on occasion utilized by NGOs in support of these departments who could train women in their roles as mothers to spot signs of radicalization in their families, raise awareness of the threats of extremism for their community, or conduct training to interject in extremist narratives or radicalization processes more generally. This category became more emphasized as CVE gained increased focus in US efforts and as concerns in relation to ISIS grew. However, more preventative efforts were required to respond to them, and to prevent thousands more persons from joining the group and supporting its ideology. This category assumed a level of agency for women that was dependent upon their status in the family: where women were viewed as oppressed in the family unit, they may be perceived as ineffective; when empowered, they could be viewed as important actors in CVE.[45] In practice, this would suggest that women's roles within their families may be of significant value, but still remained a sensitive area of engagement for government agencies. It was this work that was often done by NGOs, who could be funded by or partnered with the US government to reduce perceptions of government interference in the private sphere.

The sixth category—"victimhood"—emphasized women as victims in several senses. Firstly, this could be seen as deficits of women's rights, or highlighting women's oppression or SGBV. It was also linked to "social and economic malaise" in the Muslim world, where Bin Laden's message had gained some support.[46] As outlined from the onset of the GWOT in Afghanistan, women's victimhood could also be instrumentalized in the pursuit of counterterrorism aims. Women were recognized as victims of direct actions by these terrorist groups, often facing kidnap or either physical or SGBV at the hands of terrorist groups. In terms of counterterrorism, this category viewed women's victimhood largely as an indicator of broader challenges and shortfalls in a society that was more susceptible to extremist appeal. It also considered women as victims specifically targeted by terrorist violence. In some cases, "saving" women was also used to justify or promote specific counterterrorism practices.

The seventh category was women as "terrorist actors," which highlighted their varied roles and status in jihadist terrorist organizations, primarily in response to and focused on al-Qaeda, ISIS and their affiliates. While women are still largely viewed as either (limited) violent terrorist actors or victims duped into joining terrorist organizations, there was in fact much nuance in this category. Indeed, women were often considered within these groups as reflecting several of the six categories above. For example, in some jihadist discourses, women were discussed in terms of their rights, their roles in the family and community, or indeed their victimhood. Al-Qaeda, but particularly ISIS, demonstrated they had an increasingly nuanced understanding of these diverse categorizations, as reflected in their own discourses and practices, which increasingly reached out to and engaged women. This book expands on women as terrorist actors in each core chapter, and demonstrates that, to a notable degree, these groups became more idiosyncratic in how they understood and framed the roles of women in their own ambitions, particularly as groups like al-Qaeda and ISIS attempted to become governing actors themselves by holding and administering territory. In fact, as efforts related to governance expanded, the categories by which these terror groups described women fell in line more closely with those propagated by counterter-rorism actors. Thus, this category was particularly useful for determin-ing if/how counterterrorism parties recognized these nuances, and how both counterterrorism and terrorist discourses and practices related to women interacted and informed each other.

It is evident that these categories are neither exhaustive nor mutually exclusive, and indeed they often interact with and inform each other: women may be viewed as mothers to be empowered, victims who require rights and equality, or as practitioners who may protect wom-en's rights. However, these categories offer a starting point to help map where women became visible across the full spectrum of direct and indirect US counterterrorism efforts, and how and why these evolved. These consider women along the full breadth of counterterrorism dis-courses and practices, and from the private sphere to the front lines. While each agency drew on multiple categories, those most emphasized were also unique to each department and agency, as will be seen later in this book. For example, the DoD prioritized women as security actors, but recognized women as terrorist actors, while US State and USAID emphasized women in terms of rights, empowerment and equality; the latter groups also supported those who were victims or who worked to prevent women from joining/supporting terror groups. How these categories were understood and became visible in practice in relation to counterterrorism evolved significantly over this period, based on several discursive, operational and institutional factors.

*Key factors for women's evolution in counterterrorism discourses
and practices*

There was no single factor that informed how or why these categories related to women evolved in the DoD, US State and USAID in relation to counterterrorism. However, this book will demonstrate these have been largely influenced by eight key factors observed between 2001 and early 2019, and that each department and agency was influenced uniquely by these factors at different points in time. These factors generally relate to the specific discourses present in the wider environment at the time (the discursive milieu; that is, the discourses that guided and informed these practices), the physical operational environments in which the US was operating (the operational milieu; that is, the locations and contexts these actors operated in and the mission at hand) and features within each agency itself (the agency milieu).

This included, first, the international discourses pertaining to women in relation to security, specifically those from the UN. The UN's CEDAW (1979) and Millennium Development Goals remained important for informing how and why women were emphasized in relation to their rights and status in society immediately after 9/11. UN Security Council Resolutions also played an important role. The most important UN resolution was UNSCR 1325 (2000) on Women, Peace and Security, although multilateral institutions the US was a lead partner in (such as NATO in Afghanistan) appeared more active in utilizing this than the US itself. However, while this resolution was a landmark in advancing global discourses on women in relation to security, and remained integral to many subsequent UNSCRs, it appeared slow to catch up with and respond to contemporary security streams of effort such as counterterrorism and CVE. This issue was not addressed until 2013, when UNSCR 2129 started considering how women were impacted by terrorist acts, and the subsequent UNSCRs 2195 and 2242 which consider women more holistically in all aspects of CVE and violent extremism. These international discourses were important for shaping the global norms pertaining to women's roles and status in this period as they related to counterterrorism and CVE, and were reflected to differing degrees in US discourses and practices.

The second factor was the national discourses (that is, statements and strategies of various US presidential administrations) pertaining to women in relation to security. At the national level, this included comprehensive "whole-of-government" approaches to security, which drove interagency cooperation and efforts. It also considered specific counterterrorism-relevant discourses—whether President Bush's emphasis on the GWOT and democracy promotion, or President Obama's emphasis on the "underlying grievances" of terrorism and pre-emption through CVE efforts (Figure 2). These were most visible in presidential speeches and statements, as well as the NSS and National Strategies for Combating Terrorism. How each US president articulated what terrorism was, and how it should be responded to in national-level strategies, was directly correlated with how women were emphasized and engaged in DoD, US State and USAID efforts throughout that administration. The most noteworthy international–national juncture was seen with the NAP on Women, Peace and Security (2011), which drew directly off UNSCR 1325 and guided US efforts in those departments. This also considered "women's champions" in key positions who accelerated considerations of women, as particularly noted with President Obama and Secretary of State Hillary Clinton.

A third factor that impacted women in counterterrorism was the operational environments the US found itself in, which considered the unique historical, geopolitical and sociocultural characteristics of each country or region in which they operated. For example, Afghanistan, Iraq and Yemen all featured diverse urban and rural populations, rates of literacy and employment, levels of central government presence, prominent insurgent and terrorist actors, ungoverned spaces, and so forth. The populations in these countries were also largely Muslim (along differing sectarian lines), with diverse minority groups and differing degrees of public and private gender segregation. The gender-segregated nature of countries like Afghanistan, Iraq and Yemen prompted female-centric or gender-sensitive responses whereby it was more culturally appropriate to have women engaging with other women, particularly in public interactions and sensitive activities such as body searches when these became required. Each of these environments had to be assessed in its unique context. These considerations held as other countries such as Tunisia, Morocco and Syria gained importance and had to be assessed in their own distinct contexts.

The fourth factor that extended from this was the evolving operational objectives prompted by the environments the US were operating within, and the strategy, mission or program at hand. No environment is static, and the situations on the ground in Afghanistan, Iraq and Yemen all changed substantially during the GWOT, prompting evolving operational objectives. Both in Afghanistan and Iraq, limited initial missions soon expanded when the US started to face an increasing threat from insurgency. Thus, there was a growing emphasis on COIN, wherein the "hearts and minds" model inherent in this required increased focus on engaging with female populations. Furthermore, as AQAP began to carry out kidnappings in Yemen, the establishment of an all-female counterterrorism unit was seen as one component of an effective response to this concern. This could also be seen in the recognized need for stabilization efforts, where some areas were deemed too unsafe for civilian staff to operate, but which required development programs to achieve long-term success beyond direct operations to prevent the return of terrorist safe havens. Stabilization efforts in particular emphasized improving the rights and status of women, and considered their development and humanitarian needs in these environments. In countries at risk from growing instability, a greater emphasis on CVE was at times engaged to undercut extremist appeals, prompting a focus on families and communities where women became a key population to engage with. In short, how women were engaged was directly tied to the operational objective of the day, as well as the understood means with which to achieve this.

How counterterrorism is constructed depends largely on how the terrorist threat is understood, and this book expands notably on the women-centric actions of terrorist groups. Often embedded in broader counterterrorism efforts, this category impacted institutional considerations of, and responses to, women in their practices, as seen when AQI began using women to smuggle contraband and deploying female suicide bombers, prompting the DoD to establish Team Lioness and Daughters of Iraq to search women at checkpoints. As women increasingly traveled to Syria to join ISIS, US State and USAID also had to adjust their own CVE programming efforts to respond to this growing concern. Furthermore, as governance efforts by these terrorist groups evolved (as first seen with al-Qaeda, and most expansively and success-fully in ISIS's "caliphate"), the discourses and practices of these groups too evolved, particularly in relation to women. In many cases, whether discussing women as security actors, or highlighting their rights and empowerment, these actually often mirrored those of US government actors (though these remained underpinned by their own strategies and ideological justifications). However, women still appeared to be a lesser consideration, particularly when contrasted against male actors, who were understood as the most dominant threat from these groups and the primary focus of counterterrorism efforts.

A sixth factor was the agency's own historical knowledge, and their consideration of and emphasis on "women" and "gender" in their work. Women tended to be acknowledged more in evolving counterterror-ism programming when they had been explicitly mentioned in policy language, or when gender was considered in agency planning, frame-works and evaluations. This was evident in DoD, where limited expan-sion on women in counterterrorism or COIN literature (such as "Joint Publication 3–26: Counterterrorism" or "Field Manual 3–24: Counterinsurgency") reflected the lack of recognition of women as either threats or populations to engage. This led to a steeper and often flawed learning curve whereby women were increasingly utilized in new units, such as Team Lioness, or Female Engagement Teams (FETs) to engage women in local populations. In USAID, due to the 1979 Percy Amendment and numerous gender frameworks and consider-ations which featured historically throughout USAID, women remained more visible in discourses and practices as USAID responded more to insurgency and extremism concerns and moved into the security sphere. Despite this, there remained flaws, and it was not always evi-dent that this knowledge translated efficiently into practice. This also considered the presence of gender advisors, coordinators and other roles where women and gender concerns were prioritized, and what level of support, influence or access these had.

The seventh factor was agency limitations, where each faced distinct operational and bureaucratic limitations, or specific gaps in knowledge. These included restrictions on combat roles for women in the DoD, which led to female service members unintentionally ending up on the front lines; as a result, the DoD had to grapple with how to maneuver this limitation to achieve their mission. Agency limitations also saw competition for resources and prioritization where, unless programming was framed as counterterrorism-relevant, it risked being relegated down the chain of funding priorities, as was evidenced in US State programs in Yemen. Another element that became visible was a paucity in agency knowledge of women's roles in violence, where limited understanding of the push and pull factors related to women's roles in jihadist groups reflected gaps in CVE programming efforts in USAID and prompted belated research on this topic. Institutional memory—where knowledge generated in different places and spaces had the potential to inform new challenges or shape new practices—was at times shown to be limited and also impacted how women's roles became visible, and some of the contentions that surrounded these.

The eighth category was interagency cooperation and coordination, where various agencies worked together on certain programs. The DoD was the most prominent actor in counterterrorism efforts since 9/11, and the sheer size, scale and impact of its efforts suggested that it would be the most dominant in interagency interactions. This book demonstrates that the collaboration and interaction between these agencies in different countries and regions of interest was an important aspect to investigate and consider when assessing how women's roles or gendered considerations evolved in practice. This was highlighted in areas like civil military, stabilization and CVE programs. However, there was no single platform to facilitate these interactions, and they varied significantly across regions and in their nature of effort; moreover, they were impacted by a host of other considerations, including the personalities and priorities in each location. There was also limited analysis of how direct counterterrorism efforts were impacting on indirect counterterrorism efforts, or interrogation of the consequences that arose from this. Increasing civil military relations, joint gender advisory groups, joint training exercises and personnel exchanges also appeared to inform this to varying or limited degrees in specific locations and cases.

## Discourses to justify women's inclusion in counterterrorism

Related to these categories and factors were three prominent discourses, which are frequently referenced to justify how and why "women" should be engaged in counterterrorism efforts. They are their operational innovation and effectiveness; the "rights approach;" and their representation of half of the population. The discourses emphasized differed in each agency and context, and the justifications for this proved important for understanding the different motivations for including women.

The first discourse to justify women's inclusion was in terms of the perceived increased operational innovation and effectiveness achieved by including them. This became particularly pertinent in environments where gender segregation was a cultural norm, and where either accessing local women or carrying out operations in a culturally sensitive manner had proved problematic. For example, new units and roles for women like Daughters of Iraq or FETs were framed in terms of their strategic and operational capability, which helped the DoD overcome obstacles to achieve its mission. In US State, efforts to advance women's engagement in counterterrorism community partnerships were framed in terms of the positive operational impact this could have. This discourse particularly resonated with security actors in DoD and US State.

The second discourse was that based on the "rights approach," which saw three specific manifestations. The first was in relation to the belief that women had the right to be able to participate equally in all aspects of society, including security and counterterrorism. This was sometimes viewed alongside a specific standard required in the agency. In other words, as an equal member of society, as long as a woman could meet the agency standard (such as a physical requirement in the DoD), then it was her right to be able to participate in any role. This element appeared most prominent with practitioners. Second, women's rights were also often viewed as those most negatively impacted by terrorist violence and the broader insecurity that may accompany this, and as such it was crucial they be included in formulating and implementing responses to them. This also ensured that programming didn't in fact violate their rights unintentionally when gender-specific impacts were not accounted for, which were recognized to promote more effective counterterrorism approaches. This appeared prominent with policymakers in US State and USAID. Third, the status of women's rights and equality were also viewed in a democratic sense as an indicator of broader state stability, where responsive democratic states were less likely to foster extremism. This could be referred to as the "canary in the coalmine" approach, where changes to women's status were seen as indicative of broader negative societal changes. Here, women who had rights and were empowered were also understood to be able to more efficiently contribute to counterterrorism efforts, and their rights should thus be prioritized as part of a broader democratic-centric approach. These were emphasized in national-level discourses and by policymakers, particularly in US State and USAID. Thus, various "rights approach" discourses were utilized to advance women's roles in counterterrorism, to protect women in practice, and to use flourishing women's rights as an indication of a society resilient to extremism.

Third was what could be considered a "half the population" approach, where women should be included and considered equally in all aspects of security by virtue of representing 50 per cent of the population. This was seen, for example, when Secretary of Defense Ash Carter noted, "we cannot afford to cut ourselves off from half the country's skills and talents"[47] when opening combat roles to women. In some cases, this category also suggested that gender as a social construct shaped the roles and experiences of men and women in society differently, where women could bring unique perspectives, ideas or experiences to the table. As such, in order to have the most robust approach to direct and indirect counterterrorism efforts, the gendered roles, experiences and perspectives of the "other half of the population" (that is, women) had to be recognized and reflected in policy language and programming. This was seen most clearly in US State, for example where, when discussing "counter-messaging and other aspects of eradicating terrorism, there was a key gap if only half the audience was understood or engaged."[48] Sustainable peace also increasingly demanded the buy-in and consideration of diverse and traditionally neglected groups such as women, youth or minority populations to ensure their longevity, where women's representation gained particular emphasis.

As with the earlier factors and discourses, the three aforementioned were also neither exhaustive, nor mutually exclusive. Indeed, it often appeared that multiple justifications were drawn upon simultaneously when justifying women's inclusion in counterterrorism practices. However, as will be demonstrated, some of these justifications resonated

Figure 1. The framework: Women in US counterterrorism discourses between 2001–19

## The categories of "women" in US counterterrorism discourses

1. Security practitioners
2. Conflict prevention, reconciliation and reconstruction
3. Women's rights, empowerment, equality
    a. Democratic-centric efforts (political participation, rights and legal status)
    b. Development-centric efforts (foreign assistance and aid)
4. Public/community sphere
5. Private/domestic sphere
6. Victimhood
7. Terrorist actors

## The factors that impacted how "women" evolved at the agency level

*Discursive factors*

1. International discourses
2. National discourses

*Operational factors*

3. Operational environments
4. Operational objectives
5. Women-centric efforts of terrorist groups

*Institutional factors*

6. Institutional history of "women" and "gender"
7. Institutional limitations
8. Interagency cooperation and collaboration

## Justifications to include "women"

1. Operation and innovation
2. Women's rights as:
    a. Democratic right to participate
    b. Most impacted by terrorist violence (and responses)
    c. Indicative of a healthy society
3. Half the population

more with specific agencies, for various reasons. It was also noteworthy that when these factors and discourses did not appear to align, visible tensions arose in advancing women in counterterrorism, both within these agencies themselves and in interagency collaborations and cooperation. In short, these agencies had to be cognizant of the factors that informed how or why women became visible in relation to security by the agencies they were partnering with, and that they had to find common language and aims if they wanted to effectively advance their joint efforts. Key examples from this book are summarized in the Appendix.

## Looking at women: Telling the story of US counterterrorism

The two decades since 9/11 have highlighted particular strengths in counterterrorism efforts, alongside blunders and outright failures. While this book looks specifically at how women became visible in US counterterrorism efforts, it is noteworthy how this line of inquiry in fact highlighted broader tensions and concerns in this "whole-of-government" or comprehensive approach to counterterrorism. Four key tensions are discussed here and expanded on in the core chapters: (1) ownership and leadership of this whole-of-government counterterrorism strategy; (2) how direct and indirect counterterrorism efforts were balanced and prioritized (and the resources that accompanied this); (3) how policy discourses translated into security practice; and (4) how women's pre-existing roles were already seen to contribute to counterterrorism efforts, or were instead "securitized" or instrumentalized to bring them into the security space.

## A comprehensive counterterrorism strategy

Throughout this book, a number of concerns came up in relation to an overarching US government counterterrorism strategy. While it was evident that a comprehensive approach to terrorism has been visible and articulated since 9/11, there continued to be debates about who should lead this, and how to guide the multiple agencies and streams present in this "whole-of-government" approach. This became particularly true when discussing interagency interaction and coordination. The manner in which different policy issues related to counterterrorism were integrated into a cohesive strategy in each country of operation was not uniform in practice, and this had implications for programming that was focused on women, as this was often seen as a secondary consideration.

This tension was captured well by Dr Christopher Kolenda, a former senior advisor on Afghanistan and Pakistan to the senior leadership of DoD. Dr Kolenda noted that there tends to be a conflation of policy (that is, a course of action adopted or proposed by a government) and strategy (that is, the larger policy or plan which helps achieve an overall government aim). Yet, whether it was policy related to the status of women, counterterrorism or governance, these were often not "orchestrated and integrated into an actual strategy designed to achieve policy goals." Here, military efforts often took the limelight where other efforts (for example, those related to women in development or diplomacy) "play a secondary or tertiary role—nice-to-dos." Furthermore, there remained a lack of decision-makers who could bring these efforts together in a coordinated way, he suggested, and "as a result, each effort wants to optimize, but often progress in one area creates setbacks in others. Since the military effort is so dominant, its effect on others is generally far higher than the reverse."[49]

In looking at a comprehensive approach to CVE, Farah Pandith, the first US Special Representative to Muslim Communities (2007–14), noted: "There are things that need to be done in the soft power space that require somebody to wake up every day and to manage the programme globally, to manage all of the tools in our toolbox, and there isn't that person." As a result of this gap, "we have things happening scatter-shot all over the place that people are trying to say 'well that works, that works' and 'we'll do more this, we'll do more of that'. It's not a systematic or an effective analysis of what we must be doing."[50] That is, if different streams of effort were increasingly linked to a comprehensive approach to countering terrorism, how this was reflected and led at the strategic level could be uneven, and certain streams such as defense could overshadow others to the detriment of overall strategic objectives.

*Direct versus indirect efforts in a "whole-of-government" approach to counterterrorism*

Tension is bound to occur in any counterterrorism strategy which comprises multiple streams of effort, and diverse actors and agencies who each come with their own history, mandates and focus. Looking at direct and indirect streams of effort, how these were balanced and prioritized could be considered in terms of the significance and value that each stream appeared to hold in this comprehensive approach; the balance between short- and long-term objectives; and competition for the resources required to sustain each stream. In short, in a comprehensive approach to counterterrorism, looking at tensions between direct and indirect efforts also speaks more pointedly to how they are integrated, balanced and led. In the case of the US, however, it highlights how this has fallen severely short of what was needed in a more balanced approach.

Each administration defined a "whole-of-government", multi-stream, comprehensive approach to counterterrorism, and this book identifies these streams as being focused on defense, diplomacy and development. Yet, which stream took primacy in real and perceived terms was dependent on the sitting administration and what their strategic objectives were in relation to terrorism. Defense efforts largely under the DoD remained the most emphasized throughout the period studied, and had the most visible and arguably consequential impact on this comprehensive counterterrorism approach. This comes down to the very nature of direct efforts, which in the public imagination can recall death or injury caused in military operations, or the destruction of public and personal infrastructure and buildings (amongst others), both of which have discernible impact on civilian populations. Direct efforts thus produced the most consequential operational results in terms of perception and impact, and could have important implications for the indirect efforts carried out largely by US State and USAID. Importantly, these implications could be perceived to be conflated, whereby both direct and indirect efforts become stamped with a counterterrorism label. Furthermore, diplomatic and development streams may lose support based on this stigma. Direct DoD efforts were evidenced to have the least developed gender awareness in its programming compared with the indirect efforts of US State and USAID, suggesting particularly gendered impacts may have occurred and were not readily, if ever, identified. Former US Ambassador to Yemen Gerald Feierstein (2010–13) captured this imbalance in perception using the example of Yemen:

# INTRODUCTION

For most people when they're talking about US counterterrorism policy, they're talking about kinetic, they are talking about drones, and so forth. We really need to be able to say we have a much broader frame of reference on how to deal with these issues and that there is a broad understanding that, indeed, there is not a kinetic solution to the counterterrorism or violent extremist problem. You've got to have a well-developed strategy.[51]

To further expand on this tension, we can look at Yemen to consider an example of these competing streams of effort. Was a prioritization of drone strikes or a focus on training up counterterrorism forces (rather than police) impacting on women's rights or empowerment efforts when both were stated to be contributing to security and stability in the country? Were the primary, secondary or tertiary impacts of DoD activities being assessed and considered in terms of their impact on US State and USAID work, whereby they would have to support an increasing number of widows and families, some of whom may be susceptible to terrorist or insurgent recruitment? Development or diplomacy efforts were also noted at times to "complement" defense efforts, whereas this relationship was viewed at other times as being an area of tension. For example, dependent on the location, development efforts may be were framed in CVE terms, noting their positive contribution to addressing structural drivers of radicalization which could reduce threats from violence and terrorism. As such, they were heralded by DoD staff. Yet, in other cases, conflating development efforts with CVE could prove harmful, as they may be viewed with suspicion or resentment by the populations receiving them, thus putting aid and development workers at risk. This could be particularly accentuated where direct counterterrorism efforts were particularly prominent.

The potential impacts of these streams of effort on each other also meant that each had to be cognizant of the potential implications of their work on other departments or agencies. Diplomatic and development actors had to be alert to how defense efforts might be perceived or conflated with their work, and particularly any negative consequences that could arise from this, including targeting of their personnel or stigmatization of their programs. For defense actors, being aware of the concerns faced in other streams could help mitigate them in the first place or allow them to find ways of minimizing the impact of their operations on development and diplomatic work. In short, these three streams had to be better harmonized, where the shared impacts and implications of the activities of one department on another had to be better understood as part of a comprehensive approach. Looking more closely at how women became visible in these efforts can help make these tensions more discernible.

When looking at the direct and indirect efforts mentioned above, it became evident that there were also tensions between short- and long-term objectives. Long-term stabilization efforts to create stronger, more accountable governance or security structures, or empowering women in sociopolitical terms, could take many years (if not decades). Yet, when security demands were immediate, kinetic responses often took priority over these long-term goals. For example, if conflict was escalating in an area, defense efforts often took center stage, and stabilization or development work was seen to take a backseat until an acceptable level of security was reinstated. Yet, if military efforts became prioritized, was this seen as shifting funding or prioritization away from development or stabilization efforts? This was further compounded when short-term efforts (often defense-related) appeared to be less cognizant of women and gender dynamics, while long-term (stabilization, democracy-related) appeared more nuanced in their understanding of these.

As anyone who has worked in government will likely attest, another challenge was the constant competition for policy prioritization by each department and agency, as well as for the available space and resources. The GWOT has seen terrorism remain a key foreign policy and security issue since 2001, although this has declined somewhat under the Trump administration. Programs and efforts which hesitated to utilize a counterterrorism-relevant label were not always recognized for the work they were carrying out, even if it was in fact positively impacting security considerations. However, perpetually labeling every effort as counterterrorism or CVE-relevant also risked creating an endless cycle in which an increasing number of areas—from education to women's health—could be instrumentalized or even securitized and brought under a counterterrorism or CVE umbrella. This could also detract from recognizing the importance and value of this work in its own right. Yet, when not recognized for their contributions to counterterrorism efforts, such programs could face resource or funding challenges if the security concern was seen to be reduced alongside the relevance of their program. As Georgia Holmer, who has focused on terrorism for over twenty years in the Federal Bureau of Investigation and United States Institute of Peace, and who is currently senior adviser for anti-terrorism issues at the Organization for Security and Cooperation in Europe, noted: "[There] is an issue of resource and policy coordination, and it's a hard thing to do. How do you continue to support the kinetic where necessary, and make space for soft tools? This seems to be an endless question that nobody has quite gotten right."[52] One of the shortfalls in US counterterrorism efforts throughout this period was how direct and indirect streams of effort were balanced and integrated into a comprehensive strategy.

### Transforming policy discourses into practice on the ground

As becomes evident throughout this book, what is said in presidential statements, national strategies or even doctrine does not always translate seamlessly through the government department and agencies into practice on the ground. One of the most visible examples of this was the first NAP on Women, Peace and Security. While ambitious in its aims, how this plan became embraced and institutionalized into policy and practice was more sporadic in reality depending on each department and agency. The NAP tried to redress this concern by engraining yearly reviews on progress from each agency as an accountability mechanism. Yet, this remained just an ambition and did not necessarily require agency commitment to implement specific changes. If policy language did not become mainstreamed department-wide, or if the relevance of considering or engaging women in practice was not clear, there would be less emphasis on adopting and advancing these aims. For example, while visible effort was made by US State and USAID to embrace the NAP, this appeared less so in the case of the DoD; the reasons for this are discussed more fully in Chapter 3. There was also a tension at times between presidential and senior administration discourses and the departments and agencies, where what was articulated in government statements and strategies did not always get reflected fully in practice. For example, this was seen with specific tweets or statements outlining radical policy shifts made by Trump which faced stiff resistance from within his administration and highlighted internal debate. This could also be seen even within departments themselves where, for example, the DoD in their COIN field manual would discuss the roles of women in new and expansive ways, yet this was not immediately or consistently seen in practice. Perhaps most crucially for this book is the concept of 'all-of-government' approaches to security reinforced by each administration. In principle, counterterrorism had to consider full spectrum, multi-agency approaches to prevent, manage and respond holistically to terrorism. Yet, how this trickled down from the President and senior leadership, through mid-level management and to implementation on the ground in the various departments while working towards shared aims was much more complex (if not outright problematic) in practice. In short, what was articulated or stated in a strategy or statement had to be traced to its interpretation and implementation on the ground.

## New versus instrumentalized roles in the security space

There has been a substantive evolution of traditional roles women have held in security practices, and the significant and growing number of fields that have become considered in relation to counterterrorism aims, which has brought with it debate and controversy. These increasingly extended beyond military and defense efforts to consider political empowerment, development and community-based efforts in relation to countering extremism and terrorism, as highlighted in full-spectrum responses to these.

In some of the cases examined in this book, women were engaged in counterterrorism efforts based on new roles that were developed for a specific task or purpose. One example of this was the increased positions available to female servicewomen in the DoD in the wars in Afghanistan and Iraq. New women's units such as Team Lioness or FETs, or mixed gender teams such as CSTs, drew women from diverse backgrounds and established new positions within the DoD for them. Servicewomen in foreign forces which had been previously limited in places like Afghanistan, Iraq and Yemen also took up new roles in police and military forces. In each, they often faced resistance, discrimination and sporadic support along the way.

For fields previously viewed outside of this security space (such as political empowerment or education), programming related to this work appeared to be instrumentalized or even securitized so as to bring women into contemporary security discourses and practices in full-spectrum responses.[53] Here, the link between political empowerment or education became framed in new ways and gained relevance in the GWOT. This also brought concerns including access to funding or danger to employees and partners in the field. In US State, women's status appeared to be securitized to some extent in order to raise its status in US foreign policy (particularly as it related to state security), and to get it on the agenda more clearly and consistently, particularly under Secretary Clinton.[54] However, others would argue such concerns were always relevant to security and figures such as Clinton did what was required to finally get them to the policy table.

This was particularly visible as CVE gained prominence, focusing on areas such as education, job creation and peace-building work—areas where civil society, and indeed women, were traditionally more emphasized and active. Yet, the field of CVE itself was still flawed and evolving, and there was much to be clarified in terms of what should and should not be constituted CVE (and the implications for women's roles within this). There were also concerns of relabeling/instrumentalizing areas such as women's rights and empowerment that would otherwise fall under a development scope to fulfil counterterrorism or CVE aims, which could impact access to funding for programs, or even place their employees in harm's way if they were correlated with counterterrorism aims. In other words, women could be seen to contribute to counterterrorism efforts in new roles developed to help achieve specific aims; or women's programming traditionally outside the scope of security could now be framed as security relevant which had some impact on, or correlation with, counterterrorism. Each approach brought with it a unique set of concerns and reflected similar debates in bringing these fields into counterterrorism efforts. What new tools or efforts were required? Could current work in areas seen outside of security now be relevant to the concern of the day?

While this book hones in on women specifically, and demonstrates the importance of considering them through DoD, US State and USAID, focusing on women also highlights how counterterrorism has transformed over the years more generally. It illustrates how evolutions from military responses to terrorism, increasing emphasis on COIN and stabilization efforts, training and equipping partner forces, or emphasis on development in relation to long-term security came to be seen in relation to US national security and the specific threat of terrorism. As such, it also exemplifies how and where this overarching counterterrorism strategy has fallen short, how imbalances in this equation become visible and, most importantly, highlights the consequences that extended from this. It demonstrates the inherent complexity and breadth of the departments, agencies and actors which have a perceived stake in counterterrorism, and how long-term and multifaceted considerations to counterterrorism reflected competition and tension between diverse actors, and the approaches, tools and interests within these. It also highlights areas where these streams were integrated in more successful ways. The story of women in counterterrorism itself in many ways reflects the story of US counterterrorism efforts since 9/11.

## Limitations of this book

This book drew off publicly accessible texts and resources, and was thus limited from observing or assessing all internal processes, dynamics or personal/operational experiences. It attempted to mediate this by noting that conclusions were not indisputable and often "not evident." This was seen most frequently in relation to women in terrorist groups, where it was often not evident, according to publicly accessible resources, that the nuance of women's roles was fully understood, acknowledged or reflected in each agency. This may also have been due to intelligence, security or other concerns by these agencies, resulting in restrictions on the material or information available in the public realm; or the issue may have been addressed internally and not made evident publicly, or in some programs at a more local level.

It is also recognized that these presidential administrations, departments and agencies would try to portray themselves in a specific, positive light. Basing this book upon their own words and texts was bound to skew a positive bias towards them and their work, though I attempted to mediate this through a wide breadth of sources and perspectives. It furthermore does not engage in many of the moral, legal and ethical debates that have been raised in relation to US actions over these years, particularly those related to rendition, torture or targeted killings. Instead, it seeks to investigate how, where and why discourses and practices related to women became visible, and what implications these had. Furthermore, eighteen years is a significant period, and there may have been other texts or programs which were overlooked or simply could not be included due to spatial constraints. This book also prioritizes Afghanistan, Iraq, Syria and Yemen; as such, efforts in countries from Bangladesh to Indonesia, Niger to Mali are not considered, though they remain important cases to examine. However, this book attempted to maneuver through this by focusing on key themes across this period, such as the emphasis on stabilization, partner training and equipping, CVE and the trends that evolved from this. It also attempted to supplement these gaps with extensive primary source interviews from policymakers, practitioners, and academics, as well as utilizing multi-agency perspectives.

*Chapter outline*

This book consists of six chapters, which tell the story of how women have been actors, partners and targets of US counterterrorism policies and practices since 9/11, and demonstrates why considerations of women in counterterrorism are important to look at through the various institutions that directly contribute to security.

Chapter 1 reviews literature from three academic fields to situate current academic knowledge and debate in this space: women, peace and security; FSS; and terrorism studies. These three fields inform how we can analyze women in institutional counterterrorism discourses and practices in the case of the US, although these provide a base to do so in contexts beyond this case study alone. It also highlights some of the current strengths, shortfalls and debates of considering women in contemporary security (specifically counterterrorism) more explicitly.

Chapter 2 examines the key discourses of the Bush and Obama administrations in relation to women and counterterrorism. By first outlining how each president and other key figures in their administration articulated their approach to counterterrorism and the roles of women within these, it will inform how the DoD, US State and USAID interpreted and applied these in their own practices. It will demonstrate how President Bush emphasized three specific discourses pertinent to counterterrorism: (1) the "war on terror;" (2) democracy promotion; and (3) the "underlying conditions" or "drivers" of terrorism. Here, women became emphasized as security actors in military efforts; in democratic-driven rights, equality and empowerment efforts; and in foreign assistance efforts focused on education, health and employment training. Under President Obama, the US continued to be "at war with terrorism," emphasized the promotion of US "values" (as understood in democratic terms), and targeted "underlying grievances" which could motivate participation in violent extremism. Critically, the emphasis of CVE under Obama is highlighted as a key juncture in how women were understood in relation to upstream efforts to counter terrorism. In these discourses, women became emphasized most prominently as security actors; in terms of their rights, equality and empowerment in the communities in which they lived; and in foreign aid efforts to promote women's education, maternal health and employment training. CVE also prompted increased focus on women in family and community roles, and in societal resilience to extremism more broadly. Moreover, women were also increasingly recognized as security concerns, as seen with al-Qaeda and then more prominently with the emergence of ISIS. This chapter concludes with a chart summarizing these administration-level discourses (Figure 2).

Each of the next three chapters provides an agency-specific case study. They each begin by introducing the relevant department or agency, highlight how "women" were emphasized and understood to contribute to security where a counterterrorism aim was present, before discussing specific factors that impacted their evolution. Chapter 3 deals with the DoD, where women were consistently emphasized as females in the armed forces, and where women were fundamental to local community engagement efforts and gender to assessments of terrorist actors. Due to the operational environments in which the DoD found itself, new units such as Team Lioness and FETs were established to accommodate interaction with female populations. This also became influenced by the US operational shift to stabilization and COIN in Iraq and Afghanistan, where a focus on local communities required increased engagement with women, and where US servicewomen unintentionally ended up on the front lines (even as they were restricted from combat). Women's roles in foreign forces also evolved in this period, with the US training and equipping foreign partners in countries such as Yemen, Iraq and Afghanistan. Finally, as terrorist actors engaged new roles for women (such as suicide bombers in Iraq), DoD forces were noted to respond to this in their own efforts. The DoD will be demonstrated to have evolved women's roles largely due to the operational environments and objectives of the day as well as due to national-level discourses and the actions of terrorist groups.

Chapter 4 considers women in US State, where both counterterrorism and women's programming have a long history, although these were not often seen to overlap or interact. Early US State efforts highlight the Middle East Partnership Initiative (MEPI) established after 9/11, in which empowering women was a core component of their efforts. Yemen proved to be a critical case study, whereby women's empowerment in MEPI was framed through its contributions to challenging extremism based on several factors explicit to the country. An internal effort in the US State around 2007 also saw the agency begin to strategize about how it could better engage women in its counterterrorism community engagement efforts. Under Secretary Clinton, a "champion" for women's rights, significant evolutions were reflected in the elevation of development and diplomacy as core components of the US's approach to security and women's status. The launch of the NAP on Women, Peace and Security, as well as the establishment of the Office of Global Women's Affairs, highlighted an agency-level focus on gender-specific discourses and practical mechanisms to advance women's roles in security, although this became more complicated in implementation. Increases in efforts related to CVE and the new challenges posed by ISIS accelerated women's engagement and considerations in this field. Both al-Qaeda and ISIS were noted at times to mirror and reframe US discourses related to women's rights, yet this appeared to be neglected in US State responses. As such, US State will be demonstrated to have evolved women's roles largely due to operational requirements, national discourses of women in relation to security and "championing" by Secretary Clinton in particular, as well as the engagement of international resolutions such as UNSCR 1325 and the rise of CVE efforts.

Chapter 5 analyzes how women have evolved in relation to counter-terrorism-linked discourses and practices in USAID. USAID will be shown to have the most historical and robust gender lens of the three departments studied here. Nonetheless, USAID also proved to be the most hesitant in contributing to counterterrorism efforts, even as their work increasingly drew them into the security sphere as a result of democratization and poverty reduction being understood to address "underlying grievances" related to terrorism. However, as development became raised as a core component of security, and CVE efforts gained momentum, USAID had to then visibly demonstrate how their efforts contributed to security, and how it established or framed its long-term CVE programs. Furthermore, USAID was seen to interrogate and consider the gendered aspects of women's roles in conflict, COIN and the drivers that draw women into extremism more robustly than any other department or agency. However, this knowledge appeared more limited in practice and how it translated into interagency efforts (particularly after 2011) and rising concerns from extremism. It will also demonstrate how al-Qaeda and ISIS increasingly emphasized development efforts focused on women in their work, particularly as they evolved to focus more on governance.

Finally, Chapter 6 considers the significant changes that have occurred since 2017 and the end of the Obama administration: from the election of Donald Trump, to the loss of ISIS territory in Iraq and Syria, and significant shifts in the roles of women in both counterterrorism efforts and in terrorist groups themselves. This chapter first examines key discourses related to women and counterterrorism under the Trump administration, before looking at Afghanistan, Iraq, Yemen and Syria today. It draws on the lessons observed between 2001 and 2017, and considers these in relation to the current administration, and what significance these may have for counterterrorism going forward.

# 1

# ANALYZING WOMEN IN COUNTERTERRORISM

This book focuses on identifying and describing women in US counterterrorism policy discourses and practices, yet this cannot occur without taking a step back and considering the broad fields of knowledge that inform this topic. Before looking at the US specifically, it is important to consider the diverse body of research that has interrogated various aspects of women in international security, which help inform how, where and why women became visible as they have in US counterterrorism. This literature has been increasing at an unprecedented rate since the 1990s, and scholars from three fields in particular prove particularly relevant to inform contemporary research on women and counterterrorism: women, peace and security; feminist security studies (FSS); and terrorism studies. These three fields attempt two key things in relation to women. First, they try to locate women in relation to security, considering agency, power relations and structures, and interrogating gender binaries in the field. Second, they try to bring to light women who perpetrate or support violence in militant and terrorist groups and their agency (which has direct implications for counterterrorism practices). I draw from these three fields to see how we can better analyze women in institutional counterterrorism discourses and practices in the case of the US.

Firstly, the literature on women, peace and security has advanced the considerations and status of women generally in terms of security, and tended to emphasize the potential of women's agency in relation to peace and security from often male-dominant security regimes and practices. This literature, and specifically that related to United Nations Security Council Resolution (UNSCR) 1325 (2000) on Women, Peace and Security, remain key to guiding security policy and practice at a global level today. Yet, UNSCR 1325 was demonstrated to be ill-suited to consider women in counterterrorism practices post-9/11, and even appeared to securitize women to advance its aims, itself reflecting some of the critiques raised in the case of the US. Nevertheless, it will be demonstrated that this field remains foundational for advancing considerations and the status of women in contemporary counterterrorism today.

Secondly, FSS have aimed to make women more visible in relation to security. FSS is a more recent and growing body of work that has extended from feminist international relations scholarship to specifically consider women in relation to the construction and practices of security. Some important areas of focus for FSS have included locating women in security literature; analyzing women, 9/11 and the Global War on Terror (GWOT); and indeed, studying women as terrorist actors. Yet, FSS have often neglected the nuanced and diverse institutions related to counterterrorism, and their diverse policies and practices related to women, and thus neglected counterterrorism as a field of inquiry. There has also been a tension in this field as to whether scholars should engage in the policy realm or remain outside of this, which has again impacted the salience and influence of this field. Fields such as human rights law, and cases focused on certain countries such as the UK, also provide important insights to this discussion.

Thirdly, terrorism studies have grown exponentially, particularly since 9/11, and a growing body of work has considered women in terrorist organizations. Women have started to receive increased attention, emphasizing aspects such as women's agency and their diverse roles, specifically in al-Qaeda and more recently the Islamic State in Iraq and Syria (ISIS). Yet, while counterterrorism practices must continuously predict, assess and prevent terrorist threats in their strategies and practices, how women's roles have evolved in terrorist groups has not yet been sufficiently considered alongside those in counterterrorism practices. That is, there is scant literature which interrogates how the increasingly active roles of women in groups like al-Qaeda and ISIS have also impacted on or informed how women are viewed and engaged in counterterrorism practices (especially at the institutional level). Furthermore, there appears to be a mutually per-petuated trend whereby the increased recognition of women's diverse roles and agency in terrorism and political violence appears to cor-relate with increased efforts to recognize and engage them in coun-terterrorism efforts. This can in turn inform how (or if) institutions that may be more cognizant of the roles of women in terror groups may also be more nuanced in their engagement of women in counter-terrorism efforts.

Moreover, these fields have largely neglected women in two specific ways in relation to the institutions that contribute to security and spe-cifically counterterrorism efforts. First, there has been a lack of nuance and interrogation of the diverse agencies which increasingly have a stake in full-spectrum counterterrorism more broadly, including defense, diplomacy, development and community-based efforts. How these diverse agencies conceive of the roles of women in counterter-rorism discourses and practices is fluid, diverse and constantly evolving (including as terrorist actors). Yet, how they have framed and engaged women in practice has been largely neglected, particularly as these efforts have increasingly had to align as part of "whole-of-government" approaches to countering terrorism. Second, the specific factors that have impacted evolutions of "women" in counterterrorism have not been adequately mapped out or assessed. The experiences in the field, the interactions between agencies who have a role counterterrorism, the personalities that lead and shape these, and the other factors high-lighted in this book have all influenced how and why these efforts have emerged as they have. This book encourages increased academic com-plexity in discussions of counterterrorism in these three fields, particu-larly in relation to the various agencies which participate in "doing security." This review can also assist in facilitating increased interroga-tion/interaction between these rich bodies of literature and the poli-cymakers and practitioners on the ground (something called for by both academics and practitioners themselves). This chapter will high-light these fields and identify how this literature informs analysis of discourses and practices of counterterrorism today.

## Women, peace and security

Prior to 9/11, an international focus on women, peace and security had slowly emerged in wider academic and United Nations (UN) discourses over many decades. These had been driven by two key agendas which still inform women in security discourses and practices today, namely the women's rights agenda and the human security agenda. These culminated in the UNSCR 1325 on Women, Peace and Security (2000), which remains a foundational guide for encouraging women's roles in security around the world.[1] The UN and UNSCR 1325 are identified as a starting point in helping to shape contemporary international norms in relation to women and security, and have informed the considerations of US counterterrorism since 2001.

However, this section will demonstrate how UNSCR 1325 has fallen short in the contemporary security environment, as the document itself was flawed and not envisioned or imagined for a post-9/11 world, making it problematic as a resolution to guide women's engagement in counterterrorism in the years following. This was based on three key reasons. First, the formation of UNSCR 1325 was grounded in the security considerations of the 1990s, which remained distinct from counterterrorism concerns that emerged after 9/11 (such as transnational terrorism, or "homegrown threats"), thereby making it a stunted guide for women's inclusion in counterterrorism. Second, to advance the women, peace and security agenda, those with an interest in advancing it seemingly securitized women themselves to integrate their concerns into the wider security agenda. As such, "women's concern's" related to health, education and empowerment, for example, were poised to be instrumentalized or securitized as discussions arose around counterterrorism to make them relevant to the post-9/11 agenda. This proved problematic when a similar approach was deployed after 9/11, particularly due to the security concerns it then raised for personnel working in what was previously emphasized as development work (rather than security). Furthermore, the language of UNSCR 1325 still framed women in terms of victimhood, thus suggesting their limited roles as agents in dominant security practices, rather than emphasizing their diverse operational contributions.

Finally, UNSCR 1325 faced numerous criticisms after 9/11, including a lack of support and implementation by national governments, and in fact was itself accused of being "weaponized" in the GWOT.

## UNSCR 1325: A milestone, a missing link

The UN offers a logical starting point for understanding how the women and security agenda emerged at a global level, and one which remains relative to discussions of women and security today in national contexts around the world. Hudson noted that the UN "informs women's consideration in modern security agendas around the world," including "the process of securitization and its impact on non-traditional security concerns, such as women's rights and gender equality."[2] There have been numerous UN resolutions that have focused on women's equality and empowerment in some aspect, and these continue to be drawn on globally.[3] They include the Convention on the Elimination of All Forms of Discrimination Against Women (1979) and the Declaration on the Elimination of Violence Against Women (1993), as well as a growing emphasis on "gender mainstreaming" in the UN.[4] However, what is important for this book is how UNSCR 1325 was advanced prior to 2000, based on efforts to reduce discrimination and violence against women by promoting an agenda of equal human rights and increased focus on human security,[5] themes that became evident in US counterterrorism discourses and practices related to women following 9/11. UNSCR 1325 thus helps to somewhat explain how and why these topics were increasingly framed, first in relation to security broadly, then in terms of counterterrorism more specifically.

This work was also advanced by key US figures, such as First Lady Hillary Clinton at the UN Fourth World Conference on Women in Beijing in 1995. Here, Clinton argued that focusing on women's health, education, threats from violence (general and domestic), employment and equality made their families and communities flourish. Reflecting on conflicts of the 1990s that had emerged in countries like Rwanda and Bosnia, Clinton noted: "Women are most often the ones whose human rights are violated" and famously declared, "human rights are women's rights [...]. And women's rights are human rights."[6] This linkage between women's protection from violence, women's rights and human rights became an important driver of the women, peace and security agenda. However, as Clinton took up the role of Secretary of State, and her long-term colleague Ambassador Melanne Verveer became the first US Ambassador for Global Women's Affairs, this also informed the unique trajectory of women in the United States' (especially in the US Department of State [US State]) counterterrorism discourses and practices under the Obama administration.[7]

This was further informed by a growing emphasis on "human security" that emerged in the 1990s. Human security was defined by the UN as "freedom from fear and want,"[8] a definition King stated had occurred from the intersection of development and security literature.[9] MacLean took this further and defined human security as "security of the individual in his or her personal surroundings, community, and environment," which included "protection from crime and terrorism, political corruption, forced migration, absence of human rights; freedom from violations based on gender; [as well as] political, economic, and democratic development."[10] Human security was driven by a gap in security literature and practice that focused on security of the state and military efforts, which was common in traditional conceptions of international relations (a focus of critique for feminist international relations scholars). Human security also broadened the scope of issues which could be considered security (including non-military threats).[11] Hudson linked this increasing focus on human rights and human security more generally in the UN to a "bandwagoning" mechanism to see security from a gender perspective.[12] Proponents of the women, peace and security agenda utilized the rise of human security considerations to advance their demand for a "broader securitization of politics in general."[13] This focus on human security also allowed nontraditional concerns of the UN Security Council that related to women to be brought forward.[14] Increased global attention on human security provided an entry point for women and the women's rights agenda to become further considered in relation to security through its own "bandwagoning" and securitization at the UN.

This simultaneous emphasis on women's rights, security and protection and human security in the 1990s, alongside an active grassroots network, eventually led to UNSCR 1325, considered by many to be a global landmark resolution on women, peace and security. Hudson noted:

[UN]SCR 1325 outlines several explicit ways that the participation and protection of women further the goal of international peace and security. In other words, the resolution prioritizes women's rights by highlighting their (assumed positive) impact on durable peace and security [...]. Thus, the aim of [UN]SCR 1325 is to develop "effective institutional arrangements to guarantee their protection and full participation in the peace process" so that they "can significantly contribute to the maintenance and promotion of international peace and security."[15]

Through UNSCR 1325, global actors were encouraged to adopt a specific gender perspective when negotiating and implementing peace agreements: "Measures that ensure the protection of and respect for human rights of women and girls, particularly as they relate to the constitution, the electoral system, the police and the judiciary,"[16] suggesting early links to security actors such as the police.

UNSCR 1325 was the first UNSCR that recognized women as "agents in building peace and security."[17] Furthermore, it emphasized three key themes: women's participation in conflict prevention and resolution initiatives at country, regional and international levels; the protection of women; and finally, for the UN to adopt a gender perspective in its "peace operations, negotiations and agreements."[18] Inherent in UNSCR 1325 was the need to focus on "practical implementation" of women's roles and concerns in "armed conflict and security," thereby keeping it a "living document."[19] Hudson, too, noted why UNSCR 1325 was a useful starting point for this research on women and counterterrorism: "The world's largest international organization has now publicly declared that attention to women and gender is integral to 'doing security.'"[20] Furthermore, "ideas formed within and among UN officials change discourse, shape institutional development, and even influence state interests,"[21] and subsequently proved to be important in several US efforts. These were important and significant steps to advancing the discourses and practices of women in contemporary security. Yet, the resolution itself was flawed and still fell short post-2001, where terrorism and non-state actors offered a distinct departure from the circumstances present in the 1990s that shaped and led up to it. Furthermore, it was increasingly state actors such as the US or international coalitions that were supporting post-conflict security post-9/11 in environments like Afghanistan and Iraq, not traditional peacekeeping forces. It was also state institutions such as the US

Department of Defense (DoD), US State and the US Agency for International Development (USAID) that were increasingly implementing this from a national perspective. Furthermore, it was also non-state actors such as terrorist organizations that were increasingly the focus of US foreign policy concerns related to security.

This resolution has been heavily critiqued and itself remains flawed, making it a problematic base from which to extend to women and counterterrorism. For example, Hudson emphasized that UNSCR 1325 relied on "the utilitarian assumption that these issues [human security and women's security] need to be addressed because they are essential elements to establishing international peace and security."This justification had been debated by scholars who "have made a practice out of securitizing issues that are not conventionally seen as such."[22] Furthermore, UNSCR 1325 appeared to in fact securitize women's concerns through contemporary security issues in order to advance them in the international agenda, or in fact be securitized by women themselves to advance their own interests.[23] Pratt has noted that some women "choose to use this essentialized identity to leverage themselves into [security] spaces historically dominated by men," demonstrating a variety of approaches used to advance women's concerns in relation to security. This became particularly problematic after 9/11 as similar strategies appeared utilized in national efforts, with controversial results. Sjoberg and Gentry have highlighted how human security discourses may appear to become a "protection racket" actually putting citizens at risk instead of protecting them.[24] This has particular pertinence to this book, as there has also been growing considerations of human security (and its components) as a tool to fight terrorism and violent extremism.[25]

Women were also associated with "those in need of protection" in UNSCR 1325, which negatively impacted their perceived agency in relation to security as empowered, security-relevant actors, and therefore in relation to counterterrorism more specifically.[26] Furthermore, UNSCR 1325 did not provide explicit guidance for how diverse actors could involve women further into security-relevant institutions themselves, or in security practices and decision-making so that they could directly participate in contributing to security (a task which was delegated to the state level to adapt to their own context as appropriate).

It was also not evident what specific operational benefits women's inclusion in security would bring, making its relevance to policymakers and practitioners obscure. This raised the question of why policymakers and practitioners would be motivated to emphasize women's inclusion or participation without this. Furthermore, the UN itself did not enforce such efforts in practice, often resulting in "tokenism" whereby "the central problem of bridging security and development with a gender-sensitive understanding of security is not addressed."[27] Tickner noted the impacts of UNSCR 1325 have been "somewhat disappointing in terms of its impact on the international policy community," even as it "provided an important framework for feminists and women activists seeking to bridge the policy/activist/academic divide."[28] This suggested there was something missing in this equation; clearly, the framework was not speaking to the policy community or practitioners, those who guide policy in the government and implement security on the ground. Neither was it demonstrating its relevance to the practice of contemporary international security, and therefore it was not generating the momentum required post-9/11 as counterterrorism moved to the forefront of global security concerns.

Highlighting the importance of women's inclusion also did not equal commitment or response by the national actors highlighted above. The Boston Consortium on Gender, Security and Human Rights captures this well, noting that a focus on women's rights and gender equality as situated in a "human rights frame or even a moral frame" was "simply not as effective in generating awareness, response and commitment."[29] It noted of UNSCR 1325:

> The idea is that *security needs women, as much as women need security*. The security language serves as a framework for action through discursive positioning that situates women as central, or at least part of, the security agenda. This frame highlights how women's rights and gender equality can contribute to international peace and security, and therefore constitute vested interest for many national and international leaders.[30] [emphasis added]

This statement suggested that for governments around the world, women's rights and gender equality directly contributed to security. However, it was not clear what this meant in practice, and the link remained ill-defined. The UN Security Council itself cited "efforts [to increase women's role in global security] have lacked coordination and have been hampered by the lack of measurable results."[31] Baldwin has referred to traditional notions of military statecraft: "Paradoxical as it may seem, security has not been an important analytical concept for most security studies scholars;"[32] Blanchard echoed that this was "particularly true from the perspective of feminist security theory,"[33] as well as those, according to Axworthy, advocating human security.[34] That is, the traditional notions and practices of security related to the military were neglected in UNSCR 1325 and by some of those advancing the women, peace and security agenda, helping explain why it did not resonate as strongly in post-9/11 practices that became dominated by the DoD and wars in Afghanistan and Iraq.

While gender equality at the UN, and increasingly in foreign policies and international institutions, was becoming more visible, "ideal" gendered notions of women persisted in these institutions and indeed in contexts of women's engagement in violent conflicts.[35] This suggested a gap between the perceived and actual roles of women in providing security, as well as in their potential roles in violence as well. The language used in UNSCR 1325 was also limited to UN roles such as "military observers, civilian police, human rights and humanitarian personnel,"[36] but did not explicitly expand to key roles that would come to dominate in counterterrorism at the national level, such as counterterrorism-specific units, or other military actors. As such, the scope of security practices encompassed by UNSCR 1325 remained limited in, and even irrelevant to, contemporary counterterrorism practices. This point is emphasized by Ní Aoláin, who critiqued recent efforts to broaden UNSCR 1325 to counterterrorism efforts, which she argued may in fact cause greater gender insecurity and essentialism to women's status. She stated efforts by women, peace and security actors around 2015 to bring women further into the counterterrorism domain "does not mean that women will be included in widening what constitutes terrorism and what counterterrorism strategies are compliant with human rights and equality, or that all the harms inflicted on women as a result of terrorism and counterterrorism strategies will be addressed even-handedly."[37] While this is an important critique of UNSCR 1325, it still emphasized women's rights and victimhood in relation to terrorism and counterterrorism, and demonstrated that these considerations remain relatively new.[38] Other critiques include a lack of emphasis on gender and intersecting social categories, which impacted on how women's agency was perceived in the years following,[39] and the postcolonial salience of such narratives.[40]

## UNSCR 1325 and the GWOT

We will now discuss academic critiques of how UNSCR 1325 has been utilized in the GWOT since 2001. Pratt observed that in the GWOT, UNSCR 1325 itself has been "weaponized," and that many feminist have themselves become complicit within this trope.[41] Specifically, Pratt argues that UNSCR 1325 works "in tandem with dominant security practices and discourses in the post-9/11 moment, normalizing the violence of counterterrorism and counterinsurgency measures."[42] That is, instead of pushing back against this political violence, which has been a strong theme in women, peace and security literature historically, these scholars have now in fact normalized or legitimized these state practices. Perspectives of female vulnerability, victimhood, and inherent peacefulness that have already been problematically highlighted in relation to UNSCR 1325 have also often been viewed as excluded from the post-9/11 world. Yet, as Huckerby argues, because of the proliferation of soft or indirect counterterrorism practices that became increasingly visible post-9/11 these also "mobilized and reinforced such gendered images of vulnerability, innocence and care."[43] Furthermore, according to Huckerby, there have been an increasing number of ways in which the women, peace and security agenda has intersected with national security discourses post-9/11. This has been prompted in part because of the perceived relationship between conflict and terrorism. Here, women's rights issues, women as peacemakers, and the promotion of women's participation in all aspects of public and private life that became so visible in the women, peace and security agenda in relation to conflict pre-9/11, also thus began incorporating these concerns into counterterrorism responses and considerations post-9/11.[44] Though a more positive perspective, Cohn has noted that UNSCR 1325 has been used as an "organizing tool" by women's nongovernmental organizations (NGOs) in conflict zones to participate in "peace-making and political decision-making more generally" or "as a lever for attaining political access and influence with their own local and national governments."[45] Yet, these perspectives still neglect women in the actual policies and practice of security, and do not interrogate specific institutional utilization of UNSCR 1325 in counterterrorism. In the United States, UNSCR 1325 has been a foundational resolution of the National Action Plan (NAP) on Women, Peace and Security, and in some agency-level counterterrorism-linked discourses. However, its inherent flaws have made it a problematic platform to advance women in contemporary counterterrorism efforts, including those explored throughout this book.

While UNSCR 1325 provided a framework where "women's experience of conflict and their ability to prevent or end it could be substantially transformed,"[46] there has been a lack of analytical, critical, qualitative analysis of how this emerged in counterterrorism discourses and practices post-9/11. The women, peace and security trajectory offered incomplete understandings of how women become considered and integrated in practical terms, and neglected how women themselves could be security threats. This also impacted upon the roles perceived for women in various contexts: from militarized approaches to counterterrorism, or prevention approaches in the community (that is, countering violent extremism [CVE]). Indeed, the "weak" language used in UNSCR 1325 was suggested to have been one reason it was largely rejected by the military,[47] which proves vital when considering they have been a primary tool for hard counterterrorism efforts.

In short, while the UN laid important groundwork for the inclusion and expansion of women in the global security agenda, there was still a distinct gap in how this evolved in everyday security practices, particularly in the field of counterterrorism post-9/11.[48] Works by Perera and Razack also highlight how much of the scholarly research on the GWOT since has neglected the voices of indigenous women and women of color,[49] which has particular implications for how women in countries like Afghanistan or Yemen may be considered in or experience counterterrorism. Furthermore, it appeared that in global policy discourses related to women and security at the UN, securitization of women in various forms was utilized to get women and their concerns practically involved in the security agenda (albeit in unconvincing ways), which remained relevant to debates that later emerged in relation to US counterterrorism.

*FSS: Finding women in contemporary security*

While FSS itself remains a relatively young field, it has developed from rich feminist scholarship on international relations.[50] This section will highlight how key themes in FSS inform this book's research, includ- ing: dichotomous thinking in relation to feminine and masculine roles in security; gendered assumptions of security; and considering where/ how women become visible in security practice. It will expand FSS into the neglected field of counterterrorism, moving from theory to empir- ical case studies and policy relevance. However, as will be revealed in the following discussion, while FSS formed around a critique of gender structures in security, the significant question relevant to this book is whether FSS can still inform the question of women in relation to security policy. While some in FSS call for engagement with policy, others reject this notion, highlighting a tension in the field. This book demonstrates that it is crucial for this field to engage in the policy and practice of security, and particularly that of counterterrorism.

Foundational feminist international relations figures such as Cynthia Enloe critically asked, "where are the women?"[51] and challenged the perceived notion that women were not present in international rela- tions. She interrogated notions that women and gender were not found in traditional high security (that is, national security issues such as the military and diplomacy), and called into question these notions by examining the "ordinary," such as women's peace movements.[52] Enloe has noted that "as the salience of women's rights increases, so does the salience of women's gender,"[53] emphasizing the continual flux of gender and gendered relations to policy issues discussed in this book. Cohn considered how men and women are positioned in security discourses, and how this lends to how they are implicated in and constituted through these discourses.[54] Stiehm, meanwhile, pointed out how women were often denied roles as "societal protectors" by the state, and are often instead deemed "the protected,"[55] suggesting there exists some early (though limited) interrogations of both discourse and practice of security in relation to women. Tickner has argued that, aside from notable examples like Enloe and Cohn, much of the early research into gender and international relations avoided national security issues.[56] These early figures rejected realist approaches to security, instead combining "[a]n interrogation of the abstractions of strategic discourse, an awareness of the connection between women's everyday experience and security, a critique of the state, and the recognition of the effects of structural violence with a strong normative and transformative vision, evidenced by its focus on inequality and emancipation."[57]

Feminist interrogations of the international have also often viewed gendered relations on a spectrum where stereotyped "female" traits (passive, private) are considered in opposition to "male" traits (powerful, public), and where feminists attempt to challenge and destabilize these binaries. They have noted that gender discourses "regulate global politics: in interstate relations, international development and international security,"[58] and highlight how feminists look for women (biological or "female bodies"), gender ("characterizations of traits assigned on the basis of perceived membership in sex groups") and genderings ("application of perceived gender tropes to social and political analyses") in global politics.[59] Such foundational themes remain critical for interrogating "women," "gender" and "gendering" in counterterrorism, but have not yet adequately extended to national or agency levels of analysis, as has been seen in policy and practice.

These feminist international relations scholars have often interrogated women in relation to war, conflict and the military. Tickner has suggested that feminists focus on "what goes on during war and on individuals, both civilian and military, and how their lives are affected by conflict,"[60] while Shepherd noted how these issues have "gained recognition in policy circles."[61] Furthermore, feminist international relations scholars emphasized women's "wartime roles as victims, protesters, promoters, and participants,"[62] or women as peace-builders and leaders of social movements.[63] Sjoberg and Gentry highlighted that while gender was increasingly recognized in military situations at domestic, national and international levels of political analysis, "womanhood is more recognized rather than more integrated in these situations,"[64] suggesting a gap between considerations of "women" and practice. Furthermore, for women who entered these masculine institutions, they were often expected to adopt masculine values, despite their womanhood.[65] Security policy has proven important to interrogate, and rather imperatively for Tickner, "feminists have claimed that the way we frame policies about national security and the language used in formulating them is important in legitimating certain policies and delegitimizing others."[66] These insights, which extend to counterterrorism, prove useful for considering how "women" or feminist traits may gain policy salience, and how women's or gendered roles and expectations are inherent within these. Yet, there has still been little empirical research in this field in relation to contemporary security concerns such as counterterrorism.

Emerging in the early 2000s, FSS, according to Wibben and Stern, was located at "the crossroads of security studies, feminist international relations and feminist theory" while challenging international relations and security study notions to "add gender and stir."[67] Sjoberg, Cooke and Neal demonstrated how a gender analysis in global politics transforms ways of "being and knowing," power relations and understanding international processes, as well as the consequences of women's "unequal social positions."[68] Blanchard highlighted how feminist security theory has made four key theoretical contributions: first, feminists "question the supposed nonexistence and irrelevance of women in international security politics;" second, it "questions the extent to which women are secured by state 'protection' in times of war and peace;" third, it "contests discourses wherein women are linked unreflectively with peace;" and fourthly, "feminists have troubled the assumption that gendered security practices address only women and have started to develop a variegated concept of masculinity to help explain security."[69] Such points prove useful for this book, which demonstrates how and where women became viewed as relevant to counterterrorism, and interrogates the spaces between "war" and "peace" where counterterrorism often lies.

Sjoberg expanded three additional tenets of FSS: (1) "what counts as a security issue, and to whom the concepts of security should be applied;" (2) "an understanding of the gendered nature of the values prized in the realm of international security," which "influences how scholars and policy-makers frame and interpret issues of national security;" and (3) how gender plays out in "theory and practice of international security." She identified three ways this happens: first "conceptually, for understanding international security;" second, "in analyzing causes and predicting outcomes;" and third, in "thinking about solutions and promoting positive change in the security realm."[70] It is evident from the points above that FSS offers a rich lens by which to interrogate and critique how "women" may emerge specifically in counterterrorism discourses and practices, and how this is understood to contribute to counterterrorism for this book. It also provides a strong theoretical base to extend from and demonstrate women's relevance to counterterrorism. However, as will be expanded on below, in Blanchard and Sjoberg's assesssments of the contributions of FSS, a tension of sorts becomes visible—namely, that between the more theoretical and conceptual contributions of FSS, and those of a more policy-oriented nature.

### Constructing gender in the GWOT

These gendered assumptions in security became visible in the GWOT, as will be further elaborated on throughout the book. For example, Shepherd interrogated constructions of gender in the discourses of President Bush, and emphasized that "hard" military efforts taken in Afghanistan had to be framed alongside "soft" humanitarian efforts (which are feminized). This "feminization" of intervention efforts impacted negatively upon female soldiers and "worked to diminish their symbolic power as a militarized security force."[71]

Tickner noted four relatively unexplored lessons in relation to gender which emerged out of 9/11 yet are relevant to analysis of counterterrorism. First, in times of war, new definitions of both masculinity and femininity may find new space. Second, "women bear the burden of religion and culture" and the West has only exasperated this by focusing on "the place of women in its depiction of Islam as repressive and backward." Third, she encouraged "gender-sensitive conceptions of development, security and peace." Fourth, "women's gains from war may not last," such as efforts focused on women's rights in Afghanistan,[72] which can also be assessed in efforts prompted by counterterrorism-linked aims and interests. Tickner also helpfully highlighted how the GWOT is viewed as a "new kind of war" against a terror network, and asks "if there are other, more gendered ways in which this war is unlike the other wars Americans fought in the twentieth century?" Furthermore, Tickner highlighted how gender relations have become a key point of distinction between the West and groups like al-Qaeda (shaped as cultural and religious differences), and asks whether 9/11 reflects "a globalization of gender politics, a clash of gendered orders usually hidden by the normalizing practices of unequal societies?"[73] She has also pointed out that "feminists have been ambivalent about women as war-fighters—whether they should join men's wars in the name of equality or resist them in the name of women's special relationship with peace."[74]

This research posits that counterterrorism policies and practices themselves represent one key aspect of this "new kind of war," while recognizing previous interrogations of gender and gender relations in the GWOT. It also considers how women as "war fighters" (in both direct and indirect efforts) become visible, and suggests the importance of understanding how and why the discourses and practices related to these have evolved since 9/11.

As will be discussed further in the following section, there are some in FSS, such as Blanchard and Wibben, who appear to place more emphasis on the theoretical components of this field, considering aspects such as gender structures and gender relations in terms of security, while others, such as Sjoberg and Tickner, highlight the more policy-oriented aims of the field. While this research acknowledges these tensions, it will speak directly to where women are in relation to counterterrorism discourses and practices (and not the gender relations within these) and highlight the importance of doing so.

## FSS and the question of policy engagement

As highlighted in the previous section, FSS reveals gendered structures and discourses; for example, assumptions relating to women and peace, or women and violence, or assumptions relating to the roles of mothers in security practices (see counterterrorism policies discussed below). Alongside this increased work in FSS, a number of scholars, policymakers and international organizations (as highlighted with the UN and UNSCR 1325 above) are increasingly calling for greater roles for, and considerations of, women in security. However, the relationship between theorizing women's roles in relation to security and how this interacts with the policy world remains unclear and a topic of debate. While there is evidence of some focus on policy and practice in FSS, this increasingly prevalent policy orientation also reveals a "tension" within the field. On the one hand, there is a focus on the critique of gender structures and relations in security; on the other is a focus on engaging those very structures (particularly the policy and practice components of these).

Some dimensions of this debate were first explored by Sylvester, specifically the shift from research that emphasized women in relation to peace, to more security-focused interrogations of women and war in international relations. Feminism, she highlights, has "traditionally associated itself with peace and nonviolence," whereas war has not historically been seen as a feminist topic in international relations (except when positioned in "opposition mode"). She notes: "feminism has positioned itself outside war, above it, and in ethical belligerence to it, despite also expressing commitment to gender- and women-inclusive research." However, referencing authors such as Sjoberg and Gentry (2007), and Parashar (2009), amongst others, she challenges a "new generation of feminist security thinking," which is "exposing the tensions around studying war by bringing once-neglected women into security research: women who participate in the political violence of war." These actions of "war women comprise a differentiated politics that some feminist security work now investigates in the spirit of bringing all manner of gender politics and women into the study of international relations."[75] That is, there was an increased emphasis on considering women not just in traditional opposition to war, but as actors in various dimensions of war themselves.

This tension becomes more visible when emphasizing how the study of women plays out in relation to theoretical versus more policy-oriented focus in this field. This is highlighted in a 2011 special edition of *Politics and Gender*, for example, which raised questions such as: "What is the relationship between theory and practice in Feminist Security Studies?"[76] This edition notes how some authors in this field emphasize "'Feminist Security' Studies" while "others emphasize Feminist 'Security Studies.'"[77] Here Tickner, who has spent much time and effort challenging traditional notions of "security," highlights "the importance of efforts to connect scholars and practitioners," particularly those extending from UNSCR 1325. She highlights that as far back as a 2002 conference in New York, "policymakers and activists at the conference emphasized the need for more scholarly research on the implications and implementation of 1325," offering a nod to more research focusing on the resultant policy and practice that extended from UNSCR 1325, namely the inclusion of "women." Tickner further notes: "It is vitally important that we support the work of those in the policy and activist communities who are trying to get feminist issues onto the security agenda of states and international organizations. It is often a frustrating and uphill battle."[78] However, this appears to be resisted by academics such as Wibben who believe that by drawing FSS into the security studies field more broadly risks "the securitization of ever more issues while relinquishing input into addressing them." Instead, she proposes locating FSS "in the borderlands of security studies, so that our discussions can remain embedded in feminist debates within and outside of feminist [international relations]."[79] Yet she also calls for "feminists' long-standing engagement with issues of peace, war, and violence to make an impact on the field of security studies."[80]

This tension is also highlighted in a 2009 special edition of *Security Studies*, which brings to light some important insights for this book.[81] For example, Sjoberg notes the "growing influence of feminist thought and practice in the policy world;" this was seen with UNSCR 1325 and other international institutions which demonstrate "gender is a salient concern in global governance."[82] Also, citing international phenomena like female suicide bombers, women as soldiers and sexual violence in conflict, Sjoberg notes these "show not only women's significance in international security, but also the relevance of gender as a factor in understanding and addressing security matters." Gender sensitivity, too, has shown growing importance for practitioners who focus on areas such as "protecting non-combatants in times of war" or the "study of management of refugees."[83] Feminist scholars are increasingly influencing policy and practice in the international policy realm, and gender is a growing topic of concern for international actors working in zones of conflict.

However, the ways in which diverse feminist scholars approach the various aspects of international relations through different perspectives—whether their theoretical position (liberal, realist, critical, etc.), or their causational versus constitutive arguments[84]—also has implications for their awareness and emphasis on more theoretical or policy-oriented research and findings. Here, "these perspectives yield different, and sometimes contradictory, insights about and predictions for global politics;" for example, liberal feminists may call attention to "the subordinate position of women in global politics" and argue that "gender oppression can be remedied by including women in the existing structures of global politics."[85] However, this could be contrasted against critical feminists who may explore "the ideational and material manifestations of gendered identity and gendered power in world politics."[86] In FSS, the author's own approach to international relations highlights where the emphasis will fall—whether on theoretical or policy orientation.

This book places emphasis on demonstrating how the increased inclusion and consideration of women in these security structures has had very real and evident implications for how women feature in global politics. In other words, this research will highlight, through the case of the US, why the inclusion of, and emphasis on, women in counterterrorism was viewed as important for these counterterrorism policies and practices, and why this has occurred. That is, how women's roles and inclusion in counterterrorism has been understood to serve a specific function and cause a specific outcome. Furthermore, while acknowledging such tensions in the field between theoretical-focused and policy-oriented aims, this book's aim is not to resolve such tensions, but to utilize the case of the US to specifically ask: where are the women in security discourses and practices, particularly in counterterrorism? It also aims to highlight the importance of policy orientation, and engagement with the actors and institutions who operate in this space, to inform this question. This the case study of the US to specifically ask: where are the women in security discourses and practices, particularly counterterrorism? It also aims to highlight the importance of policy orientation, and engagement with the actors and institutions who operate in this space, to inform this question. This section will highlight that there remains a lack of empirical investigation into key areas critical to FSS, such as counterterrorism, the various institutions which are increasingly contributing to counterterrorism efforts, and a closer interrogation of their policies and practices, and highlight the importance of honing in more actively on these areas.

Counterterrorism offers an imperative new area not yet adequately considered by FSS. Furthermore, though the wars in Iraq and Afghanistan offer traditional war and insurgency cases to analyze through a feminist lens, an increasing number of countries are not "at war", yet have still been primary to counterterrorism concerns (Yemen being a key example). Counterterrorism practices themselves may create new forms of (in)security, but the factors that may be considered within these (interagency influences or the actions of terrorist groups, for example) are not always clear. Furthermore, assessing how institutions themselves have distinct histories and experience unique trajectories related to how women are engaged (or not) isn't adequately considered in relation to counterterrorism. There also remain gaps related to women in relation to "military hardware and weaponry" and the relationship between war, gender and technology; the rise of AI [artificial intelligence] in military operations and planning; science and war; information technology and enabled networks which this book may help inform.[87] Crucial aspects of counterterrorism, which have increasingly expanded to include drones and cyber efforts (such as managing ISIS propaganda), have furthermore been neglected. This suggests that tools and approaches critical to contemporary counterterrorism have largely been neglectful of how women and gender may be relevant to these. Blanchard too emphasized:

> The vital, often gendered, negotiation of cultural relations between the West and Islam and the effects of state antiterror campaigns on civilians are problems that military campaigns in Afghanistan or Iraq are not designed to address and traditional non-feminist theories of IR [international relations] are not entirely equipped to handle. The US-led global war on terror seems to exemplify the type of gendered, multilevel insecurity that IR feminists have raised to our critical attention.[88]

Blanchard posits that FSS is well-positioned to address the post-9/11 challenges that have arisen. However, and in support of this research, she also notes that "[i]ronically, the policy world of nation-states has recently begun to outpace the academic discipline of IR in its acceptance of feminist issues." Referencing UNSCR 1325, she stated this was a "watershed that should provide those interested in gender and security with many new research opportunities to study the ways the incorporation of a gender perspective and female participation affect peacekeeping and the security of women and men."[89]

While evidently noting the increasing importance of policy to this field, this further step was not sufficiently taken. These early leaders in FSS focused largely on international relations critiques related to concepts of war, power and the military. However, as approaches to counterterrorism have evolved, drawing on military, governance, diplomacy, development and community efforts (both direct and indirect), a chasm has emerged from this original work that neglects new and specialized or niche counterterrorism efforts. While sporadically visible, engagement with practitioners and policymakers in the field of security are not yet sufficient, and can miss out on the discursive, operational or agency-specific factors which may inform why some discourses and practices emerge in relation to women while others are repressed. It further gives the impressions of academic apathy to the often unique, complex and sometime dangerous experiences, tensions and challenges faced by agencies and their personnel, which limits the impact and resonance of research in policy and practice.

Wibben notes that future FSS needs to "engage with and debate the merits of the scholarship of all who have been conducting research along a multidimensional continuum of violence, spanning peace and war, as well as domestic and international realms, regardless of their disciplinary home."[90] This book opens a new conversation about counterterrorism and the domestic–international, multi-agency approaches considered within these; it also draws upon women, peace and security, and terrorism studies.

There are hopeful signs that these deficits are being increasingly recognized, though this development has been recent and sporadic. Sjoberg has questioned the accessibility of FSS and "our potential responsibility to include policy analysis in our work" even while she states it is the purpose of FSS to "raise problems, not to solve them."[91] However, this appears to contradict her assertion that it is not the role of FSS to outline "problems that need to be solved or divides that need to be crossed, healed or closed."[92] Tickner most pointedly noted, "it is important that [FSS] speak with (and to) the policy world."[93] While there proves to be some debate in FSS as to whether to engage more in policy-relevant research, this book starts from the position that this engagement is essential. If indeed FSS has a "responsibility" to include policy analysis, then this book provides an important contribution by engaging directly with those shaping and implementing these policies. How can FSS expect to make an impact on security practice or policy when it does not engage with the very actors and agencies responsible for security practices?

There has been some growing analysis of how women have become engaged as counterterrorism actors/agents, particularly in Afghanistan and Iraq. Some early works called for the US to "pay particular attention to women when attempting to counteract terrorism and encourage more peaceful and democratic political systems in Afghanistan and through the world."[94] Development efforts have also at times been viewed as a means to "counterbalance [the US's] image as a country that funds violence by supplying military arms, it would also address some of the root causes of terrorism" in regions such as the Middle East.[95] Pratt has noted that in this "post-9/11 moment, Muslim women are being targeted by Western governments as agents of counterinsurgency/counterterrorism,"[96] though this was expanded upon minimally. Gender has also been identified in post-9/11 identity conflicts.[97]

Encouragingly, there has been an increasing interrogation by feminist authors into specific security practices that the US has carried out following 9/11. This has largely considered women in the military as soldiers,[98] "deviant" examples like that of the female soldiers in Abu Ghraib in Iraq,[99] or gendered considerations of counterinsurgency,[100] and specifically FETs in Afghanistan,[101] all of which are discussed in more detail in this book. Yet, specific units related to counterterrorism trained by the US, such as Yemen's elite female counterterrorism unit, or early programs such as the Daughters of Iraq or Sisters of Fallujah programs, have not been assessed in a more comprehensive, chronological fashion since 9/11. This work offers important insights, but neglects the larger picture that has been developing since 9/11 which so significantly impacted how and why these new units were established. This also remains woefully neglectful of post-2014 efforts to combat ISIS.

Furthermore, noting the growing importance of gender in the policy world, and the political agendas of state governments, the UN and other international institutions, Tickner and Sjoberg note, "how to impact both the policy world and the discipline of IR [international relations] remain challenging questions." They discuss two missions which have become apparent for gender in international relations: "to rewrite [international relations], and to provide advice, guidance, reformulation, and restructuring in the policy field."[102] They highlight four key impediments to this: first, "doing policy relevant work within the constraints of the structures and ideas of global politics, as currently constituted." Second is in "convincing the policy world that gender issues are important, a painstaking task that often must be done by arguing that gender analysis will make policymakers and bureaucrats better able to perform a wide range of policy tasks, rather than arguing that gender analysis is valuable independently, in and of itself." Third is in ensuring feminist work is both "intellectually accessible and normatively compelling." Finally, "feminists need to understand more about how the policy world (both in its formal and informal structures) works in order to communicate with and transform that world,"[103] suggesting that, over time, figures like Sjoberg increasingly recognized the importance of considering the policy world.

These points are crucial for this book. Feminist international relations and subsequent FSS literature have only recently started to engage/frame their relevance to security policy. This book locates women in counterterrorism discourses and practices, and draws on policymakers themselves to highlight and inform these, thus bridging the gap between theory and practice. This book aims to be both intellectually accessible and normatively compelling, and brings to FSS policy-informed work with key figures in these practices to clarify further research. Furthermore, though FSS appear to interact to an extent with terrorism studies, terrorism studies has thus far largely not engaged with the FSS literature, despite the fact analysis of women in relation to security practices and as terrorist actors can interact and inform each other. This book posits that to positively impact these agencies and practices, they (and relevant fields like terrorism studies) must be better engaged and interrogated by FSS. This section also highlighted a tension in FSS between more policy-responsive approaches and those focused on more theoretical debate and critique. This research disputes this notion, and asserts that unless the challenges that policymakers and practitioners face in relation to security (particularly terrorism) are better understood, then FSS will not find a common dialect with, or impact upon, the policy world. Furthermore, if FSS hopes to contribute to aspects of empowerment, emancipation and broader social justice,[104] then it must begin to bridge this academic policy gap, even if this remains a single aspect of FSS more broadly.

## Women and counterterrorism: Beyond FSS

There has only very recently been an increase in scholarship which examines women in direct relation to counterterrorism, and what is available is often based in the field of law and human rights. Most notably, this scholarship has often highlighted how the legal and institutional spaces in which security is defined and developed has often neglected women, or produced inadequate, contemporary feminist responses. For example, Huckerby has stated that feminist legal analyses and feminist international law have generally fallen short post-9/11. This is particularly true in the examination of holistic approaches to counterterrorism and including 'soft' (often CVE) efforts and its "impacts on the development and implementation of international law on gender equality."[105] This is further the case with analyses of how gender features more broadly in international law responses to terrorism.[106] Ní Aoláin notes that female scholars too have "generally not articulated a feminist perspective on the ways in which states respond to violent challengers," which also extends to legal responses to terrorism.[107] Furthermore, women remain "marginal to the conversations in which definitions of security are agreed upon and generally peripheral to the institutional settings in which security frameworks are implemented as policy and law,"[108] which extends to counterterrorism. When considering legal and practical understandings of how women fit into this picture, "[t]he legal quandaries that result from the use of law as a management tool to address terrorism [have] not generally garnered a feminist response."[109] Crenshaw also highlighted how as the "threat of terrorism changes, so too does jurisdiction,"[110] and how women are considered in relation to terrorism thus has direct implications for how, and by which institution, it is addressed.

So, while it appears there has been a greater interest in demonstrating that women are relevant to security, and that they can indeed be violent/terrorist actors, their roles in the specific processes to counter these has received comparably less academic scrutiny. Indeed, numerous authors have lamented that counterterrorism "is where the gender analysis has been especially lacking" and attempted to start filling this gap by considering gender "perspectives", "apparatuses and techniques in counterterrorism measures," and "silences, erasures and voids" in accounts of counterterrorism.[111] In wider and continuing debates over what terrorism is and how it should be responded to, women have generally lacked influence or consideration. For example, women do not typically "occupy governmental positions with authority over terrorism policymaking."[112] This generally includes three relevant departments. First, the defense department or ministry which would "manage the military as related to terrorism." Second, a state department which would be responsible for "diplomacy and foreign policy related to terrorism." And lastly, "interior ministries which deal with policing and immigration as related to terrorism." Women are instead generally more reflected in ministries that are considered feminine (for instance, family, culture, education and social services) rather than masculine (such as defense, the economy, finance, security and agriculture).[113] This also reflects on the acceptance (or lack thereof) of their roles in relation to the practices by which counterterrorism often functions, and is useful for assessing how this informs analysis of women in counterterrorism in DoD, US State and USAID. That is, when fields viewed as traditionally "feminine" (such as education, or which focus on the family) become increasingly linked to indirect counterterrorism efforts, then women may appear to be more readily accepted in this space, albeit in limited circumstances or proscribed roles. However, when they take up arms on the front lines of combat, or define national security strategies, this is more likely to be resisted.

Early work by Cunningham identified six deficits in how counterterrorism specialists "anticipate, respond to, and interact with female militants,"[114] yet did not assess how women were considered as counterterrorism specialists in fields like CVE, which have evolved since. Other work in the field has considered female politicians formulating counterterrorism policy and public behavior (such as voting),[115] or has attempted to situate women more distinctly in counterterrorism discourses, whereas men have often been the most primary and visible referents in counterterrorism.[116] Most contemporary work encouraging women's consideration and inclusion in counterterrorism and CVE has in fact largely been driven or carried out by NGOs and think tanks (some of which contain academics).[117] Their work has largely emphasized women in CVE (highlighting how women are still most often highlighted in "preventing" rather than managing violence in society), and the bulk of this research has only come out since 2015, largely in response to ISIS. This work has increasingly considered country-specific case studies, and appears to be assisting in filling the gap in academic literature and bridging the policy-practitioner–researcher divide more consistently than current academics.[118] This book attempts to help bridge this further in the academic sphere.

There have been attempts to better categorize or analyze the framework by which women are considered in response to counterterrorism,[119] and suggest that in order to engage in and maneuver the field of counterterrorism policy itself, women policymakers might have to emphasize or enact different gendered frames to demonstrate agency.[120] This is a useful starting point to consider how women within these US agencies may themselves enact agency in different ways in relation to counterterrorism (for example, emphasizing their role as mothers or peacemakers to leverage influence). These authors argue for increased representation of women in "masculine" policy areas.[121] Yet, this research neglects to interrogate and emphasize how different institutions who support counterterrorism efforts themselves engage women, thereby highlighting a significant gap: namely that although women's agency is increasingly emphasized in relation to counterterrorism and even terrorism, there is inadequate assessment of how the institutions themselves conceive of this agency and how this is operationalized in practice.

In addition, there is a gap in how the framing of women by these institutions may influence how women themselves engage in or influence counterterrorism processes or practices. Gendered impacts of counterterrorism practices have also only sporadically been assessed, and only then in limited case studies considering aspects such as detention, collateral damage or rights abuses;[122] gendered dimensions and impacts of Islamophobia which may have a counterterrorism dimension;[123] or other forms of discrimination against women, including "overcorrection" of a gender focus in counterterrorism.[124] Herman has highlighted how "[t]he fact that counter-terrorism efforts seem to be premised on the assumption that terrorists are male can certainly undermine their effectiveness. Limiting the pool only to men leaves a significant gap in counterterrorism strategy." Furthermore, disproportionately profiling men may actually "lead to increased pressure on women to assume a more active role as a means of circumventing myopic anti-terrorism strategies,"[125] suggesting that by neglecting how women are understood in terrorist groups has very real implications for counterterrorism efficacy, and may too in fact be gendered.

The roles of women in US counterterrorism specifically has been interrogated to some degree in law. Indeed, a 2011 report by the NYU Center for Human Rights and Global Justice (of which Jayne Huckerby was the lead author) has proven to be one of the most comprehensive analyses of gender in US counterterrorism.[126] It focuses on bringing to light "gendering impacts" of US counterterrorism efforts (including on lesbian, gay, bisexual, transgender and intersex rights), and attempts to create a "gender framework" for counterterrorism. In so doing, it considers aspects such as development activities and CVE (focused on USAID); militarized counterterrorism; gender and anti-terrorism financing regimes; intelligence and law enforcement measures and cooperation (tactical counterterrorism); border securitization and immigration enforcement; and diplomacy and strategic communication in counterterrorism. It is practice-oriented, and has proscribed specific recommendations and tools for gender inclusion and assessment in counterterrorism practices. This report is an exceptional piece of work that drew off regional stakeholder workshops from numerous countries, as well as primary source interviews with government agencies such as DoD, US State, USAID and Department of Homeland Security, amongst others.

This quintessential piece of research can be used to inform or guide other case studies, or to extend analysis to other departments with a focus on counterterrorism. Indeed, there are several points from this report that will be drawn on throughout the course of this book. However, this book branches off from the report in several ways. First, this report still prioritizes interrogation of counterterrorism practices in terms of its gendered impacts, as driven by a human rights and legal perspective. While I acknowledge these, this book considers instead how women have been conceived of in the formation of discourses and practices of counterterrorism at the agency level, the factors that impact these, while also bringing in new and extensive perspectives of policymakers and practitioners. Second, much has happened since the report's 2011 publication, including the release of the US NAP on

Women, Peace and Security, and the emergence of ISIS (to name a few), each of which demand urgent attention. Third, this book expands on some of the specific cases discussed in the NYU Center for Human Rights and Global Justice report (such as Yemen, Iraq and Afghanistan). Since this report, there has been some sign that diverse agencies are being assessed in relation to counterterrorism. For example, Satterthwaite has interrogated USAID's development assistance in CVE, encouraging and proscribing specific gender tools or evaluations to better assess the gendered impacts of counterterrorism-related programming.[127] However, this remains an exception, and the extent to which other studies exist remains limited.

Country-specific case studies have also proved useful to inform this work. In the UK, several examples of research that interrogates domestic counterterrorism policy and practice has been carried out, focusing in particular on the Home Office's counter-extremism strategy Prevent and its attitude to women in the Muslim community.[128] Prevent proved to be particularly prolific and problematic for framing women in discourses and practices. Rashid highlighted some of the institutional thinking in this trajectory, noting that inclusion of women in community engagement efforts by the UK government had been notably neglected prior to Prevent. Due to recognition of these past failures in practice, institutions evolved in their community engagement and in their perceptions of women.[129] Women had been excluded from "talking about 'the real counter-terrorism side of things and the political side of things'," instead often only given a voice as "[v]ictims or survivors, who were prepared to disclose their personal stories," and diminished "the multiple roles that women have in communities" which may contribute directly to counterterrorism aims, or more complementary aspects such as integration.[130] Specific critiques related to gendered assumptions of women's agency in relation to security became visible, and women were "essentialized" as participants in "good—or liberal, modern, moderate, and empowering—Islam," or via their roles in the family (particularly their relationships with male relatives).[131] This suggested that institutions with different agendas (for instance security or integration) should be better at interacting in security efforts and in informing one another, and highlighted how framing in one policy area may inform/impact another.[132]

According to Brown, Muslim women are often seen as "the 'missing link'" in UK counterterrorism and counter-radicalization projects, yet "the gendered impact of securitization discourses in the U.K. is largely ignored by policy-makers and by academics."[133] Brown's work highlights the implications of flawed policies and problematic relations between the British government and the British Muslim community. Most scathingly, she noted, "the instrumental use of gender by government has had the impact of relegating Muslim women's political activism to a sideshow."[134] More broadly, the UK government demonstrated basic presumptions about Muslim women when they developed counter-radicalization policies, including believing they were disempowered in their communities, questioning their "loyalty to the U.K. state,"[135] and were often simply viewed in an "instrumental sense" as a means of access to "vulnerable men."[136] Allen and Guru also highlighted that in relation to women and mosques—which were presented as "politicized and problematized spaces" which simultaneously excluded women and allowed radicalism—the UK government was able to "find resonance between specific community issues and wider governmental policies: to rationalize and justify intervention."[137] Though focused on domestic practices within the UK, these suggest it is important to assess how competing agency-specific policy priorities may impact on how women become visible in counterterrorism, but also encourages closer interrogation at the agency-level to inform this further.

Rashid usefully assessed the impacts of diverse government policy alongside the counterterrorism policy trajectory, noting: "The association between initiatives to empower Muslim women and Prevent is only intelligible through an understanding of a wider policy trajectory in which an imagined, essentialized [/stereotyped] Muslim community is pathologized. This pathologization can be observed in the conflation of different policy concerns associated with Muslim communities." These included policy issues such as forced marriage, female genital mutilation, gendered violence and homophobia, which are frequently and problematically described as "cultural practices." Likewise, Muslim women's perceived absence from the political sphere becomes reduced to a simplistic notion of "cultural difference."[138] This suggests "conflation" of diverse policy issues (such as cultural issues or propensity for violence) has weakened the counter-frame of the practitioners trying to engage women, and highlights concerns about how, where and to what purpose policy areas can overlap when drawn on for shared aims.

This work provided a rich (albeit small) body of literature informing how women are conceived of in some government counterterrorism discourses and practices. Rashid's extensive analysis of UK government discourse has proven to be original, empirical and insightful in its findings.[139] Furthermore, in line with Brown, Rashid noted that in these discourses, "Muslim women are discursively produced within the wider policy landscape as in need of empowerment as victims of oppression. At the same time (some) Muslim women emerge as potential agents of change."[140] This book extends from such research to consider additional and more recent cases where women have been engaged in US counterterrorism efforts internationally to consider similar policy and practice questions.

*Women as militant and terrorist actors*

Despite the aforementioned aims and focus of this book, we cannot fully assess how women have been conceived of in US counterterrorism discourses and practices without finally considering how their roles in terrorism (particularly within al-Qaeda and ISIS) have been understood thus far. Needless to say, these groups were also gendered, with idealized roles for members espoused and enacted, and recruitment narratives targeted separately at men and women. Schmid points to the government as "the principal 'defining agency' that holds de facto 'definition power'" as to who a terrorist is and what constitutes a terrorist act.[141] Governments therefore also inform and influence how women are perceived in terrorist groups and in solutions to address them, and ideally these too should acknowledge and reflect gender dynamics within the organization. Furthermore, the neglect of women and gender dynamics in terrorism and related processes is increasingly posited alongside their lack of consideration in counter-efforts. Brown notes "very little of the analysis on radicalization considers women as potential radicals at all, nor are they considered to be impacted by state interventions in counter-terrorism."[142] Fink, Zeiger and Bhulai, meanwhile, emphasize that "ignoring women's active participation and agency in terrorism could result in unintended consequences in counterterrorism or CVE programs," or neglect areas such as intervention opportunities, deficits in analysis of push/pull factors[143] to recruitment and radicalization, criminal justice or practitioner strategies.[144] This section will demonstrate that though the study of women in political violence has been around for decades, there has only very recently been a growing focus on women as terrorist and violent actors (particularly in jihadist terrorism). In doing so, it highlights how this recognition has resonance with how women have been analyzed in counterterrorism practices.

It also posits that while both FSS and terrorism studies[145] focus on women in relation to security (including as threats), they rarely appear to interact, so that knowledge exchange and possible synergies are not yet optimized between these fields. This starting point assumes that women's engagement in counterterrorism is to some extent predicated and shaped by their roles in terror organizations (and vice versa). This assumption is in line with precedents within FSS, which noted women are often assessed in binary terms (violent/peaceful, strong/weak); this may then extend to agency considerations in their roles countering/participating in terrorism. Furthermore, there has been some acknowledgement by critical terrorism studies that feminist research can contribute to this literature, including justifications of counterterrorism policies (including wars in Afghanistan and Iraq), and how American and non-American women become represented in terrorism discourses.[146] This book will help to better assess how or if these evolutions of women's roles in jihadist terrorism have impacted upon women's roles in counterterrorism practices.

Terrorism has not been a tactic restricted to male actors; women too have long been engaged in terrorism and political violence, although to differing degrees dependent on the group, ideology, aim and context. Some core FSS themes—such as emphasizing women's agency, or assessing women in complex terms—also mirror assessments of women in terror groups. Indeed, many authors appear to ask where women are in relation to terrorism. Sjoberg highlighted how particular gendered stereotypes of women in terrorism are often framed in sexualized terms in relation to violence, "robbing them of agency and betraying a larger problem with our understandings of women's roles in politics and international relations."[147] However, "[w]omen are active in social movements, and overlooking them means scholarship neglects ways women are agentic as related to terrorism and political violence."[148] Furthermore, feminist interrogations of women in relation to terrorism are often inspired to some extent by "gender subordination in global politics,"[149] such as noting that women's agency in political violence is often denied to maintain "idealized notions" of women and femininity.[150] In other words, some of the same gendered stereotypes and practices that maintain gender inequality in international politics more broadly are also reflected and reinforced in analysis of terrorist organizations, thus limiting a full recognition of women's roles in all aspects of international politics.

This theme of locating women's agency in political violence is increasing in focus,[151] suggesting recognition of women's agency in this field may also impact their perceived agency in other aspects of global politics, including counterterrorism. Auchter asserted that "those who write on the topic of women and terrorism are driven by the desire to emancipate women by inscribing agency into their subjectivities," and that the "concept of agency remains largely unexplored, especially in terms of how agency frames the way scholars, journalists, and policy-makers view issues such as women and terrorism."[152] This point in particular supports the assertion that how women are assessed in terrorism can have clear counterterrorism policy implications. Violent women themselves also attempt to "write agency into themselves, to make themselves intelligible according to a framework of violence which will gain them entrance into the political community of those who are visible, intelligible and therefore agentive."[153] While women as violent actors are increasingly assessed in relation to their roles and agency, and how these are enacted or restricted, how these have also impacted or informed female actors in counterterrorism discourses and practices has not yet been adequately assessed.

Research on women in terrorist groups additionally tends to be based on secondary data and specific themes, such as portrayal in the media, group roles, motivation, recruitment and environmental enablers.[154] Women are often assessed in terms of male–female characteristics and their propensity to violence in order to identify how similar or different they are to men in practice. For example, research by Jacques and Taylor across diverse terror groups compared several traits, including male and female terrorists' age, immigration profile, employment, education, marital status and familial connections.[155] Bloom has noted that "women have overwhelmingly been portrayed as being motivated by emotion, or desire to seek revenge, whereas men tend to be portrayed by ideology, religion or nationalism." Yet, Bloom emphasized that "both men and women are motivated by many similar things, perhaps at different points in time."[156] This notion was confirmed by an anonymous senior Canadian security analyst, who noted "[w]omen are not motivated differently from men in terrorism."[157] Even when men and women are motivated by similar things, the opportunities for them to act may not occur in the same timeframe, or may be restricted or enabled by other factors, including the locus of counterterrorism efforts, the tactics, strategies and objectives of groups, or their ideological position (amongst others).

Several prominent themes remain visible in the study of female terrorists that inform this book. These include a lack of analysis by counterterrorism experts of women's motivations in terrorist organizations;[158] assessing women's violence and motivations as different from men's; women's emotional and ideological support within terror groups;[159] in terms of biological determinism,[160] or their distinct psychology or psychopathology.[161] Feminist scholars who analyze war often still focus on "masculine violence" in the international arena and its impact on women's lives and the protection of "women-and-children" (which may be viewed as a singular and indistinguishable category), but still neglect women's violence.[162] Women are also often viewed as dehumanized "weapons," where terrorist actors' use of them suggests a degree of desperation or of a last resort; similarly, their use can often be viewed as "fundamentally different to men's fighting."[163] As Sjoberg and Gentry have highlighted in relation to violent women (in contrast to "peaceful" women): "So long as a spectrum which limits women's capabilities exists, then women (and traits associated with femininity) will be less than men in society, even were they to achieve actual (rather than rising) equality in political, social and economic indicators."[164] Indeed, considering women's violence in al-Qaeda and ISIS can also inform how these discourses reflect on the roles of women in counterterrorism practices, and to women's status as agentic actors in all aspects of global politics, including political violence.

Women's militancy in terrorism and political violence often remains poorly understood in policy and practitioner circles, yet the history of this trope suggests this should not be the case. Women have been active in racialized terrorism in the US,[165] in left-wing terrorism in Italy as part of the Italian Red Brigades[166] and in Germany (where, in the case of the Red Army Faction, they were also group leaders),[167] and environmental and animal rights terrorism.[168] They have been violent actors such as militants or suicide bombers in Islamist groups in Chechnya,[169] the Liberation Tigers of Tamil Eelam in Sri Lanka,[170] in Boko Haram in Nigeria,[171] in the Kurdistan Worker's Party in Turkey,[172] in al-Qaeda in Iraq,[173] and even in al-Shabaab in Somalia (though these roles were particularly limited).[174] Women have also acted as assassins, paramilitaries and militants in various organizations, including during the Troubles in Northern Ireland (for loyalist paramilitaries, the Irish Republican Army [IRA] and the Provisional IRA),[175] the Revolutionary Armed Forces of Colombia—People's Army (otherwise known as the FARC) in Colombia,[176] Shining Path in Peru,[177] the Basque separatist movement in Spain (otherwise known as ETA),[178] in Palestine (particularly in Hamas, Hezbollah and Palestinian Islamic Jihad) and Lebanon.[179] They have played militant and support roles in civil conflicts in Eritrea, Nepal[180] and Sierra Leone.[181] Women have also been actively recruited by groups such as Harakat ul-jihad-i-Islami in Bangladesh,[182] and jihadist groups in Kashmir.[183] Throughout these, they have also acted in support roles in logistics, financing, health and aid, recruitment, as disseminators of propaganda, and even as operational leaders. Regardless of group, ideology, location or period, it can be safely stated that women have played various roles in diverse capacities in all political violence, even if they have not been the most visibly violent actors.[184] A growing number of authors have now explored this in a detailed and comparative manner,[185] and the literature cited above is only a snapshot of that which is increasingly available.

In 2007, when analyzing cross-regional trends in female terrorism, Cunningham stated that regardless of region, "female involvement with terrorist activity is widening ideologically, logistically, and regionally."[186] Women were also often assessed to offer operational benefits, particularly in terms of "actor innovation."[187] An anonymous senior Canadian intelligence analyst also confirmed women are more generally getting involved in "supporting, facilitating, organizing, and financing terrorism."[188] In terms of jihadist groups, Bloom has noted that "women now provide both the symbols of jihad and their actual operatives,"[189] which has important implications for counterterrorism practices. Sjoberg highlighted the importance of women's roles in often overlooked support networks and care labor which contribute to the ability of others to carry out violence.[190] While the specifics would certainly differ depending on group, location and context, it is noteworthy that women's overall participation in terrorist groups appears to be both growing and increasingly recognized.

## Women in jihadist groups

As demonstrated above, women have been active members of terrorist organizations for many years, yet "the prominence that the question of women in terrorism has achieved as a result of women's involvement in al-Qaeda is unprecedented."[191] This concept has extended even further with the emergence of ISIS. More recently, there has been a much-welcomed heightened focus on women's roles in al-Qaeda and ISIS, which supports this book's focus on counterterrorism responses specifically to contemporary Salafi jihadist terrorism, of which al-Qaeda and ISIS are examples. Much of this recent research has highlighted women's agency in its analysis and is focused primarily on ISIS. It has aimed to highlight or identify women's operational and support roles in these organizations (suggesting these were neglected or not visible previously);[192] how they've been represented in the media;[193] women's online recruitment and radicalization;[194] assessing women's motivations for joining ISIS including personal and political grievances,[195] or indeed creating an evidence base for determining how many women have joined contemporary groups like ISIS.[196] Arguably the most common theme in current literature is the organization's proscribed or real operational roles related to women (including those in relation to combat) and acts of terrorist violence (including suicide bombing).[197] How women's roles may evolve over time in groups such as these is also a common theme. For instance, Parashar noted that the lengthy conflict in Kashmir was impacted by al-Qaeda's "pan-Islamic ideology," which affected "how women have tried to articulate their political voices and, more specifically, their support for militant activities."[198]

Much of this literature is policy-oriented, and specifically encourages policymakers and practitioners to recognize women's roles and agency in violent non-state groups. However, what is still missing is this bridge in the analysis between women in terrorist groups and distinct agency discourses and practices of counterterrorism related to their roles in al-Qaeda and ISIS. These include not only military, development and diplomatic efforts, but also specific considerations of female members as returning "foreign fighters," as well as in deradicalization processes, counter-narratives, CVE and other counterterrorism-relevant work, which still remains highly neglected by scholars.[199] Due to the very gendered and gender-segregated nature of these Salafi jihadist groups, this has significant implications for women in counterterrorism-linked efforts.

By not understanding the roles that women can and do play in terrorism and political violence detracts from fully understanding these groups or how to respond to them. As Georgia Holmer noted:

> We need to be careful not to advance stereotypes on both sides of the coin as well, and not to assume women are always agents of peace. Certainly, I think there can be a dark form to empowerment as well. Some of the research has shown that some of the reasons women become terrorists themselves is because of the kind of opportunities it has given them for their own roles. I think that the gender stereotyping applies to both sides: women as terrorists and women as preventers of terrorism.[200]

That is, assessing women's roles in counterterrorism must also be cognizant of the flaws present in understanding and analyzing their roles in violence.

FSS itself has also only more recently begun to actively interrogate women as militant and terrorist actors.[201] Gentry and Sjoberg lament that "[w]omen are underrepresented in the study of terrorism, as scholars and as subjects."[202] "Gender blinders" also neglect the fact that "terrorism and insurgency *take place in a gendered world*"[203] and must be analyzed as such. Gentry and Sjoberg continue to call for "the growth of a feminist research programme on women's violence."[204] Sjoberg additionally calls for a feminist approach which may assess "the manipulation of gender perceptions and gender roles in terrorism and counterterrorism."[205] Feminist interrogations of terrorism could additionally examine "differential impacts of terrorism and counterterrorism on those understood as men and those understood as women," all of which "does not even get into counterterrorism—where civilian women are often the 'collateral damage' in counterterrorist attacks."[206] In addition, feminists may consider the "manipulation of gender perceptions and gender roles in terrorism and counterterrorism," as often "belligerents use gendered perceptions and language about terror/terrorism against their enemies"[207]—themes that also become apparent in US counterterrorism practices. This book assists in highlighting such perceptions.

Sjoberg and Gentry also importantly point out that women's violence is often framed in specific categories they distinguish as "mother," "monster" or "whore;" these may themselves subordinate gender, but additionally portray "the state or political organization making the characterizations in a certain light."[208] They additionally reference Moon and note the "key is to pinpoint which women at what time in what gendered way are identified with the politics of a foreign policy issue."[209] This offers a particularly useful consideration for this book, namely how different government agencies framing of women in their discourses and practices also reflects how these agencies portray themselves in relation to women. Such considerations may additionally help identify implications for framing women in certain ways. One assertion they made has particular salience for this research:

> Each person engaging in, or reacting to, actions classified as terrorism, lives in a community structured by gender hierarchy within a gendered state in a gender-hierarchical international system. Thus, if terrorism studies fail to account for the complexities of gender, it provides an incomplete account of the factors that go into producing and countering political violence.[210]

As noted by Parashar, the study of women's militancy will offer "better understandings not only of the individual participants in these conflicts but also of the conflicts in these regions writ larger than the national security discourses or realist 'high' politics."[211]

This suggests that the link between women's violence and understanding conflicts more substantially is also poorly assessed, and also has implications for post-conflict processes. For example, Parashar highlighted that not recognizing women's varied roles in violence may marginalize them from peace negotiations or other political processes.[212] Failing to recognize women's roles in militant organizations has also seen them excluded or neglected in demobilization, disarmament and reintegration (DDR) processes, such as in Angola, Mozambique[213] and Sierra Leone, where even female minors associated with militants were neglected, further problematizing their reintegration into society post-conflict.[214] While distinct from DDR, a similar concern has also thus far largely been visible in counterterrorism considerations: the lack of literature which considers former "violent women" who may disengage from terrorist organizations, and the gender-conscious judicial responses and deradicalization approaches this may entail.[215] While there has been focus on concerns such as male radicalization in prisons,[216] this too has neglected the potential for women to pose similar concerns or the uniquely gendered considerations that may be required. This becomes particularly problematic as countries around the world grapple with how to manage the thousands of women who became affiliated with ISIS, many of whom are currently returning to their countries of origin or being detained throughout the region.

This above-mentioned research is very welcome, as it increasingly interrogates the borders and assumptions of women and gender in both security and political violence. However, few of these have extended to how agencies who practice security and respond to such threats themselves view women in their practices, or how understandings of the roles of women in terrorist groups impacts/influences women's engagement in counterterrorism practices. An assumption of this research suggests that as women have become increasingly visible in terrorist groups, this has also been reflected in considerations of responses to them in counterterrorism practices. This will be outlined in the remainder of this book by focusing on al-Qaeda and ISIS discourses and practices more directly.

2

# COUNTERTERRORISM FROM BUSH TO OBAMA

*"We have some planes."*

Hijacker pilot on American Airlines Flight 11,
as overheard by a controller on 11 September 2001

Terrorist actors, the nature of the threat they pose, and responses to them have evolved significantly since 2001 and the mass casualty attack carried out by al-Qaeda on 9/11. From al-Qaeda to the Islamic State in Iraq and Syria (ISIS), concerns of the proliferation of weapons of mass destruction (WMDs) to "homegrown threats," lone actors and the utilization of online communication platforms, each evolution in actors and their capabilities has prompted a unique response. This chapter provides an overview of what this looked like under the Bush and Obama administrations, how they articulated their strategies to counter terrorism, and how women became visible within these. The first section will briefly discuss terrorism in the United States prior to 9/11, demonstrating that many of the discourses related to women and security that became visible in the subsequent years were not new, but reflected broader trends already underway, and that these were increasingly framed in relation to counterterrorism. The second section will analyze the Bush administration (Republican, 2001–09) and its strategic approach to counterterrorism over his tenure. It highlights where women become visible in this, and how 9/11 in particular became a catalyst for how these discourses evolved in relation to security in practice. The third section will analyze the Obama administration (Democrat, 2009–17) in a similar manner. The primary texts used as the starting point for this are the National Security Strategies (NSS) from the years 2002, 2006, 2010 and 2015, as well as the key White House-commissioned or -produced documents, speeches or other "texts" which prioritized terrorism as a key concern in the senior administration. These include the 9/11 Commission, the National Strategy for Combating Terrorism (NSCT; 2004) and the US National Security Strategy for Counterterrorism (2013), amongst others.

This chapter starts at the White House to trace the presidential discourses which inform how the US Department of Defense (DoD), US Department of State (US State) and US Agency for International Development (USAID) viewed their contributions to this security strategy. It helps better explain how, where and why women become visible over the following sixteen years of counterterrorism discourse and practice under these administrations. It should be emphasized at the outset that the strategies articulated in the documents discussed did not always translate seamlessly into practice. In fact, at times tensions between the strategies articulated in the senior administration appeared to be outright resisted by the aforementioned departments and agencies. Indeed, an interrogation of the specific language and approach communicated by each administration has to be assessed within the wider environment in which it was articulated. It also has to be measured against the practices that developed and those that were either carried out or resisted on the ground.

This chapter demonstrates that the Bush administration emphasized a "whole-of-government" approach to counterterrorism, with a strategic aim to defeat international terrorism through destroying the groups themselves, denying them sponsorship and support, and diminishing the underlying condition terrorists sought to exploit. This saw a "boots-on-the-ground" military-driven approach take precedence, as seen in the wars in Afghanistan and Iraq, alongside democratization and development efforts, amongst others. Within this, the primary counterterrorism-linked discourses that become visible were the Global War on Terror (GWOT); the promotion of democracy; and addressing underlying drivers of terrorism. Within these, three primary discourses related specifically to women were emphasized: (1) women as security practitioners; (2) women's rights, empowerment and equality; and (3) women's victimhood.

Following this, Obama drew down the wars in Iraq and Afghanistan, where the strategic aim was focused more on disrupting, dismantling and defeating al-Qaeda, their networks and affiliates. This saw a shift to a "lighter footprint" approach, which emphasized drone and air strikes, the use of special forces, and training and equipping foreign forces to better manage their own counterterrorism concerns internally. Obama too engaged a "whole-of-government" approach (often referred to as "smart power"), and there was a renewed emphasis on the importance of aligning defense, diplomacy and development streams as part of his strategy. Countering violent extremism (CVE) was a stream of effort which emphasized indirect approaches and reduced the pool of persons susceptible to violent extremist and terrorist appeals. While this had its roots in the Bush administration, CVE gained increased and accelerated prominence under Obama, and women in particular became emphasized in these efforts. The primary counterterrorism-linked discourses that became visible included being "at war" with terrorism; the promotion of US values; addressing underlying grievances; and CVE. Within these, three specific categories related to women become evident: (1) women as security practitioners; (2) women's rights, equality and empowerment; and (3) women's roles in the family and community. Figure 2 summarizes these and provides examples from each administration.

This chapter demonstrates that terrorism remained a primary foreign policy and security concern for the US in every year between 2001 and 2017, and was framed in a multi-departmental, comprehensive approach. This emphasized that women must be assessed in both direct and indirect counterterrorism discourses and practices. In fact, it was most often in indirect counterterrorism efforts—particularly those related to democracy promotion, development and aid—where women were most frequently emphasized.[1] This chapter provides the foundation for identifying the categories in which women feature in each department and agency, and the factors that inform how and why these changed.

## US counterterrorism before 9/11

The US has had a long history of dealing with and responding to terrorism, and continues to deal with a diverse breadth of domestic and international threats today.[2] However, 9/11 stood apart as the most deadly and sophisticated terror attack, and the US's response—in the form of the GWOT—impacted almost every corner of the globe.

The US approach to counterterrorism had been evolving for decades based on the perceived threat from terrorism during each administration. Incidents such as the 1970 hijacking of four international planes, and destruction of three, by the People's Front for the Liberation of Palestine, followed in 1972 by the hostage crisis at the Munich Olympics, prompted the Nixon government to establish more systematic and intergovernmental efforts to counter terrorism.[3] A number of attacks on US servicepersons and citizens by Muammar Gaddafi also saw the first US military operation in response to terrorism—Operation El Dorado Canyon—which targeted the Libyan government and military targets in 1986. States who sponsored terrorism or supported or hosted terrorists, such as Libya, Syria and Cuba, began to face sanctions, and these state actors maintained an important focus in the GWOT.

Another shift that became more evident in the GWOT—the promotion of US "values"—had roots that long preceded 9/11. Reflective of the Cold War period and the long-standing ideological power struggle that defined it, the promotion of US values in the country's foreign policy was seen to underpin the liberal international order. This became particularly important as the Cold War came to an end, and drove its continued strategic values throughout the 1990s. As Tankel notes, these instruments of foreign policy included military, economic, foreign aid and diplomatic efforts, and were enacted in order to influence how states behaved, particularly on the international stage, rather than in their own domestic spheres.[4] These instruments came to be understood and adopted in new foreign policy terms as the promotion of democracy, and were framed in terms of their contribution to countering and preventing terrorism. Democratic states who adopted them were viewed to be the most stable and least susceptible to grievances emphasized in terrorist appeals.

Prior to 9/11, the US had already been shifting towards a strategy that was better prepared for surprise attacks by groups committing acts of terror. This was due to previous large-scale attacks perpetrated against the US and its interests in the 1990s, both domestically and abroad, including the 1993 World Trade Center attack in New York; the

1995 Oklahoma City bombing by domestic terrorists affiliated with the Patriot Movement; the 1995 Khobar Tower bombings in Saudi Arabia; the 1998 US Embassy bombings in Tanzania and Kenya; and the attack in Aden on the USS Cole in 2000, amongst others. Prior to 9/11, the DoD had already been establishing a "new strategy for America's defense that would embrace uncertainty and contend with surprise."[5] Such threats from terrorism represented a distinct shift from the Cold War model, where the enemy was perceived to be a sovereign state with conventional military powers. Now the US was increasingly facing non-state, asymmetric enemies and even domestic terrorist actors.

The Clinton administration identified terrorism, particularly inter-national/transnational terrorism, as a "new threat," which would become a key national security priority. As seen in Presidential Decision Directive (PDD)-39 in 1995, terrorism was viewed as both a threat to international security and a criminal act, and the US would "pursue vigorously all acts to deter and preempt, apprehend and pros-ecute, or assist other governments to prosecute, individuals who per-petrate or plan to perpetrate such attacks."[7] This directive focused on four key areas. The first was to reduce US personnel and facility vulner-abilities to terrorism, reviewing areas where these may be weak; expanding the Federal Bureau of Investigation's (FBI) program of coun-terterrorism; and increasing legal responses to terrorism. The second area was to deter terrorism by emphasizing extradition of indicted terrorist actors to the US for prosecution, and enhancing counterter-rorism capabilities in US State, DoD, and the Central Intelligence Agency (CIA), amongst others. The third area was responding to ter-rorism with "all appropriate instruments against sponsoring organiza-tions and governments." It noted that US State was the lead agency for any international terror attack that took place beyond the US, except when the DoD was directed to use military force; moreover, it also emphasized interagency support. The fourth area, and that of highest importance, was noted to be to "detect, prevent, defeat and manage the consequences of nuclear, biological or chemical materials or weap-ons use by terrorists."[7]

Counterterrorism was dealt with largely in terms of law enforce-ment, and President Clinton focused on four major counterterrorism policy initiatives over his tenure.[8] These were economic isolation for those supporting terrorists; multilateral cooperation through organizations such as the United Nations (UN) or Group of Seven (G7); increased resource allocation (particularly for domestic security services); and retaliation, as seen in limited strikes abroad.[9] Domestically, there was some interagency rivalry to access increasing pots of funding for terrorism-related work,[10] a theme that remains today. Such increases were also reflected in the FBI's counterterrorism budget and number of personnel, which doubled between 1993 and 2000, and other agency efforts such as the establishment of the position of National Coordinator for Security, Infrastructure Protection, and Counterterrorism.[11] In these strategies, though, there was still an emphasis on state sponsors of terrorist groups, which were framed in line with existing defense structures, but which neglected a more detailed focus on non-state actors or terrorist groups.[12] Other legislative efforts saw the 1995 PDD-39 (otherwise known as the "US Policy on Counterterrorism") and the 1996 Federal Aviation Reauthorization Act. The latter recognized that the threat from international terrorism was growing, and if this was found to be state-supported or directed, "a state of war should be considered to exist or to have existed between the United States and that nation."[13] The 1998 PDD-62 entitled "Combating Terrorism" further outlined terrorism as an increasing national priority.

In the years immediately prior to 9/11, terrorism remained a national security focus: it was referenced twenty-nine times in the 1999 NSS,[14] and sixty-eight times in the 2000 NSS.[15] This was in terms of domestic terrorism and international terrorism directed at US targets abroad, and the role of state-sponsored terrorism by nations like Iran or North Korea. As such, counterterrorism operations had begun to emerge as a more prominent tool and component of US security and defense operations.

Concurrently, US defense, law enforcement and intelligence agencies remained the primary actors in counterterrorism efforts, although defense efforts were viewed more as an "extra-ordinary step."[16] For example, in retaliatory strikes against al-Qaeda training camps in Afghanistan and a chemical factory attack in Sudan, the military was a key component, though not a lead organization for counterterrorism efforts.[17] There was also a sense that US security more broadly depended on a multi-stream approach. For example, President Clinton's 2000 NSS noted that America's financial, diplomatic and military resources must be used to "stand up for peace and security, promote global prosperity, and advance democracy and human rights around the world."[18] Issues such as democracy, human rights promotion and responsible governance had a long history in US development efforts abroad, and were understood to positively contribute to both US and global security. This had direct implications for how aspects such as women's political participation, women's rights and women's political leadership training—areas previously emphasized outside the traditional security space—became considered in broader security discourses and practices following 9/11.

Similar to the NSSs under Bush and Obama following 9/11, women were discussed in both the 2000 and 2001 NSSs as largely falling into two categories. First, and most frequently, they were seen as the "men and women in uniform." It is noteworthy that this was one discourse that remained consistent prior to 9/11 and throughout the Bush, Obama and Trump administrations: in any reference to US security forces, there has appeared to be (without any visible exception by the author) the "men and women" in the armed forces, security services, intelligence services and other security services. Indeed "women" have been visible as American security actors in all discourses which highlight efforts to address security and terrorism. Secondly, women were discussed in terms of development considerations and rights, which were emphasized under categories such as "promoting sustainable development." Here, aspects such as women's health, education or empowerment were highlighted as components of "true and lasting social and economic progress."[19] Full respect for women's rights were noted alongside human rights when discussing the promotion of democracies, where the NSS noted: "Our security depends upon the protection and expansion of democracy worldwide."[20] This was not referenced in relation to terrorism directly, but in terms of "repression, corruption and instability" which could threaten regional stability.[21] Promoting women's status and rights was thus framed in terms of broader democratic rights and equality for citizens, which contributed to global stability and consequently US security. Women were also highlighted as one of the "most vulnerable or traditionally oppressed groups in the world," and aspects such as violence against women, or trafficking of women were noted as "international problems with national implications."[22]

Key themes in international documents at this time—such as the UN's Millennium Goals, which emphasized gender equality and empowerment,[23] or UN Security Council Resolution (UNSCR) 1325 in 2000, which emphasized women's roles in all aspects of security— were also mirrored in national security discourses in the US prior to 9/11. The security and status of women was linked to national security, albeit through streams of effort such as democracy promotion and development, which at that time remained more separate from military, law enforcement and intelligence efforts to combat terrorism. As seen above, women were also framed as vulnerable and oppressed actors, and victims of violence and trafficking in the context of international security. However, following 9/11, women's rights and oppression became directly linked to terrorism in ways not seen prior. The 9/11 Commission has received relatively little academic scrutiny in this regard, but is essential for informing how women became visible in counterterrorism discourses and practices in the years following 9/11.

## The 9/11 Commission

The 9/11 Commission was an independent, bipartisan commission established by President Bush in late 2002, and its findings were published in 2004. The Commission responded to the questions "How did this happen, and how can we avoid such tragedy again?" and aimed to offer a complete account of the circumstances and events that led up to the 9/11 attack.[24] The Commission was significant for its breadth and scope: it reviewed 2.5 million pages of documents, held nineteen days of hearings, taking testimony from 160 witnesses, and interviewed over 1,200 persons, including almost every senior official covered in the topics of inquiry. This made it an important document to be considered, as it summarized key policy and practitioner thinking at this time. It is noteworthy, however, that only one woman—Jamie S. Gorelick, a lawyer who had previously served as the Deputy Attorney General—was represented amongst the ten members of the Commission (although women were more visible on the Commission staff). It was also significant in how it highlighted and expanded the links between the status of women, terrorism and US strategies to counter terrorism. Many of these points were echoed in political discourses immediately after 9/11 and in the war in Afghanistan, as will be shown.

The Commission offered a strategy to counter not just terrorism, but the ideological movement that contributed to Islamist terrorism. The three dimensions of this strategy also informed how and where women would be emphasized in international efforts: first were offensive operations to attack terrorists and their organizations (a defense focus); second was to prevent the continued growth of Islamist terrorism (a focus that required the US to "engage with the struggle of ideas," and emphasize reform, freedom, democracy and opportunity); and third was to protect against and prepare for future attacks, which would consider aspects like interrupting terrorist travel and border screening and security, and more closely reflected the work undertaken by the Department of Homeland Security.[25] There were clear defense, diplomatic and development aspects in these first two dimensions, themes which were emphasized under Bush and Obama in a comprehensive strategy to counter terrorism.

"Women" were referenced seventeen times in the Commission in four general contexts: (1) as family members or other close relations of the attackers (for example, the sick mother of Musahib al Hamlan who impacted his decision not to return to training in Afghanistan, or Aysel Senguen, the girlfriend of hijacker Ziad Jarrah); (2) as members of the public who were impacted by terrorism, both in the US and abroad; (3) as professional US servicewomen working in areas such as intelligence and security—the "brave men and women using advanced technology" for the mission of US war fighters, or the men and women in the CIA; and (4) women were imperatively framed in terms of repression and victimhood in the Muslim world. This last context was discussed in terms of al-Qaeda's treatment of women, how women in the Islamic world more generally were oppressed, and how this was linked as circumstantial to the events culminating in the 9/11 attacks. It stated al-Qaeda's purpose was "to rid the world of religious and political pluralism, the plebiscite, and equal rights for women." Referencing the broader social and economic malaise of the Islamic world that Osama bin Laden appealed to, it noted "the repression and isolation of women in many Muslim countries have not only seriously limited individual opportunity, but also crippled overall economic productivity."[26]

The report discussed "a global strategy" to address terrorism, "defines the threat," and reflected on the "generational challenge," whereby women's rights appear to emerge as one of many wider deficits in the Muslim world: "Because the Muslim world has fallen behind the West politically, economically and militarily for the past three centuries, and because few tolerant or secular Muslim democracies provide alternative models for the future, Bin Laden's message finds receptive ears." It noted: "Tolerance, the rule of law, political and economic openness, the extension of greater opportunities to women—these cures must come from within the Muslim community itself." Such an assessment, though made after the onset of the war in Afghanistan, informed and supported the larger Bush strategy of democratization, development and reform that became focused on the Islamic world as a means to undercut future threats from terrorism, and informed the focus on improving women's rights and status within these.

Gains that had been made in Afghanistan were measured in terms of how the coalition had been able to bring freedom to women in the country: "Most Afghans enjoy greater freedom, women and girls are emerging from subjugation, and 3 million children have returned to school." With this, success against terrorist groups and their supporters could be assessed by the improved levels of education and freedom for women. This was posited against Saudi Arabia, which was noted to be "a problematic ally in combating Islamic extremism," with a poor record on women's rights, yet still an important ally of the US in terms of combating terrorism. Despite this, the Commission perceived the country as "an autocratic government that oppresses women." Furthermore, it noted that "Saudi Arabia is a troubled country" where "women find their education and employment sharply limited."[27] Here, a country which had proved important as a counterterrorism partner was also assessed alongside its treatment of women, particularly in education and employment terms, and while this was critiqued, it was seemingly subsumed by the primacy of counterterrorism concerns. There was a visible and increasing conflation of women's status in society alongside both success against terrorism, and in assessments of healthy counterterrorism partnerships that has been continuous since 9/11.

In the broader Muslim world, the US would encourage "reform, free-dom, democracy, and opportunity [...]. Muslims themselves will have to reflect upon such basic issues as the concept of jihad, the position of women [...]." The setting was framed as difficult: "Forty percent of Arabs are illiterate, two-thirds of them women [...]. In short, the United States has to help defeat an ideology, not just a group of people, and we must do so under difficult circumstances."[28] A broad range of development, rights and empowerment issues related to women, particularly educa-tion, access to employment and their broader legal and social status thus became folded more concretely into broader counterterrorism dis-courses and efforts. It also highlighted how women's rights and status became a cultural marker in the war of ideas, and gave early indication that women had to be engaged in this space. Such language neglected that such a blanket approach to the "Muslim world" was exceptionally prob-lematic; where women's positions were diverse, nuanced and complex; and appeared to neglect or recognize preexisting indigenous efforts by women in the region that could be otherwise supported.

By 2004, women's rights and status in society had become seen as a marker between the West and the Muslim world, and emerged as a prominent theme in the global counterterrorism strategy and its ideo-logical battle. In particular, improving the status of women's rights alongside other "deficits" in the Muslim world were seen to detract from the strength of Bin Laden's ideology amongst some populations. The rights and status of women in the Muslim world (narrowly defined) were highlighted as a key area that had to be "cured" in the Muslim community, and the US needed to be seen to support these efforts. This was linked to the reason extremism had found appeal amongst repressed populations, and why terrorism such as that seen on 9/11 was able to occur. There was little doubt that women's status was a critical issue to address in numerous Muslim-majority nations at that time. A major World Bank report analyzed women's status in the Middle East and North Africa (MENA) between 2000 and 2006, high-lighting that women's economic and political participation and repre-sentation there were some of the lowest in the world, and women's legal rights remained an area of significant concern.[29] Yet, in the post-9/11 context, improving women's status became specifically linked to a society's resilience or susceptibility to terrorism, and not just in its support of a liberal democratic order, suggesting these would be conflated in security efforts focused on the GWOT.

The Implementing Recommendations of the 9/11 Commission Act of 2007 is also of some relevance here. Expanding on the 9/11 Commission's findings of 2004, this Act emphasized women's rights, for example in relation to scholarships being provided in predominantly Muslim countries, where these would support "protections for internationally recognized human rights, including the rights of women." In Afghanistan, one notable success included "improving the protection of human rights, including women's rights." In Saudi Arabia, it was noted:

> It is in the national security interest of the United States to support the Government of Saudi Arabia in undertaking a number of political and economic reforms, including increasing anti-terrorism operations conducted by law enforcement agencies, providing more political and religious rights to its citizens, [and] increasing the rights of women [...].[30]

This focus on women's rights and status in the Muslim world seemingly neglected where such concerns may exist in other contexts and locations, and did not adequately reflect on the potential implications of conflating efforts directed at improving women's position in society with counterterrorism-related aims. It furthermore appeared to lend to the utilization of women's status in political discourses for broader counterterrorism objectives, or preview how agencies focused on women's status in areas such as employment or human rights would now have to assess or frame their relevance in counterterrorism terms. It is also noteworthy that women's roles as security or legal practitioners in these countries—for example in roles which could help enforce or ensure such rights for women, or as actors themselves who could contribute to counterterrorism-specific efforts—was not visible. This reflected a common theme: women's rights and status in the "Muslim world" were emphasized and assessed in socio-economic and development terms by US actors, while their roles as security actors or individuals otherwise empowered in relation to security were often neglected. As such, the 9/11 Commission proved critical for highlighting and informing the themes that became visible under the Bush and Obama administrations.

## COUNTERTERRORISM FROM BUSH TO OBAMA

*Bush and the GWOT (2001–09)*

The Bush approach to counterterrorism articulated over his tenure was presented as multifaceted, as seen in his key NSSs (2002, 2006) and the NSCT (2004). This approach to US security was referenced in the 2002 NSS as utilizing "every tool in our arsenal," which included military power, better homeland defenses, law enforcement, intelligence and efforts to cut off terrorist financing.[31] It reinforced the primacy of terrorism as a key concern, particularly threats from "terrorists and tyrants."[32] To challenge these "free and open societies" were key, particularly through the extension and promotion of democracy. This democratic focus was emphasized as "poverty, weak institutions, and corruption can make weak states vulnerable to terrorist networks and drug cartels within their borders."[33] The promotion of democracy and economic openness was noted to be "the best foundations for domestic stability and international order," and nations which protect human rights, and guarantee political and economic freedoms (specifically referenced as "values of freedom") were to be "protected from enemies."[34] The 2002 NSS expanded "the scope of US foreign and security policy to encompass forward-reaching preventive activities, including preemption, against hostile states and terrorist groups."[35] Other aims were focused on political and economic freedom, and respect for human dignity, where specific efforts included focusing on building coalitions. Women were referenced three times in the 2002 NSS: in terms of education for male and female children (and their mothers and fathers who seek this); freedom from poverty and violence; and championing aspirations for human dignity, which emphasized "respect for women."

In 2003, the US introduced its first NSCT, which was established to support the NSS.[37] This strategy noted that the fight against international terrorism could not be won primarily through military might, but would instead require fighting terrorism networks and those who support them through "every instrument of national power—diplomatic, economic, law enforcement, financial, information, intelligence, and military."[37] It intended to utilize these instruments to defeat the terrorist groups; deny them support, sponsorship or sanctuary; diminish the underlying conditions terrorists seek to exploit (for example,

by fostering economic, social and political development, good governance and rule of law, and winning the "war of ideas"); and defend the
US at home and abroad. The NSCT emphasized liberal democracy as
"the antithesis of terrorist tyranny," while democracy and its inherent
values (such as human rights and the empowerment of people) strongly
emerge.[38] Women were not explicitly mentioned in these, but as indicated previously, women were generally understood in terms of liberal
democratic norms such as rights and equality, and thus in the "underlying conditions" of terrorism through deficits in their rights and socio-
economic status. This initial lack of explicit conflation to counterterrorism would prove to be helpful, yet also suggested that women were
generally understood as peripheral to early counterterrorism strategies
and efforts.

By 2005, there was a growing recognition (prompted by the military
no less) that it was necessary to extend counterterrorism efforts
beyond military means and address the issue more expansively. General
Richard B. Myers, chairman of the Joint Chiefs of Staff, stated the
threat instead should be defined as violent extremists, with the recognition that "terror is the method they use." Although the military is
heavily engaged in the mission now, he said, future efforts require "all
instruments of our national power, all instruments of the international
communities' national power." The solution is "more diplomatic, more
economic, more political than it is military," he concluded.[39] A similar
stance was taken in the "wartime" 2006 NSS, where the greatest danger
faced was that of terrorism: in it, the US was seen to be "fighting and
winning the war on terror and promoting freedom as the alternative
to tyranny and despair." It was also growing the global community of
democracies and multilateral efforts, which they hoped would employ
the "full array of political, economic, diplomatic, and other tools at our
disposal," and were viewed as a counterbalance to terrorism.[40]

Up until 2005, US policymakers had been attempting to shift the
discourse from the "bellicose" term GWOT to a more preferred term:
Struggle Against Violent Extremism (SAVE). It had been recognized
that some non-violent yet still extremist groups may become helpful
partners in counterterror efforts, even while others were recognized
to in fact propagate ideas that created more terrorists. Such a pivot in
terminology tried to reflect this nuance.[41] The introduction of this

concept also saw more emphasis on violent extremism rather than solely fixating on terrorism. This would allow practitioners to address related issues such as the promotion or justification of violent ideas and acts without the same politicization that the term "terrorism" held.[42] This shift also previewed early steps towards CVE as a core component of counterterrorism strategy. This would become particularly emphasized under Obama, and sought to emphasize more upstream and preventative measures that fed into support and membership of violent extremist and terrorist organizations.

It was evident under Bush that broad US counterterrorism efforts continuously emphasized numerous streams and included various agencies. Women were referenced four times in the 2006 NSS under the heading "champion aspirations for human dignity," thus mirroring the 2002 strategy, where women's "rights," "freedom," "dignity and worth" were highlighted. Jihadist terrorism would remain the driving thrust behind the 2006 NSS, which took into consideration the lessons that had been learned in Afghanistan and particularly in Iraq, notably the necessity of post-conflict reconstruction and stabilization in maintaining military success in the long term. This NSS was founded upon two pillars: firstly, promoting freedom, justice and human dignity; and secondly, leading a growing community of democracies.[43] The 2006 NSS was also noteworthy due to the attacks in London on 7 July 2005 (in which fifty-six people were killed), which highlighted the fact that homegrown radicalization in democratic societies now represented a marked evolution in terrorism, whereby threats had to be assessed from one's own citizens as well as those of foreign "strangers."

While analysis of the Bush administration's approach to counterterrorism has been well-documented elsewhere,[44] there were three key counterterrorism-relevant discourses under the Bush which had implications for how women became visible within the discourses and practices of the DoD, US State and USAID: (1) the "war" on terror and military efforts; (2) democracy promotion; and (3) addressing the underlying conditions of terrorism. Within these, government discourses largely framed women in relation to counterterrorism in three primary categories. First, as security practitioners in US forces, where "men and women" in uniform were presented consistently alongside each other. Second, in terms of rights, empowerment and equality, which were framed as "women's rights," "women's empowerment," "women's dignity" and "women's equality." Here, improving the status of women was understood in democratic and development terms, and represented healthy societies in which extremism would face difficulty taking root.[45] Thirdly, in terms of victimhood, oppression and inequality (predominantly in the Muslim world), where women were seen as victims of terrorist actors and oppressive regimes. This category was often placed in binary terms against those of the second category, with the ultimate aim of the US helping to improve the status of women in these countries.

This section will now expand on these broader discourses, with specific examples over the course of the Bush administration used to demonstrate how women featured in these and what this suggested for their roles in practice. In the subsequent chapters, these will be explored in relation to the DoD, US State and USAID, considering how the departments and agencies themselves interpreted the roles for women in their own discourses and practices on the ground, and the specific factors that impacted how those evolved.

## The GWOT

After 9/11, terrorism was framed as both a tactic and a strategy, but also, more significantly, as an act of war. Within days of 9/11, Bush made clear:

> On September the 11th, enemies of freedom committed an act of war against our country [...]. We will pursue nations that provide aid or safe haven to terrorism. Every nation in every region now has a decision to make: either you are with us or you are with the terrorists. From this day forward, any nation that continues to harbor or support terrorism will be regarded by the United States as a hostile regime.[46]

This response was put into law via the Authorization for Use of Military Force (AUMF), introduced on 18 September 2001, which authorized the president to use:

> All necessary and appropriate force against those nations, organizations, or persons he determines planned, authorized, committed, or aided the terrorist attacks that occurred on September 11, 2001, or harbored such organizations or persons, in order to prevent any future

acts of international terrorism against the United States by such nations, organizations or persons.[47]

This AUMF was focused on the Taliban and al-Qaeda specifically, but is noteworthy for the long-term significance that it has maintained in terms of the breadth and scale the GWOT would take (even up to the present day). A second AUMF was introduced in 2002 and focused on Iraq, particularly emphasizing its perceived processing and develop-ment of a WMD program (a claim that was later debunked); and the aid and harboring of al-Qaeda members in the country. As such, the 2002 AUMF against Iraq authorized the president to "use the Armed Forces of the United States as he determines to be necessary and appropriate in order to—defend the national security of the United States against the continuing threat posed by Iraq."[48] These two AUMFs have proved crucial for shaping how the GWOT has continued to this day, with the list of organizations affiliated with al-Qaeda, and their locations, ever expanding: there have been at least thirty-seven occur-rences (eighteen under Bush; nineteen under Obama) involving coun-tries ranging from Djibouti to Somalia, Georgia to Kenya, that the AUMF has referenced to initiate or continue military-related action, as well as any action later taken against ISIS.[49] In relation to the Bush administration, this "war" also justified foreign military training and equipping in countries like Yemen and the Philippines, and demon-strated the extent to which the GWOT would inform women in rela-tion to terrorism around the world.

There was a tension in the United States after 9/11 as to whether terrorism should be dealt with through a criminal justice model or a war model. However, by framing terrorism as an act of war, terrorism was recategorized; this had significant repercussions for how the coun-try tackled the threat,[50] and indeed how women would be framed within these responses. Boyle highlighted how counterterrorism itself became militarized, securitized and became "a form of warfare in its own right."[51] After 9/11, how women would be framed in counterter-rorism discourses would be influenced dominantly by this military approach and its increasing role in counterterrorism, even as a broader "whole-of-government" approach was articulated.

Within these efforts, women's roles became evident in two binary categories: those of US forces (which remained most consistent throughout both the Bush, Obama and Trump administrations); and those who were oppressed and in need of saving. The former were "the men and women in our military" sent to Afghanistan, who have the "full confidence" of the president,[52] or the men and women of the United States Armed Forces in Iraq where "the peace of a troubled world and the hopes of an oppressed people now depend on you."[53] Given that the war in Afghanistan began with the US at the forefront, discourses related to "human dignity" were engaged by the Bush administration in relation to women. For example, in a radio address to the nation given by Laura Bush (at the insistence of her husband) on 17 November 2001, she stated: "The brutal oppression of women is a central goal of the terrorists [...]. The fight against terrorism is also a fight for the rights and dignity of women."[54] This address was unique as it was exceptionally rare for the spouses of acting presidents to address the nation, and having a woman speaking to the audience in this context would have lent additional weight to the urgency and importance of the status of Afghan women, and therefore more justification for US intervention.

This narrative proved to be particularly controversial. Some authors argued the plight of Afghan women was used to "supplement" the justification for going into Afghanistan,[55] pointing to this theme as exceptionally problematic where intervention was framed in terms of "saving" or "protecting" them, as well as in the racialized, masculine language the Bush administration adopted.[56] This theme of "saving" women is one that has been used to justify intervention in other locations and periods. Ahmed has highlighted how colonizers' use of feminism to "promote the culture of the colonizers and undermine native culture" has served as a tool of colonial domination.[57] Spivak referenced this as "white men saving brown women from brown men" when discussing British intervention in India in the abolition of *suttee* (widow sacrifice) in the nineteenth century.[58] Given this historical context, such narratives only proved to reinforce perceptions of American imperialistic ambitions in the region. There has been a fair body of feminist literature that has assessed gendered discourses and images post-9/11, particularly in terms of its hypermasculinity, Orientalism,[59] and how the US conceives of itself in the formation of state identity in relation to "the other."[60] Tickner has considered gendered dimensions of civilizational discourses ("dangerous men" and "helpless women"), and the responsibility of both academics and policymakers to recognize and listen to women in many of these countries who have been on the front lines of human rights efforts for decades prior to 9/11.[61] By having foreign women portrayed as victims in presidential discourses, this could directly negate the value and history of their efforts prior to US interventions.

Over the years, the US had promoted a multilateral, alliance-driven approach to defeat global terrorism, including supporting and training nations "that need our assistance in combating terror,"[62] because some nations "need military training to fight terror, and we'll provide it."[63] Yemen, for instance, became a key focus in these efforts. There was also an assumption that terrorism would become more localized as pressure was applied to certain groups. As terrorist efforts became more localized, unorganized and "relegated to the criminal domain, [the US] will rely upon and assist other states to eradicate terrorism at its root."[64] However, in order to do so, partners would need to be able to adequately respond to these concerns, so there was also a significant focus on foreign military assistance, training and equipping foreign partners to ensure they were capable of dealing with threats in their own backyards. Nonetheless, women were largely absent in these discourses. This, however, started to change around 2006 as the US started shifting to counterinsurgency (COIN) efforts in Iraq, providing new roles for both US and foreign female forces.

Women, too, were occasionally referenced in terms of violent actors themselves, particularly in Arab states: "All parties have a responsibility to stop funding or inciting terror. And all parties must say clearly that a murderer is not a martyr; he or she is just a murderer."[65] It is noteworthy that women did not generally feature in key political discourses as, for instance, "the men and women" of al-Qaeda or other terrorist organizations, and there was an assumption that "the terrorists" remained largely male-dominated in this period.

It is worth highlighting here that women have often been slow to be recognized as potential security threats, when it is obvious that they could in fact be perpetrators of violence: women conducted suicide bombings on at least three occasions in Iraq as early as 2003,[66] while al-Qaeda also claimed to have female squads of suicide bombers ready to attack the US.[67] Women such as Aafia Siddiqui (otherwise known as "Lady al-Qaeda"), a Pakistani national with a PhD in neuroscience, had been placed on the FBI's most wanted list in 2004 for her role as an al-Qaeda operative. By 2010, Siddiqui had been convicted of the attempted murder of US nationals in Afghanistan. When she was detained, she had also held plans for a mass casualty attack in the US, targeting sites such as the Empire State Building, and also allegedly had information on how to weaponize the Ebola virus. These highlight the implications of the slow responses to recognizing that women could pose as big a security threat as men in some cases.

*Promoting democracy*

While the US had a long history of advancing global stability and security through democratization, democracy promotion was not part of the initial efforts envisioned in Afghanistan or Iraq. Despite this, they did eventually become a key feature in George Bush's GWOT. Discourses emphasizing "respect for women" and "women's rights" featured most prominently in discussions related to democracy. For example, the 2002 NSS listed eight key components that would lead to national security, including championing aspirations for human dignity. The Bush administration focused on the "dignity of women" and "women's rights," though largely with the aim to "protect the freedoms that face particular peril around the world: religious freedom, women's rights, and freedom for men, women, and children caught in the cruel network of human trafficking." Women's rights in this sense were not only to be protected, but were posited alongside references to their victimhood. Women were also referenced in terms of "human dignity" and the promotion of effective democracy, where the US would use foreign assistance to "support the development of free and fair elections, rule of law, civil society, human rights, women's rights, free media, and religious freedom." Furthermore, in 2006 the NSS noted: "No nation can be free if half its population is oppressed and denied fundamental rights. We affirm the inherent dignity and worth of women, and support vigorously their full participation in all aspects of society."[68] This would include using foreign aid to promote freedom and to support those who struggle non-violently for it, making positive governance and development key themes in bilateral relations. This concept of liberty through democracy was framed as transformational: "Young women across the Middle East will hear the message that their day of equality and justice is coming. Young men will hear the message that national progress and dignity are found in liberty, not tyranny and terror."[69] "Human dignity" was attained through the "freedom" inherent in democracy, and was also directly posited against extremists who deliver "repression of women," particularly highlighted in the Muslim world.[70]

This discourse on women's equality and dignity directly mirrored CEDAW,[71] the UN's Millennium Development Goals,[72] and the enshrined rights and equality for all seen in the US Declaration of Independence,[73] thus highlighting the areas where international and national discourses aligned. However, in the case of the US, this was now being articulated within a GWOT. In 2003, this started focusing primarily on the Middle East, where democracy was "the only path to national success and dignity," and where a deficit of this had contributed to the lack of women's rights in the region. In essence, democracies recognized "the rights of women,"[74] which suggested that both democracy promotion and aid were increasingly linked to improving women's status in efforts which contributed to national security. This also suggested that increasingly diplomatic/political and aid activities had to interact in order to achieve this in practice.

Women's rights that were framed in democratic terms featured continuously in relation to the GWOT over the years in various speeches by Bush. In these, the US fought for the day when "women have full rights" in the Middle East, because "the security of our own citizens depends on it."[75] In Iraq, "[t]he systematic use of rape by Saddam's regime to dishonor families has ended. He sits in the prison cell. The advance of freedom in the greater Middle East has given new rights and new hopes to women."[76] Iraqi women were discussed in terms of "playing an essential part in rebuilding the nation" where they were "already using their new political powers to guard against extremism and intolerance in any form." Furthermore, Yemen's 2004 elections were held up as an example of the growing liberty in the Middle East, and through programs like MEPI, "[w]e're building women's centers in Afghanistan and Iraq that will offer job training and provide loans for small businesses and teach women about their rights as citizens and human beings."[77] As Bush noted in 2004, women's dignity was at times directly linked to terrorism: "men and women with hope and purpose and dignity do not strap bombs on their bodies and kill the innocent."[78] This line of discourse in relation to women's rights and equality appears most evidently in democracy promotion, where women became symbolic of free and open societies resilient to extremism and terrorism.[79]

The framing of women's rights during Bush's presidential terms has been highly disputed and challenged by academics. McBride and Wibben point out that, in the GWOT, "women are used as symbolic markers in the struggle between cultures,"[80] which becomes problematic when focused on the context of women's rights and empowerment and viewed as a western agenda. Attempts to enhance the status of women also faced significant challenges, and even "blowback" in cases such as Iraq and Afghanistan: "The invocation of women's rights for political expediency in the context of the 'war on terror' has tended to breed skepticism, if not outright resistance."[81] Some have even referred to Bush's tenure as "a war on women," particularly in terms of women's access to reproductive rights and services,[82] while others have argued the Bush administration demonstrated "a certain dedication to improving the rights and status of women more generally throughout his tenure."[83] Furthermore, the discourses in the GWOT continued to often frame women in terms of needing protection.[84] Satterthwaite and Huckerby have highlighted how analyzing such discourses through a gendered lens helps identify "when, where and how women's rights are mobilized in both terrorism and counterterrorism responses across time and in different contexts."[85] In particular, such an approach can scrutinize "why and how rights narratives are mobilized in respect of some women's rights and not others."[86] It can also highlight contradictions such moves can generate—for example, by instrumentalizing women's rights, states may "ostensibly seek to protect women but on their very terms deny women's rights enjoyment." This is where a tension arises: specifically, whether women's rights directly contributed to state stability and thereby reduced threats from terrorism indirectly; or whether they are potentially instrumentalized or even securitized in counterterrorism efforts.

## Addressing the "underlying conditions of terrorism"

The underlying conditions of terrorism overlapped with democratic discourses to some extent, but were distinguished by an emphasis on development and humanitarian aid which was focused on health, literacy, job creation and poverty reduction. Both rights discourses and those focused on development and humanitarian aid would thus be considered soft or "indirect" counterterrorism efforts. Poverty itself was noted not to cause terrorism, but was understood to be exploited by terrorist groups as a way to take power in certain regions, or for ideological promotion and recruitment purposes: "In Afghanistan, persistent poverty and war and chaos created conditions that allowed a terrorist regime to seize power. And in many other states around the world, poverty prevents governments from controlling their borders, policing their territory, and enforcing their laws."[87] In Afghanistan and Iraq, the improved status of women was consistently pointed to in terms of the success of the GWOT. In Afghanistan, for "25 million women and girls, liberation has a special significance," where women were now voting and going to school.[88]

Aid was also noted as a counterbalance of sorts to terrorism: "by helping the developing nations of the world, we offer an alternative to resentment and conflict and terror,"[89] where for terrorists, the "only way they can recruit to their hateful ideology is by exploiting despair."[90] This point was also highlighted in the NSCT, which listed as one of its primary goals, "diminishing underlying conditions that terrorists seek to exploit:"

> Ongoing US efforts to resolve regional disputes, foster economic, social, and political development, market-based economies, good governance, and the rule of law, while not necessarily focused on combating terrorism, contribute to the campaign by addressing underlying conditions that terrorists often seek to manipulate for their own advantage. Additionally, diminishing these conditions requires the United States, with its friends and allies, to win the "war of ideas," to support democratic values, and to promote economic freedom.[91]

Development efforts could thus be considered in terms of their indirect contribution to counterterrorism, and were recognized as distinct from democratization efforts alone. This "war of ideas" was also particularly significant in terms of women's rights, and emphasized areas such as women's and girls' literacy and access to education.[92] Hudson and Leidl have highlighted that UNSCR 1325 positively influenced Bush in the administration's approach to women in foreign aid,[93] yet this suggested women were still believed to adhere to traditional gender norms related to protection or in need of aid.

In 2008, while discussing a three-track approach to the Middle East, Bush suggested that the US took "the offense to the terrorists overseas," including areas such as security cooperation, addressing hostile regimes pursuing WMDs, and addressing "the lack of freedom in the Middle East," which was viewed as "a principal cause of the threats coming from the region." This "broader vision" for the region included addressing "economic prosperity, quality health care and education, and women's rights" and "encouraging Middle Eastern women to get involved in politics and to start their own businesses and take charge of their health."[94] Yemen, in particular, received specific recognition. Both democratic and development lines of effort in pursuit of this drew on discourses of "respect for women" and "women's rights:"

> [I]n our development aid, in our diplomatic efforts, in our international broadcasting, and in our educational assistance, the United States will promote moderation and tolerance and human rights. [...] America has a greater objective than controlling threats and containing resentment. We will work for a just and peaceful world beyond the war on terror.[95]

Diplomacy and development were increasingly linked to counter-terrorism aims, and viewed as contributing to this approach, yet sectors that emphasized women remained on the periphery of primary counterterrorism efforts. A government's perceived action against terrorism would also now impact their access to aid, becoming both a carrot and a stick approach to cooperation: "A state's stand on terrorism will be considered when providing aid to that country."[96] Non-governmental organizations were also increasingly recognized as "important in combating international terrorism,"[97] and would seemingly be engaged in counterterrorism efforts highlighting shifts later seen in USAID.

Falling between the categories of "underlying conditions of terrorism" and discourses related to women's rights, Huckerby has highlighted a nexus between human trafficking and counterterrorism efforts in this period, which has remained visible in discourses pertaining to national security beyond Bush's tenure.[98] Transnational organized crime networks had historically received attention, particularly for highlighting the vulnerability of state borders and state identity; to mitigate this concern, an emphasis needed to be placed on international cooperation and border control, including in the trafficking of drugs and persons. In 2000, the UN established its first Protocol to Prevent, Suppress and Punish Trafficking in Persons, Especially Women and Children (otherwise known as the UN Trafficking Protocol), which the US had been key in forming. Prior to 9/11, the US had also established its own domestic efforts in relation to this, as highlighted by the Victims of Trafficking and Violence Protection Act of 2000.

After 9/11, human trafficking became framed as a "transnational threat," as exemplified in President Bush's National Security Presidential Directive 22 on Combating Trafficking in Persons. This was focused on the profits generated from trafficking, which could fuel "other illegal activities," and the "destabilizing effect" it could have on nations, which could also lend itself to "violence."[99] This, Huckerby points out, linked terrorism and trafficking in terms of their transnational border threats, the contribution of trafficking profits to potentially finance terrorism, and trafficking's contributions to state instability.[100] When assessed at the macro level, in which women's rights become promoted in terms of their contribution to national security goals (including in how this narrative was deployed in the invasion of Afghanistan), she notes that "both relied on notions of gendered vulnerability and were explicitly characterized as having a nexus to counter-terrorism or national security, representing a fundamental elision of national security and gender-equality goals."[101]

Huckerby notes that there were two distinct consequences for the rights of trafficked persons that came about as a result of this nexus. Firstly, by bearing in mind the forms of insecurity generated in conflict, this focus on trafficking may "obscure the ways actions taken in the name of countering terrorism can be inimical to the rights of trafficked persons, including by contributing to the phenomenon of trafficking." Second, in cases where counter-terrorism conflicted with anti-trafficking initiatives, the rights of trafficked persons may become secondary to national security goals.[102] This consideration of trafficking's link to US national security highlights a "specific and striking instance of the strategic or instrumentalist use of gender under the rubric of countering terrorism."[103] This consideration is important in highlighting how the instrumentalization of women and gender in relation to counterterrorism is something that, while present from the onset of the GWOT, remained visible up to the Trump administration.

*Obama at war with terrorism (2009–17)*

When Barack Obama entered office in January 2009, the US approach to counterterrorism was marked by both continuity and shift. Obama's tenure was interspersed with significant events, including the death of Osama bin Laden on 2 May 2011 in Abbottabad, Pakistan, the Arab Spring and the emergence of ISIS. Throughout his time in office, Obama declared that terrorism was a primary security concern of the United States, and stated that it needed to be tackled using multistream efforts. Furthermore, CVE and an emphasis on preventative, indirect efforts were increasingly highlighted, previewing the wider shift in focus that would occur under his administration. Obama's presidency also oversaw the country's first NAP on Women, Peace and Security in 2011, which fundamentally broadened discourses on women and security across the US government (even as its implementation in practice proved inconsistent) and informed how they were considered in counterterrorism aims.

The 2010 NSS continued to cite the disruption, dismantlement and defeat of al-Qaeda and its affiliates as a key US intention. Within this strategy, an increasing level of interaction between defense, diplomacy and development in the service of US security interests was highlighted. Obama noted that while the armed forces were always "the cornerstone of our security, they must be complemented. Our security also depends upon diplomats who can act in every corner of the world [...] development experts who can strengthen governance and support human dignity [...]." These efforts were referenced as a "whole-of-government" approach, and as "every tool of American power to advance our objectives—including enhanced diplomatic and development capabilities with the ability both to prevent conflict and to work alongside our military," suggesting that these three fields were all be seen to be contributing to US security. This also reflected the expansion of stabilization and reconstruction efforts in key countries like Iraq and Afghanistan that had been underway and which drew these three agencies closer together. In relation to counterterrorism specifically (a key security concern), this suggested it would be approached through both direct and indirect means (including preventative efforts).

The NSS also suggested that this interaction between agencies had previously been an area of concern: "work remains to foster coordination across departments and agencies" including "effectively ensuring alignment of resources with our National Security Strategy." Terrorist groups would be addressed through "a comprehensive strategy that denies them safe havens, strengthens front-line partners, secures our homeland, pursues justice through durable legal approaches, and counters a bankrupt agenda of extremism and murder with an agenda of hope and opportunity."[104] Security would also be gained by strengthening alliances and partnerships, and focusing on renewing American leadership in the world.[105] The 2010 NSS previewed Obama's increased emphasis on women in his security discourses: women were referenced twenty-two times, most dominantly as security practitioners, and in terms of rights, dignity and education.

The 2011 National Strategy for Counterterrorism highlighted Obama's policy to "dismantle networks that pose a direct danger to us, and make it less likely for new groups to gain a foothold, all the while maintaining the freedoms and ideals that we defend."[106] Obama also highlighted a "whole-of-government" approach to counterterrorism, where the strategy "integrates the capabilities and authorities of each department and agency, ensuring that the right tools are applied at the right time." However, this explicitly distinguished two areas to be utilized; specific "tools," which were to be complimented by "broader capabilities:"

> US counterterrorism efforts require a multi-departmental and multi-national effort that goes beyond traditional intelligence, military, and law enforcement functions. We are engaged in a broad, sustained, and integrated campaign that harnesses every tool of American power—military, civilian, and the power of our values—together with the concerted efforts of allies, partners, and multilateral institutions. These efforts must also be complemented by broader capabilities, such as diplomacy, development, strategic communications, and the power of the private sector.[107]

This suggested several important points. Above all, it recognized that intelligence, military and law enforcement efforts had historically been understood to be primary to counterterrorism efforts, but long-term efforts required every tool the US had at its disposal. This "campaign" would also directly harness US "values" as a source of power, where diplomatic and development efforts would be viewed as "complementary," although they were still recognized within an holistic effort. Furthermore, it noted that responsive government through democracy also "directly contributes to our counterterrorism goals," suggesting democracy promotion would remain consistent and be assessed in complimentary terms with broader counterterrorism efforts. There was also an increased focus on countering al-Qaeda's ideology, and efforts to "diminish the specific drivers of violence that al-Qa'ida [sic] exploits," where the US would apply "focused foreign and development assistance abroad." The 2011 Nation Strategy for Counterterrorism also emphasized the "need to build foreign partnerships and capacity," and continued to focus on the responsibility and capabilities of the US's partners.[108] "Drivers of violence"—the specific grievances of and discontent felt by a population, particularly towards their government—continued to be understood as exploitable by al-Qaeda, and could be countered through foreign assistance, as well as development funding and programming.

Obama's entry to office also aligned with a broader trend that had been developing since around 2005—both within the US and globally—which distinguished and emphasized CVE. This was arguably driven by a number of factors, including: the recognition that military-led efforts alone were not sufficient to reduce concerns from terrorism; an increased decentralization of terror groups and emphasis on "lone actors" or smaller cells; the recognized need to further counter hostile ideology; the increased use of online/social media, which reached further into the less accessible private sphere; smaller more frequent terrorist plots now being harder to detect, therefore requiring more partnership/assistance from communities to interject or identify risks; and the expansion of western-targeted, English-language propaganda, as seen with Anwar al-Awlaki and *Inspire*, the online magazine of al-Qaeda in the Arabian Peninsula (AQAP). CVE efforts not only increased in response to the global rise of ISIS and the increasing numbers of foreign fighters, as well as to combat those inspired to act independently, but also due to rising support for the group, and the unprecedented production and dissemination of its propaganda on social media. It was increasingly recognized that counterterrorism efforts could not just be responsive to threats, but had to try to pre-empt them and prevent their emergence; as such, CVE was an integral part of this. Yet, as was seen throughout this period (and beyond), there is often contention by CVE actors in conflating these soft power approaches with counterterrorism, instead emphasizing their distinctive CVE focus in preventative and non-kinetic terms.

As a founding member of multilateral initiatives such as the 2011 Global Counterterrorism Forum, which focused on civilian counterterrorism cooperation, the US continued to take an active role in both counterterrorism and increasingly CVE. This allowed closer work with civil society, governments and youth, and importantly emphasized women in some aspects of their work. The US was also involved in multilateral initiatives that focused on women in CVE in organizations such as the Organization for Security and Co-operation in Europe.[109]

In 2011, the White House announced a new strategy entitled "Empowering Local Partners to Prevent Violent Extremism in the United States." It noted that the government was trying to prevent "all types of extremism that lead to violence, regardless of who inspired it," but stressed in particular countering al-Qaeda and its ideology.[110] There were three areas prioritized in this strategy: first, enhancing federal engagement with, and support of, local communities that may be targeted by violent extremists; second, building government and law enforcement expertise to prevent violent extremism; and third, countering violent extremist propaganda while promoting American ideals. It notably stated that, in contrast to what al-Qaeda "violently rejects" (that is, religious freedom and pluralism), the US had instead "emphasized a paradigm of engagement with Muslim communities around the world, based on mutual respect [...] and opportunities for women." This engagement model was based on other areas of interest that communities faced, such as gang violence, school shootings and hate crimes: "so must we address radicalization to violence and terrorist recruitment through similar relationships and by leveraging some of the same tools and solutions."[111] While focused on the US domestically, this document still echoes themes seen in international efforts.

By 2013, the terrorist threat had notably evolved into "lethal yet less capable al Qaeda affiliates; threats to diplomatic facilities and businesses abroad; [and] homegrown extremists. This is the future of terrorism."[112] Expansive approaches to counterterrorism remained consistent throughout Obama's tenure, such as discussing the US approach to developing issues of global concern: "We have to broaden our tools to include diplomacy and development; sanctions and isolation; appeals to international law; and, if just, necessary and effective, multilateral military action."[113]

Yemen gained an increased focus during the Obama administration as a country where AQAP was noted to be "the most active in plotting against our homeland."[114] Partnering with the Yemeni government, efforts to defeat al-Qaeda would include "information-sharing, law enforcement cooperation, and establishing new practices to counter evolving adversaries." Another key effort would be building partner capacity for "responsible governance and security through development and security sector assistance."[115] Alongside efforts to "support Yemen's stability and the aspirations of the Yemeni people," defeating AQAP remained "our counterterrorism priority in the region, and we will continue to leverage and strengthen our partnerships to achieve this end." This would be further embedded in a "broader effort to stabilize the country and prevent state failure." The US would work with regional and international partners to advance a number of political and economic development initiatives that addressed "[u]nderlying conditions that allow Yemen to serve as a safe haven for AQAP. These broader efforts complement those counterterrorism initiatives that are focused on building the capacity of Yemeni security services so they are able eventually to disrupt, dismantle, and defeat AQAP with only limited US involvement."[116]

It was not just training and equipping that Obama considered important for countries like Yemen that wished to "provide for their own security;" he also felt that through a range of capabilities, including drone and air strikes, "[the US] will continue to take direct action against those terrorists who pose the gravest threat to Americans." Alongside this, Obama noted "we must enlist our values in the fight," which was understood to represent a legal and policy framework relevant to these efforts.[117] Given that Yemen was a country facing a plethora of issues related to domestic security, politics and development, and where counterterrorism was a key concern for the US, it would prove to be a unique country by which to assess where many of Obama's counterterrorism practices would take shape and interact.

The final NSS of Obama's administration in 2015 echoed similar language, highlighting a "comprehensive agenda that draws on all elements of our national strength." This "comprehensive national security agenda" would "lead with all the instruments of US power," including the military, diplomacy and development.[118] This was also referenced in relation to ISIS, who had formally announced its so-called "caliphate" in mid-2014: "Our comprehensive strategy against ISIL [Islamic State in Iraq and the Levant] is harnessing all elements of American power, across our government—military, intelligence, diplomatic, economic, development and perhaps most importantly, the power of our values."[119] There was a clear assertion that groups like al-Qaeda and ISIS had been able to emerge from unstable countries with weak governance: "Our foreign policy has to be focused on the threat from ISIL and Al Qaida, but it can't stop there. For even without ISIL, even without Al Qaida, instability will continue for decades in many parts of the world," and "our answer needs to be more than tough talk or calls to carpet-bomb civilians." Obama noted the US required "a smarter approach—a patient and disciplined strategy that uses every element of our national power."[120]

In focusing on Obama's key discourses in relation to women, Jackson has noted that Bush and Obama shared many of the same discourses related to 9/11: this included the terrorist threat; the terrorist "other;" and the employment of the word "war" in relation to "terrorism" (even if this was distinguished from "the war on terror").[121] How women emerged in these discourses remained somewhat consistent, albeit with some important and notable departures. While analysis of Obama's approach to counterterrorism has been documented elsewhere,[122] there were four key discourses related to counterterrorism under his administration which had implications for how women became visible in counterterrorism discourses and practices in the DoD, US State and USAID: (1) being "at war with terrorism;" (2) the "promotion of our values;" (3) "addressing underlying grievances;" and (4) CVE.

Within these, government discourses largely framed women in relation to counterterrorism in four primary categories. First, as security practitioners, where again they were referred to as the "men and women" of the US forces. Under Obama, the first comprehensive COIN strategy in Afghanistan was established in 2009; later, as the wars in Iraq and Afghanistan were drawn down, focus shifted to training and equipping foreign forces and targeted strikes (drone and air), all of which had important implications for how security practices engaging women evolved in both US and foreign forces.

The second was related to "values," which emphasized women's rights, equality and empowerment, and which was advocated by the US in many of its efforts. Here, the US stated it would lead by example through the "power" of its values, which was also a component of democracy promotion. This was encouraged in order to provide an alternative to extremism, and to encourage more responsive, accountable government. In doing so, the US hoped their efforts to promote women's equal status would contribute to stronger, more stable societies.

Third were "underlying grievances," again drawing on elements of democracy promotion, but which emphasized aspects that were noted to lessen the motivations for persons to join or support terrorist groups. Within this category, features such as women's education, maternal health and job training continued to be emphasized in US aid and foreign assistance.

Fourth, CVE efforts suggested that as threats became harder to predict and intercept, the government should partner with communities so as to empower them to interject and resist extremism themselves in more preventative efforts. Here, women became visible as family members or members of the community in CVE efforts both at home and abroad.

Women in relation to security were more frequently and expansively referenced under Obama, as seen in the 2010 and 2015 NSSs. The next section will expand on these broader discourses, including how women featured within these throughout the Obama administration. First, however, it will briefly discuss the NAP, which represented an important and marked shift in US discourses on women and security, and highlighted a clear juncture for how women subsequently evolved in the department and agency discourses and practices related to security in DoD, US State and USAID.

## The NAP on Women, Peace and Security

Between 2005 and 2011, twenty-nine countries eventually established NAPs on Women, Peace and Security (Denmark being the first of these). NAPs were a sort of toolkit for countries to draw on UNSCR 1325 and other international commitments, and to help them identify the key priorities and means of implementing women, peace and security priorities at the national level. Civil society actors also often took an active part in the development of NAPs. There was a recognition by the Obama administration that efforts to advance UNSCR 1325 had been stunted, so he issued Executive Order 13595 in December 2011[123] to establish an NAP on Women, Peace and Security and to recommend specific activities to support this.[124] The NAP was based on consultations with DoD, US State and USAID (amongst other US agencies), though implementation was focused largely on these departments and agency. Each had designated personnel responsible for the coordination and implementation of this plan, and the White House National Security Council staff also chaired an Interagency Policy Committee that prioritized women, peace and security.

The NAP was launched in 2012, a full twelve years after UNSCR 1325 (2000), and represented a significant shift with how women were emphasized in security discourses under the Obama administration. It drew directly off the UN's document, and aimed to "empower half the world's population to act as equal partners in preventing conflict and building peace in countries threatened and affected by war, violence, and insecurity."[125] The NAP described the course the US government would take to "[a]ccelerate, institutionalize, and better coordinate our efforts to advance women's inclusion in peace negotiations, peacebuilding activities, conflict prevention, and decision-making institutions; to protect women from gender-based violence; and to ensure equal access to relief and recovery assistance, in areas of conflict and insecurity."

The NAP highlighted four areas of focus: (1) women as equal participants in conflict resolution; (2) protections for women during and after conflict; (3) women and conflict prevention efforts; and (4) women's equal access to means of recovery. There were also five high-level commitments in the NAP: (1) national integration and institutionalization; (2) participation in peace processes and decision-making; (3) protection from violence; (4) conflict prevention; and (5) access to relief and recovery. Discussing the announcement of the NAP, Secretary Clinton stated:

> Women are too often excluded from both the negotiations that make peace and the institutions that maintain it. Now of course, some women wield weapons of war—that's true—and many more are victims of it. But too few are empowered to be instruments of peace and security. That is an unacceptable waste of talent and of opportunity for the rest of us as well.[126]

This demonstrated woman's perceived exclusion from the security space, and an inferred benefit from empowering women and bringing them into peace and security efforts; this contrasted with the view that their neglect was "a waste of talent and opportunity." It also highlighted a focus on agency-level policy and practice pertaining to women's roles in contributing to peace and security to better institutionalize and operationalize these efforts in the relevant branches of the US government. This was also supported by a growing body of research that demonstrated women's inclusion in peace processes made them less likely to fail and more likely to last at least fifteen years, as well as their demonstrated lower propensity for conflict and their ability to gather intelligence about potential security threats.[127]

The 2011 NAP, while poised to inform how women could be better empowered or considered in US counterterrorism efforts, was instead largely framed in terms of "conflict" and "building peace," particularly in conflict and war zones, and neglected more counterterrorism-specific discourses. It did not reference terrorism except where sexual-based violence could be used for the purposes of terror. What's more, it did not reference extremism, terrorism, radicalization, CVE or counterterrorism in any other capacity, suggesting that women's roles in peace and security were still viewed outside these fields, thus reflecting earlier critiques of UNSCR 1325. Nevertheless, the NAP broadened considerations of how women would be assessed in US security discourses and was based on a key UN resolution now guiding US national security efforts. It encouraged recruitment and retention of women in security sectors, including for the police and military, and highlighted countries such as Afghanistan where the DoD was leading these efforts. It further highlighted efforts to "[l]everage the participation of female US military personnel to encourage and model gender integration and reach out to female and male populations in partner nations." It noted the specific needs of former female combatants in disarmament, demobilization and reintegration (DDR) programs, recognizing that women could also be violent actors, and that ways in which to address them must be conscious of gender. Moreover, it increasingly recognized men as agents of change in this field (which had been largely absent up to that point), and that males could also be victims of sexual-based violence and active agents in conflict prevention, demonstrating broadened gendered considerations in relation to security. Lastly, it provided clear guidelines for agency implementation, monitoring and evaluation of these programs.

As Melanne Verveer, the US Ambassador for Global Women's Issues from 2009–13, noted, the 2011 NAP didn't have "all the contours that [UNSCR] 1325 would eventually have, but it was a recognition that women not only faced tremendous negative impacts, but also that they had a role to play and they needed to be given agency in those situations."[128] Ambassador Verveer also highlighted the importance of this executive order:

> Basically what [President Obama] was saying is when we do our diplomatic work, when we do our development work, when we do our Homeland Security work, or our work in our military operations, we need to factor in the participation of women, and we need to factor in their perspectives. So, whether it's in the training we do of peacekeepers, or it's in the work that our diplomats and ambassadors do in areas of conflict, that we are factoring in the pivotal role that women have to play.[129]

The accountability mechanism inherent in this NAP—where each agency was to provide an annual update on their progress—was also highlighted as an important step. But what progress was, or how it should be measured, was not clear-cut:

> One of the hardest things was figuring out what would be the indicators if you will; if you do monitoring and evaluation; what would be the indicators that demonstrate we are on the road to progress? What would work in the State Department? What would make a difference in the DoD? Those could be the measurable indices of how we were doing and the reporting that we were doing on ourselves in those spaces.[130]

The NAP still fell short in an environment where terrorism and violent extremism remained the primary concern of the United States, and related areas such as deradicalization or CVE were still in their infant stages, demonstrating a gap between contemporary security concerns and efforts to promote women in peace and security more broadly. Even so, the NAP represented the most advanced US government document to date in terms of identifying institutional steps and accountability mechanisms for making women and gender more integral to considerations spanning a wide range of security concerns. Such actions often took time to start shifting in practice, and thus the speed, extent and breadth of utilizing the NAP varied significantly across the DoD, US State and USAID.

## The 2016 NAP

In 2016, the US released its second NAP, wherein violent extremism now featured heavily throughout. The goal of the 2016 NAP was "to empower half the world's population as equal partners in preventing conflict and building peace in countries threatened and affected by war, violence, and insecurity. Achieving this goal is critical to our national and global security."[131] It also expanded the scope of the women, peace and security agenda to integrate climate change concerns (an issue also reflected in the 2015 NSS). Considerations of sexual minorities (including lesbian, bisexual and transgendered persons) were also prevalent throughout the document, recognizing how such persons can be particularly vulnerable to violence and undermined by attitudes and practices which discriminate against them.

There was also a notable expansion in the focus of this NAP, which was more explicit about women's roles in CVE. The document noted the "engagement and protection of women as agents of peace and stability are central to the United States' efforts to promote security; prevent, respond to, and resolve conflict; combat violent extremism; and rebuild societies."[132] It also recognized women as "perpetrators to victims of violence," noting that limitations on how their varied roles are understood "limits policy options and perpetuates strategic blind spots," including the potential securitization of women in this space, and their potential as violent actors or mitigators of violence.[133] It also recognized that women who act as combatants (or who possess other roles within armed forces) are often overlooked in DDR programs, as well as "those involving reintegration and rehabilitation for violent extremists," which "often fail to take into account their distinct needs."[134]

The 2016 NAP introduced a number of actions explicit to CVE, particularly in the areas of conflict prevention, stabilization and economic recovery. This included actions directed at DoD, US State and USAID to "[s]upport women's participation in efforts to de-radicalize men and women who have supported violent extremism, promote tolerance and pluralism in their communities, and advance stabilization and reconstruction activities."[135] The language in the document clearly emphasized "violent extremism" in its focus, whereas terrorism and indeed counterterrorism were not discussed to any notable extent. This increased emphasis on women who had been impacted by violent extremism and as actors who could counter this is commendable. However, the gap between efforts to advance women, peace and security aims as separated from those of counterterrorism efforts specifically represented a continuation of previous shortfalls to comprehensively assess and discuss women in all aspects of contemporary security. Nevertheless, the implementation of the NAP was mainstreaming and also very distinct in practice at the department level, as will be demonstrated in the following chapters.

*"At war with terrorism"*

Returning to the four themes emphasized in the Obama administration's approach to counterterrorism, Obama too retained the war narrative, although he took visible and expansive efforts to distinguish this to be more focused on specific organizations as opposed to terrorism writ large. Obama also made efforts to distinguish his administration from that of the past, noting "we are not at war with the tactic of terrorism or the religion of Islam. We are at war with a specific organization—al-Qa'ida [sic],"[136] a criticism that had been leveled at the Bush administration. He recognized that "the language we use matters" and "we cannot paint with a broad brush a faith as a consequence of the violence that is done in that faith's name." As such, his administration would be "very clear in distinguishing between organizations like al

Qaeda—that espouse violence, espouse terror and act on it—and people who may disagree with my administration and certain actions."[137] This was a clear marker of the efforts to separate the violence of terror actors from those who may be labeled "extremist" for their beliefs, and allowed for space to engage with those extremists who may in fact be viewed as partners in CVE work. US agencies which addressed this would also have to be modernized where they had previously fallen short: "We are indeed at war with al Qaeda and its affiliates. We do need to update our institutions to deal with this threat."[138] This "war" was similar to the one Bush had emphasized in legally justified terms: "this is a just war—a war waged proportionally, in last resort, and in self-defense."[139]

When it came to ISIS, Obama emphasized the use of "more firepower and Special Operations forces"[140] as part of these new actions. This included the use of drones at a rate of ten times that of President Bush.[141] Obama's emphasis on targeting terrorist leadership had seen the rise of US Special Operations Command (SOCOM) as the favored lead in US counterterrorism activities (this was previously led largely by the CIA's National Counterterrorism Center).[142] SOCOM is a command whose core activities include counterterrorism, direct action, unconventional warfare and security force assistance (amongst others).[143] SOCOM's Joint Special Operations Command (JSOC), which resides within SOCOM, also became a key resource to combat ISIS. Its roles included conducting drone strikes and carrying out conventional attacks,[144] and as the lead in countering ISIS external operations, targeting ISIS leadership and tracking ISIS fighters leaving the battlefield.[145]

Like Bush, women in US forces under Obama were without exception always referred to in either gender-neutral terms—such as "professionals"—or in terms of "the men and women" of the security forces, and Obama took efforts to recognize their participation in and contributions to security efforts. For example, he referenced "the patriotic men and women who defend our national security,"[146] or the "extraordinary efforts of America's sons and daughters here in Afghanistan."[147] He also noted these "men and women in uniform, all of you represent the same spirit of service and sacrifice."[148] Obama specifically praised the efforts of female soldiers: "our women in uniform play an indispensable role in our national defense. And time and again, they have proven themselves to be role models for our daughters and our sons—as students and as soldiers and as leaders in the United States armed forces."[149] He also acknowledged shifts in women's security roles had been occurring during his tenure: discussing Iraq, he noted the US saw "more women tested by combat than in any war in American history," and that the US had been improving care for "female veterans"[150] or creating "more tailored care for our women veterans."[151] At West Point, he commended the first all-female command team and female Rhodes scholars.[152] As the GWOT continued (now facing ISIS), US servicewomen continued to receive recognition: "We give thanks to our men and women in uniform—especially our brave pilots and crews over Iraq who are protecting our fellow Americans and saving the lives of so many men, women and children that they would never meet."[153]

However, discussions of foreign partners did not share the same level of recognition for the men and women in their armed forces, with Obama instead referencing in broader terms "Iraqi forces,"[154] "Afghan security forces"[155] or "security forces in Yemen."[156] This essentially retained another practice, started under Bush, which suggested a lack of emphasis on foreign women as security actors in their own right. Moreover, while women remained highly visible and praised in US forces, these discourses also now reflected increased gender considerations for female veterans and gay service members. For the first time in US history, Obama repealed "Don't ask, don't tell" in 2010, and opened military service to openly gay persons: "yes, we know that some of them are gay. Starting this year, no American would be forbidden from serving the country they love because of who they love."[157] In 2016, this also extended to lifting a ban on transgendered persons from serving openly in the military.

ISIS proved to be a game changer for global counterterrorism concerns, becoming a leading focus for US military efforts once their notoriety was established. As it carried out its reign of terror and continued to acquire land and resources at a shocking speed, Obama initiated air strikes against the organization in August 2014, referencing the 1973 War Powers Resolution. In September 2014 as thousands of Yazidis became trapped by the group on Mount Sinjar, Obama announced the formation of the Global Coalition to "degrade and ultimately defeat" ISIS, which eventually included seventy-four member states and four partner organizations. Referencing the 2001 AUMF in September 2014, Obama informed Congress of the commencement of anti-ISIS and anti-terror operations in Iraq and Syria.[158] Five reinforcing lines of effort to defeat the group were subsequently introduced by former Secretary of State John Kerry and Secretary of Defense Chuck Hagel. These included providing military support to US partners; impeding the flow of foreign fighters; stopping ISIS's financing and funding; addressing humanitarian crises in the region; and exposing the group's true nature.[159] As with al-Qaeda, ISIS were similarly discussed in terms of waging war: "we are not at war with Islam. We are at war with people who have perverted Islam."[160] Additionally, Obama vowed to "degrade and ultimately destroy the terrorist group known as ISIL" which have "exploit[ed] grievances for their own gain."[161] This also suggested that humanitarian considerations, and a battle of ideas relevant to exposing ISIS's "true nature" amidst its onslaught of online propaganda, were inherent in efforts to counter this terror group.

Alongside this, the increasing number of foreign fighters, including those from the US and Europe, made the group of particular concern for potential attacks outside of the Middle East. By 2017, at least 41,490 foreigners—men, women and minors—had traveled to Iraq and Syria and become affiliated with ISIS. This proved to be the largest and most diverse mobilization of foreign fighters in history.[162] While these fighters were predominantly viewed as male, thousands of family members including women and minors taken or born into the group, became recognized for their affiliation to ISIS. To counter this, ISIS were to be subjected to a campaign of air strikes and increased support for their opponents on the ground. In addition, humanitarian assistance was to be provided to displaced civilians, and counterterrorism streams utilized such as funding, intelligence and counter-ideology, as well as stopping fighters from entering the region in the first place. It was also deemed important to give a voice to former extremists: "We need to lift up those voices."[163]

ISIS were particularly notorious and noted for their executions, barbarism, killing of children, and how they "enslave, rape, and force women into marriage."[164] Indeed, Obama highlighted how "[m]others, sisters, daughters have been subjected to rape as a weapon of war."[165] With 24/7 news coverage showing the plight of thousands of Yazidis and other women under ISIS, there was little dispute that SGBV was a particular and unique concern under ISIS, and had to be integrated in efforts to respond to the group.

*"The power of our values:" Creating alternatives to extremism*

US "values" more generally—and those that referenced women specifically in terms of equal legal rights and opportunities—were emphasized under Obama, largely in the sense that these "provide alternatives" to extremism, thereby suggesting they undercut "push" factors towards extremism. While these were not framed in specific reference to counterterrorism, they continued to be emphasized in the context of democracy promotion in a contributory capacity, as well as in longer-term efforts to promote US security and to challenge extremist narratives (in other words, indirect efforts). For example, in the 2010 NSS, promotion of and respect for human rights and democratic values were noted as "efforts to advance security and prosperity [which] are *enhanced* by our support for certain values that are universal" [emphasis mine].[166]

These "values", both broadly and specifically, were consistently framed in terms of their contribution to long-term security. Obama stated:

> I believe with every fiber of my being that in the long run we also cannot keep this country safe unless we enlist the power of our most fundamental values [...]. They are the foundation of liberty and justice in this country, and a light that shines for all who seek freedom, fairness, equality, and dignity around the world.[167]

This emphasis on rights in particular was consistent throughout his tenure: "a fundamental part of our strategy for our security has to be America's support for those universal rights that formed the creed of our founding."[168] This was viewed as conducive to the security interests of the US, where the country had been willing to "bear the burden" of "promoting liberty and human dignity overseas, understanding its links to our own liberty and security."[169] These values were often contrasted alongside those of terrorists such as Bin Laden, who "rejected democracy and individual rights for Muslims in favor of violent extremism; his agenda focused on what he could destroy—not what he could build."[170] In referencing attempts to close the detention camp at

Guantanamo Bay in Cuba, and reforming the US's surveillance programs, Obama also noted: "we counter terrorism not just through intelligence and military action, but by remaining true to our Constitutional ideals, and setting an example for the rest of the world."[171] US values thus continued to be held up against those of the terror groups they were fighting. This in itself should not be surprising; but when such values were not considered to be upheld by the US (as was often pointed to in cases of rendition, torture or the Guantanamo Bay detention facility), then this could be seen to bolster extremist narratives and challenge the salience of "US values."

In line with some of the discourse of Bush, there were also references to "human dignity" more broadly, and a certain sense of US moral authority, exceptionalism and global leadership within this. Obama also offered a definition of "human dignity" which had been rarely defined in key discourses: "We were founded upon a belief in human dignity— that no matter who you are, or where you come from, or what you look like, or what religion you practice, you are equal in the eyes of God and equal in the eyes of the law,"[172] thus emphasizing the foundational principles of US equality. Discussing components of American leadership in the world, Obama noted one key element: "Our willingness to act on behalf of human dignity. America's support for democracy and human rights goes beyond idealism—it is a matter of national security." He continued: "Democracies are our closest friends and are far less likely to go to war. Economies based on free and open markets perform better and become markets for our goods. Respect for human rights is an antidote to instability and the grievances that fuel violence and terror."[173]

These discourses, and an emphasis on women's rights in particular, were renewed after 2011 as the Arab Spring started sweeping across the MENA region, thus offering the US an opportunity to reset troubled relations with the Islamic world. After years of mistrust of US motives, and in acknowledgement of their core interests in the region pertaining to counterterrorism and stopping the spread of nuclear weapons, Obama stated "we must acknowledge that a strategy based solely upon the narrow pursuit of these interests would not fill an empty stomach or allow someone to speak their mind."[174] By admitting that US counterterrorism efforts were problematic, off-balance and insufficiently addressing long-term concerns, Obama highlighted the tension between indirect and direct efforts in a comprehensive approach to security. As such, the Arab Spring presented an "historic opportunity. We have the chance to show that America values the dignity of the street vendor in Tunisia more than the raw power of the dictator." It became a moment when "after decades of accepting the world as it is in the region, we have a chance to pursue the world as it should be." As a result, the US sought to become a positive influence in the ever shifting region, including promoting universal rights and "equality for men and women under the rule of law." Such efforts would become "a top priority that must be translated into concrete actions, and supported by all of the diplomatic, economic and strategic tools at our disposal." But how did women feature in these considerations? One quote from Obama is worth highlighting in full:

> What is true for religious minorities is also true when it comes to the rights of women. History shows that countries are more prosperous and more peaceful when women are empowered. And that's why we would continue to insist that universal rights apply to women as well as men—by focusing assistance on child and maternal health; by helping women to teach or start a business; by standing up for the right of women to have their voices heard, and to run for office. The region would never reach its full potential when more than half of its population is prevented from achieving their full potential.[175]

Obama appeared to draw on a growing evidence base for this inclusion: countries were increasingly shown to be more prosperous and peaceful when women were empowered actors with protected and enforced rights, and were less likely to engage in inter- and intrastate violence; peace agreements that included women were also seen to be substantially more durable and long-lasting.[176] This helps explain why women features so prominently in US foreign policy under Obama.

Support for women was highlighted in three realms: (1) the equal rights of women in society, which constitutes more legally defined rights; (2) aid; and (3) women's rights, empowerment and participation in political, economic, educational and broader social terms. This was also embedded in wider efforts to emphasize women's concerns throughout Obama's presidency, for instance in his trying to promote equal pay for women in the Paycheck Fairness Act (2017), or by creating the White House Council on Women and Girls in 2009. The promotion of the rights and status of women under Obama was increasingly emphasized as a US foreign policy objective, and women's status was primed to become increasingly visible in the DoD, US State and USAID, with each of these then assessing how it aligned with areas of their own programming. This suggested that as different departments interpreted and translated this line of effort into their own strategies and programming, such language would increasingly be integrated into agency program designs, assessments and proposals for funding (including those that also had counterterrorism or CVE objectives).

"Dignity" also carried a particular value, where "we [the US] respect human dignity, even when we're threatened" and why the country:

> Defends free speech, and advocates for political prisoners, and condemns the persecution of women, or religious minorities, or people who are lesbian, gay, bisexual or transgender. We do these things not only because they are the right thing to do, but because ultimately they would make us safer.[177]

These discourses linked to values were increasingly expanded to include lesbian, gay, bisexual, transgender and intersex (LGBTI) issues and gender considerations more broadly, and were actively embedded in how state security was understood.

US "values" which were "lived" in the US were referenced as "one of our weapons against terrorists like ISIL—a critical part of our strategy." According to Obama: "One of the best antidotes to the hateful ideologies that try to recruit and radicalize people to violent extremism is our own example as diverse and tolerant societies that welcome the contributions of all people, including people of all faiths."[178] This was also referenced specifically in terms of "universal truths" inherent within democracy: "No woman should ever be abused with impunity, or a girl barred from going to school." This "inclusive democracy" made countries stronger: "When girls can go to school, and get a job, and pursue unlimited opportunity, that's when a country realizes its full potential."[179] The rights and empowerment of women were understood in terms of their status in healthy, democratic societies, and were believed to make societies stronger and more resilient to terrorism, although were still understood in long-term, forward-reaching efforts which would "ultimately make us safer."

*Addressing "underlying grievances"*

The third significant discourse related to women and counterterrorism under the Obama administration was that of "underlying grievances," which were noted to feed extremism and in some cases lead to violence. Many of these themes overlapped with the second category of "values" but were distinguished by their focus on foreign aid and development. These "deep-rooted problems" included poverty and sectarianism, and were reflective of growing concerns in the MENA region, particularly in the aftermath of the Iraq War, the turbulence created by the Arab Spring, and a wider acknowledgment that greater efforts had to be made to engage with and address factors which may contribute to extremism. These efforts were noted as long-term and tumultuous: "But our security and our values demand that we make the effort."[180] Here, aid efforts, particularly in terms of poverty reduction, and increased literacy/education, employment training and opportunities, were suggested to lessen the appeal of terrorist groups (interpreted here as factors that, when absent, may "push" individuals towards extremism).

Obama articulated this in terms of a broader approach to security focused on root causes or "well springs of extremism:"

> The use of force must be seen as part of a larger discussion we need to have about a comprehensive counterterrorism strategy—because for all the focus on the use of force, force alone cannot make us safe. We cannot use force everywhere that a radical ideology takes root; and in the absence of a strategy that reduces the wellspring of extremism, a perpetual war—through drones or Special Forces or troop deployments— would prove self-defeating, and alter our country in troubling ways.[181]

Addressing these underlying grievances would take a number of paths, including supporting democratic transitions, "because the peaceful realization of individual aspirations would serve as a rebuke to violent extremists." Other efforts included modernizing economies, advancing education and promoting entrepreneurship. The foreign assistance required to support these efforts "cannot be viewed as charity. It is fundamental to our national security. And it's fundamental to any sensible long-term strategy to battle extremism." Moreover, it was framed thusly:

A tiny fraction of what we spend fighting wars that our assistance might ultimately prevent. For what we spent in a month in Iraq at the height of the war, we could be training security forces in Libya, maintaining peace agreements between Israel and its neighbors, feeding the hungry in Yemen, building schools in Pakistan, and creating reservoirs of good-will that marginalize extremists. That has to be part of our strategy.[182]

In these discussions, women were referenced largely in terms of health, education and employment efforts. For example, Obama noted, "it is no coincidence that countries where women are well educated are far more likely to be prosperous," and that "[o]ur common prosperity would be advanced by allowing all humanity—men and women—to reach their full potential." Therefore the US would "partner with any Muslim-majority country to support expanded literacy for girls, and to help young women pursue employment through micro-financing that helps people live their dreams." This was framed in terms of "a responsibility to join together on behalf of the world that we seek—a world where extremists no longer threaten our people [...]." In cases such as these, improving aspects of women's lives were described as "mutual interests."[183]

Development, aid and women's empowerment was also linked to "a common interest in development that advances dignity and security," where "we should advance the truth that nations prosper when they allow women and girls to reach their full potential." Particularly in the context of the Arab Spring, this call for democracy was a "rebuke to the worldview of al Qaeda, which smothers the rights of individuals, and would thereby subject them to perpetual poverty and violence." It was recognized that "societies are more successful when their citizens are free, and that democracies are the closest allies we have."[184] Further-more, "[t]he future must not belong to those who bully women—it must be shaped by girls who go to school, and those who stand for a world where our daughters can live their dreams just like our sons."[185] Obama highlighted the Equal Futures Partnership—a US-led multilat-eral initiative established in 2012 to empower women economically and politically—as one step to ensure that women and girls could fully participate in politics and pursue opportunity. Discourses related to development continuously reinforced the inclusion of women: "We've talked about development and how it has to include women and girls—because by every benchmark, nations that educate their women and girls end up being more successful."[186]

Discussing Boko Haram's kidnapping of the Chibok schoolgirls in April 2014 at West Point, Obama made a clear assertion of this link between defense, diplomacy and development in countering violent extremism:

> No American security operation can eradicate the threat posed by an extremist group like Boko Haram, the group that kidnapped those girls. And that's why we have to focus not just on rescuing those girls right away, but also on supporting Nigerian efforts to educate its youth. This should be one of the hard-earned lessons of Iraq and Afghanistan, where our military became the strongest advocate for diplomacy and development. They understood that foreign assistance is not an afterthought, something nice to do apart from our national defense, apart from our national security. It is part of what makes us strong.[187]

Obama was clear to distinguish poverty from terrorism, but suggested it had a potential contributory element:

> Poverty alone does not cause a person to become a terrorist, any more than poverty alone causes someone to become a criminal. But when people—especially young people—feel entirely trapped in impoverished communities, where there is no order and no path for advancement, where there are no educational opportunities, where there are no ways to support families, and no escape from injustice and the humiliations of corruption—that feeds instability and disorder, and makes those communities ripe for extremist recruitment. And we have seen that across the Middle East and we've seen it across North Africa. So if we're serious about countering violent extremism, we have to get serious about confronting these economic grievances.[188]

This too referenced women's education as a component: "And as we go forward, let's commit to expanding education, including for girls. Expanding opportunity, including for women. Nations would not truly succeed without the contributions of their women."[189] Addressing "underlying conditions" was also specifically linked to ISIS: "Our strategy recognizes that no amount of military force would end the terror that is ISIL unless it's matched by a broader effort—political and economic—that addresses the underlying conditions that have allowed ISIL to gain traction."[190] These particularly referenced the ongoing civil conflict in Syria, and the shortfalls in effective, accountable governance in Iraq. The larger refugee crisis in this period was also increasingly framed in terms of both assistance and shared security: "Today, our concern for them is driven not just by conscience, but should also be driven by self-interest. For helping people who have been pushed to the margins of our world is not mere charity, it is a matter of collective security."[191]

Under Obama there was a consistent link to foreign assistance in terms of its contributions to security:

> If we're going to prevent people from being susceptible to the false promises of extremism, then the international community has to offer something better. And the United States intends to do its part. We would keep promoting development and growth that is broadly shared, so more people can provide for their families.[192]

Here, women's empowerment was again highlighted:

> Countries have to truly invest in the education and skills and job training that our extraordinary young people need. And by the way, that's boys and girls, and men and women, because countries would not be truly successful if half their populations—if their girls and their women are denied opportunity.[193]

Empowering women, particularly in education, employment and political streams, was suggested to lend to state stability and success so that extremism would be less likely to find resonance, and were consistently and actively emphasized over the duration of the Obama administration. These efforts were clearly long-term and preventative in their nature, suggesting that even while they were recognized and demanded, they would have to find balance with immediate, short-term counterterrorism and security aims in order to become part of an overarching comprehensive strategy. These three themes of defense, governance and development are also themes that were emphasized in both COIN and stabilization work, and were stressed throughout Obama's tenure, as will be seen in the following chapters.

## CVE: Engaging families and communities

Unlike the three preceding discourses, which focused predominantly on international US aims, CVE-specific discourses focused on both domestic and international US efforts to prevent terrorist action. The distinction between international and domestic concerns was reductive, however, as terrorist groups now increasingly engaged English-language online media to recruit members. Consequently, the perceived threat was viewed not only from those radicalized outside the US, but also by those within its borders. Moreover, with the rise of ISIS, increasing numbers of westerners (including Americans) were traveling abroad to join terror organizations, making preventative measures more necessary, where these could also act to limit or reduce cases of the US engaging its own citizens in places like Iraq, Syria and Yemen.[194] CVE was already gaining prominence in domestic and international discourses throughout Obama's tenure, although it was substantially broadened to combat the growing influence and impact of ISIS. Families, communities and community leaders were increasingly urged to interject to prevent radicalization, and hence viewed as partners in these efforts.

While CVE and counterterrorism share many similar aims (such as the prevention of violent acts), CVE can extend beyond specific law enforcement efforts into the pre-crime space to consider aspects such as counter-narratives, and discouraging recruitment or other means of encouraging or inciting violence.[195] Obama discussed what would be considered in CVE efforts:

> By "violent extremism," we don't just mean the terrorists who are killing innocent people. We also mean the ideologies, the infrastructure of extremists—the propagandists, the recruiters, the funders who radicalize and recruit or incite people to violence. We all know there is no one profile of a violent extremist or terrorist, so there's no way to predict who would become radicalized.[196]

Emphasis was specifically placed on anticipatory activities such as "preventing these groups from radicalizing, recruiting or inspiring others to violence in the first place."[197] Here too, the breadth of specific actors and tools now considered to challenge violent extremism was evidently broadening (counter-ideology, counter-propaganda, etc.), and provided new streams by which to assess how women were framed in counterterrorism-related discourses and practices. This was also part of a larger trend under Obama to go further upstream of the terrorist threat and focus more on preventative work which emphasized family and community roles, both domestically and in international, multilateral efforts.

Both within the US and abroad, there was a clear shift to empower families and communities to counter radicalization from homegrown threats: "Our best defenses against this threat are well informed and equipped families, local communities, and institutions."[198] The family was often referenced in general terms (versus specific roles for mothers and fathers) and noted to play an important part in CVE efforts: "we have to recognize that our best partners in all these efforts, the best people to help protect individuals from falling victim to extremist ideologies are their own communities, their own family members."[199] There appeared to be efforts by the Obama administration to avoid language which emphasized women in specific gendered roles, instead often emphasizing "family" efforts, or including women in more general terms. However, there were limited cases of more specific references to the roles of mothers in CVE efforts. For example, speaking at the YALI Regional Leadership Center in Kenya in 2015, Obama stated:

> The idea of women being actively engaged in countering violent extremism is absolutely critical. Mothers tend to be more sensible. (Laughter.) I'm just telling the truth. (Laughter and applause.) And obviously the younger we're reaching children and giving them the sense that violence is not the right path, and that's being reinforced by their primary caregiver, which typically is the mother, and the idea of peer-to-peer support but also some peer pressure in terms of making sure that mothers are involved in steering their children in the right way—I think that's a wonderful model.[200]

In domestic US efforts, community engagement was highlighted as a priority area: "supporting community leaders and influential local stakeholders as they develop solutions tailored to their own particular circumstances is a critical part of our whole-of-government approach that contributes to our counterterrorism goals," which would include communities, and governments at the state, local and federal level.[201] This would also include working more closely with communities to help identify when someone may be on the path to radicalization: "the best way to prevent violent extremism inspired by violent jihadists is to work with the Muslim American community—which has consistently rejected terrorism—to identify signs of radicalization and partner with law enforcement when an individual is drifting towards violence."[202] It was also increasingly recognized that global narratives were having domestic resonance and impacts: "Deranged or alienated individuals—often US citizens or legal residents—can do enormous damage, particularly when inspired by larger notions of violent jihad," making such efforts more important.[203] This also highlights how Obama viewed these CVE efforts in the context of their contribution to counterterrorism goals as part of a "whole-of-government" approach to counterterrorism.

Engagement and empowerment of individuals and community groups at a local level was thus seen as a key means of countering radicalization and violent extremism, particularly in terms of building societal resistance to extremism, which occurred alongside law enforcement efforts. Obama emphasized the government did not intend to take a lead in community CVE efforts, or securitize their relationship with the Muslim community; instead, they would provide resources and "engage with partners and raise awareness so more communities understand how to protect their loved ones from becoming radicalized."[204] Communities were to be assisted to protect themselves according to a more "self-help" model, with the federal government acting as facilitator, convener, and source of information, drawing off existing structures to do so.

There were also pointed efforts to counter extremist narratives of disenfranchisement by drawing on notions of the American family: "these partnerships can only work when we recognize that Muslims are a fundamental part of the American family."[205] This was opposed with terrorist efforts which were trying to exploit domestic US grievances: "As extremists try to inspire acts of violence within our borders, we are responding with the strength of our communities, with respect for the rule of law, and with the conviction that American Muslims are a part of our American family."[206] These domestic-focused statements are important to highlight: by demonstrating that the American Muslim community were fellow citizens, allies and partners in this work could resonate internationally, encouraging similar partnerships and relationships abroad.

Supporting youth around the world was also highlighted as a key way to address violent extremism. In one instance, Obama discussed a

letter he had received from Sabrina, an eleven-year-old who was growing up in the US who was worried about people hating Muslims:

> We have to remember that 11-year-old girl. That's our hope. That's our
> future. That's how we discredit violent ideologies, by making sure her
> voice is lifted up; making sure she's nurtured; making sure that she's
> supported—and then, recognizing there are little girls and boys like
> that all around the world, and us helping to address economic and
> political grievances that can be exploited by extremists, and empower-
> ing local communities, and us staying true to our values as a diverse and
> tolerant society even when we're threatened—especially when we're
> threatened.[207]

Obama outlined the four key steps that had been taken to protect
the homeland from attacks such as that in San Bernardino in 2015. The
first three were going after terrorists abroad; preventing terrorists
from entering the US; and stepping up efforts to prevent attacks at
home. The last entailed:

> Continu[ing] to strengthen our partnership between law enforcement,
> high-tech leaders, communities, faith leaders, and citizens. We've got
> to keep on building up trust and cooperation that helps communities
> inoculate themselves from the kind of propaganda that ISIL is spewing
> out, preventing their loved ones—especially young people—from suc-
> cumbing to terrorist ideologies in the first place.[208]

Internationally, Obama highlighted the role of Muslim communities
who "explicitly, forcefully, and consistently reject the ideology of organizations like al Qaeda and ISIL."[209] CVE had both distinct domestic
and international dimensions, but the increasing use of English-
language propaganda targeting western audiences by groups like ISIS
was increasingly erasing any clear separation between domestic and
international concerns.

In February 2015, Obama held the White House Summit on
Countering Violent Extremism in Washington, DC, with the aim of
addressing the drivers that fuel the growth of violent extremism through
education, economic opportunity, good governance and security solutions, particularly in areas "close to active terrorist conflict where populations are vulnerable to the spread of violent extremism," such as Syria
and Iraq. Women featured in CVE in this context both as victims of Boko
Haram and ISIS, and in terms of their education and access to opportu-

nity: "Nations would not truly succeed without the contributions of their women."[210] CVE thus incorporated and reflected many of the values and developmental and aid streams present in ongoing government initiatives. This was expanded in the 2015 Leaders' Summit on Countering ISIL and Violent Extremism, which highlighted new efforts to engage women in countering extremist narratives both online and offline, and in building community resilience to violent extremism.[211]

In comparison with earlier activities, which were viewed more on the periphery of counterterrorism efforts, women were now seemingly being encouraged to participate in more immediate and active efforts to challenge violent extremism (which could lead to terrorism) in preventative capacities. Many earlier discourses related to "dignity" also became folded into those of CVE:

> Around the world, we're also going to insist on partnering with Muslim communities as they seek security, prosperity and the dignity that they deserve. And this larger battle for hearts and minds is going to be a generational struggle. It's ultimately not going to be won or lost by the United States alone. It would be decided by the countries and the communities that terrorists like ISIL target. It's going to be up to Muslim communities, including scholars and clerics, to keep rejecting warped interpretations of Islam, and to protect their sons and daughters from recruitment.[212]

Community leaders also had an important role to play:

> Muslim leaders here and around the globe have to continue working with us to decisively and unequivocally reject the hateful ideology that groups like ISIL and al-Qaeda promote; to speak out against not just acts of violence, but also those interpretations of Islam that are incompatible with the values of religious tolerance, mutual respect, and human dignity.[213]

Other efforts in this period included countering propaganda and messaging (that is, contesting spaces that terrorists occupy), and "offering alternative visions." Obama challenged countries around the world to "counter extremist ideologies in our own countries—by getting intolerance out of schools, stopping radicalization before it spreads, and promoting institutions and programs that build new bridges of understanding."[214]

The Arab world was called on to recognize the potential of their people, where women were a focal point: "Where women are full participants in a country's politics or economy, societies are more likely to succeed. And that's why we support the participation of women in parliaments and peace processes, schools and the economy."This course of action was contrasted with places where:

> [If] the only option is between the dictates of a state, or the lure of an extremist underground, then no counterterrorism strategy can succeed. But where a genuine civil society is allowed to flourish—where people can express their views, and organize peacefully for a better life—then you dramatically expand the alternatives to terror.[215]

These steps would "increase efforts to lift up those who counter extremist ideologies and who seek to resolve sectarian conflict. And we would expand our programs to support entrepreneurship and civil society, education and youth—because, ultimately, these investments are the best antidote to violence."[216] Consequently, CVE increasingly incorporated governance and development streams of work more centrally as a primary (versus complimentary) effort in security. With this came a transition from efforts promoting women peripherally to viewing them as integral in core security efforts, which were emphasized both quantitatively and qualitatively.

In a 2015 visit to Mulberry School for Girls in Tower Hamlets, London, then First Lady Michelle Obama also echoed this CVE theme in direct relation to girl's education: "the world needs more girls like you growing up to lead our parliaments and our board rooms and our courtrooms and our universities. We need you. We need people like you tackling the pressing problems we face—climate change and poverty, violent extremism, disease."[217] This was particularly significant in both timing and location. Tower Hamlets had a population with the highest percentage of Muslims in England and Wales (38 per cent; the national average was 5 per cent), and so the First Lady was likely speaking to an audience full of young British Muslim women.[218] Tower Hamlets was also the borough from which three British schoolgirls had left in February 2015 to join ISIS, and where at least five other schoolgirls had had travel bans imposed on them.[219] There appeared to be a visible effort to avoid directly conflating girls' education and extremism in discourses, suggesting recognition of the controversy that securitization (or perceived instrumentalization) of these areas could bring. As such, it appeared that educated, empowered women were increasingly recognized as having an important role in CVE efforts.

Violent actors, however, were still largely recognized as male in these discussions, which proved to be a significant shortfall in how the US initially recognized and understood emerging parties like ISIS. Accordingly, it was believed that "[a]l Qaeda and its affiliates are small men on the wrong side of history,"[220] or that US intelligence agencies could now track "who a terrorist is in contact with, and follow the trail of his travel or his funding."[221] This suggested that women were also still not largely recognized in terms of the roles they were playing in al-Qaeda, and not really viewed as threats. Yet the emergence of ISIS started a shift in the recognition that women may also be potentially radicalized:

> When someone starts getting radicalized, family and friends are often the first to see that something has changed in their personality. Teachers may notice a student becoming withdrawn or struggling with his or her identity, and if they intervene at that moment and offer support, that may make a difference.[222]

In the US, this radicalization became visible in December 2015 when Tashfeen Malik, the "female terrorist," and her husband Syed Rizwan Farook killed fourteen people in San Bernardino, California. The couple had "gone down the dark path of radicalization"[223] and become the first jihadist terrorist couple to commit an act of terror in the US. The successful violence and impact of this attack likely gained it more attention than previous domestic cases of women involved in jihadist terrorist plots. For example, American citizen Colleen LaRose, otherwise known as "Jihadi Jane," had plead guilty to conspiracy to murder for her role in a 2009 plot to kill Lars Vilks. However, her case had been framed in the media as "farcical" and "absurd," and LaRose herself had been portrayed as both gullible and having come from a difficult background.[224] The case of Jamie Paulin-Ramirez, otherwise known as "Jihad Jamie," was portrayed similarly, and was also linked to LaRose and the Vilks plot. Though being convicted of providing material support to terrorists following her arrest in 2010, and allowing her young son to be trained to commit violence, in public portrayals of these women, neither were really viewed as violent threats. Instead, Paulin-Ramirez was noted to be a lonely woman who got "sucked into extremism."[225] It was not until a successful attack had been perpetrated in San Bernardino that the issue of female terrorism appeared to gain serious attention.

## Final points

This chapter has demonstrated the areas in which women became emphasized in key counterterrorism discourses throughout the Bush and Obama administrations in multifaceted, comprehensive approaches to security, where counterterrorism retained a primary focus. We have seen how these discourses were historically situated in the broader US strategies, the GWOT specifically, and subsequent US responses to terrorism, while reflecting on how different factors, such as the actions of terrorist groups, or distinct administrative approaches to counterterrorism, also impacted upon the evolution of women in these discourses.

There were similarities in the presidential discourses related to women and counterterrorism, but also some divergence (as summarized in Figure 2). There has been a consistent emphasis on women as security actors, though these expanded in scope under Obama to reference both gender, LGBTI persons, and the diverse roles that women could take up. There were also consistent efforts to improve women's rights, status and empowerment, which could also extend to areas such as women's dignity. However, the frequency and emphasis of these specific references proved far greater under Obama, who also appeared to draw on UN discourses more frequently than Bush. Women's status in society was viewed and referenced in peripheral terms in relation to security under Bush; however, under Obama, improving the status of women became a central policy aim. Moreover, it was increasingly linked to security, and was particularly evident in the NSS, CVE and preventative efforts. This also reflected the more overarching shift in counterterrorism efforts that moved from emphasizing military efforts under Bush, to also expanding CVE efforts under Obama. Women's victimhood was also recognized and responded to by Bush when discussing the Taliban in Afghanistan, and particularly with Obama as Boko Haram and ISIS engaged in horrific (and visible) sexual and physical violence against women. However, in the case of Obama, this appeared less instrumental to justify US policies, but instead acted as an important concern to be folded into counterterrorist policy. Finally, women were increasingly, though still not adequately, recognized in relation to terror groups, often in direct relation to jihadist terrorism, which was emphasized more under Obama with the emergence of ISIS as thousands of men, women and minors began traveling to Iraq and Syria.

The following chapters will now demonstrate where and how these national-level discourses impacted on women at the agency level in the DoD, US State and USAID in both their discourses and practices. In each chapter, I will emphasize specific factors which further informed how or why these shifted. While this multi-stream, multi-agency approach to counterterrorism demonstrates an overlap of programming and aims between agencies, each stream of effort has been placed under the chapter where that agency was seen to take the lead.

Figure 2: Summary of key discourses pertaining to women in the Bush and Obama administrations

| | Counterterrorism-pertinent discourse | Relevant agencies | Categorization of women most emphasized | Expression in discourses (select examples) |
|---|---|---|---|---|
| Bush | GWOT | – DoD | Women as security practitioners | Men and women of the military / armed forces |
| | Democracy promotion | – US State<br>– USAID | Women's rights, empowerment and equality (rights and legal status) | – Respect for women, women's rights, equality and dignity of women<br>– Women's participation in society / politics |
| | Underlying conditions / drivers of terrorism | – US State<br>– USAID | Women's rights, empowerment and equality (foreign assistance and aid) | – Women's education<br>– Women's health<br>– Employment training |
| Obama | At war with terrorist groups | – DoD | Women as security practitioners | – Men and women of the armed forces / in uniform<br>– America's sons and daughters in Afghanistan<br>– Role models<br>– LGBTI |

| | | | |
|---|---|---|---|
| US values and democracy promotion | – US State<br>– USAID | Women's rights, empowerment and equality (rights and legal status) | – Equality for women (rule of law)<br>– Women's empowerment<br>– Women in political office |
| Underlying grievances | – US State<br>– USAID | Women's rights, empowerment and equality (foreign assistance and aid) | – Women's education<br>– Maternal health<br>– Job training and employment |
| CVE | – US State<br>– USAID | Women's roles in communities | – Community members<br>– Community leaders<br>– Counter-narratives<br>– Societal resilience to extremism<br>– Civil society |
| | – US State<br>– USAID | Women's roles in families | – Mothers and fathers<br>– Well-informed and equipped families<br>– Family members |
| NAP on Women, Peace and Security | – DoD<br>– US State<br>– USAID | Women in all categories | – Police<br>– Conflict prevention<br>– Protect women from gender-based violence<br>– Women who wield weapons of war |

3

# THE DEPARTMENT OF DEFENSE

*"We're so conditioned as a people to think that a military campaign has to be cruise missiles and television images of airplanes dropping bombs, and that's just false. This is a totally different war. We need a new vocabulary. We need to get rid of old thinking and start thinking about this thing the way it really is."*

US Defense Secretary Donald Rumsfeld, 9 October 2001[1]

The US Department of Defense (DoD), US Department of State (US State) and US Agency for International Development (USAID) are discussed in the following chapters to show how each played a key role in US security and foreign policy efforts throughout this period. Each was a distinct entity, with its own unique history, culture and mandate. Dependent on the administration in office, each also saw changes in funding, operations and programming based on the evolving nature of the conflict at hand and that administration's proposed method for responding. As was seen in the previous chapter, both the Bush and Obama administrations emphasized a "whole-of-government," full-spectrum approach to security, but military and defense efforts remained the most prominent of these. This chapter will demonstrate the important ways that women became visible as actors, partners and targets of US defense efforts where counterterrorism was a primary or related component.

The DoD is the US department responsible for providing the military forces required to deter war and protect the United States' security, training and equipping their personnel in war-fighting activities, peace-keeping and humanitarian/disaster assistance. DoD engages most visibly in direct action and is the US agency most often associated with counter-terrorism-specific and broader security efforts abroad. Headquartered in the Pentagon, the DoD consists of three key military departments: the Department of the Army, the Department of the Navy (which houses the United States Marine Corps [USMC]) and the Department of the Air Force.[2] They are the country's largest employer (and the largest department of analysis), with over 3 million employees and an annual budget in 2016 that reached $580 billion.[3] As such, how DoD considers women and gender in their discourses and practices has significant implications that extend far beyond the department itself and are bound to dispropor-tionately impact a comprehensive approach to security.

In terms of the DoD's militarized or direct counterterrorism efforts, these more generally involve diverse operations and activities that occur "in isolation or combined with conventional force opera-tions," and include five principal activities: "counter-terrorism, uncon-ventional warfare, counter-insurgency (COIN), stability operations, and foreign internal defense." These also include civil military opera-tions, coordinating with US State and USAID in stability operations, security assistance programs and building partner capacity, amongst others.[4] The activities emphasized by the DoD have evolved since 9/11, and their emphasis has differed in each country and region of focus. This chapter will focus primarily on counterterrorism; counter-insurgency (COIN); stability operations (further expanded on in Chapters 4 and 5); and building partner capacity. These three chapters highlight how women were specifically understood and operationalized in each department/agency, as seen through their own discourses and practices, and as part of a "whole-of-government" approach to security, where counterterrorism remained a leading focus.

Female service members have a history in the DoD that stretches back to 1775, with the first woman accepted for duty in the Marine Corps Reserves in 1918. During World War II, women's roles further expanded significantly. Established in 1951, the Defense Department Advisory Committee on Women in the Services has provided advice and recommendations on "matters and policies relating to the recruit-ment and retention, treatment, employment, integration, and well-being of highly qualified professional women in the Armed Forces."[5] The Office of Diversity Management and Equal Opportunity also promotes equal opportunities for all US service members and civilian personnel, including women. These are focused on the roles and status of US servicewomen within the DoD itself, rather than how women are understood in DoD operations abroad or within foreign forces.

Women became particularly visible within the DoD via four primary categories pertinent to counterterrorism between 2001–17, and primarily under operations within the US Central Command's (CENTCOM's) areas of responsibility.[6] First, women were further integrated as servicewomen in US forces, with their roles as security actors evolving due to three primary factors. The first was due to the operational environments they were in, namely gender-segregated communities in countries such as Afghanistan and Iraq, which demanded operational adaptation. This was seen, for example, via the need for female soldiers who were able to engage with and search local women, which led to the establishment of new women's units such as Team Lioness. Second, as military operations in both Iraq and Afghanistan increasingly emphasized reconstruction, stabilization and COIN operations (an operational requirement due to growing insurgencies), there was an increased emphasis on engagement of women in local communities, with units such as Provincial Reconstruction Teams (PRT), Female Engagement Teams (FET) and Cultural Support Teams (CST) established to facilitate this outreach and engagement. Third, due to a combination of the increasing emphasis on promoting gender equality under the Obama administration, and the de facto front-line combat roles and experiences that women had in Iraq and Afghanistan, roles open to women expanded across the DoD, as highlighted in 2015 when all combat roles were finally opened up to them.

The second category in which women became increasingly visible was as security actors or servicewomen in foreign forces that the US partnered with, particularly through training and advising/equipping roles, and the specific counterterrorism units that were established. This was seen, for example, in the all-female elite counterterrorism unit in Yemen's Central Security Organization/Special Security Unit; the Daughters of Iraq program, supported and established by the US to enable local women to take up roles in security forces; or the training and support of women in the Afghan National Security Forces (ANSF) and Bangladesh's Rapid Action Battalion (RAB).[7] Each were intended to fulfil operational gaps that previously existed and to improve mission success in terms of standing-up partner forces to effectively manage security in their own backyard. They were also framed at times in terms of the empowerment they brought to women as communities of interest, their alignment with the principles of the United Nations Security Council Resolution (UNSCR) 1325 on Women, Peace and Security, as well as financial opportunities they provided to women, which overlapped with efforts emphasized in US State and USAID.

The third category was the increased attention paid to women in foreign populations as communities of interest. This demographic gained particular attention under COIN and stabilization efforts, and was driven by the increasing need to understand and respond to the communities being targeted and engaged with by insurgent groups, as emphasized in attempts to win the "hearts and minds" of civilian populations. This was also informed by a broader evolution in defense efforts, which increasingly engaged in stabilization work alongside US State and USAID to help countries recover from past armed conflict and prevent its return. The increased emphasis of the UNSCR 1325 on Women, Peace and Security also informed this, as there was growing recognition that women were disproportionately impacted by violence and conflict, and should be considered and included in all aspects of improving the status of these three fields. This was reflected in the 2011 National Action Plan (NAP), which had specific streams of effort for DoD. Finally, women were increasingly considered to be potential security threats, necessitating increased awareness of women in terrorist and insurgent forces.

The DoD Joint Publications (JPs) are useful to assess how and where women and gender became relevant to DoD operations. Published by the Joint Chiefs of Staff, JPs provide joint doctrine to plan, execute and assess the topic of their focus across a range of relevant military operations. They also reflect changes in doctrine that developed over the years and consider new administrative approaches to their topics. Furthermore, they take into account any lessons learned so that they can be updated and integrated into DoD doctrine. Three JPs in particular will be considered throughout this chapter: "JP 3–26: Counterterrorism"

(2009, 2014), "JP 3–24: Counterinsurgency" (2006, 2014) and "JP 3–07: Stability Operations" (2003, 2008, 2014).

It will be demonstrated that discourses and practices related to women were largely driven internally within the DoD based on operational requirements and "learning" in these environments. UNSCR 1325 and the 2011 NAP also influenced the DoD to some extent by integrating the "women, peace and security" agenda into DoD activities. There also appeared to be agency limitations based on a lack of gender knowledge in DoD doctrine and operations, but also tensions between the DoD, US State and USAID in terms of interagency prioritizations, and the impacts and implications of one stream on another.

Expanding on these four categories, this chapter will illustrate how counterterrorism efforts conceived of women in the DoD's discourses and practices, and what factors drove these changes. The first section considers women in US forces in Afghanistan, Iraq and Yemen; it provides a brief overview before discussing the extensive programs and lines of effort that proved significant for the evolving roles of women in relation to security. It follows these in a linear fashion, in the order of their development. In Iraq, these included both Team Lioness and the troubling cases of US soldiers' actions in relation to women in Iraq. After considering programs that traversed Iraq and Afghanistan, it then discusses Human Terrain Systems, stabilization efforts, PRTs and FETs. These also included CSTs, evolutions in COIN and counterterrorism doctrine, and the 2011 NAP on Women, Peace and Security. This section ends with a summary of the evolving roles of US women that found their foundation in the Global War on Terror (GWOT).

The second section considers women in foreign forces in relation to US defense efforts where these units were directly trained, equipped or otherwise supported by US forces. It examines the all-female counterterrorism unit in Yemen; the Sisters of Fallujah, Sisters of Ameriyah/Ferris and Daughters of Iraq programs; women who served on the front lines against the Islamic State in Iraq and Syria (ISIS); and women in the ANSF and Afghan National Police (ANP). The final section considers how women have evolved as "security actors" or militants in jihadist groups (primarily al-Qaeda and ISIS), thus necessitating DoD consideration and response. This is the longest chapter in this book, and speaks to the significant changes that US women, their partners and indeed the organizations they were countering have experienced since 9/11, particularly in relation to defense.

## Women in US forces

President Bush led the US into war on two occasions, first in Afghanistan (2001) and then in Iraq (2003). At their peaks, these wars saw approximately 45,000 US troops (Afghanistan, 2009) and 165,000 US troops (Iraq, 2007) on the ground. In total, over 2.7 million uniformed Americans served in these two wars. Significant resources were allocated to the DoD during Bush's tenure, which between 2001 and 2009 saw their base budget increase by 70 per cent, as well as an increased ground force, the use of unmanned aerial vehicles and Special Operations Forces.[8] Women proved significant to this war effort, and comprised a substantial 14.3 per cent of active-duty US armed forces by September 2009 (a figure similar to that in 2000).[9] In 2015, there were 201,400 active-duty female military service members.[10]

Throughout this period, US women featured heavily in security discourses as the "men and women" of the armed forces, a theme that remained consistent under President Obama. They were "America's men and women in uniform,"[11] or the "disciplined, skilled, dedicated and professional service men and women."[12] According to the 2004 National Military Strategy, "Success depends on the dedication, professionalism and skills of the men and women in uniform."[13] The "selfless service and heroism of the men and women of the well-trained all-volunteer Total Force"[14] was also recognized. Women were consistently discussed as security actors during this time, and their roles in US security forces were constantly emphasized. Although seemingly in terms of equal status and value to their peers, in practice many roles (such as combat) were still limited for them. Moreover, even as new units and programs were established, these often relied on flawed or limited assumptions about women's roles in defense efforts. The first indication of this was seen in 2003 combat operations in Iraq.

## Combat operations in Iraq: The establishment of Team Lioness

Team Lioness was a unique initiative formed in Iraq in 2003 that consisted of groups of female US personnel who offered support services to all-male combat units, particularly for searching and facilitating inter-action with Iraqi women.[15] This included specifically engaging Iraqi women in local communities and searching them for concealed weapons and other contraband. Team Lioness was noted as an operational neces-sity as the US military adapted to overcome cultural sensitivities and security concerns in the country. It drew on diverse women from vari-ous roles across the US forces. As Lieutenant Colonel Richard Cabry, Commander 1/5 Field Artillery, who established the unit, noted: "I didn't foresee the need or circumstances to set [it] up as such, [where] we would utilize female soldiers in the roles we did. The goal [was] to ensure that nobody was smuggling anything, but we knew that male soldiers could not search women with our hands."[16] Some of the practi-cal roles Team Lioness members undertook were noted by Specialist Rebecca Sava, a supply clerk with the US military who served with Team Lioness: "They needed women to go out on the missions to calm the women and children. We gave the kids candy, toys, [and] school sup-plies, so in the beginning the army didn't look so bad to them."[17] Another member noted how women were placed at traffic points and entry and exit points where cordon searches were taking place. Specialist Rebecca Nava noted: "We were just supposed to sit out there at the traffic control points comforting the females and I think just our pres-ence made them feel better."[18] Team Lioness thus played two roles: searching Iraqi women (prompted by local cultural norms and security requirements unique to this operational environment, in which women may be moving weapons or other contraband) and softening interactions between US soldiers and the local community.

The history and evolution of this team was captured in a 2008 docu-mentary *Lioness*. The unit emerged out of the 1st Engineer Battalion through its commander Lieutenant Colonel William Brinkley, who thought the ad hoc roles women were playing should become more institutionalized:

> As we started playing around with it I said "Hey, this is sort of a special type [of] situation. We should come up with something that develops an *esprit de corps*, makes it a neat thing, something [they] want to look forward to," and so we initially came up with the idea of Lionesses.[19]

Team Lioness was noted to be successful in "increasing security, infor-mation operations, and relations building."[20] Specific combat training was not given regularly to these combat support troops, even though it was often assumed these women had already received some, which made this particularly dangerous for some of its members. There were also changes in organizational culture where female military personnel who were embedded with USMC units were noted to have faced steep learning curves without preliminary preparation or training before going out with combat troops.[21]

These roles evolved for Team Lioness in Ramadi in April 2004, when the USMC were sent in to deal with escalating violence. Captain Lori Manning USN (retired) of the Women's Research and Education Unit noted: "These women in Ramadi would become the first to engage in offensive ground combat operations in this country's history."[22] Women were embedded with USMC units in specific operations, protecting unarmed interpreters, and dealing with women and children during home searches and invasions. However, at times they were also included with USMC firing teams, both coming under and at times returning fire. Lieutenant Colonel Cabry noted: "It really was not an ideal situation to have the Lioness team out there because we had now transitioned from a benign search operation into semi-urban conflict."[23] Lioness member Major Kate Guttormsen also referenced some of these concerns as "grey lines," which in Iraq included a lack of a demarcated front line and raised concerns about women's roles in front-line combat:

A lot of people are concerned about women overstepping or going outside of their legal positions on what they can be doing and what roles they are supposed to be fulfilling in the army. When we go outside of the wire the enemy doesn't care what gender you are. You all run the same risk of an IED [improvised explosive device] ambush or a small arms ambush.[24]

Discussing this gap between legality and the reality on the ground, Captain Manning noted a 2005 Congressional and Armed Services debate that planned to discuss the roles of women in combat:

During the debate in Congress word came down to the Armed Services Committee from very high up the administration saying, "withdraw that question right now, don't go there" because if we were to obey the policy we would probably have to pull out most of the women in Iraq and Afghanistan from Iraq and Afghanistan and our ability to wage those wars would fall about. They do not want that question coming up again or catching the public interest while operations in Iraq are still going on.[25]

This pointed to internal debates and tensions in the DoD that continued between 2001 and when combat positions were fully opened to women in 2015, namely that there was seemingly an operational need for women's roles in these units and missions in this specific environment. However, the DoD faced institutional limitations which restricted women from combat roles, which limited their participation in operations. It also illustrated how the locations the US was operating in were no longer traditional wars with clearly demarcated front lines, previewing broader shifts that would occur such as a growing emphasis on COIN.

It was argued in a 2009 report by the Defense Advisory Committee on Women in the Services that women in Team Lioness had helped accomplish missions in the field, had not negatively impacted on unit cohesion, and in their roles more "closely emulate the conventional combat roles of male counterparts than did those of their predecessors." The presence of women during these missions had also allowed for "greater sensitivity to cultural issues surrounding gender," had brought with them "unique perspective or approach" and were "more careful with details," suggesting they were viewed as providing a positive contribution (albeit in stereotypical feminine forms).[26]

Team Lioness also highlight a point of debate in the DoD throughout these years: that the inclusion of women in such units would negatively impact on unit cohesion. Indeed, there were debates between those who viewed women's roles in combat positively, negatively or in more gender-neutral terms. Team Lioness indicated the GWOT was expanding the roles of women in US forces. This was due initially to the present cultural norms that restricted men from accessing women, as well as the shift in combat environment. It highlighted how such roles for women were initially based both on very gendered assumptions and battlefield practicalities (for instance, where women could help calm women and children), but also suggested they could provide an important role in operations. However, these appeared to be responsive rather than proactive initiatives, while considerations of how to initially access and address the concerns or needs of women in the local community, or to recognize their roles as potential threats or supporters of insurgencies, were overlooked.

Other programs were also established, such as the Iraqi Women's Engagement Program, a US State outreach program which partnered with the USMC. Civil Affairs Marines began the program in al Anbar Province in 2006 to build trust with local women over cups of tea, sewing circles and medical engagements,[27] and to open lines of communication with local women. It was also understood as a way to identify influential women in the community who could act as leaders in women's committees.[28] This program reflected what later emerged prominently in FETs. Although there is very little information available about this program, it highlights early interagency efforts to further engage with women in local populations, even as the proximity to the front line seemingly discouraged any promotion or recognition of the unit.

### Women and controversy in Iraq

The US war in Iraq proved controversial for many reasons. However, several incidents involving US soldiers—both male and female—proved questionable if not outright damaging to US forces. These included the abduction of Private Jessica Lynch, events at Abu Ghraib prison, and the murder of fourteen-year-old Abeer al-Janabi. Each of these cases highlight a number of important considerations, including how female soldiers were portrayed in public and political discourses in this period, as well cases of US forces directly contravening their image of aiding the people of Iraq, including with the protection of women.

### Jessica Lynch

One of the most publicized cases involving a female US soldier was that of then nineteen-year-old Private Jessica Lynch of the Army's 507th Maintenance Company, who was hailed as a hero and became a household name across America. On 23 March 2003, the convoy she was traveling in was ambushed in the town of al-Nasiriyah. Eleven personnel were killed, and Private Lynch, along with five of her colleagues, were taken as prisoners of war (POW) by Iraqi forces. On 1 April 2003, she was retrieved from a hospital in al-Nasiriyah by US Special Forces after a tip-off from an Iraqi lawyer who had happened upon her location and witnessed abuse against her by Iraqi forces. While in Iraqi custody, she was also sexually assaulted. The case of Lynch received significant media attention, but has been criticized for the public portrayal of the event (which proved to be highly inaccurate) and the implications for female soldiers in Iraq.

Early official accounts of the ambush turned out to have been embellished, and were eventually debunked in a House Report produced by the Committee on Oversight and Government Reform in 2007. The controversy began with an article in the *Washington Post* on 3 April 2004, which quoted an anonymous official who claimed that Lynch had been "fighting to the death" during a gunfight, receiving significant wounds in the process. A CENTCOM public affairs officer, Navy Captain Frank Thorp, later noted: "Reports are that she fired her (M-16 rifle) until she had no more ammunition," suggesting she was actively fighting until capture. Her rescue operation also detailed significant resistance against US forces whilst being removed her from the hospital. The story and video of her rescue was noted by Lieutenant Colonel John Robinson as "an awesome story"[29] and was broadcast heavily in the days following the event.

However, it was later demonstrated that Lynch had not picked up a weapon or engaged in a gunfight, and had sustained injuries as part of the initial hit by a rocket-propelled grenade on the convoy. Furthermore, the rescue operation was more dramatized in public portrayals. Reports also neglected the care and attention that the Iraqi nurses provided her and the attempt they had made to get Lynch returned to US forces. The House Report noted a tough political environment during the early days of the war, and that "the misinformation might be part of a deliberate propaganda strategy."[30] It also suggested that Lynch's story had been doctored to draw attention away from other debates the war was raising. Lynch later testified about the impact that period and portrayal had on her physically and emotionally. Though still "unwavering" in her support of US troops, she had experienced a "personal struggle" and wondered "why they chose to lie and tried to make me a legend" instead of just another soldier and POW. She highlighted women like her best friend Lori Piestewa, who had also been in the convoy, had assisted fellow soldiers, and who later died from her injuries but received little media attention and recognition.[31]

This episode received much scrutiny for how Lynch as a female soldier had been constructed in these official discourses, and why her story in particular received so much attention. These included sensa-tionalism about her portrayal fighting (in one instance she was even referred to as "little girl Rambo"), though this would be expected of soldiers more generally, thereby making the acts of female soldiers viewed as exceptional. The emphasis on her being "fought for" and "saved" also detracted from the perception of her as a regular soldier, and highlighted how such emphasis marginalized and neglected the stories of other female soldiers in this episode, including Shoshana Johnson (an African-American soldier) who was injured and also became a POW in the same incident, instead seeing Lynch's role as ideal and worthy of mainstreaming.[32] The story of a "vulnerable" female soldier being "rescued" in a period when the US war was facing many challenges was also critiqued for reframing discussions about the con-flict in emotional rather than rational terms, and was accused of being strategically used to win support for the war.[33] The story of Lynch demonstrates how official discourses around female soldiers could also be used to shape public impressions of US war efforts and reinforce problematic stereotypes related to women's perceived roles in battle, wherein the "men and women" of US forces were viewed distinctly.

*Abu Ghraib*

On 28 April 2004, a number of pictures taken inside the Abu Ghraib prison complex in Baghdad became public, highlighting detainee abuse conducted at the hands of US forces. In these photos, detained men were pictured in a number of disturbing and humiliating positions: they were hooded, injured, naked, piled on top of one another, and being intimi-dated by military dogs. The 2004 Taguba Report, commissioned by the army to investigate these events, also recorded that detainees had expe-rienced beatings; there were cases of men who had been sodomized, threatened with rape and forced to wear women's underwear; both female and male detainees who had been photographed naked; and a male military police (MP) guard having sex with, and recording, female detainees. It scathingly recorded, "numerous incidents of sadistic, blatant, and wanton criminal abuses were inflicted on several detainees."[34] George Bush noted the Abu Ghraib scandal as "the biggest mistake" made by the US in Iraq.[35] Abu Ghraib, alongside other detention facilities such as Guantanamo Bay in Cuba, became a *cause du jour* and lightning rod for recruiting insurgents into combat to fight against American forces. What is more, women featured heavily throughout this scandal.

The US internment and resettlement operations, including detainee operations at Abu Ghraib, were overseen at this time by Army Reserve Brigadier General Janis Karpinski and the 800th MP Brigade. Karpinski was the only female commander in the war zone at this time, and had noted she had no experience or prior training to run a detention facility. A report following an investigation into the abuses at Abu Ghraib noted her "complete unwillingness to either understand or accept that many of the problems inherent in the 800th MP Brigade were caused or exacerbated by poor leadership and the refusal of her command to both establish and enforce basic standards and principles among its soldiers."[36] However, Karpinski had countered this and stated it was because she was a woman and a reservist that she had been labeled the scapegoat, but also that she was being used to produce a "new image of what happens when women go to battle."[37] Karpinski was relieved of command of the 800th MP Brigade and rotated out of Iraq. However, in an inquiry into the treatment of detainees in US custody released in 2008 by the Senate Committee on Armed Services, it was proven that the administration had opened the door to considering aggressive techniques against Taliban and al-Qaeda detainees, a point of significant critique about US actions and conduct during the GWOT.[38]

Other women embroiled this scandal included Private First Class Lynndie R. England, and Specialists Sabrina Harman and Megan Ambuhl of the 372nd MP Company, who all faced prosecution and conviction for their roles in crimes committed at the detention center. The role of Lynndie England in particular gained significant attention both in the media and amongst scholars. Captured in these images was the soldier holding a leash placed around the neck of a naked and bloodied male prison; in another, she was seen smoking a cigarette, smiling and gesturing towards naked, hooded, male detainees. The then twenty-one-year-old soldier was dishonorably discharged for her actions, and was given a sentence of three and a half years for one count of conspiracy, four of maltreating detainees, and one of committing an indecent act.

The particular notoriety of England was due largely to the perceived transgression of traditional gender norms that she represented, which was particularly captured in media coverage of the event. Howard and Prividera argue that England was objectified in the media, her agency in these actions problematically presented, and that she became represented as an embarrassing and "fallen woman" for failing to adhere to military codes of ethics.[39] In this male-dominated and masculinized military sphere, Enloe also questioned whether some of these women may have decided to join in these activities and play these roles as a way of gaining male acceptance.[40] For example, England had a sexual relationship with the "ringleader" of this abuse, Charles Graner, and it was suggested that he "used" her at the time and that she participated in the abuse to please him. Others have also raised the more significant concern that US forces both here and in Guantanamo Bay were using strategic sexual violence through sexual torture or humiliation as a form of terror and punishment against a targeted group.[41]

From sexual violence committed or threatened against male detainees, to the particularly noted humiliation of having a female soldier emasculate a male detainee, such actions were directly intended to exploit gendered male roles in Iraqi society and exploit these for the purposes of humiliation. The case also demonstrated the women in US forces could be actors in its transgressions, though in distinctly gendered ways.

## Abeer al-Janabi

The case of fourteen-year-old Abeer al-Janabi proved to be one of the most disturbing cases to come out of the Iraq War. As is discussed in the final section of this chapter, the crimes committed against her and her family at the hands of US soldiers has since been a call to arms for diverse jihadist groups throughout the region, and highlights the gendered relationship between the actions of both US forces and the groups it countered. On 12 March 2006, Steven D. Green of the 502nd Infantry Regiment of the 101st Airborne (air assault) led fellow unit members Paul Edward Cortez, James Paul Barker and Jesse Von-Hess Spielman in multiple crimes against the al-Janabi family in the town of Yusufiyah near Mahmudiyah. The four soldiers approached the isolated home and drove Abeer's father, Kassem Hamza Rachid al-Janabi, and six-year-old daughter Hadeel inside the home. They then divided the family, including her mother, Fakhriya, into another room, before executing them at close range. Abeer was meanwhile sexually assaulted and raped, before she was killed at close range. The horrific act was finalized when the group lit Abeer's corpse on fire and initiated an explosion at the house to destroy the evidence before returning to their post.[42]

Green was later diagnosed with a personality disorder and received early release from his duties in Iraq. Yet it was only following his honorable release from the military that the crime was uncovered and he and his four unit members charged. Green was convicted in a civilian court of rape and murder, and sentenced to multiple life sentences in prison. Barker, Cortez and Spielman were tried in a military court and each pleaded guilty to murder, conspiracy, obstruction of justice, arson and housebreaking; they received sentences of ninety, one hundred and 110 years of confinement, respectively (although they are each eligible for parole in ten). Bryan Lee Howard, another member of this unit who remained at their post to keep watching during this event, was convicted of being an accessory after the fact for his role in the cover-up, and of conspiring to obstruct justice. He was demoted, dishonorably released and received a twenty-seven-month sentence.[43]

The case raised important concerns about the implications of US forces contravening their stated aims: if they were there to install democracy and promote women's rights and empowerment while simultaneously engaging in the horrific abuse of local women, then such incidents were not only ripe for terrorist propaganda, recruitment and calls for action, but also detracted from the strength and resonance of US discourses and support for these practices.

While these cases represent a mere fraction of all US forces, they did highlight diverse examples of how the image of women in US forces could be manipulated and doctored for political aims; that women could themselves be involved in disturbing violations and violence in times of war; and that they could also be victims at the hands of US forces. Such cases also directly impacted the female-centric discourses the US themselves espoused; for how seriously could the US claim to be dedicated to women's rights and protections if they themselves were committing violence? What did it mean for other female soldiers if they were continuously framed in idealized roles instead of just as soldiers? Taking a step back from these specific cases, a wider trend which increasingly emphasized a COIN approach in Iraq and Afghanistan marked another turning point for women in the DoD.

## COIN: Gain the women, undermine the insurgents

In both Iraq and Afghanistan, what were initially meant to be limited military operations eventually evolved into COIN operations. Counterterrorism remained an aspect of this, particularly as the threat from insurgency began to overshadow that from terrorism. Insurgencies differ from terrorism in that terrorists use the tactic of terrorism (and the fear and coercion that come with it) to influence political agendas to suit their own aims. In contrast, insurgencies try to overthrow or substantially weaken existing government structures while increasing their own control, and work to gain the support of populations under their sphere of influence. Insurgents tend to use all available tools, including "political (including diplomatic), informational (including appeals to religious, ethnic, or ideological beliefs), military, and economic—to overthrow the existing authority."[44] The most evident example of this in the GWOT was the Taliban in Afghanistan, who, once removed from power, have continued to fight and undermine the internationally recognized Afghan government that replaced them. Others included ISIS in Iraq and Syria after 2014, who simultaneously engaged in insurgent and terrorist activities.

Terrorist organizations can participate in insurgencies, engage in guerilla tactics, and may be assessed in their potentially hybrid nature. In response to insurgents, who often engage in terrorism as a "tool" or "tactic," both counterterrorism and COIN can be considered or carried out simultaneously. Terrorist groups can also take advantage of the instability caused during insurgencies to advance their aims, thereby bridging COIN and counterterrorism considerations.[45] In 2010, David Kilcullen (a senior COIN advisor to General Petraeus from 2007–08) suggested the GWOT was "a defensive war against a worldwide Islamic jihad, a diverse confederation of movements that uses terrorism as its principal—but not its sole—tactic".[46] As a result, COIN became more relevant than just counterterrorism, with each viewed as interlinked or mutually reinforcing, and approaches to them in Afghanistan and Iraq occurring concurrently.[47] Aspects such as security of populations, effective governance (civil services, health, education) and perceived political legitimacy are central to COIN efforts, and were increasingly relevant in the same operational space at times as counterterrorism operations.

COIN is the "comprehensive civilian and military efforts designed to simultaneously defeat and contain insurgency and address its root causes."[48] As such, it encompasses offensive (eliminating insurgents), defensive (protecting the population and infrastructure) and stability operations (civil security and control, essential services, governance, and economic and infrastructure development).[49] The general approach taken in COIN is "clear, build, and hold:" clearing enemy forces from an area and eliminating resistance; securing the population (including with local forces) and infrastructure, and then re-establishing government capacity and authority; and building support of the local populations for their government while continuing to ensure civilian protection until the government can sufficiently resume its governance role. COIN efforts increasingly considered and emphasized women in the communities being engaged, and broadened roles for US female service members. Meanwhile, COIN doctrine considered how engaging and assisting women in local populations could lend to wider COIN objectives; it also considered them as insurgents themselves. The US Army and USMC's "Army Field Manual 3–24: Counterinsurgency" (FM 3–24) was key to this, but it had been decades since the US had engaged in COIN operations, and it had to be updated to suit these contemporary operational environments, first in Iraq and then Afghanistan amidst the broader GWOT.[50]

FM 3–24 was revamped under the supervision of General David Petraeus in 2006. This period was one of heightened violence in Iraq, with civilian casualties increasing and over 1,200 sectarian murders a month in December 2006. Over 1,000 weekly attacks were targeted at Iraqi civilians, security forces and coalition forces by insurgents, including the most extreme of these—al-Qaeda in Iraq (AQI).[51] The 2006 FM 3–24 was based on "lessons learned in previous counterinsurgencies and contemporary operations," and provided "techniques for generating and incorporating lessons" into contemporary COIN efforts.[52] The development of FM 3–24 was driven by past US experience in the field and contemporary COIN literature.

It noted: "Knowledge of the history and principles of insurgency and COIN provides a solid foundation that informed leaders can use to assess insurgencies. This knowledge can also help them make appropriate decisions on employing all instruments of national power against these threats."[53]

For COIN operations to be successful, they had to "thoroughly understand the society and culture within which they are being conducted," including how key groups are organized in society (including leadership systems); ideologies and narratives that resonate with key groups; and values, interests and motivations of populations, amongst others.[54]

The manual highlighted some specific gendered aspects of COIN operations, such as understanding social norms in terms of "the appropriate treatment of women and children" or how engaging women could help gain the support of communities and families.[55] It also highlighted the role of female counterinsurgents, and how the women embedded in their families and local communities could assist in undermining them. In the most expansive discussion of women, a section entitled, "Engage the women; be cautious around the children," it notes:

> Most insurgent fighters are men. However, in traditional societies, women are hugely influential in forming the social networks that insurgents use for support. When the women support COIN efforts, family units support COIN efforts. Getting the support of families is a big step toward mobilizing the population against the insurgency. Co-opting neutral or friendly women through targeted social and economic programs builds networks of enlightened self-interest that eventually undermine the insurgents. Female counterinsurgents, including interagency people, are required to do this effectively.[56]

However, overall considerations specific to women proved minimal in this 2006 manual.

Discussing the development of FM 3–24, General Petraeus suggested that previously established programs like Team Lioness informed the manual in terms of what role such teams could play when helping to establish brigade combat teams and a broader host of "augmentees that are provided to a unit when it is going to deploy, and the types of those augmentation elements are determined by what mission we are going to ask that unit to perform."[57] In other words, the inclusion (or exclusion) of programs comparable to Team Lioness was based on mission-specific requirements the US Army was being asked to perform in COIN operations, and if/how the inclusion of something akin to a women's unit would help them achieve their mission. Discourses related to the broader women, peace and security agenda had no impact on the development of the manual:

> I don't ever recall reflecting on, or even reading UNSCR 1325, much less thinking about how it should apply in writing to the COIN field manual or guiding us. Candidly, it's the same with, to some degree—I mean don't get me wrong the NSS [National Security Strategy] and these matter—but they are generally written at a very elevated level and what you are trying to do is very specific campaigns, for very specific countries, for very specific circumstances. And even the COIN field manual can therefore only be general principles, guidelines, thoughts, paradoxes, constructs and so on. At the end of the day, you have to apply it in a specific country, and applying it in Afghanistan for example was very different from applying it in Iraq and so on.[58]

Instead, for General Petraeus, resolutions such as UNSCR 1325 could "inform the context in which people are making decisions about how to develop policies, principles and guidelines," but should not necessarily be singled out in their significance. Applying this to the case of Iraq, he noted the primary aim was to establish security in a given environment, as directed by his superior:

> I was just concerned with what my boss, my higher headquarters, was telling us to do, and then trying to figure out for ourselves what the right thing to do was when we were basically sent up to Mosul on very short notice and told to establish security, stability, governance and everything. We weren't even told that; we were basically told to go up and get the place under control because it was out of control.[59]

This quote is indicative for several reasons. First, UNSCR 1325 has been held up by proponents of the women, peace and security agenda to drive global efforts and considerations for women's roles in all aspects of security, yet it was not reaching or resonating with those who were shaping military efforts and specific security operations in countries like Iraq and Afghanistan, where UNSCR 1325's aims would be particularly important. It also elucidates the chasm between international resolutions, national-level strategies, and how these would be interpreted and applied in very unique operational environments. Even if women were emphasized in national-level discourses, this was not necessarily guaranteed to trickle down into practice. Unless considerations of women could be integrated into mission aims from the onset, or viewed as significant in their application on the ground in even the most violent operational environment, then they were likely to be relegated to a lesser concern.

Limited consideration of women in COIN was reinforced by both the notable absence of women in FM 3–24 (five mentions across 282 pages) and the lack of detail on how efforts to engage women could lead to broader campaign success. Instead, women were considered generally in FM 3–24 in relation to how they might be co-opted in social and economic terms so that their "enlightened self-interest" could eventually undermine insurgents. This also suggests that a core field manual did not perceive a necessity to expand on women's roles or status to a significant degree when addressing insurgencies, implying it would prompt minimal consideration when guiding or informing COIN operations. In comparison, gender considerations that would highlight differential impacts for (or on) women in development efforts in USAID were pointedly integrated into the planning, execution and evaluation of all its programming for decades, demonstrating how this lack of gender analysis could impact practices on the ground.

While women had featured in many insurgencies and guerilla movements historically, including in Algeria, El Salvador, Cuba, South Africa, Vietnam and more recently Nepal (amongst others), the scholarship interrogating women's roles has tended to be particularly limited, especially prior to 2006.[60] This also highlighted a broader shortfall in research which could be drawn on to inform doctrine at this time. Numerous authors have rightly pointed out flaws in the construction of women in COIN operations in Afghanistan (which will be discussed later),[61] yet these tended to be responsive in nature (that is, after COIN activity was already underway). There appeared to be little institutional or doctrinal debate within the DoD on women's engagement early on; unless it was demonstrable how or why broadening engagement or consideration of women proved significant to achieving success in COIN operations (as seen in past COIN campaigns, for example), it did not appear to gain much focus in early post-9/11 DoD doctrine and field manuals.

However, in practice this shift to COIN was an important factor that began to impact how women in local communities were considered, in terms of both winning the "hearts and minds" of counterinsurgents or, inversely, as potential insurgents (albeit minimally at first). It suggested that identifying women's interests and grievances, their power relations and status in society, and their areas of need would gain more focus as COIN operations further developed. This focus was also pointed to by Kilcullen, who echoed much of FM 3–24 as it related to women, and noted of COIN practice that winning over women assisted in winning the rest of the family unit. In doing so, it brought you closer to winning over and mobilizing the population, and could be targeted through social and economic programs: "You need your own counterinsurgents, including interagency people, to do this effectively." Kilcullen also highlighted that addressing the role of women in constitutional reforms, alongside education and governance more broadly, could be a key element to counter global jihad.[62] David B. Des Roches, who focused on COIN in the DoD and was formerly the Deputy Director for Peacekeeping and Stability Operations in the Office of the Secretary of Defense (2003–05), also assessed women in COIN in terms of their role as "influence leaders in the broader community," which could be important for gaining or losing support of that community. He further noted: "women are a subset of the bigger issue that is COIN" where "COIN has to be conducted in the cultural context of the battlefield." To do so would require, for example, "cultural sensitivity" in Iraq and Afghanistan, including sensitivities specific to women.[63]

The increased relevance of COIN therefore began to expand the DoD's scope and consideration of women to areas such as economic and social development—areas traditionally served by US State and USAID, but which were also increasingly recognized for their COIN function in winning the "hearts and minds" of populations in conflict zones. As COIN operations became a leading approach in Iraq and Afghanistan, a number of new programs were developed which supported broader COIN aims and streams of effort, including stability operations.

*Human Terrain Systems*

The need to better understand the local culture(s) in the operational environments highlighted in COIN was reflected in the establishment of the US Army program HTS in 2006. COIN practice prior to this had been viewed as heavy-handed; what was needed was referred to by some as a "gentler" COIN, which engaged a "cultural turn" now emphasizing cultural knowledge and ethnographic intelligence.[64] In 2007, the first HTS team was deployed in Afghanistan, joining a brigade of the 82nd Airborne Division; it would later go on to deploy operational support in Iraq. Teams of anthropologists were deployed alongside the DoD to help better understand the cultures and societies they were operating within, and how this could be leveraged at the tactical and operational level in full-spectrum operations.[65] Specifically, they were an "intelligence enabling capability" whose mission was to "[r]ecruit, train, deploy, and support an embedded, operationally focused sociocultural capability; conduct operationally relevant, sociocultural research and analysis; develop and maintain a sociocultural knowledge base to support operational decision making, enhance operational effectiveness, and preserve and share sociocultural institutional knowledge."[66]

The HTS handbook noted each HTS should have at least one female member to "to allow the team access to the 50% of the population frequently overlooked in military operations,"[67] and should also seek out women to interview. Women should also be assessed in local populations, for example, as to their general status in society and their health, considering questions such as "are there high rates of visible pregnancy?"[68] If efforts were focused on facilitating reconciliation in the community, women's groups were also identified as a potential institution for this.[69]

A case study by a HTS team in the Greater Zangabad area of Afghanistan highlighted the kind of gendered analysis these teams would conduct in order to gain a comprehensive understanding of the communities and environments coalition forces were operating within. It considered the limited political involvement of local women, as well as concerns they faced from coalition planes flying over their compounds and seeing them in immodest dress; it also highlighted the economic impact of women and considered the function of marriage dowries. Tying marriage dowries to the potential eradication of poppy fields, it considered how secondary and tertiary impacts in changes to local economic states could specifically impact women. The social and hierarchical status of women was also considered as influenced by age, wealth, childbearing abilities, education, marriage, family lineage and social networks. Women's concerns related to access to healthcare or fear of sending girls to school due to targeting by insurgents were also raised.[70]

Another HTS team pointed out that the Haqqani network, an anti-American group of insurgents, was gaining strength because an uncommonly large number of Afghan widows depended on their sons for support (echoing themes also seen in Iraq). On their recommendation, soldiers started a job training program that put the widows to work and cut the insurgents' supply of recruits.[71] Other topics in practice included promoting women's health and access to health services.[72] One HTS member noted in reference to a women's health project: "There is value in raising the military's awareness of definitions of security outside those of its traditional paradigm,"[73] highlighting considerations more frequently associated with human security which were becoming increasing relevant to DoD operations.[74]

While the cases above highlight important concerns related to better understanding the status and situation of women in areas in which the US was operating, this program proved highly controversial. Academics and anthropologists in particular raised concerns related to the ethics of this work, the use of academic research to support military missions, and the danger posed to the researchers and study populations;[75] one even suggested the HTS program was likely developed as an espionage project.[76] Consequently, research that had previously been carried out which may have been more relevant to development or aid work now took on an explicit security angle, highlighting controversies that arose with this shift in emphasis to COIN.

This threat to researchers became all too apparent with the deaths of a number of HTS members. On 4 November 2008, Paula Lloyd was interviewing an Afghan male who poured oil on her and lit her on fire. Her colleague Don Ayala then killed the assailant, Abdul Salam, after he found out the extent of her injuries. Two months later, Lloyd died from complications caused by her injuries. Ayala would later plead guilty to the voluntary manslaughter of Salam and served five years on probation.[77] The same year, two other HTS members were also killed on the job: Michael Bhatia was killed by a roadside bomb in eastern Afghanistan along with two soldiers; and Nicole Suveges was killed in an explosion at the Sadr City District Council building in Iraq, in which eleven others were also killed. Beyond the physical danger that they faced, a former HTS member also highlighted concerns related to flawed recruitment processes, poor training and deployment (particularly as it pertained to operating in a combat zone, where training and even use of firearms may be expected of HTS members). Other critiques included sexual harassment within the unit, and a broken leadership and organizational culture.[78] While recognizing these teams demonstrated the DoD was attempting to better understand the sociocultural environment it worked with and impacted (including female populations therein), the program itself was generally viewed with more criticism than praise.[79] The program ran until 2014, and proved to be the largest investment in a single social science project by the DoD, costing nearly $750 million.[80]

*Women and stabilization efforts*

The US had been providing stability and support operations throughout its history; for example, in the Philippines (1898–1902), Algeria (1954–62) and Vietnam (1967–75). These had historically been led and dominated by the military, and conducted generally in the midst of insurgencies, though operations increasingly included non-military stakeholders, particularly USAID and other non-governmental actors.[81] A number of changes to the way conflict evolved after the Cold War, as well as growing emphasis on areas such as civilian protection in conflict, and conflict prevention more generally, influenced themes that became emphasized in post-9/11 stability operations. These changes included the "new wars" of the 1990s;[82] a policy emphasis towards conflict prevention; increased recognition of the right to protect civilians in conflict and the need to better manage stability and security post-conflict; and increasing considerations focused on human security. These shifts prompted defense, diplomacy and development actors to better mitigate the occurrence of conflict, manage conflict itself, and to prevent it from returning.

Stabilization and post-conflict reconstruction became increasingly important themes in US foreign policy and security, and drew civil-military actors closer together in integrated efforts to achieve these aims. These now reflected concerns related to terrorism that had gained prominence after 9/11. The wars in Afghanistan and Iraq high-lighted the importance of long-term stabilization and recovery for regions impacted by armed conflict to prevent violence and instability from returning, including the re-emergence of terrorist safe havens. The importance of highlighting complimentary and coordinated secu-rity, political, economic and social aspects of this could not be under-stated, and these fields became emphasized in their contribution to state stability and the prevention of terrorism. Women gained particu-lar attention in stabilization efforts, based on their roles and status in the local communities where these efforts were focused.

It is worth taking a moment to define civil-military operations, as these describe the kind of operations being undertaken by DoD, US State, USAID and other non-governmental actors: "The activities of a commander that establish, maintain, influence, or exploit relations between military forces, governmental and nongovernmental civilian organizations and authorities, and the civilian populace in a friendly, neutral, or hostile operational area in order to facilitate military opera-tions, to consolidate and achieve operational US objectives." These would include activities and functions "normally the responsibility of the local, regional, or national government" that may occur "prior to, during, or subsequent to other military actions. They may also occur, if directed, in the absence of other military operations." Civil military operations may be "performed by designated civil affairs, by other mili-tary forces, or by a combination of civil affairs and other forces."[83]

In the "FM 3–07 Stability Operations and Support Operations" (FM 3–07) manual of 2003, stability operations were divided into ten gen-eral categories (and their "subordinate forms"): (1) peace operations; (2) foreign internal defense; (3) security assistance; (4) humanitarian and civic assistance; (5) support to insurgencies; (6) supporting coun-ter-drug operations; (7) non-combat evacuation operations; (8) arms control; (9) show of force; and (10) combating terrorism (both anti-terrorism and counterterrorism).[84] Stability operations were noted to "complement and reinforce offensive, defensive, and support opera-tions, or they may be the decisive operation," and could occur before, during or after a conflict.[85] Support operations included both domestic support operations, foreign humanitarian assistance and combating terrorism features. Foreign humanitarian assistance relieved or reduced the impact of "natural or man-made disasters or other endemic conditions such as human pain, disease, hunger, or privation that might seriously threaten life or result in great damage to or loss of property."[86]

Due to their focus on some of the "softer" aspects of security and humanitarian assistance, it was perhaps less surprising that women were considered in numerous aspects of stabilization and support operations. For example, practitioners of negotiations were encouraged to consider "what role do women play in society? How is status defined in the culture?"[87] However, women were most prominently considered as a special category of displaced person—"vulnerable groups" who required special attention and effective protection measures. Women's security in camps and settlements was noted and their input was signified as a key requirement: "involving the women in ways to improve their security, ensuring basic services are accessible, and improving lighting."[88]

Stabilization efforts required significant interagency coordination and effort, which is often easier said than done. The 2005 presidential directive "NSPD-44: Management of Interagency Efforts Concerning Reconstruction and Stabilization" was one step to better coordinate these. This called for increased coordination between US agencies, as well as the planning and implementation of these efforts, which would be led by US State. This directive further noted the US should aim to "enable governments abroad to exercise sovereignty over their own territories and to prevent those territories from being used as a base of operations or safe haven for extremists, terrorists, organized crime groups, or others who pose a threat to US foreign policy, security, or economic interests."[89] This focus on combating terrorism as part of stability operations is a feature unique to the post-9/11 terrain. It meant that interagency efforts—including the diplomatic and development actors within these—would now be obliged to consider how combating terrorism was relevant to their stabilization work. It also meant that areas of operation would become particularly crowded, complex, and require the alignment of many diverse fields, actors and interests.

In July 2005, the Office of the Coordinator for Reconstruction and Stabilization was established within US State under President Bush. The Office housed representatives from USAID, DoD, the Central Intelligence Agency, the Army Corps of Engineers, Joint Forces

Command and the Department of the Treasury. US State's role in this was to guide the development of stabilization programming. The Office had five core functions: (1) monitoring, early warning and planning; (2) mobilization and deployment; (3) building surge capacity; (4) learning from experience; and (5) coordinating with the international community.[90] This took shape in the DoD as directive "3000.5 on Military Support for Stability, Security, Transition, and Reconstruction Operations" (2005). This directive confirmed: "Stability operations are a core US military mission that the Department of Defense shall be prepared to conduct and support. They shall be given priority comparable to combat operations and be explicitly addressed and integrated across all DoD activities." Civil military efforts were "key to successful operations" and civil military teams were "a critical US Government stability operations tool." Their functions were noted to be "security, developing local governance structures, promoting bottom-up economic activity, rebuilding infrastructure, and building indigenous capacity for such tasks."[91]

There appeared to be a broader gender awareness visible in stability operations over the years, as seen in FM 3–07 from 2008. It highlighted women as those most often displaced by conflict; how important it was for women to engage in humanitarian assistance; gender equality in governance and civic participation; gender considerations in employment opportunities; and how demobilization, disarmament and reintegration (DDR) efforts must consider women and children as potential active members and supporters of armed groups.[92]

The 2014 FM 3–07 update continued to link reconstruction and development to terrorism:

> US leaders must engage failed states while understanding the potential correlation between fragile states and instability related to terrorism. Effective engagement requires the use of the tools of diplomacy, development, and defense in a collaborative fashion. The success of US military strategy and development assistance policy in these countries have become mutually reinforcing.[93]

Similar considerations pertaining to women remained. Army units supporting foreign humanitarian assistance were encouraged to "consider the special needs of women, children, the elderly, infirm, and handicapped who may have a difficult time accessing supplies." Units should also be careful not to "overlook or marginalize important groups such as women or minorities," and recognize that women may be considered a vulnerable civilian group in some contexts. In DDR programs, service support providers to armed groups, which were recognized as mostly women, would also have to be demobilized and provided with basic infrastructure such as women's latrines. This recognized that "[f]ighters are not the only former combatants that process through disarmament, demobilization, and reintegration," and that in DDR efforts "during in-processing, disarmament, demobilization, and reintegration personnel must identify women who are victims of sex slavery and forced marriage and place them in secure barracks."[94] Perhaps most importantly, effective engagement of populations was now highlighted to include women, and to consider gender norms in a society and the practical requirements to achieve this. In FM 3–07 (2014), women are described in terms of information related-capabilities:

> Army leaders account for effective engagement that includes females in the population. Leaders consider how gender norms differ by culture. They plan and prepare to include female teams and interpreters, which are critical to effectiveness. In some situations, a trained female team can interact with the population, develop an understanding of gender and family issues, provide care to victims, and influence a significant but often inaccessible part of the population. Female teams require special training as these functions will likely differ from their normal responsibilities. Female teams have been known to experience difficulties with integration into military units; therefore, commanders emphasize their importance and integration to avoid problems.[95]

There was clearly a broadening of how women were considered in US stability operations over the years, as reflected in the new female teams utilized to engage women. While stability operations still generally mirrored broader trends where women were assessed according to "softer" aspects of security (that is, as victims or as a vulnerable group in need of protection, which could prove reductionist and problematic), it also increasingly recognized them as fighters and service support providers to armed groups that had to be dealt with in a gender-sensitive manner. The following section will highlight a number of examples where women became more concretely visible in stability efforts, including those embedded in COIN operations.

## Provincial Reconstruction Teams

In Afghanistan, the establishment of PRTs in 2002 proved an early example of integrated civil military relations and efforts between DoD, US State and USAID (the Department of Agriculture was also represented). PRTs were established to "bridge the gap between major combat operations and civilian-led reconstruction and development efforts" and embraced the "3D" concept; that is, including representatives from defense, diplomacy and development. DoD generally focused on security operations; US State on political oversight, coordination and reporting; and USAID on reconstruction.[96] PRTs were used to implement projects by the DoD, US State and USAID, and were noted to be "one component of a full spectrum operation that ranged from combat to midwife training." They were described not as a physical entity, but "a platform for components of US National Security to coordinate larger political missions, while jointly developing and implementing a targeted stability operation." The structure of each PRT was based on a number of factors, including the political, development and security situation in each province.[97] They were intended to help the governments of Afghanistan, and later Iraq, build government capacity, legitimacy and effectiveness, and to deliver efficient government services.[98]

In Afghanistan, these teams focused on improving security, extending the reach of the Afghan government and facilitating reconstruction. PRTs would often number between fifty and one hundred personnel, where between 5 and 10 per cent were civilian, and the rest came from defense. While these were meant to have significant leadership and input from civilian actors, in practice these were often military-led (particularly in areas experiencing higher security threats). It was noted at times that many USAID positions in PRTs remained unfilled, or were filled by contracted personnel with limited knowledge of USAID or the US government's regulations and requirements.[99] Defense personnel were represented by a variety of specialized army units, including "two Army civil affairs teams; a military police unit; a psychological operations unit (PSYOP); explosive ordnance/demining unit (EOD); intelligence team; medics; force protection unit, normally composed of a 40-man infantry platoon; and administrative support and personnel."[100]

Defense actors had two roles in PRTs: the first was to support each PRT mission (housing, transport, medical support, base operations, etc.); the second was divided by military leadership positions. The Force Protection Commander was responsible for securing the mission both on the base and outside it; the Civil Affairs Officers would run "hearts and minds" campaigns, identifying needs and capacities in each area, and developing programs to address these. Military commanders were tasked with "managing a joint, combined task force; planning and executing tactical missions; overseeing non-lethal systems including Information Operations, Civil Affairs Activities, Public Affairs and Police Training Advisory Team; engaging, mentoring and advising the provincial leadership on security issues; and ultimately responsible for all PRT operations."[101] Initially starting with nineteen PRTs in 2004, there were twenty-six by 2008,[102] and in 2006 PRTs were brought under the operational control of the International Security Assistance Force (ISAF). In conflict environments, PRTs were noted by some to be focused largely on COIN efforts.[103] For example, PRTs were noted to have tried to use development aid "to neutralize local sources of conflict and to provide incentives for Afghans to oppose the Taliban."[104] The role of civilian actors in Afghanistan increased alongside troop numbers after a surge announced in 2009, which took the number of US civilian actors from 261 in January 2009 to 1,040 by June 2011.[105]

Many PRT activities either engaged women directly or considered gender dynamics in their work. Up to 2007, USAID had implemented 440 projects through PRTs, including "gender-related activities," though what this meant explicitly was not clear.[106] More general activities of female-focused PRTs included enhancing women's political participation, vocational training and micro-grants.[107] However, organizations like the Afghan Women's Network argued that issues to do with gender, women's participation and gendered insecurity had generally been neglected by PRTs. It was important to recognize that the activities and aims outlined differed very much on their perceived level of impact, importance and implementation on the ground. In other words, stating programs had a gender component did not necessarily translate to meaningful change. They recommended particular areas of improvement such as promoting women's attendance at provincial and regional level meetings with PRTs; incorporating gender into all reforms, including security sector reforms, defense reform and DDR; making use of female operators to improve access to women; better engaging women's civil society organizations; and better operationalizing gender mainstreaming in stability and security operations.[108]

In 2005, PRTs were established in Iraq based on the "need to develop the infrastructure and build the capacity necessary for the Iraqi people to succeed in a post-conflict environment."[109] They carried out tasks similar to those of PRTs stationed in Afghanistan, such as helping improve governance, reconstruction and security, strengthening rule of law, and promoting reconciliation. By 2007 there were twenty-five PRTs operating in Iraq, ten of which were uniquely embedded with military brigades. Activities carried out by the PRTs included training women in literacy, government (including achieving 15 per cent female representation in a local governance program), leadership, sewing and constructions trades. Other activities included promoting women's radio programming and establishing microloans for women. Programming considerations still reflected concerns from terrorism in some cases, however. One example of this was a large-scale program set up in Ramadi to pay youth $10 per day to help clear rubble from the streets to "make it less likely they will accept money to carry out Al Qaeda's attacks," and also to help identify weapons caches under the rubble.[110]

Some of the critiques of PRTs included a lack of clear lines of authority and command to ensure smooth military–civilian coordination; a lack of development knowledge amongst defense actors; poor coordination with aid agencies; individual PRTs being driven by the personalities of its members; a lack of institutional memory; and a lack of clear mandate, structure and purpose.[111] These were further viewed, particularly by aid actors, as militarizing and politicizing assistance and "blurring the lines between aid actors and the military,"[112] thus putting the former at risk. It was also not clear what "effectiveness" meant in terms of PRTs, as there was no shared metric for success, and there often appeared to be a shortfall of civilian actors and capabilities, who were unable to keep up with demand.[113] For PRTs that operated in forward operating bases, US military escorts were also critiqued in the early years for providing protection to PRTs and then standing and fighting when under attack, rather than protecting the PRTs and removing them from the area. In some cases, PRTs also combined their escort services with COIN patrols.[114] While USAID and US State had embedded advisors at the brigade, division and corps levels in the DoD, the DoD did not have advisors in USAID or US State, suggesting military dominance in PRTs. There was also a lack of integrated forward planning engaging the various actors, and future planning for operations was often led by military actors.[115] Finally, for DoD civilians embedded in PRTs, their lack of combat status also restricted them from benefits if they were wounded from combat injuries.

While PRTs have received much praise generally, there were still a number of concerns that were evident in operation, particularly in how development considerations and actors were integrated into PRT activities. As will be further highlighted in Chapter 5, USAID—the primary development actor in PRTs—had the most complex, integrated and operationalized gender knowledge in its programming of DoD and US State. If USAID was not prominent or influential in PRTs, this perhaps explains why some of the critiques related to women's participation and gendered insecurity were initially raised.

*Female Engagement Teams*

Reflecting the increased emphasis on understanding and engaging local populations through the "hearts and minds" approach in COIN, FETs were established in Afghanistan in 2009 and further impacted women in US forces, as well as women in local populations. Of all the new roles established for women in defense efforts since 9/11, FETs have been the most visible internationally and, as such, the most assessed, interrogated and critiqued.[116] This section will expand on these discussions of FETs and look beyond their roles in Afghanistan (which ended in 2012) to discuss how FETs have taken on new roles and responsibilities since 2015, particularly in training and equipping foreign female forces in the Middle East.

ISAF efforts in Afghanistan had faced critiques due to neglected engagement with and lack of consideration for Afghan women, which was well captured in a Senate testimony by Ambassador Verveer in 2010. She noted, "In the face of so many deeply entrenched problems and barriers to progress, it would be tempting to see Afghan women as little more than the victims of the enormity of their circumstances, who have nothing to do with waging a successful counterinsurgency." However, while the US COIN strategy in Afghanistan addressed issues of "security, economic and social development, good governance, and rule of law," Verveer noted "the future security, stability, and development of Afghanistan depends in large part on the degree to which women have an active role in rebuilding its society and a voice in their nation's political process."[117]

From a military perspective, such focus on women was also impacted by political limitations; for example, tensions between agencies for resources, and competing priorities and agendas. As General Petraeus noted of Afghanistan: "It was interesting that members of Congress would constantly say 'who was going to ensure the rights of Afghan women in the new Afghanistan?' and they were often the same members of Congress who were asking why we weren't drawing down our forces more rapidly?" He stated this was influenced by the main objective in Afghanistan, which was understood not to prioritize objectives related to women:

> Our core objective in Afghanistan in particular was very straightforward: it was to ensure that Afghanistan was never again a sanctuary for al-Qaeda or other transnational extremists the way that it was when the 9/11 attacks were planned on Afghan soil, where the initial training for the actors was conducted. To accomplish that mission, and indeed to do it without our forces performing it forever, there was only one solution, and that was to enable Afghan forces over time to secure their own country, with continued assistance to be sure, and to enable select Afghan institutions to govern their country to an Afghan 'good enough' standard.[118]

He noted that they certainly wanted to "see and foster the progress in a host of other areas across the board," including in development or women-specific programming. However, this mission in Afghanistan was not all about "women's rights or better treatment for women, or all about education:"

> I mean we didn't go there for that reason frankly [...]. Although we liked to see that, again that wasn't the raison d'etre for the mission. You've got to focus on the main effort, [and] the main effort does not have to do with advancing certain gender objectives or any host of any other worthy [issues], and don't get me wrong, these are worthy.[119]

However, while a focus on improving the status of women was noted to not be the primary operational aim in Afghanistan, General Petraeus acknowledged the importance of engaging with women:

> Women are 50% of the population and can't be ignored. In some places they play very important roles, the roles vary from culture to culture, tribe to tribe, sect, ethnic group, and so forth, but there needed to be engagement of them. Obviously, in Afghanistan in particular, we could not engage them because it was not the norm societally, at least not in the rural areas. Of course, this is the reason for the genesis of the Female Engagement Teams that were started and that were employed to good effect, I thought, in Afghanistan, to the point that we had a number of them augmenting every brigade combat team that we sent out there.[120]

This suggested that unless gender-specific objectives, including those related to women and their status, were considered, inherent or defined in DoD missions from the onset, or appeared to have direct operational impact in achieving the DoD operational aims, such concerns remained particularly vulnerable to conflicting priorities and resource battles between different agencies.

FETs served a distinct operational role, with this lack of engagement with women a shortcoming the insurgents inevitably took advantage of. As Des Roches noted:

> The FETs was an ad-hoc reaction to the problem where we would have guys going in to homes or buildings to search suspected insurgents, and would also search women, which in that culture was tantamount to raping them, or we would not search women. Of course, the enemy would understand this, and women would hide weapons, things like this, knowing we were hesitant to have men search them.[121]

FETs were distinct units in the US Army and USMC, where members were recruited on a voluntary basis as an additional role to their primary occupation. The roles of FETs were described within the USMC as "utilizing female influence" to engage the population. They "provided another weapon," contributed a unique information and messaging capability, increased operational awareness in the field, and helped gain intelligence from, and engage with, half the population who had previously been inaccessible.[122] Foreign female soldiers in units such as FETs may also be viewed as a "third sex" in some societies—distinct from male soldiers and local women. As such, they could be seen to facilitate "softer" interactions with males in that community who may otherwise be hesitant to engage male soldiers. FETs further directly contributed to reconstruction and development efforts in the areas of education, economic development, medicine and infrastructure.[123] They were described as a combination of "the Lioness Program's efforts to search women with the Iraqi Women's Engagement Program's efforts to address underlying causes of instability, merging them into even broader operational roles."[124] Practical tasks of FETs included conveying information, tapping into local knowledge, performing security searches (particularly for men traveling in burqas), and winning the support of Afghan mothers and daughters, who were believed to have influence over their husbands and sons. They would also conduct varied tasks such as supporting female-focused governance and development projects, holding key leader engagements and women-only *shuras* (consultations), and conducting medical outreach.[125]

It was the demonstrable, positive impact FETs were having in operations that earned them recognition of military leadership and increased their roles in COIN efforts. Des Roches stated: "Over time, people realized the tactical value that having women [in FETs] had, and it gained momentum over time, primarily in Afghanistan, though also in Iraq."[126] In 2010, ISAF Commander General Stanley McChrystal (an American) issued the "Engagement with Afghan Females Directive," which recommended that ISAF establish guidance for FETs in order to "standardize female engagements for ISAF units. This guidance will enable systemic collection of information from the female population in a culturally respectful manner to facilitate building confidence with the Afghan population."[127] General Petraeus noted: "We pride ourselves on being a learning organization and we tried to learn very much from [FETs]." FETs were started when he was heading CENTCOM (2008–10) and continued as he oversaw the Afghanistan initiative in 2010: "I applauded [FETs], thought it was a great idea."[128] The strategic emphasis on COIN, the DoD "learning" culture, and their demonstrable operational and tactical value positively impacted the acceptance and expansion of FETs.

FETs were eventually institutionalized by ISAF leadership, "directing all deploying military units to create all-female teams to develop and improve relationships with Afghan women."[129] However while ISAF leadership led this,[130] the North Atlantic Treaty Organization's (NATO's) earlier emphasis on UNSCR 1325 and its women, peace and security considerations also informed this. In December 2007, NATO and the European Atlantic Partnership Council established its policy on implementing UNSCR 1325. Subsequently, in September 2009, Bi-Strategic Command Directive 40–1 was issued by NATO and contributed to the establishment of gender advisors at ISAF.[131] This suggested that the push for women's engagement in COIN in Afghanistan as conducted by FETs was being informed in US forces by operational requirements, though was seemingly prompted in part by NATO's efforts to promote UNSCR 1325 and better consider engagement with Afghan women. This suggested that both demonstrable operational impact and the United Nations' (UN's) women, peace and security norms had some influence on how women's engagement developed in Afghanistan. Under the banner of UNSCR 1325, NATO had further aimed to increase the numbers of women in ISAF, viewing them as playing an important role in "promot[ing] the mutual trust that is essential in countering an insurgency" by reaching out to Afghan women.[132] FETs were understood to help bridge this gap and fulfill this role.

The gendered operational and conceptual considerations and critiques of FETs have been discussed at length elsewhere, but are also important to highlight here.[133] These have emphasized aspects such as gendered assumptions inherent in FETs and their role in US COIN efforts,[134] such as their basis on "dubious assumptions" about the role and influence of Afghan women in their families to combat terrorism;[135] FETs' lack of authority or capability to address local concerns and issues were also often raised.[136] Furthermore, their specific functions were not always clear, the lack of standardization in practice and ad hoc support was critiqued, and additional challenges facing FETs included:

> Lack of leadership support, training, and coordination; lack of respect from male colleagues; lack of real influence; lack of understanding of gender and institutional memory on women and gender programming; overly ambitious programming and no clear goals; potentially damaging FET activities; lack of good assessments; not rooted in the military; and loss of FET skills.[137]

It was also pointed out that there was little gender awareness in the military to facilitate these programs, and decades of experience with gender programming from the aid community was ignored.[138] This suggested that interactions between DoD and other agencies like US State or USAID were not informing FETs, or were perhaps limited in practice, even as there was evident overlap with socio-economic and governance programming, mandates and experience in these organizations. Finally, while women's roles in these teams was often praised from within the military, it also raised questions about if/how women's roles in the military may have been stereotyped. That is, if their "softer" roles in community interactions were so highly praised and valued, did this add or detract from seeing their full roles as soldiers, for example also on the front lines of combat, or suggest women's roles should be valued in only certain and limited ways?

Des Roches also highlighted internal challenges faced by the DoD with the establishment of FETs: "The problem is there is a mismatch between the mission and how the US military is structured. The idea that we, as the US military, would set up a unit full of women, that's abhorrent to our practice." This was specifically cited in terms of its friction with gender equality norms within the US forces, where women-only units would be "seen as a ghetto, seen as stigmatizing US women who have to have the same opportunities to advance as everyone else, so we can't have a single unit distinguished by gender or ethnicity." Problematically though, this put defense forces "at a disadvantage on this battlefield," as women would also be drawn from their assigned positions to join FETs, thereby also depriving those units of their personnel. This left the US, "because of its own domestic constraints, playing a pick-up game."[139] Here, equality norms in the US were viewed in conflict with operational requirements (at least when such units were viewed as a "ghetto," a label certainly not seen with all male-combat units). Yet, these units also opened new roles for women, highlighting the importance of assessing restrictions from within each agency as well.

For women based in FETs, it was often noted that they were proud of their roles and contributions, and wanted to serve in these units, in some cases particularly due to the perceived engagement and impact on the lives of women and children in the communities they were operating within. This was made clear in a 2012 interview, for example, with two FET members. In it, Private First Class Jacqueline

Buschman stated: "I wanted to make a difference. I wanted to get out and see what the Afghan people were living like [and] help out in any way I could;" Specialist Heather Ray concurred: "I volunteered because I heard about the culture and I wanted to make a difference in the women's lives." In some cases, they also believed they could influence local women to convince their husbands to stay clear of insurgent affairs.[140]

In US government and defense circles, major discussions and assessments of COIN operations also appeared to generally neglect consideration of engagement of women in local populations, or FETs more generally, suggesting that lessons learned were not being recognized or integrated into documents that could inform further COIN operations.[141] Former Marine Intelligence Officer Claire Russo highlighted this gap between the national strategies which were increasingly emphasizing women and how this developed tactically on the ground: "We haven't gotten to the point where we're looking at national strategies and coordinating the tactical employment of females with national strategies [in Afghanistan]." In short, she stated, "the *tactical employment of women has to be married with strategy*"[142] [emphasis mine]. This indicated that there remained a chasm between DoD strategies and the tactics required to achieve these on the ground. The FET program ended in 2012 alongside a troop drawdown in Afghanistan.

## Cultural Support Teams

Along with FETs, CSTs were also established in Afghanistan, and were active within both the US Army and USMC. CSTs were units of female soldiers who served as enablers and supported Special Operations Forces (SOFs) in and around secured objective areas: "Their primary task is to engage the female population in an objective area when such contact may be deemed culturally inappropriate if performed by a male service member."[143] CSTs operated in two roles. The first was with the Green Berets in Village Stability Operations, where women would assist in understanding the political and security terrain for more effective COIN efforts and community partnerships (the "hearts and minds" approach). They would hold women's *shuras* to facilitate this dialogue with women in the communities. The second capacity supported direct action raids alongside the 75th Ranger Regiment, wherein activities to capture or clear insurgents would see CSTs engage Afghan women in the home raids to gain information.[144]

Established in 2010 by Admiral Eric Olson, leader of the US Navy Sea, Air and Land (SEAL) Teams and then leading US Special Operations Command (SOCOM), women in CSTs would go out on special operation missions beginning in 2011. Katt noted that the key difference between FETs and CSTs was that "FETs were used to soften coalition forces' footprint as they moved through an area, whereas CSTs were designed to provide persistent presence and engagement— a key tenet of population-focused operations conducted by Special Operations Forces."[145] CSTs additionally supported activities along security, governance and development lines, for example advising the Department of Women's Affairs and the Labor Union, or working with the Ministry of Education to reform education syllabi in Afghanistan.[146] Notably, attachments of CSTs to SOF units was based on demand,[147] suggesting that their inclusion was promoted only when it was seen to contribute a specific operational function.

Navy Admiral William McRaven, who commanded SOCOM from 2011–14, noted that in relation to SOFs more generally, women "broaden strategic and operational capabilities," "increases the team's ability to assess the cultural climate and understand the local environment," and increase situational awareness. Women were further noted to "view the battlespace differently, and in doing so may have the potential to observe nuances overlooked by all-male [SOF] teams,"[148] which suggested that women were still viewed in distinct roles or which could provide 'unique' gendered views and persepctives. Some SOF members also noted that women's inclusion might help facilitate communication with local populations and in conducting sensitive operations.[149] This suggested that such roles were more responsive than proactive in practice, and built off of what had been viewed as successful roles for women in the field, which were perceived to be unique operational capabilities.

The women in the CST units would at times end up facing active combat, and some were even killed in these. Such cases included First Lieutenant Ashley White, who was killed in Afghanistan on 2 October 2011 alongside two Army Rangers, when the assault unit she was attached to came under attack. Her story is well-captured in the book

*Ashley's War*, where she is identified as the first CST member to be killed in action.[150] Others, such as Captain Jennifer M. Moreno, a military nurse deployed with the Army's 75th Ranger Regiment in Kandahar Province, was killed in action alongside three other soldiers. Moreno was trying to assist an injured soldier during a raid on a Taliban bomb-making compound on 5 October 2013, when she triggered an explosive device. Beyond the concerns from active-combat CSTs, there were also certain challenges comparable with those faced by FETs, including "integrating into teams, misperceptions of their capabilities, and a lack of capable female interpreters. Special operators identified additional challenges such as site selection [for deciding where CSTs would be based], security limitations and considerations, and sexual tension between CST and SOF members."[151] CSTs were eventually tasked with working with Army Rangers and other elite teams such as US Navy SEAL teams, and were cited by Major General Bennet Sacolick of SOCOM in 2013: "They very well may provide a foundation for ultimate integration" of women into all combat roles.[152]

CSTs provided another example of the tension between the positive operational utilities and contributions of women, and DoD limitations where women were still restricted from front-line combat roles. Women were now "enablers" at the front line, yet still faced shortfalls and challenges in the establishment of their roles. Moreover, they faced gendered stereotypes and hurdles, for example those pertaining to women being seen to be the cause of sexual tension in the armed forces.

*Counterterrorism*

Figure 1 highlighted how changing operational objectives throughout the GWOT was one of the factors that impacted how and why women's roles evolved in DoD efforts in this period. The previous section outlined how this became relevant to COIN and stabilization, but looking at counterterrorism specifically, the evolving nature of terrorism also impacted on the operational environment and objectives relevant to counterterrorism. The DoD's 2009 JP 3–26 on Counterterrorism doctrine was noted to have been updated based on new requirements presented by the GWOT, such as a broader role for the military in counterterrorism operations, the need for truly unified action (otherwise known as a "whole-of-government" approach) and an emphasis on indirect approaches.[153] Counterterrorism referred to "[a]ctions taken directly against terrorist networks and indirectly to influence and render global and regional environments inhospitable to terrorist networks,"[154] and combating it required "[a]ctions, including antiterrorism and counterterrorism, taken to oppose terrorism throughout the entire threat spectrum."[155] The approach outlines five lines of operations: "erode support for extremist ideology; enable partners to combat violent extremist organizations (VEOs); deter tacit and active support for VEOs; disrupt VEOs; and deny access and/or use of WMD [weapons of mass destruction] by VEOs."[156]

Both direct and indirect approaches were emphasized in this doctrine. "Direct" action can be understood in the most kinetic sense of the word; that is, actions taken against terrorists and their organizations, with the goal to "to defeat a specific threat through neutralization/dismantlement of the network (including actors, resources, and support structures) and to prevent the reemergence of a threat once neutralized."[157] "Indirect" action expanded to a broader range of partners to influence the environment terrorists operated within. Specifically, indirect approaches helped "enable partners to conduct operations against terrorists and their organizations as well as actions taken to shape and stabilize those environments as a means to erode the capabilities of terrorist organizations and degrade their ability to acquire support and sanctuary."[158]

There were three broad types of counterterrorism activities defined in JP 3–24 (2014): (1) advise and assist activities; (2) overseas counterterrorism activities (including offense, defense and stability operations, COIN operations, peace operations, etc.); and (3) support for civil authority activities.[159] It was evident there were both defensive and offensive measures to prevent, deter and respond to in terms of terrorism in these definitions, though the specific scope and practice with which to address these evolved between 2001 and 2017.[160]

In terms of the DoD's counterterrorism doctrine in these JPs, women and gender were highlighted minimally as one of many characteristics to be conscious of when analyzing terrorist profiles. Gender was described within the 2009 JP in analytical terms, as a characteristic assessed in terrorist profiling alongside status, education and intellect, age and appearance. It stated:

The terrorists' gender is predominately male, but not exclusively male, even in groups that are rigorously Islamic. Females in these groups are used to support operations or assist in intelligence gathering. Some fundamentalist Islamic groups, however, may use females in the actual conduct of terrorist operations. In groups where religious constraints do not affect women's roles, female membership may be high and leadership roles within the group are not uncommon. Female suicide bombers have been employed with a growing frequency.[161]

In the revised JP 3–26 (2014) on Counterterrorism, gender was not discussed at all. This suggested that the planning and execution of counterterrorism operations would be most cognizant of women in assessments of potential threats (that is, terrorist characteristics) and even this was negligible. However, the experiences of the US in Afghanistan, Iraq and Yemen in this period demonstrated how counterterrorism concerns (and women's roles within these) was increasingly embedded in various streams of effort such as COIN, stabilization and countering violent extremism, all of which became particularly prominent.

## COIN gets an update

As mentioned previously, interaction between the DoD and civilian agencies increased substantially after 9/11, as seen most prominently in stabilization efforts. This was particularly true of USAID. By 2012, interactions between USAID and the DoD had become more frequent and structured, with military liaison representatives from Combat Commands (COCOM) placed in USAID, and USAID senior development advisors placed in COCOM and the Joint Chiefs of Staff. This suggested there was growing evidence of USAID's influence on DoD. Richard Byess, a USAID Foreign Service Officer who served in USAID's Office of Civilian-Military Cooperation from 2006 noted:

> The Army's [2014] Counterinsurgency Field Manual (FM 3–24) reflects a development approach to stabilization, and USAID is having increasing success in influencing core DoD policy documents, including Guidance for the Employment of the Force, the Quadrennial Defense Review, and the regional Theater Security Cooperation Plans, which are now shared with USAID regional bureaus as a matter of course.[162]

This developmental approach of USAID was noted to be particularly visible in the 2014 COIN update:

There is growing evidence of USAID's influence on DoD's broader counterinsurgency strategy. Among the themes familiar to development practitioners are the critical role of host-country ownership in countering violent extremism, the importance of integrating gender analysis into conflict, the value of effective monitoring and evaluation, and the critical necessity of understanding the host country context in program design.[163]

In the 2014 update of FM 3–24, USAID's influence was also noted. In workshops for this redraft where USAID had been present, "the [FM 3–24] authors have expressed particular interest in the role of gender in conflict analysis."[164] While USAID influence in this case was difficult to quantify (particularly when considering DoD's experience with FETs and CSTs around this time), there was a visible shift in the focus and language related to women and gender in the 2014 manual update. Women were now discussed in areas such as "Considering Culture," where it was noted that culture is not static and can change in conflict. Citing Afghanistan and Iraq, it noted:

As security declines, the threat of attack, rape, and murder forces many changes in society. The rapid decline in the status and opportunities for women in these countries, therefore, was not merely due to centuries-old tribal beliefs, but to very real and pragmatic economic and social changes over time.[165]

Gender was highlighted when assessing a cultural situation where a person's status or role may relate to this, or in times of conflict where "people may choose to emphasize certain group identities such as nationality or religion, while at other times different identities, such as one's profession or gender, may matter more."[166] It also highlighted the "Anbar Province Operational Environment," where "[r]eligion was used to justify al Qaeda in Iraq's actions, which included marriages to the local women, not allowing cigarettes, the ban of music and films, and the common intimidation tactic of beheading those that resisted."

There was also a much more nuanced approach to considering women and gender in insurgencies in the 2014 update. Discussing human intelligence sources, women were highlighted as an important population to access, who should be focused on by counterinsurgents as FETs and CSTs had done in Afghanistan. HTSs were also noted to have one woman assigned to them to "facilitate access to females within the local population."[167] It also noted how reintegration "accounts for the specific needs of women and children associated with insurgent and other armed groups."[168] The manual referenced women as auxiliary forces in terms of insurgency and human intelligence, but also in ways more expansive than seen before. In relation to women's role as auxiliary forces, it notes:

> Women can play an essential role in the auxiliary force. Insurgencies generally require a robust system of financing and supply. In many cases, a woman will have greater freedom of movement in a society than a man who is actively engaging government forces. For example, a wife, niece, or daughter of an insurgent might be able to send a message or make financial transitions much easier than the actual insurgent.[169]

Gaining human intelligence is also noted as crucial in battling insurgencies and is often used for support operations. However, such intelligence can often be filled with inaccuracies, rumors or inaccurate information. As such, it was imperative to gain information from the whole population, including women, who were viewed as a "restricted population:"

> An important part of gaining access from the whole population is gaining access to restricted populations. These populations often include women, but they can include any element that the counterinsurgent cannot access because of cultural considerations. Restricted access teams may be helpful in ensuring that information is attained from the whole population, including women.[170]

This update demonstrated the way in which DoD was integrating and reflecting lessons learned about women in COIN from its own efforts, but also reaching out to partner agencies such as USAID to gain different perspectives. This highlighted how such influence may not be readily visible externally and could not easily be measured in terms of direct impact. Nevertheless, it did indeed suggest that interagency efforts and lessons learned on the ground were impacting how women were considered, assessed and engaged in DoD efforts.

### The NAP on Women, Peace and Security

Actions taken by the Obama administration, such as the establishment of the first NAP, also directly impacted how women evolved in DoD programming. Recalling that the 2011 NAP was founded on UNSCR 1325, the NAP offered substantive guidance on how women could be framed and emphasized in DoD activities. Moreover, it emphasized how the department had directly participated in the formulation of this NAP, highlighting where international discourses were interacting more practically with DoD actors to potentially guide and inform their practices. The 2011 NAP identified eighteen representative actions for DoD which required a follow-up implementation plan, and which was released by the DoD in 2013 to measure progress on these actions. The importance of Obama's executive order to establish this NAP was reinforced in this implementation plan, which "recognizes that the goal of the NAP is critical to our national security."[171] While citing some early challenges with the DoD in advancing this plan (particularly in terms of accountability mechanisms for implementation), Ambassador Verveer highlighted the importance of the direction and support of political leadership in the NAP's advancement via an executive order:

> We had incorporated into the NAP an annual assessment of where we were, progress made, so that it wasn't just another piece of paper. Out of that also came the recommendation from the military at the table in fact—some were DoD, some were civilian—that it be accompanied by a command from the President because the military responds to its leaders, to what the Commander-in-Chief says.[172]

The NAP implementation plan expressed a gender-conscious approach to DoD activities in the five areas highlighted as objectives, namely national integration and institutionalization; participation in peace processes and decision-making; protection from violence; conflict prevention; and access to relief and recovery. Specific outcomes concentrated attention on sexual and gender-based violence (SGBV) in conflict (including early warning, in conflict, and protection of actors); improving policy frameworks to support achievement in "gender equality and women's empowerment through defense work;" and effectively engaging women in "peace negotiation, security initiatives, conflict prevention, peace-building, and decision making during all phases of conflict prevention and resolution, and transition." In total, eleven outcomes were defined. Again, NAP objectives and outcomes focused heavily on the protection and participation of women, but did begin to emphasize their explicit involvement as security actors in foreign forces.

All DoD components were instructed to "incorporate, monitor, and evaluate the outcomes and actions listed in the NAP, and report progress annually to the DoD." The implementation guide was meant to

> [s]erve as a tool for implementing the NAP objectives into DoD programs and policies within the strategic, operational, and tactical environment and aims to support military personnel in recognizing and addressing the security priorities of all sectors of the local population—men, women, and children—in a military context.[173]

The Under Secretary of Defense for Policy was the position designated as being responsible for coordinating implementation of the NAP by ensuring "the principles and objectives in the NAP inform the strategic planning process, and by monitoring and reporting DoD progress."[174] The plan largely focused externally towards the environments the US operated in and the partners with which it engaged, and did not focus action points on women in US forces.

Action points included efforts to "[a]ssist partner governments in improving the recruitment and retention of women, including minorities and other historically marginalized women, into government ministries and the incorporation of women's perspectives into peace and security policy." For example, CENTCOM engaged with Afghan women and supported programs "targeted at the recruitment and retention of women in the Afghan National Security Forces." This also extended to efforts which would fall under training and equipping, to "provide common guidelines and training to assist partner nations to integrate women and their perspectives into their security sectors." This component remained one of the weaker aspects of the NAP, where the promotion of women as security actors themselves was not frequently emphasized, nor as a population actively considered in security operations and conflict environments as potential threats or radical actors. However, this shortfall could be traced to UNSCR 1325 itself, which also neglected to frame women as security actors or concerns, suggesting that there were deficits in international UN discourses which were also informing how DoD would consider women and gender in their work.[175] Susan A. Markham, the Senior Gender Coordinator for Gender Equality and Women's Empowerment at USAID (2014–17), noted:

I think an undeveloped part of [UNSCR] 1325 was the role that women could play in providing security. In our NAP, and NAPs around the world, we have strong civil society and we have strong female negotiators. However, when it comes down to providing security, taking part in security, making sure that the forces from around the world understand gender issues, and how gender issues play into the roles that security providers are to play—I think that has been one of one our weakest parts of implementing [UNSCR] 1325 in almost every country.[176]

Engell has argued that effective military organizations perform "core tasks the political leadership asks of it" (traditionally, fighting and winning wars), and have been organized, trained and equipped to do so. This has thus also created a unique professional culture and ethos to achieve this task.[177] What this means in terms of the addition of women to combat units, or the integration of a gender perspective more generally in the DoD, is that such initiatives have to be framed in their "potential to add new capabilities and thereby also improve the effectiveness of operations,"[178] whether combat, stabilization or other operations. In other words, it had to be argued that:

Implementing UNSCR 1325 and the National Action Plans is important not only for the promotion of women's rights and gender equality, it can also help military organizations maximize their operational effectiveness in a strategic context that demands local cultural understanding and great organizational diversity to tackle the often complex tasks involved in stabilization.[179]

The US's NAP implementation plan appeared to build off roles women in US forces had already taken in Afghanistan. Here, action points encouraged the US to "[l]everage the participation of female US military personnel to encourage and model gender integration and reach out to female and male populations in partner nations,"[180] which incorporated CSTs, FETs or gender advisory roles. Other actions aimed to increase "partner nation women's participation in US funded training programs for foreign police, judicial, and military personnel, Professional Military Education (PME), as well as exchange programs, conferences, and seminars."[181] The roles of women in foreign security forces was gaining increased attention, and the DoD showed great potential to further integrate and assess gendered impacts and dynamics into their efforts at strategic, operational and tactical levels.

However, one area that remained visibly absent in this NAP was a gendered assessment of the impact of DoD activities, which still appeared to be either ignored or unassessed more broadly in terms of collateral impact, particularly where secondary or tertiary issues may have specific implications for men and women. For example, if the recipients of strike targets were predominantly male, what did the future prospects look like for the widows and families left behind? Could such strikes lead to diminished support from the population for US presence in the region or the domestic government which allowed these? Could security concerns arise (or even be compounded) in the future if these families became supported by insurgents?[182]

There have been hopeful (though delayed) signs of increased reflection on the costs and consequences of civilian casualties and societal harm in military efforts more generally in countries such as Afghanistan, and the implications of this for counterterrorism efforts and relationships with partner forces in countries such as Yemen, Syria, Iraq and Pakistan.[183] In the case of Afghanistan, this has gained momentum in part due to civil-military efforts in response to increased levels of civilian casualties and harm, and the ability of non-military actors to start expressing their concern in military terms. For example, "the adoption of COIN and its rhetoric of 'protecting the population' allowed for the creation of a new opportunity for aid actors and human rights advocates to engage on these issues." This was furthered by "strategic argumentation" where humanitarian workers framed their concerns in COIN language (particularly that of civilian harm), and evidence and data which was "critical in persuading military officials to adopt tighter controls on the use of force, as was cultivating relationships with key military officials at various levels."[184] It was such reflections that opened new opportunities to consider how women were engaged in foreign partnerships and engaged or impacted by counterterrorism efforts. Indeed, the DoD demonstrated it was becoming more aware of the necessity of engaging women in local populations, and was now accounting for women and gender in some programs. While this extended to how women were assessed in activities related to civilian harm and casualties, it also indicated that for actors trying to push reforms associated with women, peace and security within DoD, they had to speak in similar terms and shared language to demonstrate what operational effectiveness could be gained. Nonetheless, the impetus appeared to be geared more to how aid and development workers could adopt security language.

While the NAP's guidance was poised to alter how women would be considered in DoD strategies, operations and tactics, the implementation proved to be slow-moving and at times outright problematic. This NAP guide proved to be particularly limited in its impact in the field, as was seen in Afghanistan. In 2010, Colonel Sheila Scanlon (retired), a thirty-two-year veteran of the USMC, was appointed to be the first gender advisor by her commanding general, Lieutenant General William B. Caldwell, in Afghanistan. She described that it was a lack of institutional knowledge about UNSCR 1325, the NAP and gender more broadly that combined to limit the impacts of the NAP in practice, and that it was rarely referenced or understood in the field: "Between 2012–14 I never knew there was a NAP, and that it had been signed in 2013. Nobody ever talked about it or mentioned it."[185]

The NAP was also neglected at the CENTCOM level: "When I came back I talked to some people at CENTCOM to ask, 'who is handling gender?' and it was pointing fingers at each other. Who was actually responsible? There was no guidance coming out from US CENTCOM." Colonel Scanlon suggested that being an implementation guide contributed to the NAP's limited impact: "It was not an order, it was not a military action plan, it was not a directive to the general that he has to do something in Afghanistan." Instead, this gender angle was implemented using "good logic. You used your head. You had no guidance on how to do this."[186] She emphasized that a specific operational plan, policy and eventual DoD instruction would make the NAP relevant, and that the inclusion of gender advisors at the COCOM level and below would further ensure gender was considered at the strategic, operational and tactical levels.

Noting the ad hoc nature of her own gender advisory role, she stated it depended on "who the commander is whether they will put a gender advisor in, and how much of the NAP implementation guide they will take on."[187] Gender advisors were appointed due to the "forward thinking of our command sergeant major, not because of our general, or because there was a billet [a specific personnel position or assignment]." In this role as gender advisor, she would attend the Inter-Agency Working Group alongside US State, USAID and ISAF, where they would share information regarding "what they were doing, what money they had, programs which were up and coming, or just trading ideas about best practices."[188]

Other suggestions to advance both the NAP and gender considerations in DoD operations and activities included identifying "champions" at the Office of the Secretary of Defense and the Chairman of the Joint Chiefs of Staff; broader education on the NAP and UNSCR 1325; establishing platforms to share lessons between DoD, US State and USAID in relation to interagency gender working groups; and conducting joint exercises in which both military and civilian personnel participated where NAP and UNSCR 1325 had been integrated, which had thus far been limited or sporadic.[189] Gender mainstreaming—"the process of assessing the often different implications for women and men of any plans, policies, and activities of all actors involved"—has also been highlighted as important for the DoD. This is due to it having "great positive potential in terms of supporting the analysis, planning, and execution of operations,"[190] and it was important to have it recognized as such. The implementation of the NAP within DoD was also perceived by other partner agencies as a work in progress, but one where interagency relationships could positively impact this. Susan Markham of USAID noted that from a defense perspective, while the NAP was acknowledged, for some troops it was not clear how it should be implemented: "They understand it's coming from the top down, they know we have the NAP on Women, Peace and Security, but how that effects their actual, everyday lives [...] we're still getting there."[191]

By 2017 the DoD had started to take a number of steps to implement the NAP and UNSCR 1325. Anne A. Witkowsky, the Deputy Assistant Secretary of Defense for Stability and Humanitarian Affairs within the Office of the Secretary of Defense (Policy), highlighted a number of these, including women, peace and security being incorporated into Joint Professional Military Education; regular training pathways; sharing some of the Geographic Combatant Commands' Theater Campaign Plans; and DoD regional centers (which inform DoD exchange programs with other militaries). The DoD had also established a Women, Peace and Security Synchronization Group to coordinate these efforts, while the Global Peace Operations Initiative, a government security assistance program funded through US State, was helping to promote the role of women in peacekeeping operations (by

2015 5,300 women had been trained), enhance gender integration, and prevent and respond to SGBV. The National Guard State Partnership Program had established partnerships and engagements with National Guards of other countries where women would focus on leadership development, empowerment, and the integration of women into armed forces, amongst others. A number of efforts related to the protection of women from SGBV in crises and conflict zones was also recognized. Noting a direct link between women, peace and security activities and counterterrorism, it highlighted the Near East South Asia Center for Strategic Studies, which incorporated DDR into "combating terrorism elements of its in-residence and overseas workshop programs, and includes a special emphasis on the reintegration of women and child soldiers as well as the radicalization of women and youth."[192]

Ways in which to continue to improve this included demonstrating "through research, monitoring, and evaluation—the ways in which NAP implementation directly contributes to a measurable increase in security and the success of military operations." While the above painted a very positive picture of progress within the DoD, due to this being a relatively new policy initiative, Witkowsky noted, "It will take time before the effort is fully integrated into the guidance documents and training cycles of the Department's activities."[193] How this implementation would continue to progress was unclear.

*FETs evolve: Engaging women in partner forces*

While the first incarnation of FETs in Afghanistan ended in 2012, they re-emerged in 2015 with new roles within the USMC. Following increasing requests for FETs from Middle Eastern partners such as Qatar, these women-only units were ideally situated to work with women in countries that were gender-segregated to differing degrees for tasks such as training exchanges, building and fostering relations with partner security forces, and female/cultural liaisons. These were relabeled by some participants as "female partner force engagement team(s)," which in evolution from the original FETs was now being used to "forge bonds with allied nations in the Middle East."[194]

This was evident, for example, in bilateral exchanges with the Kuwait Ministry of the Interior VIP Protection Unit in 2014 and 2015, where they worked with female Kuwaiti officers. It was in these initiatives that international discourses related to UNSCR 1325 became evident: "The exchange is part of a United Nations' initiative to foster equal rights for half of the world's population."The NAP commitment to encourage and model gender integration in partner nations was cited in these efforts. Lieutenant Colonel Melody Mitchell, the program lead in Kuwait, noted that the inclusion of FETs showcased "how they enhance capabilities and interoperability on a tactical level, but also serve the great strategic goal posed by our Presidential Directive [on women, peace and security]."[195]

According to Captain Jennifer Mozzetta, an FET assistant team leader with the USMC, FETs were seen to be "[a] good capability [the Marines] should have." She described the culture of the USMC as a flexible and adaptable force, which drove the impetus of early programs in Iraq and Afghanistan, and which appeared to be "a necessity based off of mission. Whatever the mission is, we adapt to make sure that mission is accomplished."[196] Captain Mozzetta also justified the roles of FETs in terms of how they could access local women: "half the population in the world is female, and half the population is male, give or take. By opening the doors and having FETs created, [this] gives us access to that other half which we did not have access to before because of gender and cultural rules."[197] With the continued US focus on the Middle East, FETs were poised to play an increasingly prominent role: "Our focus in the Middle East, whether it be for aid, assisting in conflict, or to better foster relationships, I think there is going to be a growing need for more women to be involved in a military or security level."Aside from engaging with female security partners, FETs played a positive role in also ensuring that programming considered women's concerns in the populations they were operating within:

> By having an FET that goes out and talks with a community, the men may be saying one thing, but you'll hear more of the stories from everyone in the community. So, FETs out there, [who are] engaging the female populace, we can also report back what we see and [what] we might hear—needs or desires that are not being translated through the men. So, I think it helps, and could open up the doors more for programs or assistance they may need.[198]

Despite this, the specific structure and status FETs should have in diverse operations was not always clear. General Petraeus suggested

FETs should not necessarily become a permanently established program, but should instead be based on each individual operation and context:

> I think that it is always going to be situationally dependent, when you need FETs or not. Obviously if you are doing high-intensity conflict, certainly during the conduct of a fight you are not going to need FETs, I wouldn't think, or at least sizable numbers of them. You might need it in the post-conflict phase. Again, you learn how to establish them, train them up, equip and integrate them, but I don't think you make them a part of the so-called "table of organizational equipment" that authorizes forces.[199]

This was framed in terms of organizational restrictions—you could not necessarily give a campaign every capability they required: "FETs were one more of a menu of elements that we could stand up and attach to a brigade combat team." General Petraeus suggested that if FETs were deemed suitable for a mission, a brigade combat team and their leadership should focus on their engagement within the 6–12-month pre-deployment period. Here, FETs should be "established, integrated, [and] go through the mission rehearsal exercise that is the final activity on the so-called 'road to deployment' that has lots of activities all along it. That's how I think I would go about it. I don't think I would necessarily structure it." This preference to not structure FETs was also considered in terms of resource limitations specific to the wide variety of activities carried out in COIN operations by DoD:

> I don't know if you have the luxury to give a unit every single possible element that it could want, particularly when it comes to a COIN campaign, because of the need for so many different capabilities that often extend beyond what a normal brigade combat team is called on to do in conventional operations.[200]

Colonel Scanlon had also highlighted the idea of mixed-gender FETs, where the capability of women-only units could be accessed when required, while also providing a "role model" unit of men and women working together.[201]

There was continued debate about the status of the teams, in which engagement with women was dependent on the mission at hand, the context and the resources available, and how they were seen to help them achieve that mission. However, FETs were also recognized in terms of their importance in better understanding and engaging with "half the population," particularly in gender-segregated societies. Utilizing women in FETs meant their roles were evidently evolving within US forces, while also opening access to, and support of, local women and female security practitioners in partner countries (even if there were critiques). The use of FETs also demonstrated the evolution of these efforts was informed in part by UNSCR 1325, but still largely considered in terms of the operational utility they provided to missions. However, considering the criticisms leveled at the teams prior to this, it was yet to be seen whether lessons learned would be implemented in full in this new incarnation.

## The evolving role of women in US forces

From Team Lioness to CSTs and FETs, each initiative demonstrated how women's operational roles in US forces evolved significantly between 2001 and 2017. This was impacted by several factors, including the operational environments in countries like Iraq and Afghanistan and their gender-segregated sociocultural environments; the increased prominence of COIN and stability operations, and the requisite engagement with the population; the recognition of women's unintended but increased front-line exposure in combat operations; and a sense of "learning" in the organization, particularly when the operational benefits of these new units was evident. However, these also appeared to be hindered by a number of concerns related to the establishment and integration of these units, such as clearly defined roles, purpose, mandate and support, and particularly gendered stereotypes, as well as limited assumptions of gender knowledge in the DoD more broadly. These units, while not always framed in terms of their counterterrorism contribution, all extended from efforts embedded in the wider GWOT, and each impacted women's roles and status in US armed forces and how they interacted with, and understood, local communities.

The Defense Advisory Committee on Women in the Services was active in highlighting female services members' experiences, roles and needs in this period. By 2008, though women were not allowed to serve in combat roles, 85 per cent of women service members had reported being deployed to a combat area or an area drawing hostile/

imminent danger since 2001, and 42 per cent of women service members had been involved in combat operations, particularly due to the guerilla fighting experienced in urban war zones.[202] Servicewomen from all fields, including medical, translation, intelligence, analysis and other support and logistics roles, had also been recognized for their efforts. These included Army Private First Class Monica Lin Brown, a then nineteen-year-old combat medic with the 82nd Airborne Division, who became only the second woman since World War II, and the first in Afghanistan, to win the Silver Star for valor in war. (The Silver Star is the third highest medal for valor in combat awarded by the US government.)

On 25 April 2007 the convoy Brown was traveling in came under attack in Afghanistan. Running through enemy gunfire to reach colleagues whose vehicle had hit an improvised explosive device (IED), she assisted two severely injured soldiers while under gunfire and shelling, and got them safely evacuated.[203] Despite this, she was later pulled back from her position due to the ban on women in combat.

It was initiatives such as Team Lioness that encouraged some such as Brigadier General Thomas Draude USMC (retired) to note when some combat roles were opened to women in 2008: "We have finally over a period time come to the conclusion that we've have this tremendous asset, this tremendous force that was available to us that we had neglected for years."[204] Secretary of the Army John McHugh stated at his 2009 Senate confirmation hearing: "Women in uniform today are not just invaluable, they're irreplaceable."[205] In 2009, the House Committee on Veterans' Affairs also passed Resolution 868 honoring and recognizing the service and achievements of current and former female members of the armed forces.

In 2010, the Chairman of the Joint Chiefs of Staff, Navy Admiral Mike Mullen, noted that women had given US troops a competitive advantage in Afghanistan and Iraq, and gained insights that would have been otherwise inaccessible. Despite this, they still had many doors closed to them in US forces.[206] In March 2011, the Military Leadership Diversity Commission suggested a ban on female roles in combat be rejected, and some operational fields were subsequently opened to women in 2012. This was further supported by the introduction of the DoD Policy Guidance on Promoting Gender Equality. In the 2014 Quadrennial

Defense Review (QDR), women and gender were referenced seventeen times in new contexts, such as allowing and implementing the decision to include gay men and women into the service, eliminating gender-based barriers to service, and elevating the eradication of sexual assault on military personnel as one of its highest priorities.[207]

These steps indicated a growing recognition of both gendered issues pertaining to members of the US armed forces as evidenced from recent operations, and the contributions of both women and gay service members. There had also been increasing research on women's gendered experiences in the Iraq and Afghanistan conflicts, considering things such as combat-related exposure, military sexual trauma, separation from family and gender discrimination in the military.[208] Stories about the approximately 250,000 female soldiers that served for US forces in Iraq and Afghanistan were also increasingly common in news and media, and may have also added momentum to this shift.[209]

There had also been increasing efforts in the armed forces to combat sexual assault of both servicemen and servicewomen, particularly since 2005.[210] This suggested there were also increasingly gendered considerations throughout the DoD, though it was difficult to assess to what extent these broader considerations and discourses were directly impacted by women's operational roles in the GWOT. Indeed, while such evolutions may have already been underway in the post 9/11 environment, these were visibly impacted by military operations in Afghanistan and Iraq, by presidential executive orders,[211] and documents such as the UNSCR 1325. As highlighted earlier, some women in US forces also faced controversy and even scandal, demonstrating the complexity of their roles in this period.

On 3 December 2015, the Secretary of Defense announced that all combat roles would be opened to women, without exception, for the first time in American history. Secretary Ash Carter noted that women consisted of 50 per cent of the population, so "we cannot afford to cut ourselves off from half the country's talents and skills. We have to take full advantage of every individual who can meet our standards."[212] Carter pointed to women's combat experience in Iraq and Afghanistan as lending to this shift. By referencing women as half the population, he also suggested that a full breadth of skills and abilities was not being tapped into. Referring to the military as a "learning organization,"

Carter noted how this integration and adaptation could be traced back to 9/11: "We adapted to counter insurgency and counter terrorism missions in the wake of 9/11 and in the wars in Iraq and Afghanistan."[213]

This was echoed by General Petraeus, who noted women's experiences in Team Lioness and FETs were "certainly a factor" in opening women's combat roles. But women were also present in numerous other roles as well throughout this period:

> You had females in military police who were doing reconnaissance, security missions, and a variety of other traditional military police tasks. You had females in some engineer units that were doing counter-IED missions, you basically had females in every element of the tech brigade headquarters. You had them in basically every unit except actually infantry battalions, at that time, the tactical field artillery battalions and armor units. They were in attack aviation. Again, the reality was that women were in combat [...]. I think there was a growing awareness that women are in combat, regardless of what you want to say about laws against women being in combat—they were fighting and dying for our country and for the missions in which we were engaged.[214]

For General Petraeus, the issue of women in combat units should have come down to "whether or not they can meet certain physical standards and other standards that are established for anyone, male or female, to serve in that particular type of unit." However, it was also DoD directives such as those to open combat roles to women that were viewed as more significant than resolutions such as UNSCR 1325. General Petraeus noted: "[UNSCR] 1325 is such a general statement, 'women ought to be integrated into all aspects of peace and security.' Agreed. OK, now what?" This was contrasted with specific DoD directives:

> I mean, those matter. Those are specific directives that the military under the DoD have to implement and are implementing. I think we are way past 1325 and whatever significance it has [...]. I don't mean to say that [NAP or UNSCRs] aren't important because they do shape the overall context that nations and then departments, agencies and ministries within those governments are issuing direction. But I'd be careful not to get too hung up on something like that.[215]

While UNSCR 1325 may have been increasingly informing security discourses at the national level under Obama (as evidenced in the

NAP), it was not until these women, peace and security principles were explicated by senior DoD figures like the Secretary of Defense that any impact from these was visible. In fact, it appeared such language was viewed distinctly between policymakers and practitioners. General Petraeus noted resolutions such as UNSCR 1325 "frankly are a great deal more important to those who are developing them, fighting over every word, than to those fighting in the field, who are actually trying to execute our national policies." He noted the absence of this kind of language in the QDR or National Military Strategy did not mean that women's positions were not considered, but instead that they should be dealt with at more of a policy level:

> We didn't need the QDR or the National Military Strategy to say anything about improving the status of women in US security forces any more than we should say we should improve the lot of African Americans, or other minorities, or various of the sexual orientations, or whatever else. These were issues for policy on a variety of different social issues within the DoD, but I don't think they're necessarily appropriate for the National Military Strategy, which is focused on how you accomplish the missions in the NSS and the overall Defense Strategy.[216]

This point was noteworthy when contrasted against the Quadrennial Diplomacy and Development Review in US State and USAID (discussed in the following chapters), where there was a clear directive to consider the status of women in all aspects of programming, and where women's inclusion was framed in terms of how it contributed to the goal of security. This suggested distinctions between these agencies on where such momentum should come from, what motivated it, and why it mattered for each agency's operations. This also demonstrated divergence in how inclusion and consideration of women in both policy and practice was distinct between departments, and how international resolutions like UNSCR 1325 trickled down into operational relevance in each case.

The implementation guidelines that Carter referenced also highlighted an increased emphasis on gender-neutral roles in the defense sphere: "Leaders must assign tasks and jobs throughout the force based on ability, not gender." Citing recent surveys, he noted: "Women service members emphatically do not want integration to be based on any considerations other than the ability to perform and combat effective-ness." Carter also suggested women in the US context were perceived differently in some of the areas they had been operating in:

> We know the United States is a nation committed to using our entire population to the fullest, as are some of our closest friends and allies, we also know that not all nations share this perspective. Our military has long dealt with this reality, notably, over the last 15 years in Iraq and also Afghanistan. And we'll need to be prepared to do so going forward as it bears on the specialties that will be opened by this decision.[217]

In 2015, two women graduated from the US Army Rangers (although this did not necessarily guarantee their position in a unit). The first female accepted into US Special Forces was through the 75th Ranger Regiment in 2017, thus proving that the GWOT had been a catalyst for changes to women's roles in US forces in a multitude of ways.

## Women in foreign forces

It is clear that women's roles in US forces evolved significantly based on the trajectory and scope of the GWOT, as well as due to changes in the operational environments US forces were present in, and the evolv-ing operational objectives it faced in the field. Yet, how women's roles in foreign security forces were impacted in newfound ways is often overlooked. This section considers how US discourses and practices related to counterterrorism considered women in foreign security forces through three cases: (1) Yemen's all-female elite counterterror-ism unit in the Central Security Organization; (2) the Sisters of Fallujah and Daughters of Iraq programs; and (3) women in the ANSF.

The 2006 QDR is an important starting point to consider women in foreign forces, as it marked the need for the DoD to increasingly work by, with and through allied and partner forces which may necessitate building the capacity of partner forces. It noted: "Recent operations demonstrate the critical importance of being organized to work with and through others, and of shifting emphasis from per-forming tasks ourselves to enabling others."[218] The 2006 QDR was noted to be a "game changer" in terms of fundamental restructuring in the forces, as noted David Des Roches, former NATO Operations Director (2005–07):

[It] was a real department-wide effort that looked at what had to happen, looked at the changing world, and what it came up with was an
incorporation of building partner capacity and stability operations as
core DoD missions […]. [It] really recognized that the Cold War model
that the department was organized on was not fit for purpose.[219]

This had also been informed by training of Afghan and Iraqi security
forces from 2004, and supported in some cases through Section 1206
funding for Foreign Forces/Global Train & Equip from 2006.[220] Section
1206 funding provided the Secretary of Defense with authority to train
and equip foreign military forces for two specified purposes: counterterrorism and stability operations; and foreign security forces for counterterrorism operations.[221] Section 1206 funding was particularly
important for countries like Yemen, which was the largest recipient of
this funding and had received $386 million up to 2015.[222]

The Obama administration had also increasingly emphasized the
training and equipping of foreign partners forces who would be tasked
with addressing counterterrorism concerns within their own borders.
In 2014, this would also include the establishment of the Counterterrorism Partnerships Fund. Valued at $1.3 billion, the fund provided
resources to train, build capacity and facilitate partner countries on the
front line.[223] However, it was not clear what programs were specifically
funded to support or develop women's roles in these efforts, or how or
if gender considerations were present in the design, implementation or
evaluation of these programs. Training foreign partners also continued
as ISIS dominated the scene in 2014. In terms of integrated operations,
by 2015 the military noted that the best way to counter violent extremist organizations was "by way of sustained pressure using local forces
augmented by specialized US and coalition military strengths such as
ISR [intelligence, surveillance, reconnaissance], precision strike, training, and logistical support."[224] Women became sporadically visible in
these efforts in several countries between 2001 and 2017, and the following sections will examine cases in Yemen, Iraq and Afghanistan.

### Training and equipping Yemen's counterterrorism unit[225]

Yemen remained an important focus for both the Bush and Obama
administrations in terms of counterterrorism.[226] Following 9/11, the

Bush administration applied acute pressure on the Yemeni government to cooperate in counterterrorism efforts. Yemen was viewed as a state that could either be a partner or a target of the US.[227] Edmund Hull, US Ambassador to Yemen from 2001–04, stated: "The primary US interest in Yemen was the interest of counterterrorism, and Yemen had been identified by Al Qaeda as an important node in their international network."[228] Yemeni President Ali Abdullah Saleh, wary of being viewed as harboring terrorists, openly supported US efforts. As such, Yemeni–US security cooperation increased substantially between 2002 and 2004, and economic assistance and even arms sales, which had been suspended in 1990, were resumed.[229] A multi-stream approach was taken to tackle terrorism in the country through governance, economic assistance, development efforts in deprived areas, and military and intelligence cooperation, though defense efforts claimed the lion's share of emphasis.

Yemeni security forces were viewed as relatively immature, had "very little surgical counterterrorism capability," and were a dominant focus for US training and equipping efforts.[230] This Yemeni partner seemingly required the skills and training necessary to become what was perceived to be a "practical" partner—a counterterrorism force that could operate "agilely and effectively."[231] Core training efforts focused on the Yemeni Special Forces and their designated counterterrorism unit.[232] This was first established in 2003, with approximately 150 individuals recruited, then doubled in size by July 2007, with the US providing the bulk of equipment and sharing training responsibilities with the UK. US Ambassador Thomas Krajeski (2004–07) noted: "Yemen was a prime example of where we wanted to support the more effective forces."[233] This effort was being led by trainers from US Special Forces Command in Djibouti.

Women in Yemen had historically had senior and diverse roles in the country's armed forces and security sector, particularly in the People's Democratic Republic of Yemen (PDRY) prior to unification in 1990, where they were active in the judiciary, army and police force. The PDRY was the Arab world's only socialist state, and there was much emphasis on women's emancipation and participation in all aspects of society. After unification, many of these roles for women were significantly restricted, if not closed to them. However, in 2006, an all-female elite counterterrorism unit was established in Yemen's Central Security Organization, an initiative attributed in part to Yahya Saleh, the Commander of the Central Security Organization, and Rashed al-Alimi, the Minister of Interior. This unit was understood as a way to appeal to western donors, would likely be viewed favorably, and was an area where women were indeed practically required for counterterrorism operations.[234] Twenty women were recruited into the first intake of this unit from the military police, where they were taught activities such as shooting, driving military vehicles, English-language skills, how to enter houses by force[235] and computer skills. Nabeel Khoury, the US Deputy Chief of Mission in Yemen from 2004–07, noted the training provided reflected a basic programmatic model that the US military and some specialized police units undertook in the US. This was also reflected in Iraq and Afghanistan to some extent, though was "tailor-made" to the unique Yemeni environment.[236] A group of women from this unit also traveled to the US for an exchange with their American counterparts.

Khoury suggested one key impetus behind the establishment of this female unit was the increase of kidnappings of foreigners in Yemen by al-Qaeda at the time:

> There were always tribal kidnappings in Yemen, but those were not traditionally very dangerous situations—they could be handled through bargaining between the state and the tribe. But with al-Qaeda starting to operate, kidnapping turned into something completely different, necessitating a CTU [counterterrorism unit]-type approach to the problem. That's where the women came in.[237]

Here, women would perform reconnaissance work on homes where hostages were believed to be held, talk to individuals inside the home (women were noted to be seen as less threatening by the hostage-takers), or themselves participate in operations such as home raids with their unit.[238] US Ambassador Stephen Seche (2007–10) recalled, "the ability to integrate the forces and have the women on board at the time of the assaults and searches was a very useful element as part of an effective counterterrorism operation."[239] This unit had also been praised by Khoury as "less corrupt."[240] It was a new unit which did not carry out the same practices infamous in some other units, as it was believed that women were not associated with the same networks that drove corruption and patronage practices elsewhere. This support for

the women's counterterrorism unit was also understood to complement US political, development and economic assistance in Yemen at
the time, which was focused on advancing women's rights:

> We obviously wanted to marry these two areas so that military assistance
> encouraged or complemented political and economic assistance. So, the
> concept of involving women in the military and police forces to us meant
> that we were encouraging a more democratic approach, and a better
> approach to the rights of women in general. We were stressing that on the
> civilian side, so it made sense to stress it on the military side as well. [241]

These women were observed to be confident, professional, and
could potentially play leadership roles at home and in their communities outside of their military roles. [242] This suggested there were both
operational and broader democratic/equality norms perceived in the
US's support for this unit.

However, there was a noted lack of emphasis or promotion of this
unit, suggesting that such rights approaches were more limited in practice. Ambassador Krajeski stated: "We also didn't really promote this
[women's unit]—we didn't oppose it, but we were really focused on
that intense effort to train a couple of units in counterterrorism." [243]
While appearing professional, it was also questioned just how much
"substance" was in the program, and how much was meant to appeal to
US donors: "It was kind of like the dog and pony show—let's show the
American ambassador what we've got." [244] It was seen as one small
component of a broader efforts to improve counterterrorism capabilities in the country. According to Ambassador Gerald Feierstein (2010–
13), "we thought the woman's unit was a pretty good deal, and that
they actually had some successes in the counterterrorism fight. So that
was fine, but that in and of itself was not a focus of what we were trying
to do, but that whole CTU [counterterrorism unit] structure was
something." [245] This echoed sentiments in countries such as Iraq and
Afghanistan, where women's promotion in security forces was often
viewed as one (much less significant) component of wider security or
counterterrorism partnerships; a nice add-on to broader efforts in
certain contexts, but rarely seriously invested in or supported.

Similar to Iraq and Afghanistan, women trying to enter these forces
often faced multiple barriers to entry. These barriers could include a
lack of family support, or indeed families (particularly conservative

families) outright banning their participation. Gaining the support and respect of male colleagues, and indeed of the publics they served, could also prove challenging, where stigmas about a women's correct place in society still largely prevailed.

While this small unit was noted to have some successes, women's roles in security more generally were seemingly neglected. Ambassador Seche stated:

> I don't know if we fully utilized the opportunity to have women at the forefront of the counterterrorism fight, given the ability of women to serve a multiplicity of roles, as opposed to just the kinetic counterterrorism role—for example, women's ability to go in and work with populations in a way that's not seen as nearly as threatening. I think this is something we could have done much more effectively.[246]

What particular structure such counterterrorism units should take was also unclear, noted Ambassador Feierstein: "whether you have them as standalone units, or you have them integrated into a larger structure, is a question. But I certainly think there is an important opportunity for women to participate in these activities." However, he still believed the US could be supportive of such units, but that these efforts generally should be "organic from within those societies."[247] This comment also raises an important point that extended far beyond Yemen; a focus on the promotion and support of women's roles as security actors, particularly in the most male-dominated corners of counterterrorism, appeared exceptional and problematic. Yet, when contrasted against aspects such as women's rights or empowerment, work which may also contravene some local norms, such resistance was often absent. Women's promotion in security was seen as exceptional and a point of potential conflict and contention with partner states, which was reflected in its emphasis on training, equipping and support in other defense partnerships.

This broader focus on counterterrorism training and equipping, including of this women's unit, was also perceived to be overshadowing other US efforts in the country, demonstrating how a prioritization of "direct" counterterrorism initiatives could lend to interagency or programming disputes. According to Ambassador Seche:

> There was a fair bit of money going in to these [counterterrorism] programs, training and equipping these forces, and this became a very singu-

lar purpose to the detriment of, certainly in terms of perception, other programs. We started to focus so feverishly on objectively what was necessary, but subjectively and perceptually it became very difficult to demonstrate we were doing anything other than counterterrorism.[248]

This was also considered in terms of how a focus on women in counterterrorism may have detracted from other security roles, such as their promotion in police forces, which could have positively impacted women at the local level:

> Given the focus on specialized counterterrorism units, a lot of programs that might have gone to local police forces would be put in a second-tier category because the priority was so clearly to get the counterterrorism forces running, stood up, trained and into the field. That basically became the elephant in the room—everything else was squeezed out of the space that was available.[249]

Besides detracting from other security roles, this counterterrorism focus was also thought to depreciate other streams of US efforts in Yemen. Ambassador Barbara Bodine (1997–2001) stated: "When we shifted to al-Qaeda—the GWOT was a kind of global proxy war, and the only thing that we were interested in, and did, and talked about was specifically focused on al-Qaeda. Everything else went by the boards." In Yemen, this was noted to have detracted from broader stabilization and reform efforts: "We weren't doing anything on COIN, we weren't doing development, we weren't doing these things—we were fighting a proxy war."[250] While this spoke to broader critiques of US counterterrorism strategy in Yemen, it also highlighted evident imbalances in publicly stated comprehensive approaches to security more generally. It highlighted how a disproportionate focus on direct counterterrorism efforts could severely impact other interrelated or indirect concerns (such as those which focused on or supported women in other areas like political or development spheres). It also highlighted that where defense efforts were prioritized, women within these were not.

Even though al-Qaeda had largely been eliminated in Yemen by 2003, most jihadists from Yemen had traveled to Iraq, where they accounted for 8–17 per cent of the foreign fighters.[251] There were also four attacks on the US Embassy in Yemen between 2000 and 2008, including a 2008 attack which killed sixteen (including six assailants), which maintained US counterterrorism interest in the country. This was only escalated by the announcement of al-Qaeda in the Arabian Peninsula (AQAP) in 2009. Between 2000 and 2008, Yemen had received an average of $40 million annually in military and economic aid.[252] In 2009, the US provided $40 million in economic assistance and $120 million in military assistance.[253]

The 2011 Arab Spring marked a juncture for US engagement in Yemen. There had been an understanding that focusing predominantly on Yemen's counterterrorism unit—which was viewed as resting on a "completely dysfunctional security and military structure"[254]—was not efficient, in part because of a preoccupation with counterterrorism activity versus meaningful reform. This was part of a general reassessment of the US strategy in the country at the time by Ambassador Feierstein: "The Arab Spring opened the door for us to have a much more balanced strategy for Yemen and to really look at these other issues."[255] Part of that drive was thinking of broader COIN efforts:

> You're talking about nation-building, you're talking about building up the capacity of the security and the military, not only to eliminate the terrorist cell, but also to provide security to populations, to control territory, and we hadn't done that. We had been almost completely uninvolved in anything like that. So, one of the things that we said in this rethink is that we need to invest more in trying to build a reasonably capable regular military force, a regular security force. Simultaneously, on the development and economic side, we needed to pay attention to helping them building up their capacity in these areas.[256]

As will be discussed in the following chapters, there had simultaneously been a focus on women's political participation, development and general status in Yemen over this period by US State and USAID, which had been impacted by the prioritization of counterterrorism efforts.

Yemeni women had also played significant roles in the 2011 Arab Spring and, following the exit of President Saleh, in the National Dialogue Conference from 2013–14. However, it was suggested by Khoury that women were not generally viewed as key power brokers in Yemen, which had implications for how they were included and reflected in post-2011 efforts. This, he suggested, was in part due to their low status and visibility in the security sector: "They don't have weapons in their hands, they are not combatants. As such, they are not respected as equals by the combatants."To address this, it was suggested women had to take on increasing roles in the security sector: "In the forces on the ground, if women and young people rise to the top, you will have better representation of society at large in that [area of security]."[257] This suggested a direct perceived link between empowering women in the security sector and other streams that would fall under US State or USAID, demonstrating the simultaneous and interrelated relationship between these for advancing women's roles across defense, governance and development efforts. But it also reflected the view that power rested in the hands of security actors.

A total of $328.5 million was allocated to Yemen from the US alone in 2012. In 2013, this figure was still a significant $242.8 million, of which Section 1206 funding was the single highest contributor, at $47.3 million[258] (training of police was excluded from this funding).[259] Even with the noted concerns related to a counterterrorism-heavy focus in the country, Yemen's counterterrorism training was prematurely held up as a model by Obama to be emulated in Iraq and Afghanistan.[260] Yemen continued to retain a significant focus both in terms of counterterrorism and broader stabilization concerns, which has since been lacking in the country. By 2014, as Yemen was slipping into increasingly deadly and destabilizing conflict, efforts continued to train security forces in Yemen who had "gone on the offensive against al Qaeda."[261]

The women's counterterrorism unit had proved a unique example of women engaged in a predominantly male force, and in 2014 it was noted they were set to take on an increasing role in this sector.[262] They also, in a sense, came to represent some of the broader debates related to US counterterrorism efforts, including competing (and at times conflicting) streams of effort between agencies which could work in friction, and how women's roles as security actors in foreign forces were viewed in positive, though limited, terms. However, civil conflict overtook the country and Houthi insurgents seized the capital of Sanaa in 2014, taking control over government institutions. Women working in government security forces were removed from their positions in Houthi-controlled regions, and the country has since cascaded into a devastating conflict. Notably, by 2017 the Houthis themselves had showcased stadiums full of women willing to take up arms to defend their cause, even though this was largely perceived to be symbolic and void of women's roles as armed insurgents in the group. Women have also been reported to take up roles within Houthi forces, such as recruiting and training other women, or searching or monitoring women, demonstrating how this group saw some value in utilizing women in security roles (even if these too remained limited in practice).[263]

## Training the Sisters and Daughters of Iraq

In the early stages of the insurgency in Iraq, AQI, under the leadership of Abu Musab al-Zarqawi, began playing an increasing and even leading role in violence in the country.[264] Zarqawi aimed to provoke an all-out sectarian conflict between Shia Arabs, who now played a larger role in government, and the Sunni Arabs that had previously held this role. This strategy (which was opposed by Zawahiri in al-Qaeda's central leadership) also aimed to force US troops to depart once they had lost public support. To carry out this strategy, Zarqawi implemented a campaign of spectacular violence, including mass bomb attacks against Shia sites and targets, kidnappings, beheadings, torture and a long list of other brutal tactics, which was particularly concentrated in Anbar Province. Senior US official increasingly viewed AQI as a driving force of violence, and suicide bombings in particular.[265]

The increasingly intense conflict in Iraq had prompted President Bush to announce what was labeled as the "surge" in 2007, which was led by General David Petraeus. The surge saw an additional 20,000 troops to help contain the violence, clear and secure neighborhoods (particularly in Baghdad), further build up and equip Iraqi forces, and bolster reconstruction efforts. Announcing the surge, Bush emphasized working beside Iraqi forces, and ensuring Iraqi forces could later efficiently provide security themselves, along with a renewed emphasis on diplomatic efforts. Discussing Anbar, where US forces were "killing and capturing al Qaeda leaders" and "protecting the local population," Bush noted, "these troops will work with Iraqi and tribal forces to keep up the pressure on the terrorists. America's men and women in uniform took away al Qaeda's safe haven in Afghanistan—and we will not allow them to re-establish it in Iraq."[266] It was noteworthy that Bush's references to women as part of foreign troops was distinct from that in US discourses referencing "our fighting men and women" in Iraq, though he did note "Iraqis want to be defended by their own countrymen, and we are helping Iraqis assume those duties."[267]

Women in Iraq had a history in state security forces, particularly in the autonomous Kurdish-administered regions.[268] Yet, due to the war, Iraqi women began taking on new roles in Iraqi security forces during this period. The US-led Team Lioness activities established in 2003 were transferred to Iraqi women in newly established units tasked with carrying out similar roles, such as searching women and children for weapons and contraband at checkpoints. In 2007, the Sisters of Fallujah was formed, wherein Iraqi women would volunteer to work in paid positions alongside a USMC unit.[269] Female Marines would provide security for the Sisters of Fallujah, who expressed their desire to help bring safety to the people of their eponymous city.[270] This extended into areas such as Ameriyah and Ferris, where the first group outside of Fallujah was formed—The Sisters of Ameriyah/Ferris (an Army program). This was noted to be a response to an army-wide directive to involve more women in community affairs, and reflected national and DoD emphasis on training and equipping of foreign partners. The program was not established along tribal lines as the Sons of Iraq was; instead, the women's unit was bipartisan,[271] though it was unclear why women were engaged in this manner. Training for the program was noted to have included the study of topics such as police ethics, human rights, women's issues, working in a terrorist environment, female searches and first aid, and performed live-fire training with AK-47 rifles and 9mm pistols.[272]

The Daughters of Iraq was established in 2008 by the 101st Airborne Division and was based off the similarly named Sons of Iraq, a volunteer-driven organization which began reintegrating Iraqis into security operations in the country. However, the driving thrust for Daughters of Iraq was noted to be the increasing number of female suicide bombers in the country, particularly those carried out by AQI after 2007,[273] highlighting the impact of women's roles in AQI on women's roles in state security forces. Here, over a period of ten days, Iraqi women were being trained to find female suicide bombers, and how to search rooms and handle Kalashnikov rifles so they could conduct operations alongside their male counterparts.[274] They also prevented trafficking of weapons, explosives and dangerous materials.[275] These roles were noted to provide financial opportunities for Iraqi women,[276] and many of them participated because they wanted to protect the population.[277]

This program was also framed and justified in terms of empowering women, and in terms of helping achieve democratic norms: "The Daughters of Iraq will facilitate female empowerment and the creation of the group represents a significant step towards a properly functioning democratic society," said Sergeant Jason G. George, an intelligence officer with Company C.[278] This unit was thus perceived to empower women financially and democratically, while fulfilling a required operational function. It also demonstrated (based on its volunteer status) that some Iraqi women were keen to become security actors and contribute to national security efforts, although this appeared to be a secondary consideration. Despite their training, however, they were not allowed to carry weapons, and didn't interact with their male colleagues, suggesting that such efforts fell short of their intended aim. It was also noted by Kawakib Salih, a professor at Baghdad University, that the program "was created as a temporary solution to address the security situation and perhaps in the future it will disappear."[279]

While the Daughters of Iraq initially began in 2008 with thirty-one women, this increased to over 1,000 women by March 2009. The larger unit worked under Iraqi and coalition control, with hundreds more temporarily recruited for the January 2009 elections,[280] demonstrating the significant growth and seeming importance of the program. However, this still paled in comparison to the Sons of Iraq program, which engaged around 100,000 men.[281] Responsibility and oversight of this program and all security forces was transferred to the Iraqi government in 2011. However, by the end of the year, many of the women hadn't been paid for nearly twelve months, and their numbers had greatly reduced due to departures from their positions.[282] This mirrored wider Iraqi governance shortfalls at the time, but also highlighted that while such programs may have been initially framed in terms of empowerment, the medium- or long-term impact and sustainability of these was much more questionable. In terms of Iraqi women in the police and military, training didn't begin until 2009 with the first female graduates of Iraq's police officer training academy.[283] As reflected in Yemen, there initially appeared to be a counter-terrorism-linked operational necessity which prompted the formation or support of such units by the US; this was then followed by references to rights, empowerment or equality to subsequently justify support of these, or the recognized democratic norms such units represented. As security was being re-established around the country, particularly for gender-sensitive matters such as SGBV, aspects such as women in policing did not appear to be a significant focus, which had the potential to detract from women's ability to access security services in the country more generally.

## Female forces on the front line against ISIS

The emergence of ISIS in Iraq and Syria in 2014 prompted both local and international efforts, including locally established and supported all-female and mixed-gendered units, and women in regional forces who were supported by the Global Coalition Against Daesh. A unit of fifty women named Banat al-Haqq (Daughters of Truth) were locally established in 2014 in Anbar province, and trained in military tactics to help in the fight against ISIS. [284] Thousands of female Kurdish-led counterinsurgents in the region were also actively fighting on front lines in combat operations against ISIS in this period. These included the Syrian Women's Protection Units (YPJ), where women represented over 35 per cent of broader YPG forces, [285] and totaled up to 24,000 militias by 2017; [286] as well as the women who made up Iraq's Kurdish Peshmerga forces. [287] These female counterinsurgents often cited efforts to assist local women (particularly Yazidi women) and defending their people from this ISIS onslaught in their motivations to fight. This demonstrated the importance of understanding the more pointedly gendered impacts of conflict on women, and how this may also influence women's motivations to join or support security operations.

It is important to highlight that though these predominantly Kurdish women have received significant global attention, particularly due to their roles fighting ISIS, they too have historically faced gender-based patriarchy, including forced or child marriage, honor killings, female genital mutilation, domestication stereotypes and limited rights more generally. However, the leader of the Kurdistan Workers' Party (PKK), Abdullah Öcalan, who drew from Marxist-Leninism and socialist beliefs, including feminism, envisioned more equitable roles for women in society. In publications he produced, such as *Liberating Life: Women's Revolution*, Öcalan argued that "the solution for all social problems in the Middle East should have women's positions' as [a] focus." Though the Kurds who led the fight against ISIS did not associate themselves with the internationally recognized PKK terror group, they shared a certain ideological affinity with Öcalan's ideology.[288] As such, feminist ideology was espoused, yet it was often culturally based norms that were viewed as contributing to women's repressed status in society more generally. These women had also been restricted from front-line combat.

However, due to the significant conflict with ISIS, women took up more diverse roles in 2014. In the memoirs of Kurdish sniper Azad Cudi, he described the roles of women he fought alongside in the YPJ. He highlighted women such as General Medya, General Tolin, Zahra, and Arin Mikan, who strapped grenades to her body and ran into a group of jihadists after ordering her platoon to pull back. Others, like Yaldız, was a partner in his sniper unit, and another, Nuda, carried Cudi back to safety along with other women in the unit when he was injured. He noted with admiration: "The women fight, kill and die as hard as men, as ISIS can attest."[289] This highlights an important point: that themes highlighted in US forces, such as restricting women from front-line combat, were also visible in Kurdish forces. Yet, women's front-line roles became viewed as an operational necessity, particularly as seen in the battle for Kobane from September 2014 until January 2015, when Kurdish forces fought back against a sustained and devastating ISIS assault.

The Global Coalition Against Daesh was actively training, advising and assisting local forces, though the US did not play a large role in the support for women's training up to 2017. Italian coalition forces trained some of the 1,000 women in the Zervani unit (a branch of the Kurdish Peshmerga forces) in specialized courses for female security forces;[290] British and Dutch forces also trained 120 female Peshmerga troops in an infantry battalion in combat, medical and counter-IED skills, the laws of armed conflict and the protection of human rights.[291] Yazidi women who had suffered some of the most horrific violence at the hands of ISIS had also been active in voluntarily joining forces against ISIS, with 127 Yazidi women joining Kurdish forces for basic training in 2016.[292] Another group of Yazidi women led by former singer Khatoon Khider also established a female battalion called Daughters of the Sun, which had almost 200 members, including former survivors of ISIS and their human slave markets.[293] Such units were unprecedented, and for a population that suffered most under ISIS, a testament to the changes to roles in society and gendered relations that this conflict was driving. The significant front-line support and other roles that women took in the anti-ISIS campaign were important to their overall success. Moreover, they were local in their establishment, and shattered any perceptions that women in the region could play only limited roles in defense operations. As Kurdish-led forces seized back territory from ISIS, they sought to implement their egalitarian, utopian vision, which included renewed emphasis on women's roles in society.

Though beyond the scope of this book, it is also important to note the significant changes in roles that these female forces have taken in the region. However, whether the gains that have been made in this period in these new roles, such as the freedoms, equality and recognition their work has achieved, will translate to long-term change after the fight against ISIS is over remains unknown. The Syrian Democratic Forces, the umbrella force for these units in northeastern Syria, are currently the most powerful political and security actor in the region. However, recalling that post-conflict periods often see women's gains achieved in conflict scaled back, if or how this is to unfold is yet to be seen in local and regional forces.

## Training women in Afghan forces

Women in Afghanistan also garnered some focus in the rebuilding of the ANSF. Women had historically held varied roles throughout the Afghan security forces, but these were essentially banned under Taliban rule. Women's roles in security forces received little attention during the initial stages of the war when design decisions were being made for the force based on "establishing an ethnic, political, and regional balance among the male recruits; there was no quota established for women." This was despite UNSCR 1325 being highlighted as foundational to women's inclusion in ANSF.[294]

The DoD supported the recruitment of women in the ANP, which began in 2007, but was unified under the NATO Training Mission in 2009. However, it was not until 2010 that the DoD even began reporting on women in the ANP. In 2010, there were less than 1,000 female police in the ANP, and it suffered from "low public opinion, lack of support from male co-workers, and the dangerous nature of the job," family concerns and discrimination. A growing number of women did eventually join the forces, particularly the Family Protection Units; but although ambitious targets (including 10 per cent female representation in ANP) were established for the end of 2017, by 2015 they still only numbered around 2,200.[295]

Training of women in the Afghan National Army (ANA) began with the graduation of twenty-nine students in 2010 from the Officer Cadet School.[296] This training was supported through the NATO Training Mission as well as ANSF training and advising programs,[297] and were supported by the US–Afghanistan Bilateral Commission's Democracy and Shared Values Working Group. These efforts were embedded in the broader NATO mission and additionally supported by the European Union and UN Development Program, as opposed to being exclusively run by the US.[298]

There were a number of hurdles facing the advancement of women in these roles, including gender-related concerns related to training. This was initially noted by Colonel Scanlon, who held a number of roles while in Afghanistan between 2010–14, including Senior Advisor to the Afghan Ministers of Defense and Interior for Gender Integration, and Gender Advisor to the Commanding General of NATO Training Mission Afghanistan/Combined Transition Afghanistan. She highlighted that a lack of gender perspective contributed to problems in training up Afghan forces, where in some cases US-funded facilities for both the ANP and ANA were not even built with bathroom facilities for women, suggesting that the presence of a gender advisor would "ensure that men, women, boys and girls, were being included in operational planning."[299] Such shortfalls also highlighted where efforts such as gender mainstreaming would become most essential. Other concerns related to the ANSF more generally were high rates of illiteracy, which stood at approximately 90 per cent among Afghan forces in 2011. This was an issue as illiterate forces could not read signs, maps, directions, instructions or fill in forms, creating particular barriers for security sector assistance. Gendered considerations also become apparent when noting that up to 90 per cent of rural Afghan women and 63 per cent of Afghan men are illiterate, which meant additional burdens for female recruits.[300] In Afghanistan, women were also restricted from front-line combat roles in the ANA, limiting the roles they could take.

In the ANA, recruitment and retention of women remained low due to Afghan culture impeding the entry of women into this field, specifically its lack of centralized and structured systems to onboard female applicants; its discriminatory hiring policies; and the lack of day-care facilities or female career paths. This was despite recognition by the DoD that women's roles and participation was essential to "creating credible and respectable security forces."[301] However, there were increasing examples of interagency interactions at this time, in which such problems were being tackled through consultation with other agencies. In 2010, US State established the Interagency Gender Working Group and the Afghanistan Gender Task Force, with DoD, US State and USAID (amongst others) meeting and consulting on a regular basis. Discussing the difficulty in recruiting women into ANSF, DoD personnel sought advice from this working group, and US State and USAID provided their responses.

Such groups also facilitated discussions about how donors could coordinate and identify specific requirements for facilities to support the integration of women into the ANSF.[302] Even with an ambitious goal to have 19,500 women recruited into the ANA by 2012, there were only 350 at that deadline, and efforts to improve this into 2015 remained largely unfulfilled.[303] By 2014 there were four general challenges to integrating women into all ANSF roles according to the DoD: (1) achieving recruitment and training targets; (2) identifying permanent positions for women in the forces; (3) ensuring all administrative buildings had adequate female facilities; and (4) creating a safe work environment for women.[304]

There appeared to be some recognition from lessons learned in previous units (such as FETs or CSTs) that women could play important roles, particularly in SOFs. A small unit of women called the Family Support Platoon (FSP) were being trained in Afghan special operations units called Strike Forces, based on the successes of the US

CST program: "FSPs were developed to accompany Ktah Khas Afghan Strike Forces on missions and, working in conjunction with their CST counterparts, safeguard and interact with the women and children encountered during the conduct of special operations."[305] As noted by Colonel Scanlon, this training was carried out by SOCOM:

> The Special Operations folks understood the importance of women in that they were cultivating women in Afghan Special Ops as a field. They were doing this because they needed women going in with Afghan Special Ops in order to search homes where there were no male heads of household in the home. If there were only women or children in the home, they needed women to go in and do the searching, so they included women as part of Afghan Special Ops.[306]

Often, such programs were held up as examples of advancing women's rights and empowerment. However, Naureen Chowdhury Fink, former Head of Research and Analysis at the Global Centre on Cooperative Security and now a Senior Policy Advisor (Counterterrorism) at UK Mission to UN (New York), cautioned about such units being used as "the poster child of progress," where little progress was actually made. Fink believed these programs could instead limit other entry points for women in security roles or forces; however, she felt there could also be benefits: "There is a very practical benefit that the more women you get circulating through these kind of roles, the more alumni, the more traction you get, the more role models you have for young women."[307] Ensuring that women were looped back into areas like strategic planning were also highlighted as important, and spoke to the long-term considerations that had to be integrated into the establishment and planning of these units.

In 2014, the US announced an end to combat operations, and the US and Afghanistan signed a bilateral security agreement to define the legal status of the approximate 9,800 US forces that would remain in the country after 2014. The US reaffirmed their obligation to continue developing and equipping ANSF, and sought the funding to do so, even as there were still concerns about the capabilities, leaderships and readiness of the force. In 2014, the US allocated $25 million to continue to promote the recruitment and retention of women in the ANSF.[308] There had been some improvements and the number of women in the ANA had also increased to 833. Their male colleagues also had "behaviour and expectations of male soldiers who work with Afghan women" integrated into their basic training.[309] In 2015, 3,753 women were now accounted for in the assigned force strength of both the ANP and ANA.[310] However, additional challenges to women in these roles remained; for instance, the Taliban was said to be directly targeting women in the ANA.[311] By 2016, there were 3,945 women serving in the Afghan forces: 2,866 in the ANP, 122 in the Afghan Special Security Forces, 877 in the ANA and eighty in the Afghan Air Force, demonstrating that while slow to progress, their overall numbers were continuing to increase.[312]

The nature of the threat in the country continued to evolve as Afghanistan took an increased lead in security operations. ISIS announced the founding of the Khorasan Province (IS-K) in 2015, which was to become their strongest base outside of Syria and Iraq, thus posing a challenge to both al-Qaeda and the Taliban for overall power in the country. From April 2015, IS-K began to carry out a number of major attacks in the country, and were believed to have up to 4,000 fighters by 2016. Al-Qaeda, whose supporters numbered in the lesser hundreds, remained aligned to the Taliban "emirate" and also continued to conduct attacks.[313] The Taliban continued to challenge the government of Afghanistan and scale-up their offense following the drawdown of US and NATO forces. As a result, the future prospects for the country remained uncertain.

These cases of Yemen, Iraq and Afghanistan indicated that the GWOT was also shifting the roles of women in foreign contexts based on US counterterrorism interests. This was driven by a growing emphasis on building partner capacity and practical requirements in the field, where women were engaged as a response to increasing female threats and interaction with female populations. However, such roles were ad hoc, limited and largely not considered seriously. It was not evident that the countries' traditional roles for women in security forces was accounted for in the formation of these units, which instead appeared responsive to US counterterrorism needs, or as women, peace and security norms integrated into broader security reforms. The language used in DoD documents and statements also reflected empowerment efforts, yet this appeared to be a secondary consideration. Finally, women were not being engaged proactively in the field, but instead in response to a gap that militants had in some cases exploited by their own utilization of women.

## Al-Qaeda and ISIS: Alternative interpretations of women in "security"

Ideological debates by key jihadist figures such as Osama bin Laden and Ayman al-Zawahiri (and even his wife) around women's roles and status in jihadist organizations as combatants and suicide bombers had been ongoing for some time prior to 9/11, and continued to rage thereafter.[314] In 1996, Bin Laden had also shamed the Saudi regime for allowing US female soldiers in the country: "the Saudi regime afflicted more pain on the people by allowing women of the Christian armies to defend them and allowed the crusaders to occupy the country," in a sense also shaming those forces who would allow female soldiers to defend them.[315] While these broader internal debates on the roles of women in jihad were important and require critical attention, a full interrogation of these is beyond the scope of this book. However, this final section will demonstrate that regardless of the continued internal debates held by al-Qaeda, ISIS and their affiliates, they too evolved operational roles for women in their own practices, and highlight how in some cases this simultaneously impacted women in US counterterrorism efforts.

As far back as 2004, al-Qaeda had produced publications targeted specifically at women which outlined the debates around their roles in combat. These included the 2004 publication *al-Khansa* (*The Gazelle*), produced by al-Qaeda in Saudi Arabia, and another, *The Granddaughters of Khansa*, in February 2010.[316] *Al-Khansa* proscribed women's participation in a variety of ways, including primarily in family/domestic roles, and as propagandists and educators for the next generation. It also references women as "a female jihad warrior:" "Just as she defends her family from any possible aggression, she defends society from destructive thoughts and from ideological and moral deterioration, and she is a soldier who bears [the man's] pack and weapon on his back in preparation for the military offensive."[317] Davis also notes that al-Qaeda initiated a website in this period calling on women to encourage men to become suicide bombers.[318] Both points suggest women were still discouraged from such roles themselves, and instead were meant to act in support capacities to male family members.

The first significant evolution in violent roles for women in jihadist groups was seen in Iraq with AQI. Abu-Musab al-Zarqawi took the leading role in AQI (established in 2004) and became an important figure for ISIS later. A rogue al-Qaeda branch, AQI began using female suicide bombers (both Iraqi and foreign) with increasing regularity when other global branches of al-Qaeda had restricted this. Kilcullen noted that the use of female suicide bombers for al-Qaeda was largely tactical, as there was increasing difficulty with men being searched at checkpoints, whereas for women this was less likely to happen.[319] Muriel Degauque, a Caucasian Belgian convert who died in a suicide attack in Iraq in 2005, was one of their first female suicide bombers.[320] By 2007, seven attacks were carried out by women, and the military reported this had increased to twenty-seven by July 2008.[321] Bloom noted that many of these women (at least fifty-five) had male family members associated with AQI who killed themselves in similar missions and were directly recruited due to this relationship; others were widows, or in financial or socially dire situations. AQI would also often arrange to have the would-be suicide bombers raped, ensuring that they felt they had no other option than carrying out a suicide attack to reclaim their and their families honor, exploiting local cultural attitudes. The Dhat al Nitaqayn Martyrdom Brigade was a specific unit in AQI consisting solely of women.[322] AQI female suicide bombers resulted in much collateral damage, including the death of US servicewomen Marine Corps Corporal Jennifer M. Parcell, who was killed at a checkpoint in February 2007 in Anbar Province.[323]

This suggested that a deficit of female personnel in both US and Iraqi security forces was viewed as exploitable by AQI, who took advantage of gendered cultural considerations whereby men could not search women. This also demonstrated the tactical use of SGBV committed against women as a means to gain more female suicide bombers for the group. This highlighted the importance of considering and addressing both male and female insurgents and terrorists, and of better understanding these gendered dynamics. This involved acknowledging the significance of familial relations, and the willingness of groups to utilize women for certain strategic, tactical purposes to help the group achieve their aims, even if their ideology otherwise appeared to limit these roles.

Women's roles as suicide bombers countered the perception that al-Qaeda and affiliated groups were "male-only confederations, but also prove [women] are partners and participants in jihad."[324] These female bombers were further viewed to "discredit, damage, and possibly derail the Iraqi government's efforts to democratize a fragile state,"[325] and thus impacted on simultaneous US governance efforts in Iraq. Qazi argued these female suicide bombers "directly coincided with the timing, and the locations, of Al Qaeda in Mesopotamia's [AQI] biggest loss of manpower in Diyala, Baghdad and Anbar,"[326] emphasizing how AQI engaged women out of operational necessity.

AQI also reportedly engaged local women for marriages to al-Qaeda "emirs," and would offer religious training for women, promising that paradise awaited those who died for Islam.[327] This suggested that, as an organization, they too had a specific vision of how they could engage women in local populations throughout this insurgency, and how these roles impacted their local foothold and longevity. Marriage into local populations could also strengthen the terrorist group's position within the insurgent population, as had been visible in locations such as Afghanistan and Pakistan.[328]

Richard Barrett, the Coordinator of the Al-Qaida and Taliban Monitoring Team at the UN between 2004 and 2012, also pointed out that marriage made it much more difficult to uproot these groups, as matrimony could be viewed as a tribal alliance.[329] In Iraq though, Kilcullen argued it was in fact the rejection of marriage between women in local tribes and AQI members that in part lent to this division (tribal custom held that women could not be married to outsiders), even though tribes and AQI had previously fought together against Americans during the Iraq War prior to the "Sunni Awakening."[330] This raised larger questions about how familial relations within terror groups may be relevant to security concerns, ranging from women's potential to carry out violence, to the long-term presence and support of terror groups in a region via local marriage.

Outside of AQI, the cases of women carrying out violence either directly associated with or inspired by al-Qaeda were comparatively rare between 2001 and 2017, due seemingly to organizational restrictions, as the group simply did not condone women to take up security-related roles. Authors such as Davis have also suggested that women's roles in combat operations were often influenced by other factors, such as "group outbidding" (where multiple groups operate in the same environment), media attention, surprise factors, or because (more rarely) women themselves may pressure these groups to allow more active roles for them.[331] Women had taken up violent roles in limited situations in certain branches of al-Qaeda, such as Sajida al-Rishawi, who was part of an AQI four-person suicide operation in Amman, Jordan, targeting international hotels in 2005 (her suicide vest did not detonate). Women were also visible as "lone actors" who self-radicalized and otherwise had no formal affiliation with al-Qaeda. Rare examples included US citizen Colleen LaRose (otherwise known as "Jihadi Jane"), who was convicted in 2009 of plotting to kill Swedish cartoonist Lars Vilks; or Roshanara Choudhury, who stabbed UK MP Stephen Timms in London in 2010. While combat roles for women in the Arabian Peninsula were also exceptionally rare, AQAP still published a 2011 Arabic-language magazine specifically for women, entitled *al-Shamikhah* (*The Majestic Woman*). The magazine combined tips for clean skin with interviews with jihadi wives and female fighters.

In Afghanistan, the Taliban deployed a female suicide bomber in 2008,[332] and in 2010, female suicide bombing cells were also established in Pakistan and Afghanistan by Qari Zia Rahman, a senior regional Taliban commander and member of al-Qaeda.[333] AQAP was also reported to be training female suicide bombers in 2010 and calling women to join the group, though they were never deployed.[334] In 2012, a female bomber conducted an attack in Kabul which killed twelve people, most of whom were South African.[335] However, these relatively limited roles were not necessarily because some women had not wanted to take up violence for the jihadist cause, as author Taiel Haya emphasized in AQAP's *Inspire* magazine, in her poem "My wish: if only I was a mujahid," where she stated her wish to "pile up the bodies of the enemies."[336] It was noteworthy too that the post-conflict experiences of US servicewomen were utilized in AQAP propaganda such as *Inspire*, which highlighted higher rates of homelessness amongst female veterans or rates of sexual assault,[337] both to discredit US forces and to assumedly dissuade women from seeking combat roles.[338]

*Enter ISIS: New roles for women in "security"*

ISIS proved to be a game changer, distinguishing itself in terms of the roles that women could hold in such groups, and the significant numbers of women who traveled to join the organization. Prior to the formal announcement of the ISIS caliphate in 2014, Samir Abd Muhammad al-Khlifawi, a senior ISIS figure, had outlined a "blueprint" for how to seize territory and subjugate a country. Members of ISIS were encouraged to marry into influential families in the region to help secure its establishment and influence. Fighters in the organization had also sent al-Khlifawi "wish lists," which included wives.[339] To establish a foothold in the region, marriage offered several purposes: a political utility by helping build and maintain local relationships, offering an outlet for influence at a local and regional level; it also embedded these individuals further into the local population, making ties harder to cut and creating additional challenges to expel the group from the region.

In 2014, as part of their increasing control of territory in Iraq and Syria, ISIS demonstrated their efforts to govern, which in the most significant instance yet in a transnational jihadist group included gender-segregated policing and training, highlighting evolving operative roles for women in jihadist organizations.[340] For some local women, joining ISIS security units provided an income, some degree of movement, protection for them and their families, as well as influence and even power under ISIS's harsh control and amidst the larger Syrian conflict. While there have been five women's units reported to have trained to support ISIS activities,[341] the most visible example of this was the al-Khansaa Brigade in Raqqa. The al-Khansaa Brigade's media wing confirmed there were "all-female police brigades operating in Iraq and Syria and that, in certain circumstances, women may be called to battle, [however] policing and fighting are very low on the list of responsibilities given to women." Winter noted that the publication was aimed at recruiting women from the region to join ISIS, specifically Saudi women.[342] Acting as religious and moral police, they were involved in both the arrest and punishment of women in Raqqa. It was suggested they were initially established for the purposes of verifying that individuals were indeed women, as male anti-ISIS fighters were disguising themselves as women to pass through checkpoints.[343]

Women were noted to train eight hours a day for a fifteen-day weapons course focused on pistols, where foreigners were thought to train on Kalashnikovs. They would also assist in transporting women joining the organization to Raqqa.[344] These units "policed women's dress armed with metal prongs, sometimes poking, slapping, or even biting women for dress code breaches," and would fine or beat women, or cut their fingers for minor infractions.[345] This unit was limited to non-combat roles, and were noted to only be able to serve their communities as combatants under the provision of "Jihad (by appointment)" and only then in specific circumstances: "if the enemy is attacking her country and the men are not enough to protect it and the imams give a fatwa for it, as the blessed women of Iraq and Chechnya did, with great sadness, if the men are absent even they are present."[346] It is also noteworthy that in ISIS the different "security" roles related to women were sanctioned differently in this period, though this did evolve. While women were restricted from operations as combatants and suicide bombers, female policing units were allowed. Self-defense of women in certain circumstances was also permitted, as outlined by the Zawra Foundation (a media outlet aligned with ISIS) in August 2015: acceptable scenarios included house raids, attacks where she was already holding a suicide belt, or if she was directed by her emir.[347]

For women seeking combat roles with the organization, their wish to become militants was now partially fulfilled in select operative and policing roles, and even the prospect of more combat-specific roles in limited circumstances could offer some appeal where other groups had not done so previously. The case of Sajida al-Rishawi—the unsuccessful AQI suicide bomber later imprisoned in Jordan—problematized this further. When Jordanian pilot Muath al-Kasasbeh was captured by ISIS in December 2014, ISIS used a video message to call for the release of al-Rishawi in exchange for Kasasbeh. This was also seen in the case of Aafia Siddiqui, who was detained in the US, and whom ISIS demanded in exchange for the American journalist James Foley in August 2014,[348] and again in 2014 in the case of American aid worker Kayla Mueller.[349] Notably, the Pakistani Taliban had also demanded the release of Siddiqui in exchange for Army Sergeant Bowe Bergdahl, who had been missing since 2009.[350] These cases highlighted the purported importance and symbolic value of female militants to these organizations, even as the groups still restricted this in practice.

231

Like al-Qaeda, ISIS had received pledges of allegiance from independent terrorist organizations and set up branches in other countries; for example, Boko Haram in Nigeria and Ansar Bayt al-Maqdis in Egypt formally pledged allegiance to ISIS and were later considered *waliyats* (official provinces) of the group. By March 2015, ISIS had formally recognized seven "provinces," including in Libya and Yemen, where it was operating in direct competition with AQAP;[351] in fact, the group was noted to have over sixty groups from thirty-three regions declare allegiance to the organization.[352] The status of the affiliates and their relationship to ISIS in Syria and Iraq differed between each, which was also reflected in the diverse roles for women in each *waliyat* or affiliate. For example, while ISIS in Syria and Iraq had not used suicide bombers up to 2015 (the first was reported in 2017), Boko Haram began utilizing female suicide bombers from 2014 (although they had been engaging male suicide bombers since 2011). Boko Haram also used more women (largely young women) to carry out attacks in Nigeria than any other Islamist terrorist group, particularly as increased pressure was placed on male operatives.[353] Pearson has highlighted how such divergences in these roles allowed to women appear to be based on the "material needs and objectives of each groups,"[354] and prompted localized analysis of each to better assess how and why women were engaged as they were. In April 2016, Europol police chief Robert Wainwright noted: "For the first time we are seeing reports of [women in ISIS's Libya branch] being trained for battlefield experience," noting "hundreds" were reported to have been trained in how to use weapons and carry out suicide bombings. There were also reports of all-female units being formed for the first time,[355] which could suggest another possible terrorist innovation to overcome gender-segregated restrictions on women in combat.

While ISIS itself may have restricted women to specific roles, this had not proven the case for those affiliated with them. For their affiliates, women's roles may differ based on what may be more locally accepted (a theme reflected to an extent in US efforts, which were hesitant to promote women's security roles in locations deemed culturally inappropriate), or how local goals or dynamics of groups may clash with ISIS's global aspirations. This also highlighted broader tensions and nuances within the jihadist movement itself, where women's roles in combat and as security actors were heavily debated, and themselves evolved based on different factors such as operational environment and objectives. In locations such as Syria, where jihadist groups were competing for primacy, providing such roles and opportunities to women also appeared to gain them additional support, providing more diverse roles and membership in the organization, and helping it fulfill its state-building ambition. It is also notable this sentiment reflects that of engaging women in security practice based on operational requirements that were comparable to those seen in US forces and the foreign forces which they trained and supported. This raised interesting points about shared gendered discourses of women between state and non-state actors, even if prompted by vastly differing ideological basis.

The number of female perpetrators in separate plots around the world (both interrupted and carried out) also raised concern, even as these comprised only a fraction of those carried out by men affiliated with ISIS. Some key cases include in Paris in September 2016, where five women in a terrorist cell were arrested after being "directed" by ISIS, and had placed a faulty car bomb near Notre Dame.[356] Three women in Mombasa were killed by police after entering a police station and stabbing an officer; the women had pledged allegiance to ISIS, who acknowledged them as "supporters."[357] In October 2016 in Morocco, ten women were arrested for plotting a suicide attack during parliamentary elections, a case which reflected the aims of the Madrid bombings in 2006. Four of the women in this cell had married members of ISIS in Iraq and Syria.[358] In December 2016, Dian Yulia Novi was arrested in Jakarta, Indonesia, for her role in an attempted suicide bomb plot on the presidential palace during changing of the guard involving a pressure cooker; she later confirmed that she saw herself as engaged in jihad (she was sentenced in August 2017).[359] It is noteworthy that none of these women had appeared to have traveled to Iraq or Syria themselves, but had been guided or inspired to carry out violence from their home countries.[360]

These select cases indicate that, like al-Qaeda previously, even if ISIS wanted to contain or limit the roles of women in conflict in areas under their control, their influence was extending beyond their reach as they empowered and encouraged both affiliates and "lone wolf" individuals to act on behalf of the group. It highlights how their strategies may have evolved based on counterterrorism efforts against them, and how women's roles within these may have changed too. It also speaks to a perverse trend of female empowerment and evolution in jihadist groups, where women could perceive their agency and diverse operational and non-operational roles in new and expansive ways. Furthermore, an examination of the roles of women may also speak to the ideological alignment and control of such affiliates within the core leadership, helping inform understanding of relationships between these and any distinct local dynamics.

What roles and responsibilities does ISIS leadership allow or denounce for women? How or why have affiliates deviated from this? Both Boko Haram and ISIS in Libya confirm the importance of local context, and how these roles for women may shift over time dependent on the challenges and opportunities facing the group in specific spaces and periods, each of which are important for counterterrorism responses. Other groups also increasingly appear to be tapping into this hitherto neglected female population.

Though now part of the broader seventy-three-country Operation Inherent Resolve to tackle ISIS, it was not evident up to 2017 in DoD discourses or practices whether women as security actors in ISIS garnered much attention.[361] A gendered distinction did not appear of particular importance in US forces when understanding and responding to these groups. Highlighting possible reasons for this, General Petraeus noted:

> We are gender blind when it comes to assessing bad guys [...]. [Women] are either extremists or they're not. They're either serious terrorists that are worthy of the kind of attention that puts them on the X, or they're not. It doesn't matter if they're male or female, I don't know why that distinction matters.[362]

In terms of the value gender considerations may have had when analyzing these groups, or how this might help deepen our understanding of them, Petraeus noted: "I tend to doubt it, but again, if it turns out that it is an important consideration then I'm sure we would add it to our list of factors to consider."[363] In the most direct counterterrorism efforts against ISIS, gender concerns gained little attention, which appeared to be in contrast to indirect efforts in US State and USAID, where women and gender dynamics in extremism and insurgency were considered to a much more extensive degree.

*Final points*

As the lead department in military and defense efforts, DoD was the agency most emphasized and associated with counterterrorism activities. DoD emphasized women as security actors in its own defense forces, as security actors in partner forces, in communities to engage with, and as security threats. While DoD had a long history considering and supporting women in US forces (though these had their own shortcomings), there appeared to be limited considerations of women in foreign populations or forces, and limited gender considerations in DoD activities immediately after 9/11.

The first factor that significantly impacted how this evolved were the gender-segregated and conservative environments the DoD operated in, including in Afghanistan, Iraq and Yemen. As operational objectives evolved in these countries, so too did DoD roles for women in US forces. While this was first seen in Iraq with the ad hoc establishment of Team Lioness in 2003 to engage with and search Iraqi women, the proven value of the program carried it forward as the strategy in Iraq and Afghanistan shifted to COIN. Inherent in COIN was engaging the population so as to win "hearts and minds" to undermine the insurgency, and women in communities garnered increased attention alongside this. Here, American women emerged in FETs and CSTs, which appeared to become increasingly standardized and integrated into DoD efforts. This shift also highlighted several agency limitations for the DoD, wherein women were both restricted from combat missions yet increasingly required to partake in operations that engaged with women, which by default were also often on the front lines of combat.

The particularly limited extent of gender knowledge and history of how to engage women in these operational environments were also highlighted in DoD. This was reflected in some of the critiques of FETS and Team Lioness in relation to their roles and purpose. This appeared to be further compounded by a lack of gender advisors or gender knowledge in operational terms within the DoD itself. There were also visible "champions" within the DoD (as highlighted first in Iraq, and then in Afghanistan) who established these units and emphasized their operational capabilities and benefits, or who saw the value in gendered analysis, and therefore utilized gender advisors on their teams. Agency "learning" also saw these units become further engrained in DoD practices as an operational asset. However, some gendered assumptions also appeared inherent within these. For example, women were considered at times to "soften" local interactions or reduce tensions, particularly in military operations, although this was viewed as a positive in some operations. Key publications like FM 3–24 from 2006 also initially viewed women in particularly limited and flawed terms. However, the expansion of women-specific and broader gender considerations visible in stabilization work and the 2014 FM 3–24 update, as well as the suggested interagency influence from USAID and DoD's own institutional learning in this period, emphasized how women were deemed both important actors and insurgent threats in the GWOT.

Gendered concerns more broadly appeared to be expanding within the DoD, including addressing sexual harassment, the "Don't ask, don't tell" policy, and gender discrimination in hiring practices. A recognition of the achievements and contribution of women in DoD efforts since 9/11, alongside a growing chorus of calls to end restrictions for women in the DoD, saw more combat roles open to women from 2008, with all combat roles eventually becoming open to women in 2015. While the DoD established an implementation plan based off the 2011 NAP, this and UNSCR 1325 more broadly appeared to have minimal influence or impact on the DoD, whereas presidential or DoD directives made the most visible impact. Such "women" or "gender" lenses also appeared sporadic or absent in foreign populations or operations; for example, by not assessing the gendered repercussions of counterterrorism practices on foreign populations, or limited security roles for women in training and equipping partnerships.

As partners, women in foreign nations also gained increased focus over this period for many of the same reasons stated above, such as the operational environments and requirements of the region, as seen with the Daughters of Iraq. An acknowledgement seen in both the 2006 NSS and 2006 QDR highlighted that increased emphasis should be placed on training-up partner forces, which inevitably included women. Though training of a counterterrorism unit in Yemen had been ongoing since 2003, the US began training Yemen's first female counterterrorism unit in 2006 in response to al-Qaeda's increased kidnapping activity in the country, which saw women becoming involved in negotiations and raids. As security responsibilities also began shifting to Iraqi forces, this was additionally impacted by AQI's engagement of female suicide bombers, which prompted increased Iraqi female units, as seen in the Sisters of Fallujah and Daughters of Iraq. These units were also framed in terms of employment, empowerment and leadership opportunities, thereby also supporting broader women's rights and equality aims. Increased requests from Middle Eastern partners to train-up women's security units also saw FETs reincarnated in 2015 in the USMC.

Despite few evaluations of these programs being available, it appeared that emphasizing a women's empowerment angle was often used to gain support for the program initially, although tangible empowerment in the medium- to long-term was less evident or seemingly not measured or assessed. Furthermore, by not having clear, continuous funding and support, gains made to integrate women into national security structures appear disjointed, and these units were often viewed as optional or temporary. This was demonstrated in Afghanistan, where the lack of a gender lens impeded the development of these units (for example, overlooking the building of women's bathrooms in police and military facilities in Afghanistan); or in Yemen, where important considerations of women's roles in the counterterrorism unit could have been considered alongside women's roles in other security roles (such as the police), which could have had more impact on women's security at the local level.

There was little doubt that the driving motivation for expanding women's roles in relation to counterterrorism in the DoD was in terms of operational effectiveness in these operational environments, where engaging women in new or unique roles, units or programs was understood to lend directly to operational success. This was also supported by a mission-centric focus of the DoD and its corresponding departments of the Army and Navy. Within these, there was a distinct pride and history in learning and adapting to new environments and challenges to achieve the mission at hand, and women's new or unique roles, if proven to contribute positively to that mission, were more readily embraced. There were also secondary considerations visible pertaining to how defense efforts aligned with democracy promotion, or rights and empowerment efforts more broadly (for example, where supporting women in foreign defense forces was seen in terms of democratic norms, as seen in Yemen). There was also a visible lag in assessing gender in DoD operational considerations, such as gendered impacts of their operations on the ground. Some instances of inter-agency working groups, joint training exercises or operations were highlighted as useful for expanding this, but it was suggested that gender knowledge could be shared more usefully from partner agencies such as USAID.

While gender was considered one of several terrorist traits to be assessed (as demonstrated in the "JP 3–26: Counterterrorism"), there was limited visible expansion or understanding of what prompted such roles by women in the first place; instead, the focus appeared to prioritize addressing the terrorist threat/actor directly. However, this too suggested a certain agency limitation, with the lack of a deeper knowledge of gender throughout DoD operations (which could consider "push" and "pull" factors that may motivate women to such roles) hindering DoD assessment and response to the mission at hand. For example, the case of Iraq suggested SGBV committed against targeted women was being used to force them to become suicide bombers. ISIS proved to be a critical example of how women's roles and gender dynamics became pertinent to DoD operations and considerations, as women were increasingly affiliated with terrorist organizations, but had diverse motivations to join them or roles within them compared with earlier jihadist groups. However, it was not evident these were actively assessed in DoD discourses and practices.

Up to 2017, al-Qaeda and ISIS affiliates like Boko Haram had utilized women as suicide bombers, police and other security actors in the territory they held, and changes in these roles appeared to be based on their own strategic aims and operational requirements. There was some recognition of this, particularly in Iraq, but it became particularly visible under ISIS after 2014. Some of the gendered debates and impetus around women's inclusion in combat roles also in fact mirrored those in DoD.

# 4

# THE DEPARTMENT OF STATE

*"When we have dealt with bin Laden and his network we will then broaden the campaign to go after other terrorists all around the world."*

US Secretary of State Colin Powell, September 2001[1]

The US Department of State (US State) is the designated US lead agency on all foreign policy matters, and also coordinates military and civilian actors in foreign areas of operation. Its purview covers six key fields, including arms control and international security; civilian security and democracy; political affairs; public diplomacy and public affairs; economics, energy and environment; and assistance and development. In 2015, US State had 275 diplomatic and consular posts in 190 countries, employed approximately 69,000 persons, and had an operating budget of $47.4 billion.[2]

Both counterterrorism and women's issues have a long, though distinct, history in US State. In 1972, following the attack at the Munich Olympics, US State established its Office for Combating Terrorism, which later became the Office of the Coordinator for Counterterrorism in 1985. Since 1995, US State has been producing annual reports entitled "Patterns of Global Terrorism," revamped to "Country Reports on Terrorism" in 2004 (due to the National Counterterrorism Center [NCTC] taking a lead on compiling this data), which provide detailed analysis of global threats and trends related to terrorism.

US State has stated one of its aims is to:

Forge partnerships with non-state actors, multilateral organizations, and foreign governments to advance the counterterrorism objectives and national security of the United States. Working with our US Government counterterrorism team, S/counterterrorism takes a leading role in developing coordinated strategies to defeat terrorists abroad and in securing the cooperation of international partners. In all activities, we are guided by the National Security Strategy and the National Strategy for Combating Terrorism.[3]

US State also has a long history focusing on women's issues through the joint office of the President's Interagency Council on Women and the Office of the Senior Coordinator for International Women's Issues (both established in 1995). The Interagency Council was established on the heels of the UN's 1995 Fourth World Conference on Women in Beijing, with the aim of implementing the Platform for Action, which considered areas such as women and armed conflict, women in power and decision-making, and women and poverty.[4] Then First Lady Hillary Clinton was notably the Honorary Chair of this Interagency Council, while Ambassador Melanne Verveer (Deputy Chief of Staff to First Lady Clinton, 1993–96) worked with her to advance women's rights efforts, particularly through their joint organization Vital Voices, which trained female political leaders around the world. As such, US State has historically drawn not only from key national documents like the National Security Strategies (NSS) and National Strategy for Counter-terrorism (NSCT) to inform their counterterrorism work, but was also actively informed by United Nations (UN) discourses to advance the status of women, and had a long history of considering and assessing women's issues and gendered considerations within their programming. However, while both housed in the US State, these two streams—counterterrorism and women's issues—appeared to remain relatively siloed following 9/11. In practice, efforts were focused on improving women's status in society, with specific counterterrorism aims often overlapping. These first became visibly linked through Middle East Partnership Initiative (MEPI) in countries of interest such as Yemen.

Of the three departments and agency of focus in this book, US State considered women most broadly, in categories ranging from victims of conflict and insecurity, to rights, empowerment and equality (particularly through democratic empowerment), to security actors (and threats) themselves. The breadth of these considerations was also informed by the range of offices and bureaus situated within US State, and the scope of its mandate to lead on US foreign policy. However, particularly since the Clinton administration, the department has often struggled to exert influence in foreign-policy decisions, with the US Department of Defense (DoD) and intelligence agencies taking the de facto lead, which had implications for the impact US State could have in practice.

It became evident that women's roles evolved in US State in relation to counterterrorism based on three primary factors. First, due to the promotion of democracy and reform in the Middle East—which was understood as a long-term counterterrorism investment—women's rights, empowerment and equality became increasingly linked with programming efforts to undercut appeals of extremism in the wider population. This became evident particularly in the MEPI in countries such as Yemen, where empowering women through democratic norms was framed as directly impacting extremism. Second, counterterrorism efforts largely neglected women's inclusion or their considerations in US State initiatives more systematically until around 2007, when an institutional shift initiated their first internal policy on engaging women and counterterrorism. The third and most significant driver for change was the first US State Quadrennial Development and Diplomacy Review (QDDR), released in 2010 and driven by Secretary of State Clinton. Alongside the 2011 National Action Plan (NAP), which again accelerated these efforts, these two documents marked a significant shift in how women were conceived of in relation to security in policy language across all areas of US State programming. They also demonstrated that UN and national discourses had substantial influence on the department, and appeared to be linked to Secretary Clinton's historical work on the agenda. However, how this emphasis on women, peace and security as a US foreign-policy objective translated into practice was more mixed, and saw some resistance from certain corners of US State. The final important marker was the rise of countering violent extremism (CVE) as a field of focus under the Obama administration, which opened a new area of focus to engage women.[5]

## The Middle East Partnership Initiative

Early US State efforts focused on women in the context of security largely through MEPI. Established in 2002, MEPI was framed as a "bridge between the US and Middle East," particularly its governments and peoples, and aimed to support key reform efforts in the region. MEPI noted it was "a tool to advance US foreign policy," and supported three key pillars: (1) participatory governance; (2) economic advancement; and (3) education promotion. To do this, MEPI focused on four categories of reform: political, economic, educational (with a particular focus on girls) and women's empowerment.[6] The first funded initiative under MEPI brought a delegation of fifty-five Arab female political leaders to the US to observe mid-term elections.

Announcing the launch of MEPI in 2002, Secretary of State Colin Powell noted: "Our Middle East policy has emphasized winning the war on terrorism, disarming Iraq, and bringing the Arab-Israeli conflict to an end." Yet, to achieve these, he noted "it has become increasingly clear that we must broaden our approach to the region if we are to achieve success. In particular, we must give sustained and energetic attention to economic, political, and educational reform." Improving women's status was a key part of this: "Until the countries of the Middle East unleash the abilities and potential of their women, they will not build a future of hope."[7] However, Secretary Powell was cautious to avoid tying MEPI directly to 9/11 and counterterrorism: "I don't think 9/11 should be seen as the determining factor with respect to this program. We hope that it will make it more likely that young people will see this possibility of a better future and hope, and will not be pulled into activities of the kind that led to 9/11." However, he still suggested MEPI efforts would help reduce the pool of those who may be more susceptible to radicalization in indirect efforts:

> The programs I talked about are relevant before and after 9/11—perhaps after 9/11, somewhat more relevant because to the extent that you have populations where people are angry, people are frustrated, people do not feel that their lives are improving, then you have the possibility of additional radicalization of that population.[8]

This suggested early recognition of the potentially problematic conflation of counterterrorism concerns and political, economic or education reform efforts, which was to be avoided particularly in the foreign countries where this could hinder relations with host communities and governments. However, this appeared to be inconsistent in practice, as demonstrated in countries like Yemen, where some of these efforts were tied overtly to countering extremism, particularly when it came to justifying programs and budgets to Congress. Yemen was one of the largest recipients of MEPI funding globally, with the initiative conducting programs from voter registration to literacy programs for women. While many of these initiatives fell outside of traditional counterterrorism efforts as holistic approaches to terrorism gained prominence, indirect efforts focused on women in terms of human rights and empowerment now became sporadically framed in terms of their utility and contribution to countering the terrorist threat, particularly in relation to reducing societal susceptibility to extremism and radicalization.

MEPI aimed to fill the gaps that extended beyond the US Agency for International Development (USAID), and was viewed as key to promoting democracy in the Middle East. Between 2002 and 2005 alone, MEPI received $284 million, and in 2004 the Intelligence Reform and Terrorism Prevention Act reauthorized the initiative.[9] Between 2002 and 2009, MEPI contributed $530 million in seventeen countries across 600 projects, many of which continued to focus on empowering women in areas such as law, politics, civil society and skills training.[10] Between 2002 and 2015, MEPI funding reached upwards of $960 million.[11] Programming that focused on women included "support for the Arab Women's Legal Network; a program in Egypt to strengthen women's NGO [non-governmental organization] networks; and a number of technical training and advocacy workshops aimed at improving women's educational, economic, and social conditions."[12] The structure of MEPI was notable as it operated through US-based non-governmental organizations (NGOs) in partnership with, and through funding of, indigenous NGOs, which could also reduce US visibility during implementation and better account for local actors, dynamics and concerns in implementation.

Educational efforts, which included those focused on women, were rarely linked to counterterrorism. However, one example from 2006 was in the introduction of a bill entitled "To ensure the implementation of the recommendations of the National Commission on Terrorist

Attacks Upon the United States in the House of Representatives" by Congressman Christopher Shays. Discussing the International Youth Opportunity Fund, he highlighted programs that focused on women's education:

> The secular education programs of MEPI and the United States Agency for International Development should be components of an overall strategy for educational assistance—itself one component of an overall United States strategy for counterterrorism—targeted where the need and the benefit to the national security of the United States are greatest.[13]

MEPI's aims were understood in an indirect and contributory capacity to counterterrorism, and focused on countries and regions deemed at highest risk from instability and, in some cases, terrorism. There were concerns by some about MEPI's "lack of financial and political capital and its weak hand in departmental and inter-agency battles over authority and budget," and lack of engagement with non-English-speaking NGOs.[14] Some Islamic organizations also viewed funding from MEPI as "dirty money" and a form of "colonization," or as attempts to "reform the Middle East along US-backed lines."[15] While this programming was viewed largely in terms of democracy promotion in the context of the Global War on Terror (GWOT), programming rarely framed women explicitly in relation to counterterrorism or CVE. Yet, with new avenues of funding and support for programming related to women's rights and empowerment, efforts to frame these as relevant to counterterrorism began to appear in practice.

## Women's empowerment and challenging extremism in Yemen

The US had a long and diverse interest in Yemen, largely predicated on security. This only increased after 9/11, and was often dominated by defense efforts and particularly focused on Yemen's counterterrorism unit (see Chapter 3). Yemen was also a key country of focus for broader aid and development efforts, including as a primary recipient of MEPI programming. For example, as early as 2004, $2 million was made available for programs to address the illiteracy of women and girls in the country. It also included election assistance, a training academy for NGOs on political participation, political party development, and training and support for women and media.[16] While language related to counterterrorism remained rather muted in these documents, there was a belief that these programs helped combat extremism through complementary capacities.

US Ambassador to Yemen Edmund Hull (2001–04) noted a key approach to tackling terrorism in Yemen was addressing governance in areas such as Ma'rib, al-Jawf and Shabwa, where there was little government structure or political reach. President Saleh had requested that the US undertake economic assistance and development efforts in these deprived areas to break up what Ambassador Hull referred to as a "vicious circle" of "bad governance, insecurity, national and international neglect, [and] lack of development." It was his intent to replace this with what he deemed a "virtuous cycle" of "good governance, enhanced security, national and international support, [and] local development."[17] Ambassador Hull noted this broader view of counterterrorism extended past cooperation with intelligence agencies and military forces: "For us, equipping a hospital in Ma'rib, conducting free and fair parliamentary elections, and empowering the women of Yemen were important objectives in the struggle against terrorism."[18] One area that received significant focus was women's political participation, as demonstrated with the 2003 elections in Yemen, which were hailed to be a success. MEPI had funded two NGOs—the National Democratic Institute and the International Foundation for Electoral Systems—which raised women's voter registration by a significant 40 per cent, making them 42 per cent of total voters.[19]

This trajectory continued under succeeding Ambassador Thomas Krajeski (2004–07), who also emphasized the importance of strengthening democratic institutions and encouraging economic development in relation to countering extremism. Discussing efforts to combat extremism, Krajeski noted, "a wide range of USG [US government] programs will be essential to strengthen democratic institutions and rule of law, encourage economic growth, and widen educational access, especially for women."[20] In 2005, the US Embassy had employed "[a] number of different programs to combat extremism through strengthening democratic institutions and encouraging economic development." It was noted that support and expertise came from a wide variety of sources, including "MEPI, PD [Public Diplomacy] funds,

USAID, Department of Agriculture, and Department of Defense" and these efforts addressed "[t]wo contributing factors to extremism in Yemen—poverty and weak government institutions." One project in particular provided "[i]nformation technology training for women and community outreach to encourage girls to pursue careers in information technology." Most pointedly for this book, Ambassador Krajeski noted: "Improving girl's and women's education is also a key component of promoting tolerance and combating extremism. Small grants have been an especially successful tool, including support for a successful program to target illiteracy and develop enterprise skills for rural women in western Yemen."[21]

However, as the security situation deteriorated in many of the priority areas, these projects had to cease, with the understanding that these may restart only if Saleh improved local security,[22] thus highlighting the important relationship between development and security efforts. US actions outside of Yemen also appeared to resonate increasingly negatively with many average Yemenis. These included the 2003 Iraq War, which drew large protests in Yemen,[23] and frustration at the detainment of 117 Yemenis in Guantanamo Bay, a long-standing source of tension.[24] US counterterrorism efforts abroad thus also impacted on broader perceptions of the US and its policies and programming in Yemen, which had the potential to trickle down into diverse areas such as those focused on women.

As US Ambassador to Yemen (1997–2001) Barbara Bodine recalled, there had been significant focus on non-security areas such as development, democratization and the security of Yemenis themselves prior to 9/11, as seen with steps to establish the Yemen Coast Guard. However, this focus shifted in its nature after 9/11. This was particularly accelerated after 2004 when security was noted to be the primary focus:

> Yes, there was MEPI, and talk about democratization, "if you really want to counter terrorism you have to have democracy"—I mean, the words were beautiful, but there was nothing behind them [...]. The rhetoric was on democratization, but the rhetoric was on countering terrorism, countering al-Qaeda, and it was democracy in service of counterterrorism, it was development in service of counterterrorism. It wasn't security in order to allow development and democracy— democracy and development became instruments of a counterterrorism policy, and the counterterrorism policy was focused on what was

good for the US. These became counterterrorism tools, and at that point, it goes off the tracks entirely.[25]

Turning development and democracy projects into "tools" of counterterrorism didn't work because it was "too instrumental," Ambassador Bodine explained. This extended to programs that focused on women's development in Yemen, where this feeling of instrumentalization soured the relationship between the two countries: "This idea that 'if I give you money for development, or this girls school, or contraception, or wells, or other forms of assistance, I'm buying your love'." This was not viewed as a constructive way to engage in partnership with the country, when the overarching US interest was counterterrorism.

Ambassador Bodine's comments demonstrated that when such diverse work became linked inherently to, or repurposed in relation to, counterterrorism, it could in fact directly undermine these interrelated efforts in fields such as development and democracy, and thereby negatively impact broader efforts. These insights highlighted an important tension between policy language (where women's rights were emphasized and understood to positively contribute to security) and how such practices emerged on the ground (where these were seemingly instrumentalized and subsumed under wider counterterrorism aims). Furthermore, instrumentalizing efforts from development to democratic programs in the service of counterterrorism (where women-centric programming was prominent) could prove counterproductive to diverse US development or governance programs and thus undercut broader US aims in the country.

However, as any diplomat will likely tell you, there were also bureaucratic and budgetary realities to contend with. Unless a development or empowerment program was demonstrably able to counter terror in some way, access to funding could be at risk, particularly in a political climate dominated by the GWOT. Ambassador Krajeski noted:

> If you are looking at the long view, whether it's education, economic stability, job opportunities, infrastructure, all of this contributes to overall stability, which can only have a positive impact on CVE. This is true. However, when you are a US Ambassador on the ground, and you're competing, struggling, for limited resources, whether those are people or money, you know what gets people to read your proposals. In the Middle East, especially in places like Yemen, that is all counter-

terrorism, CVE—so you have to hook women's education to counter-terrorism, or you're not going to get the money. Some of it is just pure bureaucratic reality. You can't educate women just because educating women is a good thing.[26]

This also highlighted tension between Washington and US missions abroad, where diplomatic actors in the latter may have to utilize and exploit this counterterrorism emphasis to gain resources for other areas of programming (ones which had a recognized longer-term and indirect role in stability and security). This appeared to perpetually instrumentalize (and arguably even securitize) these humanitarian, development and traditionally non-counterterrorism-related concerns, and displayed the significant shift that had occurred since 9/11. Work recognized to reduce the threat from terrorism and contribute to long-term security and stability was being increasingly stamped with an (often contentious) counterterrorism label in order to maintain their relevance and support, but came with its own set of concerns.

There were also other factors to be considered, with broader political reform efforts in Yemen (which could positively impact areas such as governance, and indeed women's status) potentially impeded by political decisions based out of Washington that were influenced by terrorism concerns. For example, in 2007, President Saleh released Jamal al-Badawi, the organizer of the 2000 USS Cole attack, prompting the US to cut aid to the country,[27] aid that was meant as a reward for its achievements with the Millennium Challenge Corporation (MCC).[28] By threatening to, or actually cutting off, such aid, there is an assumption that recipient nation's government will adjust their behavior to retain long-term US assistance. However, in reality, US politicians accountable to their domestic audience often have distinct incentives to use aid as a "carrot" or "stick," where to local/civil society actors are often the recipients of this aid, and whose programming and operations may largely rely on such support.

US Ambassador Stephen Seche (2007–10) noted the impact that this cut in MCC funding had in the country: "This was a significant amount of money: $50–60 million would have been freed up for Yemen for identified projects." However, after the release of al-Badawi:

> There was an uproar in Washington over this, and the outcome was the MCC was suspended because people were just looking for a stick to hit

him with, and that was the closest one. It wasn't a particularly appropriate one given Saleh's lack of real interest in development as a fundamental platform of his legacy. However, this was the one Washington chose to use, and the MCC grant was taken off the table.[29]

As such, funding that would have gone to building more accountable and responsible governance in Yemen—a key stated aim of US efforts—was cut. However, this corruption was also an impediment to implementing both security and development reforms, demonstrating the interconnectivity and impacts of such counterterrorism-driven considerations on wider US efforts in Yemen. According to Khoury, "even though the concept of linking development and security was an obvious one, and an accepted one rhetorically, in reality it wasn't." The cancellation of the MCC was a clear example of this:

> It was shooting ourselves in the foot [...]. The fact that they were punishing Yemen for doing something corrupt by cutting off the program that was going to fight corruption, it made absolutely no sense, but it typified the problem of seeing counterterrorism in a very narrow-minded way, and not being genuinely committed to the broader idea of development.[30]

This suggested that while there was an increased awareness of the importance of development in reducing long-term risks from extremism (one which was not necessarily of interest to Saleh), this could be sporadic, or used as punishment where counterterrorism interests diverged, and could actually negatively impact security concerns in the long-term. This was reinforced by an American researcher who focused on American–Yemeni relations:

> The problem with US–Yemeni policy is that it is like a shiny object— you have intense focus, then it dies out, something arguably more geopolitically important occurs and then focus again shifts away from Yemen. I feel that's been one of the problems with US strategy with Yemen over the past fifteen years.[31]

In areas where terrorism was a rising and ebbing concern, counterterrorism appeared to take priority over development efforts and longer-term reforms to undercut terrorism, highlighting problems in this strategic equation. As women's empowerment and development efforts often fell under this latter category, they were at higher risk of inconsistent support and funding, even as their importance to stability and development was increasingly recognized. This highlighted how the discourses and practices directly pertaining to women in this field had to be cognizant of broader institutional and bureaucratic limitations, challenges and dynamics, including those related to US funding and support. This was further emphasized as counterterrorism became the leading focus in Yemen.

In Yemen, there were many indigenous grassroots and civil society organizations around the country conducting positive work (in which women had played active roles for many years), and small funding grants through US State could be given to them to support work in their community. However, Ambassador Seche noted: "It was always frustrating that it was not always geared up to the level of need, and that it was competing for attention with counterterrorism." Even when smaller projects applied for funding, these often had to be framed in terms of how they contributed to counterterrorism: "There was always an underlying question of, 'can this support our counterterrorism efforts?'" Such themes also resonated in work focusing on empowering female journalists, where a dual counterterrorism and empowerment aim was perceived:

> We found this was both an encouraging way of helping young women identify a career, and also develop a voice that could send the right messages out to their communities, in a way that would be beneficial to all. Again, we would try and find ways that would be "writ large" helpful and positive, and also focused to the extent possible on counterterrorism messaging. This never meant that one could not coexist with the other.[32]

Indigenous organizations also had to increasingly reflect and adopt this counterterrorism language to access program funding. At times, this was not perceived as negatively impacting an organization, but in other cases they could face local backlash for their perceived western connections, or be viewed as advancing a western agenda.[33] The American–Yemeni analyst noted: "Yemenis more often would view challenges posed by extremist groups as a criminal, not terrorism, issue, but would adopt the language of counterterrorism to access western funds."[34] This highlighted how this dynamic between US security discourses and access to funding may also indeed impact on indigenous discourses and efforts to tackle security or other concerns.

There were several points that made Yemen unique when scrutinizing this relationship and interaction between women and counterterrorism. First, discourses related to women and counterterrorism/counter-extremism did not appear largely in MEPI policy language, but were in fact actively visible in practice, as seen in programming in areas such as education and skills training on the ground. This would prove to be the opposite of what was seen after 2011, where women, counterterrorism and CVE became emphasized explicitly in US State policy discourses. Secondly, there were a number of tensions that arose through framing development support for women in relation to counter-extremism efforts, including in how it became perceived by some to be in the service of counterterrorism. Others saw the positive impact that women's empowerment in these areas could have more generally on long-term security and stability efforts, however, they had to frame development or political empowerment programming in counterterrorism terms in order to help advance these in the shorter term (and to gain the necessary resources to do so). Due to budgetary or political constraints from Washington, framing women's programming in this light at times made it more likely to be funded, thus reinforcing this view. On the other hand, this also meant that as counterterrorism concerns subsided so too could funding and support for these programs. This could also impact on indigenous discourses related to security and development to allow them to access funding. Yemen in many ways epitomized early tensions between advancing women's political rights, empowerment and equality programming in a policy environment dominated by counterterrorism.

*Women and counterterrorism policy: A shift*

Increased focus on engagement with civil society also prompted new efforts related to how US State reached out to women in relation to counterterrorism. In 2006, the concept of "transformational diplomacy" was driven by Secretary Condoleezza Rice, where the US would partner with other nations to "build and sustain democratic, well-governed states that will respond to the needs of their people,"[35] alongside governments, and increasingly with civilians and civil society, through MEPI. Outside of MEPI programs, other shifts were happening internally at US State that would impact how women's engagement in civil society emerged in indirect counterterrorism policies and practices.

This engagement of women in CVE was understood within the soft power context of the "war of ideas," as noted by Farah Pandith: "The analysis of what we needed to do on the war of ideas came from an assessment [that we had to] stand up authentic voices that had the capacity to stop the appeal of the ideology."[36] Though the original thinking behind what this initiative would look like preceded 2007, around this time, US State's Office of the Coordinator for Counterterrorism received a small grant to look at how they could encourage more women in civil society to speak out against terrorism as there was an acknowledgement that "there was a major gap in the engagement of women on the issue of terrorism and counterterrorism."[37] This initiated internal interrogation of the topic. Jane Mosbacher Morris, who was based in this office between 2007 and 2012, started drafting the first US State Women and Counterterrorism Strategy, and later helped develop the department's implementation plan for the NAP on Women, Peace and Security: "[We] really started to solidify what the different ways are that you can engage women on the issue of terrorism and counterterrorism; and what we as a department should be doing consistently to engage women; and thinking about women on the issue of terrorism and counterterrorism."[38]

Some specific areas of focus in this strategy included building partner capacity, the security sector, female inclusion in program development (including women in the development, design and evaluation of programs), and not using women's rights as a bargaining tool to interact with extremists.[39] The strategy was noted as particularly successful in its engagement with civil society. Mosbacher Morris was able to gain top-level approval for this strategy, and it was eventually integrated into the departmental counterterrorism strategy and taken global. This brought with it increased resources and support as specific successes became visible in programming.

The introduction of this "women's focus" in the larger internal counterterrorism strategy in US State was "an uphill battle" she noted: "People that traditionally had worked on counterterrorism, who hadn't thought about a specific focus on women, were very resistant to the idea of a gender focus, and resistant to the idea that women required a special focus versus men." However, Mosbacher Morris pointed out that traditional counterterrorism work had been focused on military-to-military training, and law enforcement-to-law enforcement training, which often largely consisted of men: "Just by default the way we were doing the training was not fully engaging both men and women in the population." Furthermore, in terms of counter-messaging and other aspects of eradicating terrorism, she suggested there was a key gap if only half the audience was understood or engaged. Moreover, it was important to understand how these messages and programming would be shaped when reaching out to distinct and diverse audiences, including women.

For this work, Pandith, Mosbacher Morris and others working on this initiative focused on how they could best generate grassroots movements, using Mothers Against Drunk Driving (MADD) as a helpful example to model engagement of women in US State efforts:

> [MADD] was a great program, a good example of women in particular looking at a social norm—the idea of drinking and driving—and grassroots help for people, changing policy, advocacy on the government side, raising awareness of both parents and why they should talk to their kids about this issue, but also talking directly to children about why drinking and driving is so deadly. MADD served as a model and inspiration.[40]

Pandith noted: "We said 'could we do something like [MADD] to bring women's voices forward so that they can protect their children?'"[41] US State went on to fund two pilot programs in direct relation to this work: Women Against Violent Extremism and later Women Preventing Extremist Violence, which was based in the United States Institute of Peace (USIP).[42] This first program (WAVE) later became Sisters Against Violent Extremism (SAVE) and today is known as Women Without Borders (WWB), an NGO.[43] SAVE was launched in 2008 by Dr Edit Schlaffer in Vienna, and has since operated around the world in thirty countries. It has been described as "the world's first female counter-terrorism platform." This program has one key program—"Mother's Schools"—which focuses specifically on raising awareness about extremism and creating intervention strategies for women who fear their family members are at risk of radicalization. They have also developed programs to work directly with fathers to dissuade their children from radicalization, and with police to better understand radicalization and strategies to build public trust in this field.[44] Yet, it also demonstrated that US State's initial engagement of women in relation to counterterrorism was based on a number of gendered assumptions. Specifically, that women's voices were viewed as "authentic" and could speak out positively against extremism, and that women could positively impact extremism in their family and society through their familial roles (where they may in fact be the radical influences themselves).

It was also important in the acceptance of this policy within US State to frame women's inclusion in terms of how it would positively and operationally contribute to counterterrorism, as opposed to emphasizing women's inclusion as a goal in and of itself. Establishing this policy also helped highlight some of the broader streams of thinking in the field at the time, many of which remain pertinent today. For some, trying to bring in more "gendered" approaches to security was viewed as a "ruse" to promote women's equality when the specific impact on security was not immediately evident:

> From a pragmatic standpoint, or advocacy standpoint, *it can't be about gender equality*, that's not the purpose of these programs. *It has to be about the effectiveness of integrating women*—we're not going to get anywhere unless we are advocating for programs that are more effective because they involve women, or because they consider women.[45] [emphasis mine]

Mosbacher Morris suggested this was an error of those working predominantly in the field of women's rights, highlighting two distinct (and at times seemingly conflictual) trains of thought:

> That's something that folks who have previously been in the women's rights space may have struggled with—leading with the gender equality perspective, or simply arguing it's the right thing to do. Unfortunately, in the security sector, that often doesn't resonate with people—their job is to keep people safe and alive, so they're not going to respond as well if you lead with incorporating women in the name of gender equality.[46]

This also highlighted a specific tension in security debates between discourses driving women's inclusion in programming based on women's rights or equality agendas, versus their inclusion based on improving the effectiveness of a security program. The first State Ambassador-at-Large for Global Women's Issues, Ambassador Melanne Verveer (2011–14), echoed this point:

> Whether it is dealing with CVE, or ending conflict and creating sustainable peace, the point is we can't get there without women's participation. I believe that deeply, I believe it's a human right's issue as well, but others whom we are trying to persuade are in a different place and it falls on all of us, that seems to be the case, to make that point in a very compelling way.[47]

With the first internal women and counterterrorism strategy set up, the groundwork was being laid for how women would emerge in US State counterterrorism discourses and practices in the coming years.

Though it had been occurring since 2001, engaging women more pointedly in terms of the "battle of ideas" was also an important area of work for US State at this time. Through her role as the First Special Representative to Muslim Communities between 2007 and 2014, Farah Pandith traveled to dozens of countries around the world. She noted that more women were engaging in "radical changes around identity and expression of identity," which she referred to as "*halalizaiton.*" These changes raised important questions for Pandith, which also informed how women had to be engaged in this space:

> We also were looking very critically at changes that were happening with Muslim women around the world. Their affinity for the ideology of us versus them and red flags were going off for me as I was traveling around the world seeing changes within Muslim women that we had not actually thought about. That meant that the question then became, who is actually designing programs specifically to work with women? Making sure that we build resilience for women so that they don't find this ideology appealing?[48]

Referencing extremist groups, she noted they were often more proactive in recognizing the fact that they had to engage different approaches to women, "understanding that there are different things that they needed to do, to find, to bring women on board." In contrast, "America was very much behind the eight ball in terms of understanding a more sophisticated gender-based system of tools that were going to be made [and required]."[49]

Under the Bush administration, Secretary Condoleezza Rice also helped the advancement and adoption of Resolution 1820 (2008), which established a link between the maintenance of peace and security and responses to sexual violence as a tactic of war. This in effect demonstrated that there was some recognition of the value of advancing women, peace, and security norms more generally through the UN. There was also increasing evidence of efforts abroad to engage women in counterterrorism, for example through the Ambassador's Fund for Counterterrorism, which provided resources for US embassies necessary to implement small-scale, locally relevant counter-radicalization projects. In 2008, seventeen programs were funded totaling $750,000, such as a program in India that focused on empowering women against religious violence. This was viewed as the "soft" side of counterterrorism, and aimed to "shift the perceptions of target audiences, undermine the enemy's image, delegitimize extremist ideologies, and diminish support for violent extremism."[50] In 2008, US State also referenced winning the "struggle of ideas," within which the rights of women were a key component. However, such programming remained scarce, and it was not until 2009 and the tenure of Secretary of State Hillary Clinton that women's status in relation to US security in US State was fundamentally changed, as reflected in the first QDDR and NAP.

## Secretary Clinton: Driving the women, peace and security agenda

When President Obama entered office in 2009, there was a significant shift in how women became linked to security in US foreign policy, as demonstrated in the 2010 NSS, and counterterrorism and CVE more specifically (see Chapter 2). This was particularly visibly in US State, where in 2009 he established the new position of US Ambassador for Global Women's Issues (first taken up by Ambassador Melanne Verveer); this was followed in 2010 with the establishment of the Office of Global Women's Issues and the appointment of Hillary Clinton as Secretary of State. In the wider political climate, the specific interpretation and application of this policy—that of advancing the concerns and status of women in US foreign policy—within US State was particularly shaped, advanced and championed by Secretary Clinton.

Secretary Clinton had a long history as an active proponent for the rights of women and the rights of children as First Lady (1993–2001) and as New York's state senator (2001–09). Often, such efforts remained outside the scope of "security," but it became clear that under her leadership in US State, women's concerns traditionally viewed as being outside the scope of security would be drawn closer in unprecedented ways. In a 2009 interview, when asked how she could start to transform women's issues from being perceived as a "pink ghetto", she argued: "So-called women's issues are stability issues, security issues, equity issues. The World Bank and many other analysts have proved over and over again that where women are mistreated, where they are denied equal rights, you will find instability that very often serves as an incubator of extremism."[51]

State stability, security and propensity to extremism now became directly tied to women's rights, equality, and economic and development status. Clinton further stated: "if you look at where we are fighting terrorism, there is a connection to groups that are making a stand against modernity, and that is most evident in their treatment of women."[52] In March 2010, Secretary Clinton stated: "[T]he subjugation of women is a threat to the national security of the United States. It is also a threat to the common security of our world, because the suffering and denial of the rights of women and the instability of nations go hand in hand."[53]

This line of association between women's security, state stability and national security was one echoed throughout US State. Ambassador Verveer reiterated early statements linking women's security to extremism: "The correlation is clear: where women are oppressed, governance is weak, and extremism is more likely to take hold."[54] Esther Brimmer, the Assistant Secretary at the Bureau of International Organization Affairs, reinforced this: "[W]hat happens to women and girls truly impacts the security of the United States and the international community. We know this because we see that the suffering and denial of the rights of women and the instability of nations go hand in hand."[55] This link between the status of women's personal security and their rights was increasingly emphasized in the broader national security agenda too, where women's status became viewed as an indicator of state stability, and hence in some cases an indication of its vulnerability to extremism.[56] However, what would become evident in the first QDDR was how this was altered in US State policy discourses and operational frameworks as never before.

## Women and security take the stage: The QDDR

The first QDDR in 2010 was inspired by the DoD's Quadrennial Defense Review and established by Secretary Clinton, who wanted to undertake a review and strategic plan for diplomacy and development within US State and USAID. It was recognized that diplomatic and development efforts (otherwise known as "civilian power") could be "more united, more focused, and more efficient."[57] The 2010 QDDR aimed to "elevate civilian power alongside military power as *equal pillars* of US foreign policy" [emphasis added]. This was referred to as "smart power," aimed at tackling global threats such as terrorism and violent extremism. Smart power was understood as "integrating the three Ds of our foreign policy and national security: diplomacy, development and defense."[58]

"Civilian power" was noted by the Joint Special Operations University (the educational component of the United States' Special Operations Command [SOCOM]) to be "[o]ne of the most important changes in the interagency process in recent years." The QDDR title itself "acknowledges the reality that merely clustering organizations on a chart doesn't mean they share the same strategic vision or sense of an agreed unity of effort. Interagency leadership remains an essential element." This unity of effort was driven by coordinated, rather than directed, relationships. As a concept, civilian power was recognized by defense actors as functioning "primarily within the domain of indirect action," and recognized "it is not the intent to restrict military efforts."[59] Instead, this concept was proposed as "smart power," whereby DoD, US State and USAID in particular would have to become more closely partnered in order to understand the complexities of the roles and efforts inherent in each distinct department and agency. Hillary Clinton offered an example related to tackling propaganda by groups such as al-Qaeda:

> We know we need to do a better job contesting the online space, media websites and forums where al-Qaida and its affiliates spread their propaganda and recruit followers. So, at the State Department, we've launched a new interagency Center for Strategic Counterterrorism Communications. It's housed at the State Department, but it draws on experts from the intelligence community and the Defense Department, including Special Operations Forces.[60]

This Special Operations Forces (SOF) guide quoted Clinton, who stated "we need Special Operations Forces who are as comfortable drinking tea with tribal leaders as raiding a terrorist compound [...]. We also need diplomats and development experts who understand modern warfare and are up to the job of being your [SOF] partners."[61] This emphasis on civilian power highlighted a more extensive role for civilian agencies like US State and USAID, with actions by DoD that aimed to "shape the environment," and previewed more extensive interaction and understanding between these three agencies in particular. Yet, for this this move towards common objectives to be successful, it would also require leadership coordination and buy-in from each distinct actor. In reality, such aims were particularly ambitious, complex and bound to be fraught by competing and divergent interests. The recognition by SOF of the impact this increasingly emphasized interaction would have is worth quoting in full:

> The emphasis on civilian power brought about by the QDDR, PPD-6 [Presidential Policy Directive 6 on Global Development], and subsequent guidance will have significant impact on SOF activities. Increasing roles and missions for civilian power can engage interagency assets in greater numbers and with the necessary skill sets to balance both indirect and direct resources. These can then be applied to address issues of grievance and instability that tend to nurture conditions ripe for terrorist, criminal, and insurgent activities. They are also likely to render any operational environment a more crowded place in which to operate.[62]

What further distinguished the QDDR was how women, girls and gender became tied with both US State and USAID strategies to support US foreign policy and its security aims. The QDDR noted the trend of "oppression of women" as a growing cost of conflict and state weakness, where "women and girls are denied fundamental rights and freedoms."[63] Women's issues in "humanitarian emergencies, armed conflict, and post-conflict reconstruction and governance" were elevated as key concerns of US foreign policy, alongside a focus on health and human trafficking. It noted UN Security Council Resolutions (UNSCRs) 1820 and 1888 on the prevention of rape as a tool of war would continue to be implemented, and areas such as sexual and gender-based violence (SGBV) would be addressed in strategy and planning. This also demonstrated a more active recognition and utilization of UNSCRs focused on women and security in conflict in both US State and USAID. QDDR echoed the 2010 NSS, noting terrorism was a key challenge faced by the US, and highlighted expanding the role of "civilian power" to help stay ahead of a threat described as "the combined force of civilians working together across the US government to practice diplomacy, carry out development projects, and prevent and respond to crises."[64]

The 2010 QDDR was unprecedented in terms of how women, girls and gender were explicitly, holistically and directly emphasized in diplomatic and development discourses in relation to security. Women were referenced 107 times, while gender and girls also held a significant focus (with fifty and thirty references, respectively); this constituted the most of any high-level strategy document reviewed since 9/11 (and likely prior). The QDDR noted that US diplomacy would be adapted to meet new challenges by incorporating "women and girls into all our public-engagement efforts" and to "ensure that women are integrated into our efforts to prevent conflict and respond to it." Women were also explicitly linked to state security:

> Women are critical to solving virtually every challenge we face as individual nations and as a community of nations [...] when women have equal rights, nations are more stable, peaceful, and secure. *The status of the world's women is not simply an issue of morality—it is a matter of national security*.[65] [emphasis mine]

Women's status was seemingly being integrated (or arguably securitized to an extent) into US State considerations of development and diplomatic work within the larger national security agenda, particularly in conflict prevention and responses. Put another way, women's status now became a foreign policy issue and a core consideration of all aspects of both US State and USAID work.[66] As Hudson and Leidl point out, this transition by Hillary Clinton to explicitly link the status of women and security was well-founded. From female infanticide to domestic abuse, underlying sexual politics in all extremism and patriarchal nationalism, there was a growing body of evidence that demonstrated the status and security of women in a society was directly correlated with state security.[67]

Women's agency was also recognized and emphasized, where women were not simply beneficiaries of aid, but "*agents* of peace, reconciliation, development, growth, and stability" [emphasis mine]. The QDDR highlighted how in both US State and USAID, "gender guidelines and integration will be included in all activities, project selection and design, strategic planning, budgeting, and monitoring and evaluation," where they would also develop "indicators and evaluation systems to measure the impact of our programs and policies on women and girls." This contrasted with defense strategies in DoD where gender guidelines and integration (specifically in operations related to foreign populations) were noticeably absent, suggesting that this perceived importance and application was unique to US State and USAID, though these three institutions remained the core actors in foreign policy and national security efforts.

While diplomacy and development were traditionally viewed in more indirect counterterrorism efforts, the concepts of "smart power" and "civilian power" more explicitly linked US State and USAID activities to the wider security and counterterrorism agenda in several ways. First, the 2010 NSS noted the biggest threat faced by the US was al-Qaeda and its affiliates, and its primary goal was to disrupt, dismantle and defeat these. The NSS also noted that defense initiatives were always going to be a primary tool to achieve US goals, but highlighted that diplomacy and development must also be part of this approach. In QDDR, defense, diplomacy and development were viewed in equal terms, and all had to increasingly work together to support and complement each other, working "as a unified force;"[68] this was also referred to as "an integrated 'smart power' approach to solving global problems."[69] Civilian power was noted as an often "undervalued and underused asset in the national security portfolio," which required "not only redressing the balance between military and civilian power, but also ensuring that US civilian agencies can work together cooperatively and efficiently to maximize our collective impact." This suggested there was a perceived imbalance in earlier efforts and aims to make US State and USAID more integrated.[70] Indeed, the QDDR noted: "Even the world's finest military cannot defeat a virus, stop climate change, prevent the spread of violent extremism, or make peace in the Middle East."[71]

Second, violent extremism was recognized as a key global trend, shaping international affairs, thereby placing new demands on diplomats and development experts,[72] who were increasingly acting and reacting in direct response to violent extremism. This inevitably made their work more conscious of, and thus shaped by, counterterrorism and CVE considerations. Third, there were more direct links between diplomacy and counterterrorism. It noted that US State was establishing a Bureau of Counterterrorism and Countering Violent Extremism (expanding from an office previously), "which will enhance our ability to counter violent extremism, build partner capacity, and engage in counterterrorism diplomacy."[73] Counterterrorism diplomacy would engage both multilateral and bilateral diplomacy "to advance US counterterrorism goals." The 2010 QDDR also pointedly linked women to CVE:

> By reaching out to women and girls and integrating them into our diplomatic mission, we ensure more effective diplomacy, whether in driving economic growth, resisting extremism, safeguarding human rights, or promoting political solutions, including in areas of conflict. By considering women and girls in all of our policy initiatives, including global health, food security, climate change, economic issues, human rights, and peace and security we can make those initiatives stronger and more successful.[74]

In US State, inherently considering women in all aspects of policy and programming related to extremism was seen to ensure more strong, successful initiatives. As discussed in the previous chapter, this contrasted with the defense sphere, which appeared more responsive to including women, particularly when/where it was demonstrated to improve operational effectiveness.

The QDDR was noted to have resonated with SOF in the DoD, who highlighted the unclear path by which this interagency relationship would evolve in practice. Their 2013 *Interagency Counterterrorism Reference Manual* summarized some of the challenges inherent with this equal emphasis on defense, diplomacy and development:

> It is important to realize that the USG [US government] interagency community is not a body with a fixed structure and a developed operational culture. Instead, it is a loose and often undefined process of multiple structures and cultures that is often personality and situationally dependent for its success to an extent normally unfamiliar to the special operations warrior. Stepping outside the comfort zone of military organizations and operations introduces uncertainty about the

ways and means to accomplish the mission and achieve assigned strategic objectives.[75]

This suggested that specific themes of focus in one department would not just translate to another, and from a military perspective had to be understood in terms of how it could accomplish the mission and achieve its strategic objectives. Recalling that women and gender were only holistically integrated throughout the entire approach in both development and diplomacy (which still reflected stereotypical norms related to the roles of women in the "softer," indirect side of security), this also highlighted where gaps would likely emerge in cooperation and alignment of actions and priorities with defense partners in this smart power approach.

Women were also referenced in the 2010 QDDR as security actors in foreign contexts. This was one of the first notable instances of this happening, though they remained distinct to military or counterterrorism-specific considerations: "We will boost the number of women police officers and peacekeepers who are particularly well suited to work with host country female populations and local communities." Women were also referenced as part of a more "normative" approach to peace, where their inclusion in related activities was understood to positively impact female victims, particularly in conflict zones:

> The only way [...] to reduce the number of conflicts around the world, to eliminate rape as a weapon of war, to combat the culture of impunity for sexual violence, to build sustainable peace—is to draw on the full contributions of both women and men in every aspect of peacemaking, peacekeeping, and peace building.[76]

UNSCR 1325 appeared to be directly engaged in US policy language, where women were considered actors and agents in areas such as reconciliation and reconstruction, as well as with regards to some aspects of security in key countries of focus. This also appeared to overcome some of the early critiques of UNSCR 1325, which neglected an extension to terrorism and extremism more explicitly, or to women as security practitioners, but which still had its own flaws and shortcomings.

While the language of the QDDR was certainly significant, the level to which it was applied in practice was disputed. Des Roches noted: "none of the [QDDR] diplomatic reviews have had any impact, they just validate the status quo."[77] Getting women's issues to translate into programming, and indeed to make them a central part of the discussion in countries like Iraq and Afghanistan, was also noted as a challenge. There was some resistance in US State to spending programming money on women's issues, which the head of one NGO referred to as patriarchal and chauvinistic.[78] Research by Hudson and Leidl suggested women's considerations in some settings (like Iraq and Afghanistan) had only been advanced at the instruction of senior persons in the administration, particularly in US State,[79] suggesting that this department too had a divergence of views on how (or even if) to engage women. As such, it again highlights the importance of senior champions to advance efforts focused on women.

As will be highlighted throughout this book, such "champions" are often required to get issues onto the policy agenda. However, unless such policies are successfully trickled down into the bureaucracy over time and made an established norm (or "mainstreamed"), the endeavors to advance new ideas or practices risk losing momentum. Moreover, if the "champion" is to depart their post, this limits any longer-term integration and impact. Thus, while the QDDR indeed represented a significant discursive shift in how DoD, US State and USAID would interact and coordinate, particularly in the field of counterterrorism, there were evident disparities to how this would be cohesively implemented in practice.

## The Global Security Contingency Fund

The Global Security Contingency Fund (GSCF) proved another example of increased interagency coordination and effort related to counterterrorism under the Obama administration, and was prompted by increased security and stabilization needs. Set up in 2011 as a pilot project, this fund focused on bolstering integrated, interagency funding streams and efforts between the DoD and US State in counterterrorism and security training, as well as rule of law programs. This specifically included security and counterterrorism training; coalition support; and justice sector, rule of law and stabilization assistance.[80] What made this fund unique compared with previous funding (such as Section 1207) was that US State was responsible for the budget.

However, both the countries chosen for this funding, as well as the design of the programs to be implemented, would be completed jointly by the Secretary of State and Secretary of Defense.[81] The majority of this budget was also to come from DoD, which was able to transfer up to $200 million of its funding to the GSCF, while US State was able to transfer up to $50 million.[82] Seven countries received funding from this grant: Nigeria, the Philippines, Bangladesh, Libya, Hungary, Romania and Slovakia.

The fund had been critiqued for its slow planning and implementation, which had been attributed to (among other things) definitional differences between agencies, the team responsible only comprising three persons, and the detailed interagency consultation and coordination required to establish the office and its activities.[83] However, it proved another example of the increasing unity of effort being attempted in relation to counterterrorism.

## The NAP on Women, Peace and Security

As discussed in Chapter 2, the NAP was established in 2016 by an executive order from President Obama, and was relevant to the DoD, US State and USAID. This section will expand on the institutionalization and implementation of the NAP into core US State efforts in order to highlight the impact this had. The NAP implementation plan represented the policy and practical institutionalization of women, peace and security efforts in both US State and USAID. The NAP had highlighted fifty-six objectives for the department—the most of any agency discussed in it. These actions included aspects such as working to improve the capacity of the UN to prevent and respond to SGBV, and advocating that any UN peacekeeping mission have a strong mandate on this; assisting partner governments in incorporating women's perspectives into peace and security policy; providing assistance to support women in the security sector in fragile environments and democratic transitions; and mobilizing men as allies in support of women's leadership and participation in security-related processes and decision-making.[84] It also noted US State will aim to ensure that "counterterrorism dialogues with partner governments include discussions on how to effectively protect civilians, including women and girls." While this can be construed as positive and demonstrating some extension to counterterrorism, it still reflected the sort of protective language emphasized in UNSCR 1325.

The Office of Global Women's Issues led US State efforts in integrating international women's issues in the pursuit of its strategic objectives. With a 2010 budget of only $516,000, it would seemingly be limited in its impact, but it had three ambitious priorities: (1) "effectively integrate women's issues into the overall mission of the State Department"; (2) "promote women's empowerment through political, economic, and social development"; and (3) "combat gender-based violence and discrimination." It also aimed to "[i]mprove collaboration with international and multilateral organizations on addressing women's issues."[85] Ambassador Melanne Verveer oversaw the implementation of the NAP in US State, which was carried out through a department-wide working group. In 2010, the department also started tracking women-focused funds in their programs, and in their 2012 budget had requested $1.2 billion for programs which specifically targeted women for the first time.[86]

While the NAP itself did not highlight women in direct relation to counterterrorism and CVE, US State's implementation plan explicitly highlighted and promoted women's roles through specific institutional mechanisms against these, representing the first departmental plan to do so. It highlighted how women were to be engaged and supported as security practitioners in formal security institutions, and increasingly encouraged women to engage with security practitioners on CVE initiatives. It encouraged both communities to engage with security practitioners and agencies, and practitioners to engage with communities. US State demonstrated an explicitly stated commitment to increasingly engage and support foreign women as security practitioners, while also increasingly integrating feedback from local women in the security practices they participated in. This work was directly coordinated at the time with the Office for Combating Terrorism, for example supporting women's roles in community policing. This office would also:

> Build the capacity of women in civil society and the security sector to prevent the spread of violent extremism. This includes building the capacity of local, national, and multinational women's and peace groups committed to working against violent extremism to more effectively

conduct public outreach; to provide train-the-trainer opportunities to help sensitize women to the role that they can play in countering violent extremism within their communities; and to recognize signs of radicalization.[87]

It is worth expanding in full the tasks assigned to the bureaus and embassies around the world who would be directly implementing these aims in practice, as these highlight just how substantive these aims had become. It noted that US State as a department would promote women's roles in countering terrorism and preventing the spread of violent extremism, whereas bureaus and embassies would aim to:

- Build the capacity of local, national, and multinational women's and peace groups committed to working against violent extremism to more effectively conduct public outreach.
- Provide train-the-trainer opportunities to help sensitize women to the role that they can play in countering violent extremism within their communities, and to recognize signs of radicalization.
- Seek the feedback of local civil society members, including women, in the development of countering violent extremism programs, as well as all other programs, when feasible and appropriate.
- Encourage counterterrorism and countering violent extremism program recipients to include women in their training and/or implementation, when feasible and appropriate.
- Increase the number of female participants in Anti-Terrorism Assistance programs, including the training of women-only units.
- Promote the role of women in countering violent extremism through multilateral organizations, including the Global Counterterrorism Forum.[88]

Prior to the release of this NAP, US State had already started to attempt to improve coordination mechanisms between their department and DoD and USAID in areas pertaining to gender concerns in the field. This was seen, for example, in Afghanistan in 2010, where US State created two groups—the Interagency Gender Working Group and the Afghanistan Gender Task Force—to "improve interagency coordination of efforts to support Afghan women."[89] This task force was led by the US Ambassador-at-Large for Global Women's Issues and the Assistant Chief of Mission for Afghanistan, and its members included the Secretary of State's Office of Global Women's Issues, USAID and DoD, amongst others. This task force was highlighted as an example of "successful coordination on specific programmatic and strategic, policy-level issues." Alongside this, the NAP continued to formalize and guide such interagency and coordinated efforts.

US State was active in integrating the NAP in its programming, for example "integrating gender into its strategic planning processes," including in their Counterterrorism Bureau. In 2011, both US State and USAID developed performance indicators related to gender equality and women's empowerment in all areas, including counterterrorism. This included aspects such as encouraging "partner governments to mitigate the use of women's rights as bargaining chips to achieve counterterrorism goals," and of "counterterrorism measures as vehicles to restrict civil society organizations working on women's issues." Practical examples were shown in Afghanistan, where US State was helping women in the Ministry of Interior (MOI) and in civil society in "preventing the spread of violent extremist ideologies, including educating [Afghan women] about their resources for reporting potential violent extremism activity." In addition to this, the State Countering Violent Extremism Local Grants Program provided "positive alternatives to individuals and communities susceptible to recruitment and radicalization, including local activities specifically tailored for women," where programming included "training exercises to alert women to signs of radicalization, [and] to law enforcement capacity building that offers women the opportunity to help develop community engagement programs."[90]

NAP-related activities in US State were also increasingly framed in relation to DoD and USAID efforts, and explicitly linked to counter-extremism. In a speech to SOCOM in Florida in 2012, Hillary Clinton stated:

> I'm impressed by the work of your Cultural Support Teams, highly-trained female Special Operations Forces who engage with local populations in sensitive areas like Afghanistan. This is part of our National Action Plan on Women, Peace, and Security that was developed jointly by the Departments of State, Defense, and others to capitalize on the contributions women everywhere can make to resolving conflicts and improving security. Around the world today, women are refusing to sit on the sidelines while extremism undermines their communities, steals their sons, kills their husbands, and destroys family after family. (Applause.) They're joining police forces in Afghanistan. They're writing newspaper articles in Yemen. They're forming organizations such as

Sisters Against Violent Extremism that has now spread to 17 countries. And we are committed to working with these women and doing everything we can to support their efforts as well.[91]

US State also provided extensive annual overviews and updates on its implementation of the NAP between 2013 and 2015, and it became visible that counterterrorism and CVE considerations were increasingly reflected in these.[92] For example, the overview of 2013 efforts noted US State had, under the pillar of "conflict prevention," "[s]upported networks of women to speak out against violent extremism, train other women to recognize the signs of radicalization to violence, and to mediate conflict within their communities to reduce violent extremism." It also developed "the first regional training on first response support to victims of terrorism in Southeast Asia." In Syria, where instability had started to take hold, US State had "[a]ctively integrated women as participants and agents of change in resolving the conflict in Syria by providing Syrian women's groups with training and diplomatic support to prepare for future peace processes and promote their involvement in track one negotiations." This had also recognized several external challenges in integrating the NAP, such as unstable security environments, weak governance institutions, a lack of political will and societal discrimination. Even internally within US State there were several challenges in advancing these efforts, including resourcing and staffing limitations, and "insufficient training on gender-sensitive policy and programming, and uneven monitoring and evaluation."[93] It was also noted that for some in US State, this emphasis on women and gender received pushback and was thought to be too accentuated.[94]

The 2014 review noted similar efforts, such as US State support of "networks of women to counter terrorism, especially in speaking out against violent extremism, engaging other women and religious leaders to recognize signs of radicalization to violence, and mediating community conflict to reduce violent extremism." In specific response to Islamic State in Iraq and Syria (ISIS), it had "[i]ncorporated gender perspectives into regional and multilateral cooperation frameworks to respond to crisis and counter rising threats posed by [ISIS]." Echoing the challenges of the previous year, it highlighted an imbalance in focus and capacity from intergovernmental partners in implementation: "Limited capacity among government counterparts undercuts the political will necessary to convert international commitments into action and continues to preclude the development of budgets and institutional capabilities that drive local implementation and enforcement."[95]

In 2014, women's training in direct relation to counterterrorism also became more visible at US State, such as with the Anti-Terrorism Assistance (ATA) program, a partnership between the Bureau of Counterterrorism and Countering Violent Extremism and the Bureau of Diplomatic Security. The number of women being trained in partner nations through Nonproliferation, Anti-terrorism, Demining, and Related Programs/ATA funding was now being tracked, units of female law enforcement officers were being trained in several countries, and recruitment of female instructors was attempted. It noted that "ATA is making changes to ATA curriculum to emphasize the particular need to protect women in the course of counterterrorism investigations and operations,"[96] reflecting that counterterrorism efforts in US State aimed to protect women's rights through this work.

By 2015, US State had also increasingly emphasized women's roles as security actors, particularly in policing in countries like Pakistan and Ukraine. These were framed in terms of how women as citizens may relate to law enforcement in their society. The consequences of ISIS were also being responded to, with 150 Yazidi survivors of sexual violence receiving medical and psycho-social support through US State funding. It had also funded research into women's roles in preventing or perpetrating violent extremism, and "sponsored exchange programs to help equip women CVE practitioners with tools they need to build resilient communities, and developed an international network of women practitioners to facilitate the exchange of best practices." It had further "supported the President's Summit on Countering Violent Extremist in February and his Leaders' Summit on Countering ISIL [Islamic State in Iraq and the Levant] and Violent Extremism in September," which had included "women civil society advocates from around the world and highlighted the important role of women in preventing the rise and spread of violent extremist organizations." This focus on the new challenges raised by ISIS was also seen in US State participation in the Counter-ISIS Coalition Working Group on Stabilization, which had flagged up SGBV and gender concerns related to stabilization and reconciliation in Iraq, or its focus on women's empowerment in areas vulnerable to violent extremism. Hence, including a gender perspective into existent programming was high-lighted as a key and persistent concern.[97]

These NAP implementations were visible steps by US State in signaling their dedication to women, peace and security principles. Yet, implementation was not as uniform in practice, and such reviews had to be assessed in relation to wider US efforts in this period. Mosbacher Morris, who helped develop the US State implementation of the NAP, pointed out the extent to which implementation varied widely in several areas based on:

> Personalit[ies], political dynamics, not only within the department, but political as in what was going on in a country or region, all influenced the extent to which the NAP was focused on. Resources are also a huge factor—some countries in the world get a lot more funding than others. In places that are strapped for cash, it's hard for them to establish these types of programs that are not core, basic diplomacy work that they have to do at the consulate or embassy.[98]

This highlighted the importance of assessing such positive discourses with nuance, and a need to identify the various factors that could impact their successful implementation in practice. Yet, overall, the NAP had been the driving force behind notable progress within US State. Ambassador Verveer noted:

> We can see progress, you can see it in a large number of efforts, you can certainly see this in development and our diplomatic work that really do factor in the participation of women, etc., but we have a long way to go. There's no mincing those words. We are just at the beginning of this process.[99]

It was evident that in terms of policy discourses and institutional mechanisms, women had been integrated as never before in US State. Despite this, there continuously remained a gap between policy language and practice on the ground, driven by a host of factors that had to be assessed on a country or regional basis, as well as within a broader global environment, where inevitably the issue of the day often became prioritized over others.

## CVE: Expanding space for women in security

As reflected in both the QDDR and the NAP implementation plan, the rising prominence of CVE opened further opportunities for US State to extend its policy and programming to women. Former Acting Coordinator for Counterterrorism in US State and US Ambassador to Yemen (1997–2001) Barbara Bodine noted that this important emphasis on CVE was shifting back to root causes, grievances and precursors, which also integrated further considerations of development: "[CVE is] trying to get ahead of the curve and instead of doing security, then attempting to address issues of development, 'we better start working on some of these other areas first'. [It is] shifting."[100]

Of the varied streams of effort related to counterterrorism, CVE appeared to emphasize women most expansively and directly for several reasons, including those both based on gendered stereotypes related to women, but also on practical realities that had been raised with ISIS. First, CVE efforts most frequently emphasized civil society, community or familial positions that women were commonly understood to hold (versus those such as security practitioners). This also extended to areas such as advocacy or counter-narratives, where women were seen as key conduits to disseminate messages challenging groups like ISIS, or engaging in debates to help prevent their family members from becoming radicalized.

Women were also increasingly targeted in ISIS recruitment, including by female recruiters, so women in CVE efforts were sometimes viewed as most suitable to engage other women. Women were also viewed as having particularly authentic voices able to specify when they were victims of terrorist violence or when they lost family members to such organizations, providing useful counter-narratives.[101] However, this could still problematically reinforce victimhood stereotypes of women in relation to security or limit the space by which their concerns related to security may be raised, demonstrating the continuous tensions in such efforts. Furthermore, CVE did not necessarily carry with it the same negative stigmas and grievances that had been associated with some DoD actions previously, such as extraordinary renditions, torture or other human rights violations.

CVE thus presented a new stream of counterterrorism-related work in indirect or soft power efforts where women could be engaged afresh. This aligned with the pre-existing and socially resonant roles that women had traditionally held, and which were reflective of earlier US State programming focused on women. By 2012, US State was significantly emphasizing women in its CVE efforts, noting for example in its annual globally reaching Country Report on Terrorism:

> CVE programming places particular emphasis on engaging women; women are uniquely positioned to counter radicalization both at home and in their communities and are therefore a vital component of our efforts. We continued to support the networking of CVE women activists. Lastly, we sought to amplify the voices of victims of terrorism who can credibly articulate the destructive consequences of terrorism, and can thus help to dissuade those contemplating such acts. [102]

Eileen O'Connor, US Deputy Assistant Secretary of State for South and Central Asian Affairs, also echoed these themes of women in community roles, as well as those of victims in relation to violent extremism:

> Women's voices must be heard if communities are going to be able to move past violence and victimization and invest in a shared future that rejects conflict and promotes dignity. Because women have often been the targets of the violence and the depravity that follows radicalization, we must enlist and empower them as key agents of peace and reconciliation. [103]

This notion was often also framed in female interrelationships: "Women can be the most effective actors in a community to raise awareness and to build capacity among other local women to address radicalization," O'Connor noted. This emphasis on women engaging other women in this work also raised questions about assumptions that they may not be viewed as best suited to engage men in CVE work, and could potentially limit their engagement. This was also discussed in relation to more expansive, comprehensive counterterrorism approaches, noting the "need for us to continue to refine and adapt our counterterrorism policies and programs to be more comprehensive and to be more proactive, in part by involving and incorporating women and civil society actors to the fullest extent possible." Also citing UNSCR 1325, O'Connor affirmed "we are taking a holistic approach to counter terrorism by ensuring our programs maximize gender analysis and gender integration." [104] The extent of gender focus in US State CVE efforts was also recognized in other agencies. Seamus Hughes, who worked on implementing the US government's CVE policy at the NCTC noted: "State Department has had a much more nuanced approach to CVE, especially when it comes to the role of women."[105]

However, this engagement of women was still viewed in terms of "adding women and stir"—the idea that by mentioning women in new policies would translate effectively into practice. This was a notion challenged by Pandith, who believed this was not done in a systematic and comprehensive CVE program, and had to be more meaningful. In other words, it had to be consistent and proactive, not reactive:

> You're not just adding an attachment that says "and we'll do it for women too." It is a redesign for specifically the women's component as its own thing. It can't be that today we are going to look at women because something has happened for this particular city in Nigeria and we think that we're going to do a women's program. That's not how to do this.[106]

The justification to include women was that "to stop the ideology from being appealing to young people, all of humanity has to get on board. This isn't a one gender, one element, one dissection of society that is only at risk. So the first thing to understand is that everyone, everyone, all of us have a role to play." This meant looking at the gender component in a new way in CVE work, such as the differences between how and why men and women may be attracted to certain ideologies: "That comprehensive approach is the only way that we're going to be able to win. That is the only way."[107]

## CVE: Recreating the wheel?

This CVE stream of effort became increasingly visible in countries facing significant problems from extremism. However, the skills required of women in CVE efforts were oftentimes already present in these areas, albeit visible in other fields of work not necessarily labeled as CVE. Georgia Holmer discussed some US State-funded work she was involved in that focused on women and CVE in Nigeria in 2015, which featured entry points for women's roles at the community level to help prevent violent extremism.[108] One specific project explored the challenges and opportunities there were for enhancing women's relationships with local police. Engaging women from the Jos and Kaduna region, who had already worked in interfaith and peace-building, provided two important insights in terms of women's roles in CVE: "The first big epiphany we had was the skills that these women had already forged in their peace-building and interfaith work were precisely the skills that were needed in this nascent field of CVE."[109] The second lesson was in terms of how much influence women wielded in their traditional roles in society through influential marriages (otherwise known as "flanking"); the unique traditional and indigenous tribal practices of protest such as shaming men to prevent violence; or in marketplaces or schools. This proved to be one example where work in the women, peace and security and peace-building sphere was overlapping with emerging CVE aims. In addition, these were poised to be drawn under the CVE umbrella, where women's pre-existing roles in the community could positively contribute to this growing field of CVE work.

Nevertheless, it was as though this CVE learning process had originally neglected considerations of women's pre-existing roles more broadly; the work women were doing in their community was already undercutting extremism (even if it was not recognized as such), and didn't necessarily have to be initiated as, or labeled in terms of, a CVE focus. Instead, pre-existing work could potentially inform the CVE sphere, or be supported itself without this CVE label being attached to it, which risked bringing with it other tensions and grievances that may be related to counterterrorism or CVE. It also emphasized the necessity of locally tailored, contextualized approaches required for each program, and a recognition of how communities were already addressing violence and extremism.

This also elucidated the tension of "labeling" that arose in CVE efforts, resulting in a consistent debate about the value or necessity of stating something was CVE. Fink highlighted concerns that existed in CVE more broadly that became evident as the field gained increased attention:

> There is a lack of conceptual clarity as to what CVE is [...]. It's more complicated by the fact that not a lot of CVE programming needs to be labelled as CVE in order for it to fulfil a CVE function. If you promote critical thinking among young students, boys and girls, sure it helps challenge extremism because it helps them recognize there is a marketplace of ideas and you don't have to buy into a single narrative, but it's not a CVE project, it's an education project.[110]

This raised a broader consideration that was particularly driven by the GWOT: due to the distinct fear that terrorism often creates in civilian populations, governments are pressured to always be perceived to be responding to, or addressing in some manner, critical security concerns like terrorism or extremism. However, this may drive excessive labeling of efforts as counterterrorism or CVE-relevant at the department level, or drive extensive "new" CVE programs which may already be functioning in developmental or empowerment forms. This appeared at times to promote a government approach of "policy first, evidence later," where new lines of effort seen within CVE were created without recognizing how existing work or roles held by women could, or were already, contributing to these CVE aims. It also appeared to neglect a greater understanding of the impacts such labeling of projects as CVE may have, which could affect pre-existing work women were doing in their communities, or make new ones counterproductive.[111] Adnan Ansari, the Director (Programs) for US NGO Muflehun, which carries out CVE projects in the US and eight countries internationally, suggested this "securitization" was problematic. Discussing this concern related to CVE, Ansari stated:

> [CVE] has been mainstreamed, and many other areas have been securitized, that's the problem. Gender rights existed, international governance and poverty alleviation existed, work on urban management existed, human rights existed. CVE has been brought into everything, it's not just gender programs. That's kind of polluting all those areas.[112]

Ansari suggested there instead had to be a focus on distinguishing between "CVE-relevant" efforts—which could make an environment stronger and create "stronger, more resilient communities"—and those that were CVE-specific, which targeted the "root causes" of violent extremism: "Everyone is learning in this [CVE] area." However, other aspects that could influence these were the political approach of the administration in place, and the sources of funding and what these were allocated for; that is, "who provides funding for what."[113]

US State also focused on CVE programming like community engagement and community-oriented policing, which emphasized engaging with marginalized groups such as women in public diplomacy efforts. For example, in Pakistan, US State organized a women's interfaith dialogue in Rawalpindi, which was attended by female religious leaders, teachers and civil society activists to discuss CVE.[114] In terms of CVE advocacy, US State emphasized "women and victims/survivors" who could provide counter-narratives that "highlight the destruction and devastation of terrorist attacks" and which trained women to shape and disseminate CVE messages. They also highlighted weekly radio dramas, and call-in shows targeting women to discuss CVE. They noted in their Country Report on Terrorism (2014):

> Women can act as gatekeepers to their communities, and can thus provide a first line of defense against recruitment and radicalization to violence in their families and communities. In regions such as East Africa and West Africa, women are trained to recognize signs of radicalization, deploy prevention techniques, and become personally responsible for the local promotion of security and for radicalization prevention. In partnership with local women's networks, the Department of State supports training for women civil society leaders and works with law enforcement personnel to devise CVE-prevention strategies and pilot activities.[115]

While problematically contributing to stereotypes or essentialism of women in this field, this emphasis on women's family and community roles in CVE also appeared to open a new avenue in which to bring women into US security discourses and practices in what were publicly perceived as more traditional or acceptable roles.

### Problems and limitations in practice

Established in 2012, the now expanded Bureau of Counterterrorism and Countering Violent Extremism (housed in US State) led agency policy and guidance formulation on priority areas ranging from food security to CVE, counterinsurgency and counterterrorism efforts, to women and youth, amongst others. Yet, there remained a visible absence of explicit referencing of women in the Bureau, particularly in discussions of capacity building, CVE, countering terrorist safe havens and counterterrorism engagement funding.[116] This same point later extended to testimonies from the Bureau in which discussions around disrupting the flow of foreign fighters, addressing the humanitarian crises in the region or "exposing ISIL's true nature" lacked any mention of women.[117] This is not to say that these efforts promoting women and gender in US State more broadly were not also translating into the Bureau, yet such emphasis on women in discourse was not visibly integrated into contemporary efforts within certain bureaus even within US State itself.

The Bureau also identified and sanctioned a list of foreign terrorist fighters (which included some women), who had their assets frozen, and travel to and within the US restricted. One example was Sally Jones (aka Umm Hussain al-Britani) of Chatham, UK, who converted to Islam to marry British ISIS fighter Junaid Hussain.[118] Jones "targeted American military personnel through the publication of a 'hit list' online encouraging lone-offender attacks;" she also used social media to recruit women to join ISIS and "offered guidance to individuals aspiring to conduct attacks in Britain on how to construct homemade bombs."[119] In September 2015, she was designated a "foreign terrorist fighter" by the Bureau, and she was eventually killed, reportedly in a US drone strike, in June 2017.

Women also featured largely in reference to CVE in diplomatic engagement and foreign assistance programs, where one key area of programming was "[e]nhancing civil society's role in CVE efforts, particularly among youth, women, and religious leaders."[120] This was done through the Global Women, Peace and Security Initiative, which invested $16 million in small grants across thirty countries from 2013 (although only a small portion of these focused on CVE, such as building community resilience in the Philippines in areas "vulnerable to extremism").[121] Compared to funding for security more broadly though, this amount was negligible. Evaluations and outcomes of these programs were also not often available, making it difficult to assess the impact they may have had. By 2015, US State's budget for CVE was $92 million, and this doubled to $187 million the following year;[122] nevertheless, it was not clear what proportion of programming focused exclusively on women as targets or recipients. There was also some noticeable effort by US State to better assess the roles of women in CVE, including the co-sponsoring (with USIP) of a July 2015 conference on women and CVE in Washington, DC.

While these efforts appeared to be positive, there were also several concerns that arose from women's expanding roles in US State and broader CVE efforts. Fink noted there were generally two fears that accompanied conflating women with counterterrorism or CVE practices, particularly in foreign contexts. First, by conflating the two practices, if security threats receded, women's empowerment programming could then be drawn down, where it should be considered a goal in its own right. The second concern had to do with the instrumentalization of women's empowerment: "Where women's empowerment is publicly associated with counterterrorism or CVE, it makes it easier for people to delegitimize those efforts as 'western intervention' or 'foreign values'. [For example,] the same people who bring you women's empowerment bring you drones."[123] Instead of convergence of these two fields, she highlighted how they should inform one another. So, even as women were increasingly emphasized in security discourses, there were very real concerns when implemented in practice. Programs could face budgetary re-evaluation, where funding could be facilitated or limited based on its perceived CVE contribution.

Ambassador Verveer also recognized that stereotypes of women were often purported in CVE: "when you get to CVE, you see very strongly this determination that the role that women play are very strictly gendered roles—women can do this, and that's what they do." She referenced these as a "mindset" that had to be changed: "I don't know how else to describe it, it is a mindset change that has to take place."[124] This also had to be supported by demonstrating the operational impact of women's inclusion. Some of the broader CVE conceptual and operational confusion was also tied back directly to UNSCR 1325. Ambassador Verveer noted:

> CVE is not really incorporated into the understanding of 1325 [...]. 1325 does affect this space as well, and we have got to do a better job of understanding how it fits in, and what we do about it. However, it is difficult because we hadn't exactly perfected what 1325 is about.[125]

Combined with the challenges related to defining what CVE was all about, UNSCR 1325 could not always be adequately considered or reflected in a field key to terrorism prevention. This was highlighted by both the practical and conceptual challenges in advancing or considering women in this growing field, which could directly reduce extremism that may lead to societal violence.

### CVE and the UN

This shift to consider women more expansively in CVE was also seen at the UN level, and had the potential to influence CVE at national and institutional levels as well. UNSCR 2129 (2013) on "Threats to International Peace and Security Caused by Terrorist Acts" started to make this link between women, peace and security and terrorism more evident. This resolution renewed the mandate of the UN Counter-Terrorism Executive Directorate, and reaffirmed the "intention to increase its attention to women, peace and security issues in all relevant thematic areas of work on its agenda, including in threats to international peace and security caused by terrorist acts." UNSCR 2195 (2014) on Threats to International Peace and Security, meanwhile, reaffirmed the need to "increase attention to women, peace and security issues in all relevant thematic areas of work on its agenda, including in threats to international peace and security caused by terrorist acts, and noting the importance of incorporating the participation of women and youth in developing strategies to counter terrorism and violent extremism."Yet, it was not until UNSCR 2242 (2015) that women were finally considered explicitly and expansively in counterterrorism and CVE terms: for example, in the Counter-Terrorism Implementation Task Force; in understanding drivers of radicalization for women; the impacts of counterterrorism strategies on women; how women can prevent and respond to violent extremism; and roles of women's organizations in developing counterterrorism and CVE strategies.

Discussing UNSCR 2242, Fionnuala Ní Aoláin critiqued these efforts to broaden UNSCR 1325 to counterterrorism efforts, which "brings with it real risks of creating greater insecurity and gender essentialism in the management of war, conflict and security for women."[126] She states that the efforts by proponents of women, peace and security around 2015, which sought to expand and bring women into the counterterrorism domain, "does not mean that women will be included in widening what constitutes terrorism and what counterterrorism strategies are compliant with human rights and equality, or that all the harms inflicted on women as a result of terrorism and counterterrorism strategies will be addressed even-handedly."[127] She further stated:

> [UNSCR 2242] should not be read as a remaking of this closed security space, rendering it gender-friendly and open to new ways of doing business; rather, it might prompt critical inquiry into how the interna-

tional security regime, and the states that support it, can derive legitimizing benefits from co-opting the WPS [women, peace and security] agenda to its operating framework.[128]

Finally, she questioned how the concept of women, peace and security would function as it addresses contemporary security concerns: "international security has discovered WPS, and it remains an open question whether this will serve the interests of women caught up in and affected by the new and ever-shifting battlefields of our age."[129] She highlighted the "necessity of the WPS agenda to speak directly to terrorism and counterterrorism imperatives, and not on the terms set by the CTC [Security Council Counter-Terrorism Committee] or individual states."[130]

In short, women were becoming increasingly emphasized in counterterrorism and CVE work both at the UN level and at US national and agency levels, in what may be considered a top-down approach to promoting women's involvement. What was not clear was how women on the ground who were living and experience terrorist violence, or who were on the front lines in challenging extremism in their community, could themselves feed into and inform this field's policies and practices (a more bottom-up approach). This also raised questions about whose security was identified and protected, and in what spaces. Could women who may have faced diverse security concerns define these within the present security paradigm? Or were they limited from themselves having sincere and meaningful influence in this sphere? This had significant implications for women's safety, status and impact on security, and highlighted that there were multiple perspectives and motivations behind women's inclusion in CVE in US State. At times, these appeared to clash, but weren't necessarily mutually exclusive. Regardless, the rising prominence of CVE expanded US State programming significantly, and efforts that emphasized women in relation were also increasingly visible.

## Terrorist groups and SGBV

The noted increase in SGBV perpetrated by jihadist groups that had become so visible under Boko Haram and ISIS thus became increasingly pertinent in discussions related to counterterrorism and CVE. The use of SGBV in conflict is not new, and has been visible in both intra- and interstate conflicts throughout modern history. These have ranged from World War II, as well as in Peru, El Salvador, Sierra Leonne, Liberia, South Sudan, Timor-Leste, Democratic Republic of Congo, Bosnia and Rwanda, amongst many others. In many instances, SGBV has been utilized as a systematic weapon of war. However, this concern had thus far not been as prevalent in areas prioritized in the GWOT. In Afghanistan, the Taliban's oppressive treatment of women, the lack of rights afforded to women and the violence (including SGBV) that they themselves inflicted on women was well-documented. However, the particularly systematic, direct and brutal SGBV inflicted on women (and in some cases men) by Boko Haram and ISIS raised this issue to a new level of concern. The issue of SGBV now directly became linked to the actions of terrorist groups.

This new focus on terrorist groups and their utilization of SGBV was well founded, as highlighted by the kidnapping, rape and forced religious conversion of over 300 girls in the Chibok region of Nigeria by Boko Haram. The sexual slavery inflicted on women by ISIS, particularly those of Yazidi descent, also proved a particular kind of horror. Over 7,000 Yazidi men, women and children were abducted, and ISIS had bought and sold women within these in "markets" as sexual slaves, assigning them different prices, trading them, and even giving them as "gifts" to fighters. They also regulated the treatment of Yazidi women, allowing for and justifying their rape and abuse in their publication *Dabiq*; they even regulated birth control for these women to maintain this sexual slavery.[131] ISIS also committed SGBV against men and sexual minorities, for example allegedly against Yazidi boys, or in their utilization of gang rape against new recruits.[132] While there were initial concerns that ISIS had been trafficking women for financial gain, this largely did not prove to be the case. Instead, its primary sources of income were taxations of the population, and revenues from the sale of oil and antiquities.[133]

The use of kidnapping, rape and sexual violence in conflict is something that has been studied at length, and highlights the multiple purposes SGBV can be seen to have for both state and non-state actors, as well as its implications for those countering these groups.[134] More generally, the likelihood of rape and other forms of sexual violence increases during wartime; both men and women can be both perpetrators and victims of rape, and the most commonly reported rape during war is gang rape.[135] Rape can also be used in ethnic cleansing and targeted at specific ethnic groups, to cause shame and humiliation amongst populations (including in family and social groups), and to encourage forced displacement from regions. It can also be directed by group leadership or more diffused to local leadership or even an individual level; sanctioned or discouraged; opportunistic or strategic; framed as revenge for sexual violence committed against one's own group, as an award for participation in a group, or to inflict terror in a population.[136] Goldstein has highlighted that in societies requiring "warriors," these often rest on particularly militarized notions of manhood, where domination of an enemy can be manifested in the form of sexual violence.[137] While this becomes more evident with terrorist groups, in limited cases this was also reflected by US troops, as seen in Abu Ghraib. Cohen has noted that in group dynamics, rape can be used as a socialization tool when intragroup cohesion is low, and that "bonds of loyalty and esteem from initial circumstances of fear and mistrust" can be built and rebuilt as perpetrators later recall the events, particularly when fighters are forcibly recruited into organizations.[138] It is evident that SGBV becomes extremely relevant for considering conflict today, including in relation to terrorism and responses developed to it.

However, what is important to note for this analysis is how beyond the inter- and intrastate conflicts where SGBV has most often been studied, there have more recently been large-scale and systematic incidents of SGBV—particularly with Boko Haram and ISIS—ranging from forced kidnapping and marriage, to rape and sexual slavery (amongst others). Yet, the wartime utility that SGBV has served for armed groups in other settings can mirror that of non-state actors such as jihadist groups. Wood has raised two important hypotheses that may be directly relevant to the cases studied in this book. First, when insurgent groups require support from the population—whether intelligence, supplies or so forth—they are unlikely to engage in sexual violence against civilians if there is a sound command structure in place. By focusing sexual violence on minority groups and committing such violence against Yazidis (whom they viewed as heretics), ISIS have attempted to circumvent this concern with the wider population as they attempted to gain support and influence (via fear and coercion) of local Sunni populations. Second, armed groups with a high proportion of female combatants are also less likely to engage in sexual violence. While women in ISIS are largely non-combatants, they represent a notable proportion of its affiliated persons in ISIS. This is particularly significant, as ISIS has framed itself as a state-building project which requires women at the core of this—raising the next generation of jihadists, supporting jihadist husbands, and providing gender-segregated public services to other women in areas such as health and education. Ahram also suggests that ISIS has deployed sexual violence "in ways that mirrors the states it is trying to supplant" in its efforts to construct alternative governing institutions and public services. That is, sexual violence has become intertwined with "Sunni fundamentalist, supremacist ideology, and the attendant notion of ethno-sectarian hierarchy," subordinating and degrading minorities, and reinforcing bonds between Sunni fighters.[139] As such, it is clear that SGBV must be accounted for in the tactics, strategies and operations of terrorist groups today, and integrated in responses to them.

Terrorist groups using SGBV as a tactic prompted it to be an essential aspect of prevention work, of active missions where front-line actors may come across these victims in the fields, and systematic approaches and support for these victims in stabilization and recovery efforts. SGBV was thus now folded into the GWOT and full-spectrum efforts to respond to these groups. This focus on responses to SGBV was supported by the 2012 US Strategy to Prevent and Respond to Gender-based Violence Globally, and was recognized at the US State level in testimony from Sarah Sewall, then Under Secretary for Civilian Security, Democracy, and Human Rights:

> The fight against Boko Haram requires more than just military action, it requires a comprehensive approach to improving the lives of people in Northeast Nigeria. Just as my portfolio at the State Department includes counterterrorism, law enforcement, democracy promotion, human rights, conflict response, criminal justice, refugees, trafficking in persons, and religious freedom, Nigeria needs to address all of these important, inter-related issues in its fight against Boko Haram.[140]

In testimony from Tom Malinowski, Assistant Secretary of the Bureau of Democracy, Human Rights and Labor, ISIS's persecution of

Yazidis was emphasized, as well as the horrific sexual violence being inflicted by the group.[141] Then Secretary of State John Kerry also noted, for example, "you ought to care about fighting ISIL, because ISIL is killing and raping and mutilating women, and they believe women shouldn't have an education. They sell off girls to be sex slaves to jihadists. There is no negotiation with ISIL; there is nothing to negotiate."[142] These high-level discourses extended into 2015 when Justin Siberell, the Principal Deputy Coordinator for Counterterrorism, noted: "Boko Haram shares with ISIL a penchant for the use of brutal tactics, which include public beheadings, stonings, indiscriminate mass casualty attacks, and systematic oppression of women and girls, including enslavement, torture and rape."[143]

It was crucial that such SGBV perpetrated by these groups was recognized and addressed in any holistic approach to security in these regions. How, why, and to what ends terrorist groups were utilizing SGBV in their activities had implications in everything from how to understand a group's strategies, operations and tactics, to challenging such groups holistically, to how communities and societies could best recover from such violence, and how partners could support and assist this. Yet, while the importance of recognizing the impact of SGBV on women from terrorist groups and the urgent need to address women who were victims of such groups was evident, it was not apparent if/ how this was tied to an emphasis on simultaneously recognizing how women could be supported as agents and actors in this space, or how holistic high-level counterterrorism approaches to these groups reflected these SGBV concerns.

## Women and gender in the 2015 QDDR

Now overseen by Secretary of State John Kerry (2013–17), the second QDDR published in 2015 continued emphasizing diplomacy and development as equal pillars alongside defense. However, now the QDDR was distinguished by its heavy focus on violent extremism, demonstrating the continued growth and emphasis of this concern. Linking development and diplomacy directly with CVE, it noted: "Diplomacy and development play critical roles in preventing, mitigating, and responding to threats such as instability within countries, inter-state and great-power conflict, and the spread of violent extremism in both stable and fragile countries." It further noted: "Additional adaptation and reform are required to enable State and USAID to meet the challenge of conflict and fragility within countries, and to address the underlying dynamics that fuel extremism."[144]

There were six specific lines of effort it identified for US State and USAID in terms of preventing and mitigating conflict and violent extremism: (1) CVE; (2) strengthening US and international capacity to prevent conflict; (3) preventing atrocities; (4) establishing frameworks for action in fragile states; (5) strengthening partner capacity to protect civilians and restore peace; and (6) eliminating the threat of destabilizing weapons. The 2015 QDDR also developed and expanded considerations of both women and gender uniquely in several ways. First, while women were again highlighted frequently throughout the document (with forty-nine references), as was gender (ten), the lesbian, gay, bisexual, transgender and intersex (LGBTI) community (ten references) was expanded on more than any other US government document thus far reviewed. In reference to defending human rights and promoting the inclusion of marginalized groups, there was an entire subsection focused on advancing long-term strategies to promote the rights of LGBTI persons, indicating both US State and USAID were reflecting a broadened understanding of diverse gender considerations across these agencies and their work.

The 2015 QDDR still highlighted the roles of women in addressing and ending conflict, and now also appeared to recognize women as having the potential to be extremist actors themselves. In referencing CVE messaging: "Our goal is to build a global movement offering positive, alternative pathways for vulnerable groups, especially youth and women." While it was unhelpful to mention women as a group as being "vulnerable" to extremist messaging alongside youth (as opposed to recognizing women may consciously choose to support such groups or that they may face circumstances distinct to those of youth), it demonstrated an increasing awareness of the roles women were playing in extremist and terrorist groups. Yet, as thousands of women had since traveled to join ISIS, with thousands more prevented, such sentiments rang too little, too late.

Practical examples of work by US State in this period included programs focused on women's empowerment in politics in Iraq, supporting Iraq's National Strategy and NAP on UNSCR 1325, and mobilizing Iraqi youth for peace in CVE and preventing violent extremism efforts.[145] US State's Bureau of Population, Refugees and Migration also ran women's centers that provided supports, services and programs, including psychosocial support for over 11,000 female survivors of SGBV.[146] The Bureau of Democracy, Human Rights and Labor also allocated $2.5 million for programs to support vulnerable populations, including survivors of SGBV, widows and female single-headed households.[147]

This second QDDR was highlighted by Ambassador Verveer in terms of the growing recognition that women and security had been gaining in US State:

> I think in the State Department there is a growing awareness about why this matters. When Secretary John Kerry began the process that Secretary Clinton had embarked on with the QDDR, he had just started on the second round, and made the strongest statements. If you read that QDDR, women and the integration of gender is integrated throughout that QDDR to the point that I had an official at the White House who had an embargoed copy say to me, "I can't believe how significant this is." I mean, it's there in full force. When Secretary Kerry went to announce that we are moving into the second review he said, "I want this to continue and be even stronger." So, there has been a strong push in this space, and you see it in a variety of programs.[148]

Calls to recognize women in CVE continued to emanate from the Office for Global Women's Issues. Ambassador Catherine Russell, Ambassador-at-Large for Global Women's Issues (2013–17), stated: "We cannot effectively counter violent extremist groups without engaging women."[149] However, it was not evident how this rhetoric related to integration of gender was significantly shifting US State approaches on the ground, or impacting the broader US CVE agenda in a way that reflected its discursive significance. In 2015, the February White House Summit on CVE was held in Washington, DC. With the new space and momentum established over the previous four years (that is, since the 2011 summit on CVE to advance women's concerns in the CVE space), it would be assumed that significant advances would be made to promote the roles of women. While there was notably a session dedicated to women in relation to CVE, broader themes on women and gender did not appear to be woven throughout the conference more expansively. From the perspective of Ambassador Verveer, "women really weren't on the agenda." This may be partially explained by the status of the Office of Global Women's Issues, which had itself been referred to within US State as a "pink ghetto" which had struggled to gain traction with the rest of the department, and where meaningful engagement of women in all aspects of CVE remained elusive.

There was a noted push to get women on the agenda for the September 2015 Leaders' Summit Countering Violent Extremism at the UN. However, within statements from US State at this summit, the advancement of their CVE efforts as related to women was not evidenced or promoted.[150] By the end of 2015, Ambassador Verveer acknowledged some significant concerns still persisted:

> You look at how we're doing counterterrorism: are we really adopting the best approach when your answer is totally the military, security approach, that is that classic approach? What role do women have in that space, being close to the ground, knowing what's going on, knowing not just how they're making impact, [but that] they are targets of terrorists in significant ways, whether you look at Boko Haram, or you look at ISIS, or whomever. [Women] are on the front line as targets. We're not incorporating women in a way that is not maternalistic, or that is a very gendered understanding of women, that imagines only certain roles that women can have. We're not expanding that, seeing a more holistic way in which they can operate.[151]

Ambassador Bodine also noted the shift towards focusing more on development, where CVE initiatives largely reside, was a work in progress: "It hasn't quite [fully] shifted yet, and the question is 'can we stay on this trajectory', or is our more latter-day predisposition to 'when in doubt, send in the SEAL team'? Will we revert to that? I don't know."[152]

### Al-Qaeda and ISIS: Alternative interpretations of women's rights and empowerment

The distinct language seen in US government discourses promoting women's rights, equality and empowerment were also increasingly being mirrored, responded to and reinterpreted by terrorist groups themselves for their own purposes, which in turn became factors that had to be assessed in responses to these groups. For example, al-Qaeda in the Arabian Peninsula (AQAP) in Yemen was increasingly reaching out to the English-speaking western world by drawing on the theme of women's rights, empowerment and dignity. Prior to the more overt emphasis of these in ISIS propaganda, AQAP highlighted some of the first significant emphases in Salafi jihadist groups on women's empowerment and rights. Women who were attracted to these groups could increasingly perceive these issues in the propaganda of these groups.

Discussing ongoing debates on bans on the wearing of burqas (as particularly seen in France at the time where Law of 2010–1192, an Act prohibiting concealment of the face in public space had just been passed) a 2010 edition of AQAP's online magazine *Inspire*, author Yahya Ibrahim noted: "The West is hiding behind a niqab of human rights, civil liberties, women's rights, gender equality and other rallying slogans while in practice it is being imperialistic, intolerant, chauvinistic and discriminating against the Muslim population of Western countries."[153] A 2014 edition of *Inspire* discussed a case of a US soldier in Iraq who was charged with the rape and murder of fourteen-year-old Abeer al-Janabi, and of four other US soldiers charged with the murder of her family in March 2006: "the American sordid soldiers violated honors of Muslim women, as they did in Afghanistan and more. The whole world heard and witnessed the rape cases. It is the same country that shouts, 'Women's rights! Women's rights!'" Other jihadist groups such as Jaysh al-Mujahidin and Iraq's Islamic Army dedicated actions, such as downing a helicopter, and the naming of missiles after al-Janabi in commemoration; Dhat al Nitayqayn—a female suicide bomber unit in Diyala Province—also named a new brigade after al-Janabi.[154] These groups also focused their own discourses on counterterrorism practices linked to human rights violations, and capitalized on these in their recruitment efforts and propaganda. Practices referenced included irregular renditions, illegal transfers of persons, and "torture by proxy," in which the US "transferred suspected 'terrorists' to other countries in 'black sites' in order to torture the suspects beyond the legal protection of the American law."[155]

The rape of Muslim women in conflict zones was a consistent theme in AQAP literature, often highlighted in critiques of the West and utilized in recruitment drives or calls for attacks against western targets.[156] While this theme of protecting women from rape had previously been engaged by al-Zarqawi in Iraq, bearing in mind that AQI had engaged in rape in the recruitment of female suicide bombers themselves, this appeared more to question the masculinity of men who failed to defend women and to urge them to restore their dignity by joining jihad.[157] This suggested that in AQAP discourses, human rights and women's rights were acknowledged, engaged and interpreted for their own aims. Yet, this did not necessarily appear intentioned to recruit women to AQAP as members, but more to mobilize men for fighting or justifying their actions as defenders or protectors of Muslims, and Muslim women in particular. Their emphasis on rape even echoed those in UN and US discourses and policies, which paid special attention to SGBV in conflict zones, highlighting gender-paralleled discourses between state and non-state actors, and the perceived legitimacy they hoped to gain through utilizing these gendered discourses.

ISIS also spent considerable effort, particularly after 2014, highlighting what it viewed as deficits of women's rights in the West, and offered its own interpretation of how women could regain their these in the so-called caliphate. However, this now shifted to attempts to recruit women themselves to join ISIS. These rights were framed in both classical terms, referencing rights of women from the time of the Prophet Muhammad and under classical interpretations of sharia law, and contrasted against those in secular countries. These discourses were often closely collocated with victimhood discourses, exploiting where Muslim women may have faced real or perceived discrimination or violations at home. Documents produced by ISIS demonstrated how the organization redressed women's victimhood through themes of rights and dignity. After ISIS published their first edition of *Dabiq* in 2014, they also discussed women's rights in contexts such as marriage.[158]

ISIS explicitly noted how they could support and protect women's rights: "Sunni women suffered throughout the Crusader-Shiite war when they were abducted and kidnapped, tortured, violated and murdered in many situations." However, as ISIS "fully undertook administration of the land, the people regained their rights, none more so than women." This was also extended to women's rights linked to human security, as purported by ISIS. In countries such as Saudi Arabia, women were viewed in terms of victimhood, which ISIS claimed they could redress: "In the Gulf, social security is an artificial arm that is not sufficient, with many instances of poverty, misery and sadness for families, especially harming vulnerable women."[159] For ISIS, these governance/structural failings were highlighted as a "push" factor for women, whereby the group felt they could redress women's social security concerns (a "pull" factor) to promote female recruitment to ISIS and fulfill its governance aims.

There was an alternative discourse pertaining to women's rights being purported by these groups. This at times mirrored, though challenged, US discourses, and was indeed embraced by some who joined or supported the organization. These included western "deviances" such as "feminism" and "sodomy." In a lengthy article entitled "The Fitrah of Mankind and the Near-Extinction of the Western Woman," ISIS emphasized these specific aspects of western culture as "corruptive" and key ails to be escaped. It noted of *fitrah* (human nature):

> Fitrah continues to be desecrated day by day in the West and more and more women abandon motherhood, wifehood, chastity, femininity, and heterosexuality, the true woman in the West has become an endangered creature. The Western way of life a female adopts brings with it so many dangers and deviances, threatening her very own soul. She is the willing victim who sacrifices herself for the immoral "freedoms" of her people, offering her fitrah on the altar of secular liberalism.[160]

ISIS suggested that aspects of western politics, and freedoms such as feminism, or women's or LGBTI rights, were harmful for society, particularly women. This binary of western rights for women versus those offered by ISIS under its interpretation and implementation of "governance" extended to its justifications for their treatment of Yazidi women. Through their own twisted religious interpretation, they attempted to justify enslaving and raping Yazidi women, which in their eyes was demonstrative of their reincarnation as prophetic *sunnah* (teachings, sayings of actions of the Prophet Muhammad). They saw their efforts as providing women with certain rights under Islam which could not be achieved through "pacifism, negotiations, democracy, or elections." In fact, for one woman who became a slave and converted to Islam, they purported she "found in Islam what she couldn't find in *dar al-kufr* [land of unbelievers], despite the slogans of 'freedom' and 'equality.'" They even contrasted this behavior with prostitutes in the West who "sell their honor", and scoffed: "then her [Yazidi] enslavement is in opposition to human rights and copulation with her is rape?!"[161] As such, ISIS too proved active in engaging, challenging and reinterpreting women's rights discourses to justify their own horrific activities (up to and including human slavery) in their governance efforts.[162]

Women and supporters in al-Khansaa Brigade's media wing also framed their roles in ISIS in contrast to western notions of rights and feminism. In a manifesto by the group, they noted that many women have been driven away from their true role because of gender equality in "free societies" and "liberal states." This was attributed to "the rise in the number of emasculated men who do not shoulder the responsibility allocated to them towards their ummah, religion or people, and not even towards their houses or their sons, who are being supported by their wives." They noted that the failed western model that "liberated" women from the house led to women adopting "corrupted ideas and shoddy-minded beliefs instead of religion, sharia and the methodology of life that was ordained by God." Indeed, there's no need to "flit here and there to get degrees and so on, just so she can try to prove that her intelligence is greater than a man's," but women should instead focus on their role in the home. They also highlighted activities women were allowed to carry out, such as studying "the science of religion and as female teachers or doctors."[163]

The above examples suggested several important points. First, not only were these groups conscious of western gendered discourses specific to women, but when contraventions of these stated women's rights occurred (for example, rapes by US soldiers, or violations related to niqabs), they had a particular salience and role in the propaganda, recruitment efforts and calls for action by its members or supporters. Furthermore, ISIS were taking efforts to reinterpret and challenge these shared discourses to justify their own practices. In other words, their engagement and reinterpretation of "rights" and "empowerment" were used both for recruitment purposes and to justify horrific practices such as SGBV and human slavery. This also draws attention to the increasingly mirrored discourses related to women in these areas by both state actors and Salafi jihadist groups. This was particularly relevant as AQAP and ISIS started evolving and engaging in state-building practices and establishing "caliphates," at which point they had to appeal to a wider constituent of potential members and supporters, including women. It also raised important questions about how in their own elaborate and detailed governance structures, they too engaged with western discourses and policies, particularly those that reflected development aims specific to women. If such points were not recognized or adequately responded to in counterterrorism efforts (including aspects like CVE, counter-narratives or stabilization work), then there would indeed be a critical gap in how efficient these efforts could be. However, it was not evident in US State if or how these discourses were recognized or responded to.

*Final points*

As the primary department for carrying out US foreign policy abroad, US State was evidently going to consider women most expansively in its efforts; as such, women appeared in every category, from security actors like police, to women in the community and family in CVE efforts. Yet, this scope was also supported by US State's long institutional history focused on women's programming and status, as seen with the President's Interagency Council on Women and the Office of the Senior Coordinator for International Women's Issues. These were established off the back of the 1995 UN Fourth World Conference on Women in Beijing, where women's rights and status were a key concern, suggesting that UN norms had had a long and evident degree of influence in US State.

Soon after 9/11, women were most visible as targeted recipients of US State programming, which emphasized women's rights and empowerment in society, as well as governance and democracy efforts. These had been emphasized by President Bush as important foreign policy concerns for both democracy promotion and addressing the drivers of terrorism. Drawing on the example of MEPI, Yemen was highlighted as a country which lacked a strong central government accountable to its people, and where the status of women generally was among the lowest in the world. As such, women's political empowerment, illiteracy and job training became prominent themes in MEPI programming in Yemen in particular. MEPI also highlighted some of the broader agency concerns of US State in this period, where attempts were made to keep its funding distinct from conflation with post-9/11 counterterrorism-specific efforts. Yet, recognizing that such efforts contributed to reducing the frustrations of a population and additional threats from radicalization, many of these programs in Yemen were instead often directly framed through their contribution to CVE, where women's programming appeared to be instrumentalized. In fact, in numerous cases it was suggested that this framing—that is, how the program contributed to CVE—was required to maintain support and funding from Washington. Yet, this trend of trying to avoid conflation with counterterrorism, while framing efforts as counterterrorism-relevant to maintain support for them, led to efforts by the US more broadly being perceived as counterterrorism-centric, where counterterrorism work associated with defense appeared to subsume other streams of work (such as development). By 2007, US State was also increasingly aware that it was not adequately engaging half the population in its counterterrorism-specific community engagement activities, and thus the Office of the Coordinator for Counterterrorism started drafting its first internal strategy for women's engagement. To gain support from this office in US State, it was emphasized how women's engagement had to be framed in terms of its contribution to operational effectiveness.

President Obama had also emphasized democracy promotion (also referred to as "US values") alongside efforts to address underlying grievances which may contribute to increased extremism, and thus similar streams of effort continued. However, three significant factors under Obama impacted how women were engaged by US State. First, the 2010 NSS now framed women's security as a matter of national security, raising its prioritization on the national agenda and in US foreign policy. Second, the appointment of Hillary Clinton as Secretary of State, a noted "women's champion," further drove these efforts in US State, as seen in the 2010 QDDR, a review she launched aimed at making civilian power more streamlined and efficient. The QDDR emphasized women and gender to an unprecedented degree in all US State and USAID activities, and raised the status of women's concerns in all aspects of "smart power." Lastly, the 2011 executive order in relation to the NAP on Women, Peace and Security also required concrete plans from key departments, including US State, and this appeared to be readily embraced and expanded upon.

The subsequent implementation plan and annual updates demonstrated how US State efforts were increasingly expanding to areas specific to counterterrorism, such as discussing the protection of women in counterterrorism efforts with partner governments, or building the capacity of "women in civil society and security sector to help prevent the spread of violent extremism."[164] Women became increasingly visible in prevention, reconciliation and reconstruction efforts, and as security actors in US State programs and initiatives, as was seen in Syria. Between 2011 and 2017, there were increased efforts to engage women in counterterrorism-specific efforts to promote women's roles, from partner training to capacity building and civil society engagement. However, the implementation of these efforts was noted to be inconsistent across US State in different countries, and was impacted by everything from the funding and prioritization of efforts in each location, to the personalities of various ambassadors themselves. Finally, the newfound emphasis on CVE opened new avenues for US State to consider and engage women in their efforts. Yet, CVE work also appeared at times to in fact reinforce gendered stereotypes of women in some cases (for example, women as stabilizing influences). There was also a lack of conceptual clarity as to what CVE was, how it should be applied, and bureaucratic pressures to always be seen to establish and advance counterterrorism or CVE efforts, even if this labeling may ultimately prove unhelpful or even counterproductive.

US State also demonstrated extensive interagency efforts and coordination with both DoD and USAID. As the second agency of focus in the QDDR, it appeared that US State and USAID worked in closer coordination on efforts related to women and security; however, even as there were numerous interagency efforts and interactions discussed with DoD, it was not starkly evident to what degree US State was influencing DoD efforts in relation to women's roles in counterterrorism efforts, or vice versa, though efforts like the Iraqi Women's Engagement Program (a joint US State–DoD program) suggested that such influence was occurring. In fact, it appeared that US State had been limited in leading US foreign policy concerns, where defense considerations took precedence (as seen in the case of Yemen). It was also not apparent whether the Office of Global Women's Affairs and the Bureau of Counterterrorism and Countering Violent Extremism (both housed in US State) had enough significant interaction to have extensively informed women and gender concerns in US State counterterrorism and CVE programming. Furthermore, while specific terrorist figures such as Sally Jones were recognized and sanctioned by US State, with both al-Qaeda and ISIS framing their efforts in terms of how they too were supporting and protecting women's rights it was not evident that significant emphasis was placed on recognizing or responding to women in relation to these groups, except when they were sanctioned terrorist actors. As with the US, al-Qaeda and ISIS would increasingly draw on similar discourses of women's rights and even SGBV (albeit in their own twisted terms), which had to be accounted for in responses to the group.

# 5

# THE US AGENCY FOR
# INTERNATIONAL DEVELOPMENT

"Despite the events of September 11, and the fact that we have no diplomatic relations with the Taliban, and despite their refusal to hand over bin Laden and dismantle al-Qaeda, our humanitarian assistance policies will not change. Food aid distribution will be based on need. The President has made this very clear. Accomplishing our humanitarian objectives under the current circumstances is a huge task, but I am confident that, if we follow the President's strategy, we can save many, many lives and help Afghanistan begin to rebuild itself."

USAID Administrator Andrew Natsios, 10 October, 2001[1]

The US Agency for International Development (USAID) is the lead government agency in efforts to end extreme global poverty and enable resilient, democratic societies.[2] Although an independent organization, this agency and its Administrator operate under the direct authority and policy guidance guidance of the US Department of State (US State) and coordinates closely with it due to the US State lead on US foreign policy. This contributes to a unique (and at times contentious) interagency relationship that has evolved greatly over the years. USAID has numerous supporting sectors with it, including promoting democracy, human rights and governance; working in crises and conflict; and economic growth and trade, amongst numerous others. In 2015, USAID operated in one hundred countries globally, employed just over 9,400 persons and had a budget of just over $27 billion, making it the smallest of the three bodies examined in this work.[3]

USAID evolved substantially in relation to post-9/11 coordination and efforts abroad, in part due to their increasing alignment with US foreign policy and security objectives. The agency became increasingly active and elevated in contributions to broader indirect counterterrorism strategies over the years, particularly in addressing underlying conditions or drivers of terrorism, such as grievances, poverty and political participation; aid could also be used as a "carrot" or "stick" to try to influence the actions of recipient governments. This drove much debate about the value of development and aid in and of themselves, where some argued that the instrumentalization of USAID's work for foreign policy objectives was bringing new challenges and risks.

As an agency, USAID also appeared to have the most nuanced approach to women and gender in its discourses and programming, which was seemingly informed by its focus on gender throughout its history: since the 1973 Percy Amendment to the Foreign Assistance Act, it has been a requirement for gender to be incorporated into all US governmental development efforts; this was followed in 1974 by the establishment of the Women in Development Office. Subsequent efforts saw the release of the "Women in Development" policy paper (1982), and a supplementary Gender Plan of Action (1996). Throughout the 2000s, other efforts were made to assess the status of gender integration in areas such as USAID planning, procurement and solicitation so as to continue to progress their development. This was also demonstrated in the 2009 Automated Directives System, where gender analysis became "mandatory in the development of strategic plans, assistance objectives, and project-level analyses,"[4] as well as in the 2011 Foreign Service training carried out by USAID, amongst several other efforts.[5] As such, it is clear that USAID has long considered gender across its policies and programming, which became evident as USAID increasingly contributed to efforts specific to countering violent extremism (CVE). However, as will be demonstrated, this did not always occur in an even and systematic fashion.

Of the three agencies discussed in this book, USAID was the one that initially viewed work which emphasized women in programming in the most peripheral terms in relation to security. Instead, women's status was generally discussed more indirectly, addressing underlying conditions and grievances in society. Yet, women became increasingly apparent in several categories related to broader counterterrorism efforts between 2001 and 2017, including women's rights, empowerment and equality; their roles and status in the community; the private sphere; victimhood; and as extremist actors. Their roles appeared to evolve in USAID based on several factors. First, as reflected in US national discourses and a "whole-of-government" approach, development efforts became increasingly emphasized in comprehensive approaches to security, and its work was therefore increasingly framed in relation to national security priorities. There was also an increase of civil-military cooperation in stabilization and reconstruction efforts in environments such as Iraq and Afghanistan, or in more contributory motions to support counterterrorism objectives, as seen in Yemen. In these cases, USAID focused on areas such as women's health, literacy, participation in governance and employment training. These remained a key focus between 2001 and 2017, yet how they were framed in relation to security evolved over that time. Second, the Quadrennial Diplomacy and Development Review (QDDR) of 2011 marked a turning point in how development became elevated to the realm of "high security" alongside diplomacy and defense, meaning USAID had to assess and delineate how its programming contributed directly to national security objectives. Third, as CVE gained prominence, this longer-term, preventative focus dovetailed with USAID programming based on enduring conflict prevention efforts. USAID also proved to be the agency with the most nuance and history in relation to assessing "gender" and "women" across all its programming, resulting in increased "gender analysis" as these shifts took place (although not always in uniform ways).

According to Huckerby, there were four diverse ways in which USAID programs contributed to counterterrorism: (1) those explicitly designed for CVE; (2) USAID activities with the US Department of Defense (DoD) in "kinetic or active combat" (for example, Iraq and Afghanistan) and "non-kinetic environments" where the US had a counterterrorism or counterinsurgency (COIN) objective (for example, Yemen); (3) programming that contributed to mitigating environments which may enable terrorism; and (4) those that do not state a counterterrorism or CVE objective for fear that "this could undermine the project's efficacy."[6]

While USAID efforts with a link to counterterrorism and CVE in numerous countries between 2001 and 2011 have already been expanded on well by the NYU Center for Human Rights and Global Justice—and will be drawn on throughout this section[7]—this chapter will differentiate and expand on this work by offering additional detail and analysis of efforts in Iraq, Afghanistan and particularly Yemen, and consider activities up to 2017. It will demonstrate how women were categorized in USAID discourses and what key factors impacted these. There will be a particular focus first on USAID's role in stabilization and reconstruction work in Afghanistan and Iraq, before looking at development and security in Yemen. In this earlier period, women's programming was not usually expressed explicitly through consideration of counterterrorism or extremism. Instead, as will be demonstrated, the agency's work focused more overtly on how its contribution to reducing the drivers to extremism, and more explicit work on CVE, represented a significant shift for the organization. Furthermore, several key changes took place between 2011 and 2017—for example, democratic transitions in some regions as driven by the Arab Spring, and a rise in extremism and instability in others as driven largely by ISIS—which have thus far been neglected in the literature in relation to USAID. Finally, this chapter will outline how terrorist groups such as al-Qaeda and ISIS have expanded on "women's programming" in this period, and how USAID acknowledged and responded to this.

## Development moves into the security space

After 9/11, there was an increased focus on the links between security and development. This book will not wade into the many debates concerning this, which often center on the interrelationships between these two fields (what comes first, security or development? How do they interact and advance in active conflict operations?).[8] Instead, it will demonstrate how specific development concerns in relation to women in areas such as education and health became progressively incorporated into security and defense efforts, and increasingly carried out alongside DoD in countries prioritized in the Global War on Terror

(GWOT). Moreover, counterterrorism was also increasingly considered in various streams of USAID work. For example, addressing terrorist financing had been a key priority following 9/11, particularly in terms of funding acquired through non-governmental organizations (NGOs) who may directly or indirectly support terrorist groups. In 2002, USAID established the controversial Acquisition and Assistance Policy Directive 2–19, which required that applicants for USAID assistance certify they did not "provide material support or resources for terrorist acts,"[9] thus demonstrating early (albeit limited) areas of overlap between counterterrorism concerns and USAID. That same year, the Office of Conflict Management and Mitigation was also established, which addresses "causes and consequences of violent conflict, supports early warning and early response to violent conflict, and integrates conflict mitigation and management into USAID's analysis, strategies and programs."[10] USAID's work throughout this period was often framed in terms of its recoverability or preventative contributions to conflict, which over the years was increasingly linked to counterterrorism, COIN, stabilization, reconstruction and CVE.

While gender empowerment had been a key aspect of USAID's work for decades, 9/11 acted as a catalyst for informing how gender and development more broadly would interact with security discourses. Susan Markham, USAID's Senior Gender Coordinator for Gender Equality and Women's Empowerment (2014–17), noted several interactive aspects which contributed to these increased considerations of women in wider security discourses at the time:

> If you look at the 2000 Millennium Development Goals [MDGs], obviously that coincided with 9/11 and this rise of the fight against terrorism. It was destined that this issue of gender empowerment, which we really tried to cut across all of the MDGs, would be brought up naturally at some point when we faced other issues. Whereas before 2000, even though there was the [1995] Beijing Conference, there wasn't this international pressure for gender empowerment. It was almost the timing more than a proactive attempt to "make gender part of it." It's more that gender was coming up more in every discussion we were having in development, diplomacy and defense.[11]

This latent interaction between global discourses and actions focused on women's rights and empowerment emerged in a world where terrorism had taken center stage, interacting with new ideas and proposals to challenge it in US efforts. However, its emphasis was more coincidental and ad hoc as it became increasingly considered. How these interactions between women's rights, empowerment and responses to terrorism would appear in practice were not initially evident in USAID. In 2002, an agency brief noted it supported the GWOT in two primary areas: (1) reconstruction needs in countries most impacted by counterterrorism campaigns; and (2) through "better governance, effective employment generation, and better basic health and primary education services."[12] These areas were viewed as long-term efforts to support broader security objectives, yet how this unfolded in practice was often more complex.

Alongside women's empowerment, Harborne noted that development and poverty reduction was also a larger trend in this period, while foreign aid became viewed as "part of the terrorism solution." Development aid was understood as "providing a critical instrument for engineering the behavior of both state and individual." At the geopolitical level, this focus was aimed at "preventing or shoring up failed states" and at the micro level at winning "hearts and minds," particularly in COIN efforts.[13] Early endeavors in Afghanistan did not generally discuss women's status in work in relation to extremism. In one rare 2002 example though, USAID Senior Counselor James Clad noted: "When aid for Afghan women's welfare ceased, an important social buffer against extremism also disappeared,"[14] suggesting an inherent understanding that conflation of development work with countering extremism was best avoided in policy language. Nevertheless, such statements still demonstrated that women as empowered actors in society were seen to act as bulwarks against extremism. Throughout the Bush administration, USAID largely focused on women in terms of empowerment and development, with this work supportive of, though seemingly largely separate to, direct counterterrorism efforts. As such, its link to countering extremism was not initially emphasized.

In development aid efforts linked more overtly to countering terrorism, women were emphasized in terms of their contribution to state stability, good governance and projects seen to improve the lives of those in conflict environments. However, there were also growing concerns from NGOs and aid workers after 2001 about the increased role of the military in relief and development efforts. As COIN took an increasing role in countries like Iraq and Afghanistan, the military aimed to gain local support through "hearts and minds" campaigns. Howell, however, was critical of this approach: "Military personnel have appropriated the language of development, civil society and rights to dilute their militarism and to gain support locally."[15] Many of these concerns extended to USAID in key countries in the GWOT, where increased attention on women-focused programming risked this perceived conflation between military and aid/development efforts, including by women's civil society groups and actors in the countries of focus. Yet, in some conflict zones, it was also increasingly difficult for USAID to operate, where either partnering with DoD, or indeed having DoD themselves carry out some of this work, was the only way to deliver aid and programming to those that needed it most.

USAID also increasingly attempted to better understand the evolving contexts they were operating within to refine country programming, where growing incidents of extremism were increasingly impacting their work.[16] This could be seen in their 2005 report "Conducting a conflict assessment: A framework for analysis and program development," which noted that 60 per cent of countries USAID worked in were being increasingly affected by violence, extremism or state failure, suggesting ways its interventions could play a part in prevention or how "development assistance can be used to manage the causes of violence."[17] These "new war" scenarios they were operating in included "[c]hild soldiers, gender-specific atrocities, extremist ideologies, and the targeting of aid workers."[18] Women's recruitment and mobilization by insurgent and militant groups was acknowledged here, with the report noting, for example, how Nepalese women had gained a level of authority and respect by joining the Maoist insurgency, or how Tamil insurgents offered financial incentives to women when their husbands had been killed.[19] Women's roles in civil society were also recognized: "Donors should give particular consideration to locating and supporting organizations that cross ethnic, economic, or political fault lines such as women's groups or community development associations that explicitly engage members of different communities in order to address common problems."[20]

This highlighted several points that informed USAID's considerations of women in relation to security in this early period. First, there appeared to be nuanced, gendered considerations of the impact of conflict on women (particularly sexual and gender-based violence [SGBV]), thereby reflecting broader themes such as those seen in United Nations Security Council Resolution (UNSCR) 1325. Second, women's recruitment by extremist or insurgent groups was acknowledged, though was only made apparent when women were militant actors. While understanding women in insurgencies was and still is important, many US bodies had not considered women's roles in terrorist groups such as al-Qaeda (a key government focus at this time) or in contexts specific to the GWOT. Third, it suggested that women's groups were generally viewed as mediating bodies, often able to overcome many of the cleavages wrought in conflict settings. Finally, as USAID was increasingly operating in areas affected by war and extremism, they had to increasingly understand and recognize how this impacted their own work, and thus account for it accordingly, particularly in work focused on conflict prevention.

On the back of this, early warning systems linked to state instability were developed. This was seen in the 2005 Conflict and Fragility Alert, Consultation and Tracking System, which noted male and female life expectancy and literacy rates as areas to look at when assessing state fragility, as these were particularly linked to the provision of social services and perceived state legitimacy.[21] This increased focus on development's role in conflict prevention and management also impacted civil-military relations, as seen in the establishment in 2005 of the Office for Civilian-Military Cooperation in USAID, for example. This office acted as the primary point of contact between USAID and DoD, synchronizing efforts through personnel exchanges, policy development and training. Despite this, as will be demonstrated, it was not always evident that USAID's history with gender programming translated across or informed other agencies.

Foreign assistance itself also evolved over both the Bush and Obama administrations, particularly efforts to better integrate and streamline development efforts across various agencies. For example, in 2006 the position of Director of Foreign Assistance in US State was established (which was equivalent to a Deputy Secretary position)—a role that would serve concurrently with that of Administrator of USAID, and the person who would coordinate with other bodies such as the Millennium Challenge Corporation.[22] The aim of this position was to provide "leadership, coordination and strategic direction within the US Government and with external stakeholders to enhance foreign assistance effectiveness and integrate foreign assistance planning and resource management across [US] State and USAID."[23] It would also help better prepare diplomats to "think creatively about the integration between development, diplomacy, democracy and security."[24]

This "transformational development" was noted to make foreign aid more prominent in supporting US security efforts, and act as a "tool to promote national security."[25] This suggested two noteworthy points. First, that USAID would not just deliver aid in areas most in need (an ongoing trend), but instead had to increasingly start determining in which contexts it could more effectively support US foreign-policy objectives where security was a primary concern. Second, the agencies it was coordinating with in this work also saw important changes. Both US State and USAID were asked to start thinking about their roles in contributing to security, while at the same time DoD was increasingly assessing its role in humanitarian efforts. It was clear here that foreign assistance as it related to national security efforts was evolving, and that USAID was moving into an area it had limited prior experience, also mirroring similar circumstances faced by US State and DoD. At the same time, all three were increasingly expected to coordinate with each other to support US security objectives.

There was also visible effort by USAID to better understand the varied roles of women in conflict, as reflected in the Bureau of Conflict Management and Mitigation and its 2007 guide "Women and conflict."[26] This Bureau aimed to "provide technical leadership on conflict, instability, extremism and now terrorism and insurgency to Missions and our Washington bureaus." In this guide, USAID noted it would "aggressively expand its development and implementation of programs mitigating the causes and consequences of conflict, instability, fragility and extremism." It also assessed how conflict and fragility could increase gender inequalities, and would design programs "building on the strengths of women." Women were understood in complex terms: they could be "agents of change; active participants (combatants); supporting participants or shields (forced or voluntary camp followers, cooks, wives, slaves, etc.); victims and spoils of war; and newly responsible care providers."[27]

Women's roles as "agents of change" and "peacemakers" were also recognized, and their inclusion was justified in terms of improving the effectiveness of various interventions: "When they are not active participants, the views, needs and interests of half of the population are not represented, and therefore interventions will not be as appropriate or enduring." Furthermore, USAID noted that conflict could indeed have positive impacts on women's status in society, such as increased social and economic responsibilities, which could lend to financial independence and changes in divisions of labor. In terms of programming, USAID highlighted key areas to focus on, including women's protection; increased participation in decision-making; women's roles in conflict resolution and peace; job training and employment; state policy; and women's legal rights.[28] USAID appeared to have the most advanced and nuanced understandings of women and conflict of the three institutions, which was first demonstrated in its stabilization and reconstruction efforts in Afghanistan and Iraq.

## USAID in Afghanistan and Iraq

The USAID development program in Afghanistan was the most extensive since the Vietnam War. When the US went into Afghanistan in 2001, USAID was asked to increase its country staff from one hundred to 400, and to support a massive military operation in ways it was both underprepared for and inexperienced with. USAID's aims at the onset of the conflict in Afghanistan included supporting the recovery, rehabilitation and political processes in Afghanistan in the post-conflict environment, which included a focus on areas such as "infrastructure, food security, economic development, democracy and governance, education and health."[29] Addressing the needs of Afghan women and girls as part of broader US stabilization and reconstruction efforts proved to be a significant focus in the country. Between 2003 and 2010, Congress had appropriated approximately $627 million to DoD, US State and USAID to carry out this work, focused specifically on women and girls.[30] Even from the outset of the war, however, how these stabilization efforts unfolded was deeply problematic and had specific implications for programming focused on women in practice. Two of the themes that became apparent in Afghanistan were the tensions between different actors in this work and their objectives, which evolved as the conflict in Afghanistan did: these ranged from counterterrorism objectives in the 2002–03 period, to reconstruction, stabilization and counter-narcotics, COIN and capacity building. Programming that focused on women would feature distinctly in how they were viewed as contributing to these objectives, and could thus be emphasized or de-emphasized accordingly.

This focus on women was visible as early as December 2001, when USAID Administrator Andrew Natsios highlighted that one area they would focus on was women as teachers. He noted that two-thirds of teachers were women, and thus a good way to "reintroduce women in a visible way into Afghan society would be through schools [...]. That would be very useful in terms of making a statement about women's role in Afghan society." This was also seen to improve the status for minors, as women are noted to be more likely to feed their children and assist their family when they came into extra income.[31] As such, USAID played a significant role in Afghanistan, where one of its key goals was "promoting a voice for women in Afghan society."[32]

In 2006, USAID resources for Afghanistan were $700 million, which rose to $2.1 billion by 2010. During this time, there was also an emphasis on gradually transferring the responsibility and development of USAID-funded programming to Afghan partners.[33] Women's rights developed as a cross-program emphasis, particularly in health and education. For example, the 2005–10 USAID strategy in Afghanistan noted: "USAID/Afghanistan has built gender-equity elements into every aspect of its program. It has formulated strategies and activities based on an analysis of how they affect both men and women, girls and boys, and it is making extra efforts to alter the deplorable status of women in many communities and institutions."[34] Furthermore, there was a 50 per cent target for program funding to be focused on women. Ambassador Verveer noted of the USAID Initiative to Promote Afghan Civil Society: "We are also committed to allocating at least fifty percent of the grants to female-led or female-focused organizations. The challenges remain significant, but our commitment to the women of Afghanistan must not wane."[35] One example of women-specific programming at the time included the Afghanistan Women's Business Federation to support female entrepreneurs.[36] However, differing levels of violence around the country impacted where such work could be implemented. For USAID, it became impossible to function in highly insecure areas where its staff would be at risk; and although the DoD workforce would carry out some tasks in highly insecure areas it was operating in, it lacked a strong gender-specific lens in its work (as was highlighted in Chapter 3).

There also appeared to be a lack of overarching strategy related to how this women-focused work could be integrated into an overall vision for Afghanistan. Even with this focus on women in USAID programming throughout its time in Afghanistan, it was noted in a 2005 review of USAID work: "in spite of significant support for Afghan women at the highest levels of the US administration, no coherent strategy to support Afghan females was developed by OTI [Office for Transition Initiatives]. OTI programming related to women consisted of mostly small, seemingly haphazard projects."[37] Even with an emphasis on women inherent throughout all USAID programs, how this was integrated and coordinated into a larger strategy in the country was viewed as problematic. Local organizations, such as the Agency Coordinating Body for Afghan Relief, highlighted local grievances, such as aid focused on insecure areas or those with high levels of poppy cultivation, which created "perverse incentives." Military actors who were delivering aid were also noted to lack development knowledge, including principles concerning local ownership or long-term support for community maintenance.[38] Aid and military actors were also viewed as operating in tension with each other, which could negatively impact cooperation and coordination in programming that may emphasize women. Discussing 2002–03 efforts in Afghanistan, Des Roches noted: "When we were trying to do development work on the military side in the case of Afghanistan, USAID were not quite hostile to us, but at best, grudgingly acquiescent." Women's empowerment efforts were also often engaged in Taliban propaganda, which could raise concerns from a defense perspective and also highlighted implications for other US partners operating on the ground.[39]

Such concerns extended beyond programs that focused predominantly on women, yet still had implications for programming, including which regions of the country may prioritize women's issues along-side aid more generally. Gender knowledge that may have been more evident in USAID and development work would also be lacking in areas where the military was undertaking development work—namely, the most insecure areas of the country, where women were likely fac-ing compounded concerns. This also raised important points about the balance and coordination between immediate security requirements and long-term development aims.

As Afghanistan was increasingly viewed as an insurgency, the rela-tionship between military COIN efforts and USAID humanitarian efforts became increasingly emphasized, but these did not seamlessly occur in practice. It was recognized that weak governance was being exploited by violent insurgents, and local communities were being marginalized in broader reconstruction efforts (particularly where government reach was lacking).[40] Yet, aid agencies were increasingly trying to distance their work from military activities, as this "close association with ISAF [International Security Assistance Force] and the Afghan government undermined perceptions of their neutrality and independence;"[41] others felt that civil-military and humanitarian guid-ance was overridden by COIN concerns.[42] From a defense perspective, this was attributed by some to USAID following a "pure" humanitarian agenda which was distinct from other US governmental interests; from a development perspective, aid work associated with military activities could negate things like community buy-in and trust.

That a significant portion of USAID funding was earmarked for women's empowerment was also regarded with some degree of incre-dulity by some in defense: "It sounds nice in Congress, but there wasn't the capacity to absorb it in Afghanistan," noted Des Roches.[43] Concerns related to the capacity of organizations in Afghanistan to effectively utilize and apply this funding on the ground was a wider concern that extended beyond women-specific programming. Yet, the tensions between aid and military actors also suggested that USAID and DoD may not have been operating as closely as was required to achieve their stabilization aims. Furthermore, bearing in mind that DoD was increas-ingly engaging in development work in highly insecure areas that aid workers could not access, not working as closely with USAID risked the gendered knowledge inherent in its development programming becoming less likely to translate to the areas where women would likely need it most.

Despite being restricted from the most unstable areas, USAID's staff also faced physical security risks while in Afghanistan. This was seen in 2012, for example, with the death of Ragaei Abdelfattah, who had been working with the Afghan government to develop an industrial park in Nangahar Province. Abdelfattah was killed in an explosion on 8 August 2012, en route to a meeting at a provincial governor's compound, along with three coalition soldiers and an Afghan national.[44]

This friction was noted up to 2009—eight years after the US had entered Afghanistan—when the country's "surge" strategy was announced, and DoD, US State and USAID committed to a stabilization strategy utilizing a "whole-of-government" approach that became more integrated and synchronized in practice.[45] Stabilization work also became more cognizant of its relationship to countering both the insurgency in the country and the growing levels of extremism. The stabilization strategy announced by US State invested in and advanced the rights of Afghan women, and was noted to help "strengthen Afghan communities' capacity to withstand the threat posed by extremism," creating economic benefits for the country. Key initiatives were focused on "women's security; women's leadership in the public and private sector; women's access to judicial institutions, education, and health services; and women's ability to take advantage of economic opportunities, especially in the agricultural sector;"[46] however, these areas of focus largely overlapped with those of USAID.

Programming within the various departments and agencies continued to emphasize women throughout this period. Between 2011 and 2013, DoD, US State and USAID reported spending $64.5 million on 652 projects, programs and initiatives to support Afghan women; however, due to a lack of effective mechanisms for tracking funding associated with broader projects, real figures were unclear.[47] In 2013, USAID made the largest single investment to advance women globally, with their Promoting Gender Equity in National Priority Programs Initiative (otherwise known as "Promote"). Promote was valued at $216 million over five years; it aimed to reach 75,000 women, and improve their access to jobs through training and other support, increase their access to education, and empower women who wanted to work in government. However, security concerns were noted to hamper the implementation of this program, and its sustainability was unclear, most notably for the long-term prospects of job opportunities for women in the country.[48] Moreover, it was difficult to measure the overall success of the program, and Afghan women were noted to be inadequately consulted in the implementation of the programming.

Women's welfare and aid was still rarely framed in terms of its contribution to CVE or counterterrorism, but was increasingly becoming an evident focus for USAID in stabilization and reconstruction efforts, particularly in how it could reduce drivers of the insurgency. However, in a review of stabilization work in Afghanistan, it was noted that efforts to buttress insecure and contested areas in Afghanistan between 2001 and 2017 "mostly failed." This was due to an overestimation by the US of its abilities to build and reform government institutions within its larger stabilization strategy.[49] Programming that focused on improving the status of Afghan women could be seen as one casualty of this failed stabilization work, even as some cases of successful programming were seen, and overall the status of women in Afghanistan did improve in this period.

*Iraq*

In Iraq, USAID played a significant role in stabilization and reconstruction efforts, including a focus on infrastructure (until 2006), health, education, community development, local governance capacity building, economic development and other development activities. Due to Iraq's security situation, USAID faced several concerns related to operating on the ground; despite this, it still carried out its work. Early on, their work was largely seen through the Community Action Program, and its scaled-up version, the Community Stabilization Program, which increasingly focused on women (although this too was not inherently linked with counterterrorism efforts). Between 2003 and 2005, allocations managed by USAID in Iraq peaked at $4.8 billion.[50] The Iraq Community Action Program (June 2003–March 2007) carried out activities such as training women in business skills management; building women's centers; improving facilities, training and healthcare for women (including 2,000 new jobs for women in this sector); and supporting 60,000 women and girls through the Marla Ruzicka program for unintended victims of the actions of coalition forces. USAID reported that programming focused on women's skills and job opportunities reached 180,000 beneficiaries, and that ten specialized women's centers supported 11,351 women.[51] Between May 2006 and October 2009, Community Stabilization programs saw $648 million spent to support USAID and Iraq's Strategic Objective 7—"Reduced incentives for participating in conflicts in selected communities." This represented its largest cooperative agreement to date, thus highlighting the importance of USAID in conflict prevention efforts.[52] Still, women were not initially a key focus of the Community Stabilization program, although this evolved over time.

Women and female youth participated in USAID programming in Iraq. including in youth conflict resolution programs, business grants programs, and vocational training courses in areas such as cosmetology or cell phone repair.[53] USAID noted that these training and employment services aimed to have women represent 30 per cent of participants;[54] yet as the insurgency worsened, programming for women in real terms only increased from 8 to 18 per cent between 2006 and 2008, when it was recognized that "many of these women were destitute with children—especially young boys—who would be prime recruits for insurgent activity." It was also noted that city programs that helped widows were "a quick way to reduce local suspicions about the project being a military operation and to gain wider community appreciation once the number of female suicide bombers (many of them widows) became a strategic concern in late 2008."[55]

Several important points became evident. First, by drawing USAID into stabilization efforts, they could now access funding and implement programming on a significant scale; this was important in helping ensure humanitarian and development concerns were addressed in US activities in the GWOT. Second, women's programming, while helping to improve the prospects of Iraqi women, could also be seen to mask military operations, which was particularly controversial. Finally, it pointed out that women's roles as suicide bombers further drove this effort to engage women, and that the increased numbers of widows were correlated with youth at risk of joining insurgencies. These efforts were framed in terms of stabilization and conflict prevention, and also more quietly understood to reduce terrorist threats and drivers of the insurgency. In some locations, there appeared to be increased tension from bringing humanitarian and military efforts closer.

In USAID efforts up to around 2008, women were focused on largely in terms of stabilization and reconstruction, but more specifically in relation to employment, governance, health and education. While such work was certainly admirable, it was noted by Des Roches that in these COIN environments this was not always aligned with broader efforts: where there was a "humanitarian agenda, and a military/security agenda—they should operate in tandem." However, USAID often "pursue[d] a humanitarian agenda in isolation from government," or humanitarian achievements outside those to explicitly advance government interests.[56] As Zuhur (a professor at the Strategic Studies Institute) noted of Iraq, women's issues were also often viewed as secondary to security or state-building concerns:

> It is as if the US Government planners are cognizant of women and "women's issues" as a component of social and political development and democratization, yet they do not fully recognize women's or gender issues as constituting a vital element of "security" or the "security environment." Women are extras on the set, not lead actors.[57]

While USAID had a strong understanding of gender in development work, they were not always seen by partner agencies as aligned in joint efforts in reconstruction and stabilization. There were also critiques that USAID's areas of focus were viewed as relevant to, but still outside, primary security efforts.

### Development to support counterterrorism objectives in Yemen

Differentiated from Afghanistan and Iraq in that the US was not "at war" in the country, Yemen proved a unique example of how development assistance focused on women was more overtly linked to counterterrorism aims, as evidenced in the choice of program locations and the framing of programs in counterterrorism terms. While some of this governance and democratic programming has already been discussed in the previous chapter in relation to efforts by the Middle East Partnership Initiative (MEPI), who USAID also partnered with, this section will expand more specifically on women's health and education initiatives carried out by USAID to demonstrate how what were initially viewed largely as development and aid activities became increasingly framed in terms of their contribution to undercutting extremism in the country.

Yemen's USAID office reopened in 2003, and noted that one of its crosscutting themes in terms of programming was "improved services and opportunities for women and girls." Yemen remains classified as one of the worst countries in the world to be a woman, and also arguably faces the most consistent and severe political and development challenges of any country in the MENA region.[58] Between 2003 and 2008, USAID focused primarily on four areas. The first was "governing justly and democratically", which included "enhancing women's participation" and tribal conflict mitigation programs, which also focused on the roles of women and youth as local peacekeepers. The second area was investing in healthcare, with maternal health given specific consideration. The third was investing in education, and included "improving education, especially for women and girls." The fourth was "creating economic opportunities," particularly in agriculture and herding. These efforts were centered on the five "remote, very poor, rural governorates most at-risk of generating political instability and providing possible refuge for terrorists."[59]

The five governorates of Al-Jawf, Ma'rib, Sa'ada, Amran and Shabwa had been identified for these efforts due to concerns from "inter-tribal conflicts, tribe-state conflicts, and al-Qaeda presence." It was also noted: "Populations in highly needy and unstable areas must experience a direct impact on their daily lives, see improvement in their communities, and perceive state institutions as responsive to their needs in order to develop an active stake in their futures and communities."[60] The 2009–12 Yemen strategy highlighted five crosscutting themes to be incorporated into all its programming. It noted these would "be key to addressing drivers of instability [...]. Each of these themes can serve as sources of conflict mitigation, stabilization, and longer-term development." The themes were youth, gender, good governance, institution building and natural resource conservation.[61]

This strategy indicated three things in Yemen in relation to women. First, development aid since 2003 had been considered and framed to some degree in terms of how it could contribute to US counterterrorism objectives in Yemen, particularly in terms of location choice for programming. Second, both gender and improving the status of women were considered inherently within these, with the latter linked to tackling broader instability in the country. Third, programming was developed and delivered on a very local level, and had to be visible to the population to have a direct impact on improving their lives, which stood in contrast to national-level schemes in the country in areas such as security (where such impact was not always visible).

Another important factor to impact these discourses and practices was the shift in the role of USAID itself in relation to US foreign policy, where development was now increasingly perceived in relation to security objectives. Ambassador Thomas Krajeski (2004–07) noted that previously:

> USAID was almost an independent organization, independent of US policy, and they were supposed to help the poorest of the poor, the sickest of the sick, and they really didn't give a damn about what the US Ambassador wanted to do in Uganda, or what the US policy was in Yemen. They were there to inoculate children and prevent children from dying—that's not the case anymore. For a long time now, our aid policy is overall directed by our primary US strategic goals in a country, which in the Middle East is almost always focused on counterterrorism and counter-violence, and basic stability.[62]

USAID was having to adapt to this new direction, and the US' new emphasis on foreign policy and national security in relation to counterterrorism. Yet, in some cases, development work had already been contributing to counterterrorism efforts in indirect ways. Ambassador Krajeski offered an example where development work had directly helped undercut al-Qaeda in Yemen, thereby facilitating counterterrorism goals. Discussing a sheikh in Ma'rib who had previously allowed al-Qaeda to train in his territory and had a history of kidnapping foreigners, Ambassador Hull, Krajeski's predecessor (2001–04), had a discussion with the sheikh to address this concern:

> What the sheikh wanted was a health clinic, specifically a birthing clinic, for the women in his region. Women were dying in childbirth and he wanted training for midwives, ultrasound machines for sonograms, and trained people to know how to use these. So, we did that, we built the clinic, we trained the people [...]. [We also] built another wing on a local school, as well as a girl's toilet. One of the reasons girls

were unable to go to this school is that they didn't have a separate toi-
let, so we took care of that. We also trained women teachers. We did
this to educate women, and try and reduce death in childbirth, but we
also did it because the sheikh stopped kidnapping people and stopped
supporting al-Qaeda, because he got these things. It was really transactional, and that's the way I wanted to keep going, and that's what I kept
fighting for. However, it always had to be with a focus, and again, not
just the humanitarian effort, and development work which does have
the bigger impact in the longer term, it was very much transactional in
relation to security.[63]

This illuminating example highlighted how work supporting wom-
en's development concerns could latently interact with counterterrorism, in this case acting almost like a bargaining chip or even a currency.
It also demonstrated how locals may indeed exploit or manipulate
counterterrorism concerns to gain services desperately needed where
general governance shortfalls existed. It also highlighted an almost
inverse consideration: instead of responding to terrorism-driven concerns by engaging development activities as a solution, the provision of
these services may have initially undercut support for al-Qaeda, as seen
through the need by this sheikh to gain resources through kidnapping
or the provision of land to al-Qaeda. For Yemenis such as this sheikh,
who sought to address development needs for his community, demonstrating his support for al-Qaeda may have actually assisted in having
these concerns addressed, thereby creating perverse incentives.

This link to counterterrorism was also explicated in diplomatic discourses (notably by those who often had to compete for programming
funding) from Washington. In 2005, Ambassador Krajeski stated:
"USAID's overall goal is to support USG [US government] counterterrorism objectives by helping to develop a healthy and educated
population with access to diverse economic opportunities. By improving health, education and family income, USAID helps reduce the
country's vulnerability to extremist ideas." USAID was noted to have
had limited Economic Support Funds for programming, so had leveraged this by partnering with other US governmental agencies and
programs, including MEPI (US State) and DoD,[64] thus highlighting
agency limitations and innovation to pursue funds and advance development programming. Some specific USAID activities that partnered
with the DoD in Yemen included renovating schools and health clinics,

and providing community medical and veterinary services. Ambassador Krajeski noted the DoD, through the Coalition Joint Task Force—Horn of Africa, had provided over $1.2 million for civilian affairs projects and humanitarian assistance over the previous year. In 2005, specific programs had included "visits by USG military doctors and veterinarians, which provided examinations and treatments to 3,000 people and 22,000 livestock. Projects also included the refurbishment of five schools in Sanaa, Aden, and Sa'ada, as well as two clinics in Taiz and Aden." This work was directly framed in both responsible governance and extremism prevention terms: "Helping the ROYG [Republic of Yemen Government] meet basic infrastructure and development needs strengthens the relationship between the population and the government, and reduces the community's susceptibility to extremist ideas."[65]

In Yemen, though not officially classified as a COIN environment, the DoD was also increasingly coordinating with USAID in areas like women's health, thus reflecting similar efforts in Iraq and Afghanistan. Des Roches, who was the Director for the Gulf and Arabian Peninsula Office of the Department of Defense (2010–12) and viewed Yemen through a COIN lens, noted that there had been "decades of failed COIN, and decades of failed development, and sometimes the development [was] counterproductive."[66] This COIN lens was largely due to the six Houthi wars that had raged in the country from 2004–10, causing growing human suffering and destruction of infrastructure in the northern Saada Province, while also increasingly challenging President Saleh's regime.[67] Notably, one of the Houthi grievances outlined as motivation for the first conflict was Saleh's counterterrorism cooperation with the US. Also notable is that by the later rounds of conflict, US-trained Yemeni counterterrorism forces were in fact being used to tackle this domestic conflict.

If the US was going to continue to operate in Yemen, Des Roches believed there had to be positive work done as well or the tactical mission would fail. Having learned some COIN lessons from efforts in Afghanistan, how these were translated to Yemen was noted to have improved delivery: "At this time, we were getting a lot better at cultural sensitivity, so we didn't have to deal with it in Yemen the same way we did in Afghanistan, which was initially a disaster." These civil-military efforts increasingly supported or carried out development work focused on women, such as maternal health, which was viewed as a COIN investment. Des Roches provided some practical examples of this DoD work alongside USAID:

> We had a limited amount of development assistance which was used as an adjunct to tactical aid, and generally the greatest impact you could make was in women's health. Things like fistula as a result of childbirth, or just child-birthing practices in general, that's a very low-cost area and a great way to get results [...]. Focusing on women's issues was a very cost-effective way to make an impact. There wasn't much else we could do—we could do veterinary programs, drill wells, but women's health was a big issue.[68]

For those in Special Operation Forces (SOFs) in Yemen, with limited budgets dedicated to development work, maternal health was an area that was viewed as both economical and high impact. Des Roches noted in particular of treating fistula: "You only need one set of expertise, one set of specialized equipment, and it's usually an area that is very underserved." Reflecting on his time in Afghanistan, he noted: "I personally spent more time on women's issues in Yemen than in any other country [...]. Women's health was a big issue, and I know it's a big focus for USAID. In Yemen, USAID's programs were very effective." This was due in part, he suggested, because of the close relationship between the SOF and USAID in Yemen: "It also seemed that in Yemen, USAID was more integrated with the military than anywhere else I've seen. Primarily, it was because the military operation there was so small it was run out of the embassy, as was USAID, on different floors of the same building."[69] Yemen was thus able to provide an example of interagency cooperation between DoD and USAID, where both COIN/security and development concerns were being addressed simultaneously and seemingly effectively. However, this was largely due to the unique operational environment and shared headquarters, which seemingly facilitated interaction and cooperation between the agencies.

In 2009, Yemeni military figures had also requested increased USAID assistance, specifically programming for job creation. This was driven in part by a dual concern of the emergence of al-Qaeda in the Arabian Peninsula (AQAP) alongside a worsening employment situation and a growing youth bulge. This funding was specifically requested by Major

General Mohammed al-Maqdashi, Regional Commander of the Yemeni Armed Forces Middle District, who said that Ma'rib's worsening unemployment:

> Played into AQ's [al-Qaeda's] hands by making tribal leaders more susceptible to entreaties by AQ operatives flush with cash; it also made youth recruitment easier in the absence of employment alternatives. Maqdashi pleaded for additional USG [US government] development projects in Marib and stressed that security and development went hand-in-hand.[70]

While USAID had funded a vocational institute in Marib City and numerous primary and secondary schools, this also suggested that such efforts indeed had a practical impact through indirect means on counterterrorism aims, even if not widely stated as such. Moreover, it further emphasized the preventative nature of aid in some cases related to counterterrorism concerns.

Other USAID programming, such as road repairs, was also framed in terms of its dual aid/security purpose: "USAID partners are also rehabilitating roads in underserved areas. The roads improve access to services and markets for 39,000 residents of 80 villages while preventing isolated safe havens that can be exploited by militants."[71] USAID funding in Yemen in 2010 (other than humanitarian assistance) had grown to $77.6 million, which had included "crisis-response contingency allocations from Department of Defense Section 1207 resources ($10 million) and USAID's Complex Crises Fund ($12.8 million). These resources have been critical for USAID's capacity to operate flexibly and effectively throughout the country,"[72] noted Christa Capozzola, Deputy Assistant Administrator for Democracy, Conflict and Humanitarian Assistance. This also reinforced this problematic necessity to frame programs in terms of counterterrorism benefits to access funding.

With the growing emphasis on interagency security and stabilization efforts, Section 1207 funding between 2005 and 2010 allowed up to $100 million annually to be transferred from DoD to US State for "reconstruction, stabilization, and security activities in foreign countries" in global efforts. In 2007, it was noted that this funding in Yemen "sought to promote stability by assisting in areas where the central government is largely absent in order to deter youths from joining terrorist groups,"[73] highlighting the direct perceived impact of development work and increasing interagency counterterrorism efforts (and funding). By 2010, however, Section 1207 funding authority had expired.

However, kinetic counterterrorism activities also impacted on broader US efforts in Yemen, including USAID programming. 2003 marked the first drone and air strikes against AQAP in Yemen and a marked shift away from ground operations. Ambassador Seche noted the impact this shift had on areas such as US development work in the country:

> I think we all felt it was having negative impacts, nobody thought that this was a benign activity, or that this was neutral in anybody's eyes. You could say it was an essential element in our counterterrorism toolbox, but if you were anywhere near the receiving end of this, the question would be, "What are you talking about? You wanted to do development work to improve our lives, and yet you're sending in these missiles?"[74]

This had negative implications for how US development efforts were perceived by Yemenis, noted Ambassador Seche:

> It puts a lie to the messaging we were sending, that we really want to be a development partner with you. Yet drone strikes become the headlines, and everything else is subsumed under that headline where it becomes, "oh yes, we still are a good development partner for you, don't forget that."[75]

Yemen proved to be an important example of how women's development efforts could positively impact security and stability. Nevertheless, there were still restrictions that diplomats faced on the ground, potentially forcing them to frame programs in their contribution to countering terrorism in order to maintain funding and support. Yemen also demonstrated a unique case of some successful cooperation between USAID and DoD, particularly due to the intimate US government facilities in country. Yet, it also demonstrated the delicate balance which could be easily upset when these distinct streams of effort (particularly direct or kinetic defense efforts, and indirect development efforts) appeared to operate at counter-ends.

### Countering the drivers of insurgency and violent extremism

There was a broadening understanding that while poverty was not equated directly with a person's propensity to terrorism, development efforts assisted in reducing societal frustrations or grievances which may increase the salience of extremist appeals for some, including through areas such as strengthening governance. USAID and other government partners had appeared to be aware of the thrust and contributions of development programming to address the drivers of conflict and extremism since the early 2000s, yet it appeared that such relations were often left unlabeled or discreet in some operational environments, while remained emphasized in others (such as Yemen). This focus on CVE, particularly in assessing and mitigating the root causes and "push" and "pull" drivers of extremism, became increasingly visible in USAID work and in counterterrorism-specific partnerships.[76] The role of "push" factors were defined by USAID as the "characteristics of the societal environment that are alleged to push vulnerable individuals onto the path of violence." "Pull" factors were noted to be the underestimated "appeal of a particular leader, self-appointed imam or inspirational figure, or the material, emotional or spiritual benefits which affiliation with a group may confer."[77] When looking at USAID work which contained a focus on CVE, there were four explicit ways this became distinguished from traditional development aid: "the source of funds for the development activity; the basis on which project beneficiaries are identified; modalities for the design and implementation of programs; and the monitoring and evaluation tools used."[78] This section will now look at some of the cases where USAID's work had a more overt link to counterterrorism, and where it started focusing more pointedly on the drivers of extremism and CVE.

## Trans-Sahara Counterterrorism Partnership

One rare and early example of USIAD's extension into counterterrorism efforts was working alongside DoD and US State in the Trans-Sahara Counterterrorism Partnership (TSCTP). This program was preceded by the Pan-Sahel Initiative (established in 2002), which focused primarily on training and equipping counterterrorism forces in the region. This was expanded to include public diplomacy and development assistance in 2005 with the establishment of the TSCTP.[79] The TSCTP had a $230 million budget between 2005 and 2007 across nine countries.[80] USAID noted it had been "committed to TSCTP since its inception in 2005, working to define how development assistance can most effectively be used to contribute to long-term peace and stability."[81]

In 2009, in Senate testimony in a session examining US counterterrorism priorities and strategy across Africa's Sahel region, Senior USAID Deputy Administrator for Africa Earl Gast highlighted that violent extremism was impacting the US's ability to improve governance and create opportunities. This work with TSCTP focused on identifying the drivers of violent extremism, where "root causes" such as poverty were identified as "just one of many factors that contribute indirectly to radicalization in Africa."[82] Others assessed in USAID work included socioeconomic drivers, political and rights deficits, corruption and broader cultural threats. This informed the agency's work, which was now focused on four areas: (1) youth empowerment; (2) education; (3) media; and (4) good governance. Gast noted: "These findings are critical to our policy and programming decisions and will inform what interventions will be the most effective toward preventing drivers from spiraling, how to monitor our progress, and how to integrate counter-terrorism concerns into our future efforts."[83] This is noteworthy as it highlights early consideration of how counterterrorism work would impact on USAID programming.

In practice, this work with TSCTP meant USAID focused their work on "maintaining low levels of violent extremist threat in Chad, Niger, Mali, and Mauritania by reducing the drivers we identified through activities that strengthen resiliencies and communicate messages among at-risk groups." Gast further noted: "Unlike traditional development programs, our counter-extremism efforts, when necessary, target narrow populations that generally aren't reached by other programs. We also specifically reach out to young men—the group most likely to be recruited by extremist groups."[84] This suggested that young men would be the primary focus of USAID efforts in this region and during that period, and that CVE-specific programming would be more specifically targeted based on perceived risk from extremism.

The TSCTP had faced several critiques for its lack of comprehensive, integrated strategy to guide program implementation between partners, what authorities participating agencies had, and fluctuating funds (particularly for USAID). Perhaps most importantly, USAID and US State were both noted to not actually have mechanisms or indicators to measure programming outputs, specifically how these reduced violent extremism.[85] This is a problem which remains in CVE work today: how do you measure success, particularly in the prevention space? How can you determine or measure a negative—that persons don't in fact join a violent extremist group, support its ideology, or carry out actions on behalf of a group or ideology? It was also not clear how USAID reflected gender considerations in its programming design; for example, ensuring both male and female youth were involved, or what salience this had for CVE results.[86] It was suggested by a USAID employee that in these civil-military interactions, even if gender considerations and the roles of women were being encouraged and integrated throughout USAID's own activities, "the extent to which they were taken up depended on the individual decision-maker in the field."[87] This also reflected a theme seen in DoD and US State: in interagency interactions, the personalities on the ground could directly impact the extent to which policy guidance was implemented in practice.

*Programming directed at the drivers of violent extremism*

While USAID was now contributing more directly to some counter-terrorism-specific efforts, it was not evident what measurable outcomes this was producing. It was also unclear how USAID's history with gender considerations in its programming was translating to these new efforts, where, in fact, it appeared early programming focused most dominantly on males. Critiques such as those highlighted in the TSCTP, and its experience in other locations that were being impacted by extremism, appeared to encourage USAID to identify how its programming contributed to CVE in more practical terms.

In 2008, USAID tried to better assess terrorism and extremism in the fields they operated in. They also considered women more in relation to terrorism and extremism, and developed a framework for strategy and program development entitled "Guide to the drivers of violent extremism" so they could conduct a terrorist or extremist assessment. The framework aimed to develop a profile of at-risk populations; understanding recruitment and motivations for joining organizations;

organizational factors; trends and scope of the nature of the threat; and programming implications. Their analysis considered gendered questions such as: "Are males or females over-represented among violent extremists? (If so, why might that be the case?)" and "are women playing a more active role?"[88] As USAID started conducting assessments explicitly for terrorism and extremism, it appeared that women were becoming increasingly considered in these. From 2008 onwards, USAID began to play a more active role in direct relation to counterterrorism and CVE, and appeared more poised for, and cognizant of, gender considerations in these efforts.[89]

This could also be seen in its 2009 "Guide to the drivers of violent extremism" and the 2009 publication "Development assistance and counter-extremism: A guide to programming."[90] Here, USAID's gender lens became more visible in relation to CVE, although in particularly limited ways. In the "Guide to the drivers of violent extremism," women and gender garnered some attention in the form of, for example, women who converted to Islam. Al-Qaeda in Iraq (AQI) suicide bomber Muriel Degauque was referenced to highlight the potential of women to adopt particularly conservative views, or to consider women's personal motivations for joining and supporting such groups. Gender was featured once in the 2009 "Drivers" guide as a characteristic to be aware of in assessing at-risk populations: "What are the most common characteristics (if any) of those being recruited: age range; gender; socio-economic status; level of education; employment patterns; ethnic, clan, tribal or religious affiliation; residence and geographical origins?"[91] Extensive gendered considerations were not assessed at length in terms of the drivers of violent extremism, but reflected DoD terrorist assessments where gender was considered one of many factors to be cognizant of in extremist profiling. This shortfall in assessing gender and women's roles specifically as USAID moved further into the security space was stated to be linked to two broader shifts that were occurring in USAID at this time, namely that gender analysis in its programming was being strengthened throughout this period, and that the agency increasingly framed its work in terms of national security. The NYU Center for Human Rights and Global Justice noted that despite these two shifts, gender analysis was not extending to CVE programs as it should, and that these two areas were not sufficiently intersecting at the policy or analysis level.[92]

However, by the 2009 "Development assistance and counter-extremism: A guide to programming," women and gender roles became more visible. For example, gender was seen as a characteristic to consider when identifying which populations may be particularly vulnerable to extremism and why. Cultural threats where Islam was viewed as being "under attack" were noted as the most significant driver of violent extremism in majority-Muslim countries, where feelings of incursion in "sensitive areas such as gender roles and education—can be a powerful motivation for engaging in violent behavior." In project design and implementation, it suggested a gender rights program may want to shape itself in religious terms, where implementing this "within the frame of rights granted to women within Islam might change the activities and how they are implemented and articulated but could also generate more support, less hostility and greater impact." Development responses in cultural programming were instructed to "avoid interventions—especially in such sensitive areas as gender roles or the content of education—which local populations easily may perceive as efforts by external forces to impose certain values on them."[93] This highlighted the concern that women's rights and empowerment work was seen as a sensitive area of programming, and a point of contention and distinction between the West in some of the countries USAID was operating in. Furthermore, it noted how these issues had to be better assessed and responded to in local contexts. Programming was encouraged to be cognizant of local gender dynamics, and if it was viewed to impact on or discuss gender roles, it should be avoided. This may inform why this gender angle was initially more limited in programming discourses related to counter-terrorism and CVE.

## Development becomes a core pillar of US security

The 2010 QDDR (discussed at length in Chapter 4) marked an important shift for USAID, where development was now elevated alongside diplomacy and defense as an equal pillar of security (or "smart power") to tackle global threats such as terrorism and violent extremism. This also previewed what would become another important shift in USAID discourses and practices, where development efforts became increasingly framed in terms of their contribution to security more broadly, and CVE specifically. USAID had already adopted a significant reform agenda called "USAID Forward" in 2010, which aimed to reform and innovate the agency's approach to development, focusing on partnerships (particularly local partners), innovation and results. Now with the QDDR, USAID's work would be contributing directly to US national-security objectives: "The development perspective must also be incorporated throughout US foreign policy decision-making. To ensure this broader policy role, USAID will have a consistent seat at the policy table on critical foreign policy challenges and contribute its development perspective to policy debates on national security in other forums."[94] Part of this new effort would be USAID working more closely with US State:

> As the United States elevates development, the Department of State's diplomacy is changing to reflect development's appropriate status by raising development issues from *low politics to high politics*. When a Secretary of State advocates as fiercely for food security and women's rights at the U.N. General Assembly as on proliferation of nuclear weapons [...] we improve lives in ways that reinforce almost every aspect of US foreign policy.[95] [emphasis mine]

Development was now elevated to the realm of "high politics"—a matter seen as having existential importance for the state, as it governs its very survival, and is often associated with military, diplomatic and security efforts. This was particularly significant language that indicated development was now viewed as an effort vital to US national security.

The 2010 QDDR marked an important juncture for USAID. By elevating the agency as an equal pillar of foreign policy, it previewed two shifts. First, USAID would have to become more cognizant about how their programming would directly contribute to key foreign policy issues such as terrorism and violent extremism, instead of more complimentary efforts. Second, with this historical emphasis on gender analysis already discussed, and advanced understanding of women in relation to conflict in all aspects of their programming, gender considerations would be (suggestively) inherent in terms of USAID'S contributions to US national security. The QDDR also noted: "USAID will enhance emphasis on programs to address trafficking in persons, gender-based-violence, and women, peace, and security."[96]

## THE US AGENCY FOR INTERNATIONAL DEVELOPMENT

The 2011 National Action Plan (NAP) had also focused substantially on USAID, with fifty-three actions highlighted where USAID was a significant implementing partner. Many of these related to CVE and were shared alongside US State, including action points to "[s]upport the participation and leadership roles of women from all backgrounds [...] in countering violent extremism efforts."[97] However, some were specific to USAID, such as providing updated guidance for US government partners on SGBV in humanitarian assistance programming; counter-trafficking efforts and training; and training Disaster Assistance Response Teams to protect women and girls in conflict. Many of these efforts for USAID focused on women in terms of sexual violence, and echoed UNSCR 1325's concerns related to women in conflict. The 2010 QDDR and 2011 NAP had solidified USAID's roles in US security efforts, and this continued to expand in CVE and COIN in particular, albeit with several visible tensions and shortfalls.

### Development and CVE: Gaps and debates

USAID increasingly framed their responses and programming in direct relation to CVE, but this also highlighted a number of debates and implications specifically centered on what work should be labeled CVE. Moreover, how did the agency distinguish CVE and counterterrorism in the minds of recipient populations, and what did this mean for their interagency work? In 2011, USAID established "The development response to violent extremism and insurgency" policy, which began to highlight these concerns. This foray into CVE was noted to have brought greater institutional and operational risk, but the development response was recognized as "part of a broader USG effort" in CVE and COIN. Furthermore, this was emphasized in contributory terms to counterterrorism:

> This policy does not directly address counter-terrorism approaches based on intelligence, law enforcement and military assets; other [US government] departments and agencies are generally better placed to engage in such counterterrorism programming. However, USAID's development response to violent extremism and insurgency contributes to counterterrorism goals by mitigating the specific drivers that encourage the use, advocacy of, and support for violence.[98]

There were concerns that having USAID programming labeled as counterterrorism could increase security risks for the agency's staff. As such, development workers were often active in distinguishing these streams of effort. Markham emphasized the distinction between CVE and counterterrorism and the implications for practice:

> We talk about CVE and not counterterrorism, this is key. Certainly, we don't want to put any of our colleagues or partners in the field who are doing immunization, education, or economic growth into harm's way because it may be thought they are trying to secretly infiltrate the community. We are trying to provide development, but we are also trying to look at what the drivers of extremism are.[99]

This was a point echoed by the NYU Center for Human Rights and Global Justice, who noted that the GWOT "does not occur in a vacuum, and that indelibly impacted how communities perceive the United States and their willingness to cooperate in the [US government's] current 'soft' counter-terrorism measures."[100] Even while trying to keep these areas distinct, direct or kinetic counterterrorism actions were still likely to impact on development actors who were trying to mitigate extremism. Yet, for better or worse, Markham noted that women's empowerment was often viewed as a "safe" area of programming in countries where counterterrorism may be perceived particularly negatively, emphasizing a benefit of separating the two: "we are oftentimes allowed to do work in areas such as women's economic empowerment, political empowerment, agricultural work that seems non-threatening to the government."[101] Even in terms of conflating US counterterrorism or CVE work with other programs (for example, ones that focused exclusively on women's empowerment), Markham stated: "I think women's empowerment is oftentimes the last to be put into the CVE world," suggesting that this area was viewed as the one most detached from the kinetic counterterrorism programs that are often the locus of criticism. This was due, in some cases, to the significant use of local implementing partners, where a "US face" was not necessarily put to the forefront in the programs, or an avoidance of labeling the initiative as CVE.

It was also not always clear when an existing or new program should be considered CVE, pointing to another challenge USAID faced as it moved into this field:

> I think there is a deliberate lack of clarity to protect the people and the process, but there is also a lack of conceptual clarity. There are also very good realpolitik reasons why things are not called CVE. That contributes to questions around: what should I be doing? Is my program a CVE program or is it an education, or women's empowerment program?[102]

This remained a concern up to 2017, whereby counterterrorism and CVE could at times prove unhelpful labels for those working on women's rights, empowerment and development, and where counterterrorism initiatives could also be conflated with CVE. There was continued debate about what constituted a counterterrorism or CVE practice. This extended to academic and practitioner spheres as well, particularly noting the interactive and fluid relationship between these wherein preventative efforts directly fed into and impacted the incidence of violent extremism.

Even as the field was starting to place more emphasis on a CVE approach, key programs that could assist in empowering women (such as education) were not necessarily recognized for the contribution they were already providing to CVE aims, or were simply acknowledged for their value in and of themselves. There was an increased risk that these programs would have to emphasize a CVE angle to remain relevant or access resources. However, being conflated with counterterrorism or CVE labels may in fact put these programs or participants at risk.[103] Markham pointed to specific cases where the use of a CVE label may be appropriate (such as programs in an area at significant risk of extremism) while in others such a label may be far less helpful (for instance, promoting tolerance in groups or communities).[104] However, for the populations targeted by this programming, there was also a concern that public awareness of this distinction between counterterrorism and CVE was not always present.

Other debates also extended to resources, which USAID could potentially now access, albeit if framed in security terms, poising it for competition between other government bodies. Mosbacher Morris of US State noted:

> I don't want to argue that government-related programming should never have some sort of security component or some security-intended outcome. What I don't recommend is people working in development trying to inflate a security element, because then you get into poten-

tially trying to access security-related resources for development purposes, instead of making a case for why a development program has to take place in a community and how that will have positive ramifications in itself.[105]

This also highlighted how even as USAID was trying to access more funding for its work, this could also be viewed as impinging upon budgetary funds for other partners, driving competition for resources related to US security aims. It could also be argued that it negated the importance of certain development work unless it demonstrated a strong security function.

By 2011 there was a USAID policy (versus just a "guide") for responding to violent extremism and insurgency; as with CVE in general, this tended to focus on prevention efforts (mitigating "drivers"), whereas those focused on insurgency were noted to be more reactive in nature, "seeking to contain and reduce active support for an ongoing insurgency."[106] They acknowledged that their understanding of gender in relation to extremism and insurgency on the ground still fell short:

> Gaps remain in USAID's understanding of violent extremism and insurgency. This includes the role of gender. Women may act as both a potential brake on, as well as a driver of, violent extremism. Some suggest that family ties, and women's roles in families, create psychological barriers for husbands, sons, or other male relatives to join violent extremist groups. Others have asserted that women may serve as motivators for male family members to join. Understanding the role of gender at the local level is fundamental.[107]

Furthermore, in practice, this policy noted: "Missions should consider the role of women vis-à-vis drivers of any relevant development response."[108] This suggested that women's roles would be increasingly and inherently assessed alongside USAID development programming when it related to both CVE and COIN. In following with development principles, there would also be an emphasis on efforts at a local level, through local actors promoting local ownership. This localized focus was also reflective of some women and peacebuilding work (for example, that previously highlighted in Nigeria), suggesting that there was potential for overlap in these areas. USAID's implementation of the 2012 NAP also reaffirmed that long-standing gaps still existed in understanding women and gender roles in CVE and COIN.[109]

In specific CVE, crisis response or reconstruction environments (such as the Provincial Reconstruction Teams), security and development actors had been working on the same platform, and some "micro-learning" had already occurred. Julia Billings, a program analyst with USAID, noted:

> We did see some shifts in attitude from military actors, who "didn't do gender" or know why gender mattered, who wanted to focus on addressing the military-focused [concerns] first, then worry about women's empowerment later, to noting how things like where solar lights were positioned in the camps mattered.[110]

There were some contexts where USAID's gender analysis was seemingly translating to DoD or US State partners, but these were not often specific to counterterrorism or CVE, but generally more limited in practice. As noted by Billings, it was development practitioners at the local level who often engaged with security actors the most, in areas such as community policing, systems perspectives and the responsiveness of security systems.[111] This suggested that an active place for dialogue between areas that focused on gender, women, counterterrorism and CVE often occurred in civil-military efforts, or on some specific programs related to reconstruction or community policing, whereas development and security partners interacted on a more regular basis.

CVE, meanwhile, tended to be focused at the community level and on interactions between communities and security actors, where there is often noted to be a disconnect. It also offered an important space for demographics such as women to better access these institutions, or to also be considered in these initiatives. Markham referenced this gap in terms of "building a bridge" between USAID and security actors in terms of knowledge and practice:

> We have done a lot of work around the issues of women, peace and security, [and] we are trying to help the military and other actors learn from those. I think where there is a gap is our language—when we are talking about negotiations and civil society, the military instead looks at "how does this keep our troops safe?" [...] We think that we can make the case that it makes troops safer if they engage women and talk to women who are not in the military. But, they are still at the ground level of "how many troops are there, where can we have female soldiers

engage women in civil society?" So, we are building that bridge, but are not trying to move into the security sphere—we are trying to take a bit of what we learned, and help guide them when they are creating their very own tactical, training and other engagements, that they take these issues into account.[112]

This knowledge exchange still faced much work before it would become engrained in wider practice: "There is a gap between high-level policies and micro-learning, and it's the middle we have to do a better job of systematizing," noted Billings.[113] Increased interaction between DoD, US State and USAID were evident in security discourses and in unified efforts in distinct environments, but appeared infrequent and patchy in the transfer of knowledge related to women and gender across programming.

An important factor for informing how women and gender were considered alongside USAID's work on CVE was its seemingly strong and rapid prioritization of gender in its institutional frameworks.[114] These included the integration of gender equality and female empowerment into USAID's work, as seen in the USAID Policy Framework 2011–15, and the updated 2012 USAID publication "Gender equality and female empowerment policy." The latter was designed to "enhance women's empowerment and reduce gender gaps, the policy affirms the critical role women play in accelerating progress in development and advancing global prosperity and security." In terms of programming, this policy would provide "guidance on pursuing more effective, evidence-based investments in gender equality and female empowerment and incorporating these efforts into our core development programming."[115] While this policy does not explicitly emphasize extremism or CVE, it continued to parallel both USAID and UNSCR 1325 areas of focus, such as post-conflict peacebuilding, responses to SGBV, or relief and recovery considerations, and to demonstrate the emphasis on gender awareness in continued USAID programming. Reflecting themes visible throughout UNSCR 1325, Markham noted some of the same concerns related to women's agency also became reflected in relation to CVE and needed to be challenged:

Across a lot of these issues with WPS [women, peace and security], which flow into CVE, oftentimes in the public view women are just seen as victims. In these sectors, as well as in all other sectors, women are actors in their own lives. They are decision-makers; they can also add to the work we are doing. They bring unique experiences and often time in parliament or other public roles they bring problems or ideas that hadn't been discussed before, but also solutions that hadn't been discussed before. It's the same way in CVE: women might be motivated to take part in violent extremism in different ways, there might be different things they are going for in their lives, but they also can help fight recruitment, they can provide intelligence, they can help other women who have been victims. So, women have a wide variety of roles, and in some places, they are the actual soldiers or bombers. So, we have to take a step back and look at both the roles women can play, and also the gender angle.[116]

There was also caution raised about only emphasizing women in these efforts. Ambassador Bodine pointed out that in areas where women's development concerns were particularly acute, these often reflected those of men in that society, and should not necessarily be viewed as distinct: "in societies where women are undereducated, so are the men. In societies where women get inadequate healthcare, so do the men. In societies where women are not fully part of the power structure, neither are the men."[117] As such, it was important to not only focus on improving the status of women, but those of all members of society more broadly:

If you have a political, social and economic structure where women are healthy, participating, and have a voice, you probably have a strong structure. You can't raise the women independent of raising the men, and granted you should not just be educating the men and not the women, but it's an "all boats floating" idea. This is where you start getting at it […]. Improving the situation for the mother, for the sister, simply to blunt [groups like] ISIS, that's not the reason you do it. But, if you do this well, you will blunt [groups like] ISIS.[118]

Many of the debates highlighted in this section remain today. Furthermore, they also informed the USAID response as the Arab Spring began unfolding, which inevitably required programs ranging from democracy promotion and political engagement, to supporting displaced populations, and responding to SGBV and CVE.

## USAID and the Arab Spring

In 2011, unforeseen protests dubbed the "Arab Spring" began following the self-immolation of aggrieved street vendor Mohamed Bouazizi in

Tunisia. These protests quickly spread and eventually impacted countries such as Jordan, Yemen, Bahrain, Libya, Tunisia and Egypt, amongst several others in the MENA region. People across the region demanded dignity and accountable governments. There was initially great hope for peaceful democratic transitions, and greater inclusion and opportunity for women and youth in particular. Simultaneously, there was also a growing threat from extremism, and increasing instability and conflict more broadly.

From diverse actors attempting to capitalize on this movement, to opposition clampdowns by governments under threat, women were visible in the Arab Spring at every step. Their experience became symbolic of the movement and challenged conservative stereotypes of a woman's place in this region. In Yemen, Tawakkol Karman, from the group Women Journalists Without Chains, led protests against their government alongside thousands of Yemeni men and women. Further rallies and street protests mobilized across the country, leading to then President Ali Abdullah Saleh eventually stepping down. As a result, Karman became the first Arab woman to win the Nobel Peace Prize for her efforts. Libyan human rights activists like Salwa Bugaighis took to the streets and organized protests against the Gaddafi regime, and would eventually pay for it with her life in 2014 when she was murdered in her home. In Cairo, the abuse women faced in these protests were captured in the image of the "girl in the blue bra," who had her clothes ripped off her body while soldiers arrested her for peacefully protesting. At each step, women coordinated social media campaigns and protests, and sat at the negotiating table. Their participation and energy during these protests shocked many of these governments, and were clear demonstrations of women demanding respect, dignity and a meaningful say in the way their countries were being administered. As violence unfolded in countries such as Syria, some even later joined extremist movements that began to rise as instability took hold and power vacuums were filled by non-state actors.

The Arab Spring thus presented an important case for how these two streams—USAID's newly elevated status in security, and its increased gender awareness throughout the organization—would interact in practice alongside other US government efforts as countries such as Tunisia and Egypt transitioned to democracies, while others like

Syria and Yemen descended into civil conflict. Each country faced different challenges and required a unique approach (although between 2011 and 2017, USAID tended to focus on supporting democratic transitions and emergency response). However, while important work on women's political participation and empowerment was visible across the region, women often appeared neglected from CVE-specific efforts in some of the country's most at risk from extremism.

In many of USAID's efforts at the time, women became visible within traditional areas of their work, such as political engagement, job and skills training, or peacemaking efforts. Between January 2011 and April 2013, US State and USAID allocated over $1.8 billion to support both democratic transitions in the MENA region and to respond to emerging crisis needs. In 2013, USAID Administrator Rajiv Shah specifically referenced women in these:

> Across the world, we are strengthening democracy, human rights, and governance, with a special emphasis on marginalized populations, including women and youth. Support for democratic and economic transitions enables the rise of capable new players who can help solve regional challenges and advance US national security.[119]

Approaches to each country were tailored accordingly. For example, in Libya, a 2012 request for $9.5 million under the Middle East Regional Account prioritized work developing governance and security institutions. Here, specific activities would include "promoting voter registration, especially for women and marginalized groups; supporting justice and security reform; and promoting women's empowerment and training opportunities for emerging entrepreneurs."[120]

By 2013, $115 million of non-lethal assistance had been committed to Syria, where $54 million was already flowing through US State- and USAID-affiliated mechanisms to "support, train, equip, and connect a network of civil society activists, civilian opposition leaders, and emergent democratic institutions. USAID has prioritized help for Syrian women to play a meaningful role in the country's transition through training and support for coalition-building."[121] These efforts were at times framed in terms of their broader, long-term contributions to challenging extremism, as noted by USAID Assistant Administrator Nancy Lindborg:

In Syria, we are empowering Syrian women leaders to play a more active role in transition planning and peace negotiations, in keeping with UNSCR 1325 and our objectives under the NAP for Women, Peace, and Security. We believe that support for Syrian women bolsters opposition credibility, increases pressure for a negotiated settlement, and effectively counters extremists.[122]

These efforts included training over "500 Syrian women so that they are equipped with essential advocacy and negotiation skills to contribute to high-level and community-level peacebuilding efforts," which occurred across fourteen governorates in Syria. USAID also provided support to a group of women leaders who created the Syrian Women's Network:

We supported the women from the network so that they could partici-pate in the Geneva II negotiations, where they shared compelling mes-sages about the devastating impact of the conflict and the need for peace. We also trained several women who ran in provisional local council elections in liberated areas of Aleppo last December. These advances are nevertheless constrained within the greater context of a shrinking space for civil society and nascent local governance structures inside Syria, due to the violence perpetrated by the Syrian regime, ISIL [Islamic State of Iraq and the Levant] and other terrorist groups' exploi-tation of ungoverned spaces. But I am confident that these simple acts of female empowerment are critical for Syria's future.[123]

Aside from the visible failure of peace talks that remain to this day, and the challenges from ISIS and continuing conflict, there remained a visible association and emphasis on women's assistance in conflict which aimed to empower those present in negotiations and future transition processes, which demonstrated the US's belief that a political transition would occur (however, as of 2019, this had not materialized).

Other programs in Syria which were focused on women included protection in conflict, SGBV, and other immediate emergency and humanitarian support, including in neighboring countries. Some efforts with a CVE link at the time were noted in Lebanon, such as trying to decrease tensions between host communities and refugee populations, particularly those focused on engaging youth, to reduce the appeal of violent extremism. More often though, programming for women in Syria focused on the more traditional aspects of women, peace and security, whereby "[g]ender-based violence undermines the safety, dignity, health, and human rights of survivors as well as the public health, economic stability, and security of nations."[124] These efforts were certainly important and necessary as the number of Syrian refugees rose into the millions. Simultaneously, a specific CVE angle remained largely absent at this time in USAID's work.

Tunisia was noted as being the country that contributed some of the greatest number of foreign fighters to Syria.[125] As part of its Overseas Transition Initiative between 2011 and 2014, USAID carried out significant programming focusing on areas such as youth engagement, women's political participation and CVE in the country. However, even programs focused on CVE faced numerous challenges, not least of which was identifying those at risk from extremism, where women were not often framed as potential extremists themselves.[126] Moreover, the majority of CVE programming had been based upon interviews with young men only, and most were targeted at men aged between fifteen and thirty-five years old (that is, those "most vulnerable" to joining extremist groups), even though women were actively recognized as a historically marginalized group in the country.[127] This highlighted how even in the agency where women and gender considerations were integrated most prominently into agency frameworks, guides and other key documents, an extension of this knowledge to CVE programming fell short. This proved a significant oversight, as by 2017 approximately 700 women and girls from Tunisia had been estimated amongst the 4,000 Tunisians who had joined ISIS in Iraq and Syria, while many more still had traveled to neighboring Libya.[128]

Work in Yemen focused on the constitutional transition as President Saleh agreed to step down from power. In 2014, USAID's request of $54 million represented a $9.9 million increase from two years prior, and would:

> [...] [a]llow us to assist the transition through support for constitutional review and referendum, as well as elections and voter registry reform. We are also helping the government improve its maternal and child health care services and family planning health services, as well as quality of and access to basic education and early grade reading, especially for girls.[129]

USAID was the leading supporter of development funding in Yemen, and remained the largest global provider of humanitarian aid in the country, having contributed nearly $100 million in assistance to 400,000 individuals by 2015.[130]

Other USAID efforts continued across the Sahel in this period to help prevent other areas from becoming hotspots for extremism. This was done by focusing on the understood socioeconomic, political and cultural drivers of violent extremism, including programming to strengthen local government and "local community advisory councils composed of women, youth, religious, and other representatives to ensure local governance and activities are more responsive to community needs." There was also increased interrogation of gendered drivers of extremism and research in the Sahel produced by USAID in 2015. It noted that both men and women viewed prospects of marriage or taking sexual partners as incentives to join extremist groups, as could be seen with ISIS, who had arranged marriages for both men and women who traveled to their so-called caliphate.[131] Other examples of CVE-related work that engaged women were the Somali Youth Livelihood Program (2008–11), which provided skills training and created job opportunities that aimed to "improve access to economic opportunities for young people who are particularly vulnerable to recruitment by extremist or criminalist networks." This program trained 10,900 youth, 41 per cent of whom were women, who trained in traditional areas like tailoring and non-traditional areas like cell phone repair.[132] USAID had also been active in supporting CVE work in stabilization programming in countries like Pakistan, where women and gender featured heavily.[133] It was evident that both gender and women were themes more emphasized in some CVE contexts (such as Somalia) than others (such as Tunisia), demonstrating such a consideration was not mainstreamed or inherent in USAID work.

USAID also had a long history of working in Morocco, and significant efforts had been made to increase women's civic participation in governance there, including women's leadership roles, increasing women's involvement in political parties and broader electoral reform initiatives. CVE-specific efforts in the country focused on engaging at-risk youth in political processes and economic opportunities.[134] Women were acknowledged in these efforts: "USAID recognizes that male and female beneficiaries face different barriers to employment. USAID will therefore customize activities to ensure equal access for beneficiaries with a particular attention on the actual outcomes for young men and women benefitting from project interventions."[135]

Morocco was also noteworthy because it became the third largest contributor of foreign fighters to ISIS.[136] Yet, there also appeared to be attempts to not closely conflate CVE with ongoing USAID programming in the country, even when a noticeable impact (primary or secondary) was present. Instead, there appeared to be an aim to recognize, though not emphasize, this relationship. Discussing USAID's work in Morocco, Markham discussed the importance of both youth employment and getting youth engaged in their communities: "It's trying to ensure that whatever is driving them or encouraging them to go abroad is not as strong, because they will be engaged at home, but it is so context-specific."[137] This programming differentiated from neighborhood to neighborhood to ensure that each was tailored to that unique environment. Moreover, engaging the CVE label in programming was consciously avoided in many programs when such a label was not proved necessary. Numerous programs that engaged women or had a gender focus helped ease the "drivers" of extremism, but were not necessarily labelled as CVE work.

During this time, there continued to be evident coordination between USAID and other government agencies on counterterrorism and CVE efforts. For example, USAID was viewed as one of numerous government agencies which could work with the US State's Bureau of Counterterrorism and Countering Violent Extremism to help identify and develop CVE efforts. Ambassador-at-Large and Coordinator for Counterterrorism at US State Tina Kaidanow noted:

> We ensure that our areas of focus overseas align with the areas of greatest risk by working with foreign partners and other US government agencies, such as USAID, the intelligence community, and DoD, to identify hotspots of radicalization and to design relevant programming that counters drivers of extremism in those locales.[138]

USAID was also responding directly to the actions of terrorist organizations in the region. As ISIS overran Sinjar in August 2014, and increasingly seized territory, it drove approximately 200,000 persons from Sinjar City (including 50,000 Yazidis) into the Sinjar Mountains, where they were held under siege.[139] This was only the start of the horrors that would be faced by the Yazidi people, as their targeting in killings, abductions and human slavery ramped up during this period. By 8 August, President Obama had, for the first time thus far, authorized air strikes on ISIS fighters and positions, and solidified US involvement in this conflict as part of an international coalition. USAID worked with DoD to coordinate an air drop of aid to Yazidis trapped on Mount Sinjar, as many persons including small children had been left without food and water, while local forces attempted to push ISIS back.

In 2014, USAID requested $1.5 billion to support post-Arab Spring efforts in the MENA region. USAID Administrator Rajiv Shah noted: "Of the President's $2.8 billion assistance request for the Frontline States, USAID implements $1.8 billion for long-term development assistance, continuing to work closely with interagency partners—including the [US] State and Defense departments—to move toward long-term stability, promote economic growth, and support governance reforms, including the rights of women."[140] Work also continued to support women's empowerment efforts in Afghanistan.[141]

Women were clearly integrated into programming and budgetary considerations for USAID efforts in support of longer-term stability efforts across the region. This both reduced concerns from extremism and enhanced US national security, despite only sporadically referencing counterterrorism or CVE specifically. The Arab Spring also continued to shape USAID efforts in the MENA region up to 2017.

USAID and US State continued to work together in an increasingly strategic and coordinated manner, as emphasized throughout their 2014–17 Strategic Plan, where empowering or emphasizing women in all strategic objectives was evident.[142] The 2010 QDDR had focused heavily on conflict and state weakness, and highlighted the integration of women in USAID's responses to humanitarian emergencies, armed conflict, post-conflict reconstruction and governance. However, this expanded in the 2015 QDDR to explicitly emphasize the prevention and mitigation of conflict and violent extremism. In expanding efforts, this QDDR would "identify and scale up tailored approaches that empower [...] youth and women." It would assist in "[b]uilding secure and resilient communities, by supporting civil society, governments, and communities, including youth and women, in their efforts to address social, economic, and development vulnerabilities, improve community-police relations, and expand religious and other education that promotes tolerance."[143] That same year, USAID announced it would establish the position of Secretariat on CVE at the agency to "enhance USAID's roles in the response to violent extremism."[144]

The 2015 QDDR also emphasized development as an equal pillar alongside defense. Linking this directly with CVE, it noted: "Diplomacy and development play critical roles in preventing, mitigating, and responding to threats such as instability within countries, inter-state and great-power conflict, and the spread of violent extremism in both stable and fragile countries." It went on to identify six specific lines of effort it identified for USAID and US State.[145]

USAID was evidently and increasingly a vital agency for US CVE efforts, yet such work was not always (either purposefully or negligibly) considered in CVE terms. USAID had been noted by some to be able to be quite successful at advancing gender considerations in conflict and post-conflict environments, though this was often disputed (as seen with the discussion above). Ambassador Verveer highlighted this visible impact, and the importance of its extension to contracted partners who helped implement these programs:

> [USAID has] significantly pushed the gender piece of the gender resources we bring to conflict and post-conflict societies, in a very significant way. Whether that is post-conflict work in terms of economic opportunities, whether its resources coming in to address instability, the lack of protection, the violence piece, it is strongly there. [And] because of the way our aid work goes, the fact that so much of it is contracted out, it is a significant principle that has to be represented in the way that those resources get allocated by the actor.[146]

It was evident that in USAID policy documents, plans and strategies that considerations pertaining to women, gender and violent extremism were often inherent. Yet, this was slower to take hold in practice, the consequences of which saw thousands of women from across the MENA region join ISIS in Iraq, Syria and its other locations, rising rates of female radicalization in the region, and USAID left on the back foot.

There were also renewed efforts around protection from SGBV that became evident from 2015 due to the treatment of women by groups like Boko Haram and ISIS. As USAID Assistant Administrator Nancy Lindborg aptly noted: "Women and children always bear the brunt of suffering in a conflict, but under ISIL, women and girls are suffering a special hell." One program, called Safe from the Start, aimed to help women in humanitarian emergencies. USAID had provided $10.5 million to respond to and reduce the risk of SGBV and other abuses towards women and other refugees in Syria and Iraq; humanitarian responses in this program related to relief supplies, shelter, and addressing needs related to protection and trauma. In these responses, specific considerations were given to women, and often contained broader gendered considerations, as well as attention paid to issues such as child marriage. This was informed by the level of women affected, where 80 per cent of the 3 million Syrian refugees were women and children.[147] Furthermore, 85 per cent of those killed in the conflict were male, leaving an increasingly large number of female-headed households. In 2015, the US was the largest bilateral humanitarian aid donor to Syrian efforts, with contributions totaling $4.5 billion.[148]

*Identifying the drivers of female participation in violent extremist organizations*

It was not until September 2015, however, that USAID appeared to pointedly assess the drivers of women's roles in violent extremism, as seen with its first study on women and violent extremism in the MENA region in a research brief entitled "Drivers of female participation in [violent extremist organizations] in MENA."[149] This was a notable for being fifteen months after ISIS's announcement of their "caliphate," when thousands of foreign and local women had already become affiliated with the group in locations such as Libya, Iraq and Syria. This research was produced and informed by external academics and researchers,[150] highlighting one instance of USAID's engagement with academics to inform its programming. The significant mobilization of women by ISIS had only made the topic more salient, where otherwise both research and policy had neglected this, suggesting USAID was now playing a catch-up game in response to this concern. Indeed, this focus on women as violent extremist actors appeared to be directly reactive to unfolding events, suggesting responsive versus proactive efforts to mitigate and manage this concern.

The report noted three key findings, including "the drivers of women's participation in [violent extremism] are similar to men's, with some gender specific differences;" "[violent extremist organizations] are actively recruiting women for a variety of reasons using a wide array of tactics;" and "the lack of a gendered analysis of drivers of [violent extremism] has left gaps in current CVE strategies." Notably, it also identified women's "push" and "pull" factors related to recruitment into violent extremist groups for the first time, including "push" factors such as "dissatisfaction with regime or political process; seeking security amidst instability; experience of abuse of humiliation by state security forces; death or abuse of family members; [and] gender subordination/exclusion from mainstream politics," and "pull" such as "support of [violent extremist] group ideology (eg. religious, nationalist goals, etc.); selective incentives (security services, financial gain); groups' rejection of 'Western' political and economics experiments (for Islamist groups)."[151]

Many of these "push" and "pull" factors were reflective of those of men who joined the group, such as "dissatisfaction with regime or political process" or "experience of abuse of humiliation by state security forces." Both men and women had bought into ISIS's ideology and incentives; for example, the provision of a spouse (husband or wife) or to seek some kind of security from within the group. Yet, these too could be gendered, such as if a culture placed emphasis on a woman's honor, then abuse by state forces or other non-state actors could particularly compound such motivations for women or the men who may feel obliged to protect them. The death of a family member may also have gendered implications; for example, when female-headed households were left behind and faced physical and financial insecurity. This suggested that as the drivers for men's involvement in conflict were increasingly identified, if a gender lens had been inherent at every step from the beginning, the likelihood of being able to tailor resultant programming specifically for women would have helped address this demographic. In particular, it would have further lent to a better understanding of recruitment of all persons into ISIS.

There were additional factors to consider in each context, such as the roles played by women in recruitment into these groups, as well as their "access to public space; freedom of movement; access to information (particularly European sources for Magrebi [sic] women); and previous political engagement/awareness."[152] This directly tied previous streams of effort by USAID—such as women's political participation and democracy promotion—into concerns related to recruitment into violent extremist groups. Again, if there had been more extensive and meaningful integration of gender analysis into USAID's programming and its increasing role in contributing to national security objectives, then this may have better mitigated women's participation in these groups. Its recommendations included recognizing and leveraging the diversity of roles women play in violent extremism; understanding the gender- and sex-specific push and pull factors for violent extremism organizations in MENA; and gender-mainstreaming all CVE programming. Such research was welcome and encouraging, but also suggested that even after an increase in policy discourses promoting women in USAID's work, this was slow to evolve in practice. This was particularly in relation to understanding women and gender as they interacted with violent extremist groups, and how they should be mainstreamed and appropriately responded to in CVE work, which still contained significant shortfalls.

Recognizing that women were playing increasingly diverse roles within these groups, USAID also promoted more closely analyzing women's roles in propagating and countering violent extremism, and highlighted the various myths around women's roles in this area, including women solely being victims (and men perpetrators); the need to focus programs on young disenfranchised men who were most at risk from extremism; and the lack of tools available in the international community to engage women in CVE.[153] The emergence of ISIS had proven to be of significant focus for USAID's work, even as these appeared to fall short in terms of women's considerations of violent extremist groups themselves, particularly in CVE.

*Al-Qaeda and ISIS: Alternative interpretations of development and governance*[154]

Several of the programming areas focused on by USAID—including poor governance, human rights violations, marginalization, and even development efforts such as literacy promotion or employment creation—had been increasingly considered and reflected by terrorist organizations. This was particularly visible to various degrees where these groups had controlled and administered land in proto-states (which author Lia argues allow these groups to "expand their influence and weight" vis-à-vis their Islamist competitors).[155] Women had been specifically targeted in these efforts, even though their societal positions were still largely repressed in these areas. Al-Qaeda, ISIS and their affiliates had focused on several public endeavors—from food distribution and healthcare, to "law and order" and provision of security at the local level. They did this in order to gain credibility and support from the local and wider populations, demonstrating their own ability to establish and govern an Islamic "caliphate." Such initiatives have not only prolonged the lifespans of such groups, but have in some cases drawn differing levels of support for them, particularly when such services had not been provided by the state or other international actors, or in periods of prolonged instability and conflict, illustrating the interconnected nature of service provision/development aid by governments or international actors, and the gaps which were exploitable by terrorist groups. This was particularly true when terrorist groups' strategies contained some element of governance, and thus women also had to be inherently considered within these. It also highlighted the longer-term strategies for winning "hearts and minds" in these regions, and shared a number of elements of COIN strategy more generally.

Early examples of attempts at governance by a jihadist group were seen in Iraq; these had their roots in AQI, which had been active under Abu Musab al-Zarqawi following the US invasion of the country from 2004, and represented one of the most destructive forces during the insurgency. When al-Zarqawi was killed in 2006, AQI combined with a number of smaller extremist groups and renamed itself the Islamic State of Iraq (ISI), which announced their formation on 15 October 2006. ISI had explicit aims: to gain and hold territory, establish a caliphate, and provide governance following the departure of US forces. The framework it established included small public work projects; pay and care for families of deceased martyrs; calling for foreign fighters to join from around the world; and the recruitment of persons with administrative and scientific backgrounds (a point later promoted by ISIS).[156] However, unlike ISIS, which was successfully able to hold territory and implement this governance, ISI did not appear to focus on women extensively in its efforts. Although some of their policies were women-specific—including supporting families of martyrs, enforcing public segregation of the sexes and forcing women to wear niqabs—propaganda targeted directly at women was largely absent, and programs for women limited in number and largely unimplemented. Due to the increasing pressures against ISI, including from the US and coalition forces in the surge of 2007, and the turning of Sunni tribes during the "Sunni awakening" of 2006, ISI was fractional in these early attempts. However, these efforts to govern territory would again emerge in more spectacular ways, when Abu Bakr al-Baghdadi would take over the group in 2010 and eventually evolve it into ISIS. After this, engagement with women became more systematic and overt than ever before.

One of the first successful examples of governance by a transnational terrorist group was by AQAP in the areas of Ja'ar and Zinjibar in Yemen in 2011. These cases were distinct from the case of Iraq above as they were generally beyond the reach and scope of the central government. When the Arab Spring swept the region in 2011, President Saleh withdrew what few state security forces were present in this area, and this gap was quickly filled by AQAP. The group controlled these areas for nearly a year, where they advertised and promoted their establishment of a police station, a women's literacy center, distributed food aid, established water projects, delivered electricity, and controlled garbage and sewage management.[157]

The lessons learned in the administration of governance were also shared between branches of al-Qaeda, as was seen in several letters found in 2011 in Timbuktu between top Yemeni AQAP operative Nasser al-Wahaishi and Algerian national leader of al-Qaeda in the Islamic Maghreb (AQIM) Abdelmalek Droukdel. As Wahaishi explained: "providing these necessities will have a great effect on people, and will make them sympathize with us and feel that their fate is tied to ours." Wahaishi also reflected on lessons learned in Yemen, where harsh sharia laws were first implemented, and emphasized that such punishments should only be implemented on the local community progressively.[158] In Somalia, al-Shabaab (a group largely restricted to the East African nation) had also filled humanitarian gaps left by aid organizations forced to leave, or whose presence had been restricted in the country. Similar to other organizations, al-Shabaab engaged in the abduction of women and forced marriage, and banned them from working in areas under their control,[159] and also participated in governance efforts, including financial management and welfare systems.[160]

By 2015, AQAP were reported to be supporting widows in the community, particularly when male breadwinners had been killed in US drone or air strikes. In some cases, aid such as food, money and educational materials required by these families was directly provided by AQAP,[161] building up additional support and indeed a potential future recruitment base for the group. This also pointed to how the recipients of AQAP programming efforts could evolve as female-headed households became increasingly common. Recalling that since 2015 the country had descended into a fierce conflict—and that the US had carried out over 163 drone and other air strikes in the country, resulting in the death of upwards of 1,106 persons up to 2017;[162] and that women in rural Yemen have an average of 6.75 children per family[163]—this point became increasingly important in terms of potential recruitment and support.

Yet, even when job creation did occur and was initiated by government actors, it was not always guaranteed that these employees would be actually paid, as noted by wider shortfalls in governance in Yemen at this time, where non-state actors would in fact prove to be the guarantors of this. This was highlighted by Dr Elisabeth Kendall, a Senior Research Fellow at Pembroke College, Oxford, and an expert on AQAP. She noted that in 2015 tribesmen hired for state security forces by President Hadi (under Saudi tutelage) were not being paid, and it was in fact al-Qaeda who stepped in and ensured their pay was resumed.[164] This suggested that al-Qaeda was able to identify and exploit development and employment concerns to their benefit, and could also co-opt or influence government services rather than exclusively governing. This only reinforced the necessity of considering defense, diplomacy and development streams of effort in a more holistic and balanced fashion, which had evident implications for women in each.

Within the growing conflict in Yemen, al-Qaeda had again been able to seize, hold and govern territory, though on a much larger scale than previously, and in spite of facing persistent loss of leadership. This was seen most prominently in the city of Mukallah between April 2015 and April 2016, where the group took over the city, administered the port, implemented public works, carried out sharia law and suppressed the rights of women. In this period, the group was able to amass a wealth of up to $100 million, allowing them resources to support their governance works there and elsewhere. The departure of AQAP from Mukalla was said to have been negotiated, not fought, by allied forces from the United Arab Emirates, who also recruited hundreds of members of disengaged AQAP into coalition ranks after undergoing "repentance" programs.[165] Here, Yemen offered an interesting case to consider in relation to the evolving governance model of AQAP: namely, that where initial models that had implemented harsh forms of sharia law softened, a focus on community support and public works were instead promoted that more overtly emphasized women. Supporting female-headed households also appeared to be considered in efforts and directly linked to kinetic counterterrorism policies in the country.

Demonstrating the breadth of this concern beyond Yemen, the AQIM-supported Ansar Dine took over in northern Mali in 2012. In the city of Timbuktu, women faced a harsh interpretation of sharia law and were forced to cover themselves. In some cases, women faced physical punishment for not adhering to these standards, and unrelated men and women who were seen speaking in the streets were ordered to marry (essentially forced marriage).[166] Other rebel groups in Mali during this period, such as National Movement for the Liberation of Azawad, had also been committing increased abduction and rape of women and girls. There were cases recorded by Human Rights Watch where Ansar Dine had helped women escape from these rebel groups and provided them with medical care.[167] This also pointed to how even sexual violence against women was being responded to by some groups in select cases, and may be used to differentiate or distinguish themselves from other groups, or even to gain local support.

## The ISIS governance project

While those who traveled to Syria and Iraq did so largely to join one of the many groups fighting on the ground, including ISIS (particularly those after 2014), many who traveled to the Syria earlier in the post-

2011 conflict did so claiming they wanted to provide humanitarian assistance and defend civilians who were suffering from abuses carried out by the Assad government.[168]

In June 2014, ISIS declared they had established a "caliphate" in an audio recording released by the group, which they claimed stretched from Diyala Province in Iraq to Aleppo in Syria. They would go on to control an area the size of the United Kingdom, and themselves govern over a population of 8 million. One area the group focused on was drawing people with skills in the field of medicine, education and engineering in order to provide the services that a state traditionally provided for its citizens.[169] The vast resources that ISIS gained from the land under its control allowed it to attract supporters from around the world, including women, to be part of its state-building project. Even before announcing the caliphate, the group was said to have accumulated $875 million, and by September 2014 was noted to be worth $2 billion,[170] making it the wealthiest terrorist group in history. This income was key to paying the wages of its soldiers and their families, supporting widows and the families of "martyrs," and for maintaining a system of governance and public service delivery.

This support of widows and martyrs is particularly noteworthy due to the growing number of casualties—both those driven by the conflict with civilians, and where elimination of combatants on the battlefield by the Global Coalition Against Daesh became the approach of choice. As discussed in a 2018 report by Cook and Vale, estimates of ISIS followers killed on the battlefield ranged between 25,000 and 70,000,[171] and excluded the number of civilians also widowed in this period. Here, the long-term support provided to family left behind could also act as an incentive to join the organization in an environment where death became a normal part of life. For these widows, such assistance could also solidify long-term support for the organization and ensure there was a willing next generation to support ISIS's cause.

ISIS proved it could seize, hold and maintain territory, offering its own unprecedented governance model and public services. There were also clear efforts to promote the benefits of these jobs, including salaries, wives or husbands, and housing that would be provided to those who joined them. Many of these benefits were also provided to differing degrees for locals who joined. Speckhard and Yayla have further noted that fear of rape by Assad's forces in some cases also acted as an "inducement" for some local women to join ISIS as a better alternative; moreover, these women viewed marriage into ISIS as a means of avoiding starvation and of assisting their families.[172] Governance and development considerations were thus inherent as part of the group's strategic aims, which could draw off a pre-existing sympathy pool of foreign individuals who wanted to assist civilians suffering from the conflict (many of whom had become disillusioned or traumatized as the war intensified), and attracted many persons to travel to join the group. Furthermore, for some locals, joining or supporting ISIS was seen as a means to avoid violence (including SGBV), or as a way of accessing resources required for survival. Locals who did not support this ISIS project were in many cases forced to return to their previous government posts to support ISIS governance or face harsh punishment against them and their families. In many cases, they became "coerced civilians," obliged to support the group or face severe punishment, or even death.[173] The provision of services by the group itself was a draw for potential members; for individuals traveling to Syria, their contributions and roles in state services could also be perceived to positively impact one's "citizenship" in the "state," giving them an identity and stake in this governance project. This also goes some way to demonstrate how these could lend to the recruitment and retention of female members.

Employment positions for women were also advertised and promoted in this "state" beyond roles of mothers and wives, such as nurses or teachers, which offered appeal to a wider pool of female supporters who may have sought more active roles in the jihadist group. In a June 2014 edition of *Dabiq*, the group specifically called for specific skill sets such as "scholars, *fuqaha* [experts in Islamic jurisprudence], and callers, especially the judges as well as people with military, administrative, service expertise, and medical doctors and engineers,"[174] with some of these positions open to women. As Khelghat-Doost observed, the use of "gender-segregated parallel institutions" (comparable to the gender-segregated public services seen in Saudi Arabia or Iran) offered a new mechanism for including women across its governance structure.[175] This call was not gender-specific, and in fact ISIS had confirmed that it required female medical personnel to deal specifically with women. As a result, several female medical students from the United Kingdom and other countries traveled to join the organization.[176]

The provision of these services also attracted families from around the world. One particularly egregious example saw a seventeen-year-old Indonesian girl convince twenty-six members of her family to travel to Raqqa in Syria, as the family sought to clear debts and access free education (including for female family members) and healthcare.[177] There were also indications that British women were involved in running brothels for ISIS fighters, demonstrating that women could be complicit in, or perpetrators of, SGBV themselves.[178] ISIS also boasted about its *da'wah* (proselytizing) and sharia courses set up specifically for girls and women, and stated that such courses had encouraged mothers to sign their children up as volunteers for military and suicide operations.[179] With both extensive resources and land under its control, as well as the announcement that they had formed a "state," women could now envision themselves as citizens in state-building roles, could access public services and fulfill perceived religious obligations.

Further gains in territory and resources claimed by ISIS facilitated this, and incentivized the participation of women. For women that were unmarried who wanted to travel, *maqqars* (women's hostels) were set up to facilitate their accommodation upon arrival. Bloom noted that ISIS appealed to women by providing electricity, food and a salary for each fighter's family.[180] This overlapped with empowerment themes as well, where joining this community could be understood to offer women independence or freedoms they may have believed they lacked previously in their home countries. ISIS also emphasized charitable activities, such as giving women *zakat* (charity), or offering bread and aid to women in communities they had seized. As the organization continued to expand, development structures and specific institutions focused on women's education were established, such as women's sharia institutions, where topics like sciences were also taught.[181]

The provision of public services that became embedded in the larger governance project and public image of ISIS highlighted several points. First, ISIS attempted to maintain the perception to those outside of areas under its control that governance services such as healthcare, education, food security and even varied employment opportunities would be available to those who came to join them, acting as an incentive for international recruits who may have been hesitant about traveling to an active war zone. This also further expanded the pool of those willing to travel, such as mothers with children, or families who may have otherwise been deterred from traveling to join the group. On top of this, for those from the local area that had been suffering from the humanitarian disaster driven by the Syrian conflict, such provision of services may have appeared attractive, and for a suffering population, offered some semblance of reprieve. This in fact mirrored (and indeed delivered) governance programming where local governance fell short.

These examples have not expanded on the abhorrent human rights abuses, terrorist acts, violence and other violations committed by these groups. However, they have highlighted that when there was a distinct gap in provision of key governance elements—such as food, health, employment opportunities, physical and human security (whether more generally, or in times of conflict, such as from SGBV)—this could provide a window of opportunity for non-state terrorist actors to secure a foothold and gain support, whether by co-opting pre-existing services or establishing new ones. This may prolong acceptance or even gain support for their group where such deficits were otherwise present, and increased the attraction of the group to a broader demographic of potential supporters. For those who joined such groups and provided services, this also positively impacted on their perceived "citizenship" in the "state".[182] Moreover, even though populations would otherwise largely reject these terror groups, for those that struggled to achieve even basic survival, or have faced extended conflict or insecurity, or indeed government repression and abuse, the provision of various services or stability in such publics works by terrorist actors may dilute local resistance when married with a particular ideology.

This shift to governance efforts that became increasingly visible amongst jihadist organizations (particularly where they held and administered territory) had explicit implications for how women became members, targets and even (unwilling) "citizens" affiliated with such groups; it also had explicit consequences for how women had to be understood in all efforts to counter them, including in long-term stabilization and recovery efforts, where these services would be crucial to gain support from the population.

The connotations of these development and governance efforts by terrorist groups for the US's "whole-of-government" approach to security are profound. Even as USAID was elevated to high politics in security, earlier imbalances in this equation (that is, where governance and development efforts were perceived as a lesser priority) could have lent to exploitable gaps that helped these terror groups operate and grow (even providing learning opportunities for them to share along the way). The US government can certainly not be viewed as responsible for all development and governance work in the region, the onus of which rests on regional governments and actors themselves. Yet, this evolving and increased focus on governance and development, and particularly women's "programming" by al-Qaeda and ISIS, had to be acknowledged and responded to in broader US counterterrorism discourses and practices, as seen in a comprehensive approach to security in the region in this period. This included ensuring partner nations were willing and able to provide basic standards of governance and development, and that such work was prioritized and supported in US engagement in these nations.

*Final points*

While always an independent organization, USAID operated under the policy guidance of US State, where its main mission focused on ending extreme poverty and the promotion of democracy. Traditional humanitarian and development aid efforts by USAID had been notably distinct from US foreign-policy efforts related to security. However, this began to shift as efforts by both the Bush and Obama administrations looked to better coordinate and streamline development efforts in line with US foreign policy and security aims (and as such, counterterrorism). Women became visible in USAID in categories such as conflict prevention, reconciliation and recovery; rights and empowerment; community; and victimhood.

There appeared to be early recognition that USAID programming played a role in preventing and countering conflict and extremism, even if this was not initially expressly stated. The contribution to stabilization, reconstruction and governance by USAID, and its long and broad understanding of gender impacts and assessments, was also clear. Between 2001 and 2008, an explicit focus on women in terms of counterterrorism and CVE appeared separate and peripheral to primary security efforts, even as they were quietly understood to contribute to the prevention of conflict, insurgency and terrorism (and implemented as such). This was highlighted in countries like Yemen, where USAID programming was targeted at regions labeled most at risk from extremism or framed in terms of its contribution to counter-extremism. Yet, Yemen also demonstrated agency limitations: when available funding was limited, emphasis on the perceived connection between USAID programming and counterterrorism and counter-extremism efforts could gain it support and open new funding opportunities.

As USAID took up an active role in stabilization efforts in countries such as Iraq, this appeared to prompt increased internal interrogation of the links between development and humanitarian aid and conflict, as well as stabilization, COIN and reconstruction, amongst other issues it now had to consider; inherent in these were the roles and status of women/gender. USAID was also increasingly operating alongside DoD partners in stabilization efforts, as seen in Yemen, where they supported women's health and education efforts, or the Trans-Sahara Counterterrorism Partnership, where it assessed the areas in which development efforts could make the biggest impact on counterterrorism aims. USAID was thus undergoing a broader evolution as it assessed where it felt it fit into these new roles and fields of security. Yet, this evolution also brought with it controversies and challenges, whereby the agency was at times seen by other agencies to operate outside of foreign-policy considerations, or where the its employees now faced increased concerns or danger from conflation with US security efforts (especially counterterrorism).

USAID's gender-conscious programming, which aimed to elevate women in all its efforts, had been core to its operations for decades, and it continued to be so as it increasingly contributed to US security. Similar to US State, USAID was active in utilizing UNSCR 1325 (as well as other UNSCRs related to women, peace and security) in their policies and practices. In fact, the frequency by which women were explicitly referenced in USAID policies and documentation was noteworthy in and of itself; by referencing women consistently, its policy and programming ensured that this gender angle was at least recurrently considered. The agency also had the most visibly nuanced approach to assessing women in conflict in terms of how they could be agents in all aspects of peacebuilding, prevention and recovery efforts, as well as how women could be distinctly impacted by conflict, but also could be militants or violent actors themselves. Development principles that "do no harm" also ensured a strong assessment of how USAID programming may impact negatively on any population it worked with, including women specifically.

Another core principle in USAID was that of achieving progress through ensuring half the population (that is, women) were also raised to an equal status. These principles could be seen in programs to promote voices of women in Afghanistan, where up to half of USAID programming targeted women, or Community Action programs (then called Community Stabilization) in Iraq, where women were key recipients in areas such as skills training and youth conflict resolution. Agency publications and guides such as the 2007 "Women and conflict" guide, or 2008's "Conducting an extremism or terrorism assessment," were visible markers that carried forward gender knowledge in USAID's own institutional memory as it interrogated the new challenges faced in its operations (though this was not always evident with USAID activities pertinent to ISIS).

The 2010 NAP and 2011 QDDR also marked a significant turning point for USAID whereby development now became elevated to high security as a core pillar of US security efforts alongside defense and diplomacy. It now became contingent for USAID to define how its operations directly contributed to US security efforts, as could be seen in its 2011 policy publication "The development response to violent extremism and insurgency." This foray into security occurred alongside increased focus on women and gender, with the establishment in 2011 of the Senior Gender Coordinator for Gender Equality and Women's Empowerment.

CVE also continued to develop and expand within USAID efforts, which opened new opportunities for the agency to bring increased attention to areas such as women's empowerment and gender considerations in programming, although there were also visible tensions. Several debates emerge: should women's rights and empowerment efforts be linked to counterterrorism and later CVE, or should these be kept separate? Unless development or rights programming was framed in terms of its contribution to counterterrorism or CVE, would it be funded or prioritized? Would this impact upon the safety of USAID staff and their partners in the field? This pointed to wider shortfalls in academic, practitioner and bureaucratic circles, where knowledge of and approaches to both counterterrorism and CVE were still evolving. This also highlighted some debates that had very real implications for USAID programming and personnel in the field. In fact, there had been significant resistance by some in the development sphere to engage in this work under a counterterrorism or CVE umbrella, instead viewing such work as distinct, though complimentary, to security priorities.

Following the 2011 Arab Spring, USAID's work began to focus on democratic transitions, and particularly women's roles within these. As a rising threat from extremism became visible in the region, there was increased focus on the drivers of extremism. USAID CVE efforts were visible in countries like Tunisia and Morocco, but it was not evident how women and gender were initially focused on in these efforts. In countries like Syria or Yemen, there did not appear to be any CVE angle emphasized that was pertinent to women; in fact, it appeared that it was well after women from around the world were joining ISIS by the thousands that any analysis of the drivers and brakes of women's roles in violent extremist organizations was assessed by USAID, suggesting a missed opportunity for utilizing and mainstreaming its strengths on gender in the field. Indeed, this appeared to be a point that had been taken advantage of by groups such as al-Qaeda and ISIS to some extent, who were tapping into some of these development-related drivers of extremism and reframing them for their own purposes (for example, women's rights and human security concerns), particularly as they themselves tried to become governance actors (as seen in Iraq and Syria). This suggested agency limitations remained both in assessing how CVE programming could be most efficient, and how women should be considered and engaged in these.

USAID also seemed to view itself and its history as particularly able to inform defense partners in terms of how they could better consider and engage women in their work. Certain civil-military efforts demonstrated practical cases where overlap between the defense and development spheres interacted and informed each other. As Markham of USAID pointed out: "I think military and defense forces are, across

Yemen and many countries, beginning to understand the role that development can take hand-in-hand with them."[183] However, this process was slow to evolve, and demonstrated how considerations of women and gender had not yet adequately transferred from the development and diplomacy sphere into defense. This focus of women's rights and programming at times faced tensions with DoD efforts, where perceived prioritization of defense streams were seen to attenuate from development work; however, they also faced practical difficulties in implementation unless some degree of security were present, such as security and development considerations pertaining to stabilization programming.

Finally, as al-Qaeda, ISIS and their affiliates were increasingly engaging in development and governance activities, women became increasingly emphasized and targeted in these. While there was evidence that USAID was making efforts to better understand the brakes and drivers of women's roles in violent extremism, there remained a dearth of evident research or reflection of this in USAID programming.

The final chapter will look at changes since the onset of the Trump administration in 2017. Drawing off these past sixteen years, it will demonstrate why considering a woman's place in relation to full-spectrum responses to prevent, mitigate and respond to terrorism is more crucial than ever.

# 6

## ENTER TRUMP

### COUNTERTERRORISM GOING FORWARD

*'ISIS is our number one threat [....]. I would knock the hell out of them, I would hit them so hard like they've never been hit before [....].We're fighting a very politically correct war. The other thing with the terrorists is you have to take out their families, when you get these terrorists, you have to take out their families. They care about their lives, don't kid yourself. When they say they don't care about their lives, you have to take out their families."*

Donald Trump on *Fox News Insider*, 2 December 2015[1]

By the time of publication, much had changed since 9/11 and the administrations of Bush and Obama. Students entering university today may not recall the mass casualty attacks of 9/11 because some of them had not yet been born. Instead, their dominant point of reference for contemporary terrorism is the world's most media-savvy terrorist organization—the Islamic State in Iraq and Syria (ISIS)—and the diverse global attacks perpetrated by it and its adherents. The discourses and practices pertaining to women in counterterrorism—from front-line soldiers, and community leaders countering and recovering from terrorism, to terrorist perpetrators themselves—have evolved in significant ways. The broader environment that now shapes how the next generation perceives terrorism and counterterrorism is a world apart from that of their preceding one.

There have also been significant changes in the US administration, particularly the departure of President Obama in 2017 and the surprise election of Donald Trump to the White House, who assumed office in January 2017. Understandably, these have also already had demonstrable impacts in relation to women in this space. Trump entered the White House riding on the slogan "America First"—a theme that also became reflected in his approach to domestic and foreign policy more generally. This approach raised important questions and concerns about the US as the country leading and championing the liberal world order (as it had done for decades), and what this would mean for its relations with other nations, including security partnerships, burden-sharing with partners and multilateral organizations, and the country's emphasis on democracy promotion and development aid abroad. The controversial and bombastic language often engaged by Trump, and his unprecedented use of social media (particularly Twitter) to convey policy decisions and positions, also shattered previous norms related to presidential behavior and communications. This further extended to the discourses he used pertaining to women and policy decisions related to national security, which further impacted women as actors in this space.

The Trump administration's approach to national security thus far has contained both elements of change and continuity from his predecessors. It has proven unpredictable and may evolve further as his tenure continues. Counterterrorism has lost center stage amongst national security priorities, being usurped by the great power struggles between the US, Russia and China. Other notable actions under the Trump administration thus far included reversing the country's position on the Iranian nuclear deal, and oscillating between confronting North Korea on their nuclear program while also trying to engage in discussions related to denuclearization. An election promise to build a border wall between the USA and Mexico emphasized the dangers he stated immigrants posed, claiming Mexicans coming over the border were "bringing drugs" and "rapists," earning accusations of racism and xenophobia.[2] Reminiscent of the idioms used to justify the US war in Afghanistan, Trump highlighted the gendered language he was willing to engage to achieve his policy ends and mobilize support for what he labeled a "national security crisis."[3] This border wall debate also led to the longest government shutdown in US history over disputes about Congressional funding for this structure.

The administration has continued to focus on key cases such as Afghanistan, Iraq, Syria and Yemen (as highlighted throughout the book), where the picture remains grim, long-term stabilization and peace uncertain, and the US's role and presence increasingly diminished. What specific policy the Trump administration had in the region also remained vague. There was also a notable shift in the emphasis on which departments and agencies would be brought to the forefront of US foreign policy and security efforts, with significant revitalization and investment in the US Department of Defense (DoD), and bleak budgetary and staffing cuts to both the US Department of State (US State) and US Agency for International Development (USAID), where key overseas diplomatic positions too remained unfilled.

The administration has also demonstrated points of continuity and departure from the preceding administrations in terms of specific counterterrorism discourses and practices. However—and similar to Bush and Obama prior—the domestic, security and foreign policy discourses and actions utilized by Trump also impact the salience and effectiveness of the broader security agenda. These have thus far included the controversial move of the US Embassy in Israel from Tel Aviv to Jerusalem; the April 2017 direct action against President Assad in Syria; and the apparent mainstreaming of far-right and Islamophobic discourses, and even white nationalism, by Trump and senior administration.[4] Such actions by the US both domestically and abroad also influenced the political and social climate in which counterterrorism efforts operated, and how concepts like "American values" were understood and projected abroad.

The nature of the terrorist threat itself has also continued to evolve. The increased use of encrypted, closed communications platforms like Telegram, as opposed to the previously utilized public platforms such as Twitter and Facebook, are creating new challenges in intercepting and countering terrorist and violent extremist communications. Cheap and accessible market technologies like drones have allowed for terrorist innovation, while the weaponization of everyday vehicles, and use of low-grade weapons such as knives in attacks have impacted the ability to detect and prevent such incidents. Key groups like al-Qaeda and ISIS are now more geographically dispersed, decentralized and autonomous than at any time since 9/11. An array of new regions of concern—ranging from the Philippines and Libya, to the Sinai and West Africa—have gained attention, demonstrating how threats from terrorism were also increasingly more disperse and decentralized. Countries like Afghanistan are presenting new challenges, and is the country where the largest ISIS branch outside Syria and Iraq is currently established. Worries from self-starters, homegrown radicals and increasingly far-right extremism also remained prominent on both international and domestic security agendas. Domestically, far-right ideology had already been linked to 70 per cent of extremist-related killings between 2008 and 2018.[5] However, there was a significant spike under Trump and during his first year in office, where anti-Semitic attacks rose by 57 per cent, while hate crimes rose by 17 per cent.[6] This caused many analysts to argue Trump was enabling and even mainstreaming the right-wing movements responsible for violence.[7]

Finally, the environment in which these counterterrorism efforts, and indeed terrorist and violent extremist groups are embedded within, are more interconnected and global in their scale than at any time in human history. Global migration has reached its highest levels in history: 258 million people in 2017, bringing with it many significant benefits, but also stoking fear in some populations.[8] The world's number of displaced persons currently sits at 68.5 million, including 25.4 million refugee and asylum seekers; nearly 10 million of these refugees come from Iraq and Afghanistan alone, demonstrating the impacts these conflicts have had on the movement of populations around the world.[9] The Intergovernmental Panel on Climate Change have emphasized how we now stand at a critical point in terms of irreversible consequences from climate change, and have called for a global response.[10] Many diverse countries, such as Germany, Italy and even Brazil, now face the rise of populist and far-right movements, where previously this was considered unlikely. The world was changing, and such shifts had both direct and indirect impacts on US foreign policy and security considerations.

As this book has demonstrated, each event and shift has specific implications for women as agents, partners and targets of security-related policies and practices, and therefore demand that we look beyond the headlines to identify women and gender considerations at every step—including the roles they are seen or assumed to have, and the factors that may have evolved these. In this final chapter, the counterterrorism approach taken thus far by the Trump administration will first be examined through an analysis of the key strategies and statements articulated by him, his administration, and how this has unfolded thus far in practice on the ground. This will highlight a significant disconnect and tension that has become visible between Trump's own discourses, those of his wider administration, and the departments and agencies in the US government, and what this has meant for this topic. The second section will provide an update on the situations in Afghanistan, Iraq, Syria and Yemen since the beginning of 2017, outlining key areas of concern going forward and drawing off insights gleaned from the Bush and Obama administrations to assess the significance of these for women today. This chapter will inherently consider what these may mean for how women are assessed as agents, partners and targets of full-spectrum counterterrorism going forward. As will be demonstrated, there are a number of growing concerns related to how women are considered and engaged in this space, yet their active participation and consideration are now perhaps more vital than ever.

## Trump and radical Islamic terrorism

The Trump administration's approach to counterterrorism from January 2017 to late 2018 was presented as multifaceted. In reality though, this was militarily dominated while simultaneously reducing funding and emphasis on diplomatic and developmental streams of effort. This was seen in his 2018 National Security Strategy (NSS) and National Strategy for Counterterrorism (NSCT), which are discussed below. However, his tenure thus far has also been marked by a number of controversies in this area, particularly his referencing of "radical Islamic terrorism" and the so-called "Muslim ban," which will be briefly discussed first. One key implication of such discourses and practices was that they were certain to alienate key Muslim allies and partners, including women, who could assist in direct and indirect counterterrorism efforts, even as the importance of engaging women in such moves was increasingly recognized.

There were a number of notable divergences from both Presidents Bush and Obama in the discourses around terrorism and the practices of counterterrorism under President Trump. One of the most evident of these was the label of "radical Islamic terrorism" that he personally engaged in the run-up to the election and throughout his term in office, and his general perception of the religion of Islam. This was a particularly problematic label which appeared to conflate the religion of Islam with terrorism, which differed greatly from previous administration efforts to emphasize "radical Islamists" as those who may support violence or militancy to achieve their political aims (such as ISIS or al-Qaeda).[11] For example, in 2016, Trump noted: "Containing the spread of radical Islam must be a major foreign policy goal of the United States."[12] In another example, when speaking to the Central Intelligence Agency (CIA) in 2017, President Trump noted: "Radical Islamic terrorism. And I said it yesterday—it has to be eradicated just off the face of the Earth. This is evil."[13] He noted again that the US would "unite the civilized world against Radical Islamic Terrorism, which we will eradicate completely from the face of the Earth."[14] In relation to the religion of Islam more broadly, he also linked Islam to the events on 9/11, and discussed Islam's treatment and status of women. In a 2016 Republican debate he noted:

> There is tremendous hate. Where large portions of a group of people, Islam, large portions want to use very, very harsh means. Let me go a step further. Women are treated horribly. You know that. You do know that. Women are treated horribly, and other things are happening that are very, very bad.[15]

This language was particularly problematic, and echoed Samuel Huntington's controversial "clash of civilizations" theory, which proposed that after the Cold War, western and Islamic cultures would be caught in a struggle. Such language appeared to pit the West against Islamic civilizations, as opposed to recognizing a minority fringe within Islam which engaged in violence.[16] Similar sentiments were also echoed by early figures in his administration, including Sebastian Gorka, a deputy assistant to Trump who viewed Islam as an inherently violent religion,[17] and Lieutenant General Michael Flynn (retired), a former national security advisor who also had a history of problematic comments that some viewed as Islamophobic.[18] It also offered another example of how Muslim women appeared to need "saving" in order to justify Trump's own political position, in which women were again held up as symbolic of the distinction between "us" and "them," and whose status became a cultural marker of this. While in some official strategies and publications this label of "radical Islamic terrorism" appeared absent,[19] the president's personal use of this phrase, as well as that of senior figures in the administration, overshadowed this point.

In January 2017, the first month of his presidency, Trump declared his Executive Order 13769, "Protecting the Nation from Foreign Terrorist Entry into the United States," a ninety-day restriction on entry of visa-holding citizens from Iran, Iraq, Syria, Yemen, Somalia, Sudan and Libya into the US (termed by many as a "Muslim ban"). This was defended based on the flawed argument that "the vast majority of individuals convicted of terrorism and terrorism-related offenses since 9/11 came here from outside of our country."[20] Trump noted: "We cannot allow our nation to become a sanctuary for extremists."[21] In another instance, he noted: "We have established strict new vetting procedures to keep terrorists out of the United States, and our vetting is getting tougher each month."[22] This ban appeared to conflate the broader Muslim community, including lawful immigrants and refugees, with violence and terrorism, thereby alienating the Muslim community both in the US and abroad.[23] Daniel Byman, a former staffer on the 9/11 Commission, suggested such policies were actually more inclined to increase terrorism, and aid recruitment for jihadist groups who claim the West is at war with Islam.[24]

Some of the tools and methods Trump proposed to deal with terrorists also proved controversial. Through Executive Order 13823 in January 2018 ("Protecting America Through Lawful Detention Of Terrorists"), Trump revoked Obama's order to close the Guantanamo Bay detention facility to "preserve military detention as a counterterrorism tool."[25] During his campaign prior to taking office, Trump also proposed to "take out the families" of terrorist actors, a particularly problematic statement as families would be considered civilians, and intentionally targeting civilians would be a violation of the Geneva Conventions.[26]

At their minimum, these actions served to alienate American Muslims and partner nations, particularly those with significant Muslim populations and the women that can contribute to direct and indirect counterterrorism efforts. Instead, women were framed as victims, thereby significantly limiting their perceived contributions to security. At their worst, these discourses risked feeding jihadist recruitment narratives, dividing the world into an "us" versus "them" mentality (which they referred to as eliminating the "grey zone") calls for war against the West in defense of Islam, and driving men and women into the arms of extremists. Furthermore, such narratives served to embolden right-wing extremists focused on issues such as immigration, race relations and a perceived cultural threat from Islam. Muslim women who wear visible religious symbols (such as the hijab or niqab) are often viewed as "soft" targets of Islamophobic attacks in particular, and largely face the brunt of this vitriol, highlighting the broader implications such discourses could have on public safety and security.[27]

## The 2017 NSS

Trump's first NSS was released in December 2017, and outlined US foreign policy and security priorities for the duration of his administration, much of which had already been visible during his first year in office. Trump had focused much attention on rebuilding his interpretation of American status in the world, and delineating an "America First" foreign policy. This was evident in the first outline of his foreign policy agenda in April 2016, which noted American "humiliation" from failures based on their previous focus on democratization and nation-building, as well as US allies like the North Atlantic Treaty Organization (NATO) "not paying their fair share" and rivals "no longer respecting us." Instead, America was "going to be strong again," and the US would focus on stabilization rather "nation-building," and a "a long-term plan to halt the spread and reach of radical Islam."[28]

Trump also suggested early on that many of the universal values that had been defined in previous foreign policy—where women's rights, status and equality have featured most visibly—would receive significantly less emphasis in practice now: "Instead of trying to spread universal values that not everybody shares or wants, we should understand that strengthening and promoting Western civilization and its accomplishments will do more to inspire positive reforms around the world than military interventions."[29] This perhaps helps explain why themes such as American greatness and America's "strategic confidence" became so heavily emphasized in the NSS. It also previews how programs which had focused on women's rights, status and equality in society not only faced less emphasis in foreign policy, but also in relation to US security.

Just prior to the release of the NSS, Lieutenant General H.R. McMaster, then a national security advisor under Trump, suggested that new national security challenges required a "dramatic rethinking of American foreign policy from the previous decades." There was a visible shift back to the pre-Cold War era of great power competition, where threats from non-state actors became a lesser priority. McMaster highlighted four key national interests, as outlined in the NSS: (1) protecting the American people, the homeland and the American way of life; (2) promoting American prosperity; (3) preserving peace through strength by rebuilding the military; and (4) advancing American influence. However, in order to do this, he stated the US had to reclaim "the strategic confidence necessary for implementing this strategy." This was discussed in four areas: (1) the values that defined the US; (2) the full instruments of US power; (3) the threats facing the US; and (4) the dynamic and competitive nature of the security environment.[30] These values had been described by Trump as "the dignity of every human life, protect[ing] the rights of every person, and shar[ing] the hope of every soul to live in freedom." The full instruments of power referred to "diplomatic, economic, military, informational, intelligence, and law enforcement." In the case of Afghanistan, this shift meant moving away from nation-building and back towards the 2001 goals of denying terrorist safe havens.[31] Discussing the security environment, Trump noted: "we do not base national security decisions on rigid ideology, but instead, on our core national interests and clearly defined objectives derived from these interests."[32]

Echoing similar comprehensive approaches to security as those of Bush and Obama, Trump's NSS noted America will "compete with all tools of national power to ensure that regions of the world are not dominated by one power."[33] While threats from revisionist China and Russia, and the "rogue states" of Iran and North Korea, now became prioritized over a focus on threats from jihadist groups, America was still focused on transnational terrorism and continued to "wage a long war against jihadist terrorist groups such as ISIS and al-Qa'ida [sic]." It noted: "These groups are linked by a common radical Islamist ideology that encourages violence against the United States and our partners and produces misery for those under their control."[34] This strategy, it noted, "calls for us to confront, discredit, and defeat radical Islamic terrorism and ideology and to prevent it from spreading into the United States.[35] To "prevail," it notes, "we must integrate all elements of America's national power—political, economic, and military."[36] Focusing on ensuring superior military power as related to America's ability to carry out diplomatic work, it stated: "A strong military ensures that our diplomats are able to operate from a position of strength."[37]

There was also a continued emphasis on jihadist terrorist organizations, which presented "the most dangerous terrorist threat to the Nation." It stated: "America, alongside our allies and partners, is fighting a long war against these fanatics who advance a totalitarian vision for a global Islamist caliphate that justifies murder and slavery, promotes repression, and seeks to undermine the American way of life." There were six priority actions in the NSS to specifically respond to jihadist terrorist organizations: first, by enhancing domestic and international intelligence, the US would seek to disrupt terror plots; second, the US would take direct action against terrorists and their sources of support; third, it would eliminate terrorist safe havens, both physical and online; fourth, they would sever sources of strength, such as financial, material and personnel supply chains, including a focus on online recruitment, counter-narratives and "amplifying credible voices;" fifth, it would focus on shared responsibility with partners, and help them develop capacity to fight terrorism independently; and finally, it would combat radicalization and recruitment in communities. It was evident that through direct action taken against terror groups, and an emphasis on partner capacity, the DoD would be taking the lead role in these efforts.

US development assistance—which had been an equal tool of the "3D" (defense, development and diplomacy) approach under Obama—was now seen in light of the "America First" approach, and thus had to support America's national interests even more explicitly in relation to security.[38] Development assistance would "assist fragile states to prevent threats to the US homeland. Transnational threat organizations, such as jihadist terrorists and organized crime, often operate freely from fragile states and undermine sovereign governments. Failing states can destabilize entire regions."[39] Noting specifically of Afghanistan, "engagement in Afghanistan seeks to prevent the reemergence of terrorist safe havens."[40] The role of development in US security strategies was still seen in relation to terrorist safe havens, yet the term "development" had now been excluded when discussing "all elements of America's powers." This suggested that in relation to primary military, political and economic streams of efforts, development was now delegated a lower status, and was required to demonstrate a security function.

In its discussion and inclusions of women, the 2017 NSS stands in stark contrast to that which preceded it. In the fifty-six-page document, "women" are referenced a mere eight times, while "girl" and "daughter" each receive one mention. Women are emphasized most clearly in defense terms as US servicewomen; as the "servicemen and women who defend the nation,"[41] ensuring "America's sons and daughters will never be in a fair fight,"[42] or more generalized as the "war fighters."[43] Women are also discussed in terms of their rights and empowerment; for example, in advancing American influence: "There can be no moral equivalency between nations that uphold the rule of law, empower women, and respect individual rights and those that brutalize and suppress their people. Through our words and deeds, America demonstrates a positive alternative to political and religious despotism."[44] Women are also referenced in this category under discussions of "American Values," whereby "governments that fail to treat women equally do not allow their societies to reach their potential."[45]

However, while the promotion of US values to advance American influence was highlighted, the US would not "impose its values on others,"[46] but instead try and inspire other nations to follow a similar path through their example. Perhaps most explicitly, it states empowering women and youth was encouraged: "Societies that empower women to participate fully in civic and economic life are more prosperous and peaceful. We will support efforts to advance women's equality, protect the rights of women and girls, and promote women and youth empowerment programs." America was thus demonstrating a "positive alternative to political and religious despotism."[47] The terms "gender" and "gender inequality" do not garner any mention. This appeared contradictory: if women's rights and empowerment were clearly associated with state peace and prosperity (yet as a value that would not be imposed on others), then women's rights and empowerment would likely be included in increasingly ad hoc and limited ways.

This demonstrated a significant shift in emphasis away from women's issues and programs in US foreign policy and security efforts, but largely represented obligatory and minimal lip-service to this concern. Moreover, extending from the discussion above, if diverse stated US values were being flouted by the Trump administration itself, then such values could be perceived in the wider global system as bankrupt or no longer relevant, including those pertaining to women. It is notable that alongside this, even with its reduced status, terrorism and terrorists are mentioned seventy-nine times in this strategy. It is also important to acknowledge the context within which this promotion of American values was articulated. President Trump himself had numerous recorded instances perceived as borderline, if not outright, sexist, which clearly stood in contrast to themes of women's empowerment and equality.[48] Combined with the military emphasis on direct action against terrorist groups, and a lessened emphasis on development and advancing US values, this approach to national security now emphasized defense efforts in this long war on jihadist groups, where considerations of women's status and their participation in this begins to fade.

## The 2018 NSCT

The Trump administration's explicit approach to counterterrorism was increasingly visible even prior to the release of the NSCT in 2018, with Lieutenant General H.R. McMaster stating a need for an integrated approach to counterterrorism in November 2017. Describing previous efforts as "an almost narcissistic approach to national security," he suggested, "Strategies are frequently based on what we would prefer, rather than what the situation demands." Facing non-state actors such as ISIS, he noted, required "integrated strategies to direct the purposeful employment of all instruments of power," which included "every element of national power—diplomatic, informational, military, economic, law enforcement, intelligence."[49]

## ENTER TRUMP: COUNTERTERRORISM GOING FORWARD

In October 2018, the White House released the first NSCT under the Trump administration. This strategy, similar to the NSS, reflected both continuity and divergence from the previous administrations in how it perceived terrorism and the means to counter it. What is noteworthy about this strategy though is the emphasis on diverse forms of extremism discussed in it, the use of the term "Islamist extremist," and a clear emphasis on areas like stabilization and development. There were four primary end states defined in this document: (1) eliminating the terrorist threat to the US; (2) securing borders and border entry points to the US against terror threats; (3) ensuring terrorism, radical Islamist and other violent extremist ideologies do not undermine the American way of life; and (4) emphasizing the role of foreign partners in addressing these threats. There was also an increased emphasis on countering terrorist radicalization and recruitment.

In a sign of the times in which it was written, the strategy also discussed the intervention, reintegration and counter-recidivism efforts being used in prisons, and with returning foreign terrorist fighters (FTFs), their families and children. Alongside this were efforts to combat extremist ideologies and undercut terrorist recruitment.[50] The focus on families raised another important point: that where considerations related to women do not appear explicit in the language of these strategies (which in the case of "families" was only partially so), there remains an assumption that considerations specific to women are either implicit (where women are assessed as fully agentic actors in all aspects of terrorist organizations) or irrelevant (where women are not seen as important in responses devised to terrorist groups). As responses to terrorist organizations since 9/11 have demonstrated, women remain at the margins of what we define as terrorist actors and how we account for their diverse roles in our responses.

Terrorist threats defined in this document recognized "Islamist terrorism, Iran-sponsored terrorism, and other forms of violent extremism," while the most potent transnational threat continued to be "radical Islamist terrorists." The eight official branches and two dozen networks of ISIS, as well as al-Qaeda's seemingly resilient network, were emphasized in its focus, but it also recognized more regionally focused groups such as Boko Haram, Tehrik-i-Taliban Pakistan (TTP otherwise known as the Taliban Movement of Pakistan) and Lashkar-e-

371

Taiba. There was a prominent focus on ideology, recognizing that this underpinned these terrorist groups. However, it was notable that the types of movements discussed in the strategy was expanding to recognize "a broad range of revolutionary, nationalist, and separatist movements overseas whose use of violence and intent to destabilize societies often puts American lives at risk."[51] Examples of these included the Nordic Resistance Movement (a nationalist socialist organization) and neo-Nazi groups like National Action, both of which have female membership, and both of which espouse idealized gendered roles for women, particularly in the domestic/family sphere. The document also acknowledged the diverse array of domestic terrorists motivated by other extremist ideologies, such as racially motivated extremism, and extremism related to animal rights, the environment, sovereign citizenship and militias in the US, which appeared to extend beyond Trump's own stated focus on Islamist terrorism. The use of strategic communications in this space was also highlighted in efforts to discredit terrorist narratives, deter supporters of these organizations, and try to emphasize that counterterrorism efforts extended beyond direct action alone. This is notable in that it appeared to be a divergence from how extremist ideologies were acknowledged and emphasized by Trump in broader public discourses, and those that were focused on in the national counterterrorism strategy.

A comprehensive approach to counterterrorism, which ranged from direct military action to preventative efforts, was also articulated: "We must confront terrorists with the combined power of America's strengths—our strong military, our law enforcement and intelligence communities, our civilian government institutions, our vibrant private sector, our civil society, our international partnerships, and the firm resolve of the American people." Indeed, these non-military tools such as "law enforcement, intelligence, diplomacy, financial measures, stabilization, development, prevention, and intervention and reintegration programs—are also required to prevent and counter terrorism." The US would work to better develop domestic and partner non-counterterrorism capabilities in these spheres, emphasizing "proactive diplomatic engagement, development assistance, and security assistance to help our partners act independently," and investing their own capital into counterterrorism efforts. This emphasis on balanced approaches to counterterrorism was also reflected in this discussion of partnerships: "We will also continue to work with our less resourced, non-traditional, or novel partners who may make unique contributions to help advance our shared counterterrorism efforts. Over time, this will result in a more balanced, equitable, and effective global approach to counterterrorism."[52]

The NSCT was informed by the "America First" approach, where prioritization was given to countries that posed a direct threat to the US, with "integrated actions and resources" directed at these countries. It also emphasized the roles of partner nations in dealing with these concerns domestically. The NSCT was "guided by United States interests; shaped by realistic assessments of both our challenges and our capabilities; and attuned to the important roles of our allies and partners, both foreign and domestic, in our shared counterterrorism efforts."[53] There was a particular emphasis on preventing terrorists from entering the US and a focus on border security, while cyber operations and strategic communications were also highlighted. Moreover, the NSCT signaled a range of indirect efforts:

> Broader range of non-military capabilities, such as our ability to prevent and intervene in terrorist recruitment, minimize the appeal of terrorist propaganda online, and build societal resilience to terrorism. This includes leveraging the skills and resources of civil society and non-traditional partners to diminish terrorists' efforts to radicalize and recruit people in the United States.[54]

It was evident that the Trump administration's approach to terrorism prioritized Islamist groups, emphasized military streams of effort and border security, and the roles of partners in dealing with these concerns. However, the NSCT suggested that the scope of recognized threats was widening across the ideological spectrum, and that areas also emphasized under the previous administration (such as development, countering violent extremism [CVE] and other preventative efforts) were also documented. There was also a focus on the cyber sphere, and on countering online ideologies and recruitment.

The following section will consider how this approach became evidenced in the DoD, US State and USAID, and how these parties understood the roles of women in this space. First though, it will highlight an important advancement for the women, peace and security agenda that took place in 2017, which informs how women were considered in US counterterror efforts.

## The Women, Peace and Security Act 2017

Though the Trump administration appeared to relegate women's status and empowerment in foreign policy to a lesser focus, there was still a notable change that occurred in this period. On 6 October 2017, the Women, Peace and Security Act was signed into law after several attempts to pass it in Congress between 2011 and 2017 were unsuccessful—the first law in the world of its kind. It mandated that the president would make public a Women, Peace and Security Strategy for the US within one year. Notably, Congress urged the Trump administration to "encourage increased women's participation in US-funded programs that provide foreign nationals with law enforcement, rule of law, or military education training" and "expand gender analysis to improve program design." This Act further outlined obligations for the DoD, US State and USAID specifically related to training for personnel in women, peace and security priority areas, such as conflict prevention, mitigation and resolution, international human rights law, and protecting civilians from violence, exploitation and trafficking. Notably for the DoD, it also stated training in "security initiatives that addresses the importance of participation by women" would be encouraged.[55] This was an important Act that continued to further integrate the women, peace and security agenda into US foreign policy, while also emphasizing the roles of women as security practitioners in foreign support and training.

In 2018, the DoD announced it was working with the National Security Council on an interagency strategy to incorporate and operationalize this Act. Steps taken within this included the creation of a synchronization group, with various representatives from around the armed forces who meet monthly to share and compare best practices, lessons learned, and advance future programs in the department. The DoD was aiming to have an instruction to outline how to implement women, peace and security measures into all DoD operations.[56] US State and USAID, meanwhile, also stated their commitment to the full implementation of this Act.[57]

However, annual reviews and updates on the implementation of the US NAP on Women, Peace and Security had ceased after 2016 in US

State and USAID, and by 2013 in DoD, making progress in advancing women, peace and security aims difficult to assess. This further suggested that this momentum required demonstrable action in these departments and agency, and that stated commitments had to be translated into action. The historical implementation of the NAP and women, peace and security agenda suggested that the will of influential persons in these organizations, as well as the availability of resources allocated to support this, would inform what impact this Act would have in practice. As this book was going to print this strategy was released in June 2019.

*Women in the DoD*

From the onset of his administration, Trump had emphasized the military as a lead actor in counterterrorism efforts and as a funding priority. In January 2017, he released the "Memorandum on Rebuilding the US Armed Forces," which stated that to "pursue peace through strength, it shall be the policy of the United States to rebuild the US Armed Forces,"[58] suggesting a shift in emphasis from the 3D approach to one which prioritized purely defense. Within the first budget of his administration, Trump had sought to increase the DoD budget by $54 billion, requesting a 2018 budget of $639 billion (real spending reached $700 billion). This further increased in 2019 to $686 billion, making it the highest request since 2011. The number of active-duty service members also increased in this period by 16,600 in 2018, and was set to reach an increase of 24,100 in 2019.[59]

The US had continued to focus military efforts in Iraq and Syria to defeat ISIS, and to maintain military gains against the group. Operations against ISIS in Iraq and Syria, but also Afghanistan, Libya, the Philippines, Niger and Somalia, continued to operate under the 2001 Authorization for Use of Military Force against al-Qaeda, demonstrating the longevity and reach of this authorization over the years.[60] Between August 2014 and March 2018, US military operations as part of the Combined Joint Task Force-Operation Inherent Resolve were estimated to have cost $23.5 billion,[61] and by late 2017, the number of US forces in Syria had reached approximately 2,000 personnel. These included US military advisors who were working with Iraqi national forces and Syrian Democratic Forces (SDF), with the US training 200 female volunteers in 2017 who then went on to fight ISIS on the front lines in Raqqa.[62] In an extremely rare, if not unprecedented, instance, US forces were training foreign women to operate specifically in active front-line combat operations in the Global War on Terror (GWOT). Under Trump, the US continued to emphasize the role of local and regional partners, and broadly maintained the five primary lines of efforts introduced under Obama in response to ISIS.[63] Yet some changes to US military operations and assistance programs also took place.

One visible way the military became more active in counterterrorism efforts was through the use of drone and air strikes, which increased sharply in tempo from the Obama administration (who had himself increased these greatly from the Bush administration) and also emphasized the military primacy of Trump's approach to counterterrorism. In Syria and Iraq, in the fight against ISIS, Operation Inherent Resolve had released a peak of 39,577 weapons in 2017, up from 30,743 the year prior.[64] Between January 2017 and April 2019, there had been a total of 4,852 confirmed strikes and up to 3,514 killed in Pakistan, Yemen, Afghanistan and Somalia.[65] Afghanistan was a particularly notable case, with strikes from January 2015 and the two years up to the onset of the Trump administration totaling 1,306; this more doubled to 4,582 between January 2017 and January 2019. However, in 2018, there was also a worrying trend that civilian casualties from US and Afghan strikes were also at their highest since 2010, wherein women and children accounted for 60 per cent of casualties.[66] Yemen experienced the highest concentration of strikes in its history, with fifty strikes being carried out in March 2017 (the next highest was fourteen strikes in October 2017). The US was also expanding its drone operations in West Africa, including expanding a CIA drone base in Dirkou, Niger,[67] and building a new DoD base in Agadez, Niger—a $110 million project which would cover a large part of the region, including Libya.[68]

The increasing rate of strikes and expansion of drone bases suggested that this was going to be a prominent counterterrorism tool of the Trump administration. The protection of civilians and the recording of civilian casualties in US operations had been increasingly emphasized, and was an encouraging sign that the US was becoming more transparent in this aspect of military operations.[69] However, particular considerations, such as the gender of those killed, or gender-specific impacts of civilians casualties, remained absent, suggesting there was not a clear picture of who was being targeted, or the holistic and gender-conscious civilian harm such tactics may have in practice.[70] Furthermore, in March 2019, Trump rejected the Obama-era Executive Order 13732 "United States Policy on Pre- and Post-Strike Measures To Address Civilian Casualties in US Operations Involving the Use of Force." This executive order required an annual and unclassified summary of the "the number of strikes undertaken by the United States Government against terrorist targets outside areas of active hostilities, as well as assessments of combatant and non-combatant deaths resulting from those strikes, among other information."[71] The susceptibility of the families of the enemy combatants killed in strikes to sympathize with insurgent or terrorist movements also became relevant to assessing the long-term implications of this form of military operations, particularly in areas where such groups would seek to support the families of "martyrs," but it was not clear if or how this was being assessed. While such concerns had been relevant since 2003 with the use of drones by the US, as their use in US operations increased, so too did the urgency of such aspects. Such emphasis on "eliminating" the terror threat as an end state, while reducing emphasis and funding for the agencies responsible for CVE, development and broader stabilization, risked creating a dangerous imbalance; as a result, the flow of persons joining or supporting such groups was not necessarily reduced, only targeted when perceived as a threat.

In the DoD, women continued to be discussed primarily as security practitioners. Trump appeared to largely hold to similar previous patterns by discussing the "men and women" of the armed forces, with the country "protected by the great men and women of our military and law enforcement and, most importantly, we are protected by God."[72] He recognized the "men and women serving at CENTCOM [central command] and SOCOM [US Special Operations Command] [who] have poured out their hearts and souls for this country,"[73] and "the men and women of the United States military […] the greatest fighters and the greatest force of justice on the face of the Earth and that the world has ever known."[74] He stated: "The men and women of our military operate as one team, with one shared mission, and one shared sense of purpose […]. [A]ll servicemembers are brothers and sisters. They're all part of the same family; it's called the American family."[75] In the fight against ISIS, female service members and support staff continued to die while on active duty. On 17 January 2019, four Americans were killed in a bomb attack claimed by ISIS in Manbij, northern Syria. One of the victims was Shannon M. Kent, a thirty-five-year-old Navy Chief Cryptologist Technician (Interpretative), as well as a civilian contractor, shedding light on another population of persons which are often over-looked in this space, and in which women play active roles. Up to 2018, a total of 169 active-duty female military personnel were killed on active duty, and 1,034 injured.[76]

Furthermore, under Trump, specific women were defined as unwel-come in the military. Trump announced in a tweet in July 2017 that "the United States Government will not accept or allow Transgender indi-viduals to serve in any capacity in the US Military," a decision that would impact the 250 transgendered persons openly serving in the military at this time.[77] This was followed up by a presidential memo in August which prohibited the military from enlisting transgendered persons or using funds to pay for gender-transition related surgeries.[78] This policy was struck down in multiple courts, and widely protested by lesbian, gay, bisexual, transgender and intersex (LGBTI) activists; despite this, the policy was confirmed in March 2018.[79]

Similar to his predecessors, Trump did not visibly distinguish women in foreign forces. For example, he noted of the liberation of Mosul from ISIS: "We grieve with the Iraqi people for the loss of the heroic soldiers and Peshmerga who gave their lives to restore life to their country, and we honor their sacrifice."[80] Moreover, women were refer-enced as victims of terrorist actors. Citing the 2017 attack in Barcelona, he noted, "terror groups will stop at nothing to commit the mass murder of innocent men, women and children."[81]

### Joint Publication 3–24 Counterinsurgency 2018

Within the DoD, women continued to evolve in how they were con-sidered in military doctrine and practice. In 2018, the US updated its "Joint Publication 3–24: Counterinsurgency" (JP 3–24) for the third time since 9/11. Reflecting a significant focus on the roles of women in insurgent organizations, it garnered nineteen mentions of women, and ten of female—the most of any COIN field manual thus far. It highlights gender norms as an important component of sociocultural knowledge, where US counterinsurgents should avoid imposing their ideal of normalcy on that culture.[82] The publication expands notably, and in a nuanced fashion, on aspects such as women's motivations to join insurgent movements, considering forced and volunteer recruitment, and the equality and independence provided by a movement. It notes the auxiliary roles women play in groups, ranging from combatants to cooks and suicide bombers (which is framed in terms of the tactical element of surprise), and the cultural norms which may prevent women from being searched.

Women are also discussed in terms of their potential for forced recruitment into insurgent organizations. In a welcome expansion, disarmament, demobilization and reintegration (DDR) also notably approaches women with greater nuance than previously seen:

> Females who have been associated with guerilla forces need specialized assistance during the DDR process. Females who have been raped or physically abused need counseling and medical services. Many women find, after being a guerilla, their former communities shun them for having rejected more traditional female roles. Conversely, demobilized females can be highly valuable human intelligence (HUMINT) sources, given their knowledge of their former unit and their various experiences.[83]

It also highlights considerations related to sexual violence: "DDR of females requires special considerations for medical treatment and counseling due to the high frequency of sexual assault and rape."With many lessons presumably integrated due to women's roles in ISIS, JP 3–24 offered the most advanced and nuanced expansion on women as both insurgents and in COIN activities seen since 9/11.

## Women in US State and USAID

While key documents such as the 2017 NSS did (minimally) discuss women's rights and empowerment in relation to broader security considerations, this emphasis in practice was markedly different. Themes that had been visible under Bush and Obama in relation to US State and USAID's work (for example, women's rights and empowerment) were also articulated by Trump. However, two key factors impacted what such discourses meant in practice on the ground. First, as these were considered under the rubric of US values, by emphasizing that the US would no longer seek to impose its "values" and "way of life" (or as it was referred to "principled realism") then the promotion of these within US foreign-policy objectives would likely be decreased. The US was now instead placing the onus on partner states to choose whether or not to emphasize these themes. Second, the institutions which have most directly focused their work in these areas—namely, US State and USAID—faced significant staffing and budgetary cuts, thereby limiting their own capacity to carry out programming in these fields.

This divergence between discourse and practice was first seen most prominently when speaking to leaders of the Islamic world in Riyadh at the Arab Islamic American Summit in May 2017—Trump's first foreign visit. Alongside an announcement of an agreement worth $400 billion in investment between the two countries, including $110 billion of Saudi defense purchases, and the opening of a Global Center for Combating Extremist Ideology, Trump echoed themes seen under both Bush and Obama. He noted it was in the shared interest of the US and its partners in the Arab world to "conquer extremism and vanquish the forces of terrorism." Terrorism, he noted, was a "battle between Good and Evil," which could only be overcome if "the forces of good are united and strong" and all partners did "their fair share and fulfills their part of the burden." He tied this to the girls and women in the Arab world: "Young Muslim boys and girls should be able to grow up free from fear, safe from violence, and innocent of hatred. And young Muslim men and women should have the chance to build a new era of prosperity for themselves and their peoples."[84] The US would, "wherever possible [...] seek gradual reforms—not sudden intervention."

Trump stated there was still much work to do: "That means honestly confronting the crisis of Islamist extremism and the Islamist terror groups it inspires. And it means standing together against the murder of innocent Muslims, the oppression of women, the persecution of Jews, and the slaughter of Christians."[85] Saudi Arabia was also praised for their "Vision for 2030:" a statement of "tolerance, respect, empowering women, and economic development." Middle Eastern countries should offer hope and a brighter future to their citizens: "promoting the aspirations and dreams of all citizens who seek a better life—

including women, children, and followers of all faiths. Numerous Arab and Islamic scholars have eloquently argued that protecting equality strengthens Arab and Muslim communities." Reflecting the language of the Bush administration, Trump also referenced women's dignity: "We must practice tolerance and respect for each other once again—and make this region a place where every man and woman, no matter their faith or ethnicity, can enjoy a life of dignity and hope."[86]

However, there was a practical gap between such discourses and what was unfolding in practice. In contrast to the DoD, US State and USAID faced significant budget and programming cuts, with women's programming in particular most affected. In contrast to previous administrations, language even referencing women and gender was drastically reduced at the request of the administration. There were also some worrying trends within US State and USAID under the Trump administration that suggested that these institutions would face limitations more generally, and specifically in work focused on women's issues. These related particularly to budgetary cuts within US State and USAID, which would carry out the bulk of work focused on women in security-relevant environments; a declining focus on women's rights and status more generally under the administration; and relevant posts and updates such as the NAP implementation updates remaining unfulfilled.

Prior to the release of the first budget, there were already indications that spending on diplomacy and development in US State and USAID was going to be drastically reduced from that of the Obama administration. There was significant pushback to these cuts, particularly from the armed forces themselves. In a letter to Congress in February 2017, 120 retired generals and admirals urged Congress not to cut funding to diplomacy and development aid, which they noted should be elevated alongside defense to keep America safe:

> We know from our service in uniform that many of the crises our nation faces do not have military solutions alone—from confronting violent extremist groups like ISIS in the Middle East and North Africa to preventing pandemics like Ebola and stabilizing weak and fragile states that can lead to greater instability.[87]

They noted the military would lead the "fight against terrorism on the battlefield, but it needs strong civilian partners in the battle against the drivers of extremism—lack of opportunity, insecurity, injustice, and hopelessness." It is noteworthy that the letter emphasized America's strategic investments in areas such as "the rights of women and girls," which had strong bipartisan support. It urged the government to ensure "resources for the International Affairs Budget keep pace with the growing global threats and opportunities we face. Now is not the time to retreat."[88] This suggested a key tension between the Trump administration and leading figures from the armed forces.[89]

Within the blueprint of the first budget for the 2018 financial year (released in March 2017), the Trump administration proposed cutting the budget of US State and USAID by as much 28 per cent, and proposed to further consolidate the two bodies.[90] The budget released in May 2017 indeed cut funding, and highlighted that foreign aid would be focused on US strategic objectives, including "supporting US national security in efforts to defeat the Islamic State of Iraq and Syria."[91] USAID believed they would have to cut down between 30 and 35 per cent of its field mission, and reduce its regional bureaus by up to 65 per cent.[92] Positions established under the Obama administration such as the Ambassador for Global Women's Affairs remained vacant, and there were concerns that funding for the Office of Global Women's Affairs would be cut off completely.

USAID's work was also increasingly framed in terms of its contributions to CVE. For example, USAID's Overseas Transitions Office—the office which emphasized short-term assistance focused on transitional and stabilization needs—stated that half of its country programs now focused on CVE. These programs were now framed in direct relation to the terrorist groups of the day and were global in scale. They were designed to "address the drivers of extremism and prevent the growth and expansion of the Islamic State in Iraq and Syria (ISIS), al-Qaida, and their affiliates around the globe from West Africa to South Asia." It had even established a CVE toolkit in 2018 which emphasized six streams of work: "counter and alternative narratives; reducing marginalization; youth engagement; improving government effectiveness; addressing economic drivers of extremism; supporting change agents and key influencers." Considerations of women and gender were inherent in this, even outlining a section on "working with women and girls." However, women were still viewed in terms such as playing a "moderating role against extremism" and bringing "unique perspectives" in relation to violent extremist threats. It was also recognized that these programs may have to be tailored specifically to the needs of women, and that women can also participate in violent extremism in some cases.[93] It was evident that USAID was now firmly focused on CVE work specifically, and that women were increasingly assessed within this.

Beyond this toolkit, three key documents in this period really highlighted how US State's and USAID's programming was being scaled back even while their work became increasingly concentrated and prioritized in work supportive of US security aims. These are the US State–USAID Joint Strategic Plan; the Stabilization Assistance Review and the US Strategy to Support Women and Girls at Risk of Violent Extremism, which will be briefly discussed.

## US State–USAID Joint Strategic Plan 2018–22

This prioritization of diplomatic and development resources for areas viewed in direct relation to national security became particularly evident in the US State–USAID Joint Strategic Plan 2018–22, released in February 2018. The first goal outlined in this plan was to protect America's security at home and abroad, including "[d]efeat ISIS, al-Qa'ida [sic] and other Transnational terrorist organizations, and counter state-sponsored, regional, and local terrorist groups that threaten US national security interests."[94] A second important element of this pertaining to stabilization work was to "[c]ounter instability, transnational crime, and violence that threaten US interests by strengthening citizen-responsive governance, security, democracy, human rights, and rule of law."[95] As part of their overarching objective to "degrade global terrorism threats so local governments and security forces can contain them and restore stability," one strategy would be to encourage local governments and non-governmental actors to "counter these radical ideologies, as well as to prevent and mitigate conditions conducive to instability, radicalization, and terrorist recruitment."[96]

Democratic governance would still be promoted, which would include "the voices of women and marginalized communities, to increase the trust between government authorities and local populations."[97] US State and USAID would prioritize their engagement and assistance to "stabilize areas liberated from violent extremist organizations, particularly ISIS," and work with government partners and civil society organizations to "to establish legitimate governance, restore the rule of law, and address local grievances, particularly among women, religious and ethnic minorities, and other marginalized communities."[98] Women's economic empowerment was also discussed in terms of its "transformational effects on families and communities," which could drive "inclusive economic growth that opens markets for US investments and counters violent extremism."[99] This document was notable in relation to the extent to which women's rights and empowerment programming now explicitly prioritized women's contributions to countering groups like ISIS and al-Qaeda in particular. US State was also continuing to carry out programs and efforts as related to counterterrorism and CVE that worked with women. US State's Global Engagement Centre, which was established in 2016 and led US government's efforts to counter propaganda and disinformation from international terrorist organizations and foreign countries, was reaching out to women in this CVE work.[100] In practice, however, most work was evident in US State's Anti-Terrorism and Assistance program, which, for example, trained Iraqi policewomen from the Ministry of Interior in terrorist crime scene investigation.[101]

There were some worrying concerns that women's rights were being increasingly neglected in US State's work under the Trump administration. US State was accused in this 2018 period of scaling back its reporting on women's rights, particularly that linked with violence against women and reproductive rights and discrimination, as well as its reporting on sexual and gender-based discrimination.[102] Research conducted by Oxfam and the University of Denver reported that annual Country Reports on Human Rights Practices for countries receiving US development assistance, which are delivered by US State to Congress on an annual basis, traditionally consider human rights practices in formulating US foreign policy, including development assistance. However, their research showed that reporting on women's rights issues outside of the US was down 32 per cent under the Trump administration, while reporting on LGBTI rights was down 21 per cent. In fact, countries with greater gender inequality saw greater declines in reporting; Afghanistan saw the largest reduction in reporting (56 per cent), while Yemen (52 per cent) and Iraq and both saw significant declines as well.[103]

Bearing in mind that women's status in conflict and post-conflict situations is particularly fragile, such reporting would be critical to directly informing stabilization needs and priorities, and risked significant neglect if they fell out of focus. When combined with the budget and personnel cuts in US State and USAID (which already placed challenges on existing programming) and prioritization of programs which had a direct link to counterterrorism, this raised important concerns about how women's status and rights were being reported and acted upon in US State.

*Stabilization Assistance Review*

In June 2018, DoD, US State and USAID released their Stabilization Assistance Review. It identified ways in which the US could more effectively leverage diplomatic engagements, defense and foreign assistance to stabilize conflict-affected areas, focusing on US national security interests, clearly defined outcomes, and increased burden sharing with international partners and local actors. Stabilization efforts would now be even more focused where there was a threat from terrorism which may threaten US national interests, making stabilization efforts which were targeted at women align more closely with mitigating risks from terrorism. For the first time, it also offered a clear US government-wide definition of "stabilization" as "a political endeavor involving an integrated civilian-military process to create conditions where locally legitimate authorities and systems can peaceably manage conflict and prevent a resurgence of violence." Stabilization efforts were emphasized as political at their core, and transitional in their nature, ideally lasting between one to five years. They would focus on civil security and dispute resolution, and targeted basic services, the return of displaced persons and longer-term development.[104] According to the review, focus should be on local efforts: building local support and legitimacy, and local political and social systems to begin with, and scaling-up accordingly where focus on political settlements on the national level should be synchronized.

The review continued to recognize that "[p]rotracted conflicts provide fertile ground for violent extremists and criminals to expand their influence and threaten US interests." It specifically pointed to the post-ISIS response in Syria and Iraq, where the US had to assist local partners to "secure the peace" and consolidate security gains made against the group. It also pointed to Libya and Nigeria, where the US was encountering similar concerns from ISIS and other transnational terror groups,[105] and directly outlined the impacts that counterterrorism efforts could have on stability operations:

> Counterterrorism operations are prioritized in many conflict environments today, but some operations may have destabilizing effects. Stabilization cannot be an afterthought. Rather, it needs to be fully integrated and elevated across lines of effort. It should be incorporated into campaign planning as early as possible to help shape operational design and strategic decisions.[106]

Here, civilian-military planning, joint training and coordination was emphasized, interagency input flagged as essential, and clear lines of authority between and within the US government required for an effective "whole-of-government" approach to stabilization. In short, DoD, US State and USAID had to better prepare and train for stabilization efforts together, and better institutionalize how this would work in practice towards a common and clearly defined aim. In support of better integrated civil-military operations, USAID had placed thirty staff in the Pentagon, Combat Commands and other military headquarters, and each of its missions now had an appointed Mission Civil-Military Coordinator who advised and coordinated with a DoD counterpart. USAID even had stabilization advisors at US Special Operations Command and some Theater Special Operations Commands.[107]

The link between stabilization efforts and counterterrorism aims was even more clearly explicated in relation to security training and assistance:

> In support of counterterrorism objectives, the international community is providing high volumes of security sector training and assistance to many conflict-affected countries, but our programs are largely disconnected from a political strategy writ large, and do not address the civilian-military aspects required for transitional public and citizen security. More focus needs to be placed on helping security forces to secure population centers and restore trust with local communities.[108]

This review had a number of important implications for how women would be engaged in stabilization efforts. First, there was a potential opportunity to further integrate and embed both gendered knowledge and women's participation that were historically prominent in US State and USAID into future stabilization programs, as well as the increased knowledge that DoD had developed over the years in locations such as Afghanistan, Iraq and Yemen, as highlighted in the chapters on US State and USAID in this book. These had encompassed areas of focus ranging from women's rights and political empowerment, to how women's security was assessed at the local level (and indeed how they were integrated into these security efforts themselves), women's protection in conflict (including from SGBV), or women's consultation and participation in dispute resolution. Stabilization work carried out in Iraq in 2018 that emphasized women included programs promoting community engagement and reconciliation, where women and youth were supported through advocacy training and livelihood support.[109] It also raised important considerations about how women's presence in local security forces could be vital to securing populations and restoring trust with communities.

However, this increased targeting of stabilization efforts in areas viewed as counterterrorism priorities also brought with it numerous concerns. If women's participation or women-centric programming was not recognized to have an explicit counterterrorism link then it risked being relegated to a lesser priority. This also fed into previous concerns where efforts that emphasized women would have to "securitize women" in order to make them relevant to counterterrorism concerns. For example, would practitioners (both local and US) have to demonstrate that women's rights and development programming could serve a specific stabilization or counterterrorism function? Would this jeopardize the safety of personnel working in these fields and make these women themselves targets of opposition actors? The success of better integrated approaches to stabilization would be very much dependent on how this review was operationalized and supported in practice, and if/how women were considered at each step.

### US Strategy to Support Women and Girls at Risk from Violent Extremism and Armed Conflict

In February 2019, US State's Office of Global Women's Affairs released a strategy to accelerate the incorporation of women (who were viewed as influential actors) into US counterterrorism initiatives, address their safety and empowerment to facilitate this, and respond to women as terrorist actors. This included "targeted countering violent extremism (CVE) programs to address women's disengagement, rehabilitation, and reintegration of women foreign terrorist fighters."[110] This strategy was guided by three principles and stated four key objectives. First, women and girls "leadership, participation, and agency in addressing the life-cycle of violent extremism in fragile and conflict-affected environments" was defined, and would thus consider women's radicalization, empha-size safety and access to education, and respect their human rights. Secondly, these policies and programs would be anchored in research and best practices. Thirdly, localized approaches, research and analysis across CVE policies and activities which incorporated gender consider-ations would aim to improve the sustainability, effectiveness and buy-in among implementing agencies. This included through community-led approaches and empowered women-led organizations.

In terms of objectives, women were to be supported as "effective leaders and participants in preventing and responding to terrorism radicalization" in their societies and families. The promotion and pro-tection of the rights, safety and inclusion of women and girls in societ-ies was also promoted. This included in cases where women had sur-vived terrorist violence, including those who had been kidnapped by terror groups. Women also had to be recognized as terrorist actors who can radicalize, facilitate or perpetrate violence, and their disen-gagement, rehabilitation and reintegration had to be tailored to their needs. Finally, this strategy aimed to establish appropriate capacity building and coordination, including internally in the US government. It is noteworthy that the success of this strategy was dependent on "interagency cooperation and leveraging diverse resources."[111] While particularly brief and limited (approximately two pages in length in online format), this strategy was the most cognizant to date of the varied roles that women could play in all aspects of violent extrem-ism: as leaders and actors challenging and preventing violent extrem-ism, to drivers and actors of violent extremism themselves. While internal to US State, and defining activities specifically for US State and USAID, the impact and implementation of this strategy remains to be seen in broader agency-specific and interagency efforts. At the time of publication, the position of Ambassador-at-Large for Global Women's Issues still remained unfilled, as it had since the beginning of the Trump administration.

## Thinking about women and security today

Key countries of focus for US counterterrorism efforts since 9/11—namely Afghanistan, Iraq and Yemen—remain a priority, even as these have now been joined by locations such as Syria, Libya, the Philippines, the Sinai, and others in the Middle East and North Africa (MENA) region, and East and West Africa, amongst others. The nature of these concerns has evolved greatly in the years since 2001, but as became starkly visible, each country faced a host of interlinked challenges which had both direct and indirect security implications for the citizens of those countries, and increasingly for regional and international actors as well. The necessity of strategies that encompass holistic efforts—ranging from military to political, and development to the economy—is clear, and considerations related to women have been highlighted throughout.

The final section will look at Afghanistan, Iraq, Syria and Yemen since 2017, and will demonstrate just how important these evolutions in US strategy and policy will be for immediate security concerns, as well as the long-term stabilization and recovery of these countries. Holistic approaches to security concerns have perhaps never been as important as they are today due to the multifaceted strategies and tactics engaged by groups like ISIS and al-Qaeda. It also demonstrates that perhaps now, more than ever, women must be inherently considered and engaged in all efforts going forward. Yet, as will be demonstrated, a number of the shortfalls that have been visible since 9/11 are still prominent today, highlighting a continued divergence in policy and practice.

## Afghanistan

Since 9/11, Afghanistan has remained a focus of US foreign policy, and will remain on the agenda for the foreseeable future. The conflict has continued to evolve, as has the US's role and the nature of their efforts in the country since 2017. By 2018, the US had suffered over 2,000 casualties in the conflict, and invested $132 billion in various aid, more than it invested in the post-World War II Marshall Plan for Europe's reconstruction.[112]

When Trump entered office, he announced what he deemed a new US strategy in the country, focused on creating conditions on the ground as a guideline for US withdrawal, rather than setting a specific date to leave. Yet, the conditions on the ground that would satisfy a US withdrawal were changing. He stated previous foreign policy had spent too much "time, energy, money, and most importantly lives, trying to rebuild countries in our own image, instead of pursuing our security interests above all other considerations."[113] A fundamental pillar of this new strategy was "the integration of all instruments of American power—diplomatic, economic, and military—toward a successful outcome." However, this outcome would move away from "nation-building" to more direct efforts against terrorists: "We are not nation-building again. We are killing terrorists." This new strategy would also take a harder line against Pakistan—both a partner in counterterrorism efforts, but also one who also harbored "militants and terrorists who target US servicemembers and officials"—and also increase the role of India as a partner. Finally, Trump would "expand authority for American armed forces to target the terrorist and criminal networks that sow violence and chaos throughout Afghanistan." How victory was defined in Afghanistan for the US focused almost exclusively on terrorism: "attacking our enemies, obliterating ISIS, crushing al Qaeda, preventing the Taliban from taking over Afghanistan, and stopping mass terror attacks against America before they emerge."[114]

While economic development was discussed in this strategy, this burden was increasingly placed on the Afghan government and international partners. Trump described these efforts as "principled realism," where "we will no longer use American military might to construct democracies in faraway lands, or try to rebuild other countries in our own image. Those days are now over. Instead, we will work with allies and partners to protect our shared interests."[115] Development and diplomatic efforts became relegated to a lesser concern even as it was recognized that "[m]ilitary power alone will not bring peace to Afghanistan or stop the terrorist threat arising in that country. But strategically applied force aims to create the conditions for a political process to achieve a lasting peace."[116]

As part of Operation Freedom's Sentinel, the US has taken a two-stream approach to countering Islamic State in Khorasan Province (IS-K) in Afghanistan since 2015. The first was multilateral efforts as part of the NATO-led mission Resolute Support Mission, which focused on training, advising and assisting Afghan government forces. The second stream of effort was led by US counterterrorism forces and some partner forces engaging in direct combat operations. Perhaps most well-known of these operations was the unprecedented use of MOAB (short for "Mother of all Bombs")—one of the country's largest, most lethal non-nuclear bombs, which targeted a tunnel complex being used by IS-K in April 2017, killing ninety militants.[117] Both streams of effort have seen $134.3 billion earmarked for these since the beginning of 2015.[118] Yet, concerns related to IS-K have only continued to grow.

The Taliban remained the primary insurgent group in the country, and continued to wage an entrenched insurgency against the Afghan government, launching attacks throughout the country. Yet, some elements within the Taliban also appeared to be evolving in ways that distinguished it from the insurgent group the US has been at war with since 2001. There was an acknowledgement by some in the US government that there was a stalemate with the Taliban, with neither parties able to claim a victory in the country.[119] Even after all the years of military conflict, since the major withdrawal of foreign troops in 2014, the Taliban still controlled up to half the country, and was "openly active" in up to 70 per cent of it.[120]

The Taliban's governance was now recognized to be more coherent than ever, the influence of which extended farther in reach than their control of land. Examples highlighted by Ashley Jackson include their co-option and control of both government and non-governmental organizations, regulation of the education curriculum, and even controlling mobile service in some areas. The Taliban claimed to be trying to correct their previous positions that had gained them international condemnation, now stating that all women should have access to education. Jackson highlighted the implications this could have for international actors dealing with the Taliban:

> The question is not *whether* to engage: the Taliban are using humanitarian access and development interventions for political and military

ends, and agencies are increasingly being forced to react to this reality [...]. The challenge for the international community now is to figure out *how* to engage with the Taliban on these issues in a politically feasible and strategic way.[121] [original emphasis]

In 2014, the Taliban opened their first political office in Qatar, which presented the first official representation of the Taliban outside of Afghanistan. In November 2017, US citizens began to engage in unofficial backchannel dialogue with Taliban representatives, laying what were hoped to be foundations for future peace talks with the group.[122] The government of Afghanistan also indicated it would potentially enter into talks with the Taliban without preconditions in February 2018. Within this, President Ashraf Ghani had stipulated that the Taliban would have to recognize the Afghan government and respect the rule of law, including the rights of women.[123]

Women had made considerable gains in Afghanistan since 2001. From a Taliban government that did not allow women to work and largely kept them in the home, 78,000 had now been appointed to government positions since 2001, and 8,000 held office in 2017.[124] Women were increasingly present in the police, military and other security roles around the country, including in its 777th Special Mission Wing in Afghanistan's Special Security Forces.[125] National legislation had strengthened women's rights and protections under the law, women were increasingly present in the workforce and security forces, and were going to school at the highest rates since 2001. Yet, Afghanistan still ranked last in the world in the 2018 Women, Peace and Security Index, where it tied with Syria based on the dimensions of security, justice and inclusion, starkly outlining the challenges that still remained.[126]

In 2018, President Ghani announced a Ramadan ceasefire between 15–17 June, the first real cessation of hostilities between the two parties in seventeen years.[127] In August that year, President Ghani announced a three-month ceasefire with the Taliban in celebration of the Eid al-Adha holiday, offering some hope that a political settlement could finally be attainable (although this ceasefire failed to hold). Other contentious issues, such as the Taliban's close alliance with al-Qaeda, which is still observed,[128] make the prospects for such a settlement less clear. However, if a political settlement with the Taliban is in part a future pathway to peace and stability in the country, women would have the most at stake in any settlement with the group. Women's rights are often one of the first points of compromise in negotiated settlements, and the Taliban's record on this has not been encouraging. Women's representation and participation in such negotiations would be imperative for maintaining and continuing to build on the humble gains they had achieved. However, at peace talks held in February 2019 in Moscow (where prominent Afghan politicians, but not the Afghan government, were represented), only two women were present. The Taliban envoy noted they would protect the rights of women "in a way that neither their legitimate rights are violated nor their human dignity and Afghan values are threatened." However, he then criticized "so-called women's rights activists" for undermining Afghan traditions and customs, which he stated were "imposed on Afghan society under the name of women rights." Both a lack of women's presence in these talks, and the discourses being engaged by the Taliban, raised significant concerns that a peace deal would put women's fragile status in the country in limbo.[129]

Terror organizations also continued to be active in Afghanistan, and were evolving in both their form and the threat they posed. Established in 2015, IS-K had become the most potent ISIS branch beyond Iraq and Syria, drawing members from various regional organizations, including the Afghan and Pakistani Taliban, and groups like the Islamist Movement of Uzbekistan. IS-K has inflicted misery on local populations, including the abduction of women and minors, use of child soldiers, SGBV (including rape and sexual slavery) and the targeting of girls' schools.[130] DoD estimates have placed the membership of IS-K at around 1,200 fighters,[131] but UN estimates have stated this could be as high as 4,000.[132] Afghanistan has also proven to be a choice relocation destination for some ISIS affiliates departing Iraq and Syria, including some foreign families and women, a small number of which were reportedly training other women in Jowzan Province.[133] Notably, in August 2017, the TTP, once infamous for its treatment of women, released the publication *The Way of Khaula*, which focused on women's recruitment and active combat roles in jihad.[134] The release of this text suggested that some regional jihadist groups were targeting propaganda at women, may be seeking female membership and support, and may even be in competition for this.

Al-Qaeda has continued to maintain a firm alliance with the Taliban in the face of this ISIS rivalry, and appeared to be playing the long game; meanwhile, ISIS has continued to confront the Taliban for territorial and political supremacy. The Taliban, too, were increasingly pushing back against IS-K, even requesting a cessation of US and Afghan hostilities to facilitate an offensive against the terror group in August 2018. General John Nicholson, commander of US and coalition forces, did not confirm the US would do this, but stated: "We are going fully at Isis. We also note that the Taliban is fighting IS [Islamic State] and we encourage that because IS needs to be destroyed."[135] Due in part to an increase in attacks conducted by IS-K in the country, and its increased confrontation with other actors in the country, 2016–18 saw increasing rates of civilian casualties: the first half of 2018 saw the highest numbers since 2010 (the first year the United Nations Assistance Mission in Afghanistan started keeping records), a significant portion of which were women who were killed or injured in attacks.[136]

Afghanistan clearly faces many challenges going forward, and its prospects for long-term peace remain unclear. Yet, from a country where women were publicly executed in soccer stadiums and prevented from accessing basic education or employment, there is cause for some optimism. How women are considered, engaged and supported in all efforts related to governance, state security and stability remain crucial to maintaining the gains they have thus far made, and indeed to the long-term prospects for the country.

## Iraq and Syria

At its peak in 2015, ISIS had controlled approximately 27,000 square miles across Iraq and Syria, and governed over a population of around 8 million persons. Moreover, the group had largely continued to carry out its reign of terror in the two countries up until the end of 2017. As global efforts to degrade and defeat the group intensified, they increasingly inflicted misery and suffering on populations under their control. They also began to develop cheap, new technologies which were deployed in battle, designing and mass-producing munitions and other improvised weapons, as well as weaponizing more mainstream improvised explosive devices.[137] ISIS had also been attempting to manufacture chemical weapons at laboratories throughout the territory it held, and had used low-grade chemical weapons in attacks against Iraqi forces. ISIS finally lost its final urban strongholds in Iraq (Mosul) in July, and Syria (Abu Kamal) in December 2017. As Iraqi forces retook Mosul, between June and early July 2017, at least thirty-eight female suicide bombers (some carrying children) carried out attacks for the first time in Syria and Iraq.[138] By fall 2018, this territory had been reduced to pockets of land around the eastern region of Deir al-Zour and the eastern side of the Middle Euphrates River Valley in Syria.[139] In March 2019, ISIS had finally been physically defeated in the city of Baghouz—almost five full years after declaring their "caliphate." What were initially thought to be small numbers of foreign women and minors remaining with ISIS instead saw thousands come streaming out and surrender to SDF custody—4,000 women, 8,000 minors and 1,000 men from fifty countries (excluding Syria and Iraq) by April 2019.[140] From regional IDP camps such as al-Hawl, many were requesting return to their home nations, prompting international debate on the future and responsibility (for and of) these persons. However, even with this defeat ISIS were still reported to control between 14,000 and 18,000 militants in Iraq and Syria, including up to 3,000 FTFs. In Iraq alone, up to 13,000 minors younger than twelve years old were noted to lack nationality due to not having birth registration or paperwork, including foreign minors, which may place their future in jeopardy.[141]

Iraq and Syria remained firmly on the global agenda: two priority countries for US foreign policy and security considerations in relation to both continued threats from terrorist actors, and the long-term recovery and stabilization required to prevent the resurgence of such a scenario again. While ISIS had been defeated militarily in these two countries, it has now entered a new insurgent phase, which will continue to impact the region. The necessary stabilization, reconciliation, rebuilding and recovery from this period remain formidable long-term tasks, and a future political settlement in Syria is still elusive. The status of the foreigners that traveled to Iraq and Syria is now a point of international concern and attention. However, a closer look at the current status of the two countries demonstrate how women suffered particular horrors under ISIS, and that their participation and consideration in all efforts related to recovery, security and stabilization is more vital than ever. It also demonstrates the global responses now required to manage the thousands of women who became affiliated with ISIS, and integrations of considerations pertinent to them must be inherent in all efforts going forward.

### UN responses to ISIS

Iraq and Syria prompted notable shifts at the United Nations (UN) in relation to women who had become affiliated with ISIS. These were poised to inform wider global responses to the issue, as well as how women were accounted for and responded to in all areas of countering terrorism and violent extremism going forward. In the UN's own activities, this was particularly evident with UNSCR 2395 in 2017; this renewed the mandate of the UN's Counter-terrorism Committee Executive Directorate (CTED), which carried out the committee's policy decisions, assessed member states and offered counterterrorism technical assistance. UNSCR 2395 highlighted the importance of engaging women in CTED's work, as well as the importance of utilizing women in increasing awareness about threats and tackling them more efficiently, and in strategies aimed at countering terrorism and violent extremism. In fact, it noted gender as a crosscutting theme to be integrated in all UN/CTED activities, and encouraged CTED to conduct:

> [...] [c]onsultations with women and women's organizations to inform its work, and *urges* CTED in collaboration with UN Women to conduct and gather gender-sensitive research and data collection on the drivers of radicalization to terrorism for women, and the impacts of counterterrorism strategies on women's human rights and women's organizations.[142]

The UN had also produced a number of new resolutions to lead cooperation and coordination between member states in response to ISIS, which focused on aspects like the identification and management of FTFs, and interrupting terrorist financing.[143] These also considered women affiliated with ISIS for the first time in such detail. UNSCR 2396 (2017) recognized that women and children associated with FTFs may have served roles including as supporters, facilitators and perpetrators of terrorist acts, and therefore required tailored prosecution, rehabilitation and reintegration strategies. It also recognized that these women and children may be victims of terrorism, and so gender and age sensitivities had to be accounted for. It noted women's participation and leadership was essential in the "design, implementation, monitoring, and evaluation of these strategies," addressing returning and relocating FTFs and their families. Other notable points included gender sensitivities when investigating ISIS crimes in Iraq, including gender perspectives in risk assessment and intervention programs; and gender-sensitive strategies to address and counter terrorist narratives in prisons. The breadth of considerations related to women and gender in relation to terrorist organizations in UNSCR was unprecedented; these would now inform the UN's own activities, and had the potential to inform and shape how member states considered women and gender in their own activities and responses to terrorism and violent extremism.

## Iraq

The people of Iraq continued to suffer the brunt of ISIS rule, and the future prospects for millions remain stark. Six million Iraqis (15 per cent of the population) had been displaced since 2014 due to ISIS and operations against the group. By October 2018, 4 million of these had returned home, while 1.9 million remain displaced, a majority of which were women and children. For those who returned home, concerns related to destroyed housing and infrastructure, dim prospects for employment opportunities and ongoing security remained.[144] The government of Iraq have sought $100 billion to support reconstruction efforts across the country, as well as economic revival efforts to boost the economy post-conflict.[145] The reconstruction and stabilization of West Mosul alone is estimated to cost $700 million.[146]

The true number of civilians killed at the hands of ISIS and in the operations to defeat it will likely remain unknown. However, the most conservative estimates by the UN recorded 30,000 deaths between 2014 and 2017, as well as 55,150 injured. The actual figures are expected to be significantly higher. There is also growing evidence of what may account to war crimes, crimes against humanity and genocide being carried out by ISIS, and over 200 mass graves have now been found in Nineveh, Kirkuk, Salahuddin and Anbar, with an estimated 12,000 persons buried amidst these alone.[147] Areas that recorded atrocities by the group have highlighted that women featured prominently on ISIS execution lists, particularly those working in the fields of medicine, law, academia, media, politics and female activists, as well as LGBTI persons. Estimates of civilian casualties in the battle for Mosul alone are between 9,000 and 11,000, where at least a third of these are attributed to ISIS directly targeting and executing civilians, and using them as human shields;[148] women and children were prominent amidst these.[149] At least 1,452 Yazidi women and girls also remained in ISIS captivity as of November 2018.[150]

Beyond violence committed directly by ISIS, the insecurities that already faced many Iraqi women in their lives were also exacerbated during the conflict. Women saw increased rates of domestic abuse, trafficking, psychological traumas, honor killings, forced marriage and female genital mutilation go largely unaddressed by the state in this period.[151] Yet there are some glimmers of hope emerging in this region. Despite conservative social norms against women who experience sexual violence, as well as conversion and sexual relations outside of this tight-knit community, leaders in the Yazidi community had been challenging stigmas related to these. For example, the Yazidis' supreme spiritual leader, Khurto Hajji Ismail (also known as the Baba Sheikh), and other religious leaders created a religious ritual for persons who had experienced forced conversion or rape whereby they were blessed, declared "true Yazidis" and welcomed back to their community. Men who escaped were also being welcomed back to the community.[152] However, such welcome did not extend to children born of Yazidi mothers and ISIS fathers, leaving the status of these women and their children in limbo.

Many civilians, including women, were also killed in anti-ISIS operations. By the end of April 2018, US Central Command assessed "at least 883 civilians have been unintentionally killed since the start of Operation Inherent Resolve."[153] However, in June 2018, Airwars, an independent monitoring organization, stated a minimum of 6,321 civilians have been killed by coalition strikes.[154] Following this, the Pentagon acknowledged "no one will ever know" how many civilians were killed in operations against ISIS in Syria and Iraq.[155] As cases from other conflicts, including the earlier Iraq War demonstrate, a significant influx of widows and orphans—both of local civilians, and civilians that became affiliated with ISIS—have likely been produced as a result of this. The number of orphans generated by conflict—again, both local children and those of foreign ISIS affiliates—are currently unknown, but are estimated to be in the thousands.[156] Though exact figures remain unknown, upwards of tens of thousands of widows and orphans are not beyond the realm of possibility, highlighting the urgency of accounting for their specific needs and challenges in stabilization and long-term recovery work.

There were also many aspects about the conflict that remained unclear, but which encapsulate the severity of concerns going forward, particularly for women. Estimates for ISIS affiliates that had been killed on the battlefield ranged wildly between former UK Defence Secretary Michael Fallon's figures of 25,000,[157] and those of US Special Operations General Raymond Thomas, who noted conservative figures of up to 70,000.[158] How many of these were civilians who became coerced into supporting the organization—for example, paying taxes or returning to their civil jobs for fear of punishment under ISIS— remain unclear. Revkin has highlighted how US targeting doctrines have historically been based on groups such as al-Qaeda, where identifying militants was clearer-cut. Now, with terrorist groups taking up state-building, and in many cases forcing those under its controlled territory to support it in diverse (though sometimes non-violent) ways, it was becoming more difficult to observe and distinguish between civilians coerced into supporting the group and those who may be committed members of the organization. This lack of distinction may end up penalizing civilians in counterterrorism operations, and impact these persons in post-conflict efforts.[159] For those who had family members in ISIS, many faced the additional stigma of ISIS affiliation, which has impacted their ability to return home and reintegrate into their community. These figures also raised questions and concerns about the status of families of ISIS members—a community unlikely to receive sympathy from the populations that suffered under the group and who largely comprised women and minors. Yet, their future prospects required consideration in terms of both what this meant for potential security concerns going forward if they were committed to ISIS and its ideology, and prospects for reconciliation and reintegration into society more broadly.

Beyond such destruction, the concerns related to ISIS affiliates—both those accounted for and unaccounted for; foreign and local—continue to linger and are likely to do so into the foreseeable future. Many of these had already left the country; by July 2018, approximately 20 per cent of its estimated 41,490 foreign affiliates (men, women and minors who became affiliated with or were born into the group) had returned to their country of departure or appeared to be in the process of doing so. This prompted governments around the world to grapple with the required security, judicial and deradicalization responses of these distinct populations, making this a shared global concern. However, of these, only 256 cases of female returnees had been publicly accounted for globally.[160] In Iraq, at least 1,350 foreign women and 580 children were held by authorities in April 2018, where many have been facing trial.[161] By August 2018, at least 494 foreign women had been convicted of belonging to or aiding ISIS.[162] These numbers do not account for all foreign women still in Iraq and Syria, where they have also been held in other sites, engaged in detainee exchanges between SDF forces and ISIS fighters, and in negotiated departures from cities like Raqqa.[163]

These are only a snapshot of the full numbers: including local populations, at least 7,374 persons have been charged with ISIS-related crimes, and up to 20,000 have been held as ISIS suspects in Iraq according to Human Rights Watch, who have also raised concerns about these prosecutions and access to justice for ISIS victims.[164] The age of criminality in Iraq is nine years old, highlighting the number of children in trials and the distinct concerns in terms of rehabilitation and their future prospects. For displaced women who were suspected of being family members of ISIS, they also faced revenge attacks, retribution killings and sexual exploitation, and were denied access to services. Many refused or were unable to return home.[165] Amnesty International has highlighted "thousands" of female-headed families with a perceived affiliation to ISIS who now face dire prospects due to collective punishment.[166] The government of Iraq has recognized that "the return and reintegration of family members of suspected ISIS supporters is important to prevent future radicalization to violence."[167] Such figures prompt urgent concerns about how women affiliated with terror groups are identified, assessed and responded to in more ways than just judicially, ensuring that those who have committed crimes are brought to justice. This also raises interrelated concerns such as female detention (and the potential to radicalize in prison), and how deradicalization, rehabilitation and possible reintegration and reconciliation are conducted and supported. Addressing stigmas of those with a perceived affiliation to ISIS also becomes important.

In 2018, between 20,000 and 30,000 local and foreign ISIS supporters remained in Syria and Iraq, and were anticipated to be a medium-term threat due to ongoing conflict and stabilization concerns.[168] Some figures noted up to 17,000 ISIS fighters remained in Iraq.[169] While no longer the presence it once was in either country, and unlikely to ever hold territory as it once did, ISIS is currently morphing into a more covert, insurgent force, and will likely be an ongoing threat in terms of terror and broader instability across the region; this has hence been framed as a "generational struggle."[170] In fall of 2018, regional forces had stated that between 225–250 women originally associated with the al-Khansaa Brigade had been trained up to carry out invasive activities and attacks, and had also been directed to recruit and train women in other centers established throughout the region. Many of these women remained unaccounted for at the time of writing, and thus pose a threat in this evolution to an insurgent movement. Researcher Vera Mironova, who was embedded on the front lines with Iraqi Special Operations Forces, observed small numbers of female ISIS members appearing to engage in combat, and raised concerns about women's covert roles in the insurgency that ISIS is now morphing into.[171] ISIS must also be assessed in terms of its ability to continue to inspire those who were unable to travel to Iraq and Syria around the world, or who appear to otherwise have no formal affiliation to the group to carry out attacks. This includes a significant proportion of women.

Perhaps most worryingly, despite the horrors that ISIS inflicted, the group still maintained the support of some local populations, particularly due to their ability to govern and maintain order. Survey research conducted in 2018 amongst limited populations in Mosul after the physical defeat of ISIS highlighted that up to 65 per cent of persons still recognized some good that ISIS had done at the beginning of its rule, including "defense, commitment to religion, implementation of sharia, and provision of security, stability, and a sense of freedom." The physical and juridical subordination of women was noted by the authors in this survey work, and many locals supported this view of the role of women, particularly as it was deemed in opposition to western values. The requirement of women to wear the niqab was particularly praised.[172] Survey work conducted by Iraq's Ministry of Interior also showed that in some areas controlled by ISIS, around a third of marriage-aged women eventually married members of the organization, many of them foreign nationals. Their motivations ranged from romantic to religious and ideological, and even due to personal security as a result of the lack of social security throughout the country.[173] Increased rates of divorce have now been noted from women who may be trying to leave the stigma of ISIS marriages behind in regions where the group formerly had a strong presence.[174] This highlights the long-term challenges the region now faces, where ISIS must now be assessed in its perception as being a more effective and legitimate governing actor, and where support for the group is seen in terms of resistance to "western values," whereby women continue to face the brunt of these actions. It also highlights the particular social aspects of dealing with ISIS, where more women than ever have become associated with this terrorist organization.

Following the security challenges posed by ISIS and other jihadist-affiliated groups, Iraq also faces substantial concerns linked to the post-conflict recovery, stability and reconciliation; concerns that, if not met sufficiently, risk losing any military gains achieved during operations against the group. In now dealing with the aftermath of ISIS, thousands of trials of local and foreign men, women and minors are being carried out across the country, stretching the judicial and detention infrastructure. Iraqi Counter-terrorism Law No. 13 (2005) criminalizes broad activities related to insurgency and terrorism (such as "planning or assisting"), which means that instead of specific crimes, individual defendants can be charged for roles ranging from cooking to fighting for ISIS. This has meant thousands of local and foreign people have been charged (and increasingly convicted) with crimes, including children from age nine.

Security sector reform also remains a long-term and necessary project in the country. How women are engaged as actors in police and military forces, and how they are consulted in such reforms, will be critical to how local women are able to influence and access security forces and seek justice—factors that extend to also rebuilding public faith in the government. Yet, even with the 2016 Iraqi National Security Strategy, how women would be engaged in the security sector or how their needs would be met (through such policies as UNSCR 1325) was not evident. Women also appeared largely absent from the National Reconciliation Committee, and remain highly marginalized and excluded in this work.[175] As of 2018, a government-led national approach to community justice reconciliation process itself was absent, although some efforts were occurring on a local level.[176]

The political leadership in Iraq also remains fragile and divided. The parliamentary election results in May 2018 saw populist Shi'ite Muslim cleric Muqtada al-Sadr—a figure who mobilized the Shia militia known as the Mahdi Army against US forces during the Iraq War—lead the polls, with fifty-four seats for his Saairun (Alliance Towards Reform) party. In September 2018, in areas such as Basra, the government had been unable to provide basic services to the people; officials were accused of corruption and the city faced weeks of violent protests.[177] Such political uncertainty and the inability to provide basic services to the population stokes discontent and fear that many of the conditions that led to the emergence of ISIS in the first place may only continue to smolder.

The situation in Iraq, and the implications for future security concerns within the country, appear grim. However, in the post-ISIS recovery, women have also demonstrated they are essential to helping society recover and rebuild. Instances of women resisting ISIS influence and governance—providing education for small groups within their homes, publicly protesting against the group—are widespread but rarely covered in the media.[178] In Mosul, women are now restoring the libraries that ISIS formerly used as their headquarters;[179] female engineers are reconstructing their cities;[180] female parliamentarians are rebuilding the social fabric of areas affected by the group,[181] and are returning displaced children to their families, or supporting those now orphaned (even those believed to be the children of ISIS).[182] Women are supporting other women who suffered sexual traumas throughout the conflict,[183] and they continue to fight for women's rights and status around the country. The co-leader of the Raqqa Civil Council—thirty-year-old Leila Mustafa—is a civil engineer who has the daunting task of rebuilding this city, but is holding a role that only two years prior would have been unthinkable.[184] As highlighted with the Peshmerga forces, women were on the front lines against ISIS, directly assisted women who had been kidnapped by ISIS and had the potential to positively shape social norms and acceptance of women's roles as security actors. With so many challenges ahead facing Iraq, women will be integral to carrying the country forward and helping prevent such abuses and atrocities from occurring again. How international actors (including the US) support them will be vital to this.

### Syria

By 2019, Syria was in its eighth year of conflict, and remained one of the world's leading humanitarian crises. The conflict had produced an estimated 12.6 million displaced persons (over half the pre-war population), of which 6.3 million were refugees who had fled the country.[185] Inconceivably, these are perhaps the lucky ones: over half a million people are estimated to have been killed in the conflict.[186] Women have faced particular horrors throughout this, where gender-based crimes and their deliberate victimization is rife, and rape and sexual violence increasingly utilized as a weapon of war. This gendered violence was "destroying identity, dignity and the social fabrics of families and communities," reported UN Assistant High Commissioner (Protection) Erika Feller.[187] The long-term consequences generated by this conflict cannot be understated.

Backed by the Russian and Iranian governments, President Assad—whose departure the US had once demanded—had consolidated his control across a number of regions of the country, recapturing the cities of Aleppo in December 2016, and other key cities such as Homs. However, control across the country remained divided between a variety of actors beyond Assad's forces, including Kurdish-led SDF forces; opposition forces; and the final pockets of ISIS-controlled territory.[188] The UN-led Geneva process based on UNSCR 2254 (2015) endorsed a road map for a political settlement in Syria, but has achieved little success thus far. There has, however, been an increased effort to establish a Syrian-led committee to rewrite the constitution and pave the way for elections. UN efforts to advance these have continued to push for 30 per cent representation of women, and they have been included in these efforts.[189]

April 2018 also saw the US, UK and France launch over one hundred missiles at Syrian chemical weapons facilities following a chemical weapons attack by Assad on Douma in Eastern Ghouta on 7 April, which killed dozens of persons and injured hundreds more. This was also a noteworthy development in US activity in Syria, as it was the first time Syrian government forces were directly targeted in US efforts; moreover, this military force was claimed to be defending US national interests.[190]

The first phase of Operation Roundup was launched on 1 May 2018 by SDF forces in northeast Syria—an operation aimed at dealing with the last pockets of ISIS in the Middle Euphrates River Valley and on the Syria-Iraq border region. ISIS was estimated to have approximately 14,000 fighters in the country, and control over 5 per cent of Syria's territory by August 2018.[191] SDF forces faced similar dilemmas as those in Iraq in that they were now facing overcrowding from ISIS detainees, and did not have the capacity nor inclination to deal with the long-term detention of these persons (particularly foreign ISIS affiliates). While the US provided funding to update and secure these facilities, and to train SDF prison guards,[192] the long-term resources and will to detain or prosecute these persons was a looming concern. SDF forces are not internationally recognized state actors, which further complicated political and diplomatic relations with the group, including the management of ISIS detainees.

For those detained, deradicalization and rehabilitation services were also extremely limited, if present at all. Such services were even more rare for female detainees. For female family members of ISIS fighters, while some may have returned home, many have not been welcomed back to their communities. For those that have now moved to separated sections of internally displaced persons (IDP) camps, few efforts (if any) to rehabilitate or reintegrate them exist, and these women are increasingly of concern for radicalizing their children.[193] For those that are detained, well-funded, long-term rehabilitation and reintegration efforts remain absent. The future US support for the SDF was also uncertain: in December 2018, President Trump announced in a surprise tweet that the

US would be withdrawing its 2,000 personnel on the ground, only to later agree to a remaining force of 400.[194] He also encouraged his European partners to return and to try their citizens in SDF custody, an approach also encouraged by the SDF, who did not wish to indefinitely hold these persons, sparking international debates about how foreign nations would now manage these men, women and minors.[195]

This became particularly pertinent to discussions of returning women including Samantha Elhassani and her four children,[196] or Tania Georgelas (a UK citizen who had married an American ISIS commander) and her four children,[197] who had already returned to the US from Iraq and Syria. By early 2019, US citizens such as Hoda Muthana raised another set of concerns that transcended the country in this period. Once an active, vocal supporter of ISIS, Muthana, who was from Alabama and aged twenty at the time of traveling to Syria, wanted to return to the US, and had publicly declared repentance for her actions. She had also since had a son in Syria. Yet, while Trump requested nations to take back their citizens being held in SDF custody, in February 2019 he announced that the US would reject her citizenship and not allow her back in the country. The case reflected that of UK citizen Shamima Begum, who had traveled with two fellow schoolgirls to join ISIS in 2015 when she was aged fifteen, and had her citizenship revoked in February 2019 (though this was being legally challenged at the time of writing). Begum had given birth to (and lost) three children throughout her time with ISIS. UK sisters, Reema and Zara Iqbal, who have a total of five children under aged eight, subsequently faced a similar fate.

It was imperative in this period to serve justice to the men and women who had suffered most under ISIS. But it was also imperative to consider the long-term implications of not adequately managing these populations of ISIS families. This complex period raised important questions: should these women be considered security threats? If repatriated, they could face detention, investigation and prosecution; they may otherwise face monitoring, or may have access to deradicalization programs and be reintegrated into society. Would these appropriate steps be cognizant of the roles that these women played in the group, and would responses be gender-conscious to the unique circumstances and roles played by each? Moreover, by recognizing that these children are largely victims of their parents' choices, would these responses simultaneously address both parents and minors in a distinct and nuanced fashion? If analysis of the period since 9/11 has demonstrated anything, it's that the actions taken in a period of shift—whether evolving operational objectives in the field, operational environments, or even the women-centric efforts of terrorist groups—would have long-term implications. There remain real concerns in this period that these women may continue to be radicalized or influence their children (or others), raising questions about intergenerational scope and future security, which can only be compounded in an already fragile region.

Western stabilization efforts in Syria, which were earlier focused on support for local governance and humanitarian aid for the Syrian opposition in anticipation of the removal of Assad, have now slowed and have an unclear future. Security factors on the ground, such as the continued offensive and reclamation of territory by Assad, coupled with limited military intervention in Syria by western militaries, have left the future status of this work unclear.[198] The estimates for rebuilding the country range between $250 billion to $1 trillion,[199] but projects have been largely on hold barring a final political settlement, and remained significantly underfunded. The US has stated it will only provide reconstruction and stabilization aid (both direct and indirect, to limit it from also going through international institutions) in areas not under the control of Assad, until he engages in a political solution as defined in the H.R. 4681 No Assistance for Assad Act, which was passed by the House of Representatives in April 2018.[200] The US had also suspended $200 million worth of stabilization funding for Syria, and had pushed for additional contributions from regional parties such as Saudi Arabia and the United Arab Emirates, even as it continued to lead stabilization work.[201] As they were no longer the primary donors, consideration of women in this endeavor was at risk of not being as thoroughly integrated as outlined; for example, as highlighted in the Stabilization Assistance Review. Funding cuts to US State was viewed as damaging to local human and organizational networks that the US and coalition forces had previously supported and trained specifically for stabilization and governance activities.[202] Nonetheless, the US continued to support humanitarian assistance, which had reached nearly $5 billion by June 2018.[203]

Support for women who have lived and suffered under ISIS rule has also been limited. Some local community-led initiatives appeared to try to fill this gap, and to support communities that were exposed to ISIS ideology (for example, the Sound and Picture Organization had programs to support IDPs who had lived under the group). This organization had small-scale programs explicitly for women, and provided information on humanitarian services and psychosocial support.[204] However, such programs were rarely, if ever, acknowledged internationally. The recognition of men and boys who have suffered sexual violence in this conflict, and also as displaced and detained persons, has also lacked broader recognition; this is despite UN reports that note up to 40 per cent of men in Syria who were detained experienced sexual violence, and that men and boys in particular face multiple barriers to support services.[205]

Al-Qaeda and its affiliates have continued to remain a consistent presence in Iraq and Syria. The al-Nusra Front for the People of the Levant was determined to now be the strongest terrorist group; demonstrating a penchant for playing the long game, it has also appeared to remain stronger than its ISIS competitors in locations such as Yemen, Somalia and areas in West Africa.[206] In Syria, its presence had more recently been concentrated in Idlib Province. One key group that had their roots in al-Qaeda, but had since distanced themselves from them was Hayat Tahrir al-Sham (HTS) in Idlib, and added to the list of organizations of concern.[207] HTS is an alliance of jihadist groups that announced their formation in January 2017, and is led by the al-Qaeda affiliated Jahbat Fateh al-Sham. It is currently listed by the US as a terrorist organization, and estimates by Charles Lister suggest that there are around 20,000 members in Syria, of which 12,000 are full-time fighters.[208] Similar to ISIS, the group have also implemented some governance (though to a less invasive and expansive degree), and appear to do so in a way that is more coercive and less brutal than ISIS,[209] particularly through its civilian-led Salvation Government.

HTS has also considered women in their governance efforts, although, like ISIS, women's roles have been promoted largely in the private sphere. Due to the governing aims of the organization, and the practical ways in which HTS has thus administered territory, women affiliated with the group and those working in institutions under their control have played diverse roles in public life. Local and foreign women's participation in HTS is well captured in a report by the Stabilization Network, who recorded the roles women had been known to hold, including security and law enforcement agents at border crossings (for searching and arresting women who may be suspected of smuggling or other illegal activity); overseeing women in detention centers; or assisting court proceedings by collecting and recording women's testimonies (the authors note that these women are often relatives or wives of HTS members). Women also provided intelligence and may act as informants for the group.[210] HTS also presides over religious education centers in their territory, where theological training based on the jihadist ideology is provided. Called *du'at al-jihad*, women-only centers have ensured that female family members are not neglected in these efforts.[211]

Women have also been active in religious outreach and in recruiting other women to join the group. This is evident among women in their established social circles and IDPs, particularly widows facing financial troubles, who may gain paid employment or food aid in HTS-affiliated institutions; they may also be assisted in finding a HTS-linked husband (which can further reduce their financial burdens).[212] Education services have been provided to both male and female students, where women are instructed in Quranic studies and bent towards conservative gender roles. It argues their most visible roles are those of *hisba* (morality police): female units attached to male *hisba* who carry out patrols in public locations are able to earn up to $100 a month. Local women have also resisted the *hisba*, and have physically and verbally confronted both male and female members on patrol, or purposefully contravened dress codes in protest.[213] However, HTS had demonstrated that new jihadist groups were rising and focusing on governance; and women were important actors in this and had to thus be accounted for in all responses.

The significant role that Kurdish-led forces have played in liberating areas of Syria and Iraq from ISIS are also poised to inform regional dynamics going forward, including those related to women. Here, local women were on the front lines fighting ISIS—25,000 in the Women's Protection Units in Syria, representing 40 per cent of Syrian Kurdish forces[214]—and helping free populations under their control. These units are noteworthy for promoting female rights and equality in their ranks,[215] and are in the unique position of administering local territories where women's status has had a much less prominent standing. However, they have also faced tensions with local communities who may reject such status and positions of women, with the perceived imposition of this ideology on local populations not welcome where women's rights and equality may still be viewed in western-centric terms. But with women on the front lines helping reclaim these cities, gender roles and norms were being redefined around the region. There was also fear that many of the rights they had gained in the fight against ISIS would reverse once the group was defeated. Many women now sought social equality and social change due to their military roles and successes.[216] Meanwhile, Yazidi women had also created new spaces and initiatives in the region, establishing a female-only commune in Jinwar in Syria, offering them a chance to rebuild their lives.[217] As the US continued to fund and support Kurdish-led forces, such considerations also became relevant to programming, funding and international support.

The cases of Iraq and Syria also highlight the significant level of reconstruction and stabilization that will be required going forward. In areas that have been reclaimed from ISIS, it is now believed that the terror group is moving into its next phase and morphing into an insurgent force. Similar to discussions of COIN and stability operations throughout this book, stabilization and the provision of basic services, legitimacy in local government, and the protection of populations will continue to have a direct impact on the appeal of, and support for, terror groups. These terror groups have demonstrated, for example, that they too can offer basic governance services, jobs, security and some sense of order in a region which has faced many years of insecurity and conflict. The imperative of including women in all the post-conflict stabilization efforts was well captured by John R. Allen, a retired US Marine Corps four-star general, former commander of ISAF in Afghanistan (2011–13) and Special Presidential Envoy to the Global Coalition to Counter Daesh (2014–15). Discussing the stabilization efforts which will be required for the post-ISIS campaign in Syria and Iraq, Allen remarked:

> The process of stabilization has to leverage the full potential of women of that culture. We have to support their aspect in civil society, their

role within the stabilization. Those efforts that can capitalize on that, and leverage that, will accelerate the role of women in that society, but also leverage one of the most powerful influences in that society.[218]

While prospects for Syria remain grim, women will remain integral to carrying the country forward and, like in Afghanistan, must be represented in all aspects of final peace negotiations.

*Yemen*

Beginning in March 2015, the US-backed Saudi-led intervention in Yemen has seen the conflict persist and deepen, and human suffering soar.[219] Ali Abdullah Saleh, the former president of Yemen, who departed government in 2012 following the Arab Spring, joined forces with the Houthis in May 2015 against the Saudi-led coalition. Saleh was killed by the Houthis on 4 December 2017, further complicating the conflict and various power struggles. Though still based on local grievances and demanding a localized solution, the war had since morphed into a regional proxy battle between Iran and the Saudi-led coalition. The internationally recognized government of Yemen led by President Abdrabbuh Mansur Hadi has also now lost legitimacy to such an extent that it is questionable whether it will be able to maintain a unified Yemen.

Throughout this conflict, the US has continued to support Saudi Arabia and its Gulf allies with non-combat activities, including limited intelligence support, mid-air refueling operations, military advice and arms sales.[220] Since 2015, the US embassy in Sanaa has been closed and USAID activities in the country have ceased. However, the US has remained the largest donor of humanitarian aid to Yemen, contributing $1.46 billion between 2015 and 2018.[221] Despite this, their role in the country has also become a lightning rod for criticism, particularly as the number of civilian casualties has continued to climb, in part due to the use of US-made weapons and continued assistance to the coalition. The significant destruction of civilian infrastructure and targeting of civilians by the Saudi coalition have only compounded such criticisms. By August 2018, the UN High Commissioner for Human Rights had documented 17,062 civilian casualties (6,592 dead and 10,470 injured), though the real figures were expected to be much higher. At least 10,471 of these casualties were a result of Saudi-led strikes.[222]

The Armed Conflict Location and Event Data Project, meanwhile, has put this number of deaths at 56,000.[223] Much of the country's infrastructure has now been destroyed and estimates to reconstruct the country are estimated at $40 billion.[224] The US has stated that operations around the port of Al-Hudaydah—Yemen's second largest port, and a key lifeline for commercial and humanitarian goods—could worsen the humanitarian crisis, and "undercut US counterterrorism efforts" against Islamic militants in the country.[225]

Multiple rounds of peace negotiations attempted by UN Special Envoy to Yemen Ismaïl Ould Cheikh Ahmed (April 2015–February 2018) and Martin Griffiths (March 2018–present) have failed to produce an end to the conflict. However, in December 2018, the Stockholm Agreement was reached—the first substantial step towards peace since the beginning of the war. However, these multiple rounds of talks have also faced criticism for neglecting the meaningful inclusion of women, despite their significant participation and representation in the National Dialogue Conference in 2013–14, where they represented just under 30 per cent of the NDC members. Though the UN has pushed for increased women's participation, including with the formation of the "Yemeni Women Pact for Peace and Security," and have included them as observers and in side activities at these talks, this has still fallen short of having women in roles which could directly impact peace negotiations.[226] Even in Stockholm, only one woman was visibly present at the negotiating table.

Earlier efforts to advance women's roles in security forces have also now reversed. The women's counterterrorism unit that used to operate in the Special Security Forces no longer functions, and attempts to bring women into local police forces have been severely stunted. Instead, some women (including some armed women) have at times publicly demonstrated their support for Houthi rebels at rallies throughout the country and supported their operations on the ground in searches, intelligence gathering, policing women, and so forth.[227]

Already one of the poorest countries in the Arab world, Yemen has now infamously become the world's worst humanitarian crisis. The conflict in the country had also led to three-quarters of its population (22 million people) requiring humanitarian aid and protection. Yemen also became the global leader for cases of cholera, with over 1.1 million suspected cases; nearly 30 per cent of these were children under the age of five.[228] Women have suffered particular burdens in this conflict, with three-quarters of displaced persons being women and children. These women have also faced increased gender-based violence, and even though there are still significant social taboos against discussing such topics publicly, there has been a 30 per cent increase in the number of women accessing services for SGBV. Child marriage has also increased substantially, and two-thirds of girls are married before the age of eighteen (and even fifteen in some cases), demonstrating particular impacts of this conflict on women and girls.[229] Only Afghanistan and Syria (who are tied), ranked worse than Yemen in the Women, Peace and Security Index, thus highlighting that even with some previous efforts to improve their status, women faced incredible hurdles.[230]

Unilateral counterterrorism operations against al-Qaeda in the Arabian Peninsula (AQAP) were ramped up by the US in this period. In the first major counterterrorism operation under the Trump presidency, a US Navy Sea, Air and Land (SEAL) raid in the village of al-Ghayil was carried out in January 2017, which was thought to be targeting AQAP leader Qassim al-Rimi (though this was officially disputed). This was only the fourth ground raid in a US military operation in Yemen; it resulted in the deaths of two SEALs, fourteen suspected AQAP members, ten children (one of whom was an American citizen) and six women. In this raid, two women were stated to have taken up arms and even thrown a grenade at US soldiers—an exceptionally rare event in Yemen.[231] There were 131 recorded US strikes in the country throughout 2017—more than the four previous years combined.[232] 2018 also proved an important year in terms of counterterrorism operations, with thirty-six strikes confirmed.[233]

AQAP has been noted to be increasingly fragmented, and weaker than at any point since 2009 due to the ongoing conflict, the loss of senior leadership (including their key bombmaker Ibrahim al-Asiri in August 2018) and direct conflict with ISIS in Yemen.[234] However, some experts have stated that this perceived success against jihadist groups in the country will only last insofar as the conflict is brought to an end, and development and political stability follow.[235] The membership of AQAP is currently estimated to be between 6,000 and 7,000 persons, demonstrating that it remains a substantial focus of concern.[236] Even under this sustained pressure, AQAP has continued to publish a women's magazine, proscribing their roles in the home, and offering tasty recipes to cook for jihadist husbands. The United Arab Emirates has also unlawfully detained hundreds, and carried out torture and abuse in a number of sites throughout the country with the aim of detaining AQAP members. Women and other family members have been active in protesting these actions, and some have been intimidated or attacked while protesting.[237]

In Mukalla, a city previously under AQAP control, women who had been removed from public posts were now returning to work. Across the country, women have demonstrated that despite the current challenges, they are contributing to cohesion and the promotion of peace in their communities, supporting education gaps, and facilitating the implementation of humanitarian efforts, particularly at the local level.[238] They are also continuing to train in programs for peacebuilding in the country.[239]

The current situations in Iraq, Syria, Afghanistan and Yemen demonstrate the complexity of dealing with contemporary security concerns in these countries. While counterterrorism considerations remain prevalent in each, they are also embedded in environments rife with political uncertainties, humanitarian challenges, stabilization and reconstruction concerns, and broader insecurity. Such a vast array of issues cannot be assumed to be the responsibility of the US to manage alone, and in fact suggesting so would certainly prove counterproductive. Yet, if the US truly does want to reduce the long-term concerns from terrorism and security vacuums in these regions, then a comprehensive and long-term approach to security—both physical and human in each country—must be utilized by the US and encouraged for its partners. The full consideration and meaningful inclusion of women in these is paramount.

*Redefining a woman's place in counterterrorism*

As demonstrated in the US, overall there appeared to be an encouraging shift between 2001 and up to 2019 to think more expansively about women in relation to both counterterrorism and terrorism. Richard Barrett, the former UN coordinator of the Al-Qaida and

Taliban Monitoring Team, also highlighted the US was not unique in this, and that many countries around the world were following similar trajectories:

> I think that we are on the point of a curve here. I think we still have a long way to go, and we are still at the stage now where we think there should be more female engagement on [counterterrorism], and there should be more understanding of women in terrorism too [...] but I think what you do about it is still a bit unknown.[240]

Recalling that Tickner noted war creates new space and understanding of women and gender in relation to security,[241] this book has expanded on this, and drawn attention to the complexity of counterterrorism in the GWOT and beyond. Here, efforts such as defense, diplomacy/governance and development were increasingly interacting. It also called attention to the spaces not always clearly labeled counterterrorism but which were increasingly interacting, such as CVE, stability operations and COIN. It also demonstrated that many of the gendered roles and relations which distinguish the West from groups like al-Qaeda and ISIS often drew on similar themes, though were interpreted in distinct ways. As both terror groups demonstrated, the roles they envisioned for women often drew on similar language and categorizations, emphasizing things like women's rights or development projects, which they adapted for their own purposes, particularly as governance came to the forefront. Counterterrorism efforts which engaged women thus had to be cognizant of how their roles were evolving in terrorist groups. Yet, as figures like Brown,[242] or Fink, Zeiger and Bhulai[243] have pointed out, little of this research on women in relation to terrorism has assessed how it interacts with counterterrorism and counterterrorism-related practices, which could produce unintended consequences. Sjoberg has also pointed out that stereotypes of women in terrorism limits larger "understandings of women's roles in politics and international relations,"[244] which I argue extends as well to counterterrorism.

The growing recognition of women's roles and agency in political violence also appears to be mutually reinforced by their recognized roles and agency in efforts to challenge them, demanding further interrogation and interaction of these two fields. There is still a tendency to focus on women as partners in counterterrorism work in limited gendered roles, such as those in the community, or as peacemakers, media-tors or stabilizing influences. Yet, women's full potential as partners in all aspects of security, including the most direct roles as soldiers on the front line, or directly shaping and informing counterterrorism policy and practice itself, remained the most limited. A similar concern is also mirrored in our understanding of terror actors: there is still significant resistance to recognizing that women are not just "jihadi brides" or victims duped into joining these groups, but can play important and influential roles throughout these organizations and failing to acknow-ledge this limits our responses to them. Jihadist actors too still resist conferring power and influence on women in their organizations. In other words, a full understanding of women in all aspects of contem-porary security remains limited as long as there is incomplete recogni-tion and understanding that women can be the most empowered and visible actors in all aspects of counterterrorism, and indeed in terror groups as well. Growing research into women and gender as they per-tain to both the practices of security actors and of terrorist actors, and how women's agency is understood to enable or restrict these, offers significant potential for future research, policy and practice.

The DoD, US State and USAID have also all demonstrated that since 9/11 they have undergone momentous transformations in how their mandates, policies and practices were understood in contributions to contemporary security concerns (especially terrorism), and where or how women and gender fit into this. These have not always been easy or straightforward, but by recognizing these and the challenges they have faced, interested parties may also be more empathetic and cogni-zant of the barriers faced by institutions and their actors. Better under-standing these institutions, their histories and mandates also offers increased opportunity to interject or inform problematic practices, or learn from positive ones. This book has demonstrated that interrogat-ing factors at the institutional level in discursive, operational and institution-specific terms is imperative to better understanding women in relation to all aspects of counterterrorism. It matters to establishing holistic, synchronized and effective approaches to security, and where and how women became increasingly visible in these as active partners, agents and indeed as threats.

Perhaps the most significant contribution this book can make to the field of counterterrorism is highlighting the necessity of focus on national strategies, and the relevant institutions and actors implementing these on the ground. While organizations like NYU CHRGJ have established foundations and precedents for this area of research (particularly in the field of law),[245] this remains woefully sparse and neglected in other disciplines. A focus on the institutional level offers deeper insights that are more proactive in informing and interrogating how and why women may emerge in certain ways, at certain times, and indeed for certain purposes in counterterrorism efforts. This focus offers researchers a chance to be more proactive in engaging with contemporary security concerns via policy and practice. The histories and cultures of these diverse institutions also varies significantly in relation to how they perceive of women, gender and security, and the assumptions about women as both counterterrorism actors and terrorist threats.

It is my hope that this book has raised more questions than it has answered, and has demonstrated that the scope of future research efforts is broad and timely. While this book has examined the US in international efforts, many of these considerations extend to other countries who are currently grappling with how to best respond to increasingly shared and evolving security threats. An increasing number of fields—from women's empowerment to education; counterterrorism and CVE—are being applied to an ever-widening and growing range of threats from the extreme far-right, and even a resurgence of leftist or Antifa concerns. While this book highlighted considerations of women in jihadist-focused efforts, looking specifically at women also raises larger questions about how governments view, understand and respond to evolving concerns in other ideological fields. These can also be adopted and adapted at the domestic level, where comparable efforts related to counterterrorism are often visible (such as how domestic institutions highlight women in their discourses and practices).

While the gaps of research in women in counterterrorism, COIN and CVE have already been pointed out, a better understanding of the roles women have within these subfields is crucial, as is the gendered dynamics of these diverse streams. These could include streams of effort such as counterterrorism financing, the DoD's use of Special Operations Forces and psychological operations, to contemporary counterterrorism tools such as drones or cybersecurity.

Similar considerations can be extended to both US State and USAID. In the former, whether assisting in security sector reforms, working with refugee populations displaced by conflict, or smuggling and narcotic efforts, an increasing number of these topics (and many more under the department) have some direct or tangential link to ongoing counterterrorism concerns. Meanwhile, as USAID continues to contribute to CVE—whether through setting up radio stations to air alternative and moderate voices, youth engagement programs or job training—a stronger understanding of the gendered "push" and "pull" factors of extremism and dynamics in terrorist groups are essential. This could also extend to considerations such as counter-radicalization and deradicalization work, strategic communications and counter-narratives, and intervention efforts (amongst many others). Perhaps rather than analyzing women within counterterrorism streams alone, it should be queried how the participation and consideration of women in all aspects of peace and security can occur at the highest levels of global and state politics, and the very strategies conceived to deal with security today.

The interagency aspect of this topic may also be considered in multilateral partnerships and organizations that focus on counterterrorism in some capacity, each of which has the potential to influence and impact how the US operates within these coalitions, and how women and gender feature in these. Some examples of these include the Organization for Security and Co-operation in Europe, NATO, the Global Counterterrorism Forum, the UN Counter-Terrorism Implementation Task Force, or multi-partner coalitions such as Combined Joint Task Force which led to Operation Inherent Resolve—the global intervention to defeat ISIS. This could also extend to consider whether these international institutions influence national discourses and practices in individual countries or vice versa. Indeed, understanding both women's roles and gendered dynamics within these partnerships will be critical to holistically and robustly deliver positive programming which addresses concerns related to security.

If counterterrorism is understood to comprise distinct streams which must work cohesively together across the full counterterrorism spectrum—and its direct and indirect, short- and long-term efforts— then how these streams interact to form part of a unified strategy must be better understood and assessed. Counterterrorism cannot be viewed as isolated components: a military raid which disrupts a terrorist cell but leaves increasing numbers of female-headed households behind; a new program to train foreign women's counterterrorism units rather than local police; CVE-linked education or job training that prioritizes young men—these must be viewed holistically in terms of their complimentary, synergetic or frictional relationships. There is no question that women and gender dimensions are an essential consideration of every aspect of full-spectrum counterterrorism efforts in any contemporary security strategy.

Extending from the points already discussed in this book, there are a number of considerations that are likely to impact both how women are considered and engaged as counterterrorist actors, and indeed as terrorist threats themselves going forward. The first is counterterrorism as a key security focus. While it is unlikely to fully regress in importance in the future, how counterterrorism is prioritized amongst competing foreign policy foci remains unclear, and will thus impact funding, support and political will for this work. Other concerns that have the potential to impact this field in ways not yet decipherable include climate change and the management of the consequences thereof; the rise of populism and nationalism; the rise of right-wing extremism; increasing flows of migration; continued advances in technology; and any unexpected or unpredicted events (as the Arab Spring so aptly demonstrated).

The second is future trends in jihadist groups who have emphasized the role of governance, within which increased space, roles and consideration of women have been evident. Simultaneously, there is the recognized importance of stabilization, its inherent focus on restoring governance to local actors, and its increasing link to countering terror groups who may seek to themselves govern or operate in these spaces. These two trends bring women more clearly into this space in two important ways. First, stabilization efforts must be increasingly cognizant of how women are engaged and supported. Second, we should consider how terror groups themselves envision and engage women in their own governance projects in order to better understand their strategic aims, operations and tactics, offering better chances to interrupt these.

Looking at these groups also prompts us to consider intergroup rivalry and positioning for dominance, particularly as the scene once dominated by al-Qaeda is now also filled with ISIS and its affiliates. As diverse jihadi groups continue to form strategic alliances and partnerships with some groups, and vie for dominance and ascent over others (i.e. group outbidding), their own strategic calculations will also impact how women are engaged, and what roles they may take in these organizations. While ISIS proved its intent (and indeed success) in drawing large numbers of women from around the world to its state-building project, others such as AQAP, Boko Haram and TTP have also articulated and demonstrated what roles they envision for women in their organizations, even while being more locally focused. The challenges they face going forward (including that of resources, financing, and political and strategic opportunities) will determine if/how these evolve. This will also be impacted by the extent of direct command and control versus independence of cells and branches within these same organizations, particularly as they become more diffuse.

Women will continue to be considered, engaged and impacted in all future efforts, including as agents, partners and targets of this work. However, the question is how can we consider past flaws, shortfalls and the outright neglect demonstrated in previous efforts? More to the point, are we willing and motivated to do so? The record demonstrates the vast consequences for the very women engaged and impacted by these efforts. Nevertheless, examining women has also outlined the strengths and shortfalls of counterterror efforts more generally. Indeed, continuing to do so may prove a barometer of sorts for measuring the efficacy and success of this work more generally.

Similarly to the post-9/11 period, we are again at another crucial turning point, and the policies and lines of actions developed today will have far-reaching implications for years to come. The physical "caliphate" held by ISIS has been defeated, but its ideology lives on, now bolstered by its demonstrable ability to hold and govern territory. Due to the thousands of women that became affiliated with ISIS, thousands of minors have now been born into this organization and identity, as well as others such as Boko Haram. The youngest victims of these organizations demand care, attention, rehabilitation and reintegration, or risk becoming primed as the next generation of extremists. Groups such as al-Qaeda remain active, with the leadership torch having now seemingly been passed to Osama bin Laden's son, Hamza bin Laden, thus demonstrating the intergenerational nature of this conflict. The scale of destruction and vast number of extremist actors left behind in these jihadists' wake, and the continued ideological challenge posed by Islamist jihadist groups more generally, leaves international partners facing a formidable task. Current estimates suggest we will be dealing with current jihadist terrorist groups for the next two to three decades (not to mention any new or evolving threats), and that they will continue to evolve and innovate in new ways in order to achieve their competing aims.[246] We must demand that women are involved in meaningful and inclusive ways in all aspects of security and particularly countering terrorism and violent extremism (in its many forms) in our societies today.

# APPENDIX

## SELECT EXAMPLES HIGHLIGHTED IN THE BOOK

---

**Key factors that inform women's roles in counterterrorism**

---

*Discursive factors*

---

| | |
|---|---|
| 1. International discourses | – Convention on the Elimination of All Forms of Discrimination Against Women (1979) |
| | – UN Millennium Development goals (2000) |
| | – UNSCR 1325 (2000), 2129 (2013), 2195 (2014), 2242 (2015) |
| 2. National discourses | – National Security Strategy, National Strategy for Combating Terrorism/National Strategy for Counterterrorism |
| | – Presidential speeches, statements, executive orders |
| | – National Action Plan on Women, Peace and Security |
| | – Women's champions (for example, Secretary Clinton) |

---

*Operational factors*

---

| | |
|---|---|
| 3. Operational environments | – Country locations such as Afghanistan, Iraq, Yemen |

|  | — Country-specific socio-economic, cultural and other features such as Muslim-majority populations, gender segregation |
|  | — Diverse security concerns including active insurgency, terrorism, instability |
|  | — Lack of strong, central government |
|  | — Development and governance gaps |
| 4. Operational objectives | — Emphasis on counterterrorism, COIN, CVE, stabilization and reconstruction objectives |
|  | — Emphasis on development, governance or job creation |
|  | — Increased cultural sensitivity; engagement with women in operations |
| 5. Women-centric efforts of terrorist groups | — Women as suicide bombers, establishing policing roles, combat training in terrorist groups |
|  | — Establishment of a "caliphate," and recruiting, establishing services and roles for women |
|  | — Emphasizing women's rights in terrorist group |
|  | — Targeting women in SGBV, human slavery |

*Institutional factors*

| 6. Institutional history with women and gender | — "Women" and "gender" in frameworks, manuals and publications |
|  | — DoD: JP 3–26 Counterterrorism, FM 3–24, Advisory Committee on Women |
|  | — US State: Office of Global Women's Affairs, Office for Combating Terrorism |
|  | — USAID: Percy Amendment (1979), women/gender in guides, briefs, frameworks |
| 7. Institutional limitations | — Competition for resources, funding, support (interagency rivalry) |
|  | — Institutional personalities who may embrace or resist national discourses or interagency instruction or guidance |
|  | — Limited time to implement programs, achieve missions/objectives |

— Limited capacities/personnel to carry out programs or missions
— Agency-specific: Women limited from combat roles (DoD)
— Agency-specific: Limitations on work in unsecure environments (USAID, US State)
— Lack of gender advisor; lens by which to consider women and gender in planning, programming, evaluation, or at strategic, operational and tactical levels
— Limited knowledge of women and gender roles in terrorist organizations

| | |
|---|---|
| 8. Interagency cooperation and coordination | — Stability operations<br>— Human Terrain Systems, Provincial Reconstruction Teams<br>— Interactions between US and foreign partners<br>— Interagency working groups, training exercises |

## Agency discourses to justify women's inclusion in counterterrorism

| | |
|---|---|
| 1. Operation and innovation | — Women bring new tools or operational capabilities to achieve mission<br>— Women can access other women in foreign populations and access new information<br>— Women can facilitate/soften interactions with population |
| 2. Women's rights | — If women can achieve the institutional standard, they have a right to participate in different aspects of counterterrorism<br>— Women's status and rights are most impacted by terrorism and violence, and should be included in efforts to address these<br>— Women's rights and status in society as equated with democratic values, state stability |
| 3. Half the population | — Women are half the population and must be considered/involved in efforts<br>— Women have unique gendered experiences and unique perspectives they can contribute |

# NOTES

## INTRODUCTION:  WOMEN AS AGENTS, PARTNERS AND TARGETS OF COUNTERTERRORISM

1. Islamic State in Iraq and Syria (ISIS) is also referred to as Islamic State (IS), Islamic State in the Levant (ISIL) and simply ISIS. ISIS, IS and ISIL are self-proclaimed names given to the group. The term Daesh (Dawlat al-Islamiyah f'al-Iraq w Belaad al-Sham) is similar to the Arabic word *das*, which translates as "to trample down" or "crush," and avoids the legitimization of conferring upon this organization the status of a "state." This book uses the term ISIS.
2. Rineheart 2010, 38.
3. Wilson III 2008, 114.
4. Ibid.
5. Rineheart 2010, 38.
6. Priest and Arkin 2010.
7. Williams and Epstein 2017.
8. Crawford 2018. Other attempts to capture the real cost of the post-9/11 response included the National Priorities Project, which put spending on defense and homeland security between 2001 and 2011 alone as high as $7.6 trillion. See National Priorities Project 2011.
9. This figure comprises US casualties from Operation Enduring Freedom (Afghanistan: 2,347 killed; 20,094 injured); Operation Iraqi Freedom (Iraq: 4,410 killed; 31,958 injured), Operation New Dawn (Iraq: 73 killed; 295 injured); Operation Inherent Resolve (multiple locations: 67 killed; 72 injured); and Operation Freedom's Sentinel (Afghanistan: 52 killed; 318 injured). See DeBruyne 2018.
10. Watson Institute of International and Public Affairs 2015.
11. UN Women 2012.
12. Tickner 2011, 579.

427

13. For an excellent summary of the various agencies throughout the US government, and their explicit contribution to counterterrorism in individual and inter-agency capacities, see Special Operations Forces 2013.
14. Watson Institute of International and Public Affairs 2017b.
15. Tickner 2002, 343–8.
16. Crelinsten 2009, 39; Gentry and Sjoberg 2014, 127.
17. Crelinsten 2009,135.
18. Alison 2003, 38.
19. Davis 2017, Annex.
20. In this research, less than half of the countries examined had publicly available figures for women, thus highlighting the potential scope of this concern well beyond 13 per cent. See Cook and Vale 2018, 16–19. This data set is set to be updated in 2019 and will be available at icsr.info
21. This book recognizes there are practical and semantic differences between the terms "agency," "department," "institution," "bureau," "office" and other titles specific to distinct government institutional bodies. Indeed, both the DoD and US State are executive agencies while USAID is considered an independent government agency, and is in fact directed by US State. Each contain numerous departments, offices, bureaus, agencies and so forth within these. See Government Publishing Office 2017 for more details.
22. Jackson 2005, 1–2.
23. Jackson 2011, 393.
24. Richardson 2007, 175.
25. Ibid., 177–8.
26. Ibid., 1.
27. Biddle 2005, 179, as cited in NBC News 2003.
28. For detailed elaboration of these bodies and their roles, see Kraft and Marks 2011.
29. For more on the history of ISIS, see Stern and Berger 2015; McCants 2015; Gerges 2017.
30. While Yemen has officially been at war since March 2015, this was not directly in relation to terrorism, but rather based on internal dynamics which saw Houthi rebels from the north oppose the democratically elected (though disputed) President Hadi. See Hokayem and Roberts 2016; International Crisis Group 2013; 2016; Baron 2015; Al-Dawsari 2017.
31. For more detailed history of al-Qaeda in Yemen, see Johnsen 2013; Koehler-Derrick 2011; Murphy 2010.
32. For more details on Al-Awlaki, see Meleagrou-Hitchens 2011.
33. Fairclough 1992, 4.
34. Shapiro 1988, as cited in Hansen 2013, 19.

35. Jackson 2005, 8.
36. Ibid.
37. Weinberg, Pedahzur and Hirsch-Hoefler 2004, 786; Schmid 2004, 385; Crenshaw 2011. This debate has also since expanded to what constitutes "radical" and "extremism" even when non-violent, as particularly seen in the UK. See Kundnani 2009; Richards 2011.
38. Pillar 2008; Crelinsten 2009; Davis and Cragin 2009; Richards 2015.
39. Pillar 2008, 458.
40. Crelinsten 2009, 236.
41. Crenshaw 2001, 330.
42. Satterthwaite and Huckerby 2013, 5.
43. H. Clinton 2010c.
44. Blears et al. 2008; Brown 2008; 2013; Cook 2017a.
45. This discussion of "mothers" in particular is explored by numerous authors in Fink, Zeiger and Bhulai 2016.
46. Kean 2011, 53.
47. Carter 2015.
48. Mosbacher Morris interview 2015.
49. Kolenda interview 2015.
50. Pandith interview 2019.
51. Feierstein interview 2015.
52. Holmer interview 2015.
53. The term "securitization" was expanded on most notably by Buzan, Wæver and De Wilde, and places importance on "determining how an issue becomes a security issue, by how it is articulated." That is, examining why we think of something as a security issue, and how the elites (such as political leaders) convince us that it represents a threat to our very survival. It looks at expanding what we view as "security issues" beyond traditional political and military sectors, and also helps us to understand and analyze when and how issues are deemed security issues. In considering women as being securitized in some counterterrorism efforts, this suggests that the status and security of women in areas such as education or their societal status became framed as fundamental to US security interests, thus requiring increased focus and attention. Others may argue that such steps instead represent instrumentalization of these areas for national security purposes. See Buzan, Wæver and De Wilde 1995.

## 1. ANALYZING WOMEN IN COUNTERTERRORISM

1. For example, UNSCR 1325 is the foundational document of the National Action Plans for the implementation of UNSCR 1325 in seventy-nine countries, including the US (2011). See Peace Women 2018.

2. N. Hudson 2009.
3. UN Women 2017.
4. On gender mainstreaming, see Cohn 2008, 185, footnotes 3 and 4.
5. It is beyond the scope of this research to fully assess the trajectory leading up to UNSCR 1325, though some useful sources for this include Shepherd 2008; Cohn 2008.
6. H. Clinton 1995.
7. This work throughout her career was coined by Hudson and Leidl as the "Hillary doctrine," which is explored at length in Hudson and Leidl 2015.
8. Gomez and Gasper 2013.
9. King and Murray 2001, 585.
10. MacLean 1998.
11. King and Murray 2001, 588; Del Rosso 1995.
12. N. Hudson 2009, 14.
13. Ibid., 14.
14. Ibid., 15.
15. N. Hudson 2009, 44.
16. UN Security Council 2000, 8b-c.
17. Pratt and Richter-Devroe 2011, 490.
18. Ibid., 492.
19. Cohn 2008, 2–5.
20. N. Hudson 2009, 4.
21. Ibid., 5–6.
22. N. Hudson 2009, 2.
23. Pratt 2013a, 775.
24. Sjoberg and Gentry 2007, 202.
25. Jebb and Gallo 2013; Cook (forthcoming).
26. Puechguirbal 2015, 255.
27. Ibid., 254.
28. Tickner 2011, 579.
29. N. Hudson 2009, 9.
30. Ibid.
31. Norville 2010.
32. Baldwin 1997, 9.
33. Blanchard 2003.
34. Axworthy 2001, as cited in N. Hudson 2009, 4.
35. Gentry and Sjoberg 2015, 4.
36. N. Hudson 2009, 4.
37. Ní Aoláin 2016, 276.
38. See footnote 46, which expands on UNSCR 2242 (2015).
39. Pratt and Richter-Devroe 2011, 494.

40. Pratt 2013a.
41. Pratt 2013b, 329.
42. Pratt 2013a, 2.
43. Huckerby 2016, 555.
44. Huckerby 2016, 572–575.
45. Cohn 2008, 6.
46. Cohn 2004, 8.
47. Swaine 2009, 410
48. It is important to note—though beyond the scope of this book to expand upon—how UNSCRs post-9/11 have furthered the importance of considering women in aspects of violence, conflict and, finally, terrorism and extremism. These include UNSCRs 1820 (2008), 1888 (2009), 1889 (2009), 1960 (2010), 2106 (2013), 2122 (2013) and 2242 (2015) which were all adopted under the title "Women and Peace and Security," while many other resolutions recall it in their introduction. Yet many of these only occur after 2008, and it's not until 2015 that a distinct emphasis on women in counterterrorism and CVE emerges. UNSCRs 1820, 1888, 1890, 1960 and 2106 focused on women, peace and security, particularly in terms of sexual violence in armed conflict and the adverse, often disproportionate, impacts that conflict had on the lives of women. UNSCR 2122 focused more attention and concrete measures on women's leadership and participation in conflict resolution and peace-building. It was not until UNSCR 2242 (2015) that women were considered in counterterrorism and CVE terms. UNSCR 2242 extends to women's efforts in counterterrorism, for example in the Counter-Terrorism Implementation Task Force; understanding drivers of radicalization for women; impacts of counterterrorism strategies on women; how women can prevent and respond to violent extremism; and roles of women's organizations in developing counterterrorism and CVE strategies. These are discussed briefly later in the book.
49. Perera and Razack 2014, 6.
50. This is particularly well surveyed in Blanchard 2003; Shepherd 2013b; V. Hudson 2013, 99, footnote 20.
51. Enloe 1993, Chapter 1.
52. Enloe 1989.
53. Enloe 2000.
54. Cohn 1993, as cited in Blanchard 2003, 1294.
55. Stiehm 1983, as cited in Blanchard 2003, 1297.
56. Tickner 2011, 577.
57. Blanchard 2003, 1298.
58. Sjoberg and Gentry 2015, 4.

59. Ibid., 24.
60. Tickner 2011, 578.
61. Shepherd 2013b, 437.
62. Blanchard 2003, 1300.
63. Cheldelin and Eliatamby 2011.
64. Sjoberg and Gentry 2007, 9
65. Ibid., 10.
66. Tickner 2011, 578–9.
67. Stern and Wibben 2014, 2.
68. Sjoberg and Gentry 2011, 6.
69. Blanchard 2003, 1290.
70. Sjoberg 2009a, 4–5.
71. Shepherd 2006, 31.
72. Tickner 2002, 343–8.
73. Ibid., 348.
74. Tickner 2014, 142.
75. Sylvester 2010, 609.
76. Lobasz and Sjoberg 2011, 574.
77. Ibid., 575.
78. Tickner 2011, 576.
79. Wibben 2011b, 594.
80. Wibben 2011a., 7.
81. Sjoberg 2009c.
82. Ibid., 185.
83. Ibid.
84. This point on causational versus constitutive arguments is based on a definitional discussion by Wendt 1998.
85. Sjoberg 2009c, 187.
86. Ibid., 188.
87. Blanchard 2003, 1305–6.
88. Ibid.
89. Ibid., 1307.
90. Wibben 2014, 755.
91. Sjoberg 2011, 601.
92. Ibid., 602.
93. Ibid.
94. Caiazza 2001, 1.
95. Ibid., 5.
96. Pratt 2013a.
97. Parashar 2010.
98. Early examples of focus on US soldiers who were women include analysis of "gendered coverage" of women's deployment in the Gulf War. See Enloe 1993.

99. Sjoberg and Gentry 2007, Chapter 3; Kaufman-Osborn 2005; McKelvey 2007.
100. Khalili 2011; 2012.
101. Dyvik 2014; 2016; McBride and Wibben 2012; Mehra 2010; Welland 2016; Pratt 2013b.
102. Tickner and Sjoberg 2013, 232.
103. Ibid.
104. Wibben 2011, 592.
105. Huckerby 2016, 588.
106. Huckerby 2014.
107. Ní Aoláin 2013, 1086.
108. Ibid.
109. Ibid.
110. Crenshaw 2001, 330.
111. Satterthwaite and Huckerby 2013, 9.
112. Poloni-Staudinger and Ortbals 2013, 70.
113. Ibid.
114. Cunningham 2007, 114.
115. Ortbals and Poloni-Staudinger 2016, Poloni-Staudinger and Ortbals 2013.
116. Ní Aoláin 2013, 1086.
117. A growing number of institutes and think tanks globally have increasingly focused on or engaged women in work related to counterterrorism and CVE, including the Global Center on Cooperative Security (US); The Georgetown Institute for Women, Peace and Security (US); The Institute for Inclusive Security (US); the US Institute of Peace (US); Muflehun (US); Women Without Borders/ Sisters Against Violent Extremism (Austria); Inspire (UK); al-Sakinah (Saudi Arabia); and Hedayah (UAE). These also emphasize the US/ western nature of this field.
118. Some useful examples from think tanks/NGOs include: Fink, Zeiger and Bhulai 2016; Winterbotham and Pearson 2016; United States Institute of Peace 2015.
119. Poloni-Staudinger and Ortbals 2013, 70.
120. These are expanded on in full in Table 5.3 in Poloni-Staudinger and Ortbals 2013, 80–2.
121. Poloni-Staudinger and Ortbals 2013, 88.
122. Herman 2009; NYU Center for Human Rights and Global Justice 2011; Cook 2017b.
123. Pantazis and Pemberton 2009; Allen, Isakjee and Young 2013.
124. Sjoberg 2013, 232–4.
125. Herman 2009, 265.

126. It in fact proved an inspiration in many ways for this research. See NYU Center for Human Rights and Global Justice 2011

127. Satterthwaite 2013. Duke Law International Human Rights Clinic and Women Peacemakers Program 2017.

128. Brown 2008; Rashid 2014; 2016; Cook 2017a.

129. Rashid 2014.

130. Ibid., 599–600.

131. Brown 2013, 40–1

132. Rashid 2014, 601.

132. Brown 2008, 472.

134. Ibid., 486–7.

135. Brown 2013, 42.

136. Ibid., 45.

137. Allen and Guru 2012.

138. Rashid 2014, 592.

139. Rashid 2016, xii.

140. Ibid., xiii.

141. Schmid 2004, 385.

142. Brown 2013, 38.

143. The term "push and pull factors" refers generally to the factors in one's life which may "push" them out of their former environment and condition and "pull" them towards a specific group or ideology.

144. Fink, Zeiger and Bhulai 2016, 10.

145. For a selection of literature on terrorism studies, see Andrusyszyn 2009; Tinnes 2014.

146. Stump and Dixit 2013, 65.

147. Sjoberg and Gentry 2008b, 6.

148. Poloni-Staudinger and Ortbals 2013, 107.

149. Sjoberg 2009b, 69.

150. Sjoberg and Gentry 2007.

151. Auchter 2012; Cheldelin and Eliatamby 2011; Gentry and Sjoberg 2015a; 2015b; Hunt and Rygiel 2013; Parashar 2010; 2011; Sjoberg and Gentry 2007; 2008a.

152. Auchter 2012, 121–3.

153. Ibid., 130.

154. Jacques and Taylor 2009.

155. Jacques and Taylor 2013.

156. Bloom interview 2015.

157. Interviewee 2 interview 2014.

158. Sjoberg and Gentry 2011, 3.

159. Ibid., 5.

160. Sjoberg and Gentry 2007, 14.

161. Crenshaw 2000, 408.
162. Sjoberg and Gentry 2007, 4.
163. Sjoberg 2013, 234.
164. Sjoberg and Gentry 2007, 221.
165. Blee 2005.
166. Weinberg and Eubank 1987.
167. Jamieson 2000; Varon 2004.
168. Liddick 2006, 83.
169. Speckhard and Akhmedova 2006; Bloom 2007; Davis 2017.
170. Bloom 2007; Schrijvers 1999; Davis 2017.
171. Zenn and Pearson 2014; Bloom and Matfess 2016; Matfess 2017;
     Ladbury et al. 2016.
172. Ergil 2000.
173. Davis 2013, 2018; Bloom 2011.
174. Davis 2017, 113.
175. Alison 2004, 451; Eager 2008, 163; McEvoy 2009; Dowler 1998.
176. Stanski 2006.
177. Palmer 1992.
178. MacDonald 1991; Hamilton 2013.
179. Margolin 2016; Berko and Erez 2007; Erez and Berko 2008; Eggert
     2018a; Holt 2010; Israeli 2004; Bloom 2007.
180. Gautam Banskota and Manchanda 2001; Eliatamby 2011.
181. MacKenzie 2012.
182. US Department of State 2013.
183. Parashar 2011.
184. It is also interesting to note that the majority of those who research
     female political violence tend to be women themselves.
185. For example, see MacDonald 1991; Ness 2007; Gonzalez-Perez 2008;
     Cragin and Daly 2009; Jacques and Taylor 2009; Bloom 2011; Poloni-
     Staudinger and Ortbals 2013; Ladbury 2015a; Davis 2017; Wood and
     Thomas 2017; Handyside 2018; Darden, Henshaw and Szekely 2019.
186. Cunningham 2010, 171.
187. Poloni-Staudinger and Ortbals 2013, 172.
188. Interviewee 2 interview 2014.
189. Bloom 2010a, 96.
190. Sjoberg interview 2015.
191. Sjoberg and Gentry 2011, 14.
192. Alexander 2016; Cook 2005; Saltman and Smith 2015.
193. Conway and McInerney 2012.
194. Pearson 2015; 2017.
195. Cottee 2016; Bradford 2015.
196. Cook and Vale 2018.

197. Lahoud 2014; 2017; Khelghat-Doost 2017; Winter 2015a; Musial 2016; Peresin and Cervone 2015; Tarras-Wahlberg 2017; Winter and Margolin 2017; Ladbury 2015a.
198. Parashar 2011, 301.
199. One of the few, though limited, examples found was Saripi 2015.
200. Holmer interview 2015.
201. Some earlier examples included Sjoberg and Gentry 2007; Alison 2004.
202. Gentry and Sjoberg 2014a, 125
203. Sjoberg and Gentry 2011, 237.
204. Gentry and Sjoberg 2015, 17.
205. Sjoberg 2009b, 72.
206. Ibid, 70.
207. Ibid., 72.
208. Sjoberg and Gentry 2007, 204.
209. Moon 1997, 56, as cited in Sjoberg and Gentry 2007, 205.
210. Gentry and Sjoberg 2015, 125.
211. Parashar 2010, 181.
212. Parashar 2011, 312.
213. Mazurana and Cole 2013.
214. Betancourt et al. 2008. Women's more active inclusion and consideration in DDR processes has been noted in Burundi and Liberia (Knight 2008).
215. This literature also emphasizes far-right extremism over Islamist extremism in its analysis. See Glaser 2017; Gielen 2018; Schmidt 2018; Van der Wetering Zick and Mietke 2018; Eggert 2018b.
216. Hamm 2009; 2013; Jones 2014; Veldhuis 2016.


## 2. COUNTERTERRORISM FROM BUSH TO OBAMA

1. CHRGJ 2011, 13.
2. For a list of domestic terror attacks in the US prior to 9/11, see Kushner 1998, Chapters 5 and 6. For a more expansive history of US counterterrorism efforts, see Tankel 2018, Chapter 2.
3. Tankel 2018, 35.
4. Ibid., 39.
5. Rumsfeld and Shelton 2001, 3.
6. B. Clinton 1995.
7. Ibid.
8. Badey also acknowledged that definitions of terrorism in this period, particularly in these multilateral efforts, remained ill-defined and without clear consensus, which became problematic in some efforts. See Badey 1998, 62.

9. Badey 2006, 308.
10. Badey 1998, 66.
11. B. Clinton 2000.
12. Badey 1998, 53.
13. US Congress 1996.
14. B. Clinton 1999.
15. B. Clinton 2000.
16. For example, the 2000 NSS highlights "military activities" as a key stream of counterterrorism effort, even while referencing briefly diplomatic and economic sanctions or tools, or other preventative efforts.
17. Badey 2006, 318.
18. B. Clinton 2000, Preface.
19. Ibid.
20. Ibid.
21. B. Clinton 1999.
22. B. Clinton 2000.
23. The eight Millennium Development Goals were (1) eradicate extreme hunger and poverty; (2) achieve universal primary education (boys and girls alike); (3) promote gender equality and empowerment (education-centric); (4) reduce child mortality; (5) improve maternal health (mortality focused); (6) combat HIV/AIDS, malaria and other diseases; (7) ensure environmental sustainability; and (8) develop a global partnership for development. These eight goals were derived from United Nations 2000.
24. Kean 2011, xv.
25. Ibid., 363.
26. Ibid., 53.
27. Ibid., 374.
28. Ibid., 376
29. World Bank 2009.
30. US Congress 2007.
31. Bush 2002f.
32. Ibid.
33. Ibid.
34. Ibid.
35. Stated in US Department of Defense 2005b.
36. Office of the Coordinator of Counterterrorism 2003.
37. Ibid., 29.
38. Office of the Coordinator of Counterterrorism 2006.
39. Schmitt and Shanker 2005.
40. Bush 2006a, 6.
41. Schmid 2013, 10.

42. Romaniuk 2015, 7.
43. Ibid.
44. Silberstein 2004; Jackson 2005; 2006a; 2007; 2009; 2011; Croft 2006.
45. CHRGJ 2011, 18–19.
46. Bush 2001b.
47. Bush 2001c.
48. Bush 2002.
49. Weed 2016.
50. Tembo 2014, 88.
51. Boyle 2010, 342.
52. Bush 2001a.
53. Bush 2003a.
54. Full text of speech available at Hudson and Leidl 2015, 37–8.
55. Young 2003; Kandiyoti 2007, 505. This is expanded on further in this chapter.
56. Tickner 2002; Ayotte and Husain 2005; Cooke 2002.
57. Ahmed 1992.
58. Spivak 1988.
59. Gentry 2016.
60. Nayak 2006; Thobani 2007.
61. Tickner 2006, 389.
62. Bush 2002f.
63. Bush 2002e.
64. Office of the Coordinator of Counterterrorism 2003, 2.
65. Al-Qaeda did not use its first female suicide bomber until 2005 in Iraq, suggesting they had been influenced by Palestinian and Chechen female suicide bombers who were active at that time. See Bush 2002c.
66. Davis 2017, 147.
67. Bloom 2007, 98.
68. Bush 2006a.
69. Bush 2004b.
70. Bush 2007a.
71. According to CEDAW: "Discrimination against women violates the principles of equality of rights and respect for human dignity, is an obstacle to the participation of women, on equal terms with men, in the political, social, economic and cultural life of their countries, hampers the growth of the prosperity of society and the family and makes more difficult the full development of the potentialities of women in the service of their countries and of humanity." See United Nations General Assembly 1979.
72. Specifically, the goals to "Promote gender equality and empower women" and "improve maternal morality." United Nations 2000.

73. The Declaration of Independence specifically states, "We hold these truths to be self-evident, that all men are created equal, that they are endowed by their Creator with certain unalienable Rights, that among these are Life, Liberty and the pursuit of Happiness." See Jefferson et al. 1776.

74. Bush 2003b.

75. Bush 2006b.

76. Bush 2004a.

77. Ibid.

78. Bush 2004b, footnote 45.

79. CHRGJ 2011, 18–19.

80. McBride and Wibben 2012, 202.

81. Kandiyoti 2007, 514.

82. Nayak 2006, 53–4.

83. Hudson and Leidl 2015, 44–6. Hudson and Leidl expand on several other women's-focused foreign policy matters under Bush in Chapter 1 of their book.

84. Hunt and Rygiel 2013.

85. CHRGJ 2011, 18–19.

86. Satterthwaite and Huckerby 2013, 3.

87. Bush 2002b.

88. Bush 2004a.

89. Bush 2002a.

90. Bush 2008a.

91. Office of the Coordinator of Counterterrorism 2003, 23.

92. Bush 2008a.

93. Hudson and Leidl 2015, 44–6. Hudson and Leidl expand on several other women's-focused foreign policy matters under Bush in Chapter 1 of their book.

94. Bush 2008b.

95. Bush 2002e.

96. Office of the Coordinator of Counterterrorism 2003, 23.

97. Ibid.

98. Huckerby 2013.

99. The White House 2002.

100. Huckerby 2013, 108.

101. Ibid., 110.

102. Ibid., 120–1.

103. Ibid., 122.

104. Obama 2010d.

105. Ibid.

106. Obama 2013b.

107. Obama 2011d.
108. Ibid.
109. While this book does not extend to these multilateral efforts, it should be noted that many of these had diverse levels of "gender awareness," and women were distinctly considered and engaged with in each.
110. Obama 2011e.
111. Ibid.
112. Obama 2013b.
113. Obama 2014c.
114. Obama 2013b.
115. Obama 2010d.
116. Obama 2011d.
117. Obama 2013a.
118. Obama 2015b.
119. Obama 2015f.
120. Ibid.
121. Jackson 2011, 402.
122. Jackson 2011; Gilmore 2011; Mullin 2011; McCrisken 2011; Woodward 2011.
123. Executive orders are direct orders by the president which carry the full weight of the law. It is noteworthy that this executive order called only for a "plan," and not necessarily implementation by the agencies, a point of significance later.
124. Obama 2011f.
125. The White House 2011.
126. Clinton 2011.
127. Council on Foreign Relations 2019.
128. Verveer interview 2015.
129. Ibid.
130. Ibid.
131. Obama 2016.
132. Ibid., 2.
133. Ibid., 10.
134. Ibid., 15.
135. Ibid., 28.
136. Obama 2010d.
137. Obama 2009a.
138. Obama 2009d.
139. Obama 2013b.
140. Obama 2015i.
141. Purkiss and Serle 2017.

142. See comment by General Carter in Gibbons-Neff and Lamothe 2016.
143. United States Special Operations Command 2017.
144. A 2016 report by the *Washington Post* noted that upwards of 50,000 ISIS operatives have been killed in drone strikes and conventional attacks under the purview of JSOC. See Ignatius 2016.
145. Carter and Le Drian 2016.
146. Obama 2009c.
147. Obama 2010b.
148. Obama 2010e.
149. Obama 2010c.
150. Obama 2010f.
151. Obama 2012a.
152. Obama 2014c.
153. Obama 2014e.
154. Obama 2009b.
155. Obama 2010a.
156. Obama 2014c.
157. Obama 2011a.
158. Weed 2016, 9.
159. US Department of State 2014d.
160. Obama 2015d.
161. Obama 2014f.
162. Cook and Vale 2018.
163. Obama 2015d.
164. Obama 2014f.
165. Obama 2014g.
166. Obama 2010d.
167. Obama 2009c.
168. Obama 2010c.
169. Obama 2010g.
170. Obama 2011b.
171. Obama 2014b.
172. Obama 2015i.
173. Obama 2014c.
174. Obama 2011b.
175. Ibid.
176. Hudson et al. 2009; Hudson and Leidl 2015; Cook 2015a, 150; Our Secure Future 2018.
177. Obama 2015a.
178. Obama 2015c.
179. Obama 2015h.
180. Obama 2013b.

181. Ibid.
182. Ibid.
183. Obama 2009d.
184. Obama 2011c.
185. Obama 2012c.
186. Obama 2012b.
187. Obama 2014c.
188. Obama 2015e.
189. Ibid.
190. Obama 2015f.
191. Obama 2015h.
192. Obama 2015d.
193. Ibid.
194. Cook and Vale 2018.
195. For example, the FBI defines violent extremism as "encouraging, condoning, justifying, or supporting the commission of a violent act to achieve political, ideological, religious, social, or economic goals." Some of these components were not offenses punishable by law, though they could contribute to the continuation or support of violent extremism more broadly. "Terrorism prevention" on the other hand was noted as "a documented instance in which a violent act by a known or suspected terrorist group or individual with the means and a proven propensity for violence is successfully interdicted through investigative activity" (see www.fbi.gov). However, it should be recognized that CVE and counterterrorism efforts not only feed into one another, but there often remains a problem of conceptual and practical overlap, where violent extremism and terrorism are used almost interchangeably. For more on this, see Neumann 2017, 19–25.
196. Obama 2015d.
197. Ibid.
198. Obama 2010d.
199. Obama 2015d.
200. Obama 2015j.
201. Obama 2011d.
202. Obama 2013b.
203. Ibid.
204. Obama 2015d.
205. Obama 2013b.
206. Obama 2011a.
207. Obama 2015d.
208. Obama 2015g.

209. Obama 2014g.
210. The White House Office of Communications 2015.
211. The White House 2015.
212. Obama 2015f.
213. Obama 2015i.
214. Obama 2014g.
215. Ibid.
216. Ibid.
217. M. Obama 2015.
218. Borough of Tower Hamlets 2015.
219. Bowcott 2015.
220. Obama 2010c.
221. Obama 2014a.
222. Obama 2015d.
223. Obama 2015i.
224. Shiffman 2012.
225. Nasaw and McDonald 2010.

3. US DEPARTMENT OF DEFENSE

1. Harnden 2001.
2. See the Appendix for full DoD organizational structure.
3. Chief Financial Officer 2018.
4. Joint Chiefs of Staff 2009, vi; NYU Center for Human Rights and Global Justice 2011, 54.
5. Defense Advisory Committee on Women in the Services 2017.
6. The DoD distinguishes ten combatant commands, six of which have a regional focus (for instance, CENTCOM, US Africa Command, etc.), and three of which have a thematic focus (US Special Operations Command, US Strategic Command, etc.). CENTCOM's areas of responsibility cover eighteen countries focused in the Middle East, North East Africa, and Central and South Asia, including the key cases of Afghanistan, Iraq and Yemen.
7. NYU Center for Human Rights and Global Justice 2011, 59
8. White House Office of Communications 2015.
9. Rutgers Institute for Women's Leadership 2010.
10. US Department of Defense 2015c.
11. Rumsfeld and Shelton 2001.
12. Myers 2004.
13. Ibid.
14. The White House 2006a.
15. Kennedy, Santiago and Torres 2009.

16. Sommers 2008.
17. Ibid.
18. Ibid.; Nava 2009.
19. Ibid.
20. Beals 2010.
21. These points are expanded on with interviews of Team Lioness in Sommers 2008, and Kennedy, Santiago and Torres 2009.
22. Sommers 2008.
23. Ibid.
24. Ibid.
25. Ibid.
26. Kennedy, Santiago and Torres 2009.
27. Katt 2014.
28. Torres 2008.
29. United States Congress 2008.
30. Ibid.
31. Oversight Committee 2007.
32. Sjoberg 2007, 85–7.
33. Kumar 2004, 297; Howard and Prividera 2004.
34. Federation of American Scientists 2004, 16.
35. White House 2006b.
36. Federation of American Scientists 2004, 40.
37. Karpinski and Strasser 2005, 106–8, as cited in Sjoberg 2007.
38. Committee on Armed Services 2008.
39. Howard and Prividera 2008.
40. Enloe 2004, 99.
41. Wood 2006, 331.
42. US Court of Appeals 2011.
43. Ibid.
44. US Army 2006, 1.
45. US Army 2006.
46. Kilcullen 2010, 127. This relationship between links and cooperation between terrorist and insurgent groups is discussed in Moghadam 2017, 50–54.
47. Boyle 2010, 343 & 345.
48. US Department of Defense 2011.
49. US Army 2006, 3 & 19.
50. This relevance of COIN in the GWOT was critiqued by some, as it was stated to now in fact be less likely to empower local populations as required in Iraq or Afghanistan. See Gilmore 2011.
51. US Department of Defense 2007.
52. US Army 2006, vii.

53. Ibid., ix.

54. Ibid., 22.

55. Ibid., A-6.

56. Ibid.

57. Petraeus interview 2016.

58. Petraeus interview 2016.

59. Ibid.

60. See Reif 1986.

61. Khalili 2011; 2012, Dyvik 2014; 2016; McBride and Wibben 2012; Mehra 2010; Welland 2016; Pratt 2013b.

62. Kilcullen 2010, 40 & 219.

63. Des Roches interview 2015.

64. Jager 2007, v.

65. McFate and Laurence 2015; Fawcett 2009.

66. Military Intelligence Professional Bulletin, 1.

67. Finney 2008, 11.

68. Ibid., 70.

69. Ibid., 42.

70. Rutledge 2011.

71. Gezari 2014.

72. McFate and Laurence 2015, 137.

73. Ibid., 195.

74. "Human security" is defined by the UN as "freedom from fear and want," a definition which King claimed was borne from the intersection of development and security literature. MacLean took this further and defined human security as "security of the individual in his or her personal surroundings, community, and environment," which included "protection from crime and terrorism, political corruption, forced migration, absence of human rights; freedom from violations based on gender; [as well as] political, economic, and democratic development." Human security was driven by a gap in security literature and practice that focused on security of the state and military efforts, which was common in traditional conceptions of international relations (although a focus of critique for feminist international relations scholars). Human security also broadened the scope of issues which could be considered security, including non-military threats. See Gomez and Gasper 2013; King and Murray 2001, 585; MacLean 1998; Del Rosso 1995.

75. American Anthropological Association 2007.

76. González 2008, 21.

77. For a deeper account of Lloyd's life and the HTS program, see Gezari 2014.

78. Evans 2015.
79. Sims 2016; Martin 2016.
80. Sims 2016.
81. Barakat et al. 2015.
82. "New wars" is a concept established by Mary Kaldor, who argued that they were defined largely by "state weakness, extremist identity politics, and transnational criminality" (in contrast to "old wars," defined as interstate or classical civil wars). See Kaldor 2013.
83. US Government 2017, 1224.
84. US Army 2003, 4.
85. Ibid., 3.
86. Ibid., 6.
87. Ibid., E4.
88. Ibid., F4.
89. Bush 2005a.
90. Buss 2005.
91. US Department of Defense 2005a.
92. US Army 2008.
93. US Army 2014b.
94. Ibid.
95. US Army 2014a.
96. US Combined Arms Centre 2011, 41.
97. Parker 2007.
98. US Combined Arms Centre 2011, 1.
99. Perito 2007.
100. Perito 2005.
101. Parker 2007, 6.
102. Haysom and Jackson 2013, 4–5.
103. Katzman 2008b, 34.
104. Perito 2007.
105. Haysom and Jackson 2013, 9.
106. USAID 2013b.
107. US Combined Arms Centre 2011.
108. Afghan Women's Network 2007.
109. US Army Combined Arms Center 2010.
110. USAID 2007c.
111. Perito 2007; Haysom and Jackson 2013, 6; Luehrs 2009.
112. Haysom and Jackson 2013, 6.
113. Oversight and Investigations Subcommittee of the Committee on Armed Services 2007.
114. Perito 2007.
115. Parker 2007, 9 & 12.

116. See Dyvik 2014; 2016; McBride and Wibben 2012; Mehra 2010; Welland 2016; Pratt 2013b.
117. Verveer 2010a.
118. Petraeus interview 2016.
119. Ibid.
120. Ibid.
121. Des Roches interview 2015.
122. Marine Expeditionary Force 2012.
123. International Security Assistance Force 2010.
124. Katt 2014.
125. Ibid.
126. Des Roches interview 2015.
127. North Atlantic Treaty Organization 2010.
128. Petraeus interview 2016.
129. Katt 2014.
130. International Security Assistance Force 2010. This leadership was notably represented by American commanders in the periods immediately prior to and following this: General David D. McKiernan (June 2008–June 2009), General Stanley A. McChrystal (June 2009–June 2010) and General David Petraeus (July 2010–July 2011).
131. North Atlantic Treaty Organization 2010, 5.2.4.
132. Rasmussen 2010.
133. Azarbaijani-Moghaddam 2014.
134. Rohwerder 2015; McBride and Wibben 2012.
135. NYU Center for Human Rights and Global Justice 2011, 57.
136. Katt 2014.
137. Rohwerder 2015, 9.
138. Azarbaijani-Moghaddam 2014, 1.
139. Des Roches interview 2015.
140. McCullough 2012.
141. Jones 2008; United States Government Interagency Counterinsurgency Initiative 2009; Meyerle et al. 2012
142. Center for Strategic and International Studies 2012.
143. United States Army Special Operations Command 2016.
144. Lemmon 2015a, 97–8.
145. Katt 2014, 109.
146. Ibid., 111.
147. Ibid., 100.
148. Clinton and Panetta 2015, 132–3.
149. Szayna et al. 2015, 79.
150. Lemmon 2015b.
151. Ibid., 112.

152. Lemmon 2015b.
153. Joint Chiefs of Staff 2009, vi.
154. US Government 2017, 1228.
155. Joint Chiefs of Staff 2009, GL5–6.
156. Ibid., xv.
157. Ibid.
158. Ibid., xv.
159. Ibid., viii.
160. For example, JP 3–26 evolves from its 2009 edition to the 2014 approach, which redefined and refocused counterterrorism, and reflected updated policy and strategy introduced under President Obama.
161. Joint Chiefs of Staff 2009, II-8.
162. Byess 2012, 64.
163. Ibid.
164. Ibid.
165. US Army 2014a, 2–3.
166. Ibid., 3.
167. Ibid., 3–6.
168. Ibid., 10.
169. Ibid., 4–17.
170. Ibid. 5–8.
171. US Department of Defense 2013, 88.
172. Verveer interview 2015.
173. US Department of Defense 2013, 4.
174. Ibid.
175. Cook 2018.
176. Markham interview 2015.
177. Engell 2016, 75.
178. Ibid., 77.
179. Ibid., 87.
180. US Department of Defense 2013, 11.
181. Ibid.
182. The gendered impacts of counterterrorism activities is discussed further in the case of Yemen and drone strikes in Cook 2017b.
183. Kolenda and Reid 2016, 9.
184. Haysom and Jackson 2013, 11.
185. Scanlon interview 2017.
186. Ibid.
187. Ibid.
188. Ibid.
189. Ibid.

190. Engell 2016.
191. Markham interview 2015.
192. Witkowsky 2016.
193. Ibid.
194. Seck 2015.
195. Pirek 2016.
196. Mozzetta interview 2016.
197. Ibid.
198. Ibid.
199. Petraeus interview 2016.
200. Ibid.
201. Scanlon interview 2017.
202. Campbell et al. 2011.
203. Clare 2008.
204. Sommers 2008.
205. Kennedy, Santiago and Torres 2009.
206. Mullen 2010.
207. The White House 2014b.
208. Mattocks et al. 2012; Street, Vogt and Dutra 2009; Fontana, Rosenheck and Desai 2010.
209. Some examples include Thompson 2013; Holmstedt 2008; Lemmon 2015a; Woodruff 2007.
210. See US Department of Defense 2015a.
211. Particularly those focused on the NAP and opening all combat roles to women.
212. Carter 2015.
213. Ibid.
214. Petraeus interview 2016.
215. Ibid.
216. Ibid.
217. Carter 2015.
218. The White House 2006a.
219. Des Roches interview 2015.
220. Belasco 2014, Table 9.
221. Serafino 2014a.
222. Sharp and Humud 2015, 3.
223. US Department of Defense 2015b, 17.
224. US Military 2015, 11.
225. This section draws in part from Cook 2017b.
226. For expansive analysis, see Cook 2017b.
227. Hull 2011, 24.
228. Hull 2005, 123.

229. Rugh 2010, 113.
230. Hull 2005, 130.
231. Ibid., 136.
232. Hull 2011, 137.
233. Krajeski interview 2015.
234. Khoury interview 2015.
235. Hill 2007.
236. Khoury interview 2015.
237. Seche interview 2015.
238. Khoury interview 2015.
239. Seche interview 2015.
240. Hill 2007.
241. Khoury interview 2015.
242. Ibid.
243. Krajeski interview 2015.
244. Ibid.
245. Feierstein interview 2015.
246. Seche interview 2015.
247. Feierstein interview 2015.
248. Seche interview 2015.
249. Ibid.
250. Bodine interview 2015.
251. Hewitt and Kelley-Moore 2009, 212; Felter and Fishman 2007, 30.
252. Knickmeyer 2008.
253. Phillips 2010, 2.
254. Feierstein interview 2015.
255. Ibid.
256. Ibid.
257. Khoury interview 2015.
258. Sharp 2014, 10.
259. This section is drawn from Cook 2017b.
260. Obama 2014d.
261. Obama 2014c.
262. Al-Moshki 2014. This paragraph is drawn from Cook 2015a.
263. Pasha-Robinson 2017.
264. The name AQI was the shorthand for Al Qaeda Jihad Organization in the Land of Two Rivers (Mesopotamia–Iraq) given to the group by Zarqawi in October 2004. Prior to this, the group had been rebranded from Ansar al-Islam, and before that the Organization of Monotheism and Jihad group. Zarqawi was killed in a US airstrike in June 2006.
265. Katzman 2008a, 11.

266. Bush 2007b.
267. Bush 2005b.
268. Women's roles in Kurdish-led forces are discussed further in Tax 2016; Valentine 2018, Chapter 9.
269. Beals 2010, 8.
270. Medina 2008.
271. Frederisk 2008.
272. Lyttle 2008.
273. Rubin 2008.
274. Nunez 2008.
275. Starz 2008.
276. Dougherty 2008.
277. Healy and Ghazi 2011.
278. Starz 2008.
279. Peter 2008.
280. Dale 2011, 120.
281. Special Inspector General for Iraq Reconstruction 2010.
282. Healy and Ghazi 2011.
283. Leland 2009.
284. Paraszczuk 2014.
285. Ghitis 2014.
286. Perry 2017.
287. Valentine 2016.
288. Öcalan 2013. The PKK is viewed by Turkey as a terrorist organization. In conflicts with ISIS, the PKK became distinguished from the Kurdish-led forces in the Syrian Democratic Forces, including the YPJ and YPG forces (People's Protection Units), amongst others, under this umbrella organization, and thus received support from the US and international coalitions. However, Turkey still accused these groups of ties to the PKK—a point of great contention between the US and its NATO ally.
289. Cudi 2019, 3.
290. McLaughlin 2016; Fine 2016, 27.
291. Ministry of Defense 2016.
292. Kurdistan 24 2016.
293. Graham-Harrison 2017a.
294. Special Inspector General for Afghanistan Reconstruction 2017, 148.
295. Ibid., 150.
296. Special Inspector General for Afghanistan Reconstruction 2018a, 247–8.
297. Caldwell 2011; Sopko 2017, 148.
298. These were expanded upon in the DoD's Report on Progress Toward

Security and Stability in Afghanistan between 2010 and 2014. Available at www.defense.gov

299. Scanlon interview 2017.
300. Special Inspector General for Afghanistan Reconstruction 2017, 142.
301. Ibid.
302. Special Inspector General for Afghanistan Reconstruction 2014b, 9–10.
303. Special Inspector General for Afghanistan Reconstruction 2017, 142.
304. Ibid., 151.
305. US Department of Defense 2012, 134.
306. Scanlon interview 2017.
307. Fink interview 2015.
308. Special Inspector General for Afghanistan Reconstruction 2014b, 12.
309. Special Inspector General for Afghanistan Reconstruction 2014a, 102–3.
310. Special Inspector General for Afghanistan Reconstruction 2015.
311. Special Inspector General for Afghanistan Reconstruction 2016, 10.
312. Ibid., 128.
313. UN Analytical Support and Sanctions Monitoring Team 2017.
314. Some particularly useful articles on these debates include Bloom 2013; Lahoud 2010; 2014; 2018; Davis 2017, 85.
315. Bin Laden 1996b.
316. Zelin 2011.
317. Bloom 2005.
318. Davis 2017, 86.
319. Kilcullen 2016.
320. National Security Criminal Investigations 2009.
321. Muir 2008.
322. This is expanded upon at length in Bloom 2011, Chapter 7.
323. Zimmerman 2007.
324. Qazi 2011, 31.
325. Ibid., 30.
326. Rubin 2008.
327. Ibid.
328. See "Bonds of Matrimony" in Bergen and Tiedemann 2012, 79.
329. Barrett interview 2016.
330. Kilcullen 2008, 1.
331. Davis 2017, Chapter 1.
332. CBC News 2008.
333. Roggio 2010.
334. Ahmed 2010.
335. Graham-Harrison 2012.

336. AQAP 2013.

337. AQAP 2014a.

338. This point is not meant to suggest that any department should change or guide their internal policies in direct relation to propaganda of such groups. However, being cognizant of how certain topics are being utilized in propaganda, and considering what impacts such propaganda may have on potential support or recruitment for the group, can ensure the most robust and holistic responses to them by all relevant parties.

339. Reuter 2015.

340. Similar roles for women in security forces have a history in groups like Hamas and Hezbollah, though these are generally viewed as distinct from transnational jihadist groups like al-Qaeda and ISIS.

341. These are outlined in detail in Speckhard and Almohammad 2017.

342. Winter 2015a, 8.

343. Gilsinan 2014.

344. Moaveni 2015.

345. Human Rights Watch 2016.

346. Winter 2015b.

347. See Winter and Margolin 2017.

348. Public Radio International 2014.

349. Revesz 2016.

350. Harris 2014.

351. Byman 2015.

352. Winter 2015a, 23.

353. Zenn and Pearson 2014, 46; Davis 2017, 108.

354. Pearson 2018.

355. Whitehead 2016.

356. Breeden 2016.

357. Akwiri 2016.

358. Rothwell 2016.

359. Costa and Kapoor 2016.

360. The roles of women as potential security threats in relation to ISIS is analyzed in more detail in Cook and Vale 2018, 53–7. Here, the distinction between those with no formal affiliation to ISIS (but who had been inspired by the group); those with direct links to militants in Syria and Iraq; and those who have carried out attacks in ISIS territory as suicide bombers are discussed.

361. This could also be informed by the phases of this campaign, where the first phase prioritized degradation, followed by counter-attack and defeat, and finally support/stabilization. Efforts that had highlighted women were often in the support/stabilization stage.

362. Petraeus interview 2016.
363. Ibid.


4. THE DEPARTMENT OF STATE

1. *The Guardian* 2001.
2. US Department of State 2015.
3. US Department of Defense 2009.
4. United Nations Entity for Gender Equality and the Empowerment of Women 1995.
5. Discussed in CHRGJ 2011, 13, Huckerby 2016, 52. Generally see: Huckerby 2014.
6. Middle East Partnership Initiative 2017.
7. Powell 2002.
8. Ibid.
9. Sharp 2005, 1.
10. US Department of State 2010b.
11. Sharp and Humud 2015, 9.
12. Rabasa 2007, 59.
13. Shays 2006.
14. Rabasa 2007, 59.
15. Abdo 2005, 15.
16. US Department of State 2004, 196
17. Hull 2005, 129.
18. Hull 2011, xviii.
19. US Department of State 2004, 196.
20. Wikileaks Cable Viewer 2005.
21. Ibid.
22. Krajeski interview 2015.
23. Hull 2011, 70.
24. Sharp 2014, 19.
25. Bodine interview 2015.
26. Krajeski interview 2015.
27. UN Security Council Resolution 678 in 1990 was to authorize Operation Desert Storm. Yemen had a seat on the Security Council at the time and voted against the initiative. As a direct consequence of that, the US largely terminated US military and economic assistance programs in Yemen.
28. Wikileaks Cable Viewer 2007.
29. Seche interview 2015.
30. Khoury interview 2015.
31. Interviewee 1 interview 2015.

32. Seche interview 2015.
33. This point is expanded on in Cook 2017b.
34. Interviewee 1 interview 2015.
35. Carpenter 2006.
36. Pandith interview 2019.
37. Mosbacher Morris interview 2015.
38. Mosbacher Morris interview 2015.
39. This had historically been an issue in Swat Valley, and was expanded on more by Mosbacher Morris in Clinton and Panetta 2015, Chapter 6.
40. Mosbacher Morris interview 2015.
41. Pandith interview 2019.
42. United States Institute for Peace 2015
43. For more expansive discussion on the initial thinking and evolution of this policy, see Pandith 2019.
44. SAVE 2018.
45. Ibid.
46. Mosbacher Morris interview 2015,
47. Verveer interview 2015.
48. Pandith interview 2019.
49. Ibid.
50. US Department of State 2009.
51. Landler 2009.
52. Ibid.
53. H. Clinton 2010b.
54. Verveer 2009.
55. Brimmer 2010.
56. CHRGJ 2011, 18–19.
57. H.Clinton 2010a.
58. H. Clinton 2012.
59. Special Operations Forces 2013, I-3.
60. H. Clinton 2012.
61. Ibid.
62. Special Operations Forces 2013, I-4.
63. Ibid.
64. Ibid.
65. H. Clinton 2010a, 23.
66. This approach was reminiscent of efforts in the 1990s leading up to UNSCR 1325, where women were seemingly securitized to get the attention and support required to advance the women, peace and security agenda. See N. Hudson 2009 for further discussion.
67. See Hudson and Leidl 2015, Chapter 2. Additional material on the links between women and security are referenced in Cook 2015a.

68. H. Clinton 2010a, ii.
69. Ibid., ii.
70. Ibid., 4.
71. Ibid., 1.
72. Ibid., iii.
73. Ibid., vii.
74. Ibid., 57.
75. Special Operations Forces 2013, I-4.
76. H. Clinton 2010a, 152.
77. Des Roches interview 2015.
78. Lemmon 2011.
79. Hudson and Leidl 2015, 33
80. Serafino 2014b, 4.
81. Serafino 2014b.
82. Ibid.
83. Ibid.
84. The White House 2011.
85. US Department of State 2010a, 108.
86. Lemmon 2011.
87. US Department of State 2012b.
88. Ibid., 37.
89. Special Inspector General for Afghanistan Reconstruction 2014b, 8.
90. US Department of State 2012a.
91. H. Clinton 2012.
92. The 2016 review would have been conducted under the Trump administration in 2017. No review was produced for 2016.
93. US Department of State 2014c.
94. Scanlon interview 2017.
95. US Department of State 2014b.
96. The White House 2014a, 40.
97. US Department of State 2016b.
98. Mosbacher Morris interview 2015.
99. Verveer interview 2015.
100. Bodine interview 2015.
101. CHRGJ 2011.
102. US Department of State 2013.
103. O'Connor 2014.
104. Ibid.
105. Though this book does not extend to domestic US counterterrorism efforts, it is worth highlighting how Hughes emphasized that domestic and international agencies often "both stay in their own lanes" for reasons that were both bureaucratic and institutional. Personnel

working on domestic issues often did not engage in international CVE efforts and vice versa. It was also noteworthy how Hughes highlighted a "weakness" in knowledge-sharing between international and domestic US CVE efforts, even as these were notably distinct contexts, though these still may have informed US domestic efforts. Hughes interview 2016.

106. Pandith interview 2019.
107. Ibid.
108. See also United States Institute of Peace 2015; Holmer and Deventer 2014.
109. Holmer interview 2015.
110. Fink interview 2015.
111. This point is also discussed in Huckerby 2015.
112. Ansari interview 2016.
113. Ibid.
114. Soneshine 2013.
115. US Department of State 2014a, 249.
116. Kaidanow 2014.
117. Bradtke 2014.
118. Meredith 2014.
119. US Department of State 2016a, 317.
120. US Department of State 2017a.
121. US Department of State 2017b.
122. Epstein, Lawson and Tiersky 2017, 5.
123. Fink interview 2015.
124. Verveer interview 2015.
125. Ibid.
126. Ní Aoláin 2016, 276.
127. Ibid.
128. Ibid., 281.
129. Ibid., 289.
130. Ibid., 290.
131. Callimachi 2016.
132. Chynoweth 2017, 15.
133. Some examples of trafficking for profit included the sales of women to ISIS fighters directly or via human markets they established. For more detail on ISIS financing see: Financial Action Task Force 2015.
134. Some excellent sources to explore this further include: Wood 2006; 2009; 2010; Cohen 2016. For an annotated bibliography of contemporary work, see Consortium on Gender, Security and Human Rights 2012.
135. Cohen 2016, 5.

136. Wood 2006.
137. Goldstein 2001.
138. Cohen 2016, 2.
139. Ahram 2015, 59.
140. Sewall 2014.
141. Malinowski 2014.
142. Kerry 2014.
143. Siberell 2015.
144. Kerry 2015, 21.
145. Fine 2016, 54.
146. Ibid., 110.
147. Ibid., 22.
148. Verveer interview 2015.
149. Russell 2015.
150. US Department of State 2015.
151. Verveer interview 2015.
152. Bodine interview 2015.
153. AQAP 2010.
154. Bloom 2010b, 446.
155. AQAP 2014b.
156. AQAP 2013; 2014b.
157. Fishman 2016, 56.
158. Islamic State Media 2015b.
159. Winter 2015, 39.
160. Islamic State Media 2016.
161. Islamic State Media 2015a.
162. A justification for the enslavement of women was also discussed in a pamphlet produced by ISIS found in a raid in May 2015 in Syria. See Fine 2015, 66.
163. Winter 2015, 19–22.
164. US Department of State 2012b, 2.1.3.

## 5. THE US AGENCY FOR INTERNATIONAL DEVELOPMENT

1. Natsios 2001b.
2. For a full organizational outline of USAID, see https://www.usaid.gov/who-we-are/organization
3. USAID 2015a.
4. NYU Center for Human Rights and Global Justice 2011, 31.
5. More detail of this history is available at USAID 2012a, 4–5.
6. NYU Center for Human Rights and Global Justice 2011, 31–2.
7. NYU Center for Human Rights and Global Justice 2011.

8. Most of this literature falls under the research field of security and development. For some useful discussions, see Cragin and Chalk 2003; Beall, Goodfellow and Putzel 2006; Keen 2008; Stern and Öjendal 2010; Spear and Williams 2012; Keen and Attree 2015.

9. USAID 2002. Due do unclear language from NGOs, this was updated in 2004 with AAPD 04–07. Preventing terrorism financing through USAID programming remained unsystematic and problematic during the Bush administration, as reported in Office of the Inspector General 2007.

10. USAID 2016b.

11. Markham interview 2015.

12. Clad 2002, 6.

13. Harborne 2012, 41.

14. Clad 2002, 2.

15. Howell 2006, 129.

16. Harborne 2012, 46.

17. USAID 2004, foreword.

18. Ibid., 7.

19. Ibid., 24

20. Ibid., 35

21. USAID 2005c.

22. Tarnoff 2015, 54.

23. USAID 2015e.

24. Rice 2006.

25. Veillette 2007, 2.

26. USAID 2007a.

27. Ibid., 2.

28. USAID 2007a, 17–22.

29. USAID 2017.

30. Special Inspector General for Afghanistan Reconstruction 2014b, 1.

31. Natsios 2001.

32. USAID Afghanistan 2005.

33. Bever 2010.

34. USAID Afghanistan 2005.

35. Verveer interview 2015.

36. USAID 2007a.

37. USAID 2005b. As highlighted in NYU Center for Human Rights and Global Justice 2011, 37. Office for Transition Initiatives is the office in USAID that implemented stabilization programming.

38. Agency Coordinating Body for Afghan Relief 2006.

39. Des Roches interview 2015.

40. USAID 2017.

41. Haysom and Jackson 2013, 10.
42. Ibid.
43. Des Roches interview 2015.
44. USAID blog 2012.
45. Special Inspector General for Afghanistan Reconstruction 2018a.
46. Office of the Special Representative for Afghanistan and Pakistan 2010, ii.
47. Special Inspector General for Afghanistan Reconstruction 2014b, 1.
48. Special Inspector General for Afghanistan Reconstruction 2018b.
49. Special Inspector General for Afghanistan Reconstruction 2018a.
50. Commission on Wartime Contracting 2010.
51. USAID 2007b.
52. McMillan et al. 2010.
53. Ibid.
54. USAID 2007a.
55. McMillan et al. 2010, 81.
56. Des Roches interview 2015.
57. Zuhur 2006, 15.
58. See Cook 2017b, 367–8.
59. USAID 2009a, 1–3.
60. Ibid., 4.
61. Ibid., 9.
62. Krajeski interview 2015.
63. Ibid.
64. Wikileaks Cable Viewer 2005.
65. Ibid.
66. Des Roches interview 2015.
67. Boucek 2010.
68. Des Roches interview 2015.
69. Ibid.
70. Wikileaks Cable Viewer 2009.
71. Senate Subcommittee on Near Eastern and South and Central Asian Affairs 2011.
72. Ibid.
73. Serafino 2011, 12.
74. Seche interview 2015.
75. Ibid.
76. It is interesting to note that while the term "push" and "pull" factors is now common parlance amidst those that study recruitment and radicalization, the term appears to have its roots in the literature on development and migration, although this has also featured in that on social movement theory. Lipton highlighted in his analysis of migra-

tion from rural areas two main streams that became apparent: those "pushed" out by inequality in villages; and those who are "pulled" out of their village to seek additional opportunities to guard their assets. Later, research on social movements by McAdam noted: "An intense ideological identification with the values of the campaign acts to 'push' the individuals in the direction of participation while a prior history of activism and integration into supportive networks acts as the structural 'pull' that encourages the individual to make good on his strongly held beliefs." Wiktorowicz expanded these ideas further in relation to recruitment into radical networks, highlighting how structural drivers, strains or frustrations may lead to a "cognitive opening" where religious-seeking may take place, where new (potentially radical) ideas could take hold, and in some cases lead the individual to take up violence. Bjørgo and Horgan discuss push and pull factors largely in relation to factors that makes it unappealing to remain with a group, where other more attractive alternatives are present. See Lipton 1980; McAdam 1986; Wiktorowicz 2005; Bjørgo and Horgan 2006. For additional discussion, see Schmid 2013 and Ranstorp 2016.

77. Denoeux and Carter 2009b, iii.
78. NYU Center for Human Rights and Global Justice 2011, 37.
79. House International Relations Committee, Subcommittee on International Terrorism and Nonproliferation 2005.
80. Government Accountability Office 2008.
81. US Congress 2009.
82. Ibid.
83. Ibid.
84. US Congress 2009.
85. Government Accountability Office 2008, 4.
86. By 2016, one of the principles outlined in the TSCTP was to "be gender nuanced" and "[i]nvest in women's capacity to prevent VE [violent extremism] in their communities and explore how concepts of masculinity can facilitate or inhibit VE." See USAID 2016a.
87. NYU Center for Human Rights and Global Justice 2011, 37.
88. Denoeux and Carter 2008, 5 & 7.
89. CHRGJ 2011, 30–31.
90. There is a distinction between "guides" which provide certain information, and specific "policy" which facilitated action.
91. Denoeux and Carter 2009a, 62.
92. NYU Center for Human Rights and Global Justice 2011, 30.
93. Ibid., 42.
94. H. Clinton 2010a, 115.
95. Ibid., 116.

96. Ibid., 93.
97. The White House 2011, 21.
98. USAID 2011, footnote 9.
99. Markham interview 2015.
100. NYU Center for Human Rights and Global Justice 2011, 14.
101. Markham interview 2015.
102. Ibid.
103. This concern was also raised in CHRGJ 2011, 108.
104. Ibid.
105. Mosbacher Morris interview 2015.
106. USAID 2011, 4.
107. Ibid.
108. Ibid.
109. USAID 2012c, 48.
110. Billings interview 2015.
111. Ibid.
112. Markham interview 2015.
113. Billings interview 2015.
114. CHRGJ 2011, 30–31.
115. USAID 2012a.
116. Markham interview 2015.
117. Bodine interview 2015.
118. Ibid.
119. House Committee on Foreign Affairs 2013b.
120. House Subcommittee on the Middle East and North Africa 2013.
121. House Committee on Foreign Affairs 2013a.
122. Senate Foreign Relations Subcommittee on International Operations and Organizations, Human Rights, Democracy and Global Women's Issues 2014.
123. Ibid.
124. Senate Subcommittee on International Operations and Organizations, Human Rights, Democracy and Global Women's Issues 2014.
125. Cook and Vale 2018.
126. USAID 2014a, 119.
127. USAID 2014b, 43.
128. Cook and Vale 2018. For more on female jihadists in and from Tunisia, see Zelin 2018a; 2018b.
129. House Subcommittee on the Middle East and North Africa 2014.
130. USAID 2015c.
131. USAID 2015b.
132. Cook and Younis 2012, 26, v.
133. USAID 2012b.

134. House Subcommittee on the Middle East and North Africa 2014.
135. USAID 2013a, 8.
136. Cook and Vale 2018.
137. Markham interview 2015.
138. Bradtke 2014.
139. BBC 2014.
140. Shah 2014.
141. US Department of State 2014c.
142. US Department of State and US Agency for International Development 2014.
143. Kerry 2015, 26.
144. Ibid., 27.
145. See Chapter 4 "Women and gender in the 2015 QDDR."
146. Verveer interview 2015.
147. Lindborg 2014.
148. House Foreign Affairs Subcommittee on Middle East and North Africa 2015.
149. USAID 2015d.
150. These were Dr Laura Sjoberg, who had previously called for more practitioner engagement by academics, and Dr Reed Wood.
151. USAID 2015d, 2.
152. Ibid.
153. Porter and Cordell 2015.
154. Portions of this section have been drawn from Cook (forthcoming).
155. Lia 2015.
156. Fishman 2016, 90.
157. Johnsen 2013, 279.
158. Associated Press 2013.
159. Fakih 2013.
160. Keatings 2014.
161. Mohsen and Al-Yarisi 2015.
162. The Bureau of Investigative Journalism 2015.
163. Oxfam and Republic of Yemen 2007.
164. Kendall interview 2015.
165. Michael, Wilson and Keath 2018.
166. Nossiter 2012.
167. Human Rights Watch 2012.
168. Briggs and Silverman 2014, 13 & 16; Neumann 2014.
169. Islamic State Media 2014.
170. Lister 2015, 2.
171. Cook and Vale 2018, 42.
172. Speckhard and Yayla 2015.

173. Revkin 2018.

174. Islamic State Media 2014.

175. Khelghat-Doost 2017.

176. Zambrana, Aydemir, and Graham-Harrison 2015.

177. Krol and Fuller 2017.

178. Marsh 2014.

179. Winter and Haid 2018, 3.

180. Sullivan and Adam 2015.

181. Islamic State Media 2015a; Winter 2015.

182. For a more comprehensive understanding of ISIS's strategy, based upon their own documents, see Reuter 2015.

183. Markham interview 2015.

## 6. ENTER TRUMP: COUNTERTERRORISM GOING FORWARD

1. Trump 2015.

2. Reilly 2016.

3. Trump 2019a.

4. Two examples of this included Trump's response to the violence in Charlottesville at the "Unite the Right" rally in August 2017, in which he did not outright condemn neo-Nazis and white supremacist groups who engaged in violence. A second example was the retweeting of Islamophobic videos by far-right extremist group Britain First's Deputy Leader Jayda Fransen. Other senior figures in his early administration—including Steve Bannon (White House Chief Strategist), General Michael Flynn (National Security Advisor) and Sebastian Gorka (Deputy National Security Advisor)—all echoed similar negative views of Islam. See Shane, Rosenberg and Lipton 2017.

5. Greenblatt 2019.

6. Lowery, Kindy and Tran 2018.

7. Tankel 2018, Tracy 2018, Harcourt 2018. Specific examples of this included the October 2018 cases of Cesar Sayoc, who sent twelve pipe bombs to Democratic figures and supporters, and the attack on the Tree of Life synagogue in Pittsburg, PA, which killed eleven persons and was the worst recorded anti-Semitic attack in US history. Also in October 2018, three Kansas militia members were convicted of plotting to bomb the mosques and homes of Somali immigrants, raising this concern. It is notable that the three men requested leniency in their sentence as they claimed were inspired by Trump's rhetoric for violence. See Burke 2018; Reuters 2018.

8. United Nations 2017.

9. United Nations High Commissioner for Refugees 2018.

10. Masson-Delmotte et al. 2018.
11. For a broader discussion of the distinction between the terms Islamism, Salafism and Jihadism, see Hamid and Dar 2016.
12. Trump 2016b.
13. Trump 2017b.
14. Trump 2017a.
15. Trump 2016a.
16. Huntington 1993.
17. Ackerman 2017.
18. Khan 2016.
19. For example, the 2018 NSS references "jihadist terrorists" and "Islamist ideology."
20. This was viewed as problematic as it misleadingly presented government data which excluded domestic terrorism, and included international terrorism in its analysis. See Panduranga and Patel 2018.
21. Trump 2017e.
22. Trump 2017j.
23. This was the first of three iterations of this policy, which was eventually revised to include North Korea and Venezuela as well. It faced several court battles up to and including the Supreme Court, before it was toned down in its scope and implementation.
24. Byman 2017.
25. Trump 2018.
26. LoBianco 2015.
27. Zahedi 2011.
28. National Security Strategy 2017.
29. Teague Beckwith 2016.
30. McMaster 2017b.
31. Ibid.
32. Ibid.
33. National Security Strategy 2017, 4.
34. Ibid., 26.
35. Trump 2017j.
36. National Security Strategy 2017, 26.
37. Ibid.
38. Ibid., 39
39. Ibid.
40. National Security Strategy 2017, 40.
41. Ibid., 25.
42. Ibid., 28.
43. Ibid., 27.
44. Ibid., 38.

45. Ibid., 41.
46. Ibid., 37.
47. Ibid., 42.
48. There were many notable public instances that supported this position on Trump. Three of these included a tape released during his election campaign that recorded him stating he would grab women "by the pussy" and stating "You can do anything" to them. He had also been recorded making a long list of sexist and crude comments about female political opponents, celebrities and news anchors, amongst others. Finally, during the Supreme Court nomination of Brett Kavanaugh, Christine Blasey Ford had accused Kavanaugh of sexual assault. In a political rally, Trump had publicly mocked Blasey Ford for her testimony. Trump 2016c; Doré and Withey 2017; Allen 2018.
49. McMaster 2017a.
50. The White House 2018.
51. Ibid.
52. Ibid.
53. Ibid.
54. Ibid.
55. US Congress 2017.
56. Broadway 2018.
57. USAID 2018, 28.
58. Trump 2017c.
59. Martinez and McLaughlin 2018.
60. Blanchard and Humud 2018, 8.
61. Ibid., 6
62. Lead Inspector General for Overseas Contingency Operations 2018b, 21.
63. These are discussed in Chapter 2 in the "At war with terrorism."
64. US Air Forces Central Command Combined Air Operations Center 2018.
65. Pakistan (six strikes; sixteen to twenty-five killed); Yemen (166 strikes; 213–278 killed); Somalia (ninety-eight strikes; 664–714 killed); Afghanistan (4,582 strikes; 2,497 killed). All strikes are minimum confirmed strikes. All data drawn from Bureau of Investigative Journalism 2019a.
66. It is important to note that these figures account for international military forces as well as the Afghan Air Force, who were also carrying out strikes at this time. United Nations Assistance Mission in Afghanistan 2018b, 6; Purkiss and Fielding-Smith 2018.
67. Penney et al. 2018.
68. Schmitt 2018.

69. Executive Order 13732 "United States Policy on Pre- and Post-Strike Measures To Address Civilian Casualties in US Operations Involving the Use of Force," of 1 July 2016 was the first significant centerpiece of this policy. For 2018 financial year reporting, see US Department of Defense 2018. For more information, see Siemion 2018.

70. Some considerations of this could include the right under International Human Rights Law to have access to a fair trial and remedies in the case of civilian deaths, which may prove more difficult to access for women in countries such as Yemen or Afghanistan, where women may also face particularly compounded financial or material loss as a result of drone strikes again civilians. See International Bar Association 2017.

71. Trump 2019a.

72. Trump 2017a.

73. Trump 2017d.

74. Ibid.

75. Trump 2017h.

76. DeBruyne 2018.

77. Kheel and Savransky 2017.

78. Trump 2017i.

79. Associated Press and NBC News 2019.

80. Trump 2017g.

81. Trump 2017h.

82. Joint Chiefs of Staff 2018 III-7.

83. Joint Chiefs of Staff 2018 III-13.

84. Trump 2017f.

85. Ibid.

86. Ibid.

87. Alexander et al. 2017.

88. Ibid.

89. This tension was also visible with US Secretary of Defense General Mattis in December 2018. Mattis resigned following the announcement that US forces were to pull out of Syria, and in a candid resignation letter also highlighted Trump's neglect of key US alliances and partnerships, and weak stance on China and Russia, views that did not align with his own. See Mattis 2018.

90. Office of Management and Budget 2017, 33.

91. Ibid., 12.

92. Harris, Gramer and Tamkin 2017.

93. USAID 2018.

94. US Department of State and US Agency for International Development 2018, 23.

95. Ibid.

96. Ibid., 26.
97. Ibid., 26.
98. Ibid., 27.
99. Ibid. 35.
100. Lead Inspector General for Overseas Contingency Operations 2017, 19.
101. US Department of State 2018.
102. Toosi 2018; Gramer 2018.
103. Gramer 2018
104. US Department of State Stabilization Assistance Review 2018, 1.
105. Ibid., 4.
106. Ibid., 9.
107. Jenkins 2018.
108. US Department of State 2018, 14.
109. Lead Inspector General for Overseas Contingency Operations 2017, 38.
110. US Department of State 2019.
111. Ibid.
112. Congressional Research Service 2019a.
113. Trump 2017h.
114. Ibid.
115. Ibid.
116. Ibid.
117. Rasmussen 2017.
118. Blanchard and Humud 2018, 8.
119. Ackerman 2018.
120. Jackson 2018, 9.
121. Ibid., 25
122. Ackerman 2018.
123. Shalizi and Mackenzie 2018.
124. Akseer and Yousufzai 2018.
125. NATO Resolute Support Afghanistan 2018.
126. Georgetown Institute for Women, Peace and Security 2018.
127. United Nations Assistance Mission in Afghanistan 2019, 50.
128. United Nations Security Council 2018, 15.
129. Farmer 2019.
130. United Nations Assistance Mission in Afghanistan 2019; Sahak 2018.
131. Nicholson Jr. 2017.
132. United Nations Security Council 2017, 16.
133. *Agence France-Presse* 2017.
134. Muhajirat fi sabeelillah in Khurasan 2017.
135. Tomlinson 2018.

136. United Nations Assistance Mission in Afghanistan 2018a.
137. Conflict Armament Research 2018.
138. Trew 2017.
139. United Nations Security Council 2018.
140. Sommerville 2019
141. Ibid.
142. UN Security Council 2017.
143. Key resolutions prior to this included 2178 (2014), which imposed obligations on member states to respond to the threat of FTFs. Others developed in this period included 2195 (2014), 2199 (2015), 2249 (2015), 2253 (2015), 2354 (2016), 2370 (2015) and 2322 (2016), which considered terrorism in relation to organized crime, weapons, cultural heritage, terrorist narratives, terrorist financing, judicial responses, sanctions and other dimensions inherent in countering this threat.
144. International Organization for Migration 2018.
145. Aboulenein 2018.
146. Otten 2018.
147. Human Rights Office of the United Nations Assistance Mission for Iraq (UNAMI) and the Office of the United Nations High Commissioner for Human Rights 2018.
148. George et al. 2017; Human Rights Office of the United Nations Assistance Mission for Iraq (UNAMI) and the Office of the United Nations High Commissioner for Human Rights 2017, 15.
149. CEDAW Committee 2016, 4.
150. Human Rights Office of the United Nations Assistance Mission for Iraq (UNAMI) and the Office of the United Nations High Commissioner for Human Rights 2018, 4.
151. CEDAW Committee 2016, Davis 2016
152. Underwood 2017; Graham-Harrison 2017b.
153. Combined Joint Task Force-Operation Inherent Resolve 2018.
154. Airwars 2018. The discrepancy in reported civilian deaths from airstrikes has also been highlighted by Khan and Gopal 2017.
155. Sonne 2018.
156. Cook and Vale 2018, 52.
157. Browne 2016.
158. Thomas 2017.
159. Revkin 2018.
160. The status and trajectory of ISIS affiliates after the fall of the "caliphate" is discussed at length in Cook and Vale 2018.
161. Coker and Hassan 2018.
162. Jalabi 2019.

163. Cook and Vale 2018, 44–9.
164. Human Rights Watch 2017.
165. Amnesty International 2018.
166. Ibid., 6.
167. US Department of State 2018b, 132.
168. United Nations Security Council 2018.
169. Lead Inspector General for Overseas Contingency Operations 2018a, 3.
170. Siddiqui 2015; Dearden 2017.
171. Mironova 2019.
172. Atran et al. 2018.
173. Khalil and Demrdash 2018.
174. Givetash 2018.
175. CEDAW Committee 2016; Abouzeid 2018.
176. Lead Inspector General for Overseas Contingency Operations 2018a, 40.
177. Al Jazeera 2018.
178. See al-Kadi and Vale, "Local voices against violence: Women challenging extremism in Iraq and Syria." Small Wars and Insurgency, forthcoming.
179. Khalil and Demrdash 2018.
180. Bellingreri 2017.
181. Kenner 2017.
182. BBC 2018.
183. Lamb 2018.
184. Hall 2018.
185. UNHCR 2017.
186. McDowall 2018
187. UN News Centre 2013.
188. Humud, Blanchard and Nikitin 2018.
189. Lead Inspector General for Overseas Contingency Operations 2018a, 48.
190. Savage 2018a.
191. Lead Inspector General for Overseas Contingency Operations 2018a, 9.
192. Savage 2018b.
193. Cook and Vale 2018, 48; Haid 2018, 34.
194. Said and Francis 2019.
195. Britton 2019.
196. US Attorney's Office Northern District of Indiana 2018.
197. Wood 2017.
198. Brown 2018, 8–213; The Project on Middle East Political Science 2018.

199. The Project on Middle East Political Science 2018, 5.
200. Humud, Blanchard and Nikitin 2018, 8.
201. Borger 2018.
202. Lead Inspector General for Overseas Contingency Operations 2018a, 5.
203. Ibid., 11.
204. Haid 2018, 29.
205. Chynoweth 2017.
206. UN Security Council 2018a, 3.
207. JaN was established in 2012 and later rebranded itself as Jabhat Fatah al-Sham (July 2016) and Hayat Tahrir al-Sham (January 2017) to separate and distinguish itself from al-Qaeda and present a more "moderate" organization.
208. BBC Reality Check 2018.
209. Haid 2017; Jawad al-Tamimi 2018.
210. The Stabilisation Network 2018, 13–15.
211. Winter and Haid 2018.
212. The Stabilisation Network 2018, 22.
213. Ibid., 25–6.
214. Khezri 2018.
215. This feminist slant is based off its ideological affinity with the Marxist-Leninist Kurdistan Workers' Party, which emphasized liberation for the Kurdish people (and thus for Kurdish women).
216. Marouf 2018.
217. McKernan 2019.
218. Sopko 2017.
219. First as Operation Decisive Storm (26 March–21 April 2015), then as Operation Restoring Hope (22 April 2015 to present).
220. Congressional Research Service 2019b, 6 & 15.
221. Ibid., 20.
222. Throssell 2018.
223. Cockburn 2018.
224. The Project on Middle East Political Science 2018, 5.
225. Nissenbaum 2018.
226. Oxfam International and Saferworld 2018, 10–11.
227. Pasha-Robinson 2017.
228. World Health Organization 2018.
229. Gutteres 2018.
230. Georgetown Institute for Women, Peace and Security 2018.
231. Craig 2017.
232. Roggio and Gutowski 2018.
233. Bureau of Investigative Journalism 2018b.

234. For more on ISIS in Yemen, see Kendall 2019.
235. Johnsen 2018.
236. UN Security Council 2018a, 9–10.
237. Amnesty International 2018.
238. Oxfam International and Saferworld 2018.
239. Kendall 2018.
240. Barrett interview 2016.
241. Tickner 2002, 343–8.
242. Brown 2013, 38.
243. Fink, Zeiger, and Bhulai 2016, 10.
244. Sjoberg and Gentry 2008b, 6.
245. Satterthwaite and Huckerby 2013; NYU Center for Human Rights and Global Justice 2011.
246. BBC Radio 4 2017.

# BIBLIOGRAPHY

*Interviews with the author*

American Yemen analyst, Interview with author, 28 July 2015.

Ansari, Adnan N., Interview with author, 13 Sep. 2016.

Barrett, Richard, Interview with author, 20 Oct. 2016.

Billings, Julia, Interview with author, 21 July 2015.

Bloom, Mia, Interview with author, 23 Jan. 2015.

Bodine, Ambassador Barbara, Interview with author, 9 July 2015.

Des Roches, David B., Interview with author, 6 July 2015.

Feierstein, Ambassador Gerald, Interview with author, 26 June 2015.

Fink, Naureen Chowdhury, Interview with author, 17 July 2015.

Holmer, Georgia, Interview with author, 29 June 2015.

Hughes, Seamus, Interview with author, 29 Sep. 2016.

Interviewee 1, Interview with author, 13 July 2015.

Interviewee 2, Interview with author, 14 Mar. 2014.

Kendall, Elisabeth, Interview with author, 7 Dec. 2015.

Khoury, Nabeel, Interview with author, 9 July 2015.

Kolenda, Christopher, Interview with author, 27 Apr. 2015.

Krajeski, Ambassador Thomas C., Interview with author, 29 June 2015.

Markham, Susan A., Interview with author, 1 July 2015.

Mosbacher Morris, Jayne, Interview with author, 13 July 2015.

Mozzetta, Jennifer, Interview with author, 29 Sep. 2016.

Pandith, Farah, Interview with author, 5 Mar. 2019.

Petraeus, General David H., Interview with author, 19 Oct. 2016.

Scanlon, Sheila, Interview with author, 24 Aug. 2017.

Seche, Ambassador Stephen, Interview with author, 9 July 2015.

Sjoberg, Laura, Interview with author, 20 Jan. 2015.

Verveer, Ambassador Melanne, Interview with author, 26 June 2015.

# BIBLIOGRAPHY

*Primary sources*

Alexander, General Keith B., et al., "Open letter to congress," 2017, http://www.usglc.org/downloads/2017/02/FY18_International_Affairs_Budget_House_Senate.pdf, last accessed 8 Mar. 2019.

AQAP, "May our souls be sacrificed for you! Shaykh Anwar al-'Awlaki," *Inspire*, Al-Malahem Media, 2010, www.jihadology.net, last accessed 9 Mar. 2019.

——, "We are all Usama," *Inspire*, Al-Malahem Media, 2013, www.jihadology.net, last accessed 9 Mar. 2019.

——, "Neurotmesis, cutting the nerves and isolating the head," *Inspire*, Al-Malahem Media, 2014a, www.jihadology.net, last accessed 9 Mar. 2019.

——, "Shattered, a story about change," *Inspire*, Al-Malahem Media, 2014b, www.jihadology.net, last accessed 9 Mar. 2019.

Armitage, Richard L., "Supporting human rights and democracy: The US Record 2003–2004," 17 May 2004, https://20012009.state.gov/s/d/former/armitage/remarks/32521.htm, last accessed 11 Mar. 2019.

Bever, James A., "Testimony," 1 Mar. 2010, https://www.usaid.gov/news-information/congressional-testimony/testimony-usaid-afghanistan-pakistan-task-force-director, last accessed 1 May 2019.

Bin Laden, Osama, *Declaration of Jihad Against Americans Occupying the Land of the Two Holiest Sites*, 1996, https://ctc.usma.edu/app/uploads/2013/10/Declaration-of-Jihad-against-the-Americans-Occupying-the-Land-of-the-Two-Holiest-Sites-Translation.pdf, last accessed 1 May 2019.

——, "Expel the Mushrikeen from the Arabian Peninsula," 1996, http://faculty.smu.edu/jclam/western_religions/ubl-fatwa.html, last accessed 1 May 2019.

Bradtke, Robert A., "Statement for the record for the Foreign Affairs Subcommittees on Terrorism, Nonproliferation and Trade, and the Middle East and North Africa: Foreign Terrorists Fighters," 2 Dec. 2014, https://2009–2017.state.gov/j/ct/rls/rm/2014/234641.htm, last accessed 1 May 2019.

Brimmer, Esther, "Women as agents of change: Advancing the role of women in politics and civil society," 9 June 2010, https://2009–2017.state.gov/p/io/rm/2010/142907.htm, last accessed 1 May 2019.

Bush, George W., "Authorization for Use of Military Force, 115 STAT. 224, Public Law 107–40, 107th Congress," 18 Sep. 2001a, https://www.congress.gov/107/plaws/publ40/PLAW-107publ40.pdf, last accessed 10 Mar. 2019.

——, "Address to the Joint Session of Congress. Washington, DC, September 20," 20 Sep. 2001b, https://georgewbush-whitehouse.archives.gov/infocus/bushrecord/documents/Selected_Speeches_George_W_Bush.pdf, last accessed 10 Mar. 2019.

————, "Address to the nation on operations in Afghanistan. Washington, DC," 7 Oct. 2001c, https://georgewbush-whitehouse.archives.gov/infocus/bushrecord/documents/Selected_Speeches_George_W_Bush.pdf, last accessed 10 Mar. 2019.

————, "Address at the Citadel. The Citadel, North Carolina," 11 Dec. 2001d, https://georgewbush-whitehouse.archives.gov/infocus/bushrecord/documents/Selected_Speeches_George_W_Bush.pdf, last accessed 10 Mar. 2019.

————, *The National Security Strategy of the United States*, Washington, DC: The White House, 2002a.

————, "Remarks at the Inter-American Development Bank," 14 Mar. 2002b, https://georgewbush-whitehouse.archives.gov/infocus/bushrecord/documents/Selected_Speeches_George_W_Bush.pdf, last accessed 10 Mar. 2019.

————, "Remarks at the Virginia Military Institute in Lexington, Virginia," 17 Apr. 2002c, https://georgewbush-whitehouse.archives.gov/infocus/bushrecord/documents/Selected_Speeches_George_W_Bush.pdf, last accessed 10 Mar. 2019.

————, "Promoting compassionate conservatism. Parkside Hall, San Jose, California," 30 Apr. 2002d, https://georgewbush-whitehouse.archives.gov/, last accessed 10 Mar. 2019.

————, "West Point commencement," 1 June 2002e, https://georgewbush-whitehouse.archives.gov/infocus/bushrecord/documents/Selected_Speeches_George_W_Bush.pdf, last accessed 10 Mar. 2019.

————, "Authorization for Use of Military Force against Iraq Resolution of 2002, 116 STAT. 1498, Public Law 107–243, 107th Congress," 16 Oct. 2002f, https://www.congress.gov/107/plaws/publ243/PLAW-107publ243.pdf, last accessed 10 Mar. 2019.

————, "Address to the nation on military operations in Iraq," 10 Mar. 2003a, https://georgewbush-whitehouse.archives.gov/infocus/bushrecord/documents/Selected_Speeches_George_W_Bush.pdf, last accessed 10 Mar. 2019.

————, "Remarks on the Freedom Agenda," 6 Nov. 2003b, https://georgewbush-whitehouse.archives.gov/infocus/bushrecord/documents/Selected_Speeches_George_W_Bush.pdf, last accessed 10 Mar. 2019.

————, "Remarks on efforts to globally promote women's human rights," 12 Mar. 2004a, https://georgewbush-whitehouse.archives.gov/infocus/bushrecord/documents/Selected_Speeches_George_W_Bush.pdf, last accessed 10 Mar. 2019.

————, "Address to the Republican National Convention, New York," 2 Sep. 2004b, https://georgewbush-whitehouse.archives.gov/infocus/bushrecord/documents/Selected_Speeches_George_W_Bush.pdf, last accessed 10 Mar. 2019.

————, "National Security Presidential Directive/NSPD-44. Management of Interagency Efforts Concerning Reconstruction and Stabilization," 2005a, https://fas.org/irp/offdocs/nspd/nspd-44.pdf, last accessed 10 Mar. 2019.

————, "Transcript: President Bush's Fort Bragg speech," NBC News, 30 June 2005b, http://www.nbcnews.com/id/8404774/ns/msnbc-hardball_with_chris_matthews/t/transcript-president-bushs-fort-bragg-speech/#.XIUCuhP7TOQ, last accessed 10 Mar. 2019.

————, *The National Security Strategy of the United States of America*, Washington, DC: Wordclay, 2006a.

————, "President discusses the global war on terror," 5 Sep. 2006b, https://2001–2009.state.gov/s/ct/rls/rm/2006/71811.htm, last accessed 30 Apr. 2019.

————, "Address to an international conference on democracy and security in Prague," 5 June 2007a, https://georgewbush-whitehouse.archives.gov/, last accessed 10 Mar. 2019.

————, "Address to the nation on the way forward in Iraq," 13 Sep. 2007b, https://georgewbush-whitehouse.archives.gov/, last accessed 10 Mar. 2019.

————, "Address to the White House Summit on International Development. Washington, DC," 21 Oct. 2008a, https://georgewbush-whitehouse.archives.gov/infocus/bushrecord/documents/Selected_Speeches_George_W_Bush.pdf, last accessed 10 Mar. 2019.

————, "Remarks at the Saban Forum. Newseum. Washington, DC," 5 Dec. 2008b, https://georgewbush-whitehouse.archives.gov/infocus/bushrecord/documents/Selected_Speeches_George_W_Bush.pdf, last accessed 10 Mar. 2019.

Byess, Richard, "Civilian-military cooperation: What's next?" USAID: Frontiers in Development (2012), pp. 62–67.

Caldwell, William B., The Afghan National Police, 2011, http://www.dodlive.mil/2011/09/27/the-afghan-national-police/, last accessed 10 May 2018.

Campbell, Nancy Duff, Margarethe Cammermeyer, Julia J. Cleckley, Ruby B. DeMesme, John L. Estrada, Holly K. Hemphill, Deborah Lee James and Maureen K. LeBoeuf, "Defense Advisory Committee on women in the services 2011 report," http://dacowits.defense.gov/Portals/48/Documents/Reports/2011/Annual%20Report/dacowits2011report.pdf, last accessed 1 May 2019.

Capozzola, Christa, "US policy toward Yemen," 19 July 2011, https://www.c-span.org/person/?christacapozzola, last accessed 1 May 2019.

Carpenter, J. Scott, "Transformational diplomacy in action: Remarks to Detroit Council for World Affairs. Washington, D.C," 15 June 2006, https://2002–2009-mepi.state.gov/68167.htm, last accessed 4 Apr. 2017.

Carter, Ash, "Department of Defense press briefing by Secretary Carter in the Pentagon Briefing Room. Press Operations," 3 Dec. 2015, http://www.defense.gov/News/News-Transcripts/Transcript-View/Article/632578/department-of-defense-press-briefing-by-secretary-carter-in-the-pentagon-briefing, last accessed 1 May 2019.

Carter, Ash, and Jean-Yves le Drian, "Joint press conference by Secretary Carter and Minister Le Drian in Paris, France," 25 Oct. 2016, https://dod.defense.gov/News/Transcripts/Transcript-View/Article/986525/joint-press-conference-by-secretary-carter-and-minister-le-drian-in-paris-france/, last accessed 1 May 2019.

Chief Financial Officer, *Defense Budget Overview*, Washington, DC: Department of Defense, 2017, https://comptroller.defense.gov/Portals/45/Documents/defbudget/fy2017/FY2017_Budget_Request_Overview_Book.pdf, last accessed 1 May 2019.

Clad, James, "USAID's role in the War on Terror," United States Agency for International Development Issue Brief, 1 (2002), pp. 1–8.

Clare, Micah E., "Face of defense: Woman soldier receives Silver Star," DoD News, 24 Mar. 2008, http://archive.defense.gov/news/newsarticle.aspx?id=49348, last accessed 1 May 2019.

Clinton, Bill, "Presidential Decision Directives 39," 1995, https://fas.org/irp/offdocs/pdd39.htm, last accessed 10 Mar. 2019.

————, *A National Security Strategy for a New Century*, Washington, DC: The White House, 1999.

————, *A National Security Strategy for a Global Age*, Washington, DC: The White House, 2000.

Clinton, Hillary, "Remarks for the United Nations Fourth World Conference on Women. Beijing, China," 5 Sept. 1995, https://www.state.gov/documents/organization/65874.pdf, last accessed 1 May 2019.

————, *Quadrennial Diplomacy and Development Review*, Washington, DC: United States Agency for International Development, 2010a.

————, "Remarks at the UN Commission on the Status of Women," 12 Mar. 2010b, https://2009–2017-usun.state.gov/remarks/4627, last accessed 10 Mar. 2019.

————, "Foreign aid: Women's progress is human progress, and human progress is women's progress," *The Globe and Mail*, 29 Mar. 2010c, https://www.theglobeandmail.com/opinion/foreign-aid-womens-progress-is-human-progress-and-human-progress-is-womens-progress/article4312696/, last accessed 10 Mar. 2019.

————, "Secretary Clinton's remarks on women, peace, and security," 19 Dec. 2011, https://2009–2017.state.gov/secretary/20092013clinton/rm/2011/12/179173.htm, last accessed 11 Mar. 2019.

# BIBLIOGRAPHY

————, "Remarks at the Special Operations Command Gala dinner, Tampa, Florida," 23 May 2012, https://2009–2017.state.gov/secretary/2009 2013clinton/rm/2012/05/190805.htm, last accessed 10 Mar. 2019.

Clinton, Hillary, and Leon Panetta (eds), *Women on the Frontlines of Peace and Security*, Washington, DC: National Defense University Press, 2015.

Combined Joint Task Force-Operation Inherent Resolve, "CJTF-OIR monthly civilian casualty report," 26 Apr. 2018, http://www.centcom.mil/MEDIA/NEWSARTICLES/NewsArticleView/Article/1504033/cjtf-oir-monthly-civilian-casualty-report/, last accessed 10 Mar. 2019.

Commission on Wartime Contracting, "Testimony by USAID Afghanistan-Pakistan Task Force Director James A. Bever before the Commission on Wartime Contracting," 1 Mar. 2010, https://www.usaid.gov/news-information/congressional-testimony/testimony-usaid-afghanistan-pakistan-task-force-director, last accessed 5 May 2018.

Committee on Armed Services, "Inquiry into the treatment of detainees in US custody," 20 Nov. 2009, https://www.armed-services.senate.gov/imo/media/doc/Detainee-Report-Final_Apri-22-2009.pdf, last accessed 1 May 2019.

Congressional Research Service, "Afghanistan: Background and US policy in brief," 26 Feb. 2019a, https://fas.org/sgp/crs/row/R45122.pdf, last accessed 6 Mar. 2019.

————, "Yemen: Civil war and regional intervention," 21 Mar. 2019b https://fas.org/sgp/crs/mideast/R43960.pdf, last accessed 1 May 2019.

Defense Advisory Committee on Women in the Services, "Homepage," https://dacowits.defense.gov/, last accessed 1 Sep. 2017.

Department of Homeland Security, "Strategy for homeland defense and civil support," June 2005, https://www.hsdl.org/?view&did=454976, last accessed 30 Apr. 2019.

Denoeux, Guilain, and Lynn Carter, "Conducting an extremism or terrorism assessment: An analytical framework for strategy and program development," 2008, http://pdf.usaid.gov/pdf_docs/pnadz582.pdf, last accessed 1 May 2019.

————, "Development assistance and counter-extremism: A guide to programming," 2009a, http://pdf.usaid.gov/pdf_docs/Pnadt977.pdf, last accessed 1 May 2019.

————, "Guide to the drivers of violent extremism," 2009b, http://pdf.usaid.gov/pdf_docs/Pnadt978.pdf, last accessed 1 May 2019.

Fine, Glenn A., "Operation Inherent Resolve: Report to US Congress," 2015, https://media.defense.gov/2017/Apr/13/2001732246/-1/-1/1/FY2016_LIG_OCO_OIR_Q1_REPORT_DEC2015.PDF, last accessed 1 May 2019.

————, "Operation Inherent Resolve: Report to US Congress," 2016, https://oig.state.gov/system/files/oir_quarterly_march2016.pdf, last accessed 1 May 2019.

————, "Operation Inherent Resolve: Report to US Congress," 2017, https://media.defense.gov/2017/Apr/13/2001732247/-1/-1/1/FY2016_LIG_OCO_OIR_Q2_REPORT_MAR20164.PDF, last accessed 1 May 2019.

Government Publishing Office, *The United States Government Manual*, 2018, Washington, DC: Government Publishing Office, https://www.usgovernmentmanual.gov/, last accessed 15 Sep. 2017.

Guterres, António, "Remarks by the Secretary-General to the Pledging Conference on Yemen," United Nations Office at Geneva, 3 Apr. 2018, https://www.unog.ch/unog/website/news_media.nsf/(httpNewsBy-Year_en)/27F6CCD7178F3E9C1258264003311FA?OpenDocument, last accessed 7 Mar. 2019.

House Committee on Foreign Affairs, "Testimony of US Agency for International Development Assistant Administrator Nancy E. Lindborg. Crisis in Syria: The US response," 20 Mar. 2013a, https://docs.house.gov/meetings/FA/FA00/20130320/100537/HHRG-113-FA00-Wstate-LindborgN-20130320.pdf last accessed 1 May 2019.

————, "Testimony of Administrator Rajiv Shah," 25 Apr. 2013b, https://2012–2017.usaid.gov/news-information/congressional-testimony/april-25–2013-testimony-administrator-rajiv-shah-house-committee-foreign, last accessed 1 May 2019.

House Foreign Affairs Subcommittee on Middle East and North Africa, "Testimony of Thomas H. Staal," 27 Oct. 2015, http://docs.house.gov/meetings/FA/FA13/20151027/104123/HHRG-114-FA13-Wstate-StaalT-20151027.pdf, last accessed 1 May 2019.

————, "Statement of Deputy Assistance Administrator Alinia L. Romanowski," 22 May 2013, https://www.usaid.gov/news-information/congressional-testimony/may-22–2013-daa-alina-l-romanowski-middle-east-north-africa-fy2014-budget-request, last accessed 9 June 2017.

————, "Statement of Alina L. Romanowski, Deputy Assistant Administrator, Bureau for the Middle East," 29 May 2014, https://www.usaid.gov/news-information/congressional-testimony/apr-9–2014-alina-romanowski-daa-middle-east-us-policy-morocco, last accessed 12 June 2017.

Human Rights Office of the United Nations Assistance Mission for Iraq (UNAMI) and the Office of the United Nations High Commissioner for Human Rights, "Report on the Protection of Civilians in the context of the Ninewa Operations and the retaking of Mosul City, 17 October 2016—10 July 2017," 2017, http://www.uniraq.org/images/factsheets_reports/

Mosul_report%2017Oct201610Jul201731%20October_2017.pdf, last accessed 7 Mar. 2019.

———, "Unearthing atrocities: Mass graves in territory formerly controlled by ISIL," 6 Nov. 2018, https://ohchr.org/Documents/Countries/IQ/UNAMI_Report_on_Mass_Graves4Nov218_EN.pdf, last accessed 7 Mar. 2019.

International Security Assistance Force, "Engaging the female populace,' 23 Feb. 2010, https://info.publicintelligence.net/ISAF-FemaleEngagement.pdf, last accessed 1 May 2019.

Islamic State Media, "The return of the Khilafah," *Dabiq*, 1, July 2014, www.jihadology.net, last accessed 1 May 2019.

———, "They plot and Allah plots," *Dabiq*, 9, 21 May 2015a, www.jihadology.net, last accessed 1 May 2019.

———, "Just terror," *Dabiq*, 12, 18 Nov. 2015b, www.jihadology.net, last accessed 1 May 2019.

———, "Break the cross," *Dabiq*, 15, 31 July 2016. www.jihadology.net, last accessed 1 May 2019.

Jefferson, Thomas, et al., "Declaration of Independence," 4 July 1776, https://www.loc.gov/item/mtjbib000159/, last accessed 30 Apr. 2019.

Jenkins, Robert, "Statement of Robert Jenkins, Deputy Assistant Administrator for the Bureau of Democracy, Conflict, and Humanitarian Assistance before the House Emerging Threats and Capabilities Subcommittee," 11 July 2018, https://www.usaid.gov/news-information/congressional-testimony/jul-11–2018-robertjenkins-daa-dcha-emerging-threats-capabilities, last accessed 6 Mar. 2019.

Joint Chiefs of Staff, "Joint Publication 3–26, Counterterrorism", 13 Nov. 2009, https://www.hsdl.org/?view&did=31130, last accessed 30 Apr. 2019.

Joint Chiefs of Staff, "Joint Publication 3–24 Counterinsurgency," 25 Apr. 2018, https://www.jcs.mil/Portals/36/Documents/Doctrine/pubs/jp3_24.pdf, last accessed 3 May 2019.

Kaidanow, Tina S., "State Department's Bureau of Counterterrorism: Budget, programs, and policies," 10 June 2014, https://2009–2017.state.gov/j/ct/rls/rm/2014/227413.htm, last accessed 1 May 2019.

Kean, Thomas, "The 9/11 Commission Report," 2011, https://www.9–11commission.gov/report/911Report.pdf, last accessed 1 May 2019.

Kendall, Elisabeth, Tweet of 25 Sep. 2018, https://twitter.com/Dr_E_Kendall/status/1044575146223312897, last accessed 9. Mar 2019.

———, "The failing Islamic State within the failed state of Yemen," *Perspectives on Terrorism*, 13, 1 (2019), https://www.universiteitleiden.nl/binaries/content/assets/customsites/perspectives-on-terrorism/2019/issue-1/kendall.pdf, last accessed 1 May 2019.

# BIBLIOGRAPHY

Kerry, John, "Opening remarks on the United States strategy to defeat the Islamic State in Iraq and the Levant," 17 Sep. 2014, https://2009–2017. state.gov/secretary/remarks/2014/09/231773.htm, last accessed 1 May 2019.

———, "Enduring leadership in a dynamic world: Quadrennial Diplomacy and Development Review," 2015, https://www.state.gov/documents/ organization/267396.pdf, last accessed 1 May 2019.

Lead Inspector General for Overseas Contingency Operations, "Operation Inherent Resolve Report to the United States Congress," 2017, https:// media.defense.gov/2018/Jan/09/2001864247/-1/-1/1/2017_LIG_ OCO_OIR_Q4_092017_3_508.PDF, last accessed 4 Mar. 2019.

———, "Operation Inherent Resolve and other overseas contingency operations," 2018a, https://media.defense.gov/2018/Nov/05/2002 059226/-1/-1/1/FY2019_LIG_OCO_OIR_Q4_SEP2018.PDF, last accessed 7 Mar. 2019.

———, "Operation Inherent Resolve Pacific Eagle-Philippines," 2018b, https://media.defense.gov//2018/Aug/07/2001951441/-1/1/1/ FY2018_LIG_OCO_OIR3_JUN2018_508.PDF, last accessed 7 Mar. 2019.

Lindborg, Nancy, "ISIL's reign of terror: Confronting the growing humanitarian crisis in Iraq and Syria," 9 Dec. 2014, https://www.hsdl.org/ ?view&did=761144Press, last accessed 1 May 2019.

Malinowski, Tom, "ISIL's persecution of religious minorities in Iraq and Syria," 10 Sep. 2014, https://2009–2017.state.gov/j/drl/rls/rm/2014/231483. htm, last accessed 1 May 2019.

Marine Expeditionary Force, "A look inside the FET," *Marines*, 6 Feb. 2012, http://www.marines.mil/News/Marines-TV/videoid/136783/dvpTag/ FET/#DVIDSVideoPlayer27131, last accessed 1 May 2019.

Mattis, James N., "Resignation letter," 21 Dec. 2018, https://www.bbc. co.uk/news/world-us-canada-46644841, last accessed 1 May 2019.

McCullough, Christopher, "Female Engagement Teams: Who they are and why they do it," 2 Oct. 2012, https://www.army.mil/article/88366/ female_engagement_teams_who_they_are_and_why_they_do_it, last accessed 1 May 2019.

McMaster, LTG H.R., "Remarks by LTG H.R. McMaster at Foundation for Defense of Democracies (FDD) National Security Summit," 2017a, https://www.whitehouse.gov/briefings-statements/remarks-ltg-h-r-mcmaster-foundation-defense-democracies-fdd-national-security-summit/, last accessed 1 May 2019.

———, "Remarks by LTG H.R. McMaster at the Reagan National Defense Forum: Reclaiming America's Strategic Confidence," 2017b, https://www. whitehouse.gov/briefings-statements/remarks-ltg-h-r-mcmaster-reagan-national-defense-forum-reclaiming-americas-strategic-confidence/, last accessed 1 May 2019.

McMillan, Della, Mamadou Sidibe, Jessica Cho and Alice Willard, "Community stabilization program: Final report," Jan. 2010, http://pdf. usaid.gov/pdf_docs/pdacr642.pdf, last accessed 1 May 2019.

Medina, Robert, "'Sisters' are doing it for themselves," 7 May 2008, http:// www.centcom.mil/MEDIA/NEWS-ARTICLES/News-Article-View/ Article/883558/sisters-are-doing-it-for-themselves/, last accessed 1 May 2019.

Middle East Partnership Initiative, "About MEPI," 2017, https://mepi.state. gov/about-mepi/, last accessed 14 Mar. 2017.

Military and Professional Bulletin, "Human Terrain System," Oct.–Dec. 2011, https://fas.org/irp/agency/army/mipb/2011_04.pdf, last accessed 30 Apr. 2019.

Ministry of Defense, "UK-trained female soldiers to take the fight to ISIS," 26 Mar. 2016, https://www.gov.uk/government/news/uk-trained-female-soldiers-to-take-the-fight-to-ISIS, last accessed 1 May 2019.

Muhajirat fi sabeelillah in Khurasan, "Sunnat E Khola," Aug. 2017, www.jih-adology.net, last accessed 1 May 2019.

Mullen, Mike, "Chairman's corner: Too many doors still closed to women," Department of Defense News, 5 Nov. 2010, http://archive.defense.gov/ News/NewsArticle.aspx?ID=61586, last accessed 1 May 2019.

Myers, Richard B., "The national military strategy of the United States of America: A strategy for today; a vision for tomorrow, 2004," 2004, archive. defense.gov/news/Mar2005/d20050318nms.pdf, last accessed 1 May 2019.

NATO Resolute Support Afghanistan, "Women of the Afghan Special Security Forces: Flying high with Special Mission Wing," 5 Apr. 2018, https://rs. nato.int/mediacenter/women—peace—and-security/women-of-the-afghan-special-security-forcesflying-high-with-special-mission-wing.aspx, last accessed 6 Mar. 2019.

Natsios, Andrew, "Press briefing USAID Administrator Andrew Natsios," 20 Dec. 2001, http://avalon.law.yale.edu/sept11/natsios_004.asp, last accessed 1 May 2019.

Natsios, Andrew. "Testimony of Andrew Natsios Administrator, USAID." 10 Oct 2001b. http://avalon.law.yale.edu/sept11/natsios_002.asp, last accessed 25 May 2019.

Nava, Rebecca I., "Statement of Rebecca I. Nava," 23 Apr. 2009, http:// archives-democrats-veterans.house.gov/hearings/Testimony_Print. aspx?newsid=379&Name=_Rebecca_I._Nava, last accessed 30 Apr. 2019.

Nicholson Jr., John W., "Department of Defense Press Briefing by General Nicholson via Teleconference from Kabul, Afghanistan," 28 Nov. 2017, https://www.defense.gov/News/Transcripts/Transcript-View/

Article/1382901/department-of-defense-press-brie ng-by-general-nich-olson-via-teleconference-fr/, last accessed 1 May 2019.

Nunez, Augustin Valerio, "Daughters of Iraq begin training," 27 May 2008, http://www.centcom.mil/MEDIA/NEWS-ARTICLES/News-Article-View/Article/883600/daughters-of-iraq-begin-training/, last accessed 1 May 2019.

Obama, Barack, "Al-Arabiya Television interview with Hisham Melhem," 26 Jan. 2009a, https://www.alarabiya.net/articles/2009/01/27/65096.html, last accessed 1 May 2019.

———, "Responsibly ending the war in Iraq. Camp Lejeune, North Carolina," 27 Feb. 2009b, https://obamawhitehouse.archives.gov/the-press-office/remarks-president-barack-obama-ndash-responsibly-ending-war-iraq, last accessed 1 May 2019.

———, "Remarks on American values and National Security National Archives, Washington, D.C.," 21 May 2009c, https://obamawhitehouse.archives.gov/the-press-office/remarks-president-national-secu-rity-5–21–09, last accessed 1 May 2019.

———, "A new beginning: Speech at Cairo University. Cairo, Egypt," *New York Times*, 4 June 2009d, http://www.nytimes.com/2009/06/04/us/politics/04obama.text.html, last accessed 1 May 2019.

———, "First Presidential state of the union address. Washington, DC," 27 Jan. 2010a, https://obamawhitehouse.archives.gov/photos-and-video/video/2010-state-union-address#transcript, last accessed 1 May 2019.

———, "Address to the troops in Afghanistan. Clamshell, Bagram Air Field," 28 Mar. 2010b, https://obamawhitehouse.archives.gov/realitycheck/the-press-office/remarks-president-troops, last accessed 1 May 2019.

———, "Remarks by the President at United States Military Academy at West Point Commencement. Michie Stadium, West Point, New York," 22 May 2010c, https://obamawhitehouse.archives.gov/the-press-office/remarks-president-united-states-military-academy-west-point-commence-ment, last accessed 1 May 2019.

———, "National Security Strategy Washington, DC: The White House," 27 May 2010d, http://nssarchive.us/national-security-strategy-2010/, last accessed 1 May 2019.

———, "Address to military personnel in Pensacola, Florida," 25 June 2010e, https://obamawhitehouse.archives.gov/photos-and-video/video/president-obama-speaks-military-personnel-pensacola-fl#transcript, last accessed 1 May 2019.

———, "Remarks at the Disabled Veterans of American Conference. Hyatt Regency Hotel. Atlanta, Georgia," 2 Aug. 2010f, https://obamawhite-house.archives.gov/the-press-office/remarks-president-disabled-veterans-america-conference-atlanta-georgia, last accessed 1 May 2019.

———, "Address to the nation on the end of Operation Iraqi Freedom. Oval Office, The White House," 31 Aug. 2010g, https://obamawhitehouse. archives.gov/the-press-office/2010/08/31/remarks-president-address-nation-end-combat-operations-iraq, last accessed 1 May 2019.

———, "Remarks by the Presidential in the second State of the Union Address. Washington, DC," 25 Jan. 2011a, https://obamawhitehouse. archives.gov/the-press-office/2011/01/25/remarks-president-state-union-address, last accessed 1 May 2019.

———, "Remarks by the President on American diplomacy in Middle East and Northern Africa. State Department, Washington, DC," 19 May 2011b, https://obamawhitehouse.archives.gov/the-press-office/2011/05/19/ remarks-president-middle-east-and-north-africa, last accessed 1 May 2019.

———, "Remarks by the President to Parliament in London, United Kingdom. Westminster Hall, London," 25 May 2011c, https://obamawhitehouse.archives.gov/the-press-office/2011/05/25/remarks-president-parliament-london-united-kingdom, last accessed 1 May 2019.

———, "National Strategy for Counterterrorism. The White House," 29 June 2011d, https://obamawhitehouse.archives.gov/blog/2011/ 06/29/national-strategy-counterterrorism, last accessed 1 May 2019.

———, "Empowering Local Partners to Prevent Violent Extremism in the United States," 3 Aug. 2011e, https://obamawhitehouse.archives.gov/ the-press-office/2011/08/03/empowering-local-partners-prevent-violent-extremism-united-states, last accessed 1 May 2019.

———, "Executive order—Instituting a National Action Plan on Women, Peace, and Security. (Executive Order 13595). The White House," 19 Dec. 2011f, https://obamawhitehouse.archives.gov/the-press-office/2011/ 12/19/executive-order-instituting-national-action-plan-women-peace-and-security, last accessed 1 May 2019.

———, "Remarks by the President to the 113th National Convention of the Veterans of Foreign Wars. VFW Convention Hall. Nevada," 23 July 2012a, https://obamawhitehouse.archives.gov/the-press-office/2012/07/23/ remarks-president-113th-national-convention-veterans-foreign-wars, last accessed 1 May 2019.

———, "Remarks by the President at the Clinton Global Initiative. Sheraton New York Hotel and Towers. New York," 25 Sep. 2012b, https://obamawhitehouse.archives.gov/the-press-office/2012/09/25/remarks-president-clinton-global-initiative, last accessed 1 May 2019.

———, "Remarks by the President to the UN General Assembly. United Nations Headquarters. New York," 25 September 2012c, https://obamawhitehouse.archives.gov/the-press-office/2012/09/25/remarks-president-un-general-assembly, last accessed 1 May 2019.

———, "Remarks of President Barack Obama—As Prepared for Delivery

State of the Union Address," 12 Feb. 2013a, https://obamawhitehouse. archives.gov/the-press-office/2013/02/12/president-barack-obamas-state-union-address-prepared-delivery, last accessed 1 May 2019.

―――, "Remarks by the President at the National Defense University. Fort McNair, Washington, DC," 23 May 2013b, https://obamawhitehouse. archives.gov/the-press-office/2013/05/23/remarks-president-national-defense-university, last accessed 1 May 2019.

―――, "Remarks by the President on review of Signals Intelligence. Department of Justice. Washington, D.C," 17 Jan. 2014a, https://obamawhitehouse.archives.gov/the-press-office/2014/01/17/remarks-president-review-signals-intelligence, last accessed 1 May 2019.

―――, "President Barack Obama's State of the Union. Address. Washington, DC," 28 Jan. 2014b, https://obamawhitehouse.archives.gov/the-press-office/2014/01/28/president-barack-obamas-state-union-address, last accessed 1 May 2019.

―――, "Remarks by the President at the United States Military Academy Commencement Ceremony. US Military Academy-West Point," 28 May 2014c, https://obamawhitehouse.archives.gov/the-press-office/2014/05/28/remarks-president-united-states-military-academy-commencement-ceremony, last accessed 1 May 2019.

―――, "Remarks by the President on the situation in Iraq. James S. Brady Press Briefing Room," 19 June 2014d, https://obamawhitehouse.archives. gov/the-press-office/2014/06/19/remarks-president-situation-iraq, last accessed 1 May 2019.

―――, "Statement by the President on Iraq. Washington, D.C," 9 Aug. 2014e, https://obamawhitehouse.archives.gov/the-press-office/2014/08/09/statement-president-iraq, last accessed 1 May 2019.

―――, "Statement by the President on ISIL. State Floor," 10 Sep. 2014f, https://obamawhitehouse.archives.gov/the-press-office/2014/09/10/statement-president-isil-1, last accessed 1 May 2019.

―――, "Address to the United Nations General Assembly. United Nations General Assembly Hall. New York," 24 Sep. 2014g, https://obamawhitehouse.archives.gov/the-press-office/2014/09/24/remarks-president-obama-address-united-nations-general-assembly, last accessed 1 May 2019.

―――, "Remarks by the President in the State of the Union Address. US Capitol," 20 Jan. 2015a, https://obamawhitehouse.archives.gov/the-press-office/2015/01/20/remarks-president-state-union-address-january-20–2015, last accessed 1 May 2019.

―――, "National Security Strategy," February 2015b, http://nssarchive.us/wp content/uploads/2015/02/2015.pdf, last accessed 1 May 2019.

―――, "Remarks by the President on request to Congress for authorization of force against ISIL. Roosevelt Room," 11 Feb. 2015c, https://obamawhitehouse.archives.gov/the-press-office/2015/02/11/remarks-president-request-congress-authorization-force-against-isil, last accessed 1 May 2019.

———, "Remarks by the President in closing of the Summit on Countering Violent Extremism. South Court Auditorium," 18 Feb. 2015d, https://obamawhitehouse.archives.gov/the-press-office/2015/02/18/remarks-president-closing-summit-countering-violent-extremism, last accessed 1 May 2019.

———, "Remarks by the President at the Summit on Countering Violent Extremism. State Department," 19 Feb. 2015e, https://obamawhitehouse.archives.gov/the-press-office/2015/02/19/remarks-president-summit-countering-violent-extremism-february-19–2015, last accessed 1 May 2019.

———, "Remarks by the President on progress in the fight against ISIL. The Pentagon," 6 July 2015f, https://obamawhitehouse.archives.gov/the-press-office/2015/07/06/remarks-president-progress-fight-against-isil, last accessed 1 May 2019.

———, "Remarks by President Obama in conversation with members of civil society, Kenya," 26 July 2015g, https://obamawhitehouse.archives.gov/the-press-office/2015/07/26/remarks-president-obama-conversation-members-civil-society, last accessed 1 May 2019.

———, "Remarks by President Obama to the United Nations General Assembly. United Nations Headquarters. New York," 28 Sept. 2015h, https://obamawhitehouse.archives.gov/the-press-office/2015/09/28/remarks-president-obama-united-nations-general-assembly, last accessed 1 May 2019.

———, "Address to the nation by the President. Oval Office. Washington, D.C," 6 Dec. 2015i, https://obamawhitehouse.archives.gov/the-press-office/2015/12/06/address-nation-president, last accessed 1 May 2019.

———, "Statement by the President after the briefing at the National Counterterrorism Center. McLean, Virginia," 17 Dec. 2015j, https://obamawhitehouse.archives.gov/the-press-office/2015/12/17/statement-president-after-briefing-national-counterterrorism-center, last accessed 1 May 2019.

———, "The National Action Plan on Women, Peace and Security," 2016, https://www.usaid.gov/sites/default/files/documents/1868/National%20Action%20Plan%20on%20Women%2C%20Peace%2C%20and%20Security.pdf, last accessed 1 May 2019.

Obama, Michelle, "Remarks by The First Lady at Let Girls Learn Event in London, UK," 16 June 2015, https://obamawhitehouse.archives.gov/the-press-office/2015/06/16/remarks-first-lady-let-girls-learn-event-london-uk, last accessed 1 May 2019.

# BIBLIOGRAPHY

O'Connor, Eileen, "State's O'Connor on Women's Roles in Countering Violent Extremism," 21 Oct. 2014, https://www.osce.org/secretariat/125722?download=true, last accessed 1 May 2019.

Office of the Coordinator of Counterterrorism, "National Strategy for Combatting Terrorism," Feb. 2003, https://www.cia.gov/news-information/cia-the-war-on-terrorism/Counter_Terrorism_Strategy.pdf, last accessed 1 May 2019.

———, "National Strategy for Combating Terrorism," Sep. 2006, https://2001–2009.state.gov/s/ct/rls/wh/71803.htm#overview, last accessed 1 May 2019.

Office of the Inspector General, "Audit of the adequacy of USAID's antiterrorism vetting procedures," 6 Nov. 2007, http://pdf.usaid.gov/pdf_docs/Pdacp338.pdf, last accessed 1 May 2019.

Office of Management and Budget, "America First: A budget blueprint to make America great again," 2017, https://www.govinfo.gov/content/pkg/BUDGET-2018-BLUEPRINT/pdf/BUDGET2018-BLUEPRINT.pdf, last accessed 6 Mar. 2019.

Office of the Special Representative for Afghanistan and Pakistan, "Afghanistan and Pakistan: Regional Stabilization Strategy," Feb. 2010, https://www.state.gov/documents/organization/135728.pdf, last accessed 1 May 2019.

Oversight Committee, "Testimony of Jessica Lynch," 2007, https://www.globalsecurity.org/military/library/congress/2007_hr/070424-lynch_2.pdf, last accessed 1 May 2019.

Oversight and Investigations Subcommittee of the Committee on Armed Services, "Testimony of Maj. Gen. Bobby J. Wilkes," 110th Congress, 1st Session, 4 Oct. 2007, https://www.gpo.gov/fdsys/pkg/CHRG-110hhrg39806/html/CHRG-110hhrg39806.htm, last accessed 1 May 2019.

Parker, Michelle, "The role of the Department of Defense in Provincial Reconstruction Teams," 5 Sept. 2007, https://cfrd8-files.cfr.org/sites/default/files/pdf/2007/09/Parker_Testimony090507.pdf, last accessed 1 May 2019.

Pirek, Lindsay, "26th MEU Female Engagement Team trains with Kuwaiti police," Marines, 4 Mar. 2016, http://www.marines.mil/News/News-Display/Article/686139/26th-meu-female-engagement-team-trains-with-kuwaiti-police/, last accessed 1 May 2019.

Pope, William P., "Eliminating terrorist sanctuaries: The role of security assistance," 10 Mar. 2005, https://2001–2009.state.gov/s/ct/rls/rm/43702.htm, last accessed 1 May 2019.

Porter, Russell, and Kristen Cordell, "3 myths about women and violent extremism," USAID blog. 20 July 2015, https://blog.usaid.gov/2015/07/3-myths-about-women-and-violent-extremism/, last accessed 14 Mar. 2019.

# BIBLIOGRAPHY

Powell, Colin L., "The US-Middle East Partnership Initiative: Building Hope for the Years Ahead," 12 Dec. 2002, https://2001–2009.state.gov/secretary/former/powell/remarks/2002/15920.htm, last accessed 1 May 2019.

Rasmussen, Anders Fogh, "Speech by NATO Secretary General Anders Fogh Rasmussen at the Conference on the Role of Women in Global Security, Copenhagen," 29 Oct. 2010, http://www.nato.int/cps/en/SID-79B6 387B-58261976/natolive/opinions_67602.htm?selectedLocale=en%20, last accessed 1 May 2019.

Rice, Condoleezza, "Remarks on foreign assistance. Benjamin Franklin Room," 19 Jan. 2006, https://2001–2009.state.gov/secretary/rm/2006/59408.htm, last accessed 1 May 2019.

Rumsfeld, Donald, and Henry H Shelton, "Quadrennial Defense Review Report," 30 Sep. 2001, http://archive.defense.gov/pubs/qdr2001.pdf, last accessed 1 May 2019.

Russell, Catherine M., "Testimony," 24 June 2014, https://www.foreign.senate.gov/imo/media/doc/Russell_Testimony.pdf, last accessed 1 May 2019.

———, "Opening statement on resources, priorities and programs for global women's issues," 5 May 2015, https://2009–2017.state.gov/s/gwi/rls/rem/2015/242328.htm, last accessed 1 May 2019.

Rutledge, Rheanna, "HTT coverage of Afghan women's perceptions and perspectives: The commonly forgotten community," *Military and Professional Bulletin*, Oct.–Dec. 2011, pp. 53–58.

Seck, Hope Hodge, "Marine Corps revives Female Engagement Team mission," *Marine Corps Times*, 5 Aug. 2015, https://www.marinecorpstimes.com/story/military/2015/08/05/marine-corps-revives-female-engagement-team-mission/30796519/, last accessed 1 May 2019.

Senate Foreign Relations Subcommittee on International Operations and Organizations, Human Rights, Democracy and Global Women's Issues, "ISIL's reign of terror: Confronting the growing humanitarian crisis in Iraq and Syria. Testimony of Nancy Lindborg," 9 Dec. 2014, https://2012–2017.usaid.gov/news-information/congressional-testimony/dec-9–2014-aa-nancy-lindborg-sfrc-international-operations-isil-reign-terror, last accessed 1 May 2019.

Senate Subcommittee on International Operations and Organizations, Human Rights, Democracy and Global Women's Issues, "Testimony by Susan Markham," 24 June 2014, https://www.foreign.senate.gov/imo/media/doc/Markham_Testimony.pdf, last accessed 1 May 2019.

Senate Subcommittee on Near Eastern and South and Central Asian Affairs, "Prepared statement by Christa Capozzola," 19 July 2011, https://www.govinfo.gov/content/pkg/CHRG-112shrg73916/html/CHRG-112shrg73916.htm, last accessed 1 May 2019.

Shah, Rajiv, "Testimony," 8 Apr. 2014a, https://www.appropriations.senate. gov/download/administrator-shah, last accessed 1 May 2019.

———, "Prepared statement of Dr. Rajiv Shah," 10 Apr. 2014b, https:// www.foreign.senate.gov/imo/media/doc/041014_Transcript_ International%20Development%20Priorities%20in%20the%20FY15%20 Budget.pdf, last accessed 30 Apr. 2019.

Shays, Christopher, "Ensuring Implementation of the 9/11 Commission Report Act," US Congress H.R. 5017. Washington, DC, 28 Mar. 2006, https://www.congress.gov/bill/109th-congress/house-bill/5017/text, last accessed 1 May 2019.

Siberell, Justin, "Statement by the State Department's Bureau of Counter-terrorism: Budget, program, and policies," 2 June 2015, https://2009-2017.state.gov/j/ct/rls/rm/243114.htm, last accessed 1 May 2019.

Soneshine, Tara, "The role of public diplomacy in countering violent extrem-ism," 27 Mar. 2013, https://2009–2017.state.gov/r/remarks/2013/ 206708.htm, last accessed 1 May 2019.

Special Inspector General for Afghanistan Reconstruction, "Quarterly report to the United States Congress," 30 Oct. 2014a, https://www.sigar.mil/ pdf/quarterlyreports/2014–10–30qr.pdf, last accessed 1 May 2019.

———, "Afghan women: Comprehensive assessments needed to determine and measure DoD, State, and USAID progress", SIGAR 15–24 Audit Report, Dec. 2014b, https://www.sigar.mil/pdf/audits/sigar-15–24-ar. pdf, last accessed 1 May 2019.

———, "Quarterly report to the United States Congress," 30 Oct. 2015, https://www.sigar.mil/pdf/quarterlyreports/2015–10–30qr.pdf, last accessed 1 May 2019.

———, "Quarterly report to the United States Congress," 30 Oct. 2016, https://www.sigar.mil/pdf/quarterlyreports/2016–10–30qr.pdf, last accessed 1 May 2019.

———, "Reconstructing the Afghan National Defense and Security Forces: Lessons from the US experience in Afghanistan," Sept. 2017, https:// www.sigar.mil/pdf/lessonslearned/SIGAR-17–62-LL.pdf, last accessed 1 May 2019.

———, "Stabilization: Lessons from the US experience in Afghanistan," May 2018a, https://www.sigar.mil/interactive-reports/stabilization/index. html, last accessed 1 May 2019.

———, "Promoting gender equity in national priority programs (Promote): USAID needs to assess this $216 million program's achievements and the Afghan government's ability to sustain them," Sep. 2018b, https://www. sigar.mil/pdf/audits/SIGAR-18–69-AR.pdf, last accessed 1 May 2019.

Special Inspector General for Iraq Reconstruction, "Quarterly report to the United States Congress," 30 Apr. 2010, http://www.sigir.mil/files/quarterlyreports/April2010/Report_-_April_2010.pdf, last accessed 1 May 2019.

Special Operations Forces, *Interagency Counterterrorism Reference Manual*, 3rd edition, Sep. 2013, http://www.soc.mil/528th/PDFs/2013SOFIACT RefManual_Final.pdf, last accessed 1 May 2019.

Starz, Mike, "Soldiers create 'Daughters of Iraq' program," 23 Apr. 2008, http://www.centcom.mil/MEDIA/NEWS-ARTICLES/News-Article-View/Article/883522/soldiers-create-daughters-of-iraq-program/, last accessed 1 May 2019.

Teague Beckwith, Ryan, "Read Donald Trump's 'America First' foreign policy speech," 27 Apr. 2016, http://time.com/4309786/read-donald-trumps-america-first-foreign-policy-speech/, last accessed 1 May 2019.

Torres, Paul, "Iraqi women stop sewing and start talking," Marines, 1 June 2008, http://www.1stmardiv.marines.mil/News/News-Article-Display/Article/541668/iraqi-women-stop-sewing-and-start-talking/, last accessed 1 May 2019.

Throssell, Liz, "Press briefing notes on Yemen civilian casualties," 10 Aug. 2018, https://www.ohchr.org/EN/NewsEvents/Pages/DisplayNews.aspx?NewsID=23439&angID=E, last accessed 7 Mar. 2019.

Trump, Donald, "Trump on beating ISIS: 'You have to take out their families,'" Fox News Insider, 2 Dec. 2015, https://insider.foxnews.com/2015/12/02/donald-trump-fox-and-friends-we-have-take-out-isis-terrorists-families, last accessed 2 May 2019.

———, "Transcript of Republican debate in Miami, full text," CNN, 15 Mar. 2016a, https://edition.cnn.com/2016/03/10/politics/republican-debate-transcript-full-text/index.html, last accessed 4 Mar. 2019

———, "Read Donald Trump's 'America First' foreign policy speech," *Time*, 27 Apr. 2016b, http://time.com/4309786/read-donald-trumps-america-first-foreign-policy-speech/, last accessed 4 Mar. 2019.

———, "Transcript: Donald Trump's taped comments about women," *New York Times*, 8 Oct. 2016c, https://www.nytimes.com/2016/10/08/us/donald-trump-tape-transcript.html, last accessed 4 Mar. 2019.

———, "The inaugural address," 20 Jan. 2017a, https://www.whitehouse.gov/briefings-statements/the-inaugural-address/, last accessed 1 May 2019.

———, "Remarks by President Trump and Vice President Pence at CIA Headquarters. Langley, Virginia," 21 Jan. 2017b, https://www.whitehouse.gov/briefings-statements/remarks-president-trump-vice-president-pence-cia-headquarters/, last accessed 1 May 2019.

———, "Presidential memorandum on rebuilding the US armed forces," 27 Jan. 2017c, https://www.whitehouse.gov/presidential-actions/presidential-memorandum-rebuilding-u-s-armed-forces/, last accessed 4 Mar. 2019

————, "Remarks by President Trump to coalition representatives and senior US commanders," 6 Feb. 2017d, https://www.whitehouse.gov/briefings-statements/remarks-president-trump-coalition-representatives-senior-u-s-commanders/, last accessed 1 May 2019.

————, "Remarks by President Trump in joint address to Congress," 28 Feb. 2017e, https://www.whitehouse.gov/briefings-statements/remarks-president-trump-joint-address-congress/, last accessed 4 Mar. 2019.

————, "President Trump's speech to the Arab Islamic American Summit," 21 May 2017f, https://www.whitehouse.gov/briefings-statements/president-trumps-speech-arab-islamic-american-summit, last accessed 1 May 2019.

————, "Statement from President Donald J. Trump on the liberation of Mosul," 10 July 2017g, https://www.whitehouse.gov/briefings-statements/statement-president-donald-j-trump-liberation-mosul/, last accessed 1 May 2019.

————, "Remarks by President Trump on the strategy in Afghanistan and South Asia," 21 Aug. 2017h, https://www.whitehouse.gov/briefings-statements/remarks-president-trump-strategy-afghanistan-south-asia/, last accessed 1 May 2019.

————, "Presidential memorandum for the Secretary of Defense and the Secretary of Homeland Security," 25 Aug. 2017i, https://www.whitehouse.gov/presidential-actions/presidential-memorandum-secretary-defense-secretary-homeland-security/, last accessed 6 Mar. 2019.

————, "Remarks by President Trump on the administration's National Security Strategy," 18 Dec. 2017j, https://www.whitehouse.gov/briefings-statements/remarks-president-trump-administrations-national-security-strategy/, last accessed 1 May 2019.

————, "President Donald J. Trump protects America through lawful detention of terrorists," 18 Jan. 2018, https://www.whitehouse.gov/briefings-statements/president-donald-j-trump-protects-america-lawful-detention-terrorists/, last accessed 1 May 2019.

————, "Untitled video posted on Twitter," 19 Jan. 2019a, https://twitter.com/realDonaldTrump/status/1086446833541570560, last accessed 13 Mar. 2019.

————, "Executive order on revocation of reporting requirement," 6 Mar. 2019b, https://www.whitehouse.gov/presidential-actions/executive-order-revocation-reporting-requirement/, last accessed 1 May 2019.

UN Analytical Support and Sanctions Monitoring Team, "8th report of the Analytical Support and Sanctions Monitoring Team," 25 May 2017, https://reliefweb.int/report/afghanistan/8th-report-analytical-support-and-sanctions-monitoring-team-submitted-pursuant, last accessed 30 Apr. 2019.

UN Security Council, "Landmark resolution on Women, Peace and Security,"

31 Oct. 2000, http://www.un.org/womenwatch/osagi/wps/, last accessed 1 May 2019.

———, "Resolution 2396: Threats to international peace and security caused by terrorist acts," 21 Dec. 2017, http://unscr.com/en/resolutions/2396, last accessed 1 May 2019.

———, "Twenty-second report of the Analytical Support and Sanctions Monitoring Team submitted pursuant to resolution 2368 (2017) concerning ISIL (Da'esh), Al-Qaida and associated individuals and entities," 27 July 2018a, https://undocs.org/S/2018/705, last accessed 6 Mar. 2019.

———, "Seventh report of the Secretary-General on the threat posed by ISIL (Da'esh) to international peace and security and the range of United Nations efforts in support of member states in countering the threat," 16 Aug. 2018b, http://www.un.org/en/ga/search/view_doc.asp?symbol=S/2018/770&referer=/english/&Lang=E, last accessed 1 May 2019.

UN Women, "Gender mainstreaming: Concepts and definitions," 2012, http://www.un.org/womenwatch/osagi/conceptsanddefinitions.htm, last accessed 12 Mar. 2019.

———, "Major resolutions," 2017, http://www.unwomen.org/en/how-we-work/intergovernmental-support/major-resolutions, last accessed 5 Apr. 2017.

United Nations, "United Nations Millennium Declaration," 18 Sep. 2000, https://www.un.org/millennium/declaration/ares552e.pdf, last accessed 30 Apr. 2019.

———, "International migration report 2017," 2017, http://www.un.org/en/development/desa/population/migration/publications/migrationreport/docs/MigrationReport2017_Highlights.pdf, last accessed 30 Apr. 2019.

United Nations Assistance Mission in Afghanistan, "Midyear update on the protection of civilians in armed conflict: 1 January to 30 June 2018," 15 July 2018a, https://unama.unmissions.org/sites/default/files/unama_poc_midyear_update_2018_5_july_english.pdf, last accessed 6 Mar. 2019.

———, "Afghanistan protection of civilians in armed conflict quarterly report," 10 Oct. 2018b, https://unama.unmissions.org/sites/default/files/unama_protection_of_civilians_in_armed_conflict_3rd_quarter_report_2018_10_oct.pdf, last accessed 1 May 2019.

——— "Afghanistan: Protection of civilians in armed conflict. Annual report 2018," Feb. 2019, https://unama.unmissions.org/sites/default/files/afghanistan_protection_of_civilians_annual_report_2018_final_24_feb_2019_v3.pdf, last accessed 1 May 2019.

United Nations Entity for Gender Equality and the Empowerment of Women, "Fourth World Conference on Women: Platform for Action," September

1995, http://www.un.org/womenwatch/daw/beijing/platform/, last accessed 1 May 2019.

United Nations General Assembly, "Convention on the Elimination of All Forms of Discrimination Against Women," 18 Dec. 1979, http://www.un-documents.net/a34r180.htm, last accessed 1 May 2019.

United Nations High Commissioner for Refugees, "Global trends: Forced displacement in 2017," 2018, http://www.unhcr.org/5b27be547.pdf, last accessed 1 May 2019.

US Agency for International Development, "AAPD 02–19. Implementation of E.O. 13224—Certification Regarding Terrorist Financing," 31 Dec. 2002, https://www.usaid.gov/sites/default/files/documents/1868/aapd02_19.pdf, last accessed 1 May 2019.

———, "USAID/OTI Afghanistan Program: Final Evaluation 8," 2005a, http://pdf.usaid.gov/pdf_docs/PDACF383.pdf, last accessed 1 May 2019.

———, "Conducting a conflict assessment: A framework for analysis and program development," Apr. 2005b, http://pdf.usaid.gov/pdf_docs/Pnadd459.pdf, last accessed 1 May 2019.

———, "Measuring fragility: Indicators and methods for rating state performance," June 2005c, http://pdf.usaid.gov/pdf_docs/pnadd462.pdf, last accessed 1 May 2019.

———, "Women and conflict: An introductory guide for programing," 2007a, https://www.usaid.gov/sites/default/files/documents/1865/toolkit_women_and_conflict_an_introductory_guide_for_programming.pdf, last accessed 1 May 2019.

———, "Community Action Program 2003–2007," June 2007b, http://pdf.usaid.gov/pdf_docs/Pdacj702.pdf, last accessed 1 May 2019.

———, "Iraq Provincial Reconstruction Teams," Fall 2007c, https://reliefweb.int/sites/reliefweb.int/files/resources/F5D2C90AFC495E664925737500050C82-Full_Report.pdf, last accessed 1 May 2019.

———, "Assistance agreement between the Government of the United States of America and the Government of the Republic of Yemen," 16 Sep. 2009, https://www.state.gov/documents/organization/135100.pdf, last accessed 1 May 2019.

———, "The development response to violent extremism and insurgency," Sep. 2011, http://pdf.usaid.gov/pdf_docs/Pdacs400.pdf, last accessed 1 May 2019.

———, "Gender equality and female empowerment policy," March 2012a, https://www.usaid.gov/sites/default/files/documents/1865/GenderEqualityPolicy_0.pdf, last accessed 1 May 2019.

———, "USAID Pakistan gender analysis and gender assessment of stabilization programing," 16 July 2012b, http://waterinfo.net.pk/sites/default/

files/knowledge/USAID%20Pakistan%20Gender%20Analysis%20 and%20Gender%20Assessment%20of%20Stabilization%20Programming. pdf, last accessed 1 May 2019.

————,"Implementation of the United States National Action Plan on Women, Peace and Security," Aug. 2012c, https://www.usaid.gov/news-information/press-releases/usaid-implementation-united-states-national-action-plan-women-peace, last accessed 1 May 2019.

————, "Implementation of the United States National Action Plan on Women, Peace, and Security," Sep. 2013, https://www.usaid.gov/sites/ default/files/US_NAP_WPS_Implementation.pdf, last accessed 1 May 2019.

————,"USAID/Morocco Country Development Cooperation Strategy 2013–2017," 2013a, http://pdf.usaid.gov/pdf_docs/pdacy250.pdf, last accessed 1 May 2019.

————, "PRT Quick Impact Projects," 23 Aug. 2013b, https://www.usaid. gov/node/51861, last accessed 1 May 2019.

————, "Tunisia Transition Initiative. Final evaluation," June 2014a, http:// pdf.usaid.gov/pdf_docs/PA00JZD7.pdf, last accessed 1 May 2019.

————, "Tunisia Transition Initiative. Final report. May 2011-July 2014," July 2014b, http://pdf.usaid.gov/pdf_docs/PA00K16C.pdf, last accessed 1 May 2019.

————, "Agency financial report. Fiscal year 2015," 2015a, https://www. usaid.gov/sites/default/files/documents/1868/USAIDFY2015AFR_ 508a.pdf, last accessed 1 May 2019.

————, "Quarterly performance report, July 1–September 30, 2015. Countering violent extremism in the Middle East & North Africa (Cove-MENA). Maghreb-Sahel Pilot (Pilot 1)," 2015b, http://pdf.usaid.gov/ pdf_docs/PA00KRGD.pdf, last accessed 3 May 2017.

————, "Yemen: Working in crisis and conflict," 18 Jan. 2015c, http:// www.usaid.gov/yemen/working-crisis-and-conflict, last accessed 1 May 2019.

————, "People, not pawns: Women's participation in violent extremism across MENA," Sep. 2015d, https://www.usaid.gov/sites/default/files/ documents/1866/CVE_RESEARCHBRIEF_PEOPLENOTPAWNS.pdf, last accessed 1 May 2019.

————, "Press release: Bureau for Foreign Assistance," 19 Nov. 2015e, https://www.usaid.gov/who-we-are/organization/bureaus/foreign-assistance, last accessed 1 May 2019.

————, "Countering violent extremism in West Africa," 25 Oct. 2016a, https://www.usaid.gov/west-africa-regional/fact-sheets/countering-violent-extremism%0B-west-africa, last accessed 1 May 2019.

————, "Office of Conflict Management and Mitigation," 3 Nov. 2016b, https://www.usaid.gov/who-we-are/organization/bureaus/bureau-democracy-conflict-and-humanitarian-assistance/office-0, last accessed 1 May 2019.

———, "Afghanistan," 1 Dec. 2017, https://www.usaid.gov/political-transition-initiatives/where-we-work/closed-programs/afghanistan, last accessed 14 Mar. 2019.

———, "Office of Transitions CVE toolkit," Feb. 2018, https://sidw.org/sites/default/files/USAID-OTI-CVE_Toolkit_June_2018.pdf, last accessed 1 May 2019.

USAID blog, "Remembering USAID's Ragaei Abdelfattah," 10. Dec. 2012, https://blog.usaid.gov/2012/12/remembering-usaids-ragaei-abdelfattah/, last accessed 14 Mar. 2019.

US Agency for International Development Afghanistan, "USAID/Afghanistan strategic plan," May 2005, http://pdf.usaid.gov/pdf_docs/Pdacf119.pdf, last accessed 1 May 2019.

US Air Forces Central Command Combined Air Operations Center, "Combined Forces Air Component Commander 2013–2018 Airpower Statistics," 30 Nov. 2018, https://www.afcent.af.mil/Portals/82/Documents/Airpower%20summary/(U)%20DRAFT%20Nov%20 2018%20APS%20Data.pdf?ver=2019–01–11–101313–977, last accessed 4 Mar. 2019.

US Army, "FM 3–07 Stability," 2003, https://www.hsdl.org/?view&did= 17929, last accessed 1 May 2019.

———, "Field Manual 3–24: Counterinsurgency," 15 Dec. 2006, usacac. army.mil/cac2/Repository/Materials/COIN-FM3–24.pdf, last accessed 1 May 2019.

———, "FM 3–07: Stability Operations," 2008b, http://usacac.army.mil/cac2/repository/FM307/FM3–07.pdf, last accessed 1 May 2019.

———, "FM 3–07 Stability," 2014a, https://www.globalsecurity.org/military/library/policy/army/fm/3–07/fm3–07_2014.pdf, last accessed 1 May 2019.

———, "FM 3–24 MCWP 3–33.5. Insurgencies and Countering Insurgencies," May 2014b, https://fas.org/irp/doddir/army/fm3–24.pdf, last accessed 1 May 2019.

US Army Combined Arms Center, "Handbook: Iraq Provincial Reconstruction Team. Observations, insights and lessons," Nov. 2010, http://www.dtic. mil/dtic/tr/fulltext/u2/a550603.pdf, last accessed 1 May 2019.

———, "Afghanistan Provincial Reconstruction Team Handbook," Feb. 2011, http://www.dtic.mil/dtic/tr/fulltext/u2/a550604.pdf, last accessed 1 May 2019.

US Army Special Operations Command, "About the Cultural Support Program," n.d., http://www.soc.mil/CST/about.html, last accessed 8 Oct. 2016.

————, "SOF core activities," n.d., https://www.socom.mil/about/core-activities, last accessed 8 May 2017.

US Attorney's Office Northern District of Indiana, "Press statement regarding Samantha Elhassani," 24 July 2018, https://www.justice.gov/usao-ndin/pr/press-statement-regarding-samantha-elhassani, last accessed 4 Mar. 2019.

US Congress, "Federal Aviation Reauthorization Act of 1996," *Public Law* 104–264, 1996.

————, "Statements on introduced Bills and Joint Resolutions. Sec. 314 International Youth Opportunity Fund," 7 Sep. 2006, https://www.congress.gov/congressional-record/2006/9/7/senate-section/article/s9113–1?q=%7B%22search%22%3A%5B%22%5C%22MEPI%5C%22+WOMEN%22%5D%7D&r=11, last accessed 1 May 2019.

————, "Implementing recommendations of the 9/11 Commission Act of 2007. 110th Congress," 3 Aug. 2007, https://www.congress.gov/110/plaws/publ53/PLAW-110publ53.pdf, last accessed 1 May 2019.

————, "H. Rept. 110–858—Misleading information from the battlefield: The Tillman and Lynch episodes," 2008, https://www.congress.gov/congressional-report/110th-congress/house-report/858/1, last accessed 1 May 2019.

————, "Written testimony by USAID Senior Deputy Assistant Administrator for Africa Earl Gast on examining US counterterrorism priorities and strategy across Africa's Sahel region," 17 Nov. 2009, https://www.gpo.gov/fdsys/pkg/CHRG-111shrg56320/html/CHRG-111shrg56320.htm, last accessed 1 May 2019.

————, "Women, Peace and Security Act, S.1141. 115th Congress (2017–2018)," https://www.congress.gov/bill/115th-congress/senate-bill/1141, last accessed 1 May 2019.

US Court of Appeals, "United States of America v Steven Green Nos. 09–6108/6123," 16 Aug. 2011, http://www.opn.ca6.uscourts.gov/opinions.pdf/11a0221p-06.pdf, last accessed 1 May 2019.

US Department of Defense, "DoD Directive 3000.05: Stabilization," 2005a, https://fas.org/irp/doddir/dod/d3000_05.pdf, last accessed 1 May 2019.

————, "Measuring stability and security in Iraq," Mar. 2007, http://archive.defense.gov/home/pdf/9010_March_2007_Final_Signed.pdf, last accessed 10 Mar. 2019.

————, "JP1–02: Department of Defense dictionary of military and associated terms," 2009, http://jitc.fhu.disa.mil/jitc_dri/pdfs/jp1_02.pdf, last accessed 10 Mar. 2019.

————, "Report on progress toward security and stability in Afghanistan," 2012, https://apps.dtic.mil/dtic/tr/fulltext/u2/a571534.pdf, last accessed 10 March 2019.

————, "Quadrennial Defense Review Report," 2014, https://archive. defense.gov/pubs/2014_quadrennial_defense_review.pdf, last accessed 30 Apr. 2019.

————, "Annual report on sexual assault in the military," 2015a, http:// sapr.mil/public/docs/reports/FY15_Annual/FY15_Annual_Report_on_ Sexual_Assault_in_the_Military_Full_Report.pdf, last accessed 1 May 2019.

————, "Fiscal year 2019 budget request: Overview," Feb. 2015b, https:// comptroller.defense.gov/Portals/45/Documents/defbudget/fy2016/ FY2016_Budget_Request_Overview_Book.pdf, last accessed 9 Mar. 2019.

————, "National women's history month," Sept. 2015c, http://archive. defense.gov/home/features/2015/0315_womens-history/, last accessed 6 Sept. 2015.

US Department of State, "Country reports on terrorism 2007," Apr. 2008, https://www.state.gov/documents/organization/105904.pdf, last accessed 11 March 2019.

————, "Country reports on terrorism 2008," Apr. 2009, https://www. state.gov/documents/organization/122599.pdf, last accessed 11 Mar. 2019.

————, "Resource Summary. D & CP—Office of the Secretary," 2010a, https://www.state.gov/documents/organization/123562.pdf, last accessed 11 Mar. 2019.

————, "Country reports on terrorism 2009," 5 Aug. 2010b, https://www. state.gov/j/ct/rls/crt/2009/, last accessed 11 Mar. 2019,

————, "Department of State commitments to advance women, peace, and security," Aug. 2012a, https://www.state.gov/documents/organiza- tion, 196726.pdf, last accessed 11 Mar. 2019.

————, "Matrix of Department of State actions to advance women, peace and security," 15 Aug. 2012b, https://www.state.gov/s/gwi/priorities/ wps/196587.htm, last accessed 11 March 2019.

————, "Country reports on terrorism 2012," May 2013, https://www. state.gov/j/ct/rls/crt/2012/, last accessed 11 Mar. 2019.

————, "Country reports on terrorism 2013," 2014a, www.state.gov/j/ct/ rls/crt/2013/, last accessed 11 Mar. 2019.

————, "Implementation of the US National Action Plan on Women, Peace and Security," 2014b, https://www.state.gov/documents/organiza- tion/244162.pdf, last accessed 11 Mar. 2019.

————, "Congressional budget justification: Fiscal year 2015," 14 Mar. 2014c, https://www.state.gov/s/d/rm/rls/ebs/2015/, last accessed 11 Mar. 2019.

————, "Overview of 2013 US implementation of the National Action Plan on Women, Peace, and Security," 1 Aug. 2014d, https://www.state.gov/s/gwi/priorities/wps/240384.htm, last accessed 1 May 2019.

————, "The global coalition to counter ISIL," 10 Sep. 2014e, https://20092017.state.gov/s/seci/index.htm, last accessed 1 May 2019.

————, "70th session of the UN General Assembly," 29 Sep. 2015, https://www.state.gov/j/cve/unga/, last accessed 1 May 2019.

————, "Country report on terrorism 2015," June 2016a, www.state.gov/j/ct/rls/crt/2015/, last accessed 1 May 2019.

————, "Overview of 2015 US implementation of the National Action Plan on Women, Peace, and Security," 15 Dec. 2016b, https://www.state.gov/s/gwi/priorities/wps/267495.htm, last accessed 1 May 2019.

————, "Programs and initiatives," 2017a, https://www.state.gov/j/ct/programs, last accessed 1 May 2019.

————, "Programs and partnerships," 2017b, https://www.state.gov/s/gwi/programs/index.htm, last accessed 30 Mar. 2017.

————, "Office of the Coordinator of Counterterrorism: Archive 2001–2009," 2017c, https://2001–2009.state.gov/s/ct/, last accessed 5 June 2017.

————, "Stabilization Assistance Review. A framework for maximizing the effectiveness of U.S Government efforts to stabilize conflict affected areas," 2018, https://www.state.gov/documents/organization/283589.pdf, last accessed 6 Mar. 2019.

————, "Department of State Antiterrorism Assistance Program graduates first all-female Iraqi police class," 27 July 2018a, https://www.state.gov/r/pa/prs/ps/2018/07/284675.htm, last accessed 1 May 2019.

————, "Country reports on terrorism 2017," Sep. 2018b, https://www.state.gov/documents/organization/283100.pdf, last accessed 1 May 2019.

————, "US strategy to support women and girls at risk from violent extremism and conflict," 13 Feb. 2019, https://www.state.gov/s/gwi/priorities/wps/289431.htm, last accessed 1 May 2019.

US Department of State and US Agency for International Development, "Strategic plan FY 2014–2017," 17 Mar. 2014, https://www.state.gov/documents/organization/223997.pdf, last accessed 1 May 2019.

————, "Joint strategic plan FY 2018–2022," Feb. 2018, https://www.state.gov/documents/organization/277156.pdf, last accessed 1 May 2019.

US Government, "United States Government glossary of interagency and associated terms," 2017, https://www.hsdl.org/?view&did=802757, last accessed 1 May 2019.

US Government Accountability Office, "Combatting terrorism: Actions needed to enhance implementation of Trans-Sahara counterterrorism partnership," July 2008, http://www.gao.gov/new.items/d08860.pdf, last accessed 1 May 2019.

# BIBLIOGRAPHY

US Government Interagency Counterinsurgency Initiative, "US Government counterinsurgency guide," Jan. 2009, https://www.state.gov/documents/organization/119629.pdf, last accessed 1 May 2019.

US Institute of Peace (USIP), "Charting a new course: Thought for action kit. Women preventing violent extremism," in *Women Preventing Violent Extremism*, Washington, DC: USIP, 2015, p. 38.

US Military, "The national military strategy of the United States of America," 2015, http://www.jcs.mil/Portals/36/Documents/Publications/2015_National_Military_Strategy.pdf, last accessed 1 May 2019.

Veillette, Connie, "Restructuring US foreign aid: The role of the Director of Foreign Assistance in Transformational Development," 23 Jan. 2007, http://pdf.usaid.gov/pdf_docs/Pcaab921.pdf, last accessed 1 May 2019.

Verveer, Melanne, "International violence against women: Stories and solutions," 21 Oct. 2009, https://2009–2017.state.gov/s/gwi/rls/rem/2009/130925.htm, last accessed 1 May 2019.

———, "Afghan women and girls: Building the future of Afghanistan," 23 Feb. 2010a, https://2009–2017.state.gov/s/gwi/rls/rem/2010/137222.htm, last accessed 1 May 2019.

———, "Women as agents of change: Advancing the role of women in politics and civil society," 9 June 2010b, https://2009–2017.state.gov/s/gwi/rls/rem/2010/142953.htm, last accessed 1 May 2019.

The White House, "National Security Presidential Directive-22," 16 Dec. 2002, http:// www.combat-trafficking.army.mil/documents/policy/NSPD-22.pdf, last accessed 4 Mar. 2019.

———, "Quadrennial Defense Review Report," 6 Feb. 2006a, http://www.defense.gov/qdr/report/Report20060203.pdf, last accessed 1 May 2019.

———, "President Bush and Prime Minister Tony Blair of the United Kingdom Participate in Joint Press Availability," 25 May 2006b, https://georgewbush-whitehouse.archives.gov/news/releases/2006/05/20060525–12.html, last accessed 1 May 2019.

———, "United States National Action Plan on Women, Peace and Security," Dec. 2011, https://www.whitehouse.gov/sites/default/files/email-files/US_National_Action_Plan_on_Women_Peace_and_Security.pdf, last accessed 1 May 2019.

———, "White House Council on women and girls, recent agency accomplishments," Mar. 2014a, https://obamawhitehouse.archives.gov/sites/default/files/docs/wh_cwg_agency_march_reports_.pdf, last accessed 1 May 2019.

———, "Leaders' summit on countering ISIL and violent extremism," 29 Sep. 2015, https://www.whitehouse.gov/the-press-office/2015/09/29/leaders-summit-countering-isil-and-violent-extremism, last accessed 1 May 2019.

————, "US strategy for counterterrorism of the United Stated of America," Oct. 2018, https://www.whitehouse.gov/wp-content/uploads/2018/10/NSCT.pdf, last accessed 1 May 2019.

White House Office of Communications, "Policies of the Bush administration 2001–2009," 31 Mar. 2015, https://georgewbush-whitehouse.archives.gov/infocus/bushrecord/documents/Policies_of_the_Bush_Administration.pdf, last accessed 1 May 2019.

Wikileaks Cable Viewer, "Yemen: Combatting extremism," 05SANAA2897, 5 Oct. 2005, http://wikileaks.ikiru.ch/cable/05SANAA2897/, last accessed 1 May 2019.

———— "Embassy follow-up to MCC signing ceremony," 07SANAA1950, 27 Oct 2007, https://wikileaks.org/plusd/cables/07SANAA1950_a.html, last accessed 1 May 2019.

————, "Yemeni military commander describes al-Qaeda presence in Marib, counterterrorism needs," 09SANAA334_a, 25 Feb. 2009, https://wikileaks.org/plusd/cables/09SANAA334_a.html, last accessed 1 May 2019.

World Health Organization, "Outbreak update—cholera in Yemen," 19 July 2018, http://www.emro.who.int/pandemic-epidemic-diseases/cholera/outbreak-update-cholera-in-yemen-19-july-2018.html, last accessed 7 Mar. 2019

*Secondary sources*

Abdo, Geneive, "Islam in America: Separate but unequal," *Washington Quarterly*, 28, 4 (2005), pp. 5–17.

Aboulenein, Ahmed, "Iraq seeks $100 billion to reconstruct transport, agriculture and oil sectors," *Reuters*, 9 Feb. 2018 https://www.reuters.com/article/us-mideast-crisis-iraq-reconstruction/iraq-seeks-100-billion-to-reconstruct-transport-agriculture-and-oil-sectors-idUSKBN1FT188, last accessed 1 May 2019.

Abouzeid, Rania, "When the weapons fall silent: Reconciliation in Sinjar after ISIS," *European Council on Foreign Relations*, Oct. 2018, https://www.ecfr.eu/publications/summary/when_the_weapons_fall_silent_reconcili-aion_in_sinjar_after_isis, last accessed 7 Mar. 2019.

Ackerman, Spencer, "FBI fired Sebastian Gorka for anti-Muslim diatribes," The Daily Beast, 21 June 2017, http://www.thedailybeast.com/fbi-fired-sebastian-gorka-for-anti-muslim-diatribes, last accessed 1 May 2019.

————, "Inside the secret Taliban talks to end America's longest war," Daily Beast, 8 Feb. 2018, https://www.thedailybeast.com/inside-thesecret-taliban-talks-toend-americas-longest-war, last accessed 6 Mar. 2019.

Agence France-Presse, "French fighters appear with Islamic State in Afghanistan," *The Local Fr*, 10 Dec. 2017, https://www.thelocal.

fr/20171210/french-fighters-appear-with-islamic-state-in-afghanistan, last accessed 1 May 2019.

Agency Coordinating Body for Afghan Relief, "Aid effectiveness in Afghanistan: At a crossroads," ACBAR Briefing Paper, Nov. 2006, https://reliefweb.int/sites/reliefweb.int/files/resources/145FA71717177C3285257234006A4105-acbar-afg-01nov.pdf, last accessed 1 May 2019.

Afghan Women's Network, "Operationalizing gender in Provincial Reconstruction Teams in Afghanistan," Aug. 2007, http://www.advocacynet.org/modules/fck/upload/file/OperationalizingGender.pdf, last accessed 1 May 2019.

Ahmed, Houriya, "The growing threat of female suicide attacks in western countries," *CTC Sentinel*, 3, 7 (2010), https://ctc.usma.edu/the-growing-threat-of-female-suicide-attacks-in-western-countries/, last accessed 1 May 2019.

Ahmed, Leila, *Women and Gender in Islam: Historical Roots of a Modern Debate*, New Haven, CT: Yale University Press, 1992.

Ahram, Ariel I., "Sexual violence and the making of ISIS," *Survival*, 57, 3 (2015), pp. 57–78.

Airwars, "Homepage," https://airwars.org/, last accessed 15 June 2018

Akseer, Tabasum, and Fahim Ahmad Yousufzai, "In Afghanistan, gender not always indicator of support for women's rights," The Asia Foundation, 13 Dec. 2017, https://asiafoundation.org/2017/12/13/afghanistan-gender-not-always-indicator-support-womens-rights/, last accessed 6 Mar. 2019.

Akwiri, Joseph, "Kenyan police find note suggesting Islamic State link to Mombasa attack," *Reuters*, 15 Sep. 2016, https://www.reuters.com/article/us-kenya-attacks/kenyanpolicefind-note-suggesting-islamic-state-link-to-mombasa-attack-idUSKCN11L136, last accessed 9 Mar. 2019.

Al-Dawsari, Nadwa, "'We lived days in hell': Civilian perspectives on the conflict in Yemen," Civilians in Conflict, 10 Jan. 2017, https://civiliansinconflict.org/publications/research/we-lived-in-hell-yemen/, last accessed 1 May 2019.

Al Jazeera, "Iraq: Calm returns to Basra after week of violent protests," 9 Sep. 2018, https://www.aljazeera.com/news/2018/09/iraq-calm-returns-basra-week-violent-protests-180909093856071.html, last accessed 9 Mar. 2019.

Al-Moshki, Ali Ibrahim, "Women's unit prepares for potentially more active role in counterterrorism," *The Yemen Times*, 15 May 2015, http://www.yementimes.com/en/1781/news/3854/Women's-unit-prepares-for-potentially-more-active-role-in-counterterrorism.html, last accessed 31 July 2015.

Alexander, Audrey, *Cruel Intentions: Female Jihadists in America*, Washington, DC: Program on Extremism, 2016.

Alison, Miranda, "Women as agents of political violence: gendering security," *Security Dialogue*, 35, 4 (2004), pp. 447–463.

———, "Cogs in the wheel? Women in the Liberation Tigers of Tamil Eelam," *CivilWars*, 6, 4 (2003), pp. 37–54.

Allen, Chris, and Surinder Guru, "Between political fad and political empowerment: A critical evaluation of the National Muslim Women's Advisory Group (NMWAG) and governmental processes of engaging Muslim women," *Sociological Research Online*, 17, 3 (2012), pp. 1–9.

Allen, Chris, Arshad Isakjee and Ozlem Ogtem Young, *"Maybe we are hated": The Experience and Impact of Anti-Muslim Hate on British Muslim Women*, Birmingham: University of Birmingham, 2013, https://www.tellmamauk.org/wp-content/uploads/2013/11/maybewearehated.pdf, last accessed 1 May 2019.

Allen, Johnathan, "Trump mocks Kavanaugh accuser Christine Blasey Ford at campaign rally," NBC News, 3 Oct. 2018, https://www.nbcnews.com/politics/politics-news/trump-mocks-christine-blasey-ford-mississippi-campaign-rally-n916061, last accessed 4 Mar. 2019.

American Anthropological Association, "American Anthropological Association's executive board statement on the Human Terrain System Project," 2007, http://s3.amazonaws.com/rdcmsaaa/files/production/public/FileDownloads/pdfs/pdf/EB_Resolution_110807.pdf, last accessed 1 May 2019.

Amnesty International, "Disappearances and torture in southern Yemen detention facilities must be investigated as war crimes," 12 July 2018, https://www.amnesty.org/en/latest/news/2018/07/disappearances-and-torture-in-southern-yemen-detention-facilities-must-be-investigated-as-war-crimes/, last accessed 7 Mar. 2019.

———, "The condemned: Women and children isolated, trapped and exploited in Iraq," 2018, https://www.amnesty.org/download/Documents/MDE1481962018ENGLISH.PDF, last accessed 9 Mar. 2019.

Andrusyszyn, Greta, *Terrorism: A Selected Bibliography*, Carlisle, PA: US Army War College, 2009.

Associated Press, "The al-Qaida papers: The Yemen letters," 14 Feb. 2013, http://hosted.ap.org/specials/interactives/_international/_pdfs/al-qaida-papers-how-to-run-a-state.pdf, last accessed 1 May 2019.

Associated Press and NBC News, "Trump order would ban most transgender troops from serving," 24 Mar. 2019, https://www.nbcnews.com/news/us-news/trump-order-would-ban-most-transgender-troops-serving-n859686, last accessed 6 Mar. 2019.

Atran, Scott, Hoshang Waziri, Ángel Gómez, Hammad Sheikh, Lucía López-Rodríguez, Charles Rogan, and Richard Davis, "The Islamic State's lingering legacy among young men from the Mosul area," *CTC Sentinel*, 11, 4 (2018).

Auchter, Jessica, "Gendering terror: Discourses of terrorism and writing woman-as-agent," *International Feminist Journal of Politics*, 14, 1 (2012), pp. 121–139.

Axworthy, Lloyd, "Human security and global governance: Putting people first," *Global Governance*, 7, 1 (2001), pp. 19–23.

Ayotte, Kevin J., and Mary E. Husain, "Securing Afghan women: Neocolonialism, epistemic violence, and the rhetoric of the veil," *National Women's Studies Association Journal*, 17, 3 (2005), pp. 112–133.

Azarbaijani-Moghaddam, Sippi, *Seeking out their Afghan Sisters: Female Engagement Teams in Afghanistan*, Bergen: Chr. Michelsen Institute, 2014.

Badey, Thomas J., "US anti-terrorism policy: The Clinton administration," *Contemporary Security Policy*, 19, 2 (1998), pp. 50–70.

———, "US counter-terrorism: Change in approach, continuity in policy," *Contemporary Security Policy*, 27, 2 (2006), pp. 308–324.

Baldwin, David A., "The concept of security," *Review of International Studies*, 23, 1 (1997), pp. 5–26.

Barakat, Sultan, Sean Deely and Steven A. Zyck, "'A tradition of forgetting': Stabilisation and humanitarian action in historical perspective," *Disasters*, 34, 3 (2010), pp. S297-S319.

Baron, Adam, "Civil war in Yemen: Imminent and avoidable," in European Council of Foreign Relations (ed.), *Policy Memo*, London: European Council of Foreign Relations, 2015, p. 9.

BBC, "Obama authorises Iraq air strikes on Islamist fighters," BBC News, 8 Aug. 2014, https://www.bbc.co.uk/news/world-middle-east-28699832, last accessed 1 May 2019.

———, "Mosul: Woman risks backlash to care for 'IS orphans'," BBC News, 13 Apr. 2018, https://www.bbc.co.uk/news/av/world-middle-east-43744747/mosul-woman-risks-backlash-to-care-for-is-orphans, last accessed 9 Mar. 2019.

———, "How many IS foreign fighters are left in Iraq and Syria?" BBC News, 20 Feb. 2019, https://www.bbc.co.uk/news/world-middle-east-47286935, last accessed 7 Mar. 2019.

BBC Radio 4, "'UK could face Islamist threat for decades', former MI5 chief warns," 11 Aug. 2017, http://www.bbc.co.uk/news/uk-40890328, last accessed 1 May 2019.

BBC Reality Check, "Syria: Who's in control of Idlib?" BBC News, 7 Sep. 2018, https://www.bbc.co.uk/news/world-45401474, last accessed 1 May 2019.

Beall, Jo, Thomas Goodfellow and James Putzel, "Introductory article: On the discourse of terrorism, security and development," *Journal of International Development*, 18, 1 (2006), pp. 51–67.

Beals, Ginger E., "Women Marines in counterinsurgency operations: Lioness and Female Engagement Teams," MA dissertation, United States Marine Corps, 2010.

Belasco, Amy, *The Cost of Iraq, Afghanistan, and Other Global War on Terror Operations Since 9/11*, Washington, DC: Congressional Research Service, 2014.

Bellingreri, Marta, "Iraq's women take the lead rebuilding after IS destruction," *The New Arab*, 26 July 2017, https://www.alaraby.co.uk/english/indepth/2017/7/26/iraqs-women-take-the-lead-rebuilding-after-is-destruction, last accessed 7 Mar. 2019

Bergen, Peter, and Katherine Tiedemann, *Talibanistan: Negotiating the Borders Between Terror, Politics, and Religion*, Oxford: Oxford University Press, 2012.

Berko, Anat, and Edna Erez, "Gender, Palestinian women, and terrorism: Women's liberation or oppression?" *Studies in Conflict & Terrorism*, 30, 6 (2007), pp. 493–519.

Betancourt, Theresa S., et al., "High hopes, grim reality: Reintegration and the education of former child soldiers in Sierra Leone," *Comparative Education Review*, 52, 4 (2008), pp. 565–587.

Biddle, Stephen D., *American Grand Strategy After 9/11: An Assessment*, Carlisle, PA: US Army War College, 2005.

Bjørgo, T., and J. G. Horgan (eds), *Leaving Terrorism Behind: Individual and Collective Disengagement*, Abingdon: Routledge, 2009.

Blanchard, Christopher M., and Amy Belasco, "Train and equip program for Syria: Authorities, funding, and issues for Congress," *Congressional Research Service Document R43727*, 2015, https://fas.org/sgp/crs/natsec/R43727.pdf, last accessed 1 May 2019.

Blanchard, Christopher M., and Carla E. Humud, "The Islamic State and US policy," *Congressional Research Service Document R43612*, 25 Sep. 2018, https://fas.org/sgp/crs/mideast/R43612.pdf, last accessed 1 May 2019.

Blanchard, Eric M., "Gender, international relations, and the development of feminist security theory," *Signs: Journal of Women in Culture and Society*, 28, 4 (2003), pp. 1289–1312.

Blears, Hazel, Jacqui Smith, Ed Balls, John Denham, Andy Burnham and Jack Straw, "The Prevent strategy: A guide for local partners in England. Stopping people becoming or supporting terrorists and violent extremists," London: HM Government, 2008.

Blee, Kathleen M., "Women and organized racial terrorism in the United States," *Studies in Conflict & Terrorism*, 28, 5 (2005), pp. 421–433.

Bloom, Mia, "Mother. Daughter. Sister. Bomber," *Bulletin of the Atomic Scientists*, 61, 6 (2005), pp. 54–62.

————, "Female suicide bombers: a global trend," *Daedalus*, 136, 1 (2007), pp. 94–102.

# BIBLIOGRAPHY

————, "Death becomes her: The changing nature of women's role in terror," *Georgetown Journal of International Affairs*, 43, 3 (2010a), pp. 91–98.

————, "Death becomes her: Women, occupation, and terrorist mobilization," *PS: Political Science & Politics*, 43, 3 (2010b), pp. 445–450.

————, *Bombshell: Women and Terrorism*, Philadelphia: University of Pennsylvania Press, 2011.

————, "In defense of honor: Women and terrorist recruitment on the internet," *Journal of Postcolonial Studies*, 4, 1 (2013), pp. 150–195.

Bloom, Mia, and Hilary Matfess, "Women as symbols and swords in Boko Haram's terror," *Prism*, 6, 1 (2016).

Boesten, Jelke, *Sexual Violence During War and Peace: Gender, Power, and Post-Conflict Justice in Peru*, New York: Springer, 2014.

Borger, Julian, "Syria: US preparing for final stage of anti-Isis push despite $200m funding cut," *The Guardian*, 15 Aug. 2018, https://www.theguardian.com/world/2018/aug/17/us-cancels-funding-syria-stablization, last accessed 7 Mar. 2019.

Boucek, Christopher, "War in Saada: From local insurrection to national challenge," Yemen on the Brink: A Carnegie Paper Series, 110, Apr. 2010, https://carnegieendowment.org/files/war_in_saada.pdf, last accessed 1 May 2019.

Borough of Tower Hamlets, "Religion in Tower Hamlets: 2011 Census update (Factsheet 2015 02)," 2015, http://www.towerhamlets.gov.uk/Documents/Borough_statistics/Ward_profiles/Census-2011/2015-04-21-Faith-key-facts-Revised-data.pdf, last accessed 17 May 2017.

Bowcott, Owen, "Travel ban for five east London girls over fears they will join Isis in Syria," *The Guardian*, 27 Mar. 2015, https://www.theguardian.com/uk-news/2015/mar/27/five-girls-barred-from-travel-same-school-three-teenagers-syria-bethnal-green-academy, last accessed 1 May 2019.

Boyle, Michael J., "Do counterterrorism and counterinsurgency go together?" *International Affairs*, 86, 2 (2010), pp. 333–353.

Bradford, Alexandra, "Western women who join the Islamic State," *Terrorism Monitor*, 13, 9 (2015), pp. 3–5.

Breeden, Aurelien, "Women in terror cell were 'guided' by ISIS, Paris prosecutor says," *New York Times*, 9 Sep. 2016 https://www.nytimes.com/2016/09/10/world/europe/france-paris-isis-terrorism-women.html, last accessed 1 May 2019.

Briggs, Rachel, and Tanya Silverman, *Western Foreign Fighters: Innovations in Responding to the Threat*, London: Institute for Strategic Dialogue, 2014.

Brimmer, Esther, "Women as agents of change: Advancing the role of women in politics and civil society," 9 June 2010, https://2009-2017.state.gov/p/io/rm/2010/142907.htm, last accessed 1 May 2019.

Britton, Bianca, "Trump tells Europe to take back ISIS fighters, warns they could be released," CNN, 22 Feb. 2019, https://edition.cnn.com/2019/02/17/politics/donald-trump-isis-fighters-europe-intl/index.html, last accessed 7 Mar. 2019.

Broadway, Chuck, "DoD works to incorporate more gender perspectives in operations," DoD News, 8 Mar. 2018, https://dod.defense.gov/News/Article/Article/1461815/dod-works-to-incorporate-more-gender-perspective-in-operations/, last accessed 1 May 2019.

Brown, Katherine, "The promise and perils of women's participation in UK mosques: The impact of securitisation agendas on identity, gender and community," *The British Journal of Politics & International Relations*, 10, 3 (2008), pp. 472–491.

———, "Analysis: Why are Western women joining Islamic State?" BBC News, 6 Oct. 2014, http://www.bbc.co.uk/news/uk-29507410, last accessed 1 May 2019.

———, "Gender and counter-radicalization: women and emerging counter-terror measures," in Margaret L. Satterthwaite and Jayne C. Huckerby (eds), *Gender, National Security and Counter-Terrorism*, London: Routledge, 2013, pp. 36–59.

Browne, Ryan, "UK puts number of ISIS fighters killed at half US figure," CNN, 16 Dec. 2016, https://edition.cnn.com/2016/12/16/politics/uk-us-number-isis-fighters-killed/index.html, last accessed 7 Mar. 2019

The Bureau of Investigative Journalism, "Bureau data sets on drone strikes in Pakistan, Yemen and Somalia," 2015, http://www.thebureauinvestigates.com/category/projects/drones/drones-graphs/, last accessed 19 January 2015.

———, "Drone strikes," 2019a, https://www.thebureauinvestigates.com/projects/drone-war, last accessed 1 May. 2019.

———, "Yemen: Reported US covert actions 2018," 2018b, https://www.thebureauinvestigates.com/drone-war/data/yemen-reported-us-covert-actions-2018, last accessed 7 Mar. 2019.

Burke, Daniel, "Pittsburgh rabbi told Trump that hate speech led to synagogue massacre," CNN, 5 Nov. 2018, https://edition.cnn.com/2018/11/03/us/pittsburgh-shooting-first-shabbat/index.html, last accessed 1 May 2019.

Buss, John C., *The State Department Office of Reconstruction and Stabilization and Its Interaction with the Department of Defense*, US Army War College, 2005, http://www.dtic.mil/dtic/tr/fulltext/u2/a436010.pdf, last accessed 1 May 2019.

Buzan, Barry, Ole Wæver and Jaap De Wilde, *Security: A New Framework for Analysis*. Boulder, CO: Lynne Rienner Publishers, 1998.

Byman, Daniel, "Comparing Al Qaeda and ISIS: Different goals, different targets," *Brookings*, 29 Apr. 2015, https://www.brookings.edu/testimonies/comparing-al-qaeda-and-isis-different-goals-different-targets/, last accessed 1 May 2019.

———, "Why Trump's policies will increase terrorism—and why Trump might benefit as a result," *Lawfare*, 30 Jan. 2017, https://www.lawfareblog.com/why-trumps-policies-will-increase-terrorism%E2%80%94and-why-trump-might-benefit-result, last accessed 4 Mar. 2019.

Caiazza, Amy, "Why gender matters in understanding September 11: Women, militarism, and violence," *Institute for Women's Policy Research*, 1908 (2001), pp. 1–6, https://iwpr.org/publications/why-gender-matters-in-understanding-september-11-women-militarism-and-violence/, last accessed 1 May 2019.

Callimachi, Rukmini, "State of terror: To maintain supply of sex slaves, ISIS pushes birth control," *New York Times*, 12 March 2016, https://www.nytimes.com/2016/03/13/world/middleeast/to-maintain-supply-of-sex-slaves-isis-pushes-birth-control.html, last accessed 1 May 2019.

CBC News, "Female suicide bomber kills 15 at crowded Afghan market," 15 May 2008, https://www.cbc.ca/news/world/female-suicide-bomber-kills-15-at-crowded-afghan-market-1.709104, last accessed 1 May 2019.

CEDAW Committee, "Mid-term Iraqi Women Network (IWN) report reviewing the Concluding Observations of the CEDAW Committee (February 2014 until the 1st of August, 2016)," 2016, https://tbinternet.ohchr.org/Treaties/CEDAW/Shared%20Documents/IRQ/INT_CEDAW_NGS_IRQ_25070_E.pdf, last accessed 7 Mar. 2019 1 May 2019.

Center for Strategic and International Studies, "The roles of women in terrorism and counterterrorism—Expert panel. Washington, DC," 19 Apr. 2012, https://csis-prod.s3.amazonaws.com/s3fs-public/event/041920 12_TheRolesofWomeninTerrorismandCounterterrorism_Panel.pdf, last accessed 1 May 2019.

Cheldelin, Sandra I., and Maneshka Eliatamby, *Women Waging War and Peace: International Perspectives of Women's Roles in Conflict and Post-conflict Reconstruction*, New York: A&C Black, 2011.

Chynoweth, Sarah, "Sexual violence against men and boys in the Syria crisis," United Nations High Commissioner for Refugees, Oct. 2017, https://data2.unhcr.org/en/documents/download/60864, last accessed 7 Mar. 2019.

Cockburn, Patrick, "The Yemen war death toll is five times higher than we think—we can't shrug off our responsibilities any longer," *The Independent*, 26 Oct. 2018, https://www.independent.co.uk/voices/yemen-war-death-toll-saudi-arabia-allies-howmany-killed-responsibility-a8603326.html, last accessed 7 Mar. 2019.

Cohen, Dara Kay, *Rape During Civil War*, Ithaca, NY: Cornell University Press, 2016.

Cohn, Carol, "Wars, wimps, and women: Talking gender and thinking war," in Miriam Cooke and Angela Woollacott (eds), *Gendering War Talk*, Princeton, NJ: Princeton University Press, 1993, pp. 227–246.

————, "Feminist peacemaking," *The Women's Review of Books*, 21, 5 (2004), pp. 8–9.

————, "Mainstreaming gender in UN security policy: A path to political transformation?" Consortium on Gender, Security and Human Rights, 2008, https://genderandsecurity.org/sites/default/files/mainstreaming_gender_in_un_security_policy-_a_path_to_political_transformation_0.pdf, last accessed 30 Apr. 2019.

————, "'Feminist security studies': Toward a reflexive practice," *Politics & Gender*, 7, 4 (2011), pp. 581–586.

Coker, Margaret, and Falih Hassan, "A 10-minute trial, a death sentence: Iraqi justice for ISIS suspects," *New York Times*, 17 Apr. 2018, https://www.nytimes.com/2018/04/17/world/middleeast/iraq-isis-trials.html, last accessed 1 May 2019.

Conflict Armament Research, "Weapons of the Islamic State," 2018, www.conflictarm.com/download-file/?report_id=2568&file_id=2574, last accessed 1 May 2019.

Conway, Maura, and Lisa McInerney, "What's love got to do with it? Framing 'Jihad Jane' in the US press," *Media, War & Conflict*, 5, 1 (2012), pp. 6–21.

Consortium on Gender, Security and Human Rights, "Sexual violence and armed conflict: Annotated bibliography," 2012, https://genderandsecurity.org/sites/default/files/Sexual_Violence_and_Armed_Conflict_Annot_Bib.pdf, last accessed 1 May 2019.

Cook, David, "Women fighting in jihad?" *Studies in Conflict & Terrorism*, 28, 5 (2005), pp. 375 384.

Cook, Joana, "Women's role in Yemen's Police Force," Saferworld, Dec. 2014, http://www.saferworld.org.uk/oldsite/resources/view-resource/897-womenrsquos-role-in-yemenrsquos-police-force, last accessed 1 May 2019.

————, "'Our main concern is security': Women's political participation, engagement in the security sector, and public safety in Yemen," in Noel Brehony and Saud Al-Sarhan (eds), *Rebuilding Yemen: Political, Economic and Social Challenges*, Germany: Gerlach Publishing, 2015a, pp. 149–173.

————, "Women and security sector reform in Yemen," *British Yemeni Society Journal*, 23 (2015b), pp. 46–50.

————, "Yemen's patronage problem," *Carnegie Endowment for International Peace*, 30 July 2015c, http://carnegieendowment.org/sada/?fa=60899, last accessed 1 May 2019.

————, "Avoiding the pitfalls of Prevent," *Peace and Security Georgetown Institute for Women Occasional Paper Series*, Dec. 2017a, https://giwps.georgetown.edu/resource/avoiding-the-pitfalls-of-prevent/, last accessed 1 May 2019.

———, "Shifting priorities: Reconstituting security agendas and security sector reforms in Yemen," in Scott Nicholas Romaniuk, Francis Grice, Daniela Irrera and Stewart Webb (eds), *The Palgrave Handbook of Global Counterterrorism Policy*, London: PalgraveMacmillan UK, 2017b, pp. 855–880.

———, "Countering terrorism after 9/11: An interrogation into the shortfalls and potential of UNSCR 1325 in CT and CVE efforts," Presentation at 2018 Gender and Terrorism Workshop, European International Studies Association, 6–7 June 2018, Groningen, Netherlands.

———, "Women, human security and countering violent extremism," in Patricia Weitsman, Gunhild Hoogensen and Richard Matthew (eds), *Women and Human Security*, Athens, OH: Ohio University Press, forthcoming.

Cook, Gayla, and Abdi Younis, "Somalia Youth Livelihoods Program. Final evaluation," 2012, http://pdf.usaid.gov/pdf_docs/pdacy127.pdf, last accessed 30 Apr. 2019.

Cook, Joana, and Gina Vale, "From ISIS to 'diaspora': Tracing the women and minors of Islamic State," 2018, https://icsr.info/wp-content/uploads/2018/07/ICSR-Report-From-ISIS-to-'Diaspora'-Tracing-the-Women-and-Minors-of-Islamic-State.pdf, last accessed 1 May 2019.

Cooke, Miriam, "Saving brown women," *Signs: Journal of Women in Culture and Society*, 28, 1 (2002), pp. 468–470.

Costa, Agustinus Beo Da, and Kanupriya Kapoor, "Indonesia police say arrest of woman in bomb plot points to new militant tactic," *Reuters*, 11 Dec. 2016, http://www.reuters.com/article/us-indonesia-security-idUSKBN1400MH, last accessed 1 May 2019.

Cottee, Simon, "What ISIS women want," *Foreign Policy*, 17 May 2016, http://foreignpolicy.com/2016/05/17/what-isis-women-want-gendered-jihad/, last accessed 1 May 2019.

Council on Foreign Relations, "Women's participation in peace processes," 2019, https://www.cfr.org/interactive/womens-participation-in-peace-processes, last accessed 12 March 2019.

Cragin, Kim, and Peter Chalk, *Terrorism and Development: Using Social and Economic Development to Inhibit a Resurgence of Terrorism*, Santa Monica, CA: Rand Corporation, 2003.

Cragin, Kim, and Sara A. Daly, *Women as Terrorists: Mothers, Recruiters, and Martyrs: Mothers, Recruiters, and Martyrs*, Santa Barbara, CA: ABC-CLIO, 2009.

Craig, Iona, "Death in Al Ghayil women and children in Yemeni village recall horror of Trump's 'highly successful' SEAL raid," The Intercept, 9 Mar. 2017, https://theintercept.com/2017/03/09/women-and-children-in-yemeni-village-recallhorror-oftrumps-highly-successful-seal-raid/, last accessed 7 Mar. 2019.

Crawford, Neta C., "United States budgetary costs of post-9/11 wars through FY2018: A summary of the $5.6 trillion in costs for the US wars in Iraq, Syria, Afghanistan and Pakistan, and post 9/11 veterans care and homeland security," Watson Institute of International and Public Affairs, Brown University, Nov. 2017, https://watson.brown.edu/costsofwar/files/cow/imce/papers/2017/Costs%20of%20US%20Post-9_11%20NC%20Crawford%20FINAL%20.pdf, last accessed 1 May 2019.

Crelinsten, Ronald, *Counterterrorism*, Cambridge: Polity, 2009.

Crenshaw, Martha, "The psychology of terrorism: An agenda for the 21st century," *Political Psychology*, 21, 2 (2000), pp. 405–420.

———, "Counterterrorism policy and the political process," *Studies in Conflict and Terrorism*, 24, 5 (2001), pp. 329–337.

———, "The debate over 'old' vs. 'new' terrorism," in Rick Coolsaet (ed.), *Jihadi Terrorism and the Radicalisation Challenge. European and American Experience*, Burlington: Ashgate Publishing Company, 2011, pp. 57–68.

Croft, Stuart, *Culture, Crisis and America's War on Terror*, Cambridge: Cambridge University Press, 2006.

Cudi, Azad, *Long Shot: My Life as a Sniper in the Fight Against ISIS*, Kindle Edition: Weidenfeld & Nicolson, 2019.

Cunningham, Karla J., "Countering female terrorism," *Studies in Conflict & Terrorism*, 30, 2 (2007), pp. 113–129.

———, "Cross-regional trends in female terrorism," *Studies in Conflict and Terrorism*, 26, 3 (2010), pp. 171–195.

Dale, Catherine, *Operation Iraqi Freedom: Strategies, Approaches, Results, and Issues for Congress*, 2 Apr. 2011 https://fas.org/sgp/crs/natsec/RL34387.pdf, last accessed 1 May 2019.

———, "The 2014 Quadrennial Defense Review (QDR) and Defense Strategy: Issues for Congress." 24 Feb. 2014, https://fas.org/sgp/crs/natsec/R43403.pdf, last accessed 1 May 2019.

Darden, Jessica Trisko, Alexis Henshaw and Ora Szekely, *Insurgent Women: Female Combatants in Civil Wars*, Georgetown: Georgetown University Press, 2019.

Davis, Jessica, *Women in Modern Terrorism: From Liberation Wars to Global Jihad and the Islamic State*, Lanham, MD: Rowman & Littlefield, 2017.

———, "Evolution of the global Jihad: Female suicide bombers in Iraq," *Studies in Conflict & Terrorism*, 36, 4 (2013), pp. 279–291.

Davis, Lisa, "Iraqi women confronting ISIL: Protecting women's rights in the context of conflict," *Southwestern Journal of International Law*, 22 (2016), pp. 27–78, https://www.swlaw.edu/sites/default/files/2017–04/SJIL%20V22,%20N1%203Iraqi%20Women%20Confronting%20ISIL-Davis.pdf, last accessed 1 May 2019.

Davis, Paul K., and Kim Cragin, *Social Science for Counterterrorism: Putting the Pieces Together*, Santa Monica, CA: RAND Corporation, 2009.

Dearden, Lizzie, "Islamist attacks will threaten UK for decades, former head of MI5 warns as police say Isis is creating terror 'cult'," *The Independent*, 11 Aug. 2017, https://www.independent.co.uk/ news/uk/home-news/ terror-threat-uk-isis-alqaeda-former-head-mi5-attacks-threaten-britain-for-decades-generational-a7889156.html, last accessed 1 May 2019.

DeBruyne, Nese F., *American War and Military Operation Casualties: Lists and Statistics*, Washington, DC: Congressional Research Service, 2018, https://fas.org/sgp/crs/natsec/RL32492.pdf, last accessed 1 May 2019.

Del Rosso, Stephen J., "The insecure state: Reflections on 'the state' and 'security' in a changing world," *Daedalus*, 124, 2 (1995), pp. 175–207.

Doré, Louis, and Josh Withey, "The 11 worst things Donald Trump has said about women," *The Independent*, 8 Mar. 2017, https://www.indy100.com/ article/11-worst-things-donald-trump-women-grab-international-womens-day-7352406, last accessed 4 Mar. 2019.

Doty, Roxanne Lynn, *Imperial Encounters: The Politics of Representation in North-South Relations*, Minneapolis: University of Minnesota Press, 1996.

Dougherty, Jill, "US trains Iraqi women to find female suicide bombers," CNN, 24 June 2008, http://edition.cnn.com/2008/WORLD/meast/ 06/24/daughters.of.iraq/index.html?iref=topnews, last accessed 1 May 2019.

Dowler, Lorraine, "'And they think I'm just a nice old lady': Women and war in Belfast, Northern Ireland," *Gender, Place and Culture: A Journal of Feminist Geography*, 5, 2 (1998), pp. 159–176.

Duke Law International Human Rights Clinic and Women Peacemakers Program, "Tightening the purse strings: What counter terrorism financing costs gender equality and security," 2017. Available: https://law.duke.edu/ sites/default/files/humanrights/tighteningpursestrings.pdf Last accessed 6 Jun 2019.

Dyvik, Synne L., *Gendering Counterinsurgency: Performativity, Embodiment and Experience in the Afghan "Theatre of War"*, London: Routledge, 2016.

———, "Women as 'practitioners' and 'targets' gender and counterinsurgency in Afghanistan," *International Feminist Journal of Politics*, 16, 3 (2014), pp. 410–429.

Eager, Paige Whaley, *From Freedom Fighters to Terrorists: Women and Political Violence*, Farnham: Ashgate, 2008.

Eggert, Jennifer Philippa, "Female fighters and militants during the Lebanese civil war: Individual profiles, pathways, and motivations," *Studies in Conflict & Terrorism* (2018a), pp. 1–30.

———, "The roles of women in counter-radicalisation and disengagement (CRaD) processes," Berlin: Berghof Foundation, 2018b, https://www.

berghof-foundation.org/fileadmin/redaktion/Publications/Other_
Resources/Berghof_Input_Paper_Women_Counterradicalisation.pdf, last
accessed 1 May 2019.

Eliatamby, Maneshka, "Searching for emancipation: Eritrea, Nepal, and Sri
Lanka," in Sandra I. Cheldelin and Maneshka Eliatamby (eds), *Women Waging
War and Peace: International Perspectives on Women's Roles in Conflict and Post-
Conflict Reconstruction*, New York: Continuum, 2011, pp. 37–51.

Engell, Robert, "Gender perspectives and military effectiveness:
Implementing UNSCR 1325 and the National Action Plan on Women,
Peace and Security," *Prism*, 6, 1 (2016), pp. 72–90.

Enloe, Cynthia, *Bananas, Beaches and Bases*, London: Pandora Press, 1989.

———, *The Morning After: Sexual Politics at the End of the Cold War*, Berkeley,
CA: University of California Press, 1993.

———, *Maneuvers: The International Politics of Militarizing Women's Lives*,
Berkeley, CA: University of California Press, 2000.

———, "Wielding masculinity inside Abu Ghraib: Making feminist sense of
an American military scandal," *Asian Journal of Women's Studies*, 10, 3 (2004),
pp. 89–102.

Epstein, Susan B., Marian L. Lawson and Alex Tiersky, "State, foreign operations and related programs: FY2017 budget and appropriations," 26 May
2017, https://fas.org/sgp/crs/row/R44391.pdf, last accessed 1 May
2019.

Erez, Edna and Anat Berko, "Palestinian women in terrorism: Protectors or
protected?" *Journal of National Defense Studies*, 6 (2008), pp. 83–110.

Ergil, Doğu, "Suicide terrorism in Turkey," *Civil Wars*, 3, 1 (2000), pp. 37–54.

Evans, Ryan, "The seven deadly sins of the Human Terrain System: An insider's perspective," Foreign Policy Research Institute, 13 July 2015, https://
www.fpri.org/2015/07/the-seven-deadly-sins-of-the-human-terrain-
system-an-insiders-perspective/, last accessed 1 May 2019.

Fairclough, Norman, *Discourse and Social Change*, Cambridge: Polity Press,
1992.

———, *Critical Discourse Analysis: The Critical Study of Language*, London:
Longman, 1995.

Fakih, Lama, "Soft measures, real harm: Somalia and the US 'War on Terror',"
in Jayne Huckerby and Margaret L. Satterthwaite (eds), *Gender, National
Security, and Counter-Terrorism: Human Rights Perspectives*, Abingdon:
Routledge, 2013, pp. 183–207.

Farmer, Ben, "Taliban say women's rights to be protected under Islam, but
must not threaten Afghan values," *The Telegraph*, 5 Feb. 2019, https://www.
telegraph.co.uk/news/2019/02/05/taliban-say-womens-rights-pro-
tected-islam-must-not-threaten/, last accessed 6 Mar. 2019.

Fawcett, Grant S., "Cultural understanding in counterinsurgency: Analysis of

# BIBLIOGRAPHY

the human terrain system," May 2009, http://citeseerx.ist.psu.edu/view-doc/download?doi=10.1.1.471.5861&rep=rep1&type=pdf, last accessed 1 May 2019.

Federation of American Scientists, "Article 15–6 investigation of the 800th Military Police Brigade," 2004, https://fas.org/irp/agency/dod/taguba.pdf, last accessed 1 May 2019.

Felter, Joseph and Brian Fishman, "Al-Qa'ida's foreign fighters in Iraq: A first look at the Sinjar records," 2 Jan. 2007, https://ctc.usma.edu/al-qaidas-foreign-fighters-in-iraq-a-first-look-at-the-sinjar-records/, last accessed 1 May 2019.

Financial Action Task Force, "Financing of the terrorist organisation Islamic State in Iraq and the Levant (ISIL)," Feb. 2015, http://www.fatf-gafi.org/media/fatf/documents/reports/Financing-of-the-terrorist-organisation-ISIL.pdf, last accessed 1 May 2019.

Fink, Naureen Chowdhury, Sara Zeiger and Rafia Bhulai, *A Man's World? Exploring the Roles of Women in Counter Terrorism and Violent Extremism*, Washington, DC: Global Centre on Cooperative Security, 2016, http://www.globalcenter.org/publications/a-mans-world-exploring-the-roles-of-women-in-countering-terrorism-and-violent-extremism/, last accessed 1 May 2019.

Finney, Nathan, *Human Terrain Team Handbook*, Fort Leavenworth, KS: Public Intelligence, 2008, https://info.publicintelligence.net/humanterrainhand-book.pdf, last accessed 1 May 2019.

Fishman, Brian, *The Master Plan: ISIS, Al Qaeda, and the Jihadi Strategy for Final Victory*, New Haven CT: Yale University Press, 2016.

Fontana, Alan, Robert Rosenheck and Rani Desai, "Female veterans of Iraq and Afghanistan seeking care from VA specialized PTSD programs: Comparison with male veterans and female war zone veterans of previous eras," *Journal of Women's Health*, 19, 4 (2010), pp. 751–757.

Frederisk, Jim, "A female security force in Iraq," *Time*, 30 May 2008, http://content.time.com/time/world/article/0,8599,1810592,00.html, last accessed 1 May 2019.

Gautam, Shobha, Amrita Banskota and Rita Manchanda, "Where there are no men: Women in the Maoist insurgency in Nepal," in Rita Manchanda (ed.), *Perspectives on Modern South Asia: A Reader in Culture, History, and Representation*, Chichester, UK: Wiley Blackwell, 2001, pp. 340–349.

Gellman, Barton, and Greg Miller, "'Black budget' summary details US spy network's successes, failures and objectives," *Washington Post*, 29 Aug. 2013, https://www.washingtonpost.com/world/national-security/black-bud-get-summary-details-us-spy-networks-successes-failures-and-objectives/2013/08/29/7e57bb78–10ab-11e3–8cdd-bcdc09410972_story.html?noredirect=on&utm_term=.8f57698bf101, last accessed 1 May 2019.

Gentry, Caron E., "The mysterious case of Aafia Siddiqui: Gothic intertextual analysis of neo Orientalist narratives," *Millennium-Journal of International Studies*, 45, 1 (2016), pp. 3–24.

Gentry, Caron E., and Laura Sjoberg, "Terrorism and political violence," in Laura J. Shepherd (ed.), *Gender Matters in Global Politics: A Feminist Introduction to International Relations*, Abingdon: Routledge, 2015, pp. 120–130.

George, Sussanah, et al., "Mosul is a graveyard: Final IS battle kills 9,000 civilians," Associated Press, 21 Dec. 2017, https://apnews.com/93f0c1b83550404f99053ed7f0474740, last accessed 1 May 2019.

Georgetown Institute for Women, Peace and Security, "Women, peace and security index," 2018, https://giwps.georgetown.edu/the-index/, last accessed 1 May 2019.

Gerges, Fawaz A., *Isis: A History*, Princeton, NJ: Princeton University Press, 2017.

Gezari, Vanessa M., *The Tender Soldier: A True Story of War and Sacrifice*, New York: Simon and Schuster, 2014.

Ghitis, Frida, "Why women fight against ISIS," CNN, 30 Oct. 2014, http://edition.cnn.com/2014/10/14/opinion/ghitis-isis-women-slavery/, last accessed 1 May 2019.

Gibbons-Neff, Thomas, and Dan Lamothe, "Obama administration expands elite military unit's powers to hunt foreign fighters globally; Joint Special Operations Command's 'Counter External Operations Task Force' will hunt terrorist networks," *Washington Post*, 25 Nov. 2016, https://www.washingtonpost.com/news/checkpoint/wp/2016/11/25/obama-administration-expands-elite-military-units-powers-to-hunt-foreign-fighters-globally/?utm_term=.c8e14866a208, last accessed 1 May 2019.

Gielen, Amy-Jane, "Exit programmes for female jihadists: A proposal for conducting realistic evaluation of the Dutch approach," *International Sociology*, 33, 4 (2018), pp. 454–472.

Gilmore, Jonathan, "A kinder, gentler counter-terrorism: Counterinsurgency, human security and the War on Terror," *Security Dialogue*, 42, 1 (2011), pp. 21–37.

Gilsinan, Kathy, "The ISIS crackdown on women, by women," *The Atlantic*, 25 July 2014, http://www.theatlantic.com/international/archive/2014/07/the-women-of-isis/375047/, last accessed 1 May 2019.

Givetash, Linda, "Divorce on the rise in Iraq as wives cut ties to ISIS militants," NBC News, 5 July 2018, https://www.nbcnews.com/news/world/divorce-rise-iraq-wives-cut-ties-isis-militants-n888541, last accessed 1 May 2019.

Glaser, Michaela, "Disengagement and deradicalization work with girls and young women experiences from Germany," in Michaela Köttig, Renate

# BIBLIOGRAPHY

Bitzan and Andrea Petö, *Gender and Far Right Politics in Europe*, Basingstoke: Palgrave Macmillan, 2017, pp. 337–349.

Goldstein, Joshua S. *War and Gender*, Cambridge: Cambridge University Press, 2001.

Gomez, Oscar A., and Des Gasper, "Human security: A thematic guidance note for regional and national human development report teams," 2013, http://hdr.undp.org/sites/default/files/human_security_guidance_note_r-nhdrs.pdf, last accessed 5 May 2017.

González, Roberto J., "'Human terrain': Past, present and future applications," *Anthropology Today*, 24, 1 (2008), pp. 21–26.

Gonzalez-Perez, Margaret, *Women and Terrorism: Female Activity in Domestic and International Terror Groups*, Abingdon: Routledge, 2008.

Graham-Harrison, Emma, "Afghanistan suicide blast kills 12 in attack on Kabul airport contractors," *The Guardian*, 18 Sep. 2012, https://www.theguardian.com/world/2012/sep/18/afghanistan-suicide-blast-kills-12, last accessed 1 May 2019.

———, "Women warriors: The extraordinary story of Khatoon Khider and her Daughters of the Sun," 12 Feb. 2017a, https://www.theguardian.com/world/2017/feb/12/women-warriors-khatoon-khider-yazidi-isis-battle-iraq, last accessed 1 May 2019.

———, "'I was sold seven times': the Yazidi women welcomed back into the faith," *The Guardian*, 1 July 2017b, https://www.theguardian.com/global-development/2017/jul/01/i-was-sold-seven-times-yazidi-women-welcomed-back-into-the-faith, last accessed 1 May 2019.

Gramer, Robbie, "Human rights groups bristling at State Department report," *Foreign Policy*, 21 Apr. 2018, https://foreignpolicy.com/2018/04/21/human-rights-groups-bristling-at-state-human-rights-report/, last accessed 1 May 2019.

Greenblatt, Johnathan, "Right-wing extremist violence is our biggest threat. The numbers don't lie," Anti-Defamation League, 24 Jan. 2019, https://www.adl.org/news/op-ed/right-wing-extremist-violence-is-our-biggest-threat-the-numbers-dont-lie, last accessed 1 May 2019.

The Guardian, "They said…," 23 Sep. 2001, https://www.theguardian.com/world/2001/sep/23/september11.terrorism4, last accessed 30 Apr. 2019.

Haid, Haid, "Resisting Hayat Tahrir Al-Sham: Syrian civil society on the frontlines," *Adopt a Revolution*, Nov. 2017, https://www.adoptrevolution.org/wpcontent/uploads/2017/12/2017_11_10_HTS_Studie-eng.pdf, last accessed 1 May 2019.

———, "Reintegrating ISIS supporters in Syria: Efforts, priorities and challenges," 2018, https://icsr.info/wpcontent/uploads/2018/08/ICSR-Report-Reintegrating-ISIS-Supporters-in-Syria-Efforts-Priorities-and-Challenges.pdf, last accessed 1 May 2019.

# BIBLIOGRAPHY

Hall, Richard, "Raqqa after Isis: Meet the 30-year-old woman rebuilding the former capital of the 'caliphate'," *The Independent*, 9 Nov. 2018, https://www.independent.co.uk/news/world/middle-east/isis-raqqa-syria-civil-warcivic-council-terror-islamic-state-leila-mustafa-a8625631.html, last accessed 1 May 2019.

Hamid, Shadi, and Rashid Dar, "Islamism, Salafism, and jihadism: A primer," 15 July 2016, https://www.brookings.edu/blog/markaz/2016/07/15/islamism-salafism-and-jihadism-a-primer/, last accessed 1 May 2019.

Hamilton, Carrie, *Women and ETA: The Gender Politics of Radical Basque Nationalism*, Oxford: Oxford University Press, 2013.

Hamm, Mark S., "Prison Islam in the age of sacred terror," *The British Journal of Criminology*, 49, 5 (2009), pp. 667–685.

————, *The Spectacular Few: Prisoner Radicalization and the Evolving Terrorist Threat*, New York: NYU Press, 2013.

Handyside, Bianca, "Women's roles in violent Islamist extremism: A comparison of Australian and international experiences," 9 Nov. 2018, https://www.churchilltrust.com.au/media/fellows/Handyside_B_2017_To_investigate_the_role_of_women_in_violent_Islamist_extremism.pdf, last accessed 1 May 2019.

Hansen, Lene, *Security as Practice: Discourse Analysis and the Bosnian War*, Abingdon: Routledge, 2013.

Harborne, Bernard, "Aid: A security perspective," in Stephen Brown and Jörn Grävingholt (eds), *Security and Development in Global Politics: A Critical Comparison*, London: Palgrave Macmillan, 2012, pp. 37–56.

Harcourt, Bernard E., "How Trump rules the fascist right," New York Review of Books Daily, 29 Nov. 2018, https://www.nybooks.com/daily/2018/11/29/how-trump-fuels-the-fascist-right/, last accessed 1 May 2019.

Harnden, Toby, "Rumsfeld calls for end to old tactics of war," *The Telegraph*, 16 Oct. 2001, https://www.telegraph.co.uk/news/worldnews/northamerica/usa/1359609/Rumsfeld-calls-for-end-to-old-tactics-of-war.html, last accessed 30 Apr. 2019.

Harris, Bryant, Robbie Gramer and Emily Tamkin, "The end of foreign aid as we know it," *Foreign Policy*, 24 Apr. 2017, https://foreignpolicy.com/2017/04/24/u-s-agency-for-international-development-foreign-aid-state-department-trump-slash-foreign funding/, last accessed 6 Mar. 2019.

Harris, Shane, "Lady al Qaeda: The world's most wanted woman," *Foreign Policy*, 26 Aug. 2014, https://foreignpolicy.com/2014/08/26/lady-al-qaeda-the-worlds-most-wanted-woman/, last accessed 1 May 2019.

Haysom, Simone, and Ashley Jackson, "'You don't need to love us': Civil-military relations in Afghanistan, 2002–13," *Stability: International Journal of Security and Development*, 2, 2 (2013), pp. 1–16.

Healy, Jack, and Yasir Ghazi, "Iraqi women work to halt bombers, but paycheck is elusive," *New York Times*, 27 Feb. 2011, http://www.nytimes. com/2011/02/28/world/middleeast/28iraq.html, last accessed 1 May 2019.

Herman, Susan N., "Women and terrorism: Keynote address," *Women's Rights Law Reporter*, 31 (2009), pp. 258–267.

Hewitt, Christopher, and Jessica Kelley-Moore, "Foreign fighters in Iraq: A cross-national analysis of jihadism," *Terrorism and Political Violence*, 21, 2 (2009), pp. 211–220.

Higate, Paul, and Marsha Henry, "Engendering (in) security in peace support operations," *Security Dialogue*, 35, 4 (2004), pp. 481–498.

Hill, Ginny, "Yemeni women sign up to fight terror," BBC News, 2. April 2007, http://news.bbc.co.uk/1/hi/world/middle_east/6510149.stm, last accessed 1 May 2019.

Hokayem, Emile, and David B. Roberts, "The war in Yemen," *Survival*, 58, 6 (2016), pp. 157–186.

Holmer, Georgia, and Fulco van Deventer, "Inclusive approaches to community policing and CVE," Sept. 2014, http://www.usip.org/sites/ default/files/SR352_Inclusive-Approaches-to-Community-Policing-and-CVE.pdf, last accessed 1 May 2019.

Holmstedt, Kirsten, *Band of Sisters: American Women at War in Iraq*, Mechanicsburg, PA: Stackpole Books, 2008.

Holt, Maria, "The unlikely terrorist: women and Islamic resistance in Lebanon and the Palestinian territories," *Critical Studies on Terrorism*, 3, 3 (2010), pp. 365–382.

Howard III, John W., and Laura C. Prividera, "Rescuing patriarchy or saving 'Jessica Lynch': The rhetorical construction of the American woman soldier," *Women and Language*, 27, 2 (2004), pp. 89–98.

———, "The fallen woman archetype: Media representations of Lynndie England, gender, and the (ab)uses of US female soldiers," *Women's Studies in Communication*, 31, 3 (2008), pp. 287–311.

Howell, Jude, "The global war on terror, development and civil society," *Journal of International Development*, 18, 1 (2006), pp. 121–135.

Hoyle, Carolyn, Alexandra Bradford and Ross Frenett, "Becoming Mulan? Female Western migrants to ISIS," Institute for Strategic Dialogue, 2015, https://www.isdglobal.org/wp-content/uploads/2016/02/ISDJ2969_ Becoming_Mulan_01.15_WEB.pdf, last accessed 1 May 2019.

Huckerby, Jayne C., "Unpacking the trafficking–terror nexus," in Margaret L. Satterthwaite and Jayne Huckerby (eds), *Gender, National Security, and Counter-Terrorism*, Oxon: Routledge, 2013, pp. 106–126.

Huckerby, Jayne C. "Feminism and International Law in the Post 9/11 Era," Fordham International Law Journal 39: 533-590.

———, "Gender, Counter-Terrorism and International Law," in Research

Handbook on terrorism and international law. Ed. Ben Saul; Edward Elgar: Cheltenham, UK, 2014.

————, "The Complexities of Women, Peace, Security and Countering Violent Extremism," Just Security, 24 Sep 2015. Available: https://www.justsecurity.org/26337/womens-rights-simple-tool-counterterrorism/ Last accessed 6 Jun 2019.

Hudson, Natalie Florea, Gender, Human Security and the United Nations: Security Language as a Political Framework for Women, Abingdon: Routledge, 2009.

Hudson, Valerie M., Sex and World Peace, New York: Columbia University Press, 2013.

————, Mary Caprioli, Bonnie Ballif-Spanvill, Rose McDermott and Chad F. Emmett, "The heart of the matter: The security of women and the security of states," International Security, 33, 3 (2009), pp. 7–45.

————, and Patricia Leidl, The Hillary Doctrine: Sex and American Foreign Policy, New York: Columbia University Press, 2015.

Hull, Amb. Edmund J., "Interview with Ambassador Edmund James Hull," in Charles Stuart Kennedy (e d.), The Association for Diplomatic Studies and Training Foreign Affairs Oral History Project, 10 Oct. 2005, www.adst.org/OH%20TOCs/Hull,%20Edmund%20James.toc.pdf, last accessed 1 May 2019.

————, High-value Target: Countering Al Qaeda in Yemen, Dulles, VA: Potomac Books, 2011.

Human Rights Watch, "Mali: War crimes by northern rebels," 20 Apr. 2012, https://www.hrw.org/news/2012/04/30/mali-war-crimes-northern-rebels, last accessed 1 May 2019.

————, "Iraq: Women suffer under ISIS," 5 Apr. 2016, https://www.hrw.org/news/2016/04/05/iraq-women-suffer-under-isis, last accessed 1 May 2019.

————, "Flawed justice: Accountability for ISIS crimes in Iraq," 5 Dec. 2017, https://www.hrw.org/report/2017/12/05/flawed-justice/accountability-isis-crimes-iraq, last accessed 1 May 2019.

Humud, Carla E., Christopher M. Blanchard and Mary Beth D. Nikitin, "Armed conflict in Syria: Overview and US response," 2018, https://fas.org/sgp/crs/mideast/RL33487.pdf, last accessed 1 May 2019.

Hunt, Krista, and Kim Rygiel, (En)gendering the War on Terror: War Stories and Camouflaged Politics, Abingdon: Routledge, 2013.

Huntington, Samuel P., "The clash of civilizations?" Foreign Affairs, 72, 3 (1993), pp. 22–49.

Ignatius, David, "A turf war over terrorism," Washington Post, 9 Dec. 2016, https://www.pressreader.com/usa/the-washington-post/20161209/281930247610714, last accessed 1 May 2019.

International Bar Association, "Legality of armed drone strikes," 2017, https://www.ibanet.org/Human_Rights_Institute/HRI_Publications/Legality-of-armed-drone-strikes.aspx, last accessed 1 May 2019.

International Crisis Group, "Yemen's military-security reform: Seeds of new conflict?" *Middle East Report*, 139, 4 Apr. 2013, https://www.crisisgroup.org/middle-east-north-africa/gulf-and-arabian-peninsula/yemen/yemens-military-security-reform-seeds-new-conflict, last accessed 1 May 2019.

———, "Yemen: Is peace possible?" *Middle East Report*, 167, 9 Feb. 2016, https://www.crisisgroup.org/middle-east-north-africa/gulf-and-arabian-peninsula/yemen/yemen-peace-possible, last accessed 1 May 2019.

International Organization for Migration (IOM), "Iraq displacement figures drop below two million for first time since 2014; nearly four million have returned home," ReliefWeb, 4 Sept. 2018, https://reliefweb.int/report/iraq/iraq-displacement-figures-drop-below-two-million-first-time-2014-nearly-four-million, last accessed 1 May 2019.

Iraq Body Count, "Year four: Simply the worst," 18 Mar. 2007, https://www.iraqbodycount.org/analysis/numbers/year-four/, last accessed 1 May 2019.

Israeli, Raphael, "Palestinian women: The quest for a voice in the public square through 'Islamikaze martyrdom'," *Terrorism and Political Violence*, 16, 1 (2004), pp. 66–96.

Jackson, Ashley, "Life under the Taliban shadow government," Overseas Development Institute, June 2018, https://www.odi.org/sites/odi.org.uk/files/resourcedocuments/12269.pdf, last accessed 1 May 2019.

Jackson, Richard, *Writing the War on Terrorism: Language, Politics and Counter-terrorism*, Manchester: Manchester University Press, 2005.

———, "Genealogy, ideology, and counter-terrorism: Writing wars on terrorism from Ronald Reagan to George W. Bush Jr," *Studies in Language & Capitalism*, 1, 1 (2006a), pp. 163–193.

———, "The politics of fear: Writing the terrorist threat in the war on terror," in George Kassimeris (ed.), *Playing Politics with Terrorism: A User's Guide*, New York: Columbia University Press, 2006b, pp. 176–202.

———, "The 9/11 attacks and the social construction of a national narrative," in Matthew J. Morgan (ed.), *The Impact of 9/11 on the Media, Arts, and Entertainment*, New York: Palgrave Macmillan, 2009, pp. 25–35.

———, "Culture, identity and hegemony: Continuity and (the lack of) change in US counterterrorism policy from Bush to Obama," *International Politics*, 48, 2–3 (2011), pp. 390–411.

Jacques, Karen, and Paul J. Taylor, "Female terrorism: A review," *Terrorism and Political Violence*, 21, 3 (2009), pp. 499–515.

———, "Myths and realities of female-perpetrated terrorism," *Law and Human Behavior*, 37, 1 (2013), pp. 35–44.

Jager, Sheila Miyoshi, "On the uses of cultural knowledge," Washington, DC

# BIBLIOGRAPHY

& Carlisle, PA: Strategic Studies Institute & US Army War College, 2007, https://www.globalsecurity.org/military/library/report/2007/ssi_jager02.pdf, last accessed 1 May 2019.

Jalabi, Raya, "Forgotten victims: The children of Islamic State," Reuters, 21 Mar 2019, https://www.reuters.com/investigates/special-report/iraq-islamicstate-children/, last accessed 1 May 2019.

Jamieson, Alison, "Mafiosi and terrorists: Italian women in violent organizations," *SAIS Review of International Affairs*, 20, 2 (2000), pp. 51–64.

Jawad al-Tamimi, Aymen, "From Jabhat al-Nusra to Hay'at Tahrir al-Sham: Evolution, approach and future," 2018, https://www.kas.de/c/document_library/get_file?uuid=8cfa4cdb-e337-820d-d0bd-4cd998f38612&groupId=252038, last accessed 1 May 2019.

Jebb, Cindy R., and Andrew A. Gallo, "Adjusting the paradigm: A human security framework for combating terrorism," in Mary Martin and Taylor Owen, *Routledge Handbook of Human Security*, Abingdon: Routledge, 2013, pp. 210–223.

Johnsen, Gregory D., *The Last Refuge: Yemen, Al-Qaeda, and America's War in Arabia*, New York: WW Norton & Company, 2013.

———, "Al-Qaeda and ISIS are on their heels in Yemen, but will return unless we help build a lasting peace," Just Security, 7 Aug. 2018, https://www.justsecurity.org/60099/al-qaeda-isis-heels-yemen-return-lasting-peace/, last accessed 1 May 2019.

Jones, Clarke R., "Are prisons really schools for terrorism? Challenging the rhetoric on prison radicalization," *Punishment & Society*, 16, 1 (2014), pp. 74–103.

Jones, Seth G., "Counterinsurgency in Afghanistan," *RAND Counterinsurgency Study*, 4 (2008), https://www.rand.org/content/dam/rand/pubs/monographs/2008/RAND_MG595.pdf, last accessed 1 May 2019.

Jørgensen, Marianne W., and Louise J. Phillips, *Discourse Analysis as Theory and Method*, London: Sage, 2002.

Kaldor, Mary, *New and Old Wars: Organised Violence in a Global Era*, Boston: Polity Press, 2013.

Kandiyoti, Deniz, "Between the hammer and the anvil: Post-conflict reconstruction, Islam and women's rights," *Third World Quarterly*, 28, 3 (2007), pp. 503–517.

Karpinksi, J., and S. Strasser, *One Woman's Army: The Commanding General of Abu Ghraib Tells Her Story*. New York: Miramax Books, 2005.

Katt, Megan, "Blurred lines: Cultural Support Teams in Afghanistan," *Joint Force Quarterly*, 75 (2014), pp. 106–113.

Katzman, Kenneth, "Congressional Research Service Report for Congress: Al Qaeda in Assessment and Outside Links," 15 Aug. 2008a, https://fas.org/sgp/crs/terror/RL32217.pdf, last accessed 1 May 2019.

————, "CRS report for Congress. Afghanistan: Post-war governance, security, and US Policy," 26 Nov. 2008b, www.dtic.mil/cgi-bin/GetTRDoc?AD=ADA490415, last accessed 1 May 2019.

Kaufman-Osborn, Timothy, "Gender trouble at Abu Ghraib?" *Politics & Gender*, 1, 4 (2005), pp. 597–619.

Keatings, Tom, "The role of financing in defeating Al-Shabaab," 2014, https://rusi.org/sites/default/files/201412_whr_2–14_keatinge_web_0.pdf, last accessed 1 May 2019.

Keen, David, *Complex Emergencies*, Cambridge: Polity, 2008.

Keen, David, and Larry Attree, "Dilemmas of counter-terror, stabilisation and statebuilding," Jan. 2015, https://www.saferworld.org.uk/resources/publications/875-dilemmas-of-counter-terror-stabilisation-and-statebuilding, last accessed 1 May 2019.

Kendall, Elisabeth, "How can al-Qaeda in the Arabian Peninsula be defeated?" *Washington Post*, 3 May 2016, https://www.washingtonpost.com/news/monkey-cage/wp/2016/05/03/how-can-al-qaeda-in-the-arabian-peninsula-be-defeated/?utm_term=.cff2b499d512, last accessed 1 May 2019.

Kennedy, Claudia J., Roberta L. Santiago and Felipe Torres, "Defense Advisory Committee on women in the services 2009 report," 23 Mar. 2010, http://dacowits.defense.gov/Portals/48/Documents/Reports/2009/Annual%20Report/dacowits2009report.pdf, last accessed 1 May 2019.

Kenner, David, "The women who could save Mosul," *Foreign Policy*, 6 Feb. 2017, https://foreignpolicy.com/2017/02/06/the-women-who-could-save-mosul/, last accessed 1 May 2019.

Khalili, Laleh, "Gendered practices of counterinsurgency," *Review of International Studies*, 37, 4 (2011), pp. 1471–1491.

————, *Time in the Shadows: Confinement in Counterinsurgencies*, Stanford, CA: Stanford University Press, 2012.

Khalil, Shaimaa, and Dina Demrdash, "The sisters rebuilding Mosul University's library," BBC, 22 Mar. 2018, https://www.bbc.co.uk/news/av/world-middle-east-43488371/the-sisters-rebuilding-mosul-university-s-library, last accessed 1 May 2019.

Khan, Azmat, and Anand Gopal, "The uncounted," *New York Times Magazine*, 16 Nov. 2017, https://www.nytimes.com/interactive/2017/11/16/magazine/uncounted-civilian-casualties-iraq-airstrikes.html, last accessed 1 May 2019.

Khan, Miriam, "Donald Trump national security adviser Mike Flynn has called Islam 'a cancer'," ABC News, 18 Nov. 2016, https://abcnews.go.com/Politics/donald-trump-national-security-adviser-mike-flynn-called/story?id=43575658, last accessed 1 May 2019.

Kheel, Rebecca, and Rebecca Savransky, "Trump to ban transgender people from all military service," *The Hill*, 26 July 2017, https://thehill.com/

homenews/administration/343847-trump-calls-for-ban-on-transgender-individuals-in-military, last accessed 1 May 2019.

Khelghat-Doost, Hamoon, "Women of the caliphate: The mechanism for women's incorporation into the Islamic State (IS)," *Perspectives on Terrorism*, 11, 1 (2017), pp. 17–25.

Khezri, Haidar, "Kurdish troops fight for freedom—and women's equality—on battlegrounds across Middle East," Public Radio International, 19 Mar. 2018, https://www.pri.org/stories/2018–03–19/kurdish-troops-fight-freedom-and-womens-equality-battlegrounds-across-middle-east, last accessed 1 May 2019.

Kilcullen, David, "Field notes on Iraq's tribal revolt against Al-Qa'idam," *CTC Sentinel*, 1, 11 (2008), pp. 1–5.

———, *Counterinsurgency*, Oxford: Oxford University Press, 2010.

———, "How we lost the war on terror," Contemporary Conflict Talk, Imperial War Museum, London, 23 Feb. 2016.

King, Gary, and Christopher J. L. Murray, "Rethinking human security," *Political Science Quarterly*, 116, 4 (2001), pp. 585–610.

Kirby, Paul, and Marsha Henry, "Rethinking masculinity and practices of violence in conflict settings," *International Feminist Journal of Politics*, 14, 4 (2012), pp. 445–449.

Knickmeyer, Ellen, "Attack against US Embassy in Yemen blamed on al-Qaeda," *Washington Post*, 18 Sept. 2008, http://www.washingtonpost.com/wp-dyn/content/article/2008/09/17/AR2008091700317.html, last accessed 1 May 2019.

Knight, W. A., "Disarmament, demobilization, and reintegration and post-conflict peacebuilding in Africa: an overview," *African Security*, 1, 1 (2008), pp. 24–52.

Koehler-Derrick, Gabriel, "A false foundation? AQAP, tribes and ungoverned spaces in Yemen," Sept. 2011, www.dtic.mil/dtic/tr/fulltext/u2/a550461.pdf, last accessed 1 May 2019.

Kolenda, Christopher, Rachel Reid, Chris Rogers and Marte Retzius, "The strategic cost of civilian harm: Applying lessons from Afghanistan to current and future conflicts," June 2016, https://www.opensocietyfoundations.org/sites/default/files/strategic-costs-civilian-harm-20160622.pdf, last accessed 1 May 2019.

Kraft, Michael, and Edward Marks, *US Government Counterterrorism: A Guide to Who Does What*, Boca Raton: CRC Press, 2011.

Krol, Charlotte, and George Fuller, "'I am very naive': Daughter of Indonesian family lured to Raqqa by Islamic State tells of ordeal," *The Telegraph*, 3 Aug. 2017, https://www.telegraph.co.uk/news/2017/08/03/naive-daughter-indonesian-family-lured-raqqa-islamic-state-tells/, last accessed 1 May 2019.

Kumar, Deepa, "War propaganda and the (ab) uses of women: Media constructions of the Jessica Lynch story," *Feminist Media Studies*, 4, 3 (2004), pp. 297–313.

Kundnani, Arun, *Spooked! How Not to Prevent Violent Extremism*, London: Institute of Race Relations, 2009.

Kurdistan 24, "Ezidi women voluntarily join Peshmerga, establish Roj Force," 4 June 2016, http://www.kurdistan24.net/en/opinion/40364a84–355b-4381-a5b5-b0eff13b24e9, last accessed 1 May 2019.

Kushner, Harvey W., *Terrorism in America: A Structured Approach to Understanding the Terrorist Threat*, Springfield, IL: Charles C. Thomas, 1998.

Ladbury, Sarah, "Women and extremism: The association of women and girls with jihadi groups and implications for programming," 2015a, https://assets.publishing.service.gov.uk/media/57a0897fed915d6 22c000245/61578_Women-Extremism-Full-Report.pdf, last accessed 1 May 2019.

————, "Women and extremism: The association of women and girls with jihadi groups and implications for programming," UK Department of International Development, 11 Jan. 2015b, https://www.gov.uk/dfid-research-outputs/women-and-extremism-the-association-of-women-and-girls-with-jihadi-groups-and-implications-for-programming, last accessed 1 May 2019.

Ladbury, Sarah, Hamsatu Allamin, Chitra Nagarajan, Paul Francis and Ukoha Okorafor Ukiwo, "Jihadi groups and state-building: The case of Boko Haram in Nigeria," *Stability: International Journal of Security and Development*, 5, 1 (2016), p. 16.

Lahoud, Nelly, "Umayma al-Zawahiri on women's role in jihad," *Jihadica*, 26 Feb. 2010. /http://www.jihadica.com/umayma-al-zawahiri-on-women's-role-in-jihad, last accessed 1 May 2019.

————, "The neglected sex: The jihadis' exclusion of women from jihad," *Terrorism and Political Violence*, 26, 5 (2014), pp. 780–802.

————, "Can women be soldiers of the Islamic State?" *Survival*, 59, 1 (2017), pp. 61–78.

————, "Empowerment or subjugation?: An analysis of ISIL's gendered messaging," June 2018, https://reliefweb.int/sites/reliefweb.int/files/resources/Lahoud-Fin-Web-rev.pdf, last accessed 1 May 2019.

Lamb, Christina, "Escape from Isis: Christina Lamb meets the Yazidi women fighting for justice," *The Times*, 29 Apr. 2018, https://www.thetimes.co.uk/article/escape-from-isis-christina-lamb-meets-the-yazidi-women-fighting-for-justice-bsxzgz867, last accessed 1 May 2019.

Landler, Mark, "A new gender agenda," *New York Times Magazine*, 18 Aug. 2009, http://www.nytimes.com/2009/08/23/magazine/23clinton-t.html, last accessed 1 May 2019.

Lazar, Michelle M., "Feminist critical discourse analysis: Articulating a feminist discourse praxis 1," *Critical Discourse Studies*, 4, 2 (2007), pp. 141–164.

# BIBLIOGRAPHY

Leland, John, "Women ascend to Iraq's elite police officer corps," *New York Times*, 9 Nov. 2009, http://www.nytimes.com/2009/11/10/world/middleeast/10iraq.html?_r=0, last accessed 1 May 2019.

Lemmon, Gayle Tzemach, "The Hillary doctrine," *Newsweek*, 6 Mar. 2011, https://www.newsweek.com/hillary-doctrine-66105, last accessed 1 May 2019.

———, *Ashley's War: The Untold Story of a Team of Women Soldiers on the Special Ops Battlefield*, New York: Harper Collins, 2015a.

———, "The army's all-women special ops teams show us how we'll win tomorrow's wars," *Washington Post*, 19 May 2015b, https://www.washingtonpost.com/posteverything/wp/2015/05/19/the-armys-all-women-special-ops-teams-show-us-how-well-win-tomorrows-wars/?utm_term=.8f9e30b4a7fb, last accessed 1 May 2019.

Lia, Brynjar, "Understanding jihadi proto-states," *Perspectives on Terrorism*, 9, 4 (2015), pp. 31–41.

Liddick, Don, *Eco-terrorism: Radical Environmental and Animal Liberation Movements*, Westport, CT: Greenwood Publishing Group, 2006.

Lipton, Michael, "Migration from rural areas of poor countries: The impact on rural productivity and income distribution," *World Development*, 8, 1 (1980), pp. 1–24.

Lobasz, Jennifer, and Laura Sjoberg, "Critical perspectives on gender and politics: The state and feminist security studies: A conversation," *Politics & Gender*, 7, 4 (2011), pp. 573–604.

LoBianco, Tom, "Donald Trump on terrorists: 'Take out their families'," CNN, 3 Dec. 2015, https://edition.cnn.com/2015/12/02/politics/donald-trump-terrorists-families/index.html, last accessed 1 May 2019.

Lowery, Wesley, Kimberly Kindy and Andrew Ba Tran, "In the United States, right-wing violence is on the rise," Washington Post, 25 Nov. 2018, https://www.washingtonpost.com/national/in-the-united-states-right-wing-violence-is-on-the-rise/2018/11/25/61f7f24a-deb4–11e8–85df-7a6b4d25cfbb_story.html, last accessed 1 May 2019.

Luehrs, Christoff, "Provincial Reconstruction Teams: A literature review," *Prism*, 1, 1 (2009), pp. 95–102.

Lyttle, Chris, "3/6 recruits 'Sisters' in Ameriyah, Ferris," *Marines*, 5 June 2008, http://www.1stmardiv.marines.mil/News/News-Article-Display/Article/541439/36-recruits-sisters-in-ameriyah-ferris/, last accessed 1 May 2019.

MacDonald, Eileen, *Shoot the Women First*, London: Random House, 1991.

MacKenzie, Megan H., *Female Soldiers in Sierra Leone: Sex, Security, and Post-conflict Development*, New York: NYU Press, 2012.

MacLean, George, *The Changing Perception of Human Security: Coordinating National and Multilateral Responses, The United Nations and the New Security Agenda*, Ottawa: UNAC, 1998.

Margolin, Devorah, "A Palestinian woman's place in terrorism: Organized perpetrators or individual actors?" *Studies in Conflict & Terrorism*, 39, 10 (2016), pp. 912–934.

Marouf, Hanar, "Peshmerga female fighters: From frontline to sideline," 10 Oct. 2018, https://www.washingtoninstitute.org/fikraforum/view/peshmerga-female-fighters-from-frontline-to-sideline, last accessed 1 May 2019.

Marsh, Stephanie, "'I can't wait to have my own jihadi baby': The British women joining Isis," *The Times*, 2 Dec. 2014, https://www.thetimes.co.uk/article/i-cant-wait-to-have-my-own-jihadi-baby-the-british-women-joining-isis-vdbckjxhpqc, last accessed 1 May 2019.

Martin, Jeff, "Army's Human Terrain System needs to be buried once and for all," *American Anthropological Association*, 11 Mar. 2016, https://www.americananthro.org/StayInformed/NewsDetail.aspx?ItemNumber=13427, last accessed 1 May 2019.

Martinez, Luis and Elizabeth McLaughlin, "Trump administration proposes big budget increase for Pentagon," ABC News, 12 Feb. 2018, https://abcnews.go.com/Politics/trump-administration-proposes-big-budget-increase-pentagon/story?id=53030358, last accessed 1 May 2019.

Masson-Delmotte, V., P. Zhai, H.-O. Pörtner, D. Roberts, J. Skea, P.R. Shukla, A. Pirani, Moufouma-Okia, C. Péan, R. Pidcock, S. Connors, J.B.R. Matthews, Y. Chen, X. Zhou, M.I. Gomis, E. Lonnoy, Maycock, M. Tignor and T. Waterfield (eds), "Global warming of 1.5°C. An IPCC Special Report on the impacts of global warming of 1.5°C above pre-industrial levels and related global greenhouse gas emission pathways, in the context of strengthening the global response to the threat of climate change, sustainable development, and efforts to eradicate poverty," 2018, https://www.ipcc.ch/sr15/, last accessed 1 May 2019.

Matfess, Hilary, *Women and the War on Boko Haram: Wives, Weapons, Witnesses*, London: Zed Books, 2017.

Mattocks, Kristin M., Sally G. Haskell, Erin E. Krebs, Amy C. Justice, Elizabeth M. Yano and Cynthia Brandt, "Women at war: Understanding how women veterans cope with combat and military sexual trauma," *Social Science & Medicine*, 74, 4 (2012), pp. 537–545.

Mazurana, Dyan, and Linda Eckerbom Cole, "Women, girls and disarmament, demobilization and reintegration (DDR)," in Carol Cohn (ed.), *Women & Wars*, Cambridge: Polity, 2013, pp. 194–214.

McAdam, Doug, "Recruitment to high-risk activism: The case of Freedom Summer," *American Journal of Sociology*, 92, 1 (1986), pp. 64–90.

McBride, Keally, and Annick T. R. Wibben, "The gendering of counterinsurgency in Afghanistan," *Humanity: An International Journal of Human Rights, Humanitarianism, and Development*, 3, 2 (2012), pp. 199–215.

# BIBLIOGRAPHY

McCants, William, *The ISIS Apocalypse: The History, Strategy, and Doomsday Vision of the Islamic State*, New York: St. Martin's Press, 2015.

McCrisken, Trevor, "Ten years on: Obama's war on terrorism in rhetoric and practice," *International Affairs*, 87, 4 (2011), pp. 781–801.

McDowall, Angus, "Syrian Observatory says war has killed more than half a million," Reuters, 12 Mar. 2018, https://www.reuters.com/article/us-mideast-crisis-syria/syrian-observatory-says-war-has-killed-more-than-half-a-million-idUSKCN1GO13M, last accessed 1 May 2019.

McEvoy, Sandra, "Loyalist women paramilitaries in Northern Ireland: Beginning a feminist conversation about conflict resolution," *Security Studies*, 18, 2 (2009), pp. 262–286.

McFate, Montgomery, and Janice H. Laurence, *Social Science Goes to War: The Human Terrain System in Iraq and Afghanistan*, Oxford: Oxford University Press, 2015.

McKelvey, Tara (ed.), *One of the Guys: Women as Aggressors and Torturers*, Emeryville, CA: Seal Press, 2007.

McKernan, Bethan, "'We are now free': Yazidis fleeing Isis start over in female-only commune," *The Guardian*, 25 Feb. 2019, https://www.theguardian.com/world/2019/feb/25/yazidis-isis-female-only-commune-jinwar-syria, last accessed 1 May 2019.

McLaughlin, E., "Women at war: Meet the female Peshmerga fighters taking on ISIS," ABC News, 16 May 2016, https://abcnews.go.com/International/women-war-meet-female-peshmerga-fighters-taking-isis/story?id=39142160, last accessed 1 May 2019.

Mehra, Sasha, "Equal opportunity counterinsurgency: The importance of Afghan women in US counterinsurgency operations," MA dissertation, US Army Command and General Staff College, 2010, www.dtic.mil/cgi-bin/GetTRDoc?AD=ADA524128, last accessed 1 May 2019.

Meleagrou-Hitchens, Alexander, "As American as apple pie: How Anwar al-Awlaki became the face of western jihad," 2011, http://icsr.info/wp-content/uploads/2012/10/1315827595ICSRPaperAsAmericanAsApplePieHowAnwaralAwlakiBecametheFaceofWesternJihad.pdf, last accessed 1 May 2019.

Meredith, Charlotte, "British female jihadist wants to put 'David Cameron's head on a spike'," The Huffington Post UK, 9 Sept 2014, http://www.huffingtonpost.co.uk/2014/09/09/british-female-jihadist-david-cameron_n_5789388.html, last accessed 1 May 2019.

Meyerle, Jerry, Megan Katt, Gerald Meyerle and Jim Gavrilis, *On the Ground in Afghanistan: Counterinsurgency in Practice*, Quantico, VI: Marine Corp University Press, 2012.

Michael, Maggie, Trish Wilson and Lee Keath, "Yemen: US allies spin deals with al-Qaida in war on rebels," Associated Press, 6 Aug. 2018, https://

pulitzercenter.org/reporting/yemen-us-allies-spin-deals-al-qaida-war-rebels, last accessed 1 May 2019.

Mironova, Vera, "Is the future of ISIS female?" 20 Feb. 2019, https://www.nytimes.com/2019/02/20/opinion/islamic-state-female-fighters.html, last accessed 1 May 2019.

Mistura, Staffan de, "Security Council briefing on the situation in Syria, Special Envoy Staffan De Mistura," 2017, https://www.un.org/undpa/en/speeches-statements/27112017/syria, last accessed 1 May 2019.

Moaveni, Azadeh, "ISIS women and enforcers in Syria recount collaboration, anguish and escape," *New York Times*, 22 Nov. 2015, https://www.nytimes.com/2015/11/22/world/middleeast/isis-wives-and-enforcers-in-syria-recount-collaboration-anguish-and-escape.html, last accessed 1 May 2019.

Moghadam, Assaf, *Nexus of Global Jihad: Understanding Cooperation Among Terrorist Actors*, New York: Columbia University Press, 2017.

Mohsen, Ahlam, and Amal Al-Yarisi, "Did a 13-year old boy join al-Qaeda?" *Yemen Times*, 31 Jan. 2015, http://www.yementimes.com/en/1855/report/4851/Did-a-13-year-old-boy-join-Al-Qaeda.htm, last accessed 1 May 2019.

Moon, Katharine H. S., *Sex Among Allies: Military Prostitution in US-Korea Relations*, New York: Columbia University Press, 1997.

Muir, Jim, "Iraq's growing female bomber fear," BBC News, 29 July 2008, http://news.bbc.co.uk/1/hi/world/middle_east/7532235.stm, last accessed 1 May 2019.

Mullin, Corinna, "The US discourse on political Islam: Is Obama's a truly post-'war on terror' administration?" *Critical Studies on Terrorism*, 4, 2 (2011), pp. 263–281.

Murphy, Caryle, "AQAP's growing security threat to Saudi Arabia," *West Point Combating Terrorism Center Sentinel*, 3, 6 (2010), pp. 1–4.

Musial, Julia, "'My Muslim sister, indeed you are a mujahidah'—Narratives in the propaganda of the Islamic State to address and radicalize western Women. An exemplary analysis of the online magazine Dabiq," *Journal for Deradicalization*, 9 (2016), pp. 39–100.

Nasaw, Daniel, and Henry McDonald, "Jihad Jamie: Racial profiling under scrutiny after second white Islamist arrested," *The Guardian*, 14 Mar. 2010, https://www.theguardian.com/world/2010/mar/14/jihad-jamie-islam-terrorism-us, last accessed 1 May 2019.

National Priorities Project, "US security spending since 9/11," 26 May 2011, https://www.nationalpriorities.org/analysis/2011/us-security-spending-since-911/, last accessed 1 May 2019.

National Security Criminal Investigations, "Radicalization: A guide for the perplexed," June 2009, http://publications.gc.ca/site/eng/431926/publication.html, last accessed 1 May 2019.

# BIBLIOGRAPHY

Nayak, Meghana, "Orientalism and 'saving' US state identity after 9/11," *International Feminist Journal of Politics*, 8, 1 (2006), pp. 42–61.

NBC News, "Meet the Press: Dick Cheney," 14 Sept. 2003, http://www.nbcnews.com/id/3080244/ns/meet_the_press/t/transcript-sept/, last accessed 1 May 2019.

Ness, Cindy D. (ed.), *Female Terrorism and Militancy: Agency, Utility, and Organization*, London: Routledge, 2007.

Neumann, Peter, "Syrian foreign fighters," Presentation at UK Parliament, 20 Oct. 2014.

———, "Foreign fighter total in Syria/Iraq now exceeds 20,000; surpasses Afghanistan conflict in the 1980s," 26 Jan. 2015, http://icsr.info/2015/01/foreign-fighter-total-syriairaq-now-exceeds-20000-surpasses-afghanistan-conflict-1980s/, last accessed 1 May 2019.

———, "Countering violent extremism and radicalisation that lead to terrorism: Ideas, recommendations, and good practices from the OSCE region," 2017, https://www.osce.org/chairmanship/346841, last accessed 1 May 2019.

Ní Aoláin, Fionnuala, "Situating women in counterterrorism discourses: Undulating masculinities and luminal femininities," *Boston University Law Review*, 93 (2013), pp. 1085–1122.

———, "The 'war on terror' and extremism: assessing the relevance of the Women, Peace and Security agenda," *International Affairs*, 92, 2 (2016), pp. 275–291.

Nissenbaum, Dion, "US deepens role in Yemen fight, offers Gulf allies airstrike-target assistance," *The Wall Street Journal*, 12 June 2018, https://www.wsj.com/articles/u-s-deepens-role-in-yemen-fight-offers-gulf-allies-airstrike-target-assistance-1528830371, last accessed 1 May 2019.

North Atlantic Treaty Organization, "Comprehensive report on the NATO/EAPC policy on the implementation of UNSCR 1325 on Women, Peace and Security and related resolutions," 20 Feb. 2010, https://www.nato.int/cps/en/natohq/official_texts_68578.htm, last accessed 1 May 2019.

Norville, Valerie, "Special report: The role of women in global security," Jan. 2011, https://www.usip.org/sites/default/files/SR264-The_role_of_Women_in_Global_Security.pdf, last accessed 30 Apr. 2019.

Nossiter, Adam, "In Timbuktu, harsh change under Islamists," *New York Times*, 2 June 2012, http://www.nytimes.com/2012/06/03/world/africa/in-timbuktu-mali-rebels-and-islamists-impose-harsh-rule.html, last accessed 1 May 2019.

NYU Center for Human Rights and Global Justice, *A Decade Lost: Locating Gender in US Counter Terrorism*, New York: NYU School of Law Centre for Human Rights and Global Justice, 2011.

Öcalan, Abdullah, "Liberating life: Women's revolution," 2013, http://www.

# BIBLIOGRAPHY

freeocalan.org/wp-content/uploads/2014/06/liberating-Lifefinal.pdf, last accessed 1 May 2019.

Oriola, Temitope B., "'Unwilling cocoons': Boko Haram's war against women," *Studies in Conflict &Terrorism*, 40, 2 (2016), pp. 99–121.

Ortbals, Candice, and Lori Poloni-Staudinger, "Women policymakers Framing their leadership and lives in relation to terrorism: The Basque case," *Journal ofWomen, Politics & Policy*, 37, 2 (2016), pp. 121–144.

Otten, Cathy, "Rising from the rubble: 'If we don't rebuild Mosul, maybe Isis will come back'," *The Guardian*, 26 Mar. 2018, https://www.theguardian.com/cities/2018/mar/26/mosul-struggles-recover-ruins-iraq-isis, last accessed 1 May 2019.

Our Secure Future, "Women, peace and security by the numbers," 2018, https://oursecurefuture.org/sites/default/files/women-peace-security-infographics-web.pdf, last accessed 1 May 2019.

Oxfam and Republic ofYemen, "Women and men inYemen. Statistical portrait 2007," 2007, https://www.scribd.com/document/52828523/Women-and-Men-Yemen-Statistical-portrait, last accessed 1 May 2019.

Oxfam International and Saferworld, "We won't wait: As war ravagesYemen, its women strive to build peace," 30 Jan. 2018, https://www.saferworld.org.uk/resources/publications/1104-we-wonat-wait-as-war-ravages-yemen-its-women-strive-to-build-peace, last accessed 1 May 2019.

Palmer, David Scott (ed.), *The Shining Path of Peru*, New York: Palgrave Macmillan, 1992.

Pandith, Farah, *HowWeWin: How Cutting-Edge Entrepreneurs, PoliticalVisionaries, Enlightened Business Leaders, and Social Media Mavens Can Defeat the Extremist Threat*, NewYork: HarperCollins, 2019.

Panduranga, Harsha, and Faiza Patel, "Trump administration's terrorism claims omit crucial available data," Just Security, 10 Aug. 2018, https://www.justsecurity.org/60294/info-needed-understand-trump-administration-terrorism-claims/, last accessed 1 May 2019.

Pantazis, Christina, and Simon Pemberton, "From the 'old' to the 'new' suspect community examining the impacts of recent UK counter-terrorist legislation," *British Journal of Criminology*, 49, 5 (2009), pp. 646–666.

Parashar, Swati, "Women, militancy, and security: the South Asian conundrum," in Laura Sjoberg (ed.), *Gender and International Security: Feminine Perspectives*, Abingdon: Routledge, 2010, pp. 168–189.

———, "Gender, jihad, and jingoism 1: Women as perpetrators, planners, and patrons of militancy in Kashmir," *Studies in Conflict & Terrorism*, 34, 4 (2011), pp. 295–317.

Paraszczuk, Joanna, "Report: Anbar tribal women form all-female force to fight IS," RFERL, 12 Nov. 2014, https://www.rferl.org/a/islamic-state-iraq-anbar-tribal-female-fighters/26686909.html, last accessed 30 Apr. 2019.

# BIBLIOGRAPHY

Pasha-Robinson, Lucy, "Female Yemeni fighters carry babies and machine guns at anti-Saudi rally," *The Independent*, 18 Jan. 2017, https://www.independent.co.uk/news/world/middle-east/yemen-female-fighters-conflict-huthi-rebels-anti-saudi-coalition-rally-sanaa-a7532486.html, last accessed 1 May 2019.

Peace Women, "Member states: National Action Plans for implementation of UNSCR 1325 on Women, Peace and Security," 2019, http://www.peacewomen.org/member-states, last accessed 10 May 2019.

Pearson, Elizabeth, "The case of Roshonara Choudhry: Implications for theory on online radicalization, ISIS women, and the gendered jihad," *Policy & Internet*, 8, 1 (2015), pp. 5–33.

————, "Online as the new frontline: Affect, gender and ISIS-take-down on social media," *Studies in Conflict & Terrorism*, 41, 11 (2017), pp. 850–874.

————, "Wilayat Shahidat: Boko Haram, the Islamic State, and the question of the female suicide bomber," in Jacob Zenn (ed.), *Boko Haram Beyond the Headlines: Analyses of Africa's Enduring Insurgency*, West Point, NY: Combatting Terrorism Centre, 2018, pp. 33–52.

Penney, Joe, Eric Schmitt, Rukmini Callimachi and Christoph Koettl, "C.I.A. drone mission, curtailed by Obama, is expanded in Africa under Trump," *New York Times*, 9 Sep. 2018, https://www.nytimes.com/2018/09/09/world/africa/cia-drones-africa-military.html, last accessed 1 May 2019.

Perera, Suvendrini, and Sherene H Razack, *At the Limits of Justice: Women of Colour on Terror*, Toronto: University of Toronto Press, 2014.

Peresin, Anita, and Alberto Cervone, "The western Muhajirat of ISIS," *Studies in Conflict & Terrorism*, 38, 7 (2015), pp. 495–509.

Perito, Robert M., *The US Experience with Provincial Reconstruction Teams in Afghanistan: Lessons Identified*, USIP Special Report 152, Oct. 2005, https://www.files.ethz.ch/isn/39612/2005_october_sr152.pdf, last accessed 1 May 2019.

Perliger, Arie, "Far-right terrorism will only increase if the Trump administration refuses to admit it exists," *Business Insider*, 29 Oct. 2018, https://www.businessinsider.com/far-right-terrorism-will-worsen-trump-doesnt-criticize-2018–10?r=UK, last accessed 1 May 2019.

Perry, Tom, "Exclusive: Syrian Kurdish YPG aims to expand force to over 100,000," *Reuters*, 20 Mar. 2017, https://www.reuters.com/article/us-mideast-crisis-syria-ypg-exclusive-idUSKBN16R1QS, last accessed 1 May 2019.

Peter, Tom A., "Daughters of Iraq: Front-line guards against suicide bombers," *The Christian Science Monitor*, 11 Sept. 2008, http://www.csmonitor.com/World/Middle-East/2008/0911/p06s01-wome.html, last accessed 1 May 2019.

# BIBLIOGRAPHY

Phillips, S., "The forest for the trees: Al-Qa'ida and 'stabilisation' in Yemen," Presentation at 2010 Exeter Gulf Studies Conference: "The 21st Century Gulf: The Challenge of Identity," Institute of Arab and Islamic Studies, Exeter University, 2010.

Pillar, Paul R., "Counterterrorism," in Paul D. Williams (ed.), *Security Studies: An Introduction*, London: Routledge, 2008, pp. 457–471.

Poloni-Staudinger, Lori, and Candice D. Ortbals, *Terrorism and Violent Conflict: Women's Agency, Leadership, and Responses*, New York: Springer, 2013.

Pratt, Nicola, "Reconceptualizing gender, reinscribing racial–sexual boundaries in international security: The case of UN Security Council Resolution 1325 on 'Women, Peace and Security' 1," *International Studies Quarterly*, 57, 4 (2013a), pp. 772–783.

————, "Weaponising feminism for the 'war on terror', versus employing strategic silence," *Critical Studies on Terrorism*, 6, 2 (2013b), pp. 327–331.

Pratt, Nicola, and Sophie Richter-Devroe, "Critically examining UNSCR 1325 on Women, Peace and Security," *International Feminist Journal of Politics*, 13, 4 (2011), pp. 489–503.

Priest, Dana, and William M. Arkin, "A hidden world, growing beyond control," *Washington Post*, 19 July 2010, https://www.pulitzer.org/cms/sites/default/files/content/washpost_tsa_item1.pdf, last accessed 1 May 2019.

The Project on Middle East Political Science (POMEPS), "The politics of post-conflict reconstruction," Sep. 2018, https://pomeps.org/wpcontent/uploads/2018/09/POMEPS_Studies_30_Post-Conflict_Web.pdf, last accessed 1 May 2019.

Puechguirbal, Nadine, "Peacekeeping, peacebuilding and post-conflict reconstruction," in Laura Shepherd (ed.), *Gender Matters in Global Politics: A Feminist Introduction to International Relations*, London: Routledge, 2015, pp. 253–268.

Purkiss, Jessica, and Abigail Fielding-Smith, "US strikes causing civilian casualties more than double in Afghanistan," *The Bureau of Investigative Journalism*, 11 Oct. 2018, https://www.thebureauinvestigates.com/stories/2018-10-11/us-strikes-causing-civilian-casualties-double, last accessed 1 May 2019.

Purkiss, Jessica, and Jack Serle, "Obama's covert drone war in numbers: Ten times more strike than Bush," *The Bureau of Investigative Journalism*, 17 Jan. 2017, https://www.thebureauinvestigates.com/stories/2017–01–17/obamas-covert-drone-war-in-numbers-ten-times-more-strikes-than-bush, last accessed 1 May 2019.

Puttick, Miriam, "The lost women of Iraq: Family-based violence during armed conflict," Nov. 2018, https://minorityrights.org/wpcontent/uploads/2015/11/MRG-report-A4_OCTOBER-2015_WEB.pdf, last accessed 1 May 2019.

Qazi, Farhana, "The Mujahidaat: Tracing the early female warriors of Islam," in Laura Sjoberg and Caron E. Gentry (ed.), *Women, Gender and Terrorism*, Athens, GA: University of Georgia Press, 2011, pp. 29–56.

Rabasa, Angel, Cheryl Benard, Lowell H. Schwartz and Peter Sickle, *Building Moderate Muslim Networks*, Santa Monica, CA: Rand Corporation, 2007, https://www.rand.org/pubs/monographs/MG574.readonline.html, last accessed 1 May 2019.

Radio International, "Full text of the last email the Islamic State sent to the Foley family," Public Radio International, 21 Aug. 2014, https://www.pri.org/stories/2014–08–21/full-text-last-email-islamic-state-sent-foley-family, last accessed 1 May 2019.

Ranstorp, Magnus, "The root causes of violent extremism," RAN Issue Paper, 4 Jan. 2016, https://ec.europa.eu/home-affairs/sites/homeaffairs/files/what-we-do/networks/radicalisation_awareness_network/ran-papers/docs/issue_paper_root-causes_jan2016_en.pdf, last accessed 1 May 2019.

Rashid, Naaz, "Giving the silent majority a stronger voice? Initiatives to empower Muslim women as part of the UK's 'War on Terror'," *Ethnic and Racial Studies*, 37, 4 (2014), pp. 589–604.

————, *Veiled Threats: Producing the Muslim Woman in Public Policy Discourses*, London: Policy Press, 2016.

Rasmussen, Sune Engel, "US 'mother of all bombs' killed 92 Isis militants, say Afghan officials," *The Guardian*, 15 Apr. 2017, https://www.theguardian.com/world/2017/apr/15/us-mother-of-all-bombs-moab-afghanistan-donald-trump-death-toll, last accessed 1 May 2019.

Reif, Linda L., "Women in Latin American guerrilla movements: A comparative perspective," *Comparative Politics*, 18, 2 (1986), pp. 147–169.

Reilly, Katie, "Here are all the times Donald Trump insulted Mexico," *Time*, 31 Aug. 2016, http://time.com/4473972/donald-trump-mexico-meeting-insult/, last accessed 1 May 2019.

Reuter, Christoph, "The terror strategist: Secret files reveal the structure of Islamic State," *Der Spiegel*, 13 Apr. 2015, http://www.spiegel.de/international/world/islamic-state-files-show-structure-of-islamist-terror-group-a-1029274-druck.html, last accessed 1 May 2019.

Reuters, "Kansas militia men blame Trump rhetoric for mosque attack plan," 31 Oct. 2018, https://www.reuters.com/article/us-kansas-crime-somalia/kansas-militia-men-blame-trump-rhetoric-for-mosque-attack-plan-idUSKCN1N500O, last accessed 1 May 2019.

Revesz, Rachael, "Isis hostage Kayla Mueller shown pleading for her life in heartbreaking final video," *The Independent*, 25 Aug. 2016, https://www.independent.co.uk/news/world/americas/isis-hostage-kayla-mueller-video-us-captivity-hostages-terrorism-syria-aleppo-a7209921.html, last accessed 1 May 2019.

Revkin, Mara R., "When terrorists govern: Protecting civilians in conflicts with state-building armed groups," *Harvard National Security Journal*, 9 (2018), pp. 100–145.

Richards, Anthony, "The problem with 'radicalization': The remit of 'Prevent' and the need to refocus on terrorism in the UK," *International Affairs*, 87, 1 (2011), pp. 143–152.

———, "From terrorism to 'radicalization' to 'extremism': Counter-terrorism imperative or loss of focus?" *International Affairs*, 91, 2 (2015), pp. 371–380.

Richardson, Louise, *What Terrorists Want: Understanding the Enemy, Containing the Threat*, London: John Murray, 2007.

Rineheart, Jason, "Counterterrorism and counterinsurgency," *Perspectives on Terrorism*, 4, 5 (2010), pp. 31–47.

Robison, Kristopher K., "Unpacking the social origins of terrorism: The role of women's empowerment in reducing terrorism," *Studies in Conflict & Terrorism*, 33, 8 (2010), pp. 735–756.

Roggio, Bill, "Al Qaeda, Taliban create female suicide cells in Pakistan and Afghanistan," *Long War Journal*, 31 Dec. 2010, https://www.longwarjournal.org/archives/2010/12/al_qaeda_taliban_create_female_suicides_cell_in_pakistan_and_afghanistan.php, last accessed 1 May 2019.

Roggio, Bill, and Alexandra Gutowski, "2017: A record year for US counter-terrorism strikes," *Long War Journal*, 3 Jan. 2018, https://www.longwarjournal.org/archives/2018/01/2017-a-record-year-for-us-counterterror-ism-strikes.php, last accessed 1 May 2019.

Rohwerder, Briggitte, "Lessons from Female Engagement Teams," 14 Jan. 2015, http://www.gsdrc.org/docs/open/hdq1186.pdf, last accessed 1 May 2019.

Romaniuk, Peter, "Does CVE work? Lessons learned from the global effort to counter violent extremism," 2015, http://www.globalcenter.org/wp-content/uploads/2015/09/Does-CVE-Work_2015.pdf, last accessed 1 May 2019.

Rothwell, James, "Morocco arrests ten female Isil suicide bombers who 'planned to strike on election day'," *The Telegraph*, 5 Oct. 2016, http://www.telegraph.co.uk/news/2016/10/05/morocco-arrests-ten-female-isil-suicide-bombers-who-planned-to-s2/, last accessed 1 May 2019.

Rubin, Alissa J., "Despair drives suicide attacks by Iraqi women," *New York Times*, 5 July 2008, http://www.post322.org/www.Post322.org/Iraq_Human_Interest_News_files/2008 07 05–Despair drives suicide attacks by Iraqi women.pdf, last accessed 1 May 2019.

Rugh, William A., "Yemen and the United States: Conflicting priorities," *The Fletcher Forum of World Affairs*, 34 (2010), pp. 109–116.

Rutgers Institute for Women's Leadership, "Women leaders fact sheet: Women in the US military services," June 2010, http://iwl.rutgers.edu/

documents/njwomencount/Women%20in%20Military%202009%20 Final.pdf, last accessed 1 May 2019.

Sahak, Abdul Matin, "'Horrors that can't be told': Afghan women report Islamic State rapes," *Reuters*, 30 July 2018, https://www.reuters.com/ article/us-afghanistan-islamic-staterape/horrors-that-cant-be-told-afghan-women-report-islamic-state-rapesidUSKBN1KK0WG, last accessed 6 Mar 2019.

Said, Rodi, and Ellen Francis, "Syria Kurds evacuate civilians from IS redoubt, hail Trump troop reversal," *Reuters*, 22 Feb. 2019, https://www.reuters. com/article/us-mideast-crisis-syria/syria-kurds-evacuate-civilians-from-is-redoubt-hail-trump-troop-reversalidUSKCN1QB1IK?feedType=RSS&f eedName=topNews, last accessed 7 Mar. 2019

Saltman, Erin Marie, and Melanie Smith, "'Till martyrdom do us part': Gender and the ISIS phenomenon," 2015, https://www.isdglobal.org/ wp-content/uploads/2016/02/Till_Martyrdom_Do_Us_Part_Gender_ and_the_ISIS_Phenomenon.pdf, last accessed 1 May 2019.

Saripi, Nur Irfani Binte, "Female members of ISIS: A greater need for rehabilitation," *Counter Terrorist Trends and Analysis*, 7, 3 (2015), pp. 26–31.

Satterthwaite, Margaret L., "Missing indicators, disappearing gender: measuring USAID's programing to counter violent extremism," in Margaret L. Satterthwaite and Jayne Huckerby (eds), *Gender, National Security, and Counter-Terrorism: Human Rights Perspectives*, Abingdon: Routledge, 2013, pp. 82–106.

Satterthwaite, Margaret L., and Jayne C. Huckerby, *Gender, National Security, and Counter-Terrorism: Human Rights Perspectives*, Abingdon: Routledge, 2013.

Savage, Charlie, "US says troops can stay in Syria without new authorization," *New York Times*, 22 Feb. 2018a, https://www.nytimes.com/2018/ 02/22/us/politics/isis-syria-american-troops.html, last accessed 1 May 2019.

———, "As ISIS fighters fill prisons in Syria, their home nations look away," *New York Times*, 18 July 2018b, https://www.nytimes.com/2018/07/18/ world/middleeast/islamic-state-detainees-syria-prisons.html, last accessed 1 May 2019.

SAVE, "Preventing violent extremism: The Women without Borders MotherSchools Model—Parenting for Peace," Presentation at World Congress for Justice for Children, May 2018, https://j4c2018.org/wp-content/uploads/2018/04/EDIT-SCHLAFFER-WOMEN-WITHOUT-BORDERS-PRESENTATION-29.05.18.pdf, last accessed 12 Mar. 2019.

Schmid, Alex, "Terrorism-the definitional problem," *Case Western Reserve Journal of International Law*, 36 (2004), pp. 375–420.

———, "Radicalisation, de-radicalisation, counter-radicalisation: A conceptual discussion and literature review," ICCT Research Paper 97, Mar. 2013, https://www.icct.nl/download/file/ICCT-Schmid-Radicalisation-De-Radicalisation-Counter-Radicalisation-March–2013.pdf. last accessed 30 Apr. 2019.

Schmidt, Rachel, "Duped: Why gender stereotypes are leading to inadequate deradicalization and disengagement strategies,"TSAS Working Paper Series, No. 18–07, Aug. 2018, https://www.tsas.ca/wp-content/uploads/2018/08/WP18–07_Schmidt.pdf, last accessed 1 May 2019.

Schmitt, Eric, "A shadowy war's newest front: A drone base rising from the Sahara Desert," *New York Times*, 22 Apr. 2018, https://www.nytimes.com/2018/04/22/us/politics/drone-base-niger.html?module=inline, last accessed 1 May 2019.

Schmitt, Eric, and Thom Shanker, "US officials retool slogan for terror war," *New York Times*, 26 July 2005, https://www.nytimes.com/2005/07/26/politics/us-officials-retool-slogan-for-terror-war.html, last accessed 1 May 2019.

Schrijvers, Joke, "Fighters, victims and survivors: constructions of ethnicity, gender and refugeeness among Tamils in Sri Lanka," *Journal of Refugee Studies*, 12, 3 (1999), pp. 307–333.

Serafino, Nina M., "Department of Defense 'Section 1207' Security and Stabilization Assistance: Background and congressional concerns, FY2006-FY2010," 3 Mar. 2011.

———, "Security assistance reform: 'Section 1206' background and issues for Congress," 8 Dec. 2014a, https://fas.org/sgp/crs/natsec/RS22855.pdf, last accessed 1 May 2019.

———, "Global security contingency fund: Summary and issue overview," 4 Apr. 2014b, https://fas.org/sgp/crs/row/R42641.pdf, last accessed 1 May 2019.

Sewall, Sarah, "Boko Haram: The growing threat to schoolgirls in Nigeria and beyond," 21 May 2014, https://2009–2017.state.gov/j/226424.htm, last accessed 1 May 2019.

Shalizi, Hamid, and James Mackenzie, "Afghanistan's Ghani offers talks with Taliban 'without preconditions'," *Reuters*, 28 Feb. 2018, https://www.reuters.com/article/usafghanistan-taliban/afghanistans-ghani-offers-talks-with-taliban-without-preconditions-idUSKCN1GC0J0, last accessed 6 Mar. 2019.

Shane, Scott, Matthew Rosenberg and Eric Lipton, "Trump pushes dark view of Islam to center of US policy-making," *New York Times*, 1 Feb. 2017, https://www.nytimes.com/2017/02/01/us/politics/donald-trump-islam.html, last accessed 1 May 2019.

Sharp, Jeremy M., "The Middle East Partnership Initiative: An overview," 8 Feb. 2005, https://fas.org/sgp/crs/mideast/RS21457.pdf, last accessed 1 May 2019.

————, "Yemen Background and US relations," 6 Feb. 2014, www.dtic.mil/get-tr-doc/pdf?AD=ADA602686, last accessed 1 May 2019.

————, "Yemen: Background and US relations," 11 Feb. 2015, https://fas.org/sgp/crs/mideast/RL34170.pdf, last accessed 1 May 2019.

Sharp, Jeremy M., and Carla E. Humud, "US foreign assistance to the Middle East: Historical background, recent trends, and the FY2016 request," 19 Oct. 2015, https://fas.org/sgp/crs/mideast/R44233.pdf, last accessed 1 May 2019.

Shepherd, Laura, "Veiled references: Constructions of gender in the Bush administration discourse on the attacks on Afghanistan post-9/11," *International Feminist Journal of Politics*, 8, 1 (2006), pp. 19–41.

————, "Power and authority in the production of United Nations Security Council Resolution 1325," *International Studies Quarterly*, 52, 2 (2008), pp. 383–404.

————, *Gender, Violence and Security: Discourse as Practice*, London: Zed Books Ltd, 2013a.

————, "The state of feminist security studies: Continuing the conversation," *International Studies Perspectives*, 14, 4 (2013b), pp. 436–439.

Shiffman, John, "Special report: From abuse to a chat room, a martyr is made—Jane's Jihad," *Reuters*, 7 Dec. 2012, https://www.reuters.com/article/us-usa-jihadjane/special-report-from-abuse-to-a-chat-room-a-martyr-is-made-janes-jihad-idUSBRE8B60GP20121207, last accessed 1 May 2019.

Siddiqui, Sabrina, "Barack Obama says fights against Isis will be 'generational struggle'," *The Guardian*, 6 July 2015, https://www.theguardian.com/us-news/2015/jul/06/barack-obama-isis-generational-struggle-pentagon, last accessed 1 May 2019.

Siemion, Rita, "Two important new civilian casualties provisions in the Defense Authorization Bill," Just Security, 24 Jul 2018, https://www.just-security.org/59695/important-civilian-casualties-provisions-congressional-bill-national-defense-authorization-act/, last accessed 1 May 2019.

Silberstein, Sandra, *War of Words: Language, Politics and 9/11*, Abingdon: Routledge, 2004.

Sims, Christopher, "Academics in foxholes: The life and death of the Human Terrain System," *Foreign Affairs*, 4 Feb. 2016, https://www.foreignaffairs.com/articles/afghanistan/2016-02-04/academics-foxholes, last accessed 1 May 2019.

Sjoberg, Laura, "Agency, militarized femininity and enemy others: Observations from the war in Iraq," *International Feminist Journal of Politics*, 9, 1 (2007), pp. 82–101.

————, *Gender and International Security: Feminist Perspectives*, Abingdon: Routledge, 2009a.

————, "Feminist interrogations of terrorism/terrorism studies," *International Relations*, 23, 1 (2009b), pp. 69–74.

————,"Introduction to security studies: Feminist contributions," *Security Studies*, 18, 2 (2009c), pp. 183–213.

————, "Looking forward, conceptualizing feminist security studies," *Politics & Gender*, 7, 4 (2011), pp. 600–604.

————, *Gendering Global Conflict: Toward a Feminist Theory of War*, New York: Columbia University Press, 2013.

Sjoberg, Laura, and Caron E. Gentry, *Mothers, Monsters, Whores: Women's Violence in Global Politics*, London: Zed Books, 2007.

————, "Profiling terror: Gender, strategic logic, and emotion in the study of suicide terrorism," *Austrian Journal of Political Science*, 37, 2 (2008a), pp. 181 196.

———— "Reduced to bad sex: Narratives of violent women from the bible to the war on terror," *International Relations*, 22, 1 (2008b), pp. 5–23.

————, *Women, Gender, and Terrorism*, Athens, GA: University of Georgia Press, 2011.

————, *Beyond Mothers, Monsters, Whores: Thinking About Women's Violence in Global Politics*, London: Zed Books Ltd, 2015.

Smith, David, "'Good riddance': Progressives hail exit of hardline Trump aide Sebastian Gorka," *The Guardian*, 26 Aug. 2017, https://www.theguardian.com/us-news/2017/aug/26/sebastian-gorka-removed-donald-trump-progressive-reaction, last accessed 4 Mar. 2019.

Sommers, Meg, and Daria McLagan, *Lioness* [video], New York: Impact Partners, 2008.

Sommerville, Quentin, Tweet of 12 Apr. 2019, https://twitter.com/sommervilletv/status/1116604815612604416, last accessed 1 May 2019.

Sonne, Paul, "Pentagon: 'No one will ever know' how many civilians US has killed in fight against ISIS", *Washington Post*, 5 June 2018, https://www.washingtonpost.com/world/national-security/pentagonno-one-will-ever-know-how-many-civilians-us-has-killed-in-fight-against-isis/2018/06/05/4b3fec306900–11e8-bbc5-dc9f3634fa0a_story.html?utm_term=.9f82749dba1c, last accessed 7 Mar. 2019

Sopko, John F., "Reconstructing the Afghan National Defense and Security Forces: Lessons from the US experience in Afghanistan," 2017, https://www.sigar.mil/pdf/lessonslearned/sigar-17–62-ll.pdf, last accessed 1 May 2019.

The Soufan Group, "Foreign fighters: An updated assessment of the flow of foreign fighters into Syria and Iraq," Dec. 2015, http://soufangroup.com/wp-content/uploads/2015/12/TSG_ForeignFightersUpdate3.pdf, last accessed 1 May 2019.

Spear, Joanna, and Paul D. Williams, *Security and Development in Global Politics:*

*A Critical Comparison*, Washington, DC: Georgetown University Press, 2012.

Specia, Megan, "How Syria's death toll is lost in the fog of war," *New York Times*, 13 Apr. 2018, https://www.nytimes.com/2018/04/13/world/middleeast/syria-death-toll.html, last accessed 1 May 2019.

Speckhard, Anne, and Khapta Akhmedova, "Black widows: The Chechen female suicide terrorists," *Female Suicide Bombers: Dying for Equality*, 84, 1 (2006), pp. 63–80.

Speckhard, Anne, and Asaad Almohammad, "The operational ranks and roles of female ISIS operatives: From assassins and morality police to spies and suicide bombers," 2017, http://www.icsve.org/research-reports/the-operational-ranks-and-roles-of-female-isis-operatives-from-assassins-and-morality-police-to-spies-and-suicide-bombers/, last accessed 1 May 2019.

Speckhard, Anne, and Ahmet S. Yayla, "Eyewitness accounts from recent defectors from Islamic State: Why they joined, what they saw, why they quit," *Perspectives on Terrorism*, 9, 6 (2015), pp. 95–117.

Spivak, Gayatri Chakravorty, "Can the subaltern speak?" in Patrick Williams and Laura Chrisman (eds), *Colonial Discourse and Post-Colonial Theory, A Reader*, New York: Columbia University Press (1988), pp. 21–78.

The Stabilisation Network, "HTS and women: A gendered approach to social influence in Idlib and Dar'a," May 2018, https://docs.wixstatic.com/ugd/28808b_4a01f0b039694f11832a11d94f52077a.pdf, last accessed 1 May 2019.

Stanski, Keith, "Terrorism, gender, and ideology: A case study of women who join the revolutionary armed forces of Colombia (FARC)," in James J. F. Forest (ed.), *The Making of a Terrorist: Recruitment, Training, and Root Causes*, Westport, CT: Praeger Security International, 2006, pp. 136–150.

Stern, Jessica, and John M. Berger, *ISIS: The State of Terror*, New York: Harper Collins, 2015.

Stern, Maria, and Annick Wibben, "A decade of feminist security studies revisited," *Security Dialogue*, 2014, https://journals.sagepub.com/page/sdi/collections/virtual-collections/feminist-security-studies-revisited, last accessed 1 May 2019.

Stern, Maria, and Joakim Öjendal, "Mapping the security—development nexus: Conflict, complexity, cacophony, convergence?" *Security Dialogue*, 41, 1 (2010), pp. 5–29.

Stiehm, Judith Hicks, *Women and Men's Wars*, Oxford: Pergamon, 1983.

Street, Amy E., Dawne Vogt and Lissa Dutra, "A new generation of women veterans: Stressors faced by women deployed to Iraq and Afghanistan," *Clinical Psychology Review*, 29, 8 (2009), pp. 685–694.

Stump, Jacob L., and Priya Dixit, *Critical Terrorism Studies: An Introduction to Research Methods*, Abingdon: Routledge, 2013.

Sullivan, Kevin, and Karla Adam, "Hoping to create a new society, the Islamic State recruits entire families," *Washington Post*, 11 Jan. 2015, https://www. washingtonpost.com/world/national-security/hoping-to-create-a-new-homeland-the-islamic-state-recruits-entire-families/2014/12/24/dbff-ceec-8917–11e4–8ff4-fb93129c9c8b_story.html, last accessed 1 May 2019.

Svendsen, Adam D. M., "Re-fashioning risk: Comparing UK, US and Canadian security and intelligence efforts against terrorism," *Defence Studies*, 10, 3 (2010), pp. 307–335.

Swaine, Aisling, "Assessing the potential of National Action Plans to advance implementation of United Nations Security Council Resolution 1325," *Yearbook of International Humanitarian Law*, 12 (2009), pp. 403–433.

Sylvester, Christine, "Tensions in feminist security studies," *Security Dialogue*, 41, 6 (2010), pp. 607–614.

Szayna, Thomas S., Eric V. Larson, Angela O'Mahony, Sean Robson, Agnes Gereben Schaefer, Miriam Matthews, J. Michael Polich, Lynsay Ayer, Derek Eaton and William Marcellino, *Considerations for Integrating Women into Closed Occupations in US Special Operations Forces*, Santa Monica, CA: Rand Corporation, 2016, https://www.rand.org/pubs/research_reports/RR1058.readonline.html, last accessed 1 May 2019.

Tankel, Stephen, *With Us and Against Us: How America's Partners Help and Hinder the War on Terror*, New York: Columbia University Press, 2018.

———, "Riding the tiger: How Trump enables right-wing extremism," *War on the Rocks*, 5 Nov. 2018, https://warontherocks.com/2018/11/riding-the-tiger-how-trump-enables-right-wing-extremism/, last accessed 4 Mar. 2019.

Tarras-Wahlberg, Louisa, "Seven promises of ISIS to its female recruits," 9 Jan. 2017, http://www.icsve.org/research-reports/seven-promises-of-isis-to-its-female-recruits/, last accessed 1 May 2019.

Tarnoff, Curt. "US Agency for International Development (USAID): Background, Operations and Issues," 21 Jul 2015, https://fas.org/sgp/crs/row/R44117.pdf, last accessed 25 May 2019.

Tax, Meredith, *A Road Unforeseen: Women Fight the Islamic State*, New York: Bellevue Literary Press, 2016.

Tembo, Edgar, *US-UK Counter-Terrorism after 9/11: A Qualitative Approach*, Abingdon: Routledge, 2014.

Thobani, Sunera, "White wars: Western feminisms and the 'War on Terror'," *Feminist Theory*, 8, 2 (2007), pp. 169–185.

Thomas, Raymond, "Aspen Security Forum 2017 SOCOM: Policing the world," 21 July 2017, http://aspensecurityforum.org/wp-content/uploads/2017/07/SOCOM_Policing-the-World.pdf#page=7, last accessed 1 May 2019.

# BIBLIOGRAPHY

Thompson, Mark, "American Amazons: Hiding in plain-Jane sight," *Time*, 28 Jan. 2013, http://nation.time.com/2013/01/28/american-amazons-hiding-in-plain-jane-sight/, last accessed 1 May 2019.

Tickner, J. Ann, "Feminist perspectives on 9/11," *International Studies Perspectives*, 3, 4 (2002), pp. 333–350.

————, "On the frontlines or sidelines of knowledge and power? Feminist practices of responsible scholarship," *International Studies Review*, 8, 3 (2006), pp. 383–395.

————, "Feminist security studies: Celebrating an emerging field," *Politics & Gender*, 7, 4 (2011), pp. 576–581.

————, *A Feminist Voyage through International Relations*, Oxford: Oxford University Press, 2014.

Tickner, J. Ann, and Laura Sjoberg, *Feminism and International Relations: Conversations about the Past, Present and Future*, Abingdon: Routledge, 2013.

Tinnes, Judith, "Literature on terrorism research," *Perspectives on Terrorism*, 8, 1 (2014).

Tomlinson, Hugh, "Taliban asks US to stop airstrikes so it can crush Isis," *The Times*, 7 Aug. 2018, https://www.thetimes.co.uk/article/taliban-asks-us-to-stop-airstrikes-so-it-can-crush-isis-5dg6rtjf5, last accessed 7 Mar. 2019.

Toosi, Nahal, "State Department report will trim language on women's rights, discrimination," *Politico*, 21 Feb. 2018, https://www.politico.com/story/2018/02/21/department-women-rights-abortion-420361, last accessed 6 Mar. 2019.

TRAC, "Female foreign fighters Syria and Iraq," 2014, www.trackingterrorism.org/article/female-foreign-fighters-syria-and-iraq, last accessed 7 June 2014.

Tracy, Abigail, "'We are at a turning point': Counterterrorism experts say Trump is inspiring a terrifying new era of right wing," *Vanity Fair*, 2 Nov. 2018, https://www.vanityfair.com/news/2018/11/trump-administration-tree-of-life-shooting-domestic-terrorism, last accessed 1 May 2019.

Trew, Bel, "Isis turns to jihadist brides in last-ditch attempt to hold off Iraqi forces in Mosul," *The Times*, 5 July 2017, https://www.thetimes.co.uk/edition/world/isis-turns-to-jihadist-brides-in-last-ditch-attempt-to-hold-off-iraqi-forces-in-mosul-v9gzndb6l, last accessed 1 May 2019.

Truax, Chris, "Trump bears moral responsibility for pipe bombs. Denying it just makes things worse," *USA Today*, 1 Nov. 2018, https://eu.usatoday.com/story/opinion/2018/11/01/donald-trump-reckless-rhetoric-cesar-sayoc-pipe-bombs-column/1821238002/, last accessed 4 Mar. 2019.

UNHCR, "Global trends: Forced displacement in 2017," 25 Jun 2018, https://www.unhcr.org/5b27be547.pdf, last accessed 1 May 2019.

UN News Centre, "UNHCR warns of humanitarian cost of Syrian conflict, especially on the displaced," 27 Feb. 2013, http://www.unhcr.org/512e2a036.html, last accessed 1 May 2019.

Underwood, Emily, "Surviving genocide: Storytelling and ritual help communities heal," Science, 16 May 2017, https://www.sciencemag.org/news/2017/05/surviving-genocide-storytelling-and-ritual-help-communities-heal, last accessed 7 Mar. 2019.

United States Institute of Peace, "'Mothers schools to working with police: Women prevent violent extremism," 18 Mar. 2015, *https://www.usip.org/publications/2015/03/mothers-schools-working-police-women-prevent-violent-extremism*, last accessed 1 May 2019.

Valentine, Simon Ross, "Meet the Peshmerga women fighting ISIS," *Newsweek*, 21 May 2016, http://www.newsweek.com/meet-peshmerga-women-fighting-isis-461282, last accessed 1 May 2019.

———— *Those Who Face Death: The Kurdish Army; Its History, Development and the Fight Against ISIS*, Kindle Direct Publishing, 2018.

van de Wetering, Denis, Andreas Zick and Hannah Mietke, "Extreme right women, (dis-) engagement and deradicalisation: Findings from a qualitative study," *International Journal of Developmental Science*, 12, 1–2 (2018), pp. 115–127.

Varon, Jeremy, *Bringing the War Home: The Weather Underground, the Red Army Faction, and Revolutionary Violence in the Sixties and Seventies*, Berkeley: University of California Press, 2004.

Veldhuis, Tinka M., *Prisoner Radicalization and Terrorism Detention Policy: Institutionalized Fear or Evidence-Based Policy Making?* London: Routledge, 2016.

Watson Institute of International and Public Affairs, "Costs of war project: Figures," 2015, https://watson.brown.edu/costsofwar/figures, last accessed 1 Mar. 2019.

————, "Costs of war project," 2017a, http://watson.brown.edu/costsofwar/about, last accessed 1 Aug. 2017.

————, "Current United States counterterror war locations," 2017b, https://watson.brown.edu/costsofwar/files/cow/imce/papers/Current%20US%20Counterterror%20War%20Locations_Costs%20of%20War%20Project%20Map.pdf, last accessed 1 Mar. 2019.

Weed, Matthew, "Memorandum: Presidential references to the 2001 Authorization for Use of Military Force in publicly available executive actions and reports to Congress," 2016, https://fas.org/sgp/crs/natsec/pres-aumf.pdf, last accessed 1 May 2019.

Weinberg, Leonard, and William Lee Eubank, "Italian women terrorists," *Terrorism*, 9, 3 (1987), pp. 241–262.

Weinberg, Leonard, Ami Pedahzur and Sivan Hirsch-Hoefler, "The challenges of conceptualizing terrorism," *Terrorism and Political Violence*, 16, 4 (2004), pp. 777–794.

Welch, Stewart, and Bailey, Kevin, "In pursuit of good ideas: The Syria train and equip program," in *Research Notes*, Washington, DC: The Washington Institute for Near East Policy, 2016 http://www.washingtoninstitute.org/policy-analysis/view/in-pursuit-of-good-ideas-the-syria-train-and-equip-program, last accessed 1 May 2019.

Welland, Julia, "Gender and 'population-centric' counterinsurgency in Afghanistan," in Simona Sharoni, Julia Welland, Linda Steiner and Jennifer Pedersen (eds), *Handbook on Gender and War*, Cheltenham: Edward Elgar, 2016, 127–146.

Wendt, Alexander, "On constitution and causation in international relations," *Review of International Studies*, 24, 1 (1998), pp. 101–122.

Whitehead, Tom, "One in three jihadists now women, warns police chief," *The Guardian*, 27 Apr. 2016, http://www.telegraph.co.uk/news/2016/04/27/one-in-three-jihadists-now-women-warns-police-chief/, last accessed 1 May 2019.

Wibben, Annick, *Feminist Security Studies: A Narrative Approach*, Abingdon: Routledge, 2011a.

————, "Feminist politics in feminist security studies," *Politics & Gender*, 7, 4 (2011b), pp. 590–595.

————, "Researching feminist security studies," *Australian Journal of Political Science*, 49, 4 (2014), pp. 743–755.

Wiktorowicz, Quintan, *Radical Islam Rising: Muslim Extremism in the West*, Oxford: Rowman & Littlefield Publishers, 2005.

van Wilgenburg, Wladimir, "Syrian Kurds call on foreign countries to take back IS fighters," Kurdistan 24, 8 Oct. 2018.

Williams, Lynn M., and Susan B. Epstein, "Overseas contingency operations funding: Background and status," 7 Feb. 2017, https://fas.org/sgp/crs/natsec/R44519.pdf, last accessed 1 May 2019.

Wilson III, Ernest J., "Hard power, soft power, smart power," *The Annals of the American Academy of Political and Social Science*, 616, 1 (2008), pp. 110–124.

Winter, Charlie, "Women of the Islamic State: A manifesto on women by the al-Khanssaa Brigade," Feb. 2015a, http://www.quilliamfoundation.org/wp/wp-content/uploads/publications/free/women-of-the-islamic-state3.pdf, last accessed 1 May 2019.

————, "Detailed analysis of Islamic State propaganda video: Although the disbelievers dislike it," 2015b, https://www.stratcomcoe.org/download/file/fid/2589, last accessed 1 May 2019.

Winter, Charlie, and Haid Haid, *Jihadist Propaganda, Offline. Strategic Communications in Modern Warfare*, Washington, DC: Middle East Institute, 2018, https://www.mei.edu/sites/default/files/publications/PP3_CharlieHaid_jihadistpropagandaCT%20final.pdf, last accessed 1 May 2019.

Winter, Charlie, and Devorah Margolin, "The Mujahidat dilemma: Female combatants and the Islamic State," *Combatting Terrorism Center*, 10, 7 (2017), pp. 23–29.

Winterbotham, Emily, and Elizabeth Pearson, "Different cities, shared stories: A five-country study challenging assumptions around Muslim women and CVE interventions," *The RUSI Journal*, 161, 5 (2016), pp. 54–65.

Witkowsky, Anne A., "Integrating gender perspectives within the Department of Defense," *Prism*, 6, 1 (2016), pp. 35–44.

Wood, Elisabeth Jean, "Variation in sexual violence during war," *Politics & Society*, 34, 3 (2006), pp. 307–342.

———, "Armed groups and sexual violence: When is wartime rape rare? " *Politics & Society*, 37, 1 (2009), pp. 131–161.

———, "Sexual violence during war: Toward an understanding of variation," in *Gender, War, and Militarism: Feminist Perspectives*, Westport, CT: Praeger, 2010, pp. 124–137.

Wood, Graeme, "From the Islamic State to suburban Texas," *The Atlantic*, *3 Nov. 2017*, https://www.theatlantic.com/politics/archive/2017/11/from-isis-to-suburbantexas/544910/, last accessed 4 Mar. 2017.

Wood, Reed M., and Jakana L. Thomas, "Women on the frontline: Rebel group ideology and women's participation in violent rebellion," *Journal of Peace Research*, 54, 1 (2017), pp. 31–46.

Woodruff, Judy, "Women's combat roles evolving in Iraq, Afghanistan," PBS Newshour, 5 July 2007, http://www.pbs.org/newshour/bb/military-july-dec07-women_07–05/, last accessed 11 Mar. 2019.

Woodward, Bob, *Obama's Wars: The Inside Story*, London: Simon and Schuster, 2011.

World Bank, "The status and progress of women in the Middle East," 2009, http://siteresources.worldbank.org/INTMENA/Resources/MENA_Gender_Compendium-2009–1.pdf, last accessed 1 May 2019.

Young, Iris Marion, "The logic of masculinist protection: Reflections on the current security state," *Signs*, 29, 1 (2003), pp. 1–25.

Zahedi, Ashraf, "Muslim American women in the post-11 September era: Challenges and opportunities," *International Feminist Journal of Politics*, 13, 2 (2011), pp. 183–203.

Zambrana, Marga, Hazar Aydemir and Emma Graham-Harrison, "Nine British medics enter Isis stronghold to work in hospitals," *The Guardian*, 21 Mar. 2015, https://www.theguardian.com/world/2015/mar/21/british-medical-students-syria-isis, last accessed 1 May 2019.

Zelin, Aaron, "Al-Fajr Media releases issue one of a new women's magazine: 'Al-Shāmikhah'," 2011, http://jihadology.net/2011/03/05/al-fajr-media-presents-a-issue-one-of-a-new-womens-magazine-al-shamikhah/, last accessed 12 Mar. 2019.

————, "The others: Foreign fighters in Libya," 2018a, https://www.washingtoninstitute.org/uploads/PolicyNote45-Zelin.pdf, last accessed 1 May 2019.

————, "Policy watch 3032: Tunisia's female jihadists," 31 Oct. 2018b, https://www.washingtoninstitute.org/policy-analysis/view/tunisias-female-jihadists, last accessed 1 May 2019.

Zenn, Jacob, and Elizabeth Pearson, "Women, gender and the evolving tactics of Boko Haram," *Journal of Terrorism Research*, 5, 1 (2014), pp. 46–57.

Zimmerman, Beth, "Honor the fallen: Marine Cpl. Jennifer M. Parecell," *Military Times*, 2007, http://thefallen.militarytimes.com/marine-cpl-jennifer-m-parcell/2542608, last accessed 3 Mar. 2017.

Zuhur, Sherifa D., "Iraq, women's empowerment, and public policy," Dec. 2006, www.dtic.mil/dtic/tr/fulltext/u2/a460829.pdf, last accessed 11 Mar. 2019.

# INDEX

# INDEX

INDEX

# INDEX

# INDEX